The Governor of Goat Hill

To Dr. Wiseman,
a legend. I'm
so proud you
bought my
book,

Eddie

"Now I pass up about twenty-five or thirty thousand of honest gain because I like being a detective, like the work. And liking work makes you want to do it as well as you can. Otherwise, there'd be no sense to it. That's the fix I am in. I don't know anything else, don't enjoy anything else, don't want to know or enjoy anything else. You can't weigh that against any sum of money. Money is good stuff. I haven't anything against it. But in the past eighteen years I've been getting my fun out of chasing crooks and tackling puzzles, my satisfaction out of catching crooks and solving riddles. It's the only kind of sport I know anything about, and I can't imagine a pleasanter future than twenty-some years more of it. I'm not going to blow that up!"

-- Dashiell Hammett, *"The Gutting of Couffignal"*

"I think this will make Watergate look like child's play."

-- Former Alabama Gov. Don Siegelman,
on Karl Rove's alleged involvement in his prosecution.

The Governor of Goat Hill

Don Siegelman, the Reporter who Exposed his
Crimes, and the Hoax that Suckered some of
the Top Names in Journalism

EDDIE CURRAN

iUniverse, Inc.
New York   Bloomington

The Governor of Goat Hill
Don Siegelman, the Reporter who Exposed his Crimes, and the
Hoax that Suckered some of the Top Names in Journalism

iUniverse books may be ordered through booksellers or by contacting:

iUniverse
1663 Liberty Drive
Bloomington, IN 47403
www.iuniverse.com
1-800-Authors (1-800-288-4677)

Because of the dynamic nature of the Internet, any Web addresses or links
contained in this book may have changed since publication and may no longer be
valid. The views expressed in this work are solely those of the author and do not
necessarily reflect the views of the publisher, and the publisher hereby disclaims
any responsibility for them.

Cover design by J.D. Crowe

Quotes from page ii are from:
Dashiell Hammett, "The Gutting of Couffignal."
Markeshia Ricks, "Q&A with Don Siegelman," *Anniston Star*, May 18, 2008.

ISBN: 978-1-4401-8939-5 (sc)
ISBN: 978-1-4401-8941-8 (hc)
ISBN: 978-1-4401-8940-1 (ebk)

Library of Congress Control Number: 2009913245

Printed in the United States of America

iUniverse rev. date: 12/16/2009

This book is dedicated to the loving memory of my mother,
Eleanor Curran,
For her encouragement of curiosity and the value of reading,

And to
Jana,
For her endless support,
And our children,
Jerry and Eva,
For the joy and laughter they bring us

Table of Contents

On the Web: At the web-site, EddieCurran.Com, readers will find a host of resources, including many of the public records cited in the book; additional photos; updates on developments in the Siegelman case; and more.

Cast of Characters

SIEGELMAN ADMINISTRATION

Don Siegelman, governor, 1999-2003

Nick Bailey, Siegelman's driver, held many titles, including "confidential assistant to governor," until November 2001 resignation

Paul Hamrick, chief of staff, until July 2001; best friend of G.H. Construction owner Lanny Young

Ted Hosp, legal counsel

Henry Mabry, finance director, known as, "Dr. No"

Carrie Kurlander, director of press office

Rip Andrews, press office and campaign spokesman

Mack Roberts, highway director until July 2001

Jim Buckalew, chief of staff, starting July 2001

G.H. CONSTRUCTION/WASTE MANAGEMENT

G.H. "Goat Hill" Construction, company formed in 2001 and picked to oversee construction of two state warehouses

Clayton L. "Lanny" Young, landfill developer and lobbyist for Waste Management; secret owner of G.H. Construction

Bryan Broderick, straw man owner of G.H. Construction

Bill Blount, investment banker on G.H. project

Fred Simpler, lawyer for Blount on G.H. project

Curtis Kirsch, architect for one of the warehouses

Roland Vaughan, president of Sherlock, Smith & Adams, the engineering firm hired to oversee the project

Andrew Nolin, Vaughan's partner in warehouse land sale

Claire Austin, Young's lobbying partner; initial source on G.H. stories

Ellis Brazeal, lawyer for Young and Waste Management; Hamrick's brother in law

Susan Kennedy, Revenue Department lawyer, backed tax cut at Emelle

Susan Copeland and Doyle Fuller, Montgomery lawyers who sued Young and Waste Management

Phillip Jordan, probate judge of Cherokee County

Charles Campagna, Waste Management official, worked on Young deals in Alabama

THE ALABAMA EDUCATION LOTTERY FOUNDATION

The foundation, non-profit set up by Siegelman to fund campaign for passage of October 1999 lottery referendum

Richard Scrushy, chairman, HealthSouth Corp., found guilty of his role in arranging $500,000 in secret donations to foundation in return for appointment by Siegelman to influential state board

Mike Martin, top Scrushy assistant at HealthSouth; played role in arranging first $250,000 contribution

Bill McGahan, New York-based investment banker for UBS; told he would be fired as HealthSouth banker if UBS didn't come up with $250,000 for foundation

Integrated Health Services, Maryland nursing home company; source of first $250,000 check given by Scrushy to Siegelman

Eric Hanson, HealthSouth lobbyist, helped broker deal for Integrated Health to make payment instead of UBS

Darren Cline, fund-raising consultant for lottery foundation

Jack Miller, Siegelman ally, Democratic Party chairman during lottery referendum

Richard Dorman, Mobile lawyer, Siegelman-appointed head of the foundation

Redding Pitt, Democratic Party chairman when the party belatedly reported secret $700,000-plus loan to foundation

THE LEGAL FEES STORIES

Cherry, Givens, Mobile-Dothan law firm where Siegelman had served as 'of counsel,' and which paid him an estimated $800,000 in 2000 and 2001

Chris Peters, partner in Cherry Givens; involved in secret December 1999 state settlement with University of South Alabama that was to result in $2.8 million going to Cherry, Givens

Jack Drake, Siegelman friend; Ethics Commission member; received legal fees from South Alabama tobacco settlement

Bobby Segall, Siegelman's long-time personal lawyer; defended him against ethics charges; had role in tobacco litigation

Gordon Moulton, University of South Alabama president at time of secret settlement of 1997 tobacco lawsuit

Jim Zeigler, Mobile lawyer/political gadfly; brought ethics charge against Siegelman relating to Cherry Givens payments

Jim Sumner, director, Alabama Ethics Commissioner

EXTRAS

Keith "Tack" Mims, Alabama roadbuilder whose company shared in $36 million no-bid contract to prepare land for new Honda plant

Lanny Vines, Birmingham trial lawyer, secret purchaser of Siegelman's Montgomery home for twice its value

Wray Pearce, Vines' Birmingham accountant; served as straw-buyer for Vines on purchase of Siegelman's home

Trava Williams, stockbroker for Siegelman, Nick Bailey and others; hired by Sterne Agee & Leach to win investment contracts with state.

Anthony Fant, Birmingham businessman; partner of Williams' in AFS Equities; Siegelman friend and supporter; played lead role in apparent insider trading scheme from which Siegelman sought to benefit

Dr. Phillip Bobo, Tuscaloosa physician whose company was given multi-million dollar Medicaid contracts by administration, later rescinded because of alleged bribery scheme

Stan Pate, wealthy Tuscaloosa developer; known for antipathy to Bob Riley and support of Siegelman; Nick Bailey's employer since early 2002

Jim Lane, Montgomery businessman, owner of Group One, company paid more than $760,000 to build and manage web-site for state agency ADECA

Joe Perkins, founder of Matrix Group, a Montgomery lobbying and political consulting firm known for hardball tactics

Jim Allen, toll bridge developer, former employer of Mack Roberts; testified to being shaken down for contribution by Siegelman; sold highway striping product RainLine to state

Mac Macarto, inventor of RainLine; testified to being shaken down for contribution by Siegelman

THE MEDIA

Paul Cloos, *Mobile Register*, edited most of the Siegelman stories

Mike Marshall, Editor, *Mobile Register*

Dewey English, Managing Editor, *Mobile Register*

Howard Bronson, Publisher, *Mobile Register*

Jeb Schrenk, *Register* reporter, now editor; assigned stories on the administration's accusations against the author

Brett Blackledge, *Birmingham News* reporter, won Pulitzer for coverage of state's two-year college scandals

Kim Chandler, *Birmingham News* reporter, teamed with Blackledge on Siegelman investigative stories

Robin DeMonia, editorial writer, *Birmingham News,* likely author of the paper's editorials on Siegelman scandals, and later, the accusations that Karl Rove directed Siegelman's prosecution

Phil Rawls, legendary Associated Press reporter

Bob Johnson, covered trial for Associated Press

Dana Beyerle, reporter for Alabama papers owned by *New York Times*

Eileen Jones, reporter for WSFA in Montgomery, covered Siegelman trial

Helen Hammonds, blogged trial for WSFA; dubbed, "The Blogger Lady"

Kyle Whitmire, covered trial for *Birmingham Weekly*

Laurence Viele Davidson, covered trial for Bloomberg News

Scott Horton, online-columnist and contributing editor, *Harper's* magazine; did as much as anyone to promote Jill Simpson's story that Rove was behind Siegelman prosecution

Adam Nossiter, wrote many of the *New York Times'* stories on Siegelman

Adam Zagorin, covered Siegelman case, post-Jill Simpson, for *Time* magazine

Bob Martin, publisher of weekly *Montgomery Independent,* which republished many of Horton's columns; rabid backer of dog track owner Milton McGregor

Scott Pelley, "60 Minutes" correspondent, reported February 2008 piece on Jill Simpson and Siegelman

Andrew Rosenthal, editorial page editor, *New York Times*

Adam Cohen, assistant editor for *Times* editorial department; penned strident pro-Siegelman op-eds and probably authored the paper's editorials arguing that Siegelman was a victim of selective prosecution; a former lawyer for Southern Poverty Law Center in Montgomery

Dan Abrams, host of MSNBC news program, among most fervent backers in national media of Siegelman's claims against Karl Rove

Roger Schuler, Birmingham conspiracy theorist and Horton acolyte who runs blog called, "Legal Schnauzer"

STATE POLITICAL FIGURES

Fob James, Republican governor, 1995-1999; lost to Siegelman in 1998 governor's race

Steve Windom, Republican Lt. Gov. 1999-2003; lost to Bob Riley in 2002 Republican primary for governor

Bob Riley, Republican governor, 2003 to present (or January 2010); defeated Siegelman in 2002; one of many blamed by Siegelman for his prosecution

Roger Bedford, scandal-plagued state senator, Siegelman ally

Lucy Baxley, Lt. Gov. 2003-2007, defeated Siegelman in June 2006 Democratic primary for governor

PROSECUTION

Bill Pryor, Alabama Attorney General when investigation began

Louis Franklin, Assistant U.S. Attorney, lead prosecutor in Siegelman case

Steve Feaga, Assistant U.S. Attorney, co-lead prosecutor

J.B. Perrine, Assistant U.S. Attorney, wrote many of government's trial briefs

Richard Pilger, with Justice Department's Public Integrity Section

Joseph Fitzpatrick, assistant attorney general, member of trial team

Jennifer Garrett, assistant attorney general, member of trial team

Debbie Shaw, administrative assistant to Louis Franklin

Keith Baker, FBI

Jim Murray, FBI

Bill Long, investigator, Attorney General's Office

Jack Brennan, investigator, Attorney General's Office

Noel Hillman, head of Justice Department's Public Integrity Section, which oversees and participates in many public corruption cases, including Siegelman's; accused by Siegelman, Scott Horton and others of directing Siegelman prosecution under orders from Karl Rove

Leura Canary, U.S. Attorney for Alabama's Middle District, based in Montgomery; accused by Siegelman of helping orchestrate his prosecution for political reasons

Alice Martin, U. S. Attorney for Alabama's Northern District, based in Birmingham; like Canary, accused of being part of the political effort to ruin Siegelman

Eric Holder, U.S. Attorney General, appointed by President Obama in January 1999; continues to be focal point of lobbying efforts by Siegelman and his backers trying to get him to dismiss the case against Siegelman and Scrushy

DEFENSE LAWYERS

For Siegelman: Vince Kilborn, David McDonald, Buzz Jordan, Redding Pitt and Notre Dame law professor Robert Blakey

For Scrushy: Art Leach, Terry Butts, Fred Gray and Fred Helmsing

For Mack Roberts: Bill Baxley, David McKnight, Josh Briskman

For Paul Hamrick, Jeff Deen and Michel Nicrosi

David Cromwell Johnson, famously bombastic Birmingham lawyer, represented Siegelman from early 2002 until his death in 2003

Doug Jones, Birmingham lawyer, represented Siegelman's after Johnson's death and until being replaced by Kilborn in early 2006

JUDGES/JURORS, ETC.

Mark Fuller, Siegelman trial judge; target of defendants after trial

Sam Hendrix, jury foreman; target of defendants after trial

Katie Langer, juror; target of defendants after trial

Charlie Stanford, known as Juror 5; was roused from house to give two affidavits critical of judge and fellow jurors, and which were drafted by Birmingham pastor Charles Winston and his wife, Debra Winston

Charles Winston, Birmingham pastor with connections to Scrushy who did Stanford's first affidavit

Debra Winston, did Stanford's second affidavit and faxed it to Siegelman lawyers Vince Kilborn and David McDonald

Stephen Hudson, pastor in Ozark who told Charles Winston about Charlie Stanford

THE HOAX

Karl Rove, long-time Republican campaign strategist with reputation for dirty politics; dubbed "Bush's Brain" for his role in helping George W. Bush win presidency; senior advisor to Bush for most of his presidency; had nothing whatsoever to do with Siegelman prosecution

Jill Simpson, unknown north Alabama lawyer whose May 2007 affidavit ignited national scandal alleging that Karl Rove, Bob Riley, Bill Canary and others conspired to prosecute Siegelman as a means of preventing his planned political comeback; told "60 Minutes" that Rove assigned her to try to catch Siegelman having extramarital sex; that she tried for several weeks, but failed

Mark Bollinger, Democratic operative, friend of Siegelman and Simpson; introduced her to the ex-governor in late 2006 or early 2007; assisted Simpson in researching finances of trial judge Mark Fuller

John Aaron, Birmingham lawyer, Siegelman operative and "political researcher;" among other things, helped Simpson with her affidavit and with researching Fuller's finances

Rob Riley, son of Gov. Bob Riley; knew Simpson from college and some shared legal cases; accused by her of participating on conspiracy

Bill Canary, Alabama Republican, wife of Leura Canary; accused by Simpson, others, of playing key role in Siegelman prosecution; often mischaracterized in media reports as a "Karl Rove protégé"

Grant Woods, old Siegelman friend; former Arizona attorney general; leader of the group of former attorneys general who wrote letters and filed briefs on Siegelman's behalf and generated substantial publicity for the Rove conspiracy claims

Robert Abrams, old Siegelman friend; former New York attorney general; leader of the group of former attorneys general who wrote letters and filed briefs on Siegelman's behalf and generated substantial publicity for the Rove conspiracy claims

Artur Davis, Alabama congressman; in 2007, became prominent advocate of Siegelman's claim that he was prosecuted for political reasons at the behest of Karl Rove

John Conyers, powerful, veteran Democratic Michigan congressman; chairman of U.S. House Judiciary Committee; wrote numerous letters to Justice Department demanding investigations of Siegelman prosecution; by far Siegelman's most powerful ally in making the case that he was a victim of Karl Rove and a politicized Justice Department

Introduction

"It's much like a puzzle. It started with this one voice saying somebody needs to look into this G.H. Construction matter."

-- Montgomery-based Assistant U.S. Attorney Louis Franklin, during October 2005 press conference announcing indictment of former Alabama Gov. Don Siegelman, former HealthSouth Corp. chairman Richard Scrushy, and two Siegelman cabinet members.

"Due to the bias and unprofessional behavior of this Mobile Register reporter, the Governor's Press Office does not respond to his requests. While we respect the Mobile Register, its other reporters and its editors, we regret the paper's decision to endorse Eddie Curran's unprofessional behavior. Among other inappropriate actions, Mr. Curran cursed a member of the governor's staff for almost five minutes, repeatedly calling him a 'fucking piece of rat shit.' Such behavior is inappropriate and unprofessional. We will not dignify it by continuing to communicate with this reporter."

-- Statement that the Siegelman administration asked the Register to include in each story by me and involving the governor, and in lieu of comments or responses to questions.

Years ago, a girlfriend and I rented a place on one of the small islands along the approach to Key West. As something of a bonus, our landlord taught me how to catch the Florida spiny lobster. This requires mask and snorkel, a net, a "tickle stick," and patience.

One takes a deep breath, submerges, and scours the man-made canals looking not for claws, since the Florida species has none, but for the two long thick antennae poking from their ocean insect heads. Our landlord made it look easy, rising from his second or third submersion with a thrashing lobster in his net. He said goodbye, wished me luck, and handed over the net and tickle stick.

In the next hour I dove down dozens of times, each time rising to blow water from my snorkel, suck in a lungful of air, and repeat, without once seeing a lobster. When finally I spied antennae protruding from the rock crevices, the finding bit became easy. It was like one of those patterns shown to children that suddenly reveals itself as something else entirely, and from that point on, reveals itself again and again.

Catching them is the fun if most difficult part. Lobster, Florida's anyway, don't so much see as sense, and this they do with their antennae. The trick is to goad the nocturnal creatures from their safe havens. One reaches over or around them, and often around rocks as well, to gently tap their tail with the tickle stick. Tap too rough, and dinner whooshes away. Play it right, and the confused lobster eases into open water and out of its element.

Hunter again reaches around prey, this time with the net, placing it open-faced and inches behind the tail. Quick, like setting a hook in a fish, you bop it in the nose with the tickle stick. The lobster, now a rocket in reverse, propels itself backwards and, one hopes, deep into the net, which must be twisted sharply to prevent the hyped up crustacean from escaping. Burning for air, you emerge from the blue water, holding high the squirming trophy.

That evening, our landlord told us how to cook the lobsters, an uncomplicated process easily summed up by saying they're boiled alive. But they should be cleaned before being dropped in the roiling water. Our landlord demonstrated how this was done. He ripped off one of the spiny antennae, shoved it in the lobster's rear, twisted it and carefully removed the vein or colon or whatever it was that, if left in, mars the taste. Then the landlord dropped it in the water. The lobster issued a high-pitched whine as it perished.

Then our landlord chuckled. "I've got this recurring nightmare," he said. "A giant lobster catches me, rips my arm off, sticks it in my behind, then throws me in boiling water."

We laughed along with him. But the image. It was hard to shake.

The final days of July 2001 were the worst of my professional life. I was as I deserved to be on the receiving end of a sharp reprimand from my editors. My only defense, that I'd been provoked, paled in comparison to my response -- an astonishing, explosive and vulgarity-laden tirade directed at a young Siegelman press aide, Rip Andrews. For several minutes, or before our city editor pried the phone from my hands, the newsroom looked on in shock as I invented cuss-word combinations at rock concert decibels

I soon found myself in the big corner office of *Mobile Register* Editor Mike Marshall, who was about as angry at me as I'd been moments before with Rip. But Mike seethed where I'd shouted. The short version: If I ever did that again, or anything close to it, I was gone. Fired, finished, no matter what.

In the days to come, Siegelman's people would call Mike to ask that he remove me from covering the administration. To my everlasting gratitude, he did not. Upset that I wasn't being removed or better yet, fired, the administration told Mike that it was putting together a list of other sins I'd committed and which it intended to present to Mike's boss, *Register* publisher Howard Bronson. Siegelman was in effect appealing Mike's decision to the paper's highest court.

Mike said I should chill out for several weeks, work on other things, and wait.

Siegelman, I knew, had skilled, ruthless opposition researchers at his disposal. These are the guys used by politicians to scour the backgrounds of opponents in search of misdeeds for use in negative campaign ads and the like. But instead of, say, Fob James, Siegelman's researchers were targeting me, or so I imagined.

The shoe's on the other foot, turnabout's fair play, call it what you want. To my way of thinking, I was being stalked by the Giant Lobster. The hunter turned prey, and not liking it one bit.

About two weeks later I was at my cubicle in the *Register's* stuffy, ages-old downtown Mobile newsroom when word came that Mike wanted to see me. I instinctively knew what for and shuffled to his corner office, wondering if a career in pizza delivery could support a wife and two young children.

Mike greeted me with a grin, and my paranoia melted away. Before he uttered the first word I knew I wasn't going to be fired or -- and it would have been equally awful – pulled off covering the administration and the bottomless pit of juicy stories waiting to be unearthed in Don's World.

"Most of this stuff is silly," Mike said, handing me the letter.

The letter, with a one-page attachment, was addressed to Mr. Bronson from Siegelman's new chief of staff, Jim Buckalew. A summary of the letter might be: "If the *Mobile Register* has an ounce of journalistic integrity, it will fire Eddie Curran."

Buckalew was an outsider, brought in the month before to provide maturity and an ethical compass to an administration lacking both. The exodus of Siegelman's first chief of staff Paul Hamrick, highway director Mack Roberts, and the demotion and eventual resignation of Nick Bailey -- gubernatorial driver, confidential assistant, state budget officer and a few other titles as well – followed a barrage of stories under my byline that began six months before and ignited a state and federal criminal investigation.

Five years later, Siegelman and former HealthSouth Corp. Chairman Richard Scrushy were found guilty of charges including bribery and extortion. Several witnesses -- most notably Bailey and the ubiquitous landfill developer/lobbyist Clayton "Lanny" Young -- had by then already pleaded guilty to bribery and other crimes. All, Scrushy included, appeared in my stories well before they were named in guilty pleas or indictments, as did Waste Management Inc., by a long shot the worst corporate actor in this story.

But in August 2001, I was the defendant. I sat down and with reddened face and bouncing knee, read the letter, then the second page entitled, "Personal and Confidential." This sheet of paper contained what amounted to a seven-count indictment against Edwin Jerome Curran III, DOB 10/21/61, WM, 6-3, 230 lb., brown hair, blue eyes.

The charges, in their entirety:

- Mr. Curran helped edit an ethics complaint filed against the governor and then reported on that complaint the next day. The Governor's Office has kept on file an edited copy of an ethics complaint Mr. Curran sent to the office and a copy of the final complaint filed with the Ethics Commission. The final version includes handwritten edits, some of which mirror the edits made by Mr. Curran. The following day, Mr. Curran wrote to Ted

Hosp, in an attempt to justify this matter. In doing so, he admitted that he had discussed the contents with Jim Zeigler, who filed the complaint, before it was filed.

- Mr. Curran engaged in an extreme display of temper during a conversation with a member of the governor's staff. He cursed at the staff member so loudly and for such a long time that another *Mobile Register* reporter felt compelled to express his embarrassment the next time he called the office. Mr. Curran's verbal attack lasted non-stop for more than five minutes. He called the staff member a "f—ing piece of rat s—t."

- During the last night of this year's Regular Session of the legislature, Ted Hosp walked into a Republican Senate office, where he found Mr. Curran drinking alcohol with a Republican senator, Claire Austin, and others. Drinking is not allowed in the Alabama State House.

- On the last night of this year's session, Mr. Curran became so inebriated at a Montgomery bar that he was not able to drive home. He had no money and asked then-Chief of Staff Paul Hamrick for $20 for a cab.

- Mr. Curran once commented to Mr. Hamrick about the breast sizes of women working in the Governor's Press Office.

- Mr. Curran called Press Secretary Carrie Kurlander at her home on a Saturday night after 9:30 p.m., in a non-emergency situation.

- After having the opportunity to interview members of the governor's staff for hours, Mr. Curran continued a pattern of harassment against certain staff members, including calling Nick Bailey once after midnight.

"Mike! This is crazy! That night at …" I went on and on, which wasn't really necessary, as Mike didn't appear concerned with the case against me.

A month later, after the Siegelman administration changed the state's public records policy to prevent me from seeing certain documents, the above charges were aired in a story in our paper. And lots of fun that was.

You can be sure that I will be addressing the charges, especially the one that troubled me most – that I helped edit an ethics complaint against the governor.

This is neither a biography of Don Siegelman nor a complete history of his first and only term as governor. It's a first person account of covering, or rather, uncovering, activities of the Siegelman administration that the governor never expected the public to learn about, much less be reported on with the level of detail and depth allowed me by my editors. It's the story of Siegelman's dark side, of the implosion of his obsessively crafted political career and in the end, of the disintegration of his character.

It's about at least $1.37 million in legal fees paid Siegelman during his four years as governor, and the use of a straw man to buy his Montgomery home for twice its value. It's about landfill giant Waste Management's use of serial briber

Lanny Young to win millions of dollars in concessions from the governor and his aides and the hick judge who ran Cherokee County, and the cynicism that had to exist for a company called Goat Hill Construction to steal from the state by forging a bogus receipt two days before it even incorporated itself.

It's the story of a New South Governor as disseminating shakedown artist.

As the scandals piled up in the final two years of his administration, one was forever hearing folks declare that Siegelman had wasted so much talent and promise. "It's such a pity," they'd say. "Don was going to be our New South governor." Or, "Don was the most talented politician of his generation."

Siegelman's fall was a greater tragedy for himself, his family and a handful of associates than for the people of Alabama. The state has not suffered in his absence.

I expect that readers will wonder if I was out to get Don Siegelman. It's a question I asked myself many times. Certainly I developed a distaste for the man. Over time these feelings mellowed into pity and a skewed admiration, or rather, astonishment that someone could day in and day out be as willfully full of it as he. At some point it becomes an accomplishment and a source of wonder.

For most of the period covered in this book, I viewed him as less man than machine – open his skull and you'd find wires. To my surprise, he and I got along well during his 2006 trial. Not until then did I witness the side I should have realized existed all along, given his success with voters over three decades.

I came to see the former governor as part Peter Pan, part Pinocchio, a 62-year-old boy whose life is a perpetual campaign, for votes and reflections of love from as many people as he can reach, whether with a handshake and a smile or a television interview. I saw a man who could no more walk past a television camera without stopping than he could answer a pointed question with the truth. Whoppers ushered from his mouth without hint of shame or recognition at the absurdity of his declarations.

After the trial, one of his co-defendants, four-time former highway director Mack Roberts, described Siegelman as being among "the nicest people I've ever been around."

"Personally, I really, really like him and he's smart, and I hope things work out for him, but we disagreed on a few things," said Roberts, putting it gently. "Most governors I worked for were kind of stand-offish – Wallace, Folsom, Governor Hunt – they were the governor and kind of stand-offish, but Siegelman was a lot more personable."

This won't be an exercise in modesty. I will go ahead and declare that, were it not for my stories, Don Siegelman would have won a second term as governor. Of that there is, in my mind, in many others' and I feel sure in Siegelman's as well, no question. Nor, though, will I minimize my mistakes and excesses. I will defend myself, but hopefully not in a way that prevents you from making up your mind about the reporter as well as the governor.

My hope is that you will come to understand not just Siegelman's descent into corruption, but also the process of researching and writing investigative news stories. Because of Watergate, most people assume there's a Deep Throat behind every such piece. Even when there is, sources rarely take a reporter all the way to the well, as Deep Throat most assuredly did not for Woodward and Bernstein.

Some of the Siegelman stories originated with tips, such as those on the G.H. Construction warehouse scandal. Others, including the reports on the sale of Siegelman's house and the series that led to Scrushy, began with hunches.

With none of those stories, regardless of origin, could the finished product have been foreseen from the initial tip or hunch.

With each there was an adventure, or in any event, my idea of one.

Preface

Fast Forward to Martyrdom

"This is like the kind of thing that would happen in Nazi Germany. You never would believe it would happen in the United States."
-- Robert Kennedy Jr., during April 2008 interview with Siegelman on his "Ring of Fire" radio program.

"It is extremely disturbing that Don Siegelman, the former governor of Alabama, was hauled off to jail this week. There is reason to believe his prosecution may have been a political hit, intended to take out the state's most prominent Democrat, a serious charge that has not been adequately investigated. The appeals court that hears his case should demand answers, as should Congress."
-- From, "Questions About a Governor's Fall," a June 30, 2007, editorial in the New York Times, and the first of three times for the paper's editorial staff to apply the phrase "political hit" to the Siegelman case.

On June 29, 2006, a federal jury in Montgomery found Siegelman and former HealthSouth chief Richard Scrushy guilty of public corruption charges.

Perhaps the most memorable response that day came from Terry Butts, the former Alabama Supreme Court justice and one of Scrushy's lawyers. With reporters and television cameras converged upon Scrushy like a rugby scrum, a cherry-faced Butts burst in and in full bullhorn voice howled that the verdict was "the worst miscarriage of justice since Sherman burned Atlanta."

It was an odd proclamation, especially considering that another of Scrushy's lawyers – famed civil rights attorney Fred Gray – had in his closing argument implored jurors to "make Dr. (Martin Luther) King's dream come true by returning a verdict of not guilty" against Scrushy.

Whether the worst miscarriage of justice since the torching of Atlanta, a repudiation of King's dream – or neither – one thing's for certain. There was no national outcry over the verdict.

Not a peep, and for almost a year.

Then along came Jill.

Seven months later, near the end of 2006, the Bush-controlled U.S. Justice Department fired eight of the country's 93 United States attorneys. The following month, after more than a decade as the minority party in both houses of Congress, Democrats returned to Washington in control of the House and Senate.

During the Clinton years, the Republican dominated Congress waged an endless series of probes into the Democratic administration, many of which seemed designed not so much to uncover wrongdoing as to sap the energies and resources of the Clinton presidency. Now it was the Democrats' turn to exercise oversight and scrutiny over a Republican president. Right out of the box, Democrats turned their attentions to the U.S. Attorney firings.

The matter appeared to reach its apogee in April 2007, following the Congressional testimony of Attorney General Alberto Gonzales. His appearance didn't unearth any bombshells, such as something that would vault the firings into the stratosphere of super-scandal. Rather, it revealed Gonzales as someone who generously could be said to have memory issues but foremost as unqualified for the job as the country's top law enforcement officer. Even administration stalwarts like Republican Senator Jeff Sessions of Alabama urged his removal.

Though Gonzales would hang on for a few more months, his fate was sealed, and the U.S. Attorneys scandal seemed to be petering out.

Then, on May 21, 2007, Rainsville, Ala., lawyer Dana Jill Simpson drove across the border to Georgia to sign an affidavit she drafted with help from John Aaron, a Birmingham lawyer and Siegelman confidante. Simpson had been introduced to Aaron and Siegelman by Mark Bollinger, a client and friend of hers and a behind the scenes operator and Siegelman pal from way back.

By late May, Simpson had been in communication with Siegelman, Scrushy and lawyers and representatives for both men going on four months. She even researched the finances of Mark Fuller, the federal judge who presided over the 2006 trial, and gave those records to defendants.

At the time, Simpson was 43, twice-divorced, more than $100,000 behind on her mortgage payments, drowning in tax liens and living with her mother. On her way to Georgia, she telephoned Richard Scrushy to give him the good news. She had completed the affidavit and was about to sign it before a notary public.

Days later the affidavit was filed, not in a court of law, but with the *New York Times* and *Time* magazine.

Simpson's affidavit opened with a statement of questionable verisimilitude, it being: "I am over the age of eighteen and *of sound mind.*"

The claims within, like her subsequent tales, are notable for their breadth, boldness and complete lack of corroborating witnesses. She placed herself, Zelig-like, at the center of the leading political events of the day, and not just as witness, but as change-agent, quietly altering the course of recent Alabama political history.

Simpson was often described in the media, primarily on the national level, as a "Republican operative." In truth she was no such thing, or in any event, not one known as such by actual Republicans. State GOP leaders used the strongest language possible to convey this to the likes of CBS News and the *New York Times*, and over and over again. It didn't do the first bit of good.

Her imaginary role as Republican *uber operative* was a necessary component of what I will call, to play it safe and avoid offense, "The Massively Brazen Incredibly Goofy Hoax That Suckered Some of the Top Names in American Journalism."

Before Simpson was finished – and she may well still be going -- arms of the anti-Siegelman octopus came to include the White House and specifically, Karl Rove; officials high and low in the U.S. Justice Department; Alabama Gov. Bob Riley and his son Rob; Fuller, the judge; Birmingham-based U.S. Attorney Alice Martin; Montgomery-based U.S. Attorney Leura Canary and her husband; all involved high and low with the Siegelman prosecution, including assistant U.S. attorneys Louis Franklin and Steve Feaga; and contracting officials and one assumes generals within the U.S. Air Force.

Her allegations were not merely uncorroborated but refuted, emphatically and convincingly, by every victim of her fertile imagination. Those for whom her story was too good *not* to be true treated these denials as speed bumps and kept on going.

In no time the prosecution of Siegelman was being portrayed, as the *New York Times* put it, applying mafia lingo, as a "political hit.'"

Post Simpson, the *Times* was to cite Siegelman's plight in 15 editorials and three op-ed pieces. The paper's news side leaped on the story too, publishing 24 articles leading readers to the same conclusions as the opinion pieces. Neither the editorial page nor the *Times'* news staff had paid any attention to the Siegelman case until Simpson's affidavit.

But the nation's paper of record was hardly alone.

"Selective Justice in Alabama?" asked a headline one of four conspiracy-fueled pieces by *Time* magazine senior reporter Adam Zagorin.

"Did Ex-Alabama Governor Get a Raw Deal?" wondered "60 Minutes."

Not surprisingly, those reports and many others delivered resounding yes verdicts such questions.

The "Free Don Siegelman" web-site, which popped up after he went to prison in July 2007, presented a biography of Simpson under the link, "Heroes."

"Life-long Alabama Republican, ex-campaign worker for Bob Riley and modern-day Joan of Arc -- a rare true believer in truth, justice and the 'American way,'" it began, and from there slid into a fantastical tale of GOP operatives trying to kill her by setting her mother's house afire and trying to run her off the road.

The primary assertion of Simpson's affidavit was that Siegelman ended his protracted recount battle and conceded the 2002 governor's race because of something she did.

Specifically, the then-governor cashed in his chips when one of Bob Riley's lawyers confronted him and his election attorneys with pictures Simpson took at a Ku Klux Klan rally in Scottsboro, Ala., held two weeks after the election. The pictures -- which almost surely never existed -- were said by Simpson to show a Democratic operative frolicking about the rally with Bob Riley for governor signs.

The upshot: Simpson had caught the Democrats and by extension Siegelman perpetrating a dirty trick designed to portray Riley as a racist – all of this, mind you, after the election, and with no possible impact on the vote total.

Simpson claimed she called the Riley campaign and many of its key players gathered on a conference call to hear her report on the KKK rally. It's her story, and hers alone, that during the call, influential Alabama Republican Bill Canary began bragging about his friends in high places and how they could ensure the end of Siegelman's political career.

Three years before likening Richard Scrushy's conviction to the defeat of the Confederacy, Terry Butts was retained by Bob Riley to assist with the election dispute. Siegelman had lost by about 3,000 votes, refused to concede, and as happens in such situations, both sides lawyered up.

In her affidavit and later statements Simpson cast Butts in the role of Riley's consigliere. She claimed the former judge met secretly with Siegelman and his lawyers, laid out the KKK shots like a straight flush, and watched the Dems' jaws drop. According to Simpson, Butts told the governor that the pictures would vanish if he would concede. It worked, so petrified was Siegelman of public release of the KKK pics.

Butts likened Simpson's affidavit to the musings of "a drunk fiction writer."

"As to Ms. Simpson's allegations about concern over a Ku Klux Klan rally involving campaign signs of Governor Riley, I simply do not know of anyone who would give a good Southern 'damn' or a 'hoot in hell' about what the KKK thinks, either before, during, or after an election on any issue. Certainly this would be particularly true as to the placing of anyone's campaign signs at a Klan rally <u>after</u> an election."

Similar if less colorful renunciations of Simpson's tale by others should have been more than enough to shatter her credibility. But her affidavit didn't stop with the KKK meeting. She added a fourth K.

K for Karl. As in Rove. As in Bush's brain.

Simpson's sworn statement placed the notoriously Machiavellian Rove at dead center of a conspiracy to destroy Siegelman for good and all time by prosecuting him on trumped up charges.

The non-KKK elements of her affidavit were formally presented to Attorney General Gonzales in a July 17, 2007, letter from John Conyers, the Michigan Democrat and chairman of the House Judiciary Committee.

Wrote Conyers:

> *"In May 2007, Jill Simpson, a Republican attorney in Alabama who had worked for Mr. Siegelman's 2002 Republican opponent, wrote in an affidavit that in 2002, a former protégé of Karl Rove told a small group of Republican political operatives that Karl Rove and two U.S. Attorneys in Alabama were working to 'take care' of Mr. Siegelman. The Rove protégé, Bill Canary, is married to Leura Canary, who President Bush appointed in 2001 to be the U.S. Attorney in the Middle District of Alabama.*
>
> *"In 2005, the U.S. Attorney's Office in the Middle District of Alabama indicted Mr. Siegelman. In her affidavit, Ms. Simpson said that Bill Canary told her and two colleagues that 'Karl (Rove) had spoken with the Department of Justice and the Department was already pursuing Don Siegelman.' The phone call that Ms. Simpson was referring to occurred in November 2002, when Mr. Siegelman was seeking a recount of the vote he had just lost, and when Republican operatives were concerned that Mr. Siegelman could be a significant political threat in future elections."*

Simpson's history-changing version of the election's end was, in addition to bizarre, disputed by everyone in a position to know. Among that number were Siegelman and his election lawyers. All said they'd never heard of the KKK pictures and recalled no such meeting with Butts.

The failure of Simpson's imaginings to match reality didn't stop Siegelman from calling her a "great American citizen."

"She is a whistle-blower who now has placed Karl Rove at the scene of a crime that the United States Congress is currently investigating," he said.

Siegelman, arguably betraying a lack of proportion, said Rove's involvement in his case would "make Watergate look like child's play."

Thanks to Simpson's affidavit, the tantalizing story sold by Siegelman and his backers and some abysmal journalism, the Rove-led plot to annihilate Don Siegelman became, but for those who knew better, fact. Her patron saint and the intellectual leader of the Free Siegelman Movement was Scott Horton, a legal affairs writer for *Harper's* and columnist for the magazine's web page.

Those who Horton viewed as doubting Simpson or contributing to Siegelman's demise invariably discovered that they'd participated in a conspiracy worse than anything even Simpson could dream up.

Members of this despicable coterie range from Rove all the way down to the lowly Alabama press. In a backhanded compliment if ever there was one, Horton wrote that Simpson's affidavit was "treated as explosive news by *Time Magazine* and the *New York Times* but met with 'awkward silence' by the *Birmingham News* and *Mobile Press Register*.

He accused the papers and its reporters (primarily myself at the *Press Register* and Brett Blackledge and Kim Chandler at the *News*) of conspiring to plot Siegelman's demise, and compared the journalism practiced at Alabama's two largest papers to that from "the Soviet press of the pre-Gorbachev age."

Through appearances on TV and radio, broad coverage on left-leaning Internet sites and back-channel discussions with the likes of CBS News and the House Judiciary Committee, Horton exerted an impact on the coverage of the case that far exceeded the real estate granted him on *Harper's* web-site.

In October 2007, the new star for one of the oldest names in American journalism declared with typical brio that Siegelman was the victim of "the most brazen political prosecution in U.S. history."

Finally, America, we had one: Our own Nelson Mandela.

Here is his story.

PART ONE:
1946 to 2001

Chapter 1
Golden Flake

"He's been focused on getting here for a long time. I don't know exactly what drives people like that, the types that were just destined for public service. But he's one of them, and I'm glad there are people out there like him."

-- The late Jim Hayes, a college friend of Siegelman's and a member of his cabinet, before the onslaught of G.H. Construction and other scandals.

"Don Siegelman, in my opinion, is one of the greatest con artists who ever served in the annals of government. He's cold, mean, ruthless and vindictive, and he wants all the power."

-- Democratic state representative Alvin Holmes of Montgomery, in July 1999, two years before scandals overwhelmed the administration.

Tacked on the press room wall in the Alabama Statehouse among dozens of political cartoons and furled, yellowed photos of reporters interviewing governors and presidents is an ad from the 1998 gubernatorial campaign. "What's The Difference Between Bill Clinton And Don Siegelman?" reads the caption.

On the top left is a photo of Siegelman. Across the page, a grimacing Clinton. Below are categories -- Military, Political, Civil Rights and Drug History -- with brief expositions that, when compared to that in the other man's column, suggests twins separated at birth.

At the bottom are six head shots, the one on the far left, Siegelman, on the far right, Clinton, with those in between reflecting a gradual metamorphosis, Siegelman's face becoming Clinton's.

"The More They Change, The More They Stay The Same," declares the big print at the bottom.

The ad's obvious intent was to transfer the almost pathological hatred of Clinton among so many white Alabamians to Siegelman. And there are remarkable parallels in the lives of the two men born six months apart, with Siegelman the elder. Both are Southerners from modest backgrounds, extroverts for whom the drive for public office – high public office – seems to have formed in the womb.

The most unfair of the frequently voiced criticisms of both men, to my mind anyway, is that they're "career politicians."

Is that really so terrible? Didn't your parents or your first grade teacher or both or in any event someone tell you that in this great country, anyone can "grow up to be president" and "change the world?" And when you heard that, didn't you, if for only a moment, but maybe for a day or a week or a year, secretly imagine, and with little person seriousness, your destiny as ... President of the United States?

Washington, Lincoln, Me?

Is it really so terrible if a little boy or girl actually takes it to heart, and says, "I can and I will?"

One imagines something like this happening to the young Clinton in Arkansas, and down in Mobile, the boy Siegelman.

Don Eugene Siegelman was born in Mobile on Feb. 24, 1946, the second and last child of Leslie Bouchet and Andrea Siegelman. Father Les was the manager a well-known downtown music store; mother Andrea worked as beautician, starting at 16 and retiring at 72.

Les Siegelman Jr., three when Siegelman was born, would in adulthood serve as one of his brother's most trusted advisors, if also his least visible.

Siegelman's father suffered three heart attacks by age 55, but lived a full life. He died in July 1999 at age 85, seven months after seeing his son become governor. Andrea Siegelman died the following year after a long battle with Alzheimer's.

The elder Siegelman's early heart troubles and the family's history of heart disease may explain Don Siegelman's legendary exercise regime. As governor and before, he was known to arrive at the Montgomery YMCA at 5 a.m. It was closed at that hour, but no matter. He had his own key. A physical during his third year as governor showed the 6-1, 190-pound governor with a resting heartbeat of 50, or about what you'd expect from a marathon runner. He also holds a black belt in Kyokushin-style karate.

In many ways, Siegelman's youth paralleled my father's, though my dad is 14 years his senior. Both grew up in the shadow of downtown Mobile, their childhood homes within a mile of one another, and at a time when downtown was still the city's center, commercially and otherwise. Siegelman, like my father, attended Leinkauf Elementary School, junior high at Barton Academy, and finished up at Murphy, still the largest high school in the city.

An old friend recalled Siegelman as being "very politically oriented" in middle school and never looking back. At Murphy, the handsome, sandy blond teen was elected class president as a sophomore and served on the student council his junior and senior years. He was a class favorite, homecoming escort and, perhaps most impressively, the first president of Mobile's Junior Jaycees. In short, he amassed the sort of extra-curricular resume one might expect from a young man with his eye on political prizes.

Siegelman graduated from high school in 1964 and that fall enrolled at the University of Alabama. Like my father before and many of my friends since, Siegelman "pledged Deke," which is to say he was asked to join the fraternity

Delta Kappa Epsilon, long-known for its many Mobile members, a reputation for partying, and its ties to "the Machine." That's the voting bloc of fraternities and sororities that's long dominated politics at the university and has served as a training ground for many of the state's leading politicians.

Siegelman immersed himself in campus politics upon arrival in Tuscaloosa. A partial list of his activities and accomplishments includes: winning election as a senator in the Student Government Association as a sophomore and junior; member of Jasons; Who's Who in American College Students; and, his senior year, as SGA president.

"All the girls tore his campaign posters down and put them in their rooms. They loved his blond hair and green eyes," said Danny Sheridan, the sports oddsmaker and a friend since childhood.

Socially, Siegelman knew how to enjoy himself but was not regarded in high school or college as a big partier. "He was a conservative guy. Not to say he never had a drink and never got drunk. He may have," said Sheridan. "But there were people you knew who raised hell, and he was definitely not one of them. Every day he woke up with his blinders on saying, 'I think I can make a difference.'"

Having risen to the greatest heights possible for a politically-minded collegian in the state of Alabama, Siegelman took the next logical step, law school. For someone intending to practice in Alabama, the university's law school was the place to go. That's where you met the people who'd become the attorneys and judges you'd practice with, against and in front of.

But Siegelman had no intention of making a career of the law. And in choosing Georgetown (where Clinton had just completed his undergraduate degree) he killed two birds with one stone. He got a law degree and spent three years near that big white house of his dreams, building connections with national-level Democrats. He served as a part-time staffer in the office of Allard Lowenstein, an anti-war Democratic congressman from New York, and worked briefly as a Capitol Hill police officer (which he later cited in campaigns to burnish his law enforcement credentials.)

He enlisted in the Alabama Air National Guard and served 19 months before being discharged for medical reasons in 1969, at age 23.

Former attorney general Charlie Graddick tried to make an issue of the discharge in the 1994 lieutenant governor's campaign, but to no discernable effect. Graddick claimed Siegelman was released for "severe psychiatric" problems. Siegelman countered that it was an honorable discharge due to severe stress. He said his father was suffering health problems and had lost his job and that concerns about his family probably brought on the stress.

"Twenty-five years ago, as an airman, I had some physical symptoms, including headaches, dizziness, high blood pressure and extreme physical discomfort," he said during the 1994 campaign. "On one occasion, I blacked out while driving a fuel truck."

One has to believe that if Siegelman had sought high national office – say, the vice presidential slot on a Democratic ticket or straight to the big-time from a perch as governor or headline-making U.S. Senator -- that the circumstances of his release would have been fleshed out. Even if all else had fallen into place, Siegelman's characterization of a war-time discharge due to stress would seem sufficient to prevent voters from placing him in the White House or within a heartbeat of it.

In March 1971, the 24-year-old law student married a Mobile woman his same age and, like him, a Catholic. The union didn't last long, was annulled, and was never an issue in Siegelman's political career.

He graduated from law school in 1972 and returned to Alabama to serve as state coordinator for George McGovern's presidential campaign. After McGovern's defeat Siegelman studied at Oxford, though not, like Clinton before him, as a Rhodes Scholar. He focused on international law, one imagines for the purpose of adding foreign policy creds to the political curriculum vitae.

He returned home in 1973 and for the next five years served as general counsel and executive director of the state Democratic Party. He also worked part-time prosecuting minor crimes for the city of Vestavia Hills, a high-income outpost of Birmingham.

In 1978, the 31-year-old Siegelman made an unusual choice for his inevitable first run at public office. In 1944, when there was almost no such thing as women holding state office, Alabamians elected Sybil Pool as secretary of state. For the next 35 years, the office whose primary function is overseeing elections was run by a woman. That streak ended when Siegelman captured 71 percent of the vote in the Democratic primary, and faced no Republican opposition in the general election.

It was also an important period for him personally. That year Siegelman stepped into a Birmingham elevator and met Lori Allen, a pretty, 27-year-old social worker with an artistic bent. They wed two years later, in October 1980, in a small ceremony at Siegelman's home in Montgomery. He must have been smitten, for in Alabama, the marriage promised risk for a young man whose sole ambition was high office. Siegelman is a Catholic in a state that had never elected a Catholic governor, and Lori Allen is Jewish.

It's a credit to the public and his opponents that religious affiliation, his or his wife's, was not an issue for him politically. Though it is not widely known, the Siegelmans raised their two children in the Jewish faith.

The new secretary of state hit the ground running. He transformed the office, adding staff and cajoling the legislature into providing budget increases. His critics accused him of spending too much on public relations staff and furniture, but acknowledged that he modernized the small agency. He advocated for increased voter registration and election turn-out and backed legislation to purge Alabama's voter rolls of the dead, incarcerated, and other ineligibles.

Siegelman used the office as a bully pulpit, slinging arrows at the legislature and the governor (first Fob James, then George Wallace) and grabbing headlines with blistering commentaries on issues that strayed from his office's purview, including one with hypocrisy relevance for this story.

The secretary of state has no role in the regulation of landfills, but that didn't stop Siegelman from making Chemical Waste Management Inc., his personal whipping boy. He accused the Waste Management subsidiary of violating environmental laws at its hazardous waste landfill in Emelle, and of paying kickbacks to un-identified politicians.

More about the southwest Alabama landfill will be said later, in the chapter chronicling ChemWaste's payment of half-a-million dollars to Lanny Young. That sum was bestowed upon Young after a secret state ruling by the Siegelman administration that slashed the taxes ChemWaste paid to bury waste at Emelle. A month after the ruling, Waste Management donated $50,000 to Siegelman's lottery campaign.

As secretary of state, Siegelman pushed hard for campaign finance reform. He made passage of the Fair Campaign Practices Act the centerpiece of his 1978 and 1982 campaigns. The much-needed legislation, when finally it did pass, required candidates to disclose their contributions and expenditures before an election, rather than at year's end, when such revelations did voters little good.

"Politics costs too much," Siegelman told a reporter during his 1978 campaign. "Not only have we priced the average person out of politics (but) people perceive politics as a dirty game."

He declared that the legislation must include "strict and severe penalties for anyone who either tries to bribe or use a public official to their own advantage and to punish people who abuse public office."

"We don't need to be sending people to Maxwell Air Force Base to play tennis" after being found guilty of public corruption, he said.

Siegelman's adherence to campaign finance laws as governor was abysmal, but he flouted them even while touting them as the state's top elections officer.

In 1985, he began unofficially campaigning for the U.S. Senate, which suggests that early on, his goals were national in scope. Senators, after all, rarely come home to be governors. It was no secret that Richard Shelby, then a Democratic congressman from Tuscaloosa, planned to challenge vulnerable Republican incumbent Jeremiah Denton. Shelby had amassed a war-chest in excess of $1 million. The federal campaign law required candidates to disclose their contributions once they accepted more than $5,000. Siegelman raised far more than that but neglected to file a report. A Shelby relative tattled on him to the Federal Elections Commission and the media.

"Don Siegelman, who has pushed for stricter financial disclosure laws for political candidates, was accused of violating federal election laws in a complaint filed Monday by his Democratic opponent's nephew," began an Associated Press story on Siegelman's unreported fundraising.

Siegelman's response should be familiar to anyone who's followed his career: He was unavailable for comment, but had an aide criticize the source of the complaint rather than its merits. It was later revealed that Siegelman raised $199,400, or about 40 times the reporting threshold.

Siegelman reluctantly faced up to Shelby's towering advantage in campaign cash, lowered his sights, and ran for attorney general.

———

Siegelman has done much to advance the notion that his convictions are skin deep, but even his harshest critics don't question his sincerity on one issue.

On a Saturday morning in February 1984, he and his wife loaded up their dogs for a drive to his parents' beach house on Dauphin Island. Wallace Manning, a career criminal with a history of drunken driving arrests was heading north on Dauphin Island Parkway. Given his blood alcohol level of almost 3.0, it's a wonder Manning could drive at all.

As Manning approached the Dog River Bridge he jerked into the southbound lane, directly into the Siegelmans' path. Manning's car climbed theirs, his bumper crashing through the windshield on the passenger side and flush into Lori Siegelman's face. Her survival was a miracle. The front of Manning's car shattered almost every bone in her face, knocked out 17 teeth, and crushed her left eye. Siegelman suffered minor injuries, and one of the dogs was killed.

It was six weeks before Lori Siegelman could return home from the hospital, and then, with a glass eye. She eventually regained her health and both the couple's children were born after the wreck.

In years to come, as attorney general, lieutenant governor, then governor, Siegelman fought for stronger DUI laws.

———

Cal Franklin met Siegelman in the 1970s and the Democratic Party chief made a big impression on the teenager. In the mid-80s, Franklin took a break from his job editing a weekly paper to join Siegelman's campaign for attorney general. Franklin served a position known in politics as "the body man," whose job it is to "make sure the candidate gets where he's supposed to be," Franklin said.

"I enjoyed my relationship with Siegelman. He instilled a work ethic in me that still carries on. There's nobody that works harder than Don Siegelman. We were like daylight to dark, and his schedule was meticulous. He had his appointments down to every 15 to 30 minutes, the drive time, how long we were going to stay there – he taught me about organization in that 1986 race," Franklin said.

"There's one thing about Don that a lot of people don't know – at times, he can have a very volatile temper. But once he's over it, he'll never think about it again and why it was he was mad at you. He's just got that flash temper. One reason he'll get on your ass is to see how strong you are. He'll challenge you just to see how strong you are. If you cower he'll lose respect for you. He likes for you to get back in his face. That's the reason why he liked (Dewayne) Freeman. Freeman (state senator, future Siegelman cabinet member) would get back in his face."

Siegelman had a thoughtful side, too, and made a habit of calling aides on birthdays and other special occasions. "He had a good sense of humor, and would laugh and crack jokes with you, but there was also the temper, especially if you worked for him. If things weren't going right, you could feel the pressure, but he rewarded you with praise when things were going right," Franklin said.

Siegelman faced three legitimate candidates in the 1986 Democrat primary and still cracked 50 percent to avoid a run-off. It was a powerful showing and reflected voters' approval of his give 'em hell, headline-making tenure as secretary of state. With no Republican candidates, the office of attorney general was his.

———

Alabama's chief elections officer faced several brushes with trouble in the mid-1980s, all of which, while unflattering, were relatively minor. His responses to these scandal speed bumps foretold a pattern that would be repeated again and again, never more so than after he became governor.

The first occurred in 1980, when reporters for the *Birmingham Post Herald* learned that Siegelman was using his state car to drive to Birmingham for karate lessons. When asked if this was so, Siegelman denied it. It was the wrong answer. The *Post-Herald* reporters had observed Siegelman's Thursday night rituals for weeks. They'd witnessed him backing his car up to the building, the better to hide his state plates.

When told he had been seen, Siegelman 'fessed up. Sort of. Yes, he had driven to six lessons in his state car, but only because he was already in town on state business. When the reporters asked him to provide evidence of state work in Birmingham on those days, he couldn't. "I think it's more of a habit than anything else. But it just looks bad. I don't like having to use a state car," he said, explaining why he had tried to hide the state plates by backing into the spot.

In the second example, Siegelman faced an ethics complaint accusing him of using his public position to arrange cut-rate flying lessons and free flying time. The complaint was filed in 1986, though the activity occurred three years before.

At issue was a 1983 letter to a local outfit called Montgomery Aviation and sent on secretary of state letterhead. "I would like very much to take flying lessons, however, the expense is holding me back. I just don't have two thousand – personal – dollars that I can commit at this time," he wrote.

He asked if the company could give him 10 hours of free time for every 100 hours accrued by state agencies that leased planes. At the time, the company offered 10 hours free for every 100 hours purchased by a client. Siegelman was suggesting that the free time be given him personally; and if that idea didn't fly, he suggested another: "What about the public relations value of me doing TV commercials endorsing Montgomery Aviation?"

Siegelman didn't return calls from the Associated Press but gave a Birmingham reporter a vague statement, something about trying to save the state money. He couldn't say more, he said, because the Ethics Commission had banned him from talking about the case. This was malarkey, and quickly refuted by Ethics Director Melvin Cooper, who said the commission had no authority to silence people accused of ethics violations.

Siegelman was cleared, but still declined comment. Instead, he criticized the political motive of his accuser and pledged that as attorney general he would "work with this commission to reform our ethics laws."

With the flying case, Siegelman established the scandal response template that served him for the remainder of his career.

Step One: Cite legal restraints in refusing to address the specifics of an accusation.

Step Two: Claim political bias on the part of accusers or prosecutors. Something like: "The people of Alabama see this for what it was – a political attack by enemies opposed to my plans to improve the lives of the citizens of this state, and especially the children."

These and another mild scrape with the ethics law involving a campaign solicitation letter to lawyers and Siegelman's responses to the allegations contributed to a wit's branding him, "Golden Flake," a play on the Birmingham-based potato chip-maker.

They also reveal Siegelman as a risk-taker, and not just in pushing the envelope of the ethics laws. Siegelman became a pilot, is a lifelong motorcycle rider, and a black belt in karate. The man likes adrenaline rushes.

––––––

Franklin, the former driver, believes Siegelman might have run into more problems during those years if not for the almost constant presence of Larry Childers, a top aide and spokesman who served Siegelman during his terms as secretary of state and as attorney general.

"Larry would get back in his face and say, 'No, you can't do that. That is politically wrong.'" said Franklin. "He was the doorkeeper, the guard who kept a lot of the BS out. In my opinion, Lanny Young would never have gotten close to Siegelman if Larry had still been around. Larry was suspicious of people and their motives and could say no to Don."

Childers and Redding Pitt – the future U.S. Attorney and a top aide to Siegelman during the 1980s -- both had more than a few opportunities to say no, said Franklin. "Don had like 10,000 ideas a day, and some of them were probably borderline right or wrong, and those guys knew what to do and what not to do."

Franklin suspects that many of Siegelman's problems to come could have been avoided but for the inability or unwillingness of Paul Hamrick and Nick Bailey to, in Franklin's words, "get in his face and say no."

―――

In mid-1989, with almost two years remaining in an unremarkable tenure as attorney general, Siegelman announced plans to run for governor. He had raised more than $600,000, but for the first time in four races, Siegelman faced a foe as known and well-funded as he in Paul Hubbert, the chief lobbyist and executive director of the state teachers' union -- the powerful Alabama Education Association.

As he would in all four of his gubernatorial runs -- 1990, 1998, 2002, and 2006 -- Siegelman campaigned on a pledge to seek a state lottery to help fund education. He polled well early and finished second in the four-candidate Democratic primary. Hubbert, though, dispensed of him easily in the run-off.

Siegelman blamed his first electoral loss on money. He ran out of it near the end and swore that wouldn't happen again, said Franklin. The defeat transformed him from an able fund-raiser to a demanding, threatening one, paving the way for his comeback as well as his eventual destruction. In nominating Hubbert, Democratic voters sentenced Siegelman to four years in the political wilderness, away from the public eye, took a four-year chunk out of his life, really. From that point on, campaign donations became to Siegelman as blood to a vampire.

"It was very tough because he'd never lost a race and everybody thought that was his political obituary," Franklin said. "In a way, it made him stronger. By beating him, Paul Hubbert taught him how to raise money – that that's what you have to do to get elected. To be honest with you, at that level, you have to do it. We got outspent, and when the next election came around, he learned how to raise funds. Before, it just killed him to make calls to people asking for money, and he had to be forced to do it. But 1990 taught him a lesson. He adapted well, let's put it that way."

After the loss Siegelman, his wife, and two young children remained in Montgomery. He practiced law, if only in the most limited sense. He made some news with an environmental lawsuit in Mobile County, but for the most part, his practice consisted of referring personal injury cases to a Mobile law firm and pocketing a portion of the proceeds if the lawsuits made money.

But his vocation wasn't law, it was politics. So what next?

Federal office was out of the question since he had no intention of running as a mere congressman. Alabama's two U.S. Senators, Howell Heflin and Shelby, were popular, well-funded Democrats. No opportunity there at all.

Hubbert had lost to incumbent Republican Guy Hunt in the 1990 general election. Hunt's win had an upside for Siegelman, ensuring there would be no incumbent in 1994.

Then along came Jimmy Evans.

In the fall of 1991, the Democratic attorney general received a referral from the Ethics Commission, which had found probable cause that Hunt violated the ethics law by using state planes to fly to preaching assignments. Following his sermons, the ordained Primitive Baptist preacher accepted payment in the form of the now famous "love offerings" collected from congregations.

During the investigation Evans' staff came across something called the Hunt Transition and Inaugural Fund Inc. This was a non-profit created to raise money for Hunt's inaugural celebration and upgrade the Governor's Mansion. Hunt, it turned out, had funneled some $200,000 out of the fund, routed it through bank accounts, and used it to pay off personal debts and buy cattle, fencing and furniture for his farm and home in Cullman.

Attorneys for the tall, slow-talking, silver-haired Hunt presented two basic defenses – that he was a simple farmer preacher without a college education who was only following advice from his lawyers; and that he was merely repaying himself for past campaign loans, the largest a $185,000 debt he claimed to have incurred during a very unsuccessful 1978 run for governor. The prosecution produced evidence indicating that the old campaign loans had been repaid long ago.

On April 13, 1993, a young Evans aide gave the opening statement in Hunt's trial. Assistant Attorney General Steve Feaga told jurors that the governor "sold his oath of office" by using $200,000 raised "for the public welfare." That money, said Feaga, "wound up in the back pocket of the defendant."

Thirteen years later, the same Steve Feaga, by then an Assistant U.S. Attorney, presented the opening argument to jurors picked to consider federal criminal charges against Siegelman, Scrushy, Paul Hamrick and Mack Roberts.

On April 23, 1993, a Montgomery County jury found Hunt guilty of misusing the transition fund money. He was removed him from office and replaced by Democrat Lt. Gov. Jim Folsom Jr.

Folsom, a political blue-blood with a fraction of Siegelman's drive and talent, not only slid into the governor's mansion, but assumed the mantle as his party's nominee in '94. If Folsom were to win that election, as most expected, he would be eligible to run again in 1998.

The result of this confluence of events: Siegelman probably couldn't mount a realistic campaign for governor until 2002, by which time he would be 56. One imagines that the young Siegelman's timeline showed him as governor or U.S. senator if not vice president by 1993. But he was neither. In fact, he was nothing. At 47, his trajectory had flat-lined.

Out of the public eye, Siegelman's stature diminished. A poll taken after Folsom's ascendance showed that Shelby would be favored in the 1994 Democratic gubernatorial primary should he choose to seek that office. A second question, this time with Shelby removed, asked respondents to choose from the remaining Democrats. Folsom led with 27 percent, followed by Hubbert with 17 percent, and 14 percent for Fob James, at the time still a Democrat.

In fourth place, with 10 ten percent, was Don Siegelman.

Three years after losing to Hubbert, the politician in exile faced reality and aimed, not at the top spot, but for the lieutenant governor's office. In planning his comeback, Siegelman tore a page from Bill Clinton's playbook. By winter 1993 – more than a year before the Democratic primary – he began touring the state, holding "listening posts" at coffee shops, restaurants, general stores and county Democratic clubs. When a reporter caught up with him in April, he had been to 60 counties with seven to go. Siegelman said he got the idea from Clinton strategist James Carville.

"At each stop, Siegelman urged Democrats to write letters to newspapers, call radio talk shows and write their congressmen urging them to support Clinton," reported the *Register's* Ralph Holmes. "Siegelman says while he and Clinton are not exactly close personal friends, he thinks they are kindred spirits and have many of the same political concerns."

With Franklin retired from the candidate driving business, Siegelman needed a replacement, preferably someone young, with all the time in the world, and with enough energy to keep up with him. In late 1993, Nick Bailey, 23 and not long out the University of Alabama, was introduced to Siegelman by his uncle, Jake Bailey, the president of Wallace State Community College and an influential figure in state Democratic circles.

Bailey was a native of Baileytown, in Cullman County, and his dad headed the county Democratic organization. He volunteered for the Siegelman campaign and soon found himself behind the wheel, driving the candidate.

Smallish, dark-haired, well-groomed and serious, Bailey idolized his boss, and for the next eight years, devoted his life to him.

Bailey wasn't the only new member of the Siegelman team.

Paul Hamrick came from a well-known Cullman County family and while still in college made a beeline to Montgomery and politics. At 21, before getting his degree, he took a job as an assistant to Alabama Public Service Commissioner Charles Martin. Three years later he became the top aide to one of the state's most colorful politicians, aging Agricultural Commissioner A.W. Todd, like Martin, a Democrat.

Hamrick was 29, bright, confident, focused and schooled in the ways of Montgomery when he hooked up with Siegelman in 1994. He served as chairman of Siegelman's campaign for lieutenant governor and after Siegelman won, became his chief of staff and spokesman. He has a sharp-tongue and a quick sense of humor which he regularly applied when the press called seeking quotes, such as about actions taken by Fob James and other Siegelman foes.

Hamrick also liked to have a good time. While working for Todd he met a running buddy who was to become his roommate and his best friend for most of the 1990s and halfway through Siegelman's term as governor. The friend's name was Clayton Lamar "Lanny" Young, Jr.

––––

In the mid-1990s, one issue – tort reform -- dominated Alabama politics, and not just the judicial races. The state was, in the words of the national business press, "Tort Hell."

The poster boys of tort hell were plaintiffs attorneys and Siegelman backers like former lieutenant governor Jere Beasley and Birmingham's Lanny Vines. It seemed hardly a week went by when an Alabama jury wasn't delivering a verdict in the millions if not tens of millions of dollars, often as not for a plaintiff gypped, defrauded or overcharged in amounts measured in the hundreds of dollars. These verdicts, even when settled for some amount less, generated astounding payouts for plaintiff's attorneys.

The Republican-led business lobby established a two-prong electoral strategy to curtail big verdicts and establish "tort reform." With the Business Council of Alabama (BCA) leading the way, legal conservatives set out to elect Republican justices to the state Supreme Court; and separately, win control of the state senate through election of pro-business senators. Most pivotal was the office of lieutenant governor.

The lieutenant governor presided over the senate, appointed the chairs of its many committees and set each day's schedule. For legislation to pass, it had to go through the senate. But if the lieutenant governor opposed a bill, he merely had to assign it to a committee chaired by one of his allies, where it would be assured of death by inactivity. It is for this reason that many said the real power in state government rested not with the governor, but with the lieutenant governor.

Siegelman was the trial lawyer candidate in the '94 race. The tort-reformers backed Tuscaloosa lawyer and Democratic State Sen. Ryan deGraffenried.

Early polls showed Siegelman trailing. With his life's calling in jeopardy, the Robo-Candidate ran ads accusing deGraffenried of defending people accused of drug crimes and drunk driving. This was something deGraffenried had done a handful of times and that honorable lawyers, not to mention Siegelman donors, did regularly. The ad was deemed later to have made the difference.

"I really think the talk about negative campaigns is really overblown," said the victor when asked to defend the ad. "Politics has always been a contact sport. There's an old saying, 'If you can't stand the heat, get out of the kitchen.'"

Siegelman met Charlie Graddick in the general election. The Republican nominee was as well known as Siegelman, having made a name for himself as an aggressive, tough-talking attorney general in the early 1980s. But his was best known for his part in the historically divisive 1986 governor's race. He won the Democratic primary only to have party officials strip him of the nomination, claiming he was in truth a Republican and had won by encouraging Republican crossover votes.

It was a pair of dirty tricks during that campaign that defined Graddick for years to come. One aide illegally acquired and disseminated the tax returns of Bill Baxley, Graddick's opponent in the Democratic primary. Another pleaded guilty to planting a bug in the state Democratic Party headquarters. Graddick claimed ignorance of both activities, but the public didn't buy it.

A dozen years later, Graddick still had what pollsters call "high negatives." The business community remained on the sidelines, Siegelman out-raised his former fraternity brother five to one, and won the lieutenant governor's race by a margin of almost 2 to 1.

November 8, 1994 was a splendid day for Siegelman, and not just because he stomped Graddick. The hapless Folsom squandered incumbency, an early lead in the polls and a towering advantage in campaign funds to lose by one percentage point to recent Republican convert Fob James.

Since replacing Hunt, the tall, attractive governor with the impeccable political pedigree had with his actions and appointments all but begged foes to brand him with the two Cs – Corruption and Cronyism. "Little Jim" still could have beaten James if he had an ounce of Siegelman in him. Instead, he defended himself with the vigor and communication skills of an old milk cow.

On election night 1994, Siegelman not only became lieutenant governor, but his party's highest ranking elected official and its de facto nominee for governor in 1998. He was almost 50, but finally, reality was catching up with destiny.

He capitalized on his new power by raising more than $1.5 million in the year after his win. The late Don Duncan, a political consultant who'd worked on Siegelman's campaign, said the lieutenant governor-elect had folks gathered outside his door, waiting their turn to hand him checks and get in his good graces.

"All the big money people," remembered Duncan.

Siegelman didn't need the money to pay off a campaign debt. He was putting on muscle for the 1998 governor's race, and by the very nature of his demands, letting people know who was boss.

Chapter 2
Ink-Stained Wretch

The classified ad promised a $9 resume, but the obese, chain-smoking regional manager of Career Resume Services Inc., said the price was "just to get them in the door."

"You're not going to make any money with a $9 resume, you hear me?" he said between drags. "You've got to talk them into the $45 expanded resume, or better yet, the $150 executive package."

With that he showed me the hardy, artsy, cloudy brown paper available only with these advanced products.

Commission only, he said, but if I was halfway decent I'd pull in $400 to $500 a week.

So it was that, with a resume that led off with a degree from one of the best colleges in the South, I accepted the position as office manager and sole employee of this suburban Atlanta branch of Career Resume Services Inc.

It was 1985 and I was almost a year out of Virginia's Washington & Lee University. I'd made all A's and was a student council type up until about sixth grade, and was frequently hailed by my mother, in front of my two siblings, as by far the best of the three when it came to doing household chores. Then puberty intervened, rendering me awkward, lazy and sloppy, and for well past puberty. I underachieved in high school but managed to get into W&L. Once there I underachieved some more, the low-point being a .9 out of a possible 4.0 the winter semester of my sophomore year.

I majored in American history, in part because I actually enjoyed writing term papers, if not completing them on time. I took a couple of journalism classes and did well, as they too involved writing. In my junior year a fraternity brother who edited the school's weekly newspaper asked me to write movie reviews. The following year I was given a regular column, a silly thing called the Eat Beat that offered the opportunity to dine at places like Long John Silvers.

To my surprise the column developed a faithful readership. People I didn't know, even professors heretofore entirely unimpressed with me, would come up and say they thought this or that was funny, and ask where I was eating next. This is called feedback, and more than 20 years later, it remains by far the most gratifying part of being a reporter.

I was about 6-3, 200 pounds, but in many situations back then, shy. There is a quality known as being "sharp," that I've always lacked, and especially so then. People who are sharp dress well and neatly, and make good first impressions. For me, keeping my shirt tucked was and remains an accomplishment.

In late 1984, at 23, I moved to Atlanta, where I had neither a place to live nor a job. To some extent I'd come to grips with what I was (lazy) and the degree of professional success I could expect from myself (none.) After months of listening to people trash their bosses, moan about unemployment and blame me for the $9 product, I spied an opportunity for change in the *Atlanta Constitution* classifieds. A weekly paper in Covington, Ga., about 45 minutes away, needed a reporter. I interviewed, got the job, and retired from resume writing.

The week before I was to begin, a college friend called to say he was quitting his job as a sports writer at the *Herald*, a paper in Big Spring, Tex., pop. 22,000, and about an hour's drive from Midland, then home to our future president, George W. Bush. The Herald was a daily paper, and there I'd be covering sports. Its chief disadvantage was location – way the hell out in the moonscape of West Texas.

I flew out on my own dime and interviewed. The editor was concerned about my lack of a journalism degree and the totality of my previous experience, the sum of which could be described in two words: Eat Beat.

I returned to Atlanta and the next day showed up for work in Covington. I was barely in the door before I was out, headed to cover a county commission meeting. I don't recall the issues discussed, but will never forget my response to them. Scared of missing a word, I took notes at warp speed. When the meeting concluded I approached the commissioners and asked detailed questions the likes of which they seemed unaccustomed to receiving. I raced back to the paper, told my new bosses about the meeting, and asked if I could do three stories instead of one. Probably it's a reflection of the paper that they said yes, and put all three on the front page.

I'd been hit by the proverbial bolt of lightning. Here was a job, an actual vocation, that inspired me to get off my butt and work. Suddenly, at age 24, I knew what I wanted to be when I grew up – a newspaper reporter.

Several weeks later I mailed a batch of Covington papers to Big Spring, and soon after got the call telling me to come on out. The job, with its starting salary of $12,000, was mine.

I spent 18 months in West Texas covering high school and junior college sports, with some news and entertainment. It was my journalism school and I learned by doing. I saw my first rodeo with pen and paper in hand, my assignment being, as I saw it, to trick people into thinking they were reading a story by someone who knew about rodeos, to do everything in my power to become an instant expert on the matter. This involves leaping into a situation or subject matter you know nothing about and observing, asking and researching your way out of ignorance. It's what reporters do every day.

In the fall of 1987 I gave my notice and returned to Mobile with the vague notion of becoming a writer. But I missed the daily action, the joking in the newsroom, and the bylines. Without them, my self-esteem plummeted.

In January 1988 I received a life-changing call from the basketball coach at the junior college in Big Spring who had, coincidentally, moved to Mobile for a job as assistant coach at the University of South Alabama. He said the *Register* had fired one of its sports writers and suggested I get down there and apply. Soon after I began what was to become almost 20 years at my hometown paper.

I wrote sports for six years and enjoyed it, but it had become like watching reruns, like the Bill Murray movie, "Groundhog Day." If marriage hadn't intervened I might still be asking coaches why they punted on fourth and two with a minute left.

In the spring of 1990 an intelligent, pretty and sweet Czechoslovakian girl, Jana Janavicova, came to Mobile to study the American legal system. We dated, and in the summer of 1991, I spent a month with her in Bratislava, the capital of Slovakia. Several months later, with parents and a college friend in tow, I returned and we married. After the birth of our first child, Jerry, I sought and was granted transfer to news.

I was and remained what is known as a general assignment reporter. I did not and have never had a full-time beat, such as covering city hall or the county commission. For this I'm grateful, since I abhor sitting through meetings.

I immediately gravitated to investigative type stories. Didn't plan on it, wasn't directed to it, just felt the pull, and soon became the paper's unofficial go-to guy for such work. I plumbed all manner of public records and read books with titles like, "You, Too, Can Find Anybody;" an IRS manual called, "Financial Investigations: A Financial Approach to Detecting and Resolving Crimes"; and, best of all, the handbook published by the Investigative Reporters & Editors (IRE.)

I was, at 34, beginning a new career. Investigative reporting fed my obsessive gene and scratched my itch for a good mystery. As a child I'd gobbled up Hardy Boys books, moved on to Agatha Christie Sherlock Holmes, and later and still, the likes of John le Carre and Bill James, who writes what the English call "police procedurals."

———

As will be seen, I became suspicious of Siegelman following a series of lies told me by his chief of staff, Paul Hamrick, in early 2001. My mistrust of the Fob James administration can be assigned to a similar lack of candor, and specifically, a cold-call made on a Sunday night in July 1995.

That spring the state Revenue Department sent audit notices to about 20 legislators, many of whom were black. When the Associated Press reported this, the governor assured legislators that the state tax agency wasn't targeting legislators as a group. But if such a project were discovered, then "heads would roll," Fob promised.

In early July, a north Alabama legislator faxed me a Revenue Department memo bearing the heading, "Operation Public Servant." It contained a list of names, all blacked out. The memo directed state tax agents to audit legislators on the list, thus confirming the existence of the very program James had denied.

The story sparked a fury that raged for months, and included demands by Siegelman, Hamrick and others for an investigation. State Rep. Alvin Holmes, never one to shy from hyperbole, called it a "mini Alabama Watergate."

Ralph Eagerton, James's aged, overzealous Revenue Commissioner, had also denied the existence of such a program. After the story, Eagerton was described by an aide as "flabbergasted." He and James swore to get to the bottom of it. Subsequent records showed that Operation Public Servants began at Eagerton's direction and was spearheaded by the chief of the income tax division, who retired in its midst. It was turned over to his replacement, Dwight Pridgen, whose sin was to pursue the assignment with gusto.

Several days after our story it was announced that Pridgen had been placed on administrative leave. The following Sunday night I called him at home, sure that he would refuse to speak with me. Instead, we talked for hours. He told of being interrogated for much of an afternoon by two agents with what he understood to be a special unit of the Alabama Department of Public Safety.

One yelled threats when he refused to sign a declaration that he was solely responsible for the audits, and accused him of being mentally unbalanced. This led to my discovery of and stories about the Special Services Group, or SSG.

Legislators were enraged to learn that the governor had authorized the creation of a private intelligence unit. Siegelman, who would be impossible to get on the phone years later, declared his interest in knowing the purpose of the SSG, what it was legally authorized to do, and "who it reports to."

I found the SSG headquarters in a strip mall on the edge of Montgomery. "We don't want the whole world to know we exist," a member of the unit said when asked why there were no markings on the door.

Soon after, the SSG was disbanded.

Facing a political disaster – the exposed, systematic auditing of legislators –James had responded not by fessing up, but by making a scapegoat of a merit system employee. From that point on, I paid attention to the James administration.

A story the next year led to the resignation or firing – it was hard to tell – of James' chief of staff, his finance director and the head of the Alabama Department of Public Safety and the removal from state bond business of an investment banker with whom the three had, most unwisely, formed an investments company.

Most of my stories involved the highway department, including several about a Montgomery-based bridge-building company called McInnis Corp. After James became governor, his three sons partnered with the two McInnis brothers in a venture to build a toll bridge in Orange Beach. After that, McInnis Corp., repeatedly benefited from rulings by James' highway director, Jimmy Butts, who over-ruled his staff and the federal highway administration in deciding to pay the company for shoddy and late work.

Researching those stories -- poring through thousands of pages of highway department project files and learning the agency's processes -- served me well in the years to come. The source of the McInnis stories, who I will call Frank, would three years later point me to my first story on the Siegelman administration.

Early in James' final year a source suggested I investigate a lobbying outfit called Capital City Consultants. The firm was said to be enjoying remarkable success winning a type of federal grant that paid for projects like sidewalks and bike and nature trails. Cities and towns submitted applications and a low-level official ranked them. But the final call was Butts' to make.

Capital City was run by Johnny Moore, a lobbyist and fundraiser for James and a friend of Butts. Also involved in the grant deals was John Teague, one of the state's leading lobbyists and a childhood buddy of Butts. He had hired the highway director's son to work for his lobbying firm.

I requested a list of grant winners and called each one. For a follow-up I called all the applicants, well over 100 -- those who sought but didn't win grants as well as those who did. All that dialing allowed me to report that every town that hired Capital City won grants. Dora, pop. 2,214, won three in one year, for almost $600,000.

The stories showed about $1 million flowing into the firm's coffers.

Butts, a short, gravel-voiced, country-boy road-builder, seemed to have walked into the highway department straight from the 1950s. He claimed he had no idea which applicants hired Capital City Consultants. But the weight of the evidence rendered those claims silly.

In December 2000 Butts, Moore, Teague and Butts' son were indicted on the Capital City Consultants scam and related matters. The three older men pleaded guilty and each served six month federal prison sentences.

In debates, interviews and faxes to the media, gubernatorial candidate Siegelman turned the phrase "cesspool of corruption" into a memorable mantra for the highway department under James and Butts. Most of the faxes were re-hashings of stories I'd written. One bore the heading: "AHHHH, REFRESHING ICE TEA/THE RICH GET A HELL OF A LOT RICHER."

"It works like this," the fax began. "Say you are a city. You apply for a grant and get turned away by the Highway Department. Then one day a Montgomery lobbyist shows up at your door and says: Hire me, and I'll try to get your grant for you. You do. He does. He gets 10 percent. Pretty Nice."

They were kind enough to footnote it, so the name Curran appeared 10 times. Recipients were told that, should they request it, the campaign would forward the stories. Again, those would be my stories, sent out by the Siegelman campaign.

Petty of me, but considering what was to transpire, it's a point I enjoy making.

Chapter 3
Off and running

"We clearly knew who the quarterback was and God bless him."
-- *State pension system chief David Bronner praising Siegelman after Honda announced it would build a $440 million car-making plant in north Alabama.*

"And people say I micromanage. When else am I going to have a stage where people have to listen to me? I'm governor, and I still have trouble getting them to listen."
-- *Siegelman, making light of his reputation as a micro-manager engrossed in every detail of state government.*

Oct. 14, 1998, the *Birmingham News* reported that toll bridge developer Jim Allen was soon to open his third bridge, over the Warrior River in Tuscaloosa County. Allen told the paper he had invested tens of millions of dollars in his three bridges, none of which was making money.

Years later, at trial, Allen testified that he was at that point exceedingly vulnerable -- a decision by a governor or highway director on a road project, such as to build a road to or around one of his bridges could make or break him. Fob James was governor, but polls showed the Republican incumbent needing a miracle to defeat Siegelman in the election then three weeks away.

The day after the Birmingham story lieutenant governor Siegelman called Allen's company and asked for Mack Roberts. The former highway director was working for Allen, overseeing construction of his bridges. Could Roberts and Allen come see him the next day in Birmingham? Though Allen had contributed to James' campaign, he had permitted Roberts to use company time and resources to raise money for Siegelman. The two, Allen testified years later at Siegelman's trial, thought Siegelman summoned them to thank them.

Allen and Roberts drove as directed to a Birmingham antique store owned by Siegelman backer Anthony Fant. Upon arrival, Nick Bailey ushered them into a parlor, where they found the candidate. The scene as described by Allen suggested a spider welcoming victims to its web.

The men shook hands. Allen and Roberts sat down but Siegelman remained standing, hovering above them. "He immediately got very angry and very upset with me. He was pointing at me, and he said, 'You have not helped me one bit in this campaign, and I'm going to remember it,'" Allen told jurors. "He raised his voice and pointed his finger at me and said that others had given (him) as much as $100,000. I said I didn't have $100,000. I said I have just invested over $20 million in my toll roads."

Siegelman dropped his demand to $50,000. Again, Allen said he didn't have it. "He said, 'Will you give me $40,000, and if you give me $40,000, I will let you pick the next highway director.'"

Siegelman was most assuredly bluffing, but it worked. Allen promised to borrow $40,000 – itself a bluff. He didn't need to borrow the money but wanted to give Siegelman the impression he was hard up to ward off more demands. After Allen agreed to contribute $40,000, Siegelman's manner changed. He became friendly and told his visitors how well the campaign was proceeding.

On the drive back to Montgomery Roberts told Allen that "throughout his career, and he'd been around government about 30 years, that he'd never been treated as such and had never seen anyone treated the way we'd just been treated."

Outside court after Allen's testimony, Siegelman ridiculed the claim that he had promised to let a donor choose the highway director for $40,000, but he didn't entirely discount Allen's account.

Siegelman allowed that he "might have gotten up on the wrong side of the bed" that day.

Siegelman had in Fob James the foe of his dreams. The former Auburn running back and self-made millionaire made headlines less with accomplishments than fire, brimstone and scandal. His first prison chief reinstated chain gangs and ordered pink uniforms for prisoners who masturbated in front of female guards. Many Alabamians loved it, but the policies drew national, even international, news coverage, and reinforced the opinion among many that we're a backwards ass rube state.

James found his calling in combative conservative Christian theology, fashioning himself as the political twin of Etowah County Circuit Judge Roy Moore. In what became a defining performance, James mocked evolution at a state school board meeting by impersonating an ape. He threatened, Wallace-like, to summon the National Guard to prevent the court-ordered removal of the Ten Commandments plaque from Moore's Etowah County courtroom, and told a national television audience that he would use "force of arms" to maintain the plaque in Moore's court.

James' opponent played the Moore card perfectly. Siegelman knew Christian conservatives weren't going to support him. At the same time, he had nothing to gain by criticizing the judge, and for the most part, didn't. Beyond an occasional, not particularly heart-felt claim to support school prayer, Siegelman dodged the religious fray.

Spring 1998 found the Robo-Candidate with $3.5 million on hand and no serious foes in the Democratic primary. James, with less money, faced a primary challenge from wealthy Montgomery businessman Winton Blount. Outrageous as Fob often was, no one could accuse him of being consultant or poll-driven. He was always his own man, never canned. With shirt-sleeves rolled-up, he appealed to many voters, especially rural ones, and defeated Blount in a run-off.

Demagoguery and grandstanding came easy to James; governing bored him. His efforts at running the state, never profound, wilted in the second half of his term. It was obvious that he preferred goose-hunting at his place in Canada to scrapping with legislators over budgets, laws and such.

James' main backers were fervent members of the anti-tax crowd, led by timber growers and the insurance company and farmer's association powerhouse ALFA. But many traditional GOP donors either sat out the election or gave to Siegelman. Here he benefited from the changing of the guard in the state Supreme Court. Pro-businesses justices had essentially instituted tort reform. It remained an issue, but one of many. This freed Siegelman to ease away from his traditional trial lawyer allies without offending them, and to develop relationships with the business folk who'd long scorned him.

Siegelman's campaign message was simple: Elect me and I'll deliver an education lottery. His campaign seemed to be about little else. In this sense, the lottery campaign began, not the following year, but in early 1998.

On Nov. 3, 1998, Siegelman rolled over James with 58 percent of the vote. On Jan. 18, 1999, a month shy of his 53rd birthday, he was sworn in as governor. Friend and fellow Mobile native Jimmy Buffett regaled the inaugural crowd with a Siegelman favorite, "Stars Fell on Alabama."

Surrounded by friends and family, the overachiever from Mobile became the first Alabamian to hold four constitutional offices -- secretary of state, attorney general, lieutenant governor, and governor.

He had badgered, begged and threatened friends, businessmen, lawyers, and lobbyists for $8.9 million to become governor.

The second campaign, for the state lottery, was already underway, and once again, the `Robo-Candidate needed cash. There was to be no reprieve, for the new governor or Alabama's donor class.

Siegelman's first order of business was neutering the new lieutenant governor.

An otherwise perfect election day was marred by the razor-thin loss of Siegelman ally Dewayne Freeman to Republican Steve Windom in a battle of state senators.

Siegelman had only to look in the mirror to see the nightmare of a lieutenant governor Windom. For the next four years Siegelman would be Fob James, and

Windom him. The lottery, like so much else, would be doomed if Windom assumed control of the senate.

In the struggle for the relevancy of his office, Siegelman had an ace in the hole – a Democratic majority in the senate. For the first time, there was a Republican lieutenant governor matched with a Democrat-controlled senate, and the senate had a large say in who ran the show.

Windom peeled off some conservative Democrats and managed to shut down the body for more than a month. The battle's enduring image is of Windom urinating in a jug beneath the podium rather than risking the loss of the senate by running to the bathroom. The episode – which I thought was to Windom's credit in more ways than one -- was a political cartoonist's dream.

Windom ceded defeat in March. Control of the senate was transferred to Lowell Barron, the cunning north Alabama legislator whose ability to keep a straight face while saying the most amazing things rivaled Siegelman.

With the Democrats in control, the lottery legislation passed. It would go to a vote of the people, on Oct. 12.

———

On a recent Friday afternoon, Gov. Don Siegelman raced to neighboring Prattville to swear in the new mayor. Then it was off to Mobile for the retirement party of the state docks director.

From there, the governor flew to Birmingham to watch daughter Dana in a dramatic performance.

For Siegelman, it was a light day.

A half-year into his job as the state's chief executive, Siegelman continues to impress observers with his work ethic and intensity.

"He's as focused as anyone I've ever seen," said Speaker Seth Hammett, leader of the state House of Representatives.

So began a July 1999 feature by veteran *Birmingham News* political reporter Michael Sznajderman that nicely captured Siegelman's whirlwind first six months.

Passage of the lottery bill was but one of the new governor's successes. The legislature backed his plan to use the $131 million a year from Alabama's portion of the national tobacco settlement to fund incentives to recruit industry to the sate and, with the rest, to pay for Children's First, a package of programs designed to help at-risk youth.

Near session's end, he won praise for guiding a package of tort-reform bills through the legislature. As the bills were being considered, Jere Beasley's firm won a $581 million verdict on behalf of plaintiffs claiming to have been overcharged

$1,200 for two satellite dishes. Everyone knew the state Supreme Court would obliterate the half-billion dollar award but it served as a perfectly timed "outrage" for tort reform interests. Once again, the chips were falling into place for the new governor.

"We have sent a message to business leaders around the world that Alabama is a world-class business state, and we have said goodbye to tort hell. Alabama is now a state that is simply good for business," declared the one-time gate-keeper to tort hell in a speech to the U.S. Chamber of Commerce.

Siegelman may have bested his wizard-like handling of the legislature when he reeled Honda away from other states vying to land the Japanese automaker's planned $440 million minivan manufacturing plant. His stealth fight for Honda – code-named Operation Bingo -- commenced within days of his November election win.

On May 1, 1999, he traveled to Nashville for a secret meeting with Koki Hirashima, the chief executive of Honda of America Manufacturing. The two clicked, and a week later, Honda announced it was coming to Alabama.

"We clearly knew who the quarterback was and God bless him," said state pension system chief David Bronner.

Sznajderman's story noted what Siegelman described as his "very much hands-on" management style.

The Siegelman archives were to reflect that as well. They contain a relative handful of what were likely hundreds if not thousands of memos dictated by the governor. Many were directed to Bailey, some asking him to handle mundane tasks, like fixing furniture. A May 2000 memo to Mack Roberts, with the subject heading, "Trimming the Roadsides," showed Siegelman's sensitive side.

"Mack, please check with the Department of Conservation to see when doves and other birds nest in the grass on side of the road. I have seen several birds nesting. If they are, we probably should delay until those little babies get hatched and take off."

The Birmingham piece also mentioned complaints that Siegelman was earning a reputation for awarding professional services contracts to friends; and mentioned a lawsuit accusing the administration of rigging bids on Medicaid contracts to help a company owned by Dr. Phillip Bobo, a major Siegelman donor. The Bobo case raised its head in a big way in 2004, but at the time, inflicted little damage. It was as if no one wanted to believe that the new governor had fleas, so early indications that he might were ignored.

The story ended as it began, on a positive note. Carl Grafton, a political science professor at the University of Auburn at Montgomery, described Siegelman as "a governor you can take to a good restaurant without being embarrassed."

Grafton agreed that Siegelman is "picking the easy ones so far." But Siegelman is proceeding in a methodical, progressive way that's remarkable compared to past governors, he said.

Grafton said Siegelman already qualifies as the New South governor Alabama has never had, a governor intent on improving the quality of life rather than protecting the status quo.

In case you missed it, here it is a second time: New South Governor.

The Holy Grail. Finally, or so it seemed, Alabama had one.

Chapter 4
Scrushy plays the lottery

"It was (Siegelman's) estimate that Richard Scrushy had given some $350,000 to Fob James' campaign, and Eric asked what he could do to help Richard make up for that. And Siegelman told him that $350,000 plus interest and they'd -- $500,000 – and they'd just call it even."

-- Grand jury testimony of Nick Bailey, referring to May 1999 conversation between Siegelman and Eric Hanson, HealthSouth's Washington lobbyist.

"The 'black box' lies in the survey. However, we will be -- as you should be -- far more interested in finding out where to go from here than in sifting through the smoking rubble. We believe this loss is a setback in this administration, but it need not be a fatal one."

-- Nov. 2, 1999, memo to Siegelman from pollster Alan Secrest, accompanying his survey analyzing the defeat of the lottery referendum.

Soon after the inauguration a group of hand-picked Siegelman backers incorporated the Alabama Education Lottery Foundation. Several months later Siegelman – in a move that caused confusion forever after -- decided for public relations reasons to drop lottery and call it the Alabama Education Foundation. (For clarity purposes, it will in most cases be referred to here by its original name.)

The foundation was designed to serve much like a candidate's campaign committee: Money from contributors would be deposited in the foundation's bank account, which in turn funded the campaign, paying for everything from political ads to salaries for what was, for seven or eight months, a full-time staff. Hamrick took a leave of absence from the administration to run the campaign.

As with a candidate's campaign, the foundation was required to report its contributions and expenditures to the secretary of state. The chief difference was that the foundation, because it was raising money for a referendum, could accept donations of unlimited size from corporations. The usual $2,000 per corporation limit did not apply.

Full disclosure was a point of pride for the foundation, with Siegelman and Hamrick frequently proclaiming that they were going the extra mile to ensure a completely transparent operation. They wanted, they said, to prove that a state lottery operated by the Siegelman administration would be pure as the driven snow.

To secure passage of his lottery Siegelman brought in the same national Democratic Party consultants he'd been using since his 1994 run for lieutenant governor. Virginia-based Alan Secrest was to oversee the polling and consulting, with Cunningham, Harris & Associates, out of West Virginia, directing the fund-raising operation.

Darren Cline, a member of the Cunningham firm who had moved to Montgomery for the governor's race, stayed on for the lottery campaign. Among his duties was the creation of donor lists which included past contributors to Siegelman and companies and individuals doing business with the state. For each Cline produced a focus sheet showing past donations and a target amount to request, with that sum determined in consultation with Siegelman. As soon as the governor arrived at foundation headquarters to raise money (a home near the Mansion co-owned by Bailey), Cline would hand him a stack of focus sheets and Siegelman would start cranking out calls.

A post-referendum chart of Siegelman's "call-time results" showed that he made 1,909 calls in 132 hours, hauled in $4.5 million, and averaged $34,542 an hour. After the chart was introduced at trial, Siegelman lawyer Vince Kilborn hailed his client as "the Muhammad Ali of fund raising."

Though Cline worked directly with Siegelman, he spent more time with Bailey. Upon his election, Siegelman had appointed his driver/Man Friday to the dual position of executive secretary and, laughably, state budget officer, with a salary topping $90,000.

When his boss became governor, Bailey developed a "God complex," Cline testified years later at Siegelman's trial. Bailey's position was "whatever the governor said was right" and didn't require explaining. "We're God and we're going to get that done," is how Cline explained it to jurors.

He tried to talk to Bailey about his Siegelman mania, but to no avail. Cline and his boss, Jim Cunningham, both came to feel that Bailey was "too far gone."

―――

The rags to riches story of Richard Scrushy's rise and run at HealthSouth offers more than enough elements for the first sitcom starring the chairman of a Fortune 500 company. Probably it would be rejected as over the top, or maybe just some of it, like the washed up former TV child star given the title of director of marketing as cover for his real job, the boss's full-time celebrity buddy. And if the child star had to go, so too would a second character, the TV actor's ex-porn-star wife.

But the story of HealthSouth and its self-absorbed founder is not fiction, and is spooky rather than funny.

Richard Marin Scrushy, born and raised in Selma, dropped out of high school after getting his girlfriend pregnant. They wed, had a second child, he worked as a bricklayer, wore his hair long, in a ponytail, and lived in a trailer park. Though no one was predicting fame and fortune, Scrushy struck friends and family as smart, driven, and a little different. "You went over to Marin's trailer, and he didn't serve Pabst, he served wine and cheese," an old friend recalled years later.

Scrushy tired of the dog's life, got his GED and at his mother's suggestion, studied and trained to become a respiratory therapist. In 1974, he started teaching respiratory therapy, divorced, and as a sign of the transformation to come, traded in his middle name Marin for his first name, Richard. He remarried, and several years later, joined and prospered at a Houston-based company called Lifemark, eventually becoming a vice president.

Aaron Beam met Scrushy in 1980, when he interviewed for a job as Lifemark's comptroller.

"That night I told my wife I felt like I'd met either the most brilliant businessman I would ever meet, or the biggest con artist I would ever meet," said Beam 26 years later, following release from a short prison sentence for his role in HealthSouth's $2.6 billion accounting fraud.

When Lifemark was sold in 1983, Scrushy recruited four co-workers, Beam included, to start a new company that was also a new kind of company. It would be based in Birmingham, in Scrushy's home state.

"Back in 1984 you had to go to a hospital to receive physical therapy, such as after a car accident," said Beam. "Richard felt like you could do it cheaper outside the hospital. With all his faults, Richard was very visionary, and he was a very good businessman. His most striking quality is he's driven. He was never really not at work. If you left the office to go have dinner with him it was still business. He would wear you down because that's all he talked about was business."

In the early years Scrushy built his company methodically, one new therapy center at a time. In 1986 he took HealthSouth public, and perhaps equally important, convinced orthopedist Dr. James Andrews to move his sports clinic to Birmingham and to associate with HealthSouth. Andrews was in the early stages of developing a reputation as the country's leading sports injury surgeon, his list of patients a who's-who of America's top athletes. So astonishing were Andrews' successes that in 1999, ESPN named him one of the 20th century's most influential sports figures. Two of his patients, major leaguers David Wells and Kenny Rogers, went on to pitch perfect games. "He has helped put us on the map," Scrushy gushed to a reporter in 1999.

It was, for HealthSouth's CEO, a rare compliment for another's contribution to his company.

"Richard managed by intimidation," said Beam. "He would call you out in front of the other employees, your peers, and call you a fool in front of everybody. He's the kind of guy you just don't want to fight with. He'd make it so unpleasant. "You've heard how if you stand up to your boss, he'll respect you more? Not Richard. He didn't want anybody standing up to him."

Beam cheerfully described Scrushy as being "charismatic in a Hitler kind of way."

Amplifying the fear and paranoia at HealthSouth was Scrushy's ever-present security detail, led by his personal body guard, former state trooper Jim Goodreau. The sleek, handsome Goodreau oversaw the placement of security cameras throughout HealthSouth's corporate office. Some were disguised, with one placed inside a smoke detector. To the discomfort of his underlings, Scrushy installed a monitor in his office so he could keep watch on his employees.

HealthSouth's growth spurt began in 1994. The company borrowed and spent billions of dollars gobbling up competitors and was by 1997 the largest rehab firm in the country. That year, annual revenues skyrocketed to $4 billion and HealthSouth entered the Fortune 500. Scrushy cashed in $93 million in stock options, and combined with salary and bonuses, took home $106 million, making him the third highest paid CEO in the country that year. "At one point I know he was worth over $600 million," said Beam, noting that some of those riches came from Scrushy's investments in other companies.

Scrushy enjoyed spending it, his own and HealthSouth's. His properties included four mansions, including a garish 14,000-square-foot palace built in a gated-community on Lake Martin; an $11 million home in Palm Beach; another in Orange Beach; and his residence in Vestavia Hills, adorned with a helicopter pad.

Among his and HealthSouth's toys were ten boats, including the 92-foot yacht, the *Chez Soiree* and a racing boat called, *Monopoly*; some 30 cars, including a Lamborghini Murcielago, a Rolls Royce Corniche and a $135,000 bulletproof BMW; a Sikorsky helicopter valued at $7.5 million; and, in the art department, three Miros, two Chagalls and a Picasso.

In 1997, he flew style maven Martha Stewart and some 150 others to Jamaica for his third wedding, to Leslie Jones, a striking brunette 16 years his junior. Scrushy met her at a private airport where she was working and offered her a job. Both were married at the time, and claimed they didn't start dating until after their respective divorces. In time she became the mother of Scrushy's seventh, eighth and ninth children.

By the late 1990s HealthSouth had more than 50,000 employees; operated more than 2,000 rehabilitation outlets; had a presence in all 50 states; and controlled almost 70 percent of the country's rehabilitation market. Like many first generation companies, HealthSouth was widely identified with its founder, and he liked it that way. Only someone afflicted with far-gone narcissism could, as Scrushy did, commission a life-sized statue of himself, which welcomed visitors to the HealthSouth complex.

The company's roaring success permitted Scrushy to get away with a level of public zaniness that would not have been tolerated at a more tradition-laden firm.

In the early 1990s, the CEO recruited musicians from the Oak Ridge Boys and Sawyer Brown to play in his band, "Dallas County Line," named after his native southwest Alabama county.

The band, fueled with HealthSouth money, put out a CD and cut a video of its lead single, "Honk if You Love to Honky Tonk," from the album, "Rich Man's Dream." The video shows guitarist and lead singer Scrushy, in black from hat to boots, belting it out to an unlikely audience of, among others, Neil Diamond, Bo Jackson, wrestler Lex Luger and NASCAR legend Bobby Allison. The song isn't as bad as might be imagined, but nor was it good enough to justify the continued existence of, "Dallas County Line."

Scrushy apparently accepted his limitations as front man but chose to remain in the biz, but as producer, not player. In the mid-1990s he became the moving force behind, "Go for It! Roadshow," a touring act aimed at educating and entertaining teenagers.

On a Go for It! tour the budding impresario spotted a trio of superficially sexy, belly-button-showing 20-year-old girls who called themselves, "3rd Faze." Research for this book reflects that 3rd Faze aspired to be the next "Destiny's Child."

It was during this phase of personal growth through artistic creativity that Scrushy met former child-actor Jason Hervey – big brother Wayne in the 1980s sitcom, "The "Wonder Years." Late in 2001 Scrushy lured Hervey to Birmingham from Los Angeles with a $300,000-plus salary and the title of senior vice president of media and communications.

"People at HealthSouth were shocked. Hervey's main job, really, was to be the latest Scrushy sidekick," chortled *Fortune* in an exhaustive and thoroughly entertaining 2003 piece on the HealthSouth collapse. "Scrushy had taken a 29-year-old movie brat with no healthcare experience and put him in charge of marketing and communications. There was even more shock when some employees discovered, while Internet surfing, that Hervey's wife was a former porn star known as Angel Hart."

Beam left in 1997, no longer able to tolerate the falsification of earnings statements, which were becoming a regular if secret mainstay of HealthSouth's financial operations. He never met Hervey but said the relationship fit a Scrushy pattern. "He always liked having a kind of boy type person around … Richard sort of has to buy friends because he's just no fun. He always had an entourage of people who wanted to get his money."

In two years time Scrushy spent more than $13 million of HealthSouth's money on 3rd Faze and the "Go for It!" roadshow. Of that, $4,600 was spent on breast-enhancement surgery for one of the 3rd Faze girls.

———

For mid-size cities like Birmingham, large public corporations are a treasure. They generate considerable sums for the economy; often and certainly in HealthSouth's case, donate generously to charities; and help create a reputation as a good place to do business. It's probably for this reason that the first hard looks at Scrushy and HealthSouth came from the national media, and specifically, *Fortune.*

"We're in Birmingham, at the home of a $4 billion company called HealthSouth, and the scent of Elvis is in the air. HealthSouth is the creation of a 46-year-old Wall Street hero named Richard Scrushy, and not unlike Graceland, it's a place positively reeking of self-worship and control," wrote Peter Elkind in a June 1999 *Fortune* piece called "Vulgarians at the Gate."

The story chronicled the 1998 collapse of another Birmingham company called MedPartners that Scrushy helped create. That firm disintegration cost investors hundreds of millions of dollars and in time came to be seen as HealthSouth's warm-up act.

"Flamboyant, natty, carefully tanned, Scrushy is almost a caricature of the modern swashbuckling CEO," Elkind wrote.

The *Fortune* writer had the foresight to use the word "hustler" to describe Scrushy more than three years before HealthSouth's implosion. The story, as so happened, was published about the time Scrushy flew to Montgomery to make amends with Alabama's new governor.

On late June or early July 1999 – the date was never quite clear -- the HealthSouth helicopter landed atop the Business Council of Alabama building a few blocks from the capitol. Joining Scrushy for the short flight from Birmingham were in-house lawyer Loree Skelton and Jabo Waggoner, the Birmingham area state senator who served as the HealthSouth's vice president for public relations and its de facto lobbyist in Montgomery.

In the coming years, Scrushy and HealthSouth were to seek and receive substantial assistance from Siegelman, and the governor and First Lady socialized with the Scrushys in ritzy settings, including, at HealthSouth's expense, for a flight and accommodations at the 2001 Grammy Awards in Los Angeles. But on that day in 1999, a distance of half-a-million dollars separated tycoon and governor.

Scrushy and HealthSouth had backed Fob James, including hosting a fund-raiser for Siegelman's opponent in the 1998 governor's race. In all, Scrushy was reported to have contributed and raised some $350,000 for James. The Siegelman campaign, and almost surely the candidate himself, had called Scrushy seeking a contribution, but the HealthSouth boss declined to take or return his calls.

Not a brilliant decision, snubbing Siegelman, especially with polls showing the lieutenant governor miles ahead of James.

Skelton, whose duties included governmental relations, testified years later at trial that Scrushy's support of James had repercussions. The company's relationship with the new governor was "probably nonexistent ... because we had openly supported his opponent," said Skelton. "I told (Scrushy) that I was concerned we would not have a voice in this administration."

Eric Hanson -- HealthSouth's Washington lobbyist and a Siegelman pal from years back -- helped broker the meeting that years later took center stage in the Scrushy portion of the trial. Neither prosecution nor defense called Hanson as a witness, though the court honored him with the title, "unindicted co-conspirator."

Hanson came to Montgomery in May 1999 to meet with Siegelman and "see what he could do to make things right between the governor and Richard," testified Bailey, who sat in on the meeting. Siegelman told Hanson that Scrushy had given and raised $350,000 for James. He told Hanson to tell Scrushy that if he came up with $500,000 the governor would "just call it even."

Of immediate concern for HealthSouth was a position on the state Certificate of Need and Review Board. The nine-person board reviewed then approved or denied hospital expansion plans and major medical equipment purchases. Scrushy sat on the board during each of the previous three administrations, but Siegelman, as governors usually did, removed CON board members who'd served under the previous governor to replace them with his own appointees.

Healthcare is a huge industry in Birmingham and the competition for patients is cut-throat. Hospitals and care providers in that city have a greater stake in the activities of the CON board than anywhere else in the state. Skelton testified that HealthSouth, as the largest healthcare company in the state, considered it vital to have a seat on the board.

Company records presented at trial showed that Skelton monitored the board's every action, especially those involving HealthSouth's competitors but also applications with no connection whatsoever to the company.

Upon their arrival at the capitol, Scrushy, Waggoner and Skelton engaged in small talk with Siegelman and Bailey. Then Siegelman motioned to Scrushy.

"The governor said, 'Would y'all excuse us for a few minutes,' and they went to an adjoining office," testified Waggoner.

Governor and CEO came out about 30 minutes later, and the visitors returned to Birmingham.

―――――

In late 2005, soon after charges were announced against Scrushy, Siegelman and their co-defendants, Terry Butts, one of Scrushy's lawyers, contacted prosecutor Steve Feaga seeking a deal. According to a 2009 affidavit by Feaga, Butts and lead Scrushy lawyer Art Leach told Feaga that after Siegelman won the election, he threatened to use his office to harm HealthSouth if Scrushy didn't make a substantial contribution to the lottery foundation. According to Feaga, Scrushy's lawyers told him that Scrushy agreed to make a large donation, but "extracted from Siegelman an appointment to the CON board in exchange for his contribution."

If so, Scrushy's actions constituted a crime, since he was offering to give money in exchange for a specific action from a public official.

The government was open to a deal, but only if Scrushy agreed to testify at trial and plead guilty to a felony. Scrushy and his lawyers balked, and the negotiations ended.

Leach has stated in affidavits that the government tried to trick him and his client into revealing their proposed strategy at trial. He claimed that the government tried to force Scrushy to give testimony consistent with the government's, not Scrushy's, version of events.

Both sides have, in court filings, called the other liars.

———

Beginning with the October 2005 indictment and continuing to this day, Siegelman, Scrushy, their lawyers and supporters have ridiculed prosecutors for spinning what they characterized as an ordinary campaign contribution into a crime.

"If this verdict is allowed to stand, the traditional ways of financing a campaign or a referendum could be turned into federal bribery charges on the whim of a federal prosecutor," wrote Siegelman in one of his post-trial mass e-mails seeking donations to help him pay his legal bills.

"This verdict infringes on everyone's First Amendment right to financially support a candidate or cause," he declared.

And on another occasion: "Every governor and every president and every contributor might as well turn themselves in, because it's going to be open season on them."

Whether legal or illegal – and a jury carefully instructed on the law chose the latter – only someone of Siegelman's gumption could pretend that the two $250,000 checks handed him by Scrushy were routine political contributions. Alone, each was larger than any of the other lottery donations. That itself raises two questions.

Why was Scrushy asked to come up with so much more than any of the other major corporations in the state, and why did he?

At $250,000 apiece, each was, even by the standards of national politics, extraordinarily large. Neither was disclosed to the secretary of state or, in any event, not until years later, and then only after the attorney general's offices, responding to revelations in our stories, compelled Siegelman to report its sources of money. As will be seen, considerable effort by Siegelman, his lawyers and others was made over a three-year period to conceal the $500,000 and about $230,000 from other sources.

Even at a fraction of its size, and assuming proper disclosure, the long strange trip of the first $250,000 check separates it from any reasonable person's notion of the "traditional ways" of contributing to political campaigns.

In the spring of 1999, investment banker Bill McGahan joined a group of Salomon Smith-Barney investment bankers who made national business news by walking out the doors of that firm and into those of another, Swiss-owned UBS Warburg. Of greatest value to UBS was the group's Fortune 500-level clientele, most of whom followed the bankers to UBS. Among those was one of McGahan's top clients, HealthSouth.

The New York-based McGahan had helped orchestrate multi-billion dollar deals for HealthSouth that generated millions of dollars in fees. For McGahan, keeping Scrushy happy -- one might even say, doing whatever Scrushy wanted -- was way up on his list of priorities.

McGahan's chief contact at HealthSouth was Mike Martin, officially the company's chief financial officer and unofficially, Scrushy's number two man. Martin, with whom McGahan sometimes socialized, was a frequent conduit of Scrushy's directives. Such was the case on the day Martin called McGahan to inform him that Scrushy wanted UBS to donate $250,000 to a charity called the Alabama Education Lottery Foundation.

Martin's demand was made shortly after Scrushy's meeting with Siegelman in Montgomery.

UBS regularly made charitable donations, but $250,000 would have been unprecedented, McGahan told jurors years later.

"I sarcastically said, 'Thanks a lot.'"

But he didn't reject Martin's demand outright. "Even if the answer is 'No,' you want to give the appearance that you thought about it and tried," he said, adding that he was "hoping it would go away."

It didn't.

"Well, over the next two weeks, Mr. Martin called me every day, or perhaps even more than that on some days, and, and would ask me how I was doing on the donation, how UBS was doing on the donation, what I was doing to get the donation done. And he increased his pressure and his rhetoric over, over that time period," McGahan told jurors.

"He – he would use profanity and increase the berating and the pressure – and yelling, telling us that we, or I, had to figure out a way to make a donation.... He said that, you, meaning me, was 'going to be fucked' if I don't figure out a way to make the donation."

Martin told jurors he used such language because he "wanted Mr. McGahan to understand the seriousness of it and the severity of it because Mr. Scrushy was definitely going to fire him....I didn't want to fire him, so I really started putting pressure on Bill."

McGahan was in a jam. His bosses at UBS refused to donate anything close to $250,000, and his de facto boss in Birmingham wasn't backing down. The pressure increased when Scrushy joined Martin on one of the calls.

"Mr. Scrushy said that he wanted UBS to make a contribution to a cause in the state of Alabama, that it was a good cause, that other companies in the state were supporting it, that he was supporting it; and he wanted us to step up and support it, too."

After two weeks, and fearing he was about to lose a major client, a solution presented itself. Hanson, the HealthSouth lobbyist, also had a relationship with UBS, and the lobbyist knew that yet another of his clients, Integrated Health Services, owed UBS about $1 million in investment banking fees.

Hanson, said McGahan, suggested that UBS forgive some of Integrated Health's $1 million debt if the Maryland-based company would make the donation. McGahan proposed what may be the only debt-swap secret political charitable donation scheme in history to his superiors, and was given the green light.

McGahan called Taylor Pickett, Integrated Health's chief financial officer. Pickett's response was not unlike McGahan's to Martin's first call. "In the first conversation, when Bill indicated that he needed help, I said to him, 'Well, what are you – what are you talking about in terms of dollars?' And he said, '$250,000.' My response was ... either it was a very long pause or basically, I said that there's no way I can do that," Pickett testified at trial.

Hanson intervened, and sold the deal to Integrated Health's chairman. The company agreed to donate $250,000 to that foundation down in Alabama. In return, UBS agreed to forgive $263,000 of the $1 million owed it by Integrated Health.

"Integrated had agreed, my understanding was, to make the contribution so that Mr. Martin then didn't, didn't continue yelling at me after that," McGahan told jurors years later.

Down in Birmingham, HealthSouth was pressing for the check. Martin testified that there was "time sensitivity of getting that in Mr. Scrushy's hand in order for him to be able to deliver it to Gov. Siegelman at a meeting that he had set up, that was on his calendar."

"(Scrushy) reminded me on more than one occasion that this was an important meeting and the check had to be delivered to us at HealthSouth so he could hand deliver it to Gov. Siegelman in their meeting," Martin testified.

Up in Maryland, Pickett issued a "hot voucher" demand for Integrated's accounting people to spit the check out fast. He was told to contact Leif Murphy, another HealthSouth executive, and to arrange for its delivery to him.

"Because it was a Friday and there was some urgency in getting the check, I gave (Pickett) delivery instructions to my personal residence for Saturday delivery," Murphy testified. "If he was not able to get the check out on Friday afternoon, then he was to go ahead and send the check to my work address on that Monday."

The check wasn't cut until Monday, and arrived in Birmingham the next day. Murphy immediately delivered it to Martin, who, as he testified years later, "walked it over and handed it to Mr. Scrushy."

Scrushy made another trip to Montgomery and again, met privately with Siegelman. After the HealthSouth chairman left, Siegelman showed Bailey the check.

"He's halfway there," Siegelman told Bailey, referring to what the governor told him was Scrushy's promise to donate $500,000 to the lottery foundation.

"I responded by saying, 'What in the world is he going to want for that?' And his response was, 'The CON Board,'" Bailey testified.

To which Bailey commented, "I wouldn't think there would be a problem with it."

"I wouldn't think so," answered Siegelman.

———

On July 26 -- almost immediately after receiving the $250,000 -- Siegelman wrote Scrushy notifying him of his appointment to the CON board. The position of chair was already committed to Margie Sellers. She was head of the Alabama Association of Nursing Homes, a long-time substantial donor to Siegelman campaigns. Scrushy, according to trial testimony, asked to be named vice-chair, and Siegelman appointed him so.

Cline, the fundraising consultant, was stunned when Bailey and Siegelman showed him the $250,000 donation from Integrated Health. It was, he told jurors, "the largest check we ever received."

That amount "in one check sets off alarm bells," he testified.

Siegelman and Bailey eventually told Cline that the $250,000 originated from Scrushy, and that the HealthSouth boss had pledged another of equal size. They asked Cline to hold on to the check. This happened occasionally when there were questions about the donor that needed to be resolved prior to depositing the money.

Cline put the check in a little lockbox in his apartment. It remained there for about six weeks, which he characterized in his testimony as "an inordinate amount of time." His concern was heightened when he learned that Siegelman planned to deposit the check into a bank account in Boston set up by Anthony Fant, the treasurer for the Alabama Democratic Party and co-owner of the brokerage firm used by Siegelman, Bailey and others for their personal investments as well as Siegelman's campaign.

The check didn't go to Boston. However, some $200,000 in other donations made out to the party was routed to Boston, to the surprise, years later, of the donors themselves.

"I told (Siegelman) he was an idiot for doing it. I told him it (would be) bank fraud," Cline testified of the Boston plan.

"I know, I know. I just need to get it done," Siegelman answered.

Cline learned about the Boston account from the top two party officials – Siegelman allies Giles Perkins and Jack Miller. The two lawyers, partners in the firm Miller, Hamilton, Snider & Odom, were horrified to discover that donations to the party had been sent to an account in Boston.

Miller – a character witness at Siegelman's 2007 sentencing -- told Cline that what Siegelman and Fant were doing "could be fraud." Perkins and Miller demanded that the checks be returned to the party's regular accounts, and they were. The ultimate intent for the Boston funds remains unknown.

Meanwhile, Cline said he and his boss, Cunningham, were fretting about the Integrated Health check.

"I kept asking folks what I needed to do with this check, because I was holding onto it," Cline told jurors "And ultimately, Governor Siegelman and Nick Bailey told me to give it back to them, that they would take care of it. And they said, more specifically, that they weren't going to deposit the check, that they were going to return it."

Cline assumed the pair returned the $250,000 to Integrated Health. He didn't learn otherwise until 2004, when the FBI came knocking to ask him about the check.

———

Though he didn't know it, I had an encounter of sorts with Siegelman during the lottery campaign. I was interviewing a Mobile lawyer for a series on class action lawsuits when his secretary stepped in to say he had a call. He told her to take a message, but she trumped him. "It's the governor."

He stiffened, and picked up the phone.

His end of the conversation went something like this: "Yes sir. Yes sir. Yes sir. I'm sorry about your father, sir. He was a fine man. Yes sir. Yes sir. Yes sir," and more of the same.

I was thinking, *Is he talking to the Governor or the Godfather?*

When the call ended, I asked what Siegelman wanted, knowing it was none of my business. "He's raising money for his lottery campaign," the lawyer said, without further comment.

When the foundation filed its next campaign disclosure, I saw the attorney's name next to a $1,000 contribution.

———

Two weeks before the lotto vote, veteran AP reporter Bill Poovey wrote the first in a series of stories reporting that numerous Siegelman aides and appointees, Bailey and Hamrick among them, had speeding tickets fixed. The governor moved into damage-control mode, firing his appointed head of the state troopers, suspending three staffers, including Bailey, and ordering an investigation into the matter.

In the administration's defense, ticket-fixing was an Alabama tradition as prevalent in local courts as it was in the upper echelons of state government. Poovey's stories did much to slow down if not stop the practice, but for Siegelman's purposes, they could not have come at a worse time.

On Oct. 12, Alabama voters, especially rural, conservative Christians, jammed the polls to vote on the governor's "education lottery." That evening, the governor on a hot streak watched in disbelief as the returns came in.

The final tally: 46 percent for, 54 percent against.

Siegelman's political love-child was dead. More than dead. It was cremated. He woke up a different man the next day. "I have no plan B," an uncharacteristically dejected Siegelman told the press.

"He has put everything on this," Brad Moody, the political science professor at Auburn University at Montgomery told a reporter. "He has made it the centerpiece of his campaign and the centerpiece of his first year in office. He has thrown all his political capital away."

Three weeks later, Secrest presented his analysis of the loss in a letter to Siegelman. The Virginia pollster wrote that the churches "emerged as a much more organized opponent" than during the 1998 gubernatorial campaign.

"The opposition television (advertisements) cleverly tapped voters' ancient cynicism about their government. The free press was as relentless as it was jaded. And our mistakes amplified all of the above."

Secrest's use of the word fatal, from the quote atop this chapter, illustrated how devastating was the loss and how in the minds of Siegelman and his staff it might as well have been the governor on the ballot that day.

Years later, at trial, I felt that the prosecutors failed to fully drive home an important narrative point, which was the live-or-die aspect of the lottery for Siegelman, and as a consequence, the manic urgency of his fund-raising. The jury's verdict proved me wrong on that count.

———

On Jan. 31, of each year, candidates and PACs file annual reports of campaign contributions and expenditures from the prior year with the secretary of state. On that date in 2000 the foundation filed what appeared to all as its first and last such report, covering 1999. The summary page reported some $5 million raised, the same spent, and a final balance of zero.

"My understanding is, the attorneys have to formally close it for the foundation to end," a foundation official told the Associated Press.

A month later, the foundation did just that, filing a one-page, "Statement of Dissolution," with the secretary of state.

Campaign over, lottery lost, stick it in the history books and move on. That was the tale told the public by the proudly pro-disclosure foundation and its de facto leader.

But it wasn't over. During the previous summer Siegelman had secretly arranged for the Alabama Democratic Party's statewide grass roots ground team to get people to the polls for the referendum. The party spent about $750,000 on the operation, the agreement being that the foundation would repay it. The foundation neglected to report this arrangement on its final report, as did the Democratic Party, which was also required to disclose its contributions and expenditures to the secretary of state.

The party, its coffers sucked dry, had to take out a loan from Colonial Bank to fund its calling and hauling voters to the polls effort on Siegelman's behalf.

During our months-long run of foundation stories in 2002 and later, at trial, Siegelman (outside court, that is, since he didn't testify) maintained that he couldn't recall much if anything about the foundation's debt to the party and the two $250,000 checks delivered him by Scrushy.

He'd been, he said, too busy campaigning for the lottery. It was Bailey, operating largely solo, who carried out these shenanigans on his own, Siegelman and his lawyers declared in keeping with their wide-ranging "blame it on Nick" defense.

They said that, straight-faced, despite memos and records we had reported on showing Siegelman cognizant of the debt and fully engaged in paying it off. Among them was a Nov. 2, 1999, memo to the governor from Cunningham, the West Virginia fund-raiser. It was titled, "Debt Retirement."

"Several of our traditional contributors are basically 'tapped out,'" Cunningham wrote. "If we can deposit the Scrushy check and perform a little clean-up call time, we can retire the Foundation debt very quickly. This will give us the needed time to rest our contributors and focus on creating a plan that will retire our party debt quickly in 2000."

Three days later, Siegelman sent his Man Friday on an errand. Bailey drove to First Commercial Bank in Birmingham and opened a checking account in the name of the Alabama Education Foundation. On that day, some four months after Siegelman received it, Bailey deposited the $250,000 from Integrated Health.

Also deposited was a $25,000 check from IPSCO, a steelmaker that had recently opened a plant in Mobile; and a $15,000 donation from a Birmingham company called SCT Software & Resource Management. Neither was disclosed in the report to the secretary of state filed two months later.

"Everyone's greatest concern is the large amount of debt incurred by the Education Lottery Campaign," Jim Cunningham wrote Siegelman in another memo later that month.

In February 2000 -- shortly after the foundation's zero balance report to the secretary of state -- Siegelman sent Scrushy a hand-written note gently reminding the HealthSouth CEO about the second $250,000 promised during the meeting the previous summer in Montgomery. "Thanks so much for your continued support. Your personal commitment to help me by March 15 is very much appreciated. Hope to see you soon. Don."

To pacify the state party, on March 9, 2000, Siegelman took out a $730,789 loan from First Commercial on behalf of the foundation. He personally guaranteed the note, meaning if the foundation couldn't repay it, he would be on the line. Siegelman eased the bank's concerns by having Merv Nabors, a wealthy long-time backer, serve as co-guarantor.

Candidates routinely borrow money for campaigns. However, they're required to disclose those loans on the secretary of state reports, the same as donations. In one such case, the foundation complied. It took out a sizeable loan, listed the guarantors (which included Siegelman supporters and members of his old law firm) and later, reported the repayment of that loan – all in contrast to the undisclosed loan that Scrushy's checks went so far in repaying.

From the moment he was charged until one supposes his final breath, Siegelman has claimed that he enjoyed no personal benefit from the $500,000 given by Scrushy. It doesn't really matter, since the bribery statutes apply to campaign contributions and don't require personal financial benefit for the public official.

In March 2009, when the 11th Circuit upheld his conviction, it addressed the "personal benefit" argument if only to knock it down. The court remarked that the $730,789 foundation loan was "personally and unconditionally guaranteed by Siegelman," adding in a footnote that there was another guarantor but "each was individually liable."

With that, the court put the personal benefit argument to rest.

On the day the foundation and its two guarantors borrowed the money, the bank transferred the same amount to the Democratic Party's account at Colonial, thus burying the party's debt there. The party – in violation of the law – neglected to report this super-sized payment on its subsequent reports to the secretary of state.

———

In early 2000, Siegelman wrote Cunningham asking the consultant to structure a plan for future fundraising and for "finishing off the money that I owe for the lottery."

Cunningham responded with a document called, "Financial Plan (for) Governor Don Siegelman Year 2000 - Year 2002."

The consultant reported that the foundation's debt had been pared to $297,321. HealthSouth, wrote Cunningham, still had the outstanding $250,000 commitment. "To reduce the stress involved in carrying this debt load, it makes sense to ask Scrushy to assume the current note at First Commercial," Cunningham advised.

On May 23, 2000, Bailey drove the boss to HealthSouth's corporate offices, and as with the meeting almost a year before, remained in an outer room while the governor and Scrushy discussed business. Siegelman returned to Montgomery with a $250,000 check from HealthSouth, made payable to the lottery foundation and signed by Scrushy.

Eight months later, on Jan. 31, 2001, the foundation accepted its final contribution – a relatively smallish $13,500 check from a PAC calling itself Alabamians for Economic Development. More than a year later, that contribution became the telltale clue to the unraveling of the second, secret life of Siegelman's lottery foundation, and Scrushy's role in it.

———

In the weeks following the lottery loss, rumors swirled that the governor was suffering from depression. If true, it didn't last long. In November Siegelman put his game face back on and summoned legislators for a special session to address a long-simmering and potentially disastrous problem.

Thousands of out-of-state corporations had sued the state claiming that Alabama's franchise tax was unconstitutional because it taxed them at a higher rate than in-state companies. The state faced the prospect of refunding more than a billion dollars in back-taxes. With their backs against the wall, legislators and business leaders joined together and settled on a replacement for the old tax. This allowed Siegelman, soon after the lotto defeat, to put something in the plus column.

That column would grow during his second year in office.

"Less than 12 hours after lawmakers ended this year's regular session in a rush for the exits, a mighty swell of self-congratulation swept over the state Capitol complex Tuesday morning," wrote *Register* reporter Sean Reilly in spring 2000.

Highlights included raising teacher pay to the national average; creating a new, less political system of governance for the Alabama State Docks; and, most important for Siegelman, agreeing to let voters decide on Amendment One, a plan to borrow hundreds of millions of dollars for public works projects.

In November 2000, Alabamians overwhelmingly passed Amendment One. The vote reflected public trust in the administration, and meant Siegelman could play Santa Claus in the run-up to the 2002 election. "This governor is going to be going to a lot of ribbon cuttings from the Tennessee line to the Florida line," said Athens State political science professor Jess Brown.

But the same election produced disappointment for Democrats. Of 11 state appeals court races, Republicans won 10. After the election, State Treasurer Lucy Baxley said that as a little girl growing up in southeast Alabama, she "did not know a Republican."

"That is the truth. To me, being in politics was being in the Democratic Party. Of course, that changed."

Baxley's comments were included in a post-election piece I'd been assigned to write. It reported grumbling among Democrats that Siegelman and the state party organization cared only about the fortunes of the governor, not the party as a whole.

The assignment – and a coincidental visit by Siegelman to the *Register's* editorial board – provided me with the first of just two interviews with Siegelman during his entire tenure as governor. "Give me a break," he said. "Whoever is saying I could have had an impact -- unfortunately for me – they're wrong. This is not original, but there's a one-word explanation – Bushwacked.' There were deep, deep coattails that probably could not be anticipated."

Grafton, the political science professor, told readers that if Siegelman played his cards right, it could be Democrats riding coattails in 2002.

"What Siegelman needs to do is take full publicity advantage of construction projects started under his administration, and he must make sure the bidding process for these projects is pristine."

Added the professor: "The slightest tinge of unfairness would hurt him severely."

———

The New Year arrived with me flailing about, producing nothing that couldn't have been done just as well by a summer intern. I'd closed out the year with a story on a cleaning business shutting its doors after 54 years, and the annual piece reporting the post-Christmas strain on the city's garbage service from all that wrapping paper.

But if 2000 crawled out like a turtle, 2001 bounded in like a hare.

Few who began their Jan. 3, 2001, with *Mobile Register* in hand will ever forget this lead from that morning's paper: "Starting Sunday, the cost of sending a first-class letter increases from 33 cents to 34 cents, meaning you'll need to either use the new stamps, or supplement the old ones with 1-cent stamps." Looking back, I'm embarrassed to have put my name on what amounted to a postal service press release. This was my pitiful way of reminding editors who might otherwise not have noticed that I'd worked the day before. Reporters in slumps do such things.

The next day found me near lifeless, battling boredom and scouring the Internet for hot news to reflect off my eyeballs and give passers bye the impression of a reporter hard at it. I was the manifestation of Newton's object at rest, mired in weeks-long inertia, when the phone rang. Wake up, loser. And see about injecting some hail fellow well met into that hello.

It had been almost three years since I'd heard the voice, not since a series of stories he put me on during the James administration. Frank – and that is not his real name – said I "wouldn't believe" what the Siegelman administration was up to at the Honda plant in Talladega County.

He didn't know it, and I sure didn't, but Frank was about to change the course of my life for the next several years, and Siegelman's for far longer than that.

Inaugural Parade: **Alabama's new governor, full of hope and promise, leads the inaugural parade on Jan. 18, 1999. On Siegelman's right is his daughter Dana, to his left, wife Lori.**

Paul Hamrick. **Paul Hamrick, Siegelman's chief of staff and his connection to Lanny Young.** *Photo courtesy of Kyle Whitmire*

Nick and Siegelman: **Gov. Siegelman and his loyal aide Nick Bailey during good times, before the G.H. Construction scandal changed both their lives. Here they are viewing documents at the state archives.** *Photo courtesy of Kevin Glackmeyer*

Lanny Young: **Lanny Young leaves the federal courthouse in November 2006, after being sentenced to two years in prison for his part in the G.H. Construction and other scandals.** *Photo by Rob Carr, Associated Press*

Nobody home. **The office of G.H. "Goat Hill" Construction – as empty as the company.** *Photo by Eddie Curran*

Invoice for surveying services on the 250 acre boundary survey of the Haardt property, Dixie Garden's per our agreement with Ran Garver.

TOTAL AMOUNT DUE --- $21,625.00

Property: North Ripley Street

    Alta Survey on 258.77 acres   COPY $32,500.00

    Geotechnical Engineer Services $37,558.00
    Test Borings, Determinations of soil
    Bearing values, Ground Corrosion and Resistivity Test

    Wetlands and Federally Endangered and Threatened $20,000.00
    Species Evaluation

                                   Total Now Due: $90,058.00

TERMS: Charges are due and payable upon receipt of invoice. Accounts are considered past due if not within 30 days from date of invoice. Past due accounts are subject to 1 ½% interest per month.

Respectfully submitted,

CDG Engineers and Associates, Inc.

Mark Pugh
Mark Pugh, P.E.
Vice President

---

ing participation of Federal-aid highway funds, and is subject to applicable State and Federal laws, both

al and civil.

12/16/99
(Date)

(Signature)

The forged bills. At the top is a portion of a legitimate bill for a boundary survey of the warehouse site by a company called Lucido & Oliver. It was turned into the state for payment by G.H. Construction. The second document is an apparent bill from CDG Engineering and also submitted to the state by G.H. Construction. The bill shows CDG charging $90,058 for three reviews of the same property, including an Alta Survey -- one and the same as a boundary survey. The *Mobile Register's* reporting of that bogus bill, among other irregularities, ended the warehouse project and led to the start of the investigation into Siegelman and his administration. The third document, at bottom, shows the real signature of Marcus K. "Mark" Pugh, from a real CDG contract with the highway department. If you compare it to the signature on the bogus bill you will see that the signature on the CDG bill for the warehouse site work is a forgery. The hen-scratch on the bills is mine.

Bill Pryor. **Within days of our first story on G.H. Construction, Alabama Attorney General Bill Pryor initiated the criminal investigation that ultimately led to Siegelman's conviction.**

Bill Blount. **The collapse of the G.H. Construction deal probably cost Bill Blount more than $500,000 in fees, but likely kept him out of prison, at least until the Larry Langford case. Here he is in August 2009, after pleading guilty to bribing Langford.** *Photo courtesy of Kyle Whitmire*

Me at work. **The author, circa 2001, no doubt working on a Siegelman story. Long-time co-worker and friend Willie Rabb is in the background of this picture, taken in the old Press Register building.** *Photo courtesy of Press-Register*

Paul FCloos. **Paul Cloos, friend and adversary, he was my primary editor on most if not all of the Siegelman stories.** *Photo courtesy of Paul Cloos*

STATE OF ALABAMA

DON SIEGELMAN
LIEUTENANT GOVERNOR

P.O. BOX 5049
MONTGOMERY, ALABAMA 36103
(334) 242-7900
FAX (334) 269-5588

7/25/96

Mr. Cunningham —

Last year I sued the State (Alabama Dept. of Agriculture) for the death of a state employee.

If I can be of any help to you in any way please do not hesitate to call —

Siegelman

261-2394
Private paging #

Not printed at government expense

Siegelman the lawyer. This is the attorney-solicitation letter then-lieutenant governor Siegelman sent the parents of Todd Cunningham, soon after Cunningham was run over and killed by inmates driving a state prison van. The tiny print at the bottom states that the stationary was "not printed at government expense."

Rip Andrews. **I wish I hadn't cussed out Rip Andrews, but I did, and it caused me, and the paper, lots of problems.** *Photo courtesy of Rip Andrews*

Brett Blackledge. **Brett Blackledge and I competed like old warhorses on the Siegelman scandals. He later won a Pulitzer Prize exposing the too outrageous to be true corruption in Alabama's two-year college system.** *Copyright, The Birmingham News. All rights reserved*

Kim Chandler. **Kim Chandler was Blackledge's partner on the News's Siegelman reports, and stayed with the story, covering the grand jury, trial, and aftermath.** *Copyright, The Birmingham News. All rights reserved*

Lanny Vines. **Many say that the stories reporting that Birmingham trial lawyer Lanny Vines was the real buyer of Siegelman's house, and for twice its value, cost Siegelman the 2002 governor's race. Here's the irrepressible Vines in 2005, back practicing law after blowing $30 million in a badly timed change of careers – from the law to day-trading.** *Copyright, The Birmingham News. All rights reserved. Photo by Charles Nesbitt*

Siegelman's house. **A side view of the house Siegelman sold to Vines for $250,000, the sale concealed by a straw man buyer – Vines' accountant, Wray Pearce.** *Photo by Eddie Curran*

This page, in the court file of Lanny Vines' lawsuit against his former accountant, Wray Pearce, proved that Pearce was acting on Vines' behalf when he bought Siegelman's house.

46. Please provide all notes, correspondence, and memorandums concerning negotiations to purchase Gov. Don Siegelman's residence in Montgomery.

47. Were any phone conversations recorded with Gov. Siegelman? If so, then please provide copies of same or transcripts.

48. Please provide each and every bit of money paid directly to Gov. Siegelman in the past five (5) years as legal fees, advances on fees, and/or for any other purpose.

49. Please provide all notes, letters, memorandums, documents, correspondence or documents of any type whatsoever concerning the purchase of Gov. Siegelman's house or the L.L.C. that owned the house.

50. Please provide any and all appraisal information or other information you relied upon to induce J. Wray Pearce to purchase the house and former residence of Gov. Don Seigelman and family for a price in excess of the fair market value.

Scrushy croons. **Richard Scrushy used HealthSouth money to fund "Dallas County Line," the country music band he fronted until the failure of the band's album, "Rich Man's Dream."** *Copyright, The Birmingham News. All rights reserved. Photo by Jeff Roberts*

Leura Canary. **The Siegelman investigation began before Leura Canary became U.S. Attorney, and soon after she removed herself from all oversight of the case. Starting in early 2002, Siegelman and his backers relentlessly attacked her as if she were directing the prosecution.**

Bill Canary. **After Jill Simpson's affidavit, Bill Canary found himself tarred in national media reports as a leader of the conspiracy against Siegelman.** *Photo used permission of Bill Canary*

Heston visits Alabama. **Charlton Heston, in one of his final public appearances, campaigning for Bob Riley and other Republicans in September 2002, in Huntsville. Unbeknownst to Riley, the night before this picture was taken, Siegelman visited Heston in his Mobile hotel room. The actor, by then almost incapacitated with Alzheimer's, signed a letter endorsing Siegelman. That stunned the Riley campaign and led to Republican accusations of a dirty trick by Siegelman on the long-time public face of the NRA.** *Photo courtesy of David Azbell*

Siegelman seeks recount. **Siegelman meets the media the morning after the 2002 election, and pledges to pursue a recount of the vote he continues to insists he won.**

Dr. Henry C. Mabry, III
State Finance Director
600 Dexter Avenue
State Capitol, N-105
Montgomery, Alabama 36130

MAY 1999
Received
Finance Director's
Office

Re: University of South Alabama

Dear Dr. Mabry:

Enclosed please find two originals of the Settlement Agreement I telefaxed to you today. The Governor advised me this morning to be sure it was in your hands as soon as possible. Please call me after you have reviewed it.

Very truly yours,

CHERRY, GIVENS, PETERS
& LOCKETT, P.C.

CHRISTOPHER E. PETERS

Siegelman initiates tobacco deal. **Siegelman claimed he took a hands off approach to the settlement with the University of South Alabama with a provision to route $2.8 million to the law firm that, during the same time frame, agreed to pay the governor about $800,000. This letter from lawyer Chris Peters to Finance Director Henry Mabry shows that Siegelman was involved from the start.**

Riley campaign flier. **In the 2002 campaign, Bob Riley had plenty to work with in muddying up Siegelman as a corrupt governor, as the flier shows.**

Governor of Goat Hill. **This J.D. Crowe cartoon, published soon after the first of the G.H. Construction stories, is the source of the book's title.** *Used courtesy of J.D. Crowe*

PART TWO:
The Stories

Chapter 5
HONDA

"I do have some concerns, however, which I bring to your attention before your decision to sign the document. As you know, this project is unusual for Alabama because the work can legally be negotiated rather than competitively bid. I feel sure that at some point during the life of the project, the media will ask about the contractor and the circumstances surrounding his selection."
-- *December 1999 memo from Ken Funderburke to Siegelman following the governor's decision to hire a little known Birmingham firm to build a $10 million worker training facility at the new Honda plant.*

"Years ago, our state took the wise step of setting up a competitive bid law to break through the rash of good-old-boy contracts. But sadly, those who seek to make easy bucks off the taxpayers have found a way to sneak around the law by quietly writing exemptions to the law in numerous bills."
-- *Lt. Gov. Steve Windom's Republican response to Siegelman's February 2001 state-of-the-state address, given two days after the Register reported that a no-bid contract to prepare the Honda site had run to almost $36 million.*

Ken Funderburke tried. In memos to the governor's office, the state's chief industrial recruiter voiced concerns about a pair of multi-million dollar no-bid construction contracts, both elements of a $64 million incentives package used to lure Honda to Alabama. The state's winning offer included pledges to prepare a 400-acre site for the plant and construction of a high-tech worker training facility, both in Talladega County and about 60 miles east of Birmingham.

Siegelman had appointed Funderburke, an investment banker, to run the Alabama Development Office, the agency responsible for recruiting industry to the state. Funderburke's memos -- one in August 1999, the second that December, and both unearthed years later in a lawsuit -- can't be described as emphatic. But in both, the message was there. And he left out what he surely had to know – that the contracts, one of which soared to $36 million, were going to Siegelman's buddies.

In the first, to Hamrick, Funderburke wrote that the governor's lawyers had determined that because of the funding source, the bid law didn't apply to the Honda projects. "Obviously, this gives us the freedom to hire whomever we choose, however we may wish to go through some bid process on selected items with a limited number of contractors of our choice," he suggested.

The second memo went straight to Siegelman, and addressed the decision to hire a company called Sherrod Construction to build a high-tech building where Honda would train people to build cars. Funderburke warned the governor that eventually, "the media will ask about the contractor and the circumstances surrounding his selection."

———

In October 2000 I wrote one of my few stories that year on state government, about the sale of bonds to fund something called the Alabama 21st Century Authority. It was informational rather than investigative, and if anything, put the administration in a positive light. As luck would have it, researching the piece educated me on an important element of what became, months later, my first stories on the administration, and that I refer to as the Honda no-bid contract stories.

The stories, while not terrifically sexy, were important for several reasons. I'm convinced that without Honda, I would not have written the first word about Lanny Young and G.H. Construction. I think it reasonable to suggest that the half-million dollars given by Scrushy to the lottery foundation would have remained a secret, and much else as well.

Honda spawned a two-year blitz of stories that drew public and legislative attention to the awarding of contracts by the administration, and, I like to think, saved the state a lot of money. For me, it served as a crash course in the administration's way of doing business. It was like the slow ride to the peak of a rollercoaster. After Honda, the wild ride began.

Had Paul Hamrick responded truthfully to my questions on Honda, these stories might have been it. He did not. That bred mistrust and from there, the small step to suspicion. I started looking under rocks that I'd have otherwise passed by without a thought.

The story in October examined a decision by the Siegelman administration for Alabama to become the first state to borrow money through the sale of "tobacco bonds," the collateral being the money due Alabama from the 1998 "Master Settlement Agreement" between the states and cigarette-makers.

This was done through the Alabama 21st Century Authority. For various legal reasons, government bodies form entities, usually called authorities, to serve as the official issuer of bonds. Alabama has many. There's one to borrow money to build prisons, another for school buildings, and so on. The 21st Century Authority was created to finance the incentives used to lure big companies like Honda to the state.

Because I had no clue to its existence, the story made no mention of a seemingly innocuous one-sentence paragraph within the 28-page bill that gave birth to the authority. It read (italics mine): "Articles 2 and 3 of Chapter 16 of Title 41, Code of Alabama 1975, and other similar laws *shall not apply* to the Authority, its directors, or any of its officers, agents, or employees in their capacities as such."

Articles 2 and 3 of Chapter 16 of Title 41 are Alabama's bid laws.

With a few words, the administration had created a loophole big enough to drive a $36 million no-bid contract through. Little wonder, then, that the governor's lawyers were able to deliver a legal opinion declaring that bids weren't required on projects paid for with authority funds.

They'd drafted the legislation.

———

The call that rattled me from professional slumber sounded promising if for no other reason than it was from Frank. During the James' administration he had more than proved his value as a source on matters involving the highway department.

Frank – again, not his real name -- said the administration had skirted the bid law by hand-picking three companies to prepare the site for the new Honda plant. The firms, Siegelman supporters all, had formed a joint venture called EPM Constructors Inc., specifically for the project. The E came from Ellard Contracting Co., of Birmingham; the P from Tuscaloosa's John Plott Inc.; and Alabama Bridge Builders Inc. provided the M, by way of its president Keith "Tack" Mims.

I'd reported on all manner of construction and road-building jobs, but site prep was a new one. It entails preparing land for something, usually a building. Think of a woodsy parcel purchased for a Wal-Mart. First, a contractor must raze the trees and level the land ("clearing and grubbing"); provide whatever earth work is necessary to ensure that the foundation is solid; build drainage ditches and roads to and about a site; and develop the infrastructure for utilities.

The contract – initially for about $800,000 -- had ballooned above $35 million, and the state's roadbuilders were irate that the administration hadn't sought bids on such a huge project. "It's unbelievable what they're doing," Frank said. "I've never seen anything like it. Ever."

And Honda, he said, was only the beginning.

Months earlier, Mercedes-Benz announced plans to expand production of its M-Class SUV, which it manufactured in Tuscaloosa County. In 1994, when Mercedes became the first automaker to locate in Alabama, it stated its intention to eventually double the size of the plant. Now it was ready to do so, and as promised, the state was providing another round of incentives. The state's package for "Mercedes II" included up to $20 million for site work. The road-building grapevine had the administration handing Mercedes to EPM without seeking bids, just as it had with Honda, and the contracting community was cussing mad.

We'd need to meet, Frank said. The stuff was too complicated to explain over the phone. When I arrived the next day he had the relevant materials laid out on a table. He showed me the $818,675 contract and some of the pricing information, which he said was where I'd want to direct my inquiries.

Frank pointed out about a dozen items in the contract, the prices for which exceeded anything he'd ever seen. There were other items – not the prices, but the items themselves – that he'd never seen. These showed payment for services historically included within other categories.

"They made up some items," said Frank, aghast. "A correlation would be having a unit price for every time you cranked your machine up."

He showed me an article from the previous January by Dana Beyerle, the veteran Montgomery-bureau reporter for the *Tuscaloosa News* and other mid-sized Alabama papers owned by the *New York Times*. Put Dana in the same room with the AP's Phil Rawls and you'd have all the institutional knowledge on Alabama politics since, say, 1980. Probably before, but first hand since.

Highway director Mack Roberts had told Beyerle that he chose the EPM companies because they were "top contractors" who could work fast, and speed was vital given Honda's rushed time-line. That may have sounded reasonable to the public, but it was an insult to other contractors who knew that the EPM firms were no more equipped to "work fast" than they.

Roberts said EPM initially sought $1.1 million but the department negotiated hard to cut the price.

Some of the elements in my story were first reported by Dana, yet his didn't have near the impact. The reason my story took off where his didn't was timing. First is best in journalism, but there are exceptions. In January 2000, EPM hadn't been paid a dime and the total they were to receive was $818,675. By the time Frank called me, the state had paid EPM about $30 million, with another $6 million on the way.

When Frank showed me all those millions, I knew I needed to get moving. After I got the project records I would have a story. But it would be stronger with comments from someone in the road-building community who could put the administration's bid-dodging in perspective. It wasn't going to be Frank, but he had a friend who knew as much about the deal as anyone and was so mad he might go on the record. His name was Keith Andrews, and he ran Tuscaloosa-based company, RaCON Inc.

Keith, said Frank, was expecting my call.

———

As soon became clear, Keith was the ideal source for the story.

He knew all there was to know about the site work for the original Mercedes plant, which until Honda was the only such project of its type in state history. That job was paid for by the state but overseen by Mercedes, as opposed to the Siegelman plan of using the highway department to manage the project.

Back in 1994, the German automaker divided the work into seven contracts. All were bid, and RaCON, which Keith owned with his mother and father, won six, as well as subsequent jobs let and paid for by Mercedes.

Keith's dad Benton – an old-time roadbuilder who went way back with Roberts – had called the highway director to ask if what he was hearing was true. Handing Mercedes to EPM without seeking bids would be particularly galling for RaCON, considering the company's performance on "Mercedes I," and its location.

"My dad asked where we stood in the running for the Mercedes Benz plant site, and Mack Roberts told him we were not in the running for the Mercedes Benz site, but that there were more projects to bid on, and that Mercedes was just a small job anyway," Keith said. "He was trying to play down the size of a $20 to $25 million job."

RaCON's proximity to Mercedes would enable it to shave costs. Anyone bidding against the company would have to take that into consideration. There was no way that eliminating RaCON and handing the job to EPM wouldn't cost taxpayers.

During our first conversation I suggested a set of commonly used ground rules. Reporter and source agree to talk off the record while preserving the possibility of deciding at a later date to use the comments with attribution, with that decision the source's to make. Often as not, comments made off the record are harmful to no one, and after I read them back, he or she agrees that the comments will both serve them and enlighten readers.

Keith's comments were of a different nature. Use of what he was telling me, with his name attached, could harm his business. I knew it, he knew it. As a rule, roadbuilders never criticize a governor or highway director. There are 110 ways that the DOT can break a contractor, especially if a petty governor or highway director demands that screws be tightened.

We agreed to put off the attribution decision. In the meantime, Keith assisted in other ways, as did Frank. They tutored me on site prep contracts, explaining the dozens of items, or units, within the EPM contract and the normal price ranges for each. This helped me understand the mounds of records I was to review in Montgomery, and prepared me for a meeting with highway department engineers assigned to the Honda project. My records from the period contain this note to myself, next to the names of Keith and Frank: "I want every possible excuse they (the highway department) will throw at me, before-hand, and want inside info to help me out there."

In late January I e-mailed assistant highway director Paul Bowlin to request all correspondence between the department and the governor's office regarding the selection of EPM for Honda. The same records were sought for Mercedes.

Instead of records, the department and the administration gave me some hard to disprove if impossible to believe hokum about everything involving EPM's selection being verbal.

The same e-mail sought correspondence reflecting price negotiations between EPM and the highway department. The contract didn't have a finite price. Instead, the company was being paid based on the total number of units the job required, multiplied by the price of each unit.

I requested negotiating records for all manner of "units," including, "unclassified excavation and related units, such as fine grading and the original clearing contract; all units related to pile driving; all units related to the concrete, or crushed aggregate base; all units related to engineering controls; and mobilization."

Not as exciting or for that matter, easy, as reporting on, say, a bank robbery, but such are the questions one must ask in trying to ascertain the reasonableness of a no-bid site-prep contract.

Several times I asked to interview Siegelman, be it by telephone or in person. This was two years into his administration, before I'd written the first hard-hitting story or made anyone mad.

"While I appreciate the opportunity to speak with Mack Roberts and Jim Hayes (Funderburke's replacement as director of the Alabama Development Office), the fact remains that the governor created the 21st Century Authority, and the buck stops with him, not Mack Roberts or Jim Hayes or even Henry Mabry," went one such request. "I think he has a responsibility to address what I think are serious questions about the administration's oversight of state funds."

Siegelman didn't see it that way, and no interview was granted.

With the story about ready to run, Keith gave me the thumbs up to use his quotes. He was a big boy, we'd talked a lot about it, and I didn't go overboard trying to dissuade him.

In the weeks since Frank called I'd interviewed dozens of people, made two trips to Montgomery, and slogged through thousands of pages of project files, payment records, legislation, and other records. The story published on Feb. 4, 2001, made a convincing case for favoritism and waste, but unlike later stories, didn't present evidence suggesting criminality.

It was the first of more than 100 stories under my byline and about the governor and his administration in the two years to come. It ran atop our Sunday front page, and began:

State-funded site preparation as part of an incentives package to lure Honda Motor Co. to Alabama is projected to cost almost $36 million-- a figure that has some contractors fuming, because the state did not seek bids for the work.

The contractors claim the state could be drastically overpaying for the work and that officials unfairly limited competition.

A year ago in January, Gov. Don Siegelman's highway director, Mack Roberts, said the state had selected a contractor and entered into an $818,675 contract to prepare a Talladega County site for the Japan-based automaker.

What wasn't said was that the contract was just one of many that would be entered into with the hand-picked, Birmingham-based EPM Constructors, a joint venture of three Alabama contractors who have supported Siegelman.

So far, EPM has reaped more than $30 million from the Honda site, paid by the state without bids, according to Alabama Department of Transportation records. The agency estimates that EPM will ultimately get $35.8 million.

"I've talked to more than 25 contractors, and everybody thinks this is just total crap," said Keith Andrews, who runs the family construction business, Tuscaloosa-based RaCON Inc.

The story reported that Siegelman's lawyers provided legal clearance for not seeking bids, but noted that their opinion didn't prohibit bids, as Keith and others pointed out in the story.

"Why would the governor or the highway director skirt bids on a job that costs over $20 million?" Andrews asked. "Why would the governor not want to open it up for bids to save the taxpayers' money?"

In the weeks before Keith permitted me to use his name, I'd been trying to pin down the situation at Mercedes. As with many stories to come, we presented these efforts – replacing me or I with "the *Register*" -- to show readers how difficult it was getting answers and information from their governor.

This from the story, me as dog chasing its tail:

When the Register tried to learn whether EPM had gained the Mercedes job, Bowlin said he didn't know. He recommended that the newspaper call Jim Hayes. As director of the Alabama Development Office, Hayes (who by then had replaced Funderburke) is the state's chief industrial recruiter and is intimately involved with the Honda and Mercedes projects, Bowlin said. The DOT was merely managing the Honda project on ADO's behalf and would be doing the same for ADO on the Mercedes expansion, Bowlin said.

Carrie Kurlander, Siegelman's chief spokesperson, also recommended that the Register call Hayes to find out about the contractor selection process and the status of it.

"I don't have a clue who it is," Hayes said Wednesday. "I'm not familiar with how the process works. I wouldn't know how to judge a good contractor from a bad one. That all comes from the DOT, because they are the engineers of the world."

As it would in stories to come, the administration was applying a bastardized version of Harry Truman's leadership adage, "The Buck Stops Here." For Siegelman, it was, "The Buck Stops Somewhere Else, and We Can't Find It."

Keith Andrews's authorization to use his comments provided the truth leverage I needed to break through the nonsense. I could now use his father Benton's statement that Roberts told him that EPM was being given the Mercedes job as well.

I called the highway department and asked for Roberts, fully expecting a secretary to screen the call. I was surprised when Roberts picked up. I introduced myself, said I had spoken with Keith and Benton Andrews, and told him what he already knew -- that the Andrews and others were angry about EPM's no-bid contract at Honda.

Then I told him what Benton had said about Mercedes. The highway director sounded surprised to learn that a fellow old-timer was complaining about department business to a reporter, and went quiet. I suspected he was doing the math, forced to choose between the truth and what he imagined the governor would prefer him to say.

"Yeah, that was pretty much the decision that was made," Roberts said after a bit. "We'll be using these same people on the Mercedes project. These guys have had the experience on it, so we are just going to go ahead with them on the next project."

That quote made the story. It was followed by this: "Hamrick, Siegelman's chief of staff, stressed that the governor had no role in suggesting the contractors for the Mercedes work. He was simply accepting Roberts' recommendation."

Hamrick also said that it was Roberts, not Siegelman, who decided against seeking bids for Honda and who put together the EPM team.

In each case, the governor put his trust in the highway director, Hamrick said.

This was nonsense, but short of Roberts saying so, there was nothing I could do but let Hamrick and Siegelman get away with it. Had I been writing an opinion piece I could have added something along the lines of, "Hamrick and Siegelman should be ashamed of themselves for blaming Mack Roberts for decisions surely made within the governor's office."

Might Roberts, chafed with his new title, Fall Guy, give a different account? There was little chance of this. The then 68-year-old highway director had spent decades in the department. He'd served as director under other governors. He knew the game. It's called Protect the Governor.

After the 2006 trial, with no more governor to protect, Roberts told me what really happened.

He had urged Siegelman to take bids on Honda, and later, Mercedes as well. The governor rejected his counsel both times.

"It all came up in a staff meeting," Roberts recalled. "The bond issue didn't call for competitive bidding so there was nothing illegal about it, and he (Siegelman) was talking about giving (Honda) to friends. I said, 'Well I don't want to have to negotiate anything that big.' I told him that at the least, solicit bids from three or four friends, and then we'll have a competitive bid situation where we will have a competitive price, and of course, the governor said, 'We're not going to do that, we're going to give it to our friends.'

"I was upset about it because I didn't want to do that."

Roberts said he was shocked to read Hamrick's statements placing the Honda and Mercedes decisions squarely on his shoulders. "I started thinking about leaving (the administration) about the time that story came out," he said.

Siegelman never apologized for Hamrick's statements, nor did Roberts express his displeasure to the governor. "I just began to think I wanted to do something else," he said.

———

Several days before our story ran I interviewed a group of department engineers overseeing EPM's work at Honda. Assistant director Bowlin, who was present, said the department had negotiated a contract with EPM for Mercedes, but it remained unsigned. It was therefore not a public record and thus not available for my review.

I put that in the story, along with a comment volunteered by one of the engineers at the meeting. He said EPM had, the day before, begun cutting down trees and clearing the area for the new Mercedes site. It's a violation of the state's public works laws for a company to start work on a project without a contract. Either there was a contract, and they were breaking the public records law by not producing it, or there wasn't a contract and they were breaking the public records law by allowing the company to start work.

———

Among the state's defenses for the ballooning costs at Honda was the unexpected presence of sinkholes at the site. EPM had to fill these holes and drive additional steel piling deep into the ground to stabilize the site upon which the car-making plant was to be built. This undoubtedly contributed to the cost, all the more so because of the exorbitant prices EPM was permitted to charge for piling-related work.

The lead to the Honda piece would have been dramatically different had I known of certain payments by EPM's Tack Mims. In 1999, he'd given $50,000 to Trava Williams, Nick Bailey's friend and business partner and Siegelman's stockbroker. At the 2006 trial, Bailey admitted to having called Mims seeking the money, then directing him to pay it to Williams. Bailey also testified – and I didn't believe him – that Siegelman was unaware of the payment.

Later, while researching Lanny Young, I came across a record showing an $86,000 loan from Mims to Lanny. By the time I found it, neither Mims nor Lanny was taking my calls. I suspect to the point of being certain that Mims, like others who benefitted from state work handed them by the administration, was asked by Bailey or perhaps Siegelman himself to help keep Lanny afloat until his next landfill bonanza paid off.

You know the one: If a tree falls in the forest and nobody's there, did it make a noise?

How about: If a newspaper exposes a rotten deal when the legislature isn't in session, does anyone notice?

Not the perfect metaphor. The legislature needn't be convened for a story to make an impact. But the same story when the legislature is in town?

Stand back. The winds of righteous indignation are about to blow.

Never could I have imagined the response to the Honda story. Lawmakers from both parties jumped all over it.

The governor's, "State of the State" address was scheduled for a Tuesday, two days after our story, and Steve Windom, as his party's highest ranking state official, was to follow with the Republican version. The lieutenant governor and his allies obviously re-wrote his speech at the last minute, as it began with a blast against no-bid contracts and a proposal for a constitutional amendment to strengthen the state bid law.

Windom excoriated "those who seek to make easy bucks off the taxpayers" by, "quietly writing exemptions to the (bid) law in numerous bills."

The lieutenant governor had opposed almost every initiative pushed by Siegelman and had relished the defeat of the lottery referendum. But with the start of the 2002 campaign a year away, Windom lacked a defining issue. Stories on no-bid contracts arrived as manna from heaven. He fashioned himself as a reformer and pummeled Siegelman with each new revelation of scandal and favoritism. Over the next two years, Windom served as an echo chamber for my stories and many others by the *Birmingham News.*

The beating administered after the Honda story took its toll, and by week's end, the administration signaled an about face on Mercedes. I wrote a follow-up quoting Hamrick claiming that Roberts was leaning toward taking bids because of recently discovered differences between the engineering plans for Mercedes and those for Honda. That was ludicrous, but it being a straight news story and not an opinion piece, I had to present their reason as given to me and hope readers figured it out.

Hamrick emphasized that the decision to bid or not at Mercedes was Roberts' to make, not Siegelman's.

I asked if the apparent decision to seek bids at Mercedes was a response to complaints by legislators, contractors and others upon learning about Honda's $36 million price-tag.

"There have been no complaints," answered Hamrick.

The usually unflappable chief of staff was becoming combative, his statements absurd. No complaints? Where had he been the previous week? Neptune?

I reminded him of Roberts statement to me that the department would not be seeking bids at Mercedes, and that it planned to use the "same people on the Mercedes project" as at Honda.

Hamrick's response caught me off guard. Roberts, he declared, never said that. A translation might go something like: Hamrick told Curran that Roberts didn't tell Curran what Roberts told Curran during a conversation to which Hamrick was not a party.

The inference was that I'd fabricated Roberts' quote. But neither Hamrick nor Roberts was accusing me of that. Nor did Hamrick's answer account for the fact that EPM had *already started working* at Mercedes.

So what to do? How to present these alternate realities to the reader?

I solved the quandary by using Roberts' quote from the first story, followed by: "On Friday, Hamrick denied that Roberts had told the *Register* that he had picked EPM to do all the work at Mercedes."

I trusted readers to figure it out.

———

The story also summarized what little I knew about the hiring of little-known company to build the Honda worker training facility. I'd come across the $10 million project while wading through the authority records and was in the early stages of researching it.

This from the story:

Last year, the 21st Century Authority bypassed the bid process otherwise required by state law for such projects and awarded the contract to Sherrod Construction Co. of Birmingham.

That building construction is being overseen by a state agency called the Alabama Industrial Development and Training Institute and Ed Castile, its longtime director. Castile said last week he has no idea how Sherrod was selected.

"That's not something I was involved in, period," Castile said. "That's way outside my range."

Last Wednesday, the Register faxed a series of questions to the governor's press office. One of those addressed the method of choosing the builder for the training center. Hamrick said Friday he didn't know how Sherrod was chosen or why.

Unlike Roberts, Castille wasn't a political appointee. "Protect the Governor" wasn't in his job description, but neither was, "Tick off the Governor." His response that the training facility contract was "way outside his range" suggested a wish to distance himself from the selection of Sherrod Construction.

As for Hamrick's profession of ignorance – well, it left us with a mystery.

Am I wrong, or did someone have to choose the company?

Chapter 6
Continuing Education

"One thing that disturbs me is that I know such records exist and are easily accessible. I just need to be told where they are, and I will drive there. All I need is a table and a couple of hours, and will pay for copies. I won't bother anyone, or take up hardly any time from anyone, other than someone pointing me to a room and showing me the file cabinet that houses what I seek to review."

-- E-mail to Paul Hamrick regarding request to review records on construction of the Honda worker training facility.

"I really don't care if any of the documents referenced are public or not – we are fine with anybody looking at them. In particular if you have any documents that indicate that someone was unhappy with the work done at the Honda site, please make those available. That way no one will have to waste their time sifting through any documents that show the work was done correctly."

-- Hamrick's response.

To its credit, the highway department maintains immaculate files, thick with memos, correspondence and the like. I was familiar with the drill from the James administration. I arrive at the big ALDOT headquarters, sign in up front, and curl around the hall to the director's suite of offices. After pleasantries with the secretaries, someone would take me into a nearby room, where boxes of files awaited on a conference table.

Typically I have other business the same day in Montgomery, so I move fast, scanning everything, including handwritten notes on folder jackets. My weapon of choice is paper clips, far superior to sticky notes in that they allow one to indicate large chunks of records to be copied, whether by me or an agency secretary. Out of fear of leaving something behind, I clip everything that even might prove useful. The downside is that I accumulate mounds of crap that slows me down at writing time.

The first Honda story examined the no-bid aspect of EPM's contract. The second scrutinized the pricing to illustrate the repercussions of that failure to bid.

With highway contracts, a company's bid is the total of what might be called bids within the bid. Circumstances always vary from the plans upon which the bids were based. If a job requires more asphalt than anticipated, then the extra cost is determined by the "unit price" for asphalt within the winning contractor's bid.

Keith and Frank told me I'd want to compare the unit prices paid to EPM against the norms for those units on competitively bid projects. Because there were so many units, I limited my review to costliest units.

I called two out-of-state suppliers who had nothing to lose from being quoted in an Alabama paper, and began the piece with their comments:

In separate interviews, sales representatives Tom deMahy and Don Vukmanic agreed to this arrangement: First, they would quote a price on a type of steel piling used at the site of the new Honda Motor Corp. plant 60 miles east of Birmingham.

Then, they'd be told by the Mobile Register what the state of Alabama had paid for the same product.

DeMahy said from his Metairie, La., office that he could arrange delivery of 300,000-plus linear feet of "H" pile from a plant in Arkansas to a site near Birmingham at a cost of $11.77 per foot.

From his Pittsburgh, Pa., office, Vukmanic said he could truck the "H" pile -- a type of steel piling driven into the ground to support buildings -- from a Virginia plant to Alabama for $11.50 a foot.

After fulfilling their ends of the bargain, the two were told what Alabama had paid: $15.40 a foot, to a three-company Alabama contractor, EPM Constructors, which had ordered it from a Birmingham supplier. In the separate interviews, the two steel salesmen reacted almost identically to the number. Each remained silent for several seconds, then burst out laughing.

"Oooooh, ahhhh," said deMahy. "Yeah, I think somebody is doing extremely well."

"How do I get into this action?" said a giggling Vukmanic. "I'm telling you, we don't operate on any margins near that, sir. I don't want to speak too freely, but in a competitive bid situation, you could get a more favorable price than that. Let me say that."

Readers were also told that EPM's price for driving the "H-pile" was $5.25 a linear foot, or about $2 more than the normal price. Examples like this, some of which had substantial impact on the overall price, others less so, abounded throughout the contract, and in our story, such as here:

"Contractors, and even Bowlin, couldn't say what 'Pile Installation Set-Up' was, when asked by the Register. EPM has been paid $1.5 million for that category. The DOT staff said that's to reimburse the company its costs of moving its machines over large areas, which they said isn't required on normal jobs."

Nonsense, said Frank and Keith. They couldn't believe the state let EPM create a name and charge extra for work already included in another unit for which the company was already being overpaid.

We reported that Mississippi was buying the materials for its new Nissan plant and bidding out the work. "Had Alabama done the same, it could have purchased the H-pile for about $12 a linear foot, and saved $3.40 a linear foot -- the difference between $12 and EPM's cost," readers were told. "Such a difference, multiplied by the steel piling used at the Honda site, could have saved the (state) about $1.2 million."

Without schooling from Frank and Keith I would have never known to examine another angle. The Federal Highway Administration partners with the state on most highway projects, with the feds footing 80 percent of the bill. The agency requires that contractors pay a 5 percent gross receipts tax on the total cost of federal projects, on labor, materials, everything. That money is returned to the state, with some of it used to fund mental health programs. Before bidding projects, roadbuilders spread that 5 percent throughout their bid, said Frank and Keith. Because the Honda job didn't involve federal funds, EPM wasn't paying the tax, so the company's costs should've been 5 percent lower across the board, or based on $36 million, by about $1.8 million.

Bowlin said the department didn't consider EPM's exemption from this tax when negotiating prices. "That just wasn't part of our thought process -- the taxes they would pay," he said.

Department officials acknowledged that the unit prices throughout the contract were high, but said they'd negotiated, often fiercely, and done their best to save taxpayer dollars. Siegelman, though, had put them in an impossible situation, as Roberts, even then, hinted at. "Once you get contractors in there, you can't switch back and forth," he said.

EPM's negotiating edge was exacerbated by the imperative of moving fast to satisfy Honda. An e-mail exchange in the project files demonstrated EPM's greed, the department's attempts to limit costs, and the end result. A state engineer, Skip Powe, wrote than EPM submitted a cost of $3,900 apiece for a unit called well closure. Powe haggled the company down substantially, to $1,933. "We can live with it," he wrote, after noting that the normal bid range was $400 to $1,300.

Separately, I was working on a story about the worker training facility Honda. Hamrick's statement that the administration hadn't a clue who selected the Sherrod Construction for this substantial job could not be allowed to stand.

Two things needed doing: Find out why this obscure firm was handed a $6.5 million contract ($3.5 million was for equipment installed post-construction); and, because of the manner of their selection, research the company's performance. If Siegelman was going to dodge the bid laws, then he had to expect a level of scrutiny far and above the norm.

The week after the first story I called Hamrick and asked again. This time he said that Sherrod was "selected by people we had confidence in."

And who might those people be?

He declined to say. Just people they had confidence in.

Fortunately I didn't depend on the administration for everything. I enlisted one of my all-time favorite search engines, the secretary of state corporations database. Within seconds of entering Blake Sherrod's name I was looking at the wedge that forced the truth out of Team Siegelman. Sherrod was shown as one of two incorporators in a real estate development company called Nereus Corp. The other was Les Siegelman, the governor's brother.

Sherrod's name didn't appear in the last eight annual reports, indicating he no longer had a role in the company, but it was still a strong connection. I called Hamrick and reported what I'd found. He said he would call me back. After a bit, he did. Our next day's story ran under the headline, "Governor selected building company," and began:

Gov. Don Siegelman didn't shop around, didn't take bids and personally chose Birmingham-based Sherrod Construction for a $6.5 million contract for a worker training facility because he knew the company could get the job done right and on time, his chief of staff, Paul Hamrick, said Tuesday.

Company president P. Blake Sherrod is a former partner of the governor's brother, Les Siegelman, in a real estate venture called Nereus Corp., Alabama secretary of state incorporation records show. That partnership ended eight years ago when Les Siegelman bought out Sherrod, and the governor was unaware of the partnership until his office was asked about it Tuesday by the Mobile Register, Hamrick said.

"They know each other, obviously," Hamrick said of Sherrod and Les Siegelman.

Hamrick said the governor was familiar with Sherrod's work going back 15 to 20 years, and that he was "somebody (Siegelman) had confidence in who could get it done right and get it done on time." Hamrick's previous responses -- that no one knew who chose Sherrod and then, that Sherrod was picked by "people we had confidence in" – were included in the story, as was the final explanation and its impetus:

On Tuesday, after the Register found the Sherrod-Les Siegelman venture listed in secretary of state records, Hamrick stated that the selection of Sherrod for the training facility was the governor's choice. Hamrick said Les and Don Siegelman did not discuss the choice.

Other research showed that after the governor's office ordered it to use Sherrod, the Alabama Development Office learned that the firm wasn't qualified. Some records indicated that the company had a D rating with the state contractors licensing board. A company with a D rating can build projects costing up to but not more than $1 million. Other records showed Sherrod with an E rating, which permits jobs up to $3 million. Neither was sufficient. For the training facility Sherrod needed a U rating – for unlimited.

The licensing files suggested that a U was going to get accomplished, hell or high water. It doubtless didn't hurt that Siegelman appointed the licensing board's five members. Three of them, including the chairman, were executives with the three firms that composed EPM.

Sherrod Construction's financial reports showed a net worth of just $57,320. That was less than the $75,000 required to maintain a D rating. Still, the board upgraded the company to an E, then bounced it to a U based on the claimed $20 million net worth of Blake Sherrod and his wife.

None of the Birmingham-area contractors I called had heard of the company. It had built some agricultural structures eight to 10 years before, gone into hibernation, and returned to life after Siegelman became governor. It also won a contract to build a state liquor store in Birmingham.

The hasty elevation of Sherrod to a U rating was an act of magic that was, unbeknownst to me, being repeated at that very moment, for a spanking new company that made Sherrod Construction look like Brown & Root.

Its name was G.H. Construction.

I'd cracked one nut by solving the Sherrod selection mystery, but remained without the project records needed to gauge the company's performance. At least twice I was given records and told that was all there was, but a goldfish could have seen otherwise. So for the first but hardly last time I had to direct the administration to its own records, a game of charades based on the cover story that they couldn't find them.

I suggested to Hamrick that he call the Birmingham architectural firm Giattina Fisher, which had designed the training center. I told him I was "absolutely certain" that someone at Giattina Fisher would know the whereabouts of the files, might even have them, and provided him with the company's phone number.

Soon after I was Birmingham-bound for the paper-clip and copy routine at Giattina-Fisher. It was quickly apparent why Team Siegelman had such a hard time locating the records. Sherrod hadn't finished the job on time – a vital component of the project, given Honda's demands to start training workers pronto. For four months workers trained elsewhere. And Blake Sherrod had enraged subcontractors by withholding pay and communicating with them, not in person, but through insulting, highly-critical letters.

"Sixteen years, and I've never seen letters like that -- so off-base, so wrong," said one sub.

The company was responsible for scheduling the job in sequence, so that as soon as one sub-contractor completed its work, another could move in and find the facility ready for its services. Project files described a Chinese fire drill, with companies bringing in workers and equipment only to find there was nothing yet to do.

Before start of work, Sherrod assured the ADO director Funderburke that his company had more than $10 million in bonding capacity with a top insurer. Either this wasn't true, or Sherrod elected not to buy the insurance. There was no such thing, at least until Sherrod, as an uninsured state construction project. Even G.H. Construction had to get a bond.

The reason for the requirement was demonstrated when three subcontractors filed liens, lawsuits or both against the state – as opposed to a bonding company – demanding about $450,000. Other subs settled prior to filing liens. The state withheld final payment to Sherrod, and the company ultimately stepped in and settled with its subcontractors. It wasn't disastrous, just a mess, and one example among many to come of the perils of the administration's proclivity for favoritism.

A year later, the Alabama Development Office was compelled to produce Funderburke's telephone messages as part of a wrongful termination lawsuit against the agency. One, dated Sept. 16, 1999, read: "Les Siegelman -- called re grading contract for Honda -- also, if you have a problem (with) Blake Sherrod's info, call him (Les)."

The message triggered our final story on Sherrod. The governor's older brother, who hadn't returned my calls the year before, didn't then, either. The message implied involvement by him in both Sherrod's selection and EPM's work at Honda. I added, with abundant fairness, that the paper had found, "no evidence ... showing Les Siegelman benefited from that involvement."

Back in late January, when I first called Siegelman's press office to ask about Honda, I assumed I would be dealing with press secretary Carrie Kurlander. And initially, I was. Soon, though, I was routed to Hamrick. He apparently decided that he would handle me, due I suppose to the potential threat posed by the inquiries into the Honda contracts, the stories I'd written on the James' administration and perhaps a feeling that Carrie was still pretty new to this game.

I knew the 38-year-old chief-of-staff, if not well. I had called him a few times when Siegelman was lieutenant governor, and later, during the 1998 campaign. Hamrick oozed self-confidence, had a sharp sense of humor, and from everything I'd heard, liked having a good time. Paul, as everyone knew, reveled in the gamesmanship of politics.

I came to see my time with Hamrick as the first of four phases in my relationship with the administration. The end was near by early March, when I e-mailed to inform Paul of the key points to be reported in the Sherrod story, so as to give the administration a final chance for comment.

"Sounds like your story is pretty much written," he shot back.

To which I responded:

Is that a 'no comment?' I mean, Paul, you know I've been working on this for a long time, too long for my taste. Of course I've written some of it. Heck, it's Friday, it's supposed to run Sunday, and the story was initially to run either a week or two weeks ago, tho I'm starting to lose track. As you know, and not alleging a conspiracy, but y'all had difficulty locating the records I requested …. It's not my fault that the obviously busy chief of staff is apparently the only one authorized to answer questions.

Later that day he sent an e-mail defending Sherrod's performance and the company's selection. I was addressed, not with the usual Eddie, but as, "Mr. Curran."

After that story, the Siegelman brain trust recognized that Hamrick's handling of me backfired, had bred mistrust and spurred more rather than less scrutiny. (I make this statement based on an assumption. During the entire two years I wrote about the administration, I never had a source within the governor's office, anonymous or otherwise.) Hamrick had tried to create an alternate reality, with Siegelman as passive bystander nodding along as cabinet members like Roberts ran the show, and it hadn't sold.

I wasn't disappointed when Carrie told me that I should begin addressing questions and record requests to her. I mentioned my problems with Hamrick, and she said something to the effect that from then on, things would be different. She didn't criticize him, but I sensed frustration on her part with the way he'd handled things.

Carrie was a 33-year-old Dothan native who'd been in television, first as a reporter, then as an anchor at one of the Montgomery stations. It was easy to imagine her on television. She was blonde, attractive and well-spoken, and exuded professionalism and self-control.

Now I would be like other reporters, communicating with Carrie, not Hamrick. In other ways, though, the second of the four phases was extraordinary. It was characterized by what, for me anyway, was an unprecedented series of meetings with cabinet members, administration lawyers, press staff and others, all for my benefit and arranged by Carrie. Not solo interviews, mind you, but gatherings of as many as eight people, all summoned by Carrie to answer Eddie's questions. I didn't give her lists and say, I want them there. Nor did I request these meetings – wouldn't have dared be so presumptuous. They just happened.

I gave this second phase a name: The Carrie Kurlander Openness Experiment.

Carrie, I think, believed that if she dealt with me in an open and truthful manner then I would come to see the Siegelman administration as she saw it – as honest, progressive and working hard for the people of Alabama.

The introduction to this new phase was prompted by questions about a proposed sale of $97 million more in tobacco bonds to refuel the 21st Century Authority, then near depletion from the Honda projects. The administration was asking the legislature to approve the bond issue so the state could complete the Honda work, keep its pledges to expand at Mercedes, and fund several other projects.

I was directed to go to the governor's suite of offices at the statehouse. There I was astonished to find a crowd – Carrie, of course, and others as well from the press office. Mack Roberts and Paul Bowlin were there from transportation, as was Siegelman's general counsel Ted Hosp. And last but not least, Finance Director Henry Mabry.

It was my first and final audience with Mabry, the boy wonder known throughout state government as "Dr. No." He gloried in the moniker, which incorporated both his doctorate in public administration (he was said to insist that underlings call him, "Dr. Mabry"), and his tough-guy reputation for rejecting requests from state agencies for hires and purchases.

He was a 31-year-old Alabama Power lobbyist when Siegelman appointed him, at power company president Elmer Harris's recommendation, to become the second youngest finance director in state history. Mabry looks like Casper after a diet – skin white to the point of bright, a stubborn layer baby fat, his pale complexion offset by dark hair and black-rimmed glasses. Many considered him rude and arrogant, a Richy Rich with a general's bearing. I found him, in my lone encounter, to be something of a character, a self-aware eccentric who overplayed seriousness to conceal his glee at being Dr. No and having all that power.

Mabry, seated at the head of a conference table, opened by lecturing on what he called the streamlined incentives package for Mercedes II. This he illustrated shuffle-board style, slinging first the thick incentives contract for Honda, then the much slimmer Mercedes document. I stopped the speeding contracts with outstretched hand, lest they slide off the end of the table.

As if the crowd assembled for my benefit didn't make me feel special enough, five floors up, the House was debating the state education budget. The deliberations were piped into the room, with Mabry frequently stopping to listen. Especially memorable was a report that Mobile's Joseph Mitchell -- Alabama's goofiest legislator, perhaps the country's -- was performing a karate kick routine on the floor.

The multi-tasking Mabry was also taking calls from upstairs. After one, he reported that someone in a House committee was trying to slap a troublesome amendment on the budget bill. He apologized, and rushed out. I remember thinking, possibly saying, that we could do this another time, since there were clearly more pressing matters. Some 10 minutes later, Mabry returned, flushed with victory and grinning.

"Excellent, thank you!" he said with a flourish, when I asked how that had gone. "The budget has passed. You have my undivided attention."

Our story reported Mabry's declaration that the contract with Mercedes marked a revolution in the way Alabama designed its incentives packages. It would, among other things, limit the amount that the state would pay for site development to $14.4 million, thus preventing another Honda.

"There are no pinholes in this document, where the state has to keep paying and keep paying," he said.

What with all the good cheer and turning over of new leafs, I refrained from noting that it was largely his boss's fault, by not seeking bids, that precipitated all that paying and paying.

For Carrie, indeed for me, Phase Two had begun promisingly. But as will be seen, the Carrie Kurlander Openness Experiment failed in spectacular fashion.

Hamrick's inability or unwillingness to tell the truth doomed Phase One, whereas something quite the opposite sunk Carrie's stab at full disclosure. The administration freed Carrie to be Carrie – that is, honest and forthcoming. But when I came asking about G.H. Construction, someone -- Siegelman? Bailey? Hamrick? All three? – sent her in clueless. The fruits of my research and questions about Lanny Young's company blind-sided her. She witnessed the unraveling of the scandal pretty much as I did.

The Openness Experiment ended on April 26, the day of the final group interview and two days before our first story on the warehouse deal. There was no announcement of a change in procedure, but I wasn't surprised when the meetings ceased. The transition to Phase Three was subtle, and it, too, was unique in terms of the administration's relationships with other reporters.

From about May 1 to July 31, 2001, stories under my byline rarely contained an actual quote from someone within the administration. I had e-mailed or faxed questions before, but in Phase Three, all meaningful correspondence was conducted in writing. This gave them greater control of the process.

Phase Three disintegrated in late July with the torrent of cuss words, from my mouth in Mobile to Rip's ears in Montgomery. This loss of self-control ushered in the final phase – near total cessation of communications.

I think all four strategies were doomed from the start.

Good public relations professionals, whether in government or the private sector, can do much to impact potentially damaging stories. They can provide facts, records or perspectives that a reporter doesn't have or appears to be ignoring, and arrange interviews with people who have first-hand knowledge of the matters being scrutinized.

There have been many occasions when I thought I was about to bop someone for this or that transgression, only to change my mind after getting the other side from a spokesperson, lawyer or, best of all, the horse's mouth. I've dropped stories after hearing strong responses from an erstwhile subject. More often, there's still a story, but it's nuanced, grey rather than black and white, less of a blockbuster, and fairer.

But there's one thing even the best public relations pros can't do.

They can't change the past.

That, ultimately, is why each approach failed.

———

Even Carrie's assumption of my records requests couldn't disgorge the files chronicling EPM's work at Mercedes. We had reported in the first story that the administration awarded the Mercedes job to EPM without seeking bids, and that the company had started the "clearing and grubbing" phase. But the revelations ended there.

In early February I'd made the first of many requests over the coming eight months to review EPM's contract at Mercedes and the project files. But the administration, in the midst of a political thrashing over Honda and then G.H. Construction, hunkered down. Team Siegelman had two options: Divulge records showing they had violated the law that prohibits letting a company start work on a public project without a contract; or disregard the public records law by withholding those records. They opted for the latter.

(The phrase Team Siegelman will appear throughout. Pat though it may sound, Siegelman habitually hid behind others, never more so than when trouble surfaced. His general practice was to have spokespersons and lawyers issue denials or blame others, with no one thrown under the bus more frequently than Nick Bailey. Team Siegelman is my attempt to convey responsibility to the governor and later, the ex-governor/defendant, for statements and actions by others on his behalf.)

The quandary bred by the decision to let EPM start work at Mercedes without a contract wasn't going away. The law also forbids the state from paying for work performed without a contract. How, then, could the administration pay EPM for the work at Mercedes without violating that law and having it winding up in our paper? I was not only repeatedly requesting such records, but every time I went to Montgomery, was checking comptroller records for new payments to EPM.

Legal bills pulled from the comptroller's office showed that the administration struggled with the issue for months as EPM demanded payment of $795,000 for work at Mercedes. That dilemma was ultimately resolved by having Mercedes pay EPM and the state reimbursing the automaker.

By mid-October, we still didn't have the records of the work for which EPM was paid that money. "I've been covering the DOT since about 1996, and I'm not aware of any DOT construction project that did not have a project file, and by that I mean a box or boxes of files," I wrote administration lawyer Ted Hosp.

Days later, and for reasons that will become clear later, they over-nighted us the records.

The project files showed that neither of the three EPM firms worked at Mercedes. EPM had outsourced the work to a Tuscaloosa company called

Buddy Jones Excavation, no doubt paying Buddy Jones less than it was charging the state.

Mercedes divided the remainder of the work into two phases and bid them out. "From our standpoint, that's the only way to get the most bang for your buck," Mercedes spokesman Austin Dare told readers, with a quote that had to make Siegelman cringe.

RaCON was low bidder for the first phase, and also for a Mercedes-funded parking lot project. "RaCON, when they got the bid, the same day they were on the site," Dare said. "They were ready to go. We're right on track with the project, and everything is moving according to plan."

A Birmingham company underbid RaCON to win the contract for the second phase. With both phases, the state reimbursed Mercedes for the work.

EPM, faced with competitive situation, didn't submit a bid for either phase. I don't think it unreasonable to suggest that, were it not for our stories, the state would have paid EPM millions of dollars more for Mercedes than it ultimately paid after seeking bids.

———

In 2002, the state was once again faced with the enviable task of preparing a site for a new auto plant, this time in Montgomery County, for Hyundai. The Siegelman administration, which started out handing such contracts to EPM, bid the work out. Newell Roadbuilders won with a low bid of $6.83 million.

Ellard Construction, the E of EPM, submitted the high bid, of $14.9 million.

Chapter 7
Lanny Landfill

"I am nobody's straw man. I am nobody's dog."
-- Lanny Young, during April 2001 interview, when asked if he served as a secret front-man for Waste Management when it wanted to build landfills.

"Harry (Alabama Department of Environmental Management lawyer Harry Lyles) stated that Waste Management should be upfront and apply for the permit and not send some agent, such as Mr. Young, to do their bidding for them. Whereupon, Mr. Campagna expressed that was the way they did permitting and that they now have no confidence in ADEM."
-- Notes taken by ADEM staffer during a 2002 meeting with Waste Management official Charles Campagna, after the G.H. Construction stories and with Young's credibility shattered.

On Dec. 1, 1998, the Cherokee County Commission voted to let Waste Management substantially expand the area from which its, "Three Corners Landfill" could accept garbage, including well into Georgia. This allowed the company to vastly increase its profits while also slashing the life of the landfill for county residents.

As if that wasn't enough, the commission also consented to the company's request to halve its "host fee." From that point on, Waste Management paid Cherokee County $1 for every ton of garbage hauled into the site rather than the $2 in the original contract.

In return for this double windfall, Waste Management gave the county a few computers.

Six days after the commission's inexplicably bone-headed decision, Waste Management wired $1 million into Lanny Young's account at Colonial Bank. That was for the host fee change. Two months later, it shot him another $2 million, for his persuasive efforts in convincing county to allow the landfill to take waste from Georgia and elsewhere.

Young didn't accomplish these feats by waving a magic wand. He had inside help. Cherokee County was largely run by Phillip Jordan. He held the dual titles of probate judge and county commission chairman and had for 15 years, since his election at the ripe age of 26.

Jordan initially worked a deal with Lanny where he would become a secret part-owner of the landfill, but Young talked him into accepting money instead.

He pledged to pay Jordan $100,000. Lanny – who shorted everybody, even, apparently, those he bribed – only gave Jordan about $65,000, the latter testified years later at the Siegelman trial. The by-then disgraced former judge said Young gave lesser amounts to two other commissioners.

Lanny's initial payments to Jordan were made with cash, amounts from about $1,000 to $6,000 stuffed in envelopes, and handed over during meetings in neighboring Etowah County. Then Lanny started paying with checks. Some were written to non-existent people, others to relatives of Jordan. On at least one, Young made a notation indicating the money was for cattle and hay.

Jordan, nervous about the checks for obvious reasons, didn't want to cash them locally. He called on an old friend, Paul Thomas, for help. Thomas was the probate judge of neighboring DeKalb County.

From 1996 to 1999, Waste Management paid Lanny about $8 million for his labors in Cherokee County. The largest chunk came first, after Lanny's company, Alabama Waste Disposal Solutions, received a permit to build and operate the landfill. Lanny's though, never built much less operated the landfill. Instead, he sold the permit to Waste Management, which built and continues to operate what is one of Alabama's busiest landfills.

His and Waste Management's next target was Lowndes County, which sits to the west of Montgomery county. At the Siegelman trial it was revealed that Lanny gave $10,000 to a close friend of Lowndes County commissioner Charlie King.

As incentive for corruption, it's hard to top Waste Management's secret contracts with Young. Here's the breakdown of the Lowndes County deal:

$4 million. Amount Waste Management was to pay Lanny after he won the permit to build and operate the landfill, then sold/transferred it to the company.

$500,000. This sum would be Lanny's on the second anniversary of the permit.

$500,000. On the third anniversary.

$1 million. Amount Waste Management was to pay Lanny when the landfill began receiving an average of 550 tons of garbage per day.

$1 million. When the average climbed to 750 tons.

$1 million. If and when the average reached 1,000 tons a day.

$2 million. Due Lanny if he could convince the Lowndes County commission to decrease its "host fee" from $2 per ton $1.25.

Total, with incentives: $10 million.

Waste Management wasn't just paying for the right to own landfills. It was also paying for a protective layer between the acts the company had to suspect Lanny might commit to make his millions and the repercussions should he be discovered.

Plausible deniability. We don't pay bribes. And if someone else does, we naturally disapprove.

It's worth noting that Waste Management, with its corruption-tainted past, was by then advertising itself as the "new Waste Management," as a clean company, ethically as well as environmentally.

On June 23, 2004, FBI agents called on Thomas, the DeKalb County judge, to ask about the checks he'd cashed years before for Jordan. The judge admitted doing so.

The next morning Thomas called work to report that he wasn't feeling well and wouldn't be coming in. The next day the state wire ran a story reporting his death from "a steep fall at his mountaintop home."

It read in part:

Thomas, who turned 60 Wednesday, apparently slipped on a high rock at his Sand Mountain home and fell about 45 feet to his death, Rainsville Police Chief Roger Byrd said.

Officials received an emergency call to Thomas' home at 12:06 p.m. Thursday, and rescue workers recovered his body from the foot of the bluff, Byrd said. Although officials believe Thomas' death was accidental, DeKalb County District Attorney Mike O'Dell requested an autopsy."

By the time the FBI met with Thomas in 2004, Lanny Young was almost a household name in Alabama. The year before he'd pleaded guilty to bribery and other crimes involving G.H. Construction and other matters. It was widely known that he was cooperating in a federal probe of the Siegelman administration.

Because of the unusual circumstances of Thomas's death, Alabama Attorney General Troy King felt compelled to issue a statement declaring it an accident. Not that anyone believed that. Most people familiar with the matter think Thomas jumped to his death. Considering how law enforcement works in such matters he was probably given the choice between pleading guilty to some lesser crime or being charged with a felony for aiding Jordan. For insurance and pension reasons and to spare his family the mess to come Thomas killed himself, correctly anticipating that it would be officially declared an accident.

That's innuendo wrapped in speculation but not unfair considering the circumstances. Nor do I think that it's unfair to suggest the following:

With the outrageous incentives it dangled before Lanny, North America's largest waste company set in motion the chain of events that led to Thomas's death.

In early March, while finishing up the Sherrod Construction story, I received a call from John Nichols, the mayor of Lowndesboro, which is seat of Lowndes County. Mayor Nichols said he was impressed with the Honda stories and wondered if I'd be interested in reporting on a shady landfill deal. He said that a pal of the governor's, a Mr. Clayton Lamar "Lanny" Young, was trying to build a large regional landfill in his county and he and quite a few others didn't want it.

Now, if the mayor had told me that this Lanny Young fellow was seeking to open a chicken processing plant or one of a dozen other environmentally hazardous enterprises, I'd have told him I was neck deep in stories and, much as I'd like, just didn't see where I was going to find the time.

But it wasn't a chicken plant. It was a landfill.

Or, as I should say, a landfill!

Some years before, while absorbed in a landfill story, my wife made a crack to the effect that I liked landfills more than her. My memory's shaky on the point but I feel certain that I tried to dissuade her from such nonsense. As a source of stories, though, dumps are close to my heart.

These gargantuan burying grounds -- actually, series of multi-acre "cells" -- serve as the final resting place for almost everything we touch that isn't nailed down. Like a priest in the confessor's box, landfills forgive us our sins. They allow us to proceed mindlessly as the most wasteful, packaging-addicted society in world history. But instead of being grateful, we demonize our dumps. We deride them as an environmental hazard, forgetting that it's our own, personally generated rubbish that's the root of the problem.

It's astonishing, really, that a single landfill – for example, Chastang Landfill in north Mobile County -- can hold all the waste that a city of 200,000-plus citizens can toss curbside in two months, to say nothing of three or more decades.

The above notwithstanding, my interest in landfills is neither philosophical nor environmental. It's professional. There's probably no non-federal government service where politics, commerce and corruption intersect as they do in the landfill business. Without landfills – and here credit must go as well to Waste Management -- there is no Lanny Young, no G.H. Construction and no career-ending investigation into Don Siegelman.

So before proceeding, a short primer on the waste business.

Lesson One: Garbage isn't garbage.

The milk cartons, the molded cheese from the back of refrigerator, the poo-filled diapers? For our purposes, think cash. Many public officials have taken payoffs in return for giving crooked operators the right to haul and bury their constituents' poo-filled diapers. It's not for nothing that the mafia long controlled the waste business in New York and New Jersey. Heroin, prostitution …. and garbage.

There are three types of landfills, the most common being what are called Construction & Demolition (C&D) landfills. They receive your bagged leaves, limbs, and the cement and steel hauled away from demolished buildings. They are of no concern here.

The least common is the hazardous waste landfill. These accept dangerous waste, byproducts of chemical companies and the like. There is only one hazardous waste landfill in Alabama, at Emelle. It will appear later in our story, but for now, the subject is solid waste landfills. That's where your household garbage goes.

These sites pose a host of environmental hazards, the most serious of which is polluted groundwater. Think of making coffee. You begin with clean water and coffee grounds. The water filters through the grounds, and what comes out below, thanks to gravity and heat, is a dark noxious liquid.

At a landfill, rain seeps through the gunk, itself heated by compaction. This landfill coffee is called leachate, which if not stopped, leaks into the ground below, and from there, into streams and lakes, harming fish, wildlife, and creating all manner of potential environmental threats.

In the late 1980s, Congress ordered the Environmental Protection Agency to draft new regulations to address the many hazards posed by landfills, and primarily, the leachate problem. These new rules, collectively known as Subtitle D, mandated that landfill cells be constructed with thick plastic liners atop layers of packed sediment, the goal being to create an impermeable bottom and prevent seepage of leachate into the groundwater.

Alabama had some 100 solid waste landfills in the late 1980s. All, at least in their current state, were doomed to extinction.

The new landfills were much safer environmentally, but far costlier to build and operate. Each city and county had to decide whether to modernize its dump or build a new one; to privatize, such as by selling to a Waste Management; or haul its waste to sites counties away, with each mile adding to the cost.

Good-sized cities like Birmingham and Mobile could better afford to upgrade since their populaces generated enough garbage to justify the expense. But small towns and counties were priced out of the landfill business. Of course, they hadn't stopped producing garbage, but what, now, to do with it?

Thus was born the regional landfill – enormous, privately owned and operated sites that accepted garbage from a dozen or more counties, and often neighboring states. It took deep pockets and a substantial waste stream to make a go of what was in effect a large industrial operation.

For a McDonald's to thrive, it needs a steady stream of people hungry for hamburgers. It's the same with landfills, but instead of hamburgers, customers buy space for the garbage they've hauled in and the service of disposing it in the environmentally mandated fashion.

The economic consequence of Subtitle D was a super-lucrative opportunity for the two biggest players in the garbage business – Waste Management and Browning-Ferris Industries (BFI). These companies already had countless well-established garbage hauling contracts with cities, counties and businesses. If they could come to own the landfills as well, they would make money disposing of the garbage as well as hauling it. Instead of paying someone else to bury it, they'd pay themselves.

With the new rules in play, the two companies – as well as some smaller players – scoured the landscape for broad expanses unserved by nearby landfills, and picked their spots. But you can't just buy land and build a landfill. One needs a permit from the Alabama Department of Environmental Management. ADEM, though, isn't the problem. Landfill firms usually have enough sense to select a geographically acceptable site. The hurdle is what's called host government approval, without which ADEM will not issue a permit.

To build a landfill in County A, a company must receive permission from County A's county commission. That's the soft underbelly to the system and the reason the likes of Lanny Young have a place in the garbage business.

In all but the largest counties, the office of county commissioner is very-much part-time. The real power, the sway, belongs to the full-time commission chairman, who often as not is also the probate judge. This person is the mark. If he's not both ethical and experienced in the ways of the landfill business – maybe the former but definitely not the latter -- then there's a good chance his county's going to suffer the consequences.

It is a given that landfill proposals will generate outrage among residents, which would include me if one was to be built near my home.

To counter the opposition, public officials and the wannabe landfill operators use financial arguments to justify the project. Chiefly, they point out that the landfill will allow citizens to bury their garbage more cheaply, since they'll no longer have to pay to haul it to other counties, and because the company gives a discount to county customers. Best of all, the prospective landfill operator pledges to pay the county (or in some cases, city) a "host fee," say, $1.50 for every ton of garbage brought in the gates.

It speaks volumes that Waste Management was willing to pay Lanny Young $2 million to win reduction of the host fee in Lowndes County and paid him $1 million for doing so in Cherokee County.

Such is the landfill business.

———

Years later at trial, Siegelman lawyer Vince Kilborn called Lanny Young a con man more times than anyone could count and asked Lanny straight up if he was a "criminal tax fraud artist."

To his credit Lanny doesn't possess a self-righteous bone in his body. "If you're looking for an angel in me, you're not going to find it," he said during my one lengthy interview with him.

I enjoyed the interview and the two times I saw him testify. You just knew that no matter how hard the lawyers tried, and they were going to try very hard, that Lanny wasn't going to crack.

Smart-ass answers? Yes.

Crack? No way.

Young's a bigger than average fellow, sturdy, with a somewhat pudgy face and a Romanesque nose. The hair he does have, on the sides, is clipped short. His eyes crinkle engagingly when he smiles.

In 1990, after being kicked out of the National Guard after for overstating his academic career, he started a business printing T-shirts, caps and the like, at one point employing more than 200 people.

Lanny's company was the official provider of T-shirts and other memorabilia for NASCAR stars including Rusty Wallace, Dale Earnhardt and Davey Allison. He was friends with many of the other drivers as well as NASCAR management and introduced Siegelman to them. Young even arranged for Siegelman to drive a few laps around Talladega Superspeedway in Dale Earnhardt's car after first buying the then-lieutenant governor a racing helmet.

In the mid-1990s, his T-shirt business collapsed into bankruptcy and he turned to landfills. As previously described, his first effort, in Cherokee County, made him rich. But he spent like a fool. The married father of three bought 560 acres of farmland on the outskirts of Montgomery County from former lieutenant governor turned trial lawyer extraordinaire Jere Beasley. Lanny built a substantial abode, top scale accessories as befitted someone with his means and more surely on its way from the pending Lowndes County deal.

In 1999, he incorporated Young Motorsports LLC, which ran a car in one of NASCAR's minor league circuits. Other purchases included boats – four of them.

Then there were his extracurricular outlays.

Two months after Siegelman's inauguration the governor's chief of staff set his eyes on a black four-door BMW valued at $47,622.09. In March, Lanny cut a $25,000 check to an area dealership as a down-payment on Hamrick's new car. Later, when a Hamrick stock bet went south and the brokerage firm demanded payment, he called on Lanny, who wrote him a check for $6,000.

Years later, at trial, Young and other witnesses testified to untold thousands of dollars given by Lanny to Hamrick. The latter would call, say he needed money, and Lanny would send his secretary to the bank. All of this was above and beyond the bar and restaurant tabs picked up by Lanny when the pair went out, which was often.

Bailey was also a major beneficiary of Lanny's largesse. From 1996 to 2000 Young gave Siegelman's Man Friday more than $90,000. He also contributed an estimated $200,000 to $300,000 to Siegelman campaigns, directly and through PACS. That included the cost of 47 trips on Lanny's plane in which Siegelman was listed as the primary passenger.

Three expenditures for Siegelman were to become part of the criminal case against him. Near the end of his first year as governor, Siegelman and his wife decided to send coffee mugs to friends and supporters as Christmas presents. Siegelman called Lanny, who paid $13,500 to buy and design the 1,000 mugs.

A month later Siegelman needed money to cover a large check he'd just written. He could have made a withdrawal out of his plentiful stock market account. Instead, he called on Lanny. Young made a cashier's check payable to Bailey for $9,200. Bailey, the same day, wrote a check for that amount payable to Lori Allen. That's the maiden name of Siegelman's wife. With the third transaction of the day, Siegelman cashed the Lori Allen check and deposited the $9,200 into his checking account.

The following Christmas, Siegelman wanted a 4-wheeler for his son and a trailer to haul it around. He had Lanny order it, pay $5,324, and deliver it to the mansion.

Lanny gave, and he received. Siegelman's election brought new opportunities for the landfill developer. Within a week of the inauguration he incorporated a lobbying and political consulting business, Austin & Young Capital Resources, with Montgomery lobbyist Claire Austin.

Claire is a tall, attractive blonde with a country twang and a big personality who calls to mind Republican firebrand Mary Matalin. She worked in the Reagan and Bush White Houses before returning to her native Alabama to serve in the James' administration. She transferred to the attorney general's office, working for Jeff Sessions, then Pryor, and ran the latter's 1998 campaign for attorney general. While a member of the Republican Party, she was also, like Hamrick and Lanny, a member of the Partying Party

Montgomery's political class all go to the same few bars, is not that large, and everyone knows everyone. Claire befriended Hamrick and actually planned to form a lobbying partnership with him. Hamrick, though, decided to stay with Siegelman as chief of staff. Instead of Hamrick, she joined forces with his best friend and together, the two had the Republican and Democratic sides covered.

In no time Hamrick and Siegelman were routing clients to the new firm. G-Tech, a company that hoped to be a vendor for a state lottery, put Austin-Young on a $3,500 a month retainer after company officials met with Siegelman and Hamrick. Austin testified at trial that Hamrick called Lanny to tell him that G-Tech had agreed to hire Austin & Young after he and Siegelman told the company to do so.

In early March 1999, Hamrick called Young to tell him that officials with 3M were coming to Montgomery to meet with Siegelman. The company's products are used by the highway department and it was seeking to interest the state in using its materials for license plates. After the meeting Hamrick called to inform Young that he and the governor had recommended to 3M that it hire Austin-

Young. The 3M folks walked from the governor's office to Claire and Lanny's office and signed them up at $3,000 a month.

It was the same story with the Huntsville Airport Authority, which engaged Lanny and Claire for $4,350 a month. Both Siegelman and Hamrick told Austin that they directed the authority to hire Austin Young.

There were others. Waste Management dropped its longtime lobbyist Johnny Crawford – who was very close to the Siegelman administration – and switched to Austin-Young. That contract was for $10,000 a month, or $120,000 a year.

CDG Engineers – which did permitting work for Lanny's landfill company – had been trying for years to win contracts with the highway department. It hired Austin-Young, Lanny met with Mack Roberts, and boom, CDG got work with the highway department.

The total of those deals came to almost $23,000 a month for the firm.

After Young formed his partnership with Austin, Hamrick and Bailey told him not to register as a lobbyist with the Ethics Commission. Hamrick said it could lead to scrutiny of their relationship and curb their ability to go places together.

The directive was typical Hamrick. In all my time covering the administration, I never saw his name on a single meaningful document. He left no traces. On his annual ethics forms, he never listed outside income, even for his 2001 report, when he spent the last half of the year working for the Matrix Group lobbying/consulting firm.

Hamrick didn't report any loans either, as is required by the ethics law. Any claim that the money from Lanny was a loan, such as the $25,000 for the BMW, was belied by his own disclosures, which were filed under penalty of perjury.

Also, lobbyists must report any expenditure on a public official of more than $250 in a day. That's a ridiculously high amount – an embarrassment for the state's ethics laws, really – but the Lanny-Paul relationship was one that occasioned Young to spend that much and more on Siegelman's number two man.

Austin registered, Lanny did not.

Claire frequently joined Hamrick and Lanny on nights out. Lanny paid for everything. "He always had tons of cash," she testified, remarking that Lanny favored $100 bills.

In August 2000 the Associated Press published two stories reporting the governor's contrasting positions on two proposed landfills, one sought by Lanny, the other by dog track magnate Milton McGregor.

Siegelman came out against the McGregor site days before the Macon County Commission was to vote on it. He pledged to "fight a landfill that is a magnet for the nation's trash."

Local black leaders enlisted Jesse Jackson to oppose the site on grounds that it was an example of environmental racism.

After the county's vote Siegelman sent a statement praising the decision. "Today, you are drawing a line in the sand. You are saying, 'Enough is enough. You are saying, 'Macon County will not become the pay toilet of America.'"

A second AP story added another wrinkle. It posed the question: Why had the governor become involved in Macon County but stayed out of a near identical landfill battle in Lowndes County?

Like Macon County, Lowndes is poor, rural and majority black.

The piece reported Young's support of Siegelman and his friendship with Hamrick. The chief of staff said the difference was that the Macon County site would take garbage from out of state, whereas the Lowndes project would not.

"We typically wouldn't and haven't gotten involved (in supporting or opposing landfill projects)," Hamrick said.

Some black leaders in Lowndes County, as with Macon County, opposed the landfill. Jesse Jackson came to Lowndes County as well, and decried the proposed landfill's proximity to the historic Selma-to-Montgomery voting rights trail.

Macon County borders Montgomery County to the east and Lowndes to the west. Had McGregor won a permit, his site would surely have competed against Young's. Had it been built first, it might well have ended Waste Management's interest in the Lowndes project – a decision that would have been financially ruinous for Lanny.

At trial, prosecutors introduced a recorded telephone conversation between Lanny and investment banker Bill Blount, which Lanny had made, he said by accident, but turned over to the government.

The two are heard making fun of McGregor by calling him Elvis, a reference to the dog-track owner's famous bouffant hairdo. Young told Blount that McGregor – keenly aware of the relationship between Lanny and Hamrick – called Siegelman's chief of staff to promise that his landfill in Macon County wouldn't compete with Lanny's landfill in Lowndes County.

Said Young, in an apparent joke: "I told Paul, I said, 'You tell Elvis that I don't give a shit what he does over there. I'm trying to get my dog track *and casinos* built in Lowndes County right now.'"

McGregor's efforts did no good, as the administration lent its weight against landfill and helped kill it.

In at least one way the administration did get involved in Lanny's project. Records showed that Chris Pitts, the highest ranking black at ADECA and a Siegelman appointee, intervened on Lanny's behalf with black officials in Lowndes County.

Because I live in Mobile, I had to make the most of my Montgomery trips. The pre-Montgomery routine required an updating of what I called the shopping list.

Headings included but were not limited to the state ethics commission, Montgomery County circuit and probate courts; federal court; the secretary of state's office; the state comptroller's office; and the state agencies from which I'd requested records.

From my computer at work I could learn quite a bit. Nexis, the database with stories from most newspapers in the country and for that matter the world, was invaluable. So too was Merlin, the name of the paper's computerized library. The Alabama Secretary of State web-site – the source of so many discoveries over the years – allows you to search corporations by name of company as well as by incorporators and names partners. I used these sources to help build and update the shopping list.

Under the ethics commission heading would be the names of public officials of interest at the time, the commission being the source of their annual financial disclosures. The commission also maintains an updated list of lobbyists and their clients that is a must for any reporter who covers state politics.

The courthouse lists contained the names and case numbers of lawsuits I was monitoring or wanted to review. The benefits of two services, then near infancy, cannot be overestimated.

The first is Alacourt, which hooks you into the state court system. You punch in a name and get everything from lawsuits to traffic violations. At the time, Alacourt only provided the dockets. If you wanted to see the court filings you had to go to the courthouse where it was filed, kindly ask a clerk for the case file, sit down with a bunch of paper clips and determine which pages you wanted copied. It was the same drill at federal court, but you found the cases with PACER, the search system for federal courts.

After deciding to go full bore into the Lowndes landfill story, I searched every record in the arsenal. I found every lawsuit against Lanny and his companies, and there were plenty, including district court cases involving small amounts. I went to courthouses in several counties to get the records.

At probate court in Montgomery County I acquired his home sale and mortgage deeds. I went to the state environmental agency and reviewed boxes of records pertaining to his landfill applications in Cherokee and Lowndes counties.

Among my favorite records are UCC (Uniform Commercial Code) filings. When loans are secured -- that is, when there is collateral put up in the case of failure to repay – lenders sometimes record their loans, as UCCs, at the secretary of state. The secretary of state's web-site allowed one to search for UCC's, but the searches just identified the lender and borrower, nothing else. If you wanted to see the actual documents you had to go to Montgomery, put in an order, pay a small fortune and, worst of all, wait days or longer for the records. I found a way around that. The secretary of state elections office maintained a computer for the public's use. The UCCs were on it, and I could print them out fast and free.

When I get a promising tip I immediately start thinking which public records will be most likely to confirm it, assuming it's true. I have two metaphors for this process. One is, "The Doctor."

A patient goes to a doctor and describes his symptoms. Usually a doctor can tell within about a minute what's wrong and how to approach it. I need longer than that, but it's the same concept. When I hear a tip, my brain automatically lines up the types of records most likely to help me get the story.

The second metaphor, admittedly on the melodramatic side, I call, "The Death Star."

In the climactic scene in the first Star Wars movie, Luke Skywalker's flying into the Death Star and must locate its lone vulnerability, the one spot where a correct shot will destroy it. Otherwise, it's the end of the world as we know it. Luke finds it, and the Death Star explodes into a million bits.

Some activities, be they corrupt or merely unethical, simply cannot be proven with public records, which is to say, metaphorically, that even with the Force, Luke could not have obliterated the Death Star if not for its weak spot.

To my recollection I have never reported or in any event broke a story reporting that Businessman A gave Public Official B a cash bribe. Rarely is something like that going to be divulged in a public record. If at all, it would be an accusation in a lawsuit. While I may be told by 10 people that it occurred, that's not the same, in the news business, as liability-proof evidence. To report such an obviously illegal transaction based on interviews would open me and the paper to a potentially catastrophic lawsuit.

Now, back to the Death Star: Sometimes there are many records or in any event obvious ones that should probably exist if the tip is correct.

My proudest moments as a reporter have come from locating the one public record that proved a tip, and the more obscure the record, the greater the sense of accomplishment.

I never wrote a story on the Lowndes landfill, but the value of the month spent investigating Lanny and his relationships with Waste Management and the administration cannot be overstated. A considerable portion of that information came from a pair of lawsuits against Lanny and involving his plans for Lowndes County.

I don't think G.H. Construction would ever have existed – would not have been necessary – but for those lawsuits. Both were brought by plaintiffs represented by Montgomery lawyers Susan Copeland and Doyle Fuller.

In 1998, when Lanny set his sights on Lowndes County, he believed construction would begin within a year and Waste Management's promised millions would start flowing his way. He had reason to think so, for initially, it was smooth sailing.

He easily cleared the biggest hurdle when he won the required approval from the Lowndes County Commission. He had little trouble passing muster with the Alabama Department of Environmental Management (ADEM), which awarded him the permit to build and operate a landfill.

However, a pair of pair of businessmen sued him. Under his deal with Waste Management, the company wouldn't pay him for the landfill permit as long as litigation clouded the project. Lanny settled the case, which should have cleared the way for transfer of the permit to Waste Management and his first and largest payday, of $4 million.

Then along came Copeland and Fuller. The lawsuit that ruined Lanny – and set in motion Siegelman's downfall – was brought by Nichols, the Lowndsesboro mayor, and owners of land adjacent to the site.

Those plaintiffs didn't want money, they wanted to kill the landfill.

I came to know Doyle and Susan quite well, and they – and especially the information from their two lawsuits -- were of great assistance. They gave me a deposition they took of Lanny which provided all manner of information. One of the best Lanny records – the $10 million incentives contract between Waste Management and Lanny – was produced by Waste Management to them and eventually became a public record. Copeland, especially, bulldogged the hell out of Young and Waste Management, and probably knew more about the Lanny-Waste Management connection than anyone outside of Lanny, Ellis Brazeal and the company.

In November 2000, Montgomery County Circuit Court Judge Sally Greenhaw ruled that ADEM had failed to adhere to its own rules regarding the permitting of the Lowndes landfill and for that matter, all others in the state. Her dramatic and news-making ruling stalled Lanny's landfill as well as all other pending projects in the state. It forced Lanny to fight Copeland, Fuller and their clients in a lengthy appeals process, and delayed, for how long he had no way of knowing, the opening of the Waste Management cash pipeline.

By then Lanny's debts were approaching $3 million. The $4 million that was to be his upon transfer of the permit would have eliminated that debt and put him on solid footing, with millions more to flow his way in the years to come.

Instead, the creditors were barking, and Lanny was desperate.

It was impossible to conduct even a cursory review of Lanny's records and not notice the name Ellis Brazeal. He was everywhere. The Birmingham lawyer represented Young in his landfill ventures, defended him in his lawsuits, and incorporated about a half-dozen companies owned or part-owned by Lanny. One of Brazeal's law partners incorporated G.H. Construction.

Brazeal represented not just Lanny, but Waste Management as well, including on matters pertaining to both Lanny and the company. One document introduced at Siegelman's trial showed Brazeal writing Tom Herrington, Waste Management's Atlanta-based regional director, to tell him that "Judge Jordan" was "obtaining the signatures" of other Cherokee County commissioners on the host fee reduction there. In the same letter, written in December 1998, Brazeal directed Herrington to have Waste Management wire $1 million to Lanny for accomplishing the fee reduction.

Brazeal was a partner in the blue-blood, very Republican Birmingham law firm of Walston, Wells, Anderson & Bains. That's where Bill Pryor practiced before going to the attorney general's office, and Pryor and Brazeal were friends. I have to believe that Pryor – an ideologue perhaps, but a true clean Gene -- was disappointed in his friend after the G.H. Construction stories.

Brazeal, despite his Republican pedigree, won a good bit of legal work from the Siegelman administration. And how?

The eye-opener was Brazeal's shared connection to Lanny and the Siegelman administration.

Brazeal was Paul Hamrick's brother-in-law.

———

I got a case of reader whiplash from two lawsuits against Lanny, one in state court in Tuscaloosa County, the other in federal court in Montgomery. They were brought by separate groups of investors in Lanny's Cherokee County venture who claimed, it seemed with good cause, that he'd cheated them out of money due them from the millions paid him on the deal by Waste Management.

I was speed-reading the Tuscaloosa lawsuit and skidded to a stop when I came across the plaintiffs claim that Lanny had told them Siegelman's brother was a 10-percent owner of his landfill company.

The plaintiffs in the federal lawsuit said Lanny provided them with a record showing that a company called Solutions Inc., held a 5 percent interest in the company. I knew, from secretary of state research, that Solutions Inc., was the name of a company owned by Les Siegelman.

Both sets of investor-plaintiffs reported that Lanny told them that having Siegelman's brother along increased the chances of winning a permit in Cherokee County and, thus, making lots of money.

Neither Les Siegelman nor the administration responded when I called to determine if this was true. Lanny denied it, but then, he would. On the other hand, he might also say Siegelman's brother was a partner just to loosen investors of their money.

In early 2002 I broached the issue in another story on Young, and this time got an e-mailed response from Les Siegelman.

"In answer to your question, I knew little of Lanny Young's project and neither I nor Solutions Inc. had anything to do with the operation of his company nor was any compensation ever received in any form from him or any of his companies," he wrote.

That Siegelman's brother knew anything about Young's landfill efforts was suspicious. However, if there had been evidence of a financial relationship it almost certainly would have been revealed at trial, and was not.

———

Lanny was to be impossible to reach once it became known that I was asking about G.H. Construction, but in early April I was only beginning to look into the warehouse deal, and my studies of his landfill business were for the time being below the radar.

I wanted to verify that his office was indeed where I believed it to be, in the same building that houses a host of state agencies, among them the ethics commission. I went up the elevator, stuck my head in the door and asked a secretary if this was Lanny Young's office. It was, he heard me, and invited me in. I filled a legal pad full of quotes that I was to use in some dozen stories over the next year.

I asked him about the lawsuits against him going back years, mostly by creditors and former business partners. "If you're looking for an angel in me, you're not going to find it."

Scoundrel, yes. Charming? That too.

When I arrived he was watching a tape of news report about a visitor to Lowndes County. I used the scene to begin a feature on Lanny that ran in mid-June, after the G.H. Stories, and which I remain proud of:

Lanny Young's friendly, slightly chubby face darkened. "Hypocrite," he muttered. There, on the television in his sixth-floor leased office in one of the Retirement Systems of Alabama's downtown buildings, was Jesse Jackson, protesting on CNN. Young, chest hair popping out of his open collar, comfortable in blue jeans and cowboy boots, stared angrily at the civil rights leader.

Jackson had arrived on the scene in Lowndes County, adding his voice to the chorus of residents -- many, it's been ironically noted, who are white -- who oppose Lanny Young and don't want his landfill near their communities.

Understandably, the 40-year-old Young is not happy with these people. They're standing between him and perhaps as much as $10 million. That amount, according to a contract offer sheet produced in a lawsuit, is what one major waste company is willing to pay Young once the wrangling ends and he has a landfill permit in hand....

"There's no question in my mind," Young said that day in early April. "When the day's over, I'll have a permit."

That day never came, for Young or Waste Management.

Chapter 8
Seeds of Destruction

"Lanny's got a little problem."
-- Paul Hamrick to Bill Blount, as recalled by Blount at trial.

"Receiving money at the end of the project."
-- Answer at trial of Insurance executive David Campbell, when asked to describe G.H. Construction's role on the state warehouse project.

Bill Blount was enjoying a resurgence. The best known and to many minds least ethical of Alabama investment bankers was again raking in fees on state bond issues, a rarity for him during the James administration. Siegelman was bond-happy, political to his core, and a Democrat – an unbeatable combination for Blount, the handsome, glib former chairman of the state Democratic Party.

Merchant Capital, another Montgomery-based, Democrat-oriented investment banking outfit, was number one in Siegelman's heart. But Blount's firm -- Blount Parrish & Co. -- was second and well cared for. It had harvested close to $1 million in fees in the 13 months since Siegelman became governor.

It went without saying that keeping Siegelman happy was of utmost importance for Blount, and on a night in March 2000, such an opportunity presented itself.

He was dining at a Montgomery restaurant when the manager approached his table to inform him that the governor was on the phone. Blount took the call in the restaurant bar. Following pleasantries, Siegelman asked Blount if he would be there a few minutes longer. Blount, as he recalled years later at trial, said he would. Siegelman told him to expect a call from Hamrick. Didn't say why, just that Hamrick was going to call. Sure enough, a few minutes later, Hamrick called.

The governor's chief of staff asked Blount if he knew Lanny Young. Met him a few times socially, but that was all, Blount answered.

"Lanny's got a little problem," said Lanny's best friend. He asked if Blount would "meet with (Lanny) and help him straighten it out."

Lanny's little problem was money. He was out of it.

Landfill Lanny was one hurdle – a pesky lawsuit -- from the Lowndes County payday. The golden ticket was going to be his, of that Lanny was sure. But he had spent himself into a hole. He was behind on his payments to Jere Beasley and the latter was threatening foreclosure.

So it was that Blount – after receiving an offer too good to refuse from Alabama's governor -- came to Lanny's rescue.

Blount called on his banker pals and arranged two mortgages. The largest, for $1.4 million, was from Birmingham-based Alamerica Bank. Blount went the extra mile, signing as guarantor, meaning if Lanny defaulted, the bank could demand payment from him. A second mortgage, for $560,000, was with the First National Bank of Brundidge, run by a college friend of Blount's.

Those two loans enabled Young to pay off Beasley and bought him time for that glorious day when the Lowndes lawsuit vanished and he would be rolling in it again.

Despite those loans, winter 2001 found Lanny, if anything, worse off. The landfill lawsuit had settled but was replaced by the two brought by Susan Copeland and Doyle Fuller. Lanny's situation was grave. To keep him from going under, the administration orchestrated a plan to shovel more than $2 million in public funds his way, through a conduit called G.H. "Goat Hill" Construction.

––––

On Feb. 1, 2001, state purchasing director Ran Garver was summoned to Nick Bailey's office in the governor's suite, a few steps from Siegelman's office. There Garver found Lanny and Bailey. The pair presented him with invoices totaling $330,258 from G.H. Construction, which had had not been incorporated and didn't have a contract with the state to do anything. The bills cited services for work by the company and others in the pre-construction phase of a $16.6 million project to build two state warehouses.

One, for the state Alcoholic Beverage Control Board, was to be the first stop for every bottle of liquor sold in Alabama. The second would be the future home of the surplus property division of the Alabama Department of Economic and Community Affairs, commonly known as ADECA.

––––

Lanny had no background in construction and consequently, no construction company. Because of his known connections to the administration and his unfortunate lack of construction experience it was decided that his role must remain a secret.

Young's name was not to be found on G.H. Construction's incorporation papers. It was, officially, a partnership of David Green of Alabaster, near Birmingham, and Bryan Broderick of Montgomery. Green is Lanny's brother-in-law. Broderick was a 27-year-old construction worker who'd worked on Lanny's house.

That day in Bailey's office Garver asked the company's real owner some questions, Lanny answered them to his satisfaction, and the purchasing director authorized payment.

––––

On Feb. 6, 2001 -- two days after our Honda no-bid story and almost a year since Siegelman called Blount at the restaurant to seek help for Lanny -- an ADECA accountant was told to issue a rushed request for payment called a "hot voucher."

Among Young's creditors was Anthony Fant, the wealthy Birmingham businessman and owner of the antique store used by Siegelman as his Birmingham fund-raising headquarters. Fant donated $90,000 to Siegelman's 1998 campaign and also supported him in the 1994 lieutenant governor's race. He was also co-owner of AFS Equities. That was a Birmingham-based brokerage firm that managed Siegelman's campaign account, his personal investments and those of others in the administration, including Bailey.

Siegelman had appointed Fant to the board that oversees the Alabama state docks, and in 1999, Fant flew the governor and his son to the Super Bowl in Miami. In short, Fant was tight with Bailey and Siegelman. Like Honda contractor Tack Mims with his $86,000 loan, Fant had come to Lanny's aid.

He had loaned $100,000 to Young, was trying to collect, and was getting stiffed. Fant asked Bailey for help.

———

A week after the $330,258 "hot voucher" payment, Lanny sent Fant $100,000. Bailey later admitted that he knew the $330,258 bill included charges for work never performed but authorized it so Young could repay Fant.

Did Siegelman know this? I suspect so. As I've stated before and will again, I don't think Nick kept any secrets from Siegelman. Make that, I know he didn't, know it like I know the sun's coming up tomorrow. But can I prove it? No.

As much as anything, the $330,258 hot voucher ended Don Siegelman's political career and wrecked his life.

Of the total, $48,433 was for unspecified "professional services" by G.H. Construction. The rest sought pay for work by other firms whose bills were attached.

The largest bill, for $90,058, cited surveying and environmental studies by CDG Engineering, the company that did work on Lanny's landfill permits and which he'd gotten state work for. It was signed by company vice president Mark Pugh. Only CDG hadn't done any work on the warehouse project and the signature wasn't Pugh's. His name had been forged.

Another receipt attached to G.H. Construction's bill, for $25,000, was submitted by a highly-regarded Montgomery engineering and architectural firm Sherlock Smith & Adams (SS&A). Company chief Roland Vaughan was the recent past president of the powerful Business Council of Alabama and the state's representative on the U.S. Chamber of Commerce.

Vaughan is tall, well-built, mustachioed – a confident, Southern gentleman businessman. He is also a Democrat, and had used his influence with the BCA to encourage state business leaders to reconsider old antipathies and support Siegelman over Fob James.

The previous summer, the administration hired Sherlock Smith & Adams to evaluate potential sites for the warehouses. At that point there were two in mind. Both were already owned by the state, on flat land and along heavily traveled byways. Vaughan suggested that the administration consider a third site, called North Ripley.

The land was not owned by the state, nor was it near a major thoroughfare – an important consideration given all the liquor trucks that would be coming and going. But of its drawbacks, terrain won hands down. North Ripley, easily visible from a perch aside Hank Williams' grave and looking due north, was a bowl-shaped 256-acre parcel, its wetlands covered bottom abutted by tree-covered slopes. Unfit for building much of anything, especially warehouses, which are simple structures that require broad expanses of flat land.

In November 2000, Vaughan's firm submitted a report recommending that the state build the warehouses at North Ripley. It was paid $25,000 for its work.

Vaughan neglected to disclose that he had become a silent half-owner of the North Ripley site. His name was not to be found on any publicly recorded deeds, just bank records, which aren't public. Within months of his firm's recommendation, G.H. Construction – acting as the state's agent -- bought the North Ripley site.

Vaughan, who hadn't had to put up any money, cleared a quick $48,434.

Construction on the warehouses had yet to begin and already the administration's chosen overseers, Lanny Young and Roland Vaughan, were making funny money.

The warehouse project was to be funded with some $21.8 million raised through the sale of bonds. Of that, $16.6 million was allotted for construction and purchase of the land. The remainder, more than $5 million was to be dished out in professional fees, the largest chunks going to G.H. Construction, Sherlock Smith & Adams and the investment banker picked for the deal. Fittingly, given Blount's role in helping Siegelman save Lanny, that plum was awarded to Blount Parrish.

––––

In late March 2001 the warehouse deal ran into a snag.

The public works law requires that contractors post a surety (performance) bond of an amount equal to the size of the contract. It's a type of insurance that protects owners in the event a contractor goes bust or otherwise fails to perform. If that happens, the bonding company must step in and complete the project.

G.H. Construction had to post a $16 million bond before it could enter into the contract. Nashville-based Gulf Insurance Company was asked to bond the job. Before agreeing to do so the firm conducted its routine due diligence on the new Alabama company.

Five years later, at the Siegelman trial, Gulf Insurance executive David Campbell testified that G.H. Construction had $31,000 in the bank. That was a fraction of the $1 million or so his company required before bonding a $16 million job. Furthermore, the warehouse project was G.H. Construction's first and there was nothing to reassure Campbell that the company was up to the task. For those reasons, Gulf Insurance refused to bond the project.

At this juncture, the solution should have been obvious: Can G.H. Construction and seek competitive proposals from the wide world of companies for whom securing a bond wasn't a problem. That this wasn't contemplated suggests that the greater motivation for building two warehouses wasn't to satisfy the state's needs, but Lanny's.

He desperately needed money to tide him over until the Lowndes landfill litigation vanished and the Siegelman administration was hell-bent on making sure he got it.

Bill Blount, Roland Vaughan and Gulf Insurance negotiated a most unusual resolution to the problem. G.H. Construction would be the construction manager of record. But Sherlock Smith & Adams -- in addition to providing architectural services for the site and one of the warehouses – was to serve as the de facto construction manager.

Only then would Gulf Insurance bond the job.

As Campbell told jurors at trial, "We took G.H. out of the equation."

Gulf Insurance, recognizing that the warehouse deal couldn't proceed without a bond, played hardball. It charged a whopping $300,000 for the policy, then placed yet another onerous condition on its Alabama customers.

The company demanded that Bill Blount personally guaranty the project. If G.H. Construction faltered and the bonding company had to step in and complete the job, then, as Campbell testified of Blount, "We would pursue him (to recoup our costs)."

This time Blount was really stepping up to the plate to help Lanny, the guy he had hardly known until being called that night at the restaurant by Siegelman and Hamrick the year before.

At trial, prosecutor Steve Feaga asked Campbell to review the contracts showing that Lanny's company was to be paid a fee equal to 12 percent of the $16.6 million construction budget.

The unsmiling witness, making no effort to conceal his contempt for G.H. Construction and, it seemed as well, the manner in which the state of Alabama conducted its business, told jurors that the industry standard for construction management contracts was three to five percent.

With his final question Feaga asked the insurance executive to describe G.H. Construction's "function" on the warehouse job.

After a short pause, Campbell sneered, "Receiving money at the end of the project."

By the time I heard those words, in May 2006, I didn't think there was anything new about G.H. Construction that could surprise me. I'd known for years – had in fact reported – that Sherlock Smith & Adams was to have baby-sat the construction manager and that Lanny's company stood to make, with bonus provisions, as much as $2.3 million.

But even for me, Campbell's answer to Feaga's question was a revelation.

Lanny's company wasn't to do – would not be allowed to do – anything.

Cash checks. That was it.

Chapter 9
Goat Hill Construction

"I don't know that they've done anything on this job. I really don't know."
-- Roland Vaughan, after being shown a bill for $90,058 from a company called CDG Engineers that was included among receipts submitted by G.H. Construction for payment from the state.

"After considering financial questions raised by the Mobile Register in relation to this project, I am ordering that all work on the project by G.H. Construction and others cease until an independent review of this matter can be completed."
-- Finance Director Henry Mabry, in April 27, 2001, memo announcing what became the end of the warehouse project.

By early April I'd been working a month on a story about a landfill outside our coverage area with nothing to show for it. My editors hadn't complained but I sensed a tug on my long leash could come any day.

Some months before I'd come to know, if by phone only, a new spokesperson for the attorney general's office. A talker and a laugher, Suzanne Smith was of a type my mother called, "a hoot." I mentioned that I was working on a story about the Lowndes landfill and asked Suzanne what if she knew anything about Lanny Young.

Her answer: A lot.

Suzanne was big pals with Lanny's lobbying partner, Claire Austin. Suzanne said I had to call Claire and write a story about a warehouse project she was sure stunk to high heaven. Team Siegelman had quietly hired a company called G.H. Construction, and Lanny was its secret owner. G.H., she said with a howl, stood for Goat Hill.

Goat Hill? If so, that was brazen indeed, like a politically connected New York company calling itself T.H. Construction, for Tammany Hall. Goat Hill is the nickname of the elevated plot chosen in the early 1800s as the site for Alabama's state capitol. It had been a goat pasture. Stubborn like its namesake, Goat Hill defied efforts to replace it with something more distinguished, including Lafayette Hill, after the 1825 visit of the Marquis de Lafayette.

By April 2001 the Claire-Lanny partnership was a wreck and weeks away from dissolution. I called Claire. She said Lanny was cutting her out of deals and hiding fees -- a grievance she shared with many of his past partners, regardless of the venture. She didn't know much about the warehouse deal, only that if it involved Lanny, it had to be dirty.

Lanny had left a few pages of the contract on the fax machine, and she copied them. These she faxed to me. The only page containing meaningful information was the front, which identified G.H. Construction as the contractor for warehouses to be built for ADECA and the state liquor board.

Nothing sent by Claire gave the financial terms of the project nor identified anyone, Lanny included, associated with the company.

Though many would guess, for five years I stayed mum, doing what I could to protect Claire's identity as my source. This is no longer necessary. Claire acknowledged as much during her testimony at the Siegelman trial.

Claire, as she testified, first told investigators with the attorney general's office about G.H. Construction, but they hadn't moved on it. I don't say this to make them look bad. Their job is to investigate crimes. The level of wrongdoing needed to justify a news story is far lower than that required to commence a criminal investigation, much less charge someone. In my business, good ole political favoritism is plenty. And that was all I saw. Nothing shown or told me by Claire indicated criminal activity. It looked like another no-bid crony contract in the Sherrod vein.

My initial attraction to G.H. Construction wasn't its potential as a major story, but an easy one. I'd need only to determine the scope and cost of the project, report the selection of G.H. Construction in the context of the other no-bid contracts, present an overview of the Lanny-Hamrick-Siegelman relationship and, as gravy, ladle on some of what I'd learned about Lanny's landfill business.

G.H. Construction would be a quick pop, something to buy time until I could finish the landfill story.

The first step seemed obvious enough. Call the two agencies. They'd surely confirm their plans. The alternative was declaring they were unaware of their intentions to spend millions of dollars on warehouses a stone's throw from downtown Montgomery.

First up was ADECA, which was to be the contracting agency for both buildings. Thus began my rocky relationship with Larry Childers. Over the next two years, we would bicker like an old married couple, me insisting that records had to exist, him invariably saying otherwise, and me always – and I mean always – winning out. (Larry's wife was dying of cancer, and this was surely a very difficult period for him.)

Larry, as previously noted, had been a top Siegelman aide going back 20 years, but was no longer in the inner circle, having been supplanted by Hamrick and Bailey. He had worked on Dwayne Freeman's failed campaign for lieutenant governor, and when Siegelman appointed Freeman ADECA director, Larry was made press office chief at Alabama's most notorious agency. ADECA's earned that distinction not because of its employees, but for its misuse by legislators as a clearing house for pork, for routing money this way and that and, not infrequently, into their or their friends' pockets.

Larry is baby-faced, prematurely grey, and resembles a young Captain Kangaroo. The first time I spoke to him was when I called to ask about the warehouses. "We don't build warehouses. We issue grants," he said, matter-of-factly.

I told him, polite as could be, that I had it on good authority that ADECA was in fact preparing to build two warehouses, one for itself, the other for the liquor board.

Couldn't be, Larry said. ADECA doesn't build warehouses. It issues and manages grants.

I might as well have told him that ADECA was developing a space program so Siegelman could become the first governor hurled into orbit.

Could he pass on my question to his superiors? You know, in the highly unlikely chance that ADECA had strayed from its mission?

He hemmed and hawed, said he'd ask, didn't convince.

The next call was to the ABC board. From a straight news standpoint, that agency's plans were a bigger story. Alabama was one of a handful of states still in the liquor business, and many wished it would get out. Scandalous or not, if the Siegelman administration was contemplating a new warehouse, it reflected a long-term commitment by the state to remain the primary source of all hard spirits sold in Alabama.

I was put through to staff attorney Bob Hill. He sounded genuinely perplexed when I asked him about ABC's plans for a new warehouse. "I'm not aware of any project," he said.

Bob said if there was such plan, he would know about it. As the board's lawyer, it was his job to draft or at the very least review all its contracts. Then as now, I believe that Bob, a short, easygoing man in his 60s, was telling the truth. He really didn't know. As I would come to see, the plans to build and finance the warehouses were to an amazing degree concealed from merit system employees, the so-called bureaucrats who remain in place administration after administration.

When I called Larry back a day or so later, the response was the same. Grants, not warehouses. He seemed to waffle when I asked if he had passed my question up the food chain.

I concluded my first trip to Montgomery since Claire's tip with an unannounced visit to Larry's office. I introduced myself and asked if he'd learned anything about the warehouses. Larry said he remained unaware of any plans for new warehouses. That wasn't a definitive no, so I asked if the director was in.

I was able to ask this with a straight face, as I didn't yet know that Nick Bailey almost never darkened ADECA's halls. He had been elevated from "state budget officer" to ADECA director in May 2000, after Freeman returned home drunk from a night out and got in an ugly row with his family. His wife called the police.

Though the charges were dropped, Freeman's political career was over. He was out at ADECA, and Bailey in, though not really.

Larry said Bailey wasn't available, so I asked who served as ADECA's number two man. Chris Pitts, said Larry. The name rang a bell from my Lanny studies. Pitts, who is black, had written black leaders in Lowndes County on Lanny's behalf, urging them to cease blocking his landfill.

I took the elevator a few floors up and entered Pitts' office. I told him I was all but certain that ADECA was planning to build a pair of warehouses, but that Larry had indicated otherwise. Did he know anything about this?

Pitts, unconvincingly, said he did not. But if there was such a project, the folks at ADECA's surplus property division would be the ones to know. Surplus property is a little-known ADECA sub-agency that warehouses all manner of used state and federal government merchandise before it's sold at auction.

I asked Pitts if he could call over there.

I sensed reluctance, but recognition that he couldn't very well say no to what was, after all, not an unreasonable request. So he called, and soon I was talking with Shane Bailey, who was – and by then the connections were piling up so fast I needed a chart – Nick Bailey's younger brother.

The Siegelman administration had bypassed the merit system of using competitive means to employ state employees and made Shane, at 28, director of the surplus property division.

After a pause, Nick Bailey's brother said that, yes, his division was overseeing a project to build the two warehouses, for itself and the ABC board.

Confirmed, finally. What a pain in the rear that had been.

———

It was easier to verify the existence of G.H. Construction.

A few minutes on the secretary of state web-site and I had that and the names of its two officer/incorporators. In the coming month I made many efforts, all fruitless, to reach the pair. On paper if not in reality, G.H. Construction was David Green, the brother of Lanny's wife; and Bryan Broderick, a young guy who'd worked on Lanny's house.

———

I don't recall the exact nature of my first inquiry to Carrie Kurlander about the warehouses, but unlike those to come, it wasn't with powerful goods in hand. I was surprised, then, when she invited me to Montgomery to meet with people involved in the project. I'm sure the administration foresaw only one such gathering, but developments during the first session and my follow-up questions begat a second, then a third.

No on associated with G.H. Construction, Lanny included, attended either gathering.

It was during these group interviews that the aforementioned Carrie Kurlander Openness Experiment flowered, then died. Comments made during the sessions, each of about three hours in length, were put to use in the many G.H. stories published in the coming month.

To my knowledge, none of the meetings were taped, at least by me. Transcribing tapes takes forever, and a recorder can breed discomfort and lack of candor among interviewees. For those and other reasons, I use tape recorders sparingly. My instruments of choice are yellow legal pads and medium point blue pens. I write big and get about a sentence a page on the tiny notebooks used by most reporters. And those medium blues – oh how they glide. To ensure accuracy, I risk sounding the fool by asking subjects to repeat themselves.

The first meeting, on Friday, April 20, was in a conference room in the legal wing of the governor's offices, across the hall from the press operation. Ted Hosp, the governor's general counsel, was there, as was Carrie and two of her aides, recent Georgetown University graduates Rip Andrews and Jasper Ward. Neither of those four knew much of anything about the project, save the talking points, one of which was recited by Carrie:

"This is something we're very proud of. Not only are we saving the state, by a conservative estimate, $20 million over 20 years, but we're also committing to an economically depressed part of Montgomery. It's a win-win for the city and a win-win for the state."

Also present was Roland Vaughan, who I was meeting for the first time and who did most of the talking. Nick Bailey joined by speakerphone soon after the meeting started.

As Vaughan explained that day, the basics of the deal were thus: Money to pay for the project was to be raised from the sale of bonds. The seller wouldn't be the state, but a little-used entity called the Montgomery Downtown Development Authority that was affiliated with the city of Montgomery. Over the years the authority had sold bonds to finance several area buildings, including the maze-like Gordon Persons Building, home of many state agencies and known as the Missing Persons Building because of its tendency to turn visitors into missing persons.

The plan was for ADECA and ABC to move their operations into the warehouses and pay rent to the authority. In turn, the authority would use the lease payments to repay investors who bought the bonds. At the end of 20 years, the bonds would be paid off and the authority would transfer ownership of the warehouses to the state. It was hardly a novel concept – gazillions of bond deals have worked much the same way -- and on its face, not at all scandalous.

It quickly became evident that my hosts believed me far more knowledgeable about the G.H. Construction deal than was the case. I was early in the research stage and knew little more than that a company by that name, owned or backed by the administration's good friend Lanny, was to be in charge of building two warehouses.

I arrived with my leatherette Super Bowl XXVII satchel, a press favor from the 1994 game in Atlanta. It was bulging with papers and legal pads, but contained nothing reflecting how much G.H. Construction was to be paid.

I may have flashed the front page of the contract, but made no attempt to trick them into thinking I had more. As the meeting proceeded, I realized they believed I had the entire contract. I did nothing to dissuade them of this.

In short, I won the pot with a pair of twos and a bluff. The payoff – the instant when my interest in the warehouses expanded beyond a quick story – came when Vaughan, obviously thinking I already knew about it, started explaining G.H. Construction's 12 percent construction management fee.

From stories on Mobile area projects, I knew that construction managers were paid based on a percentage of the construction budget. Five percent is the norm. Six percent is high, 8 percent would be outrageous. Twelve is probably a world record.

The traditional method used by government entities to hire contractors for construction projects, whether for roads or buildings or what have you, is through competitive bidding. Once a contractor is chosen, selection and payment of subcontractors is the prime contractor's business. The project owners – for example, the state – are usually represented by the architects or engineers who designed the project.

The construction manager concept caught hold in the 1990s. When used, there is no prime contractor. The construction manager, not the architect or engineer, serves as the owner's representative on a job. It is responsible for bidding out the sub-contracts, scheduling the job, and ensuring the project is built to specifications.

By law – and this is important – a construction management firm is prohibited from performing the actual work. For example, none of its employees are to use bulldozers or erect steel. That's why a five percent is the high range of the norm, and why my eyes bugged when Vaughan said G.H. Construction was getting 12 percent.

I instantly expressed incredulity. It may be that they were more surprised at my surprise than I was upon hearing the fee.

The cat was out of the bag, and they let it out.

Vaughan said the 12 percent was to be applied against total "hard construction" costs of $11.5 million for building the warehouses and a road into the site. Even by that account – way low, it turned out – G.H. Construction was to receive an alarmingly high $1.38 million. Vaughan said he had been assured by Lanny and Broderick that Lanny had no stake in the enterprise.

I wasn't holding any records that would refute that malarkey, so could do little more than give Vaughan my best Buster Keaton deadpan.

Here is how we presented the 12 percent fee in our tenth story on G.H. Construction, published May 18:

Numerous construction professionals interviewed for this story said they'd never heard of anything approaching the 12-percent construction management fee G.H. was to have been paid. Construction managers -- which by definition can't themselves perform work on a job they oversee – aren't even used on most state projects, and are considered unnecessary by many, especially on easy jobs.

That G.H. was to be paid 12 percent for overseeing construction of pre-fabricated warehouses and two "pre-engineered" office buildings only made it more incredible, they said.

"On a scale of 1 to 100, with 100 being the hardest, this would be a nine," said Henry Hagood, executive director of the Alabama General Contractors Association. "This is on the low end, the real low end. Metal building warehouses – they're not that difficult."

Vaughan, Sherlock, Smith & Adams' president, said the project was complicated, because "every component has to be bid, and every subcontractor has to have a performance bond."

Roland's defense of the fee was, as he had to know, gibberish. Bidding subcontracts with bonded companies is the minimal requirement of a construction manager.

As I was to learn, work on the project -- "clearing and grubbing" of the site -- had begun. Vaughan had picked the contractor that was to build the warehouses, and did so without seeking bids.

The upshot: The architectural firm secretly standing in for the construction manager had blown off the bidding requirements. Considering everything else, bypassing the bid law was a minor infraction, a parking violation during a bank robbery. But it was typical of the anything-goes-attitude of all involved in the warehouse deal.

My chief aim that day wasn't to determine G.H. Construction's fee, but the circumstances of its hiring. I told those gathered I knew the company was associated with Lanny, and remarked that Lanny's business was landfills, not construction.

Because construction management is a professional service, selection of such firms needn't be bid out. But a competitive process should be used when awarding such work. Why, I asked, had the state picked a company that had never built anything?

Here, as throughout, Roland fell on his sword to protect Siegelman. I suspect he was motivated by a wish to keep the good times coming for Sherlock Smith & Adams. The firm's state business had tripled under Siegelman.

Vaughan recalled meeting Lanny over drinks at Sinclair's, a popular restaurant and bar in the Cloverdale section of town and a favored hangout for the political crowd. The warehouse project came up and Lanny said he represented a couple of young contractors who could do a great job. This was good enough for Vaughan, who thereafter hired Broderick and Green for the multi-million dollar project.

Had I known Roland better I would have told him to try again. But I didn't. He was a man of consequence and reputation and I had little choice but to faithfully scribble down what he said. I could see, though, that he told the tale with some discomfort.

Several months later, Vaughan told a different story to an investigator with the attorney general's office.

He said he'd been brought in to help with the project and had another firm in mind to serve as construction manager. However, he was told that a company associated with Lanny was to get the work.

"I never knew Mr. Young before then. I'd read about him in the newspapers. That's about it," Vaughan said, referring to stories about Young's efforts to build a landfill in Lowndes County.

During my early April interview with Lanny in his office -- which was prior to my meeting Vaughan -- the gregarious one described Broderick as a highly qualified, motivated young contractor whose only drawback was a lack of contacts. He said Green and Broderick approached him for help winning state business because they "didn't know a damn thing about politics."

Lanny said he called Nick Bailey to tout Green-Broderick as a pair of up and coming construction stars. "So what if somebody knows somebody. If it's done by the law and it's good for taxpayers, then what's wrong?" he said, in a quote that was later to come in handy.

Lanny said he had no financial interest in G.H. Construction, and furthermore, that he hadn't charged Green and Broderick for delivering the multi-million dollar state construction contract.

Did it as a favor, he said.

As when researching the Sherrod story, I contacted the contractor's licensing board, curious to know how this spanking new company had managed to get the unlimited (U) rating required to oversee construction of the warehouses. The board secretary, no doubt following administration directions, refused to provide me with the documentation used to grant the U rating to G.H. Construction.

I spent weeks bugging the press office for a copy of Broderick's resume. I was told that Broderick refused out of concern that I would contact his former employers. Too bad. If he wanted to keep his *bona fides* private, he shouldn't be seeking public contracts.

Eventually it was provided. It revealed him as the owner of Broderick Construction, and listed several projects performed by this company. There was no record of any such company with the secretary of state or the contractor's licensing board.

Broderick wasn't returning my calls, so I asked the press office if it could answer questions about this person in whom the administration had entrusted so much. Readers were told that this effort bore no fruit because the press office couldn't locate the president of G.H. Construction either.

It was becoming, dare I say, funny. The Siegelman administration couldn't find its own contractor.

During the first meeting I asked Vaughan if Broderick had a staff. Vaughan said he didn't know, but that it didn't matter. What mattered were the qualifications of the head man, and he chose G.H. Construction because he was so impressed by Broderick.

When I pressed the issue of company's inexperience, Roland said Sherlock Smith & Adams had been asked to provide "quality control and value control over the construction manager."

This was like hiring a baby sitter to baby-sit the baby sitter, since quality control was one of the construction manager's primary responsibilities.

In addition to being implausible, the Sinclair's story contradicted the version of G.H.'s hiring told me by Lanny weeks before. He'd said that he called Nick to tout Broderick and Green. Lanny hadn't said the first thing about Vaughan or Sinclair's.

Vaughan also claimed to have chosen Blount Parrish to sell the warehouse bonds. He said – and this too defied belief – that he'd seen no need to inform Siegelman or Bailey of his decisions to hire G.H. Construction and Bill Blount's firm.

"I didn't approach it as, 'Here, let me run to the state and get this approved,'" Vaughan said.

———

Bailey offered little that day and would have been better served saying nothing. When I pressed Roland on the propriety of hiring a company based on little else but Lanny's word, Nick piped in through the speaker phone, pumped with righteous indignation.

"Do we know all these people? I sure hope so, because we wouldn't want to be involved in this with people we didn't know and trust."

———

If for nothing else, trips to Montgomery were worth it for records maintained by the Comptroller's Office. It is the mother lode of state records resources.

When the state pays vendors, be they construction companies, law firms, or providers of paper clips, the checks come from the comptroller's office. The payment process begins when an agency sends its request for payment to the comptroller. Attached is the supporting documentation, such as itemized receipts. Agencies are responsible for assuring that the goods or services were provided. The comptroller's staff reviews the voucher for compliance with various rules, then cuts a check.

The office maintains a computer available to the media. The unwieldy search process that led to the destruction of Siegelman's political career is as follows:

You type the name of a person or company as it would appear on a check, not in a phone book. In other words, first name first. Company names are easy, individuals often tricky. You need to know a person's formal name, including middle, as well as nickname, and it never hurts to give all the names a run. One agency might pay someone under his formal name, another under his nickname, and if a lawyer, payment could be to the firm.

Preparing the comptroller's portion of my public records "shopping list" required finding all possible names in which a person or company might get paid, as well as companies related to those people or firms, the latter connections searched for on the secretary of state corporations web-site.

Preparing the comptroller's shopping list frequently took hours.

When you get a hit on the comptroller computer, the name shows up in a column of vendors. Each has a nine number vendor code. My practice was to go through all the new names on my list, jot down their codes, then switch to a separate search where you enter the vendor codes.

There's a screen for each payment. It reveals the amount, date and paying agency and a host of record locaters, such as, "batch number." You must complete a separate form for each receipt you wish to review. The process is tedious as hell.

Once finished, and usually with anywhere from 10 to 20 voucher request forms in hand, I walked across the hall to see Myron Perdue.

If Myron wasn't glad to see me, he hid it well. I represented extra work, sometimes lots of it, since one of his many duties is fulfilling voucher requests. For this reason I began my days at the comptroller's office, and with any luck, Myron would have my stuff by day's end.

It was always with anticipation that I returned to review the goods. Often – such as when I was just fishing – there was nothing of interest. But not infrequently, I hit pay-dirt.

I knew that two of the vouchers ordered that day would contain usable information. That morning I'd given "G.H. Construction" a spin and come up a winner. There were two payments: One for $330,258 on Jan. 8, 2001; the other, for $81,237, on Feb. 22.

The state had already paid more than $411,000 to G.H. Construction.

I noticed the company's billing address: P.O. Box 59. One and the same as Lanny's landfill company. Here was confirmation by public record of his involvement with G.H. Construction.

Two other connections revealed themselves, both, like the P.O. Box, fruits of the time spent on Lanny's landfill business.

Both vouchers contained receipts from G.H. Construction for work purportedly done by the company. Attached to the vouchers were bills from other companies who'd performed pre-construction services, such as architectural work, and were billing the state through G.H. Construction.

The first voucher showed that G.H. sought $48,433 for unidentified professional services it claimed to have provided. The remaining $281,824.50 was to reimburse G.H. for paying others. Two of those companies shown as having billed and paid by G.H. were familiar. Both had been listed as creditors on a sham bankruptcy filed by Lanny's landfill company, and which was a major issue in one of the lawsuits brought by Susan Copeland and Doyle Fuller.

The smallest bill, for $5,200, was from Denton, Ponder & Edwards, a Roanoke, Ala., firm I knew to be Lanny's accountant.

The second familiar name was CDG Engineers, the company that provided engineering services for Lanny's landfill ventures and which was also named in the sham bankruptcy. The CDG bill reflected that the company had performed three studies on the chosen "North Ripley" warehouse site and billed G.H. a total of $90,058.

One was a wetlands analysis and another, a test for soil stability. Most important for our story was the third one, listed on the bill as an, "Alta survey." It accounted for $32,500 of the total.

G.H. Construction's second voucher, submitted to ADECA six weeks after the first, showed the company claiming $59,612, for unspecified professional services it provided. The remaining $21,625 was to pay a company, Lucido & Oliver, for what the attached bill called a "boundary survey" of the North Ripley site.

I'd never heard of an Alta survey, but assumed it had to be different than a boundary survey. I used Google to determine what it was. Lo and behold, Google revealed that an Alta survey and a boundary survey are essentially one and the same.

That was odd. Had there been two boundary surveys, one by CDG, the other by Lucido & Oliver?

One of the comptroller records gave a physical address for G.H. Construction. It was on Clay Street, on the outskirts of downtown Montgomery. Might this be where Bryan Broderick hangs out, and if so, might he talk to me? I found the place, knocked, but there was no response. I turned the handle, and to my surprise, the door opened.

The proprietor next door ran a one-man detective agency. A few weeks before he'd seen several men drive up in big, expensive-looking trucks and go into the office. Since then, nothing. I said I was going in for a look-see, which was OK with him. The first floor was empty, not even furniture. I walked upstairs, not wanting to report that the place was vacant only to be told later that there was a full-service office on the second floor. It also was barren, but for some architectural drawings leaning against the wall. I unfurled them and saw they were for the warehouse project.

I took pictures, inside and out, and we used one of the outside shots of the office but not those taken inside. The editors feared that could open me up to a trespassing claim. Our fifth story on the warehouse deal, published in early May, began:

A visitor's knock at 452 Clay St. in downtown Montgomery produced no response, other than the slow opening of the unlocked front door.

A notice from the telephone company, dated a week earlier and announcing that service was activated, lay just inside the door. What appeared to be rolled-up architectural drawings leaned against a corner.

Shouts of "Anyone here!" echoed through the rooms, but clearly, no one was. The office of G.H. Construction -- short for Goat Hill Construction -- was barren. No people, no furniture, no pictures on the walls.

That, readers, was G.H. Construction. A bunch of nothing.

———

Because the first meeting generated more questions than it answered, Carrie set up a second one, on Tuesday, April 24, at Sherlock Smith & Adams. Joining me on the short drive there was Rip Andrews, who I was coming to know, as he was Carrie's top assistant.

It was during this short ride that we had our first riff, minor though it was. I'd been pressing for copies of various contracts, especially the one with G.H., but been refused on the grounds that the contracts were not yet signed and wouldn't be until the bonds were sold. I argued in multiple e-mails that the state had paid G.H. Construction more than $400,000; that the basis of those payments was the G.H. contract and others; and on that basis, the contracts were public record, signed or not. They didn't see it that way.

Rip, who was almost 20 years my junior, said rather emphatically that it seemed to him that a reporter wouldn't want to write a story about a contract until he had it in hand. He implied that the proper, responsible thing was to wait until the bonds were sold, after which I would have everything and could report it accurately.

I told him, sternly but not in an ugly manner, that it wasn't his role to tell me how to do my job.

But for one major exception, the second meeting was the least eventful of the three. The chief participants were Vaughan and Jim Simon, an obviously competent engineer with Sherlock Smith & Adams who was assigned to the warehouse project. At the start of the meeting Simon gave me copies of construction schedules, quite professionally done, with graphs and other information. The thing was, he'd done it, but scheduling was one of the main responsibilities of a construction manager. Here, though, was Sherlock Smith & Adams scheduling the job, not G.H. Construction with its 12 percent fee.

The meeting's pivotal moment came when I handed Vaughan the two boundary survey bills, both of which, through G.H., had already been paid for by the state.

Vaughan was familiar with the first. He said he'd hired Lucido & Oliver to conduct the survey, and had referred to the survey in his firm's site selection report.

Here is how we presented Vaughan's response to the CDG bill in the story published five days after the meeting:

Vaughan explained that all the engineering and survey studies were authorized by him, because his architects and engineers needed that information to design the layout of the 256-acre site, including the roads, the exact sites of the buildings and other aspects of the property.

For that reason, Vaughan's firm was working closely with all the companies it hired, with the state's approval, to provide surveying studies, environmental studies and geotechnical evaluations.

On Tuesday, Kurlander arranged an interview for the Register at Vaughan's firm with Vaughan and Jim Simon, an engineer assigned to the project. Vaughan explained how he'd selected the companies providing the studies, all of which were well-regarded and approved by the state.

The Register showed Vaughan the $90,058 bill from CDG Engineers. The former BCA chairman looked at it for some time, then said quietly, "I don't know that they've done anything on this job. I really don't know."

Vaughan said he could not imagine why G.H. Construction would have hired CDG and authorized the three studies. The work of such firms and the fruits of those studies didn't fall within the scope of the construction manager's duties, he said.

At that moment I knew they were screwed. They knew it too.

The final meeting, like the gathering two days before, was at Sherlock Smith &Adams, though neither Vaughan nor anyone else with the firm attended. It was the most memorable of the three, largely owing to the live-in-person appearance of Nick Bailey and his side-kick for the show, state purchasing officer Ran Garver. Others seated around the conference table were Carrie, Nick's brother Shane, and long-time ADECA lawyer Eddie Davis.

Garver came to the administration from Sherlock Smith & Adams after Vaughan recommended him to Siegelman. It was my first time to meet him, and with the exception of several court appearances years later, the last. And that's fine, with both of us.

This short, balding man remains one of the most arrogant, unpleasant people I have ever dealt with in state government. The colonel – his rank in the U.S. Army Corps of Engineers -- seemed unaccustomed to having his word questioned. He didn't understand that I get paid to question what I'm told so as to ensure accuracy and my understanding of matters, both necessary elements for a reporter seeking to educate readers. When people tell you something and you don't immediately accept it as gospel you are by your very act questioning their word or their memory or understanding of affairs. Many people – and this can include me -- don't appreciate it.

In any event, making people mad with fair, politely asked questions is an occupational hazard. Garver just got madder, more irritated, than most.

We were still in the pleasantries stage and awaiting Nick's arrival when I excused myself to go to the bathroom. I was walking down the hall when I spotted Bailey. He was speaking animatedly into a cell phone, and talking about, of all things, the warehouse bond issue.

There was a water fountain close by. I took a long drink, and another. Just kept drinking. Bailey either didn't know what I looked like or didn't see me. He was wound up, oblivious to his surroundings. The bonds had to be sold Friday, he was saying, to whom I couldn't tell.

Not that I had to be sneaky. Upon entering the conference room Bailey apologized for having to keep his cell phone on. "We're trying to close this on Friday. We've been doing everything we can to get him (authority lawyer Sam Kaufman) everything," he said.

Two days before I'd suffered the admonishment from Rip for not waiting to write the story until after the bonds were sold, and now this. If I hadn't known for certain they were trying to get the bonds to market before my story, I did now.

One problem, I knew, was rounding up the members of the Montgomery Downtown Development Authority. The husband of one of the members was in the hospital and almost surely couldn't be available Friday. Monday was looking like the soonest the bonds could be sold. With that the case, our plans to run a story Sunday was an obstacle that needed removing.

I came to liken the third meeting to a detour on a highway. I was motoring down the road, long journey almost over, when I came across a sign – actually several of them – saying "detour." Placing these signs along the highway were Bailey and Garver.

Before I'd asked the first question, Bailey looked down the table at Garver. "Tell him about the 8.4 percent," he said.

Like an actor taking a cue, Garver proceeded to report that the 12 percent construction management fee was actually 8.4 percent.

With gusto, the Garver-Bailey tag-team explained that upon sale of the bonds, G.H. Construction was to be reimbursed the $562,000 it had paid months earlier for the land. For whatever reason, that sum and some other costs had erroneously been included when calculating the construction management fee.

If what they were saying was true, a focal point of the story – the vast overbilling represented by the 12 percent – was diminished. Now, 8.4 percent was still outrageous, but it wasn't as far out of the ballpark as 12 percent.

I was suspicious, but not holding any cards – say, the contract -- that could trump this new tale. I tried to press them on several fronts. Why, I asked, hadn't I been told this in two long interviews with Vaughan, including the one in which Bailey participated by speakerphone? After all, Vaughan had tried mightily to explain the fee, without once offering that defense.

I asked Garver and Bailey if they'd seen the contract showing that fee was actually 8.4 percent. Both replied that they had not, but stuck with their story. It was an 8.4 percent fee, not 12 percent.

When I asked Bailey if I could see the contract, he said, as we later reported, that there was no contract with G.H. Construction. "I guess you could call it a handshake agreement," he said.

The purpose of a contract is to put down in writing the obligations for each party to the other, in part to force both sides to stick to an agreement or face the legal consequences. State law requires the existence of contracts before payment. The phrase "handshake agreement" is not to be found in the state law on public contracts.

This same astonishing explanation – sealing deals with the merging of palms -- was given by Bailey for the administration's inability to produce contracts with other firms working the job, such as those who'd billed the state through G.H.

About an hour after the meeting ended, I called Carrie to express doubts about the 8.4 percent solution. Could she call Bailey to ask if he was sure that the fee wasn't really 12 percent?

She said she could, did, and called me back. "He (Nick) did not know that for a fact, but I believe that's how he said it was explained to him," she said. "He said that's what Roland told him."

Roland had been kind enough to give me his cell number. I reached him and asked if the $562,000 payment for the land had been calculated as part of the 12 percent construction management fee; and if so, did that reduce the rate to 8.4 percent?

He said that the cost of the land was a separate component from the construction management fee. He said he had never heard of the 8.4 percent figure.

This prompted another call to Carrie for another round of Team Siegelman truth tennis, Carrie not as opponent, but umpire. I reported Roland's response, and she said she would call Nick again.

"He absolutely stands by what he told me, that that's what Roland told him," Carrie said, when she called back.

I wasn't able to fit this silliness into any of the stories – it was too back and forth. But I did report some other tall tales spun that day by the Garver-Bailey tandem. Team Siegelman had to learn once and for all that if they were going to fib and get caught, I was going to tattle on them, not to the teacher or their Mama, but to readers.

Such was the case with their attempt to snow me on the $90,058 bill from CDG and the smaller one from the Denton, Ponder accounting firm.

Garver and Bailey said the accountants had prepared an analysis of the state rental payments that were to be used to repay bond-holders. Such a study, declared Bailey-Garver, was required by the investment bankers and the lawyers, who needed it to compile the bond document for investors.

Sounded plausible enough, and at the time they fed it to me, I'd no proof otherwise. Just in case, what with their track record and all, it seemed a good idea to verify. In Sunday's paper, readers were provided the explanation of the accounting bill as sold by Bailey-Garver, then this:

On Thursday, the Register called Montgomery lawyer Sam Kauffman, who represents the authority and who is reviewing all the bond documents. Kauffman said he was unaware of any such study and said there would be no need for one. Kauffman said he'd never heard of Denton, Ponder.

Calls by the Register to Denton, Ponder were not returned. After the Register reported Kauffman's response to Siegelman's press office, Rip Andrews, a member of Kurlander's staff, contacted the Denton, Ponder firm asking it to provide documentation of its work product and requesting that Denton explain the purpose of his firms work, Kurlander said.

On Friday, a company partner faxed the administration a copy of the $5,200 bill. It shows that from Nov. 9 to Jan. 5, firm partner David Denton worked 52 hours at $100 per hour and listed the client as G.H. Construction. According to Kurlander, Denton told Andrews that G.H. Construction had hired his firm to study the budget on the project to "demonstrate how the project would work."

Such a study, Kurlander said, would seem to be a payment that G.H. Construction would absorb as its own cost. "Rip requested that they provide their work product, and it wasn't provided."

Carrie and Rip deserved credit for trying, and at a time when they knew things weren't looking good for their team's warehouse project.

During that final meeting, Bailey and Garver tried to shovel an even larger load my way to explain away the CDG bill.

They claimed the three CDG studies were authorized by the architectural firm hired to design the ADECA warehouse. (Vaughan's firm, in addition to its other roles, designed the ABC warehouse and the project site, but not the ADECA warehouse.)

Samuel Donze owned the Birmingham-based firm and employed W. Curtis Kirsch, a Montgomery architect known less for the quality of his work than questions about how he obtained it. Two years later Kirsch would plead guilty to bribing Bailey to get the warehouse design contract, an act unknown to Donze.

Here is how we reported Bailey-Garver's account of the CDG bill, with me as, "the *Register*":

During the meeting, Garver and Nick and Shane Bailey said it was their understanding that Donze's architectural firm, which was designing the ADECA warehouse, had commissioned CDG to do the three studies. Garver explained that Donze would have needed the studies, including the endangered species study, to draft plans for the warehouse, especially for the foundation of the structure.

The Register asked why an architectural firm hired by the state would authorize three expensive studies without first consulting with the state, which would be paying for those studies.

The Register noted that records provided by the administration showed that Donze and his partner had been working with Vaughan's firm on the project for some time and that it didn't seem to make sense that Vaughan wouldn't know about the studies.

"When we get what CDG did, we'll see if there was some duplication," Nick Bailey said.

The Register asked the three Siegelman appointees if they knew Donze's firm had hired CDG or if they were merely speculating. They acknowledged that they were speculating.

On Thursday, the Register called Donze and asked if his firm authorized the three CDG studies. Donze said he'd heard of CDG but was unaware of any work they'd done on this project. He said he hadn't hired them. He said he would have no need for a survey of the entire 256 acres just to draft plans for one of the two warehouses.

"The site work is being done by Sherlock, Smith & Adams, and all we're doing is the building, so we're not really concerned with the site itself," Donze said. The architect laughed when asked if he needed an endangered species evaluation to draft plans for the ADECA warehouse.

Garver was all innocence – truly so – on another matter.

I'd gone to probate court and pulled the sales history of the warehouse site. It had been owned for an eternity by a wealthy Montgomery family, which sold it in December to C&H Investments. That company was incorporated shortly before by local businessman Andrew Nolin. It paid $460,000 for the land.

A second deed, dated two months later, showed C&H selling the land to G.H. Construction for $562,000. (Subsequent records reflected that the two sales, or in any event, the payments on both, occurred on the same day in February.)

I handed the deeds to Garver and said it appeared that C&H had made a quick $102,000, possibly after benefitting from some inside information.

Garver gazed at the deeds, and after a spell, emitted a sarcastic chuckle. He read from the top paragraph of one of the deeds, where it was written that the buyer had paid the seller "$100 and other valuable considerations" for the property. Garver said both deeds contained that phrase. According to his reading, C&H purchased the land for $100 and sold it for the same tiny sum to G.H. Construction.

In my early days as a news reporter I was confused by the "$100 and other valuable considerations" when first coming upon it. For some ancient legal reason, many real estate deeds contain the phrase. It is not, however, a reflection of the sales price. That's revealed on the deed tax stamps of the warranty deeds and, if there is one, the mortgage. I tried to explain this to Garver, but he huffed and stood his ground.

I didn't want to put Eddie Davis, the ADECA lawyer, in a position contrary to a higher-up in the Siegelman administration. But I saw no choice. I sensed that Eddie was thinking to himself that Garver was a fool, but he was all poker face.

When I put it to him, Davis said that the sales prices on the deeds were reflected by the deed tax, and that the $100 phrase was irrelevant.

Garver ceded defeat. He said he found it "hard to believe he (Nolin) made a $102,000 profit."

"I was unaware of it, and either somebody is very shrewd or misrepresented the facts to us," Garver said, in a quote used a month later in story exploring the land sale.

As Garver knew, his old boss Roland Vaughan had helped Nolin market the land to the state and, through Sherlock Smith & Adams, recommended it over two other parcels for the warehouses.

In the first meeting, Vaughan had talked about his efforts to help Nolin market the land at a time when Nolin had signed an option on the property. Initially Nolin tried to interest a commercial buyer, but found no takers. Vaughan said Nolin never paid him for his assistance, which included bringing the land to the state's attention in the first place.

Now, it appeared that Vaughan hadn't come clean with Garver and others about the financial details of Nolin's buy and sell deal.

The day's final conflict arose after I said that as construction manager, G.H. was prohibited by law from performing actual labor on the job. It wasn't a major issue, but Garver wasn't having it. He declared that I was wrong, and as if to prove it, whipped out his U.S. Army Corps of Engineers identification card, showing him as a colonel. Garver, sneering, said he had worked on construction projects as far away as the Middle East.

Take that!

As I hope the reader will see, when I act up, I don't hide it here. I was at this meeting, like the others, polite, not the least combative. Neither, though, was I playing pushover. I told Garver that I'd recently interviewed the head of the state building commission, was as a result familiar with the law regarding construction managers, and even had in my possession a copy of the law.

Garver stood his ground. He was right, I was wrong. I couldn't concede and told him as nice as could that the law was as I'd described it. This back and forth went on until Carrie, frustrated with the both of us, asked if I could produce the citation.

It was in my satchel, but so too were hundreds of other records, and disorganized as hell. I was red-faced with exertion when I came up for air, Alabama's law on construction managers in hand. I slid it over to Garver.

I watched his face as he read it. I saw, not embarrassment or humility, but anger. Checkmate, Col. Garver. You lose again.

The meeting concluded, and with it, the Carrie Kurlander Openness Experiment.

———

Late that afternoon I sent an e-mail not just to the press office but Mabry and Siegelman as well. I complained about the administration's continued failure to provide the G.H. Construction contract and other records and summarized what I intended to report in Sunday's paper. I made particular note of the rush to sell the bonds. I had, as I told them, become aware that the administration was racing to sell the bonds before publication of our story. And then:

"I put the source's tip in the back of my head and didn't think too much of it until today, when Nick opened the meeting by apologizing for his cell phone ringing, and explaining the apparently frantic attempt to sell the bonds that was going on. I should have thought to ask then what was on my mind: Why Friday? What's the rush? Why not, say, next Wednesday?

"Rip has on several occasions sought to sway me from running the story on Sunday, using the argument that if I wait until the bonds are sold, then all the contracts and such will be public record and I'll 'have everything.' I haven't decided whether or not my story will reflect those requests on the part of the administration to hold the story until after the bond sale, but am considering doing so."

Bonds are of course sold to investors. A seller of bonds, same as a publicly traded company, must disclose risks to securities bearing its name. What might happen if investors learned that the contractor overseeing the project they were funding had already submitted fraudulent bills? Might they cut and run?

Could I do it over again, I'd be more businesslike, more judicious in my choice of words and phrases, less of a smart-aleck. But I wasn't and here it is, where I connected their refusal to provide the contract to their rush to sell the bonds:

"I'm led to believe there's only one copy (of G.H. Construction's contract) and that no one can find it or something like that. I take that explanation as an insult to my intelligence. Since I have no other choice but to accept this explanation -- this being Alice's Wonderland -- I'll play along and assume there's just one copy. Now, I propose a novel solution: Stick it on a copier and make another copy. To clarify – maybe that's been the problem – I don't actually need the ORIGINAL, but a COPY OF THE ORIGINAL.

So I ask: Is the failure to provide this public record motivated in part to keep me from writing the story by Sunday, or to prevent readers, and possibly investors in the bonds, from learning things which might possibly appear unfavorable to the people running this bond deal, and by extension, raise doubts about the bonds themselves?

From talking to Rip, I believe he would call it a conspiracy theory. I present it merely as a question that I'm hoping will be answered.

The purpose of the e-mail was to pry free the G.H. contract. I wasn't trying to kill the bond issue and the warehouse project. Couldn't imagine such an outcome. It was, then, with amazement that I read a fax sent us the next morning and dated the day before – written, it would seem, within hours of reception of my e-mail.

It was a one-page memo from Mabry to Bailey, as ADECA director, and to ABC boss Randall Smith. Siegelman was cc'd. The chief bits are as follows:

After considering financial questions raised by The Mobile Register in relation to this project, I am ordering that all work on the project by G.H. Construction and others cease until an independent review of this matter can be completed.

Former Chief Justice C.C. "Bo" Torbert, Jr., has agreed to conduct this independent review on behalf of my office. All financial records relating to this project should be delivered to Judge Torbert with all deliberate speed so that he may begin his review as soon as possible.

G.H. Construction, the warehouse project, the $393,870 fee that was to be Blount Parrish's upon the sale of the bonds -- that and more, vaporized. And before we'd written the first word.

Chapter 10
The Warehouse Stories

"We've received several requests to open an investigation into the matter of G.H., or Goat Hill, Construction."
-- *Attorney General Bill Pryor, on May 1, 2001, announcing the start of what became not just an investigation into Lanny Young's company, but much else as well.*

"Finally, I want to thank the Mobile Register for bringing this issue to my attention. Public officials and the press often seem at odds, but both serve the public in different ways. It's the job of reporters to uncover problems and find things that are wrong. When they do, it's the job of elected officials to solve the problems, and set things right. That is exactly what I am doing today."
-- *From statement issued by Siegelman on May 4, in conjunction with release of the report on G.H. Construction deal by former Alabama Supreme Court Chief Justice C.C. "Bo" Torbert Jr.*

We naturally had to report Mabry's memo, meaning I had to write a story explaining that a project the public didn't know about was being canceled because of a story that hadn't yet been written. We quoted the memo and summarized the warehouse project and the findings to be reported in detail in the next day's paper.

Carrie told readers the state expected to build the warehouses, though possibly without G.H. Construction. She said the bond sale was cancelled in part because Nick "had some tremendous discomfort because your questions could not be answered."

To which I did not add: "Actually, Nick's discomfort wasn't due to a lack of answers, but a failure on the part of the reporter to fall for them."

The story caused me some discomfort as well. Bo Torbert, the former state Supreme Court chief justice, is much revered. More problematic, he was a partner in Maynard Cooper & Gale, the firm of Siegelman's chief legal advisor Boots Gale, and the state was giving Maynard Cooper mountains of legal business. I felt uncomfortable asking someone of Torbert's reputation if he believed he had a conflict that could limit the scope of his inquiry, but saw no choice. My greater source of discomfort was my brother Greg. He was (and remains) a partner in the firm whose own brother was asking such questions. I cringed to think about it.

Torbert, to my relief, was most gracious. I expressed my unease at asking about a potential conflict, and he told me it was a fair question. "They just have to take what they see and what they get and make an evaluation of it," he said.

The warehouse deal smelled in many ways, but the silver bullet was the $90,058 payment to CDG. There was just no explaining it away. At the last minute, a final effort was made. The administration sent a courier to Mobile to deliver a stack of paper three pounds heavy but practically speaking, weightless. The cover page declared it to be the, "Engineering Report: Proposed Warehouse Building Site," by CDG Engineers. The document was composed almost entirely of pages yanked off the Internet, a bundled together glop of state laws and geological information unrelated to the North Ripley site.

I called Carrie and, part bluff, told her I wasn't buying it and wouldn't be mentioning it in the story. She didn't put up fight, as she would have had the report been genuine. To my knowledge it was never again offered, such as to law enforcement, as evidence of actual work done by CDG.

It's rare for a story to establish beyond question that a crime has been committed. Our Sunday story did that. It didn't prove bribery, since that would have required access to banking records, but theft from the state. That was plenty.

Here are the opening paragraphs of the story that started the investigation into the Siegelman administration. There's one error – reporting the bond sale at $16 million, rather than $20.7 million. That was their fault for failing to provide me with the correct numbers and the documents.

Tomorrow morning, officials in the Siegelman administration were to meet with members of the Montgomery Downtown Redevelopment Authority, a passel of lawyers and investment bankers with the firm of Blount, Parrish & Co.

The purpose: To sign the many documents required for the proposed sale that day of more than $16 million in bonds to investors. The proceeds of those bonds were to finance construction of two massive state warehouses on a 256-acre site just north of downtown Montgomery.

That meeting has been canceled. The bond deal, which almost certainly will go through at some point in the future, is on indefinite hold.

The reason involves questions raised by the Mobile Register about a fledgling two-man company, G.H. Construction of Montgomery, chosen by the state to act as "construction manager" over the project, state Finance Director Henry Mabry stated when he halted the project Thursday evening...

Though Mabry cited concerns about the entire project, the primary factor in his decision involved questions about two bills -- one for $90,058 submitted by G.H. Construction on behalf of CDG Engineers and Associates of Andalusia; and another, for $5,200 by Denton, Ponder & Edwards, a Roanoke, Ala., accounting firm.

"As of right now, we do not have a work product document, nothing," Siegelman spokeswoman Carrie Kurlander said of the CDG bill. "There may be a perfectly reasonable explanation for that. That's exactly what we hope Judge Torbert will find."

Like many of my Siegelman stories, it demanded considerable space, as there was much to tell. Readers had to be introduced to the warehouse project, Lanny Young, CDG, our discovery of the two boundary surveys, the administration's failed efforts to explain it away, and much else. There was, for example, the omnipresent Ellis Brazeal. I had called him to ask about CDG since he was listed as the firm's lawyer in the dubious bankruptcy filing by Lanny's landfill company, and CDG wasn't returning my calls.

"My understanding is that they've done substantial work on the (warehouse) project and that there is substantial work ongoing at this point," Brazeal told readers.

I couldn't let that go uncontested. Brazeal's statement was followed thusly: "Asked for comment on Brazeal's claim that CDG is presently doing substantial work on the project, Vaughan and state officials repeated earlier statements that they're unaware of any work by CDG on this project, ever."

I slept in Monday and was awakened mid-morning by a call from Tim Fuhrman, then the number two man at the FBI's Mobile office. Fuhrman said that some Montgomery-based agents and Jack Brennan, a much-respected former FBI agent then with the attorney general's office, wanted to talk to me. Soon. As in that afternoon.

He said it was clear from Sunday's story that I'd gathered all manner of records. The FBI wanted to move fast and it would save them a bunch of time if they could talk to me and copy those records. If it was okay with me, he would tell them to get in the car and come on.

I knew Tim, if not well, and liked and trusted him. But I'd never had a request like that, and it came with me in bed, groggy with sleep.

Pluses: The chance to meet with FBI agents, get a first-hand taste of how they operate, and, what the heck, get my ego stroked by a bunch of pros wanting my stuff. Also, did I have an obligation as a citizen to provide investigators with evidence of a crime if I possessed it?

Minuses: I wasn't supposed to actively participate in the prosecution of someone I was writing about.

But: Reporters can and should try to develop a rapport with prosecutors and investigators. There's almost no such thing as a national political scandal story that doesn't cite un-named, "Justice Department sources," and such relationships inevitably involve some give and take.

Was I on the verge of developing such sources for what promised to become a criminal investigation into the Siegelman administration? And if so, wouldn't this benefit our readers by availing me of information and insights?

Tell them to come on, I said. I'd meet with them.

And started having second thoughts after coffee and a shower. I arrived at work and knew I had one option. Tell Paul Cloos, my editor. I suspected he would scotch the meeting on the grounds cited above. If not, and the meeting went ahead, I'd at least have covered my ass.

Paul was against it and I made no attempt to change his mind. I called Fuhrman, apologized, and said I couldn't meet. He tried to change my mind, and I sought refuge in the reporter's trick known as "blame the editor," the most common variant being, "I hate to have to ask this next question, but my editor says I have to."

The meeting, which I would have enjoyed, was off, the advantage being I could focus on the next day's story. The night before I called Torbert to get a sense of what he was thinking. He said that on Friday, shortly after his appointment, the administration had provided him with all manner of documents. Among them: The G.H. Construction contract, located, he said, at Blount Parrish.

Soon as we said our goodbyes I was e-mailing Carrie. I told her what Torbert told me – that the contract had been found, and at Blount's office, where I'd been telling them to look for weeks. I told her I expected to be provided, immediately, with a copy of the contract.

The next morning she delivered a response: The administration would not be releasing the contract – not now, not ever.

Not ever? As in, never ever?

Like hell!

———

I'm not fond of the old saying, "Never pick a fight with people who buy ink by the barrel," though will acknowledge some truth to it.

As on this occasion. It was time to pour a few barrels on their heads.

The refusal of government agencies to turn over records bothers me more than the activities I'm seeking to uncover. I recognize that Lanny Young's theft from the state is a worse act than the administration's decision to hide, lie about and withhold the G.H. contract. But it's the denial of records that makes my blood boil.

We needed the contract. They could deny us, but at their peril.

The purpose of the next day's story was less to provide new information as to warn readers that if their paper couldn't get its hands on the contract, they would never learn the truth about G.H. Construction. Their paper was trying, but their governor was playing keep away.

We reported that the contract had been found late Friday, "where the newspaper had suggested the state look in the first place: with a firm handling bonding for the project."

Here is some of what followed:

Siegelman spokeswoman Carrie Kurlander said Monday that the administration was truthful during the past weeks when it reported, almost daily, that it couldn't locate the G.H. contract in any form ... Kurlander was reminded that the Register had suggested several times that the Blount firm be contacted, since it seemed logical that the investment banking firm handling the bond sale would have the proposals or contracts involving G.H. Construction.

Asked Monday why the administration hadn't contacted Blount, Parrish to locate the records for the Register, but had done so for Torbert, Kurlander did not respond.

I didn't take pleasure in putting Carrie on the spot. She was an innocent in this. But she was the governor's spokesperson and well compensated for it. If they were going to stick her out there to get run over, that was their call, not mine.

In the story we recited applicable portions of the public records law and quoted Ted Hosp saying he couldn't provide a citation or case law to support the decision to restrict the contract from public review. He said the contracts were un-signed drafts, and as such, not public. As the story stated – and as I'd been telling the administration for weeks – signed or not, the contract served as the basis for payments of more than $400,000 to G.H. Construction. Even if Hosp was correct that contract drafts weren't public record, the payments voided his argument.

The story gave Bailey's explanation for the lack of contracts with G.H. and other firms -- that there were no contracts because the administration was conducting business with "handshake agreements." In truth, there were contracts, but the revelations in those documents were so appalling that the administration was willing to supplant the truth with the humiliating lie about handshake agreements.

The AP picked up our stories from the start, meaning they were getting statewide play, as was the source of the reporting – the *Mobile Register*. We were, I was, smoking hot, and only getting started. I was busy as hell and having a blast. Couldn't wait to get to work, hated to leave.

The first two stories generated considerable response, but nothing like Tuesday's piece. Siegelman's refusal to release the warehouse contract ignited a wave of outrage from readers and lawmakers. Steve Windom wrote a letter to Bill Pryor, attached our story, and asked the attorney general for an opinion "as to whether the contract referred to in the attached article constitutes a public record that should be turned over to the *Mobile Register*."

Over at Camp Siegelman, this was no doubt seen as further proof of a burgeoning Curran-Windom conspiracy.

With Fuhrman's call I knew that the FBI and attorney general's office were looking into the matter, and on the day we reported the administration's refusal to turn over the contract, Pryor made it official. He announced that he had assigned the white-collar crime and public corruption divisions of his office to investigate the warehouse deal.

Hamrick said Siegelman had no objections to the investigation, since the governor, too, had been unable to get satisfactory answers. "That's certainly fine for (Pryor) to review it and appropriate for him to review it," Hamrick told Jeff Amy, one of our Montgomery reporters, who wrote our story.

One imagines the chief of staff thinking: Will they find out about the $25,000 Lanny gave me in March 1999 to I could drive a brand new BMW? What about the $6,000 check last fall, to make that margin-call demand from my bad stock deal? The trips to the strip club in Anniston? All those bar tabs and cash payments?

Amy's story reported another major development: The administration had agreed to provide us with the G.H. Construction contract.

We had, in addition to spilling ink, enlisted the help of the paper's attorney. Ed Sledge, a reporter's lawyer if ever there was one, called Hosp and made the same argument I'd been making – that the state paid money to G.H.; therefore, signed or not, the contract was a public record.

That afternoon Hosp wrote Ed to say he wasn't certain the argument was correct. He would, though, "concede that the documents have essentially become public records because they have been the basis for State action (payment)."

Ted concluded by telling Ed that the press office "will continue to work with Mr. Curran to provide him with all requested documents, and I hope that will end the involvement of the lawyers."

This was too much. I wrote Ted to tell him that there had never been a need for lawyers in the first place; told him that for weeks I'd been making the same argument used by Ed to win the day. Ted shot back a brief reply telling me I needed to read his letter to Ed "more closely." I did, several times, and still couldn't see the difference between Ed's argument and mine.

Hosp, a Rhode Island native, graduated from Brown, then Fordham law school. He served two years as a lawyer on the U.S. Senate Judiciary Committee and came to Montgomery in the mid-1990s to clerk for a federal judge. He subsequently married an Alabama girl and joined Maynard Cooper. He left in 1999 -- surely with the promise that his seat would remain warm – to become Siegelman's general counsel.

Ted has brown hair and eyes not merely blue but brightly so. He is, or so several women have told me, nice looking. He's also a nice guy, though that won't be the impression one gets in the coming pages. Ted can play hardball, which I suppose he would say of me as well. For the most part, though, I count him among Siegelman's victims. One supposes that Ted, like Carrie, Rip and others, saw New South all over Siegelman and came to government expecting to help a great man change Alabama.

Hosp could not have anticipated spending the second half of Siegelman's term as a white collar criminal defense lawyer, which is to a considerable degree what he had to become.

———

In an unusual confluence of events, the legislature's ADECA oversight committee was scheduled to meet Wednesday. The question on everyone's mind: Would director agency director Nick Bailey appear and take lawmakers' questions?

He did not. Instead, the administration sent Chris Pitts to squirm on the hot seat. It was left to Pitts to report that Siegelman had at the last minute called Bailey to meet on an important matter. Pitts said ADECA wouldn't be answering questions about the warehouse project until Torbert concluded his review.

Bill Armistead, the Republican state senator, told Pitts it was "obvious (Bailey) was called off and told not to come with all the headlines right now." He called the handling of the G.H. contracts, "deplorable."

At week's end the administration released Torbert's report. Good to his word, Torbert didn't sugarcoat the mess. During his brief investigation – truncated by Pryor's announcement – Torbert met for an entire day with Vaughan, Bailey, Lanny, Bill Blount and Blount's sidekick, bond lawyer Fred Simpler. Even the elusive Bryan Broderick made an appearance.

Torbert's report criticized the selection of G.H. Construction, the firm's qualifications, the 12 percent fee, even the need for a construction manager. The former state Supreme Court chief justice wrote that "substantial questions (exist) as to the propriety of" the state's payments to the company.

The press office released a statement from Siegelman expressing disappointment in the way the project was handled. He announced the termination of G.H. Construction and pledged to work with Pryor to "recover any money that may be proven to have been misspent."

"I will fully support Attorney General Pryor as his office looks at this matter," the governor said.

Our story on Torbert's findings, written by our Montgomery reporters, ended with a thumbs up for Bailey.

"I have talked to Nick about (the warehouse project), and he has expressed to me his regret in how the matter went forward," Siegelman said. "But I have full confidence in him. He has reassured me that he knew nothing of this G.H."

Nick "knew nothing of *this G.H*"?

Hell, I'd been in meetings with Bailey. He hadn't even claimed that. And you can be damn sure if Nick knew about it, so had Siegelman.

As Bailey said so memorably in that first meeting, "Do we know all these people? I sure hope so, because we wouldn't want to be involved in this with people we didn't know and trust."

Already, Siegelman was fashioning his criminal defense. Keeping Nick in the fold – that was job one.

———

It was going to take time to analyze the contracts and seek documents referred to but not provided. But even a rapid read and write, all I had time for that first day, revealed why Siegelman fought so hard to prevent release of the contracts. And there were two – one per warehouse – as opposed to the one suggested by the front page provided weeks before by Claire, apparently from an early draft.

Both of the nearly identical documents contained provisions to pay G.H. Construction bonuses of $250,000 for completing the warehouses ahead of schedule – a double farce since the company wasn't going to have a thing to do with the project. I suppose the drafters figured that two times $250,000 was more palatable than a one-shot chunk o $500,000, so they divided the contract in two.

We'd already reported the 12 percent fee, though had assumed, according to the norm for construction manager arrangements and what Vaughan said, that the fee was to apply to the costs of construction. Most astonishing was the revelation that G.H. was to capture 12 percent on top of every dime spent on the project.

As spelled out in the contracts, the 12 percent was to be applied as well to all "architectural, engineering, legal, insurance, consulting, and other costs reasonably incurred in connection with the project."

Among the more egregious examples of the Lanny tax was its application to the Sherlock Smith & Adams' contract. Here, as presented in a story on May 18:

A draft of the state's contract with Sherlock, Smith & Adams showed that firm was to be paid $740,000 for drafting plans for the ABC warehouse, designing the site, and to conduct much, if not most, of the duties ascribed to G.H. in its contracts.

The $740,000 included a $270,000 "lump sum" fee to oversee construction, monitor scheduling and budgets, and perform other duties described in G.H.'s contract. Vaughan explained that the entity selling the bonds, the Montgomery Downtown Redevelopment Authority, insisted that his firm act as an overseer of unknown G.H.

Given the terms of the contract, G.H. would have received $32,400 -- or 12 percent of $270,000 -- to be overseen, bringing costs of overseeing the construction manager to $302,400.

Goat Hill Construction was also to receive the extra 12 percent on a job that wasn't to commence until after completion of the ABC warehouse, and with no role, even a pretend one, for Lanny's company. A firm that specializes in such work was to install an automated system for tracking and warehousing the state's liquor supply. The cost of this work: $2 million.

G.H.'s ABC contract listed the $2 million as a line item in the construction budget. "As such," readers were told, "the firm was to be paid $240,000 as a percentage of the $2 million cost of the conveyor system, even though it would have no role in installing it."

Soon after producing the G.H. contracts, the administration turned over others. One was the $21,000 survey contract with Lucido & Oliver, the bill for which was included in G.H. Construction's second voucher to the state. The contract had been signed in November 2000, prior to incorporation of G.H. Construction.

"When we submitted our bill to the state, they had G.H. pay us," said firm president Vince Lucido.

This was done to make it appear that G.H. Construction provided oversight work, and thus earned its 12 percent. It was the same with the $90,000 in phantom services listed on the forged CDG bill. Lanny's 12 percent on top of that came to almost $11,000.

Ditto for the $25,000 site study by Roland Vaughan's firm and the exorbitant $161,566 in architectural fees paid to Curtis Kirsch's for designing the ADECA warehouse. With each, the work was completed before G.H. Construction was even a sparkle in Lanny's eye.

I pulled out a Ran Garver quote from that contentious final meeting and let him tell readers why all payments on the project were routed through G.H. Construction.

"We decided that we had to have one central point that took all of those things,"
Garver said last week.

It was noted that most state construction projects involve numerous firms and vendors, and the departments responsible for overseeing and paying for the work assign numbers to projects, to keep track of the costs. It's not standard practice to pick one firm out of many, then route all payments on that project through one firm.

"If we had to do this again, we probably would have done it the normal way,"
Garver said.

What role Garver had in these decisions, I don't know. Despite my low opinion of his personality, Garver didn't strike me as the type to countenance bribes. I suppose he was doing what his old boss (Vaughan) and his new one (Siegelman) wanted him to do, then hoped against hope that this conspiracy to shove large sums into Lanny's pockets wasn't as crooked as it appeared.

One curious line item in the contracts listed a total of $3 million for "reimbursables." This was explained as the source for payments to non-construction vendors, such as lawyers and consultants.

The contracts cited a series of exhibits, including an "Exhibit C," that purportedly named these firms and the amounts they were to receive. I begged, prodded, demanded, whined and begged some more for the Exhibit Cs from the two contracts. The answer kept coming back that Bill Blount had them.

Here was déjà vu all over again. Well, could you call Mr. Blount and ask him to fax you a copy, and once acquired, fax it to us?

It was then that the administration concocted a pretext to deny access to further records on the project. In an e-mail, the press office stated that because of the criminal investigation, it would be "inappropriate for our office to continue seeking information and documents related to this project from third parties."

A public record doesn't cease being a public record just because the FBI or the attorney general's office wants to look at it. But there was little I could do but complain and let readers know we tried. We reported a statement by Blount that the Exhibit Cs were in Simpler's possession and didn't yet show the amounts to be paid for various professional services. Therefore the lists were just "drafts," and "probably not available now," Blount said.

Lacking subpoena power, I had to eat these insults and move on.

———

A comparison of the budgets before and after the hiring of G.H. Construction showed construction costs climbing from $11.5 million pre-Lanny to $14.6 post-Lanny, for a difference of $3.1 million.

So who was responsible for these fiascos masquerading as contracts?

For weeks I'd been asking the administration to identify the lawyers who drafted and approved the contracts. "As we have made clear, lawyers from the state did not review the contracts," the press office explained in one if its unsigned, e-mailed replies. "They should have been more involved. This was not an active decision. They just didn't review the contracts. This and other unanswered questions, raised by *The Mobile Register*, are precisely why the governor froze this project. "

I believed Hosp and the staff attorneys for ADECA and the ABC board who said they hadn't seen the contracts. So who had? I asked if the administration could identify the lawyer for G.H. Construction. "We do not know who G.H. Construction's attorney is," came the response, suggesting they made no effort to learn.

In mid-May I told the press office in an e-mail that it was "inconceivable that y'all can't identify the lawyers involved, on both sides, in drafting this contract."

This time they gave me a name. Blount's man Simpler had authored the contracts.

This seemed an unusual role for Simpler, who was the "bond counsel." It's the bond counsel's job to review all the documents with an eye toward protecting the investors. Simpler didn't return my calls, so I couldn't ask him if he thought it a conflict to serve as bond counsel while also drafting contracts devoted to funneling millions of dollars in investors' money to Lanny.

I didn't take pleasure in it, as he had been a gentleman, but concluded a story on the contracts with a quote by Roland Vaughan, given during the first meeting and since rendered absurd.

"Everything we've tried to do is to not have this thing gouged by fees, so those savings will be passed on to the state," he'd said.

By early May Vaughan knew trouble lay ahead. We'd published several stories and Pryor had announced the investigation. In one of my last conversations with him, he acknowledged the pain that the warehouse project was causing him and expressed concern about its impact on the legacy of his three generation company.

Despite some wild stretchers – especially the one about hiring G.H. after meeting Lanny at Sinclair's -- I'd initially viewed Vaughan as the straightest shooter on the deal. We had a cordial relationship – near the end he told me I'd been "very fair" and said he appreciated my "civility." But as I neared publication of a story on the land sales he stopped taking my calls and answering e-mailed questions.

Before the cessation of communications I asked him straight out if he had a financial relationship with Andrew Nolin, the middle-man who bought the land then sold it at a tidy profit to G.H. Construction.

Vaughan responded by e-mail that he had not been paid by Nolin and that he had no financial stake in the 256-acre parcel. I didn't learn otherwise until the following October, when he was indicted for failing to disclose his half share in the property.

Even without that nugget, the land story raised troubling questions about the former BCA chairman's role in pushing the North Ripley site. We reported the basic facts: That Nolin, with Vaughan's help, had been trying to market the land to commercial customers; that Nolin's C&H Investments had taken out a $20,000 option on the land and stood to lose its money; and that shortly after C&H bought it for $460,000, Nolin flipped it to the state for $562,000.

Vaughan said Nolin earned $102,000, minus real estate fees for acting as a straw man for the state. Had the long-time owners been informed of the state's interest, they'd have sought more, he said. It wasn't an unreasonable point, nor was Nolin's complaint – also presented in the story.

"Is the problem that I made a profit?" he asked, irritated. "I didn't know that was something you weren't supposed to do. The state was under no obligation whatsoever to buy it. If the price was too high they could have passed on it."

The problem was that Nolin wouldn't have made a dime – would have lost money – without Vaughan's help. Worse, Vaughan concealed his half-ownership in land that he had introduced to the state, then recommended in his firm's $25,000 study. He had a fiduciary duty to the state, not Andrew Nolin.

The cost of leveling and preparing the land (the old "site prep" work) was among the main factors for the state to consider. The two state-owned parcels were largely flat. North Ripley, which I visited, was covered with trees and on a steep incline, below which were wetlands. It was entirely unsuitable for warehouses.

A comparison of cost projections by Sherlock Smith & Adams during three stages in the process was particularly damning.

In the $25,000 study delivered to the state in mid-December 2000, Sherlock Smith & Adams estimated site preparation costs at North Ripley at $430,800.

A month before, in a proposal to provide engineering services for the project, Sherlock Smith & Adams estimated the same work at hundreds of thousands of dollars more than the figure presented in the site recommendation study.

The firm's third and final projection for the cost of site prep -- made in early 2001, when fashioning the construction budget – topped s $1.5 million.

The bottom line: In the study used to convince the state to buy Nolin's land, Vaughan's firm vastly underestimated the cost of preparing the land. Considering what would later be revealed – that Vaughan secretly pocketed $48,434 from the sale of the land – it's hard not to conclude that this much-revered businessman made a decision to screw the taxpayers so he could make a fast buck.

———

The last major piece during the May 2001 flurry of G.H. stories examined the fees that were to have been disbursed immediately upon sale of the bonds. This was the Bill Blount story.

Seeing the name Blount Parrish on a bond issue should give anyone pause. And if Simpler is listed as bond counsel, it's time to put on the reading glasses and head for the fine print. Blount, with Simpler as bond counsel, has been involved in a host of bond deals that have gone south, leading to lawsuits by investors claiming fraud, conflicts of interest and other shenanigans.

I had considerable experience with Blount and Simpler from a series of stories in the late 1990s regarding two bond issues in Mobile, one for the city's landfill, the other for an "affordable housing program." The landfill deal contained a $350,000 "development fee" shared by three men, including one of the true larger than life scoundrels in south Alabama history -- Lowell Harrelson, aka the "Garbage Barge Man." Neither Blount nor Simpler could explain the development fee. The IRS revoked the tax exempt status of the bond issue, causing major headaches for the city.

The affordable housing deal, which involved many of the same players, went bust, costing the city more than $2 million. (One of the stories led to a federal prison term for Harrelson.)

During the same period, Blount's firm, with Simpler as lawyer, handled bond issues for junior colleges throughout Alabama. In each, cronies received the indefinable "development fees."

I think Blount and Simpler, and for that matter many others in that business, view money borrowed through the sale of bonds as somehow different than that generated through tax collections. But there is no difference. Money raised through bond issues is public money that must be repaid with public funds. It should not be treated as the special candy fund, though too often that's exactly what happens.

For the warehouse bond story I called two well-regarded investment bankers, provided each with copies of the bond documents, and asked them to analyze the fees and language within. Because of the political nature of that business and the possibility of retribution, both commented on the condition that they not be identified.

The Bill Blount story, which ran on May 27, 2001, began:

Layers of fees -- possibly in the millions of dollars -- would have been generated for investment professionals, lawyers and insurers upon the signing of a now-derailed $20.7 million bond issue to pay for state warehouses, documents provided by Alabama Gov. Don Siegelman's administration show.

The politically connected investment banking firm of Blount, Parrish & Co. would have reaped almost $400,000 -- a fee described as outrageously high by two veteran investment banking professionals who reviewed the bond records at the Mobile Register's request.

The Montgomery-based firm also would have been paid separately for helping G.H. Construction get bonded, or insured, to oversee the building of the warehouses. The $300,000 insurance premium listed on the bond documents is about five times the going rate for a surety bond on a warehouse project of that size, according to prices provided by insurance and construction experts.

Chief among the questions raised by the investment banking professionals who reviewed the bond records for the Register: Why was it necessary to generate $21.8 million -- the amount of the bond deal and about $1.2 million in interest on the money prior to the project's completion -- to pay for what construction budgets show was a $16.6 million project?

Blount Parrish's fee was to equal 1.9 percent of the bond issue, which one of the bankers said was about three times what it should have been. To put the fee in perspective, I asked the finance department to provide a list of 45 state-related bond issues since 1995. Only once had the underwriter's discount – the name for the investment banker's fee – exceed one percent, and then barely.

The two investment bankers pointed to another figure, called cost of issuance, which included a host of other fees, and totaled $220,440. "Add those two together, and you're talking about $610,000 for a $20 million bond issue. That's astronomical," said one.

Included in the cost of issuance was a $100,000 legal fee for Simpler.

The story addressed in some detail G.H. Construction's $300,000 performance bond. A line in the prospectus for the bond issue stated that someone with Blount Parrish (Blount, as trial testimony showed) assisted G.H. in obtaining the performance bond and was to be "reimbursed for such services outside of the compensation" of selling the bonds.

This raised two questions. The first: Why were taxpayers paying $300,000 for a performance bond on a job of a size that should be bonded for about $60,000?

I speculated, correctly as it turned out, that the outlandish premium was a consequence of G.H. Construction's lack of qualifications. "That suggests," we told readers, "that by choosing G.H., the state immediately increased the cost of the job, and the burden on taxpayers, by hiking the costs for the construction manager's bonding."

Another mystery involved Blount's role as an insurance agent. We quoted an insurance department lawyer saying the language appeared to show Blount selling insurance, though he wasn't licensed to do so. I was covering every base I could think of – all valid, mind you – and felt a well of bitterness rising in the administration.

The nature of Blount's insurance work was exposed at trial when the Gulf Insurance executive testified that G.H. Construction wasn't to be permitted to do any work and, what's more, if the bonding company had to step in, then Blount was to be personally liable for financing the completion of the job.

Simpler didn't return calls. I traded e-mails with Blount, but he ignored the specific questions. Wouldn't say the first word about the size of his firm's fee or explain the performance bond. Instead, he declared that "in broad terms (the) project was a good deal for bondholders and Alabama taxpayers" because it provided a fixed rent on the warehouses and at the end of the day, the buildings would belong to the state.

The Goat Hill Construction stories were in many ways a triumph for the paper. We killed off a comically corrupt project and saved the state millions of dollars. It had to hurt Lanny, Blount, Simpler and others to see all that money, so close to being theirs, wiped off the table because of a reporter's questions.

For all that, there's a selfish part of me that wishes I'd come across G.H. Construction a few months or even a year later.

Considering that Lanny stole several hundred thousand dollars before the project started, there's no telling what he would have pulled off and who he would have paid off with a whole year and all that bond money.

Siegelman's protestations of ignorance about the participation of Blount and Lanny in the project would not have been plausible, or in any event, only so to his most glassy-eyed admirers.

Had the stories come later, the above-named would have been truly cooked. Lanny, Blount, Siegelman, Bailey and others as well should be grateful to me for busting it when I did.

―――

After the warehouse stories, and for some time to come, I received e-mails from several fans who assumed, because I was investigating a Democrat, that I was a member of the John Birch Society. One used the e-mail tag, Rebellen, as in, Rebel, as in Confederate Ellen. Another far right fan was certain she saw communist logos in a state-funded report I wrote about later.

They had nothing but nice things to say about the stories and nothing encourages me more than feedback, but they were, to say the least, mistaken about my motivations.

Chapter 11
Night on the Town

"During the last night of this year's Regular Session of the Legislature, Ted Hosp walked into a Republican Senate office, where he found Mr. Curran drinking alcohol with a Republican senator, Claire Austin, and others. Drinking is not allowed in the Alabama State House."
-- Portion of Aug. 17, 2001, letter sent from Siegelman chief of staff Jim Buckalew to Register publisher Howard Bronson.

"On the last night of this year's session, Mr. Curran became so inebriated at a Montgomery bar that he was not able to drive home. He had no money and asked then-Chief of Staff Paul Hamrick for $20 for a cab."
-- From the same letter.

I was seeking neither drink nor trouble but enlightenment when I entered the Alabama Statehouse on the evening of May 21. I would get all three in a night that concluded with a 2 a.m. cab ride from a bar called Bud's.

By tradition, the legislature concludes each year's session on a Monday evening, often not finishing until the midnight deadline, and then after a flurry of last minute shell games orchestrated by lobbyists and the craftier and therefore more influential lawmakers. The rest of the world finds out later, fingers are pointed, no one can prove anything, and projects no one ever heard of get funded.

Or so I'm told. First hand, I wouldn't know because I've never covered the legislature. The bulk of my Montgomery coverage involves the executive branch and the state agencies under its control. I've attended a handful of committee meetings, retrieved records from legislative offices, interviewed many lawmakers, and written a reasonable number of stories about legislation. But in terms of seeing the process in action, I was a neophyte.

So I felt it would be interesting, even beneficial, to watch the sausage makers on their busiest night of the year. For that reason I scheduled meetings and record review appointments on Monday and Tuesday. Our Montgomery reporters didn't need me. I'd be off the clock, free to roam and watch, a tourist with a pass to the show.

I ate alone and at about 8:30, walked from my hotel – the aging landmark Statehouse Inn – to its namesake, a few blocks away.

The Statehouse – not the hotel, but the place where Alabama's laws are made – is a white rectangular eight story building across from the Capitol. Within the top four floors, as if carved from its innards, are the two chambers, with the Senate above the House. There's something incongruous about the relative sprightliness of the chambers residing within what is now, with the impressively modern Bronner buildings, among the plainer structures on Goat Hill. On their respective floors are the offices, with the senators – of which there are 35 – enjoying roomier accommodations than the 105 members of the lower house. I chose to start with the Senate, the more exciting and mischievous body.

Exiting the elevator was like being dropped on a downtown Mobile street at Mardi Gras, with legislators, lobbyists, reporters, support staff, and hangers on racing about, some huddled talking strategy, others calling out for this or that cohort. It was a world unto itself, its inhabitants without a trace of self consciousness and wired with energy. I was dodging people, winding my way toward the stadium seating above the senate when Claire Austin rushed out the door I was entering. "Guess who's here? Suzanne! You've got to meet her. Come on!" said Claire.

Sure! And why not?

Claire was off, me tagging along. A turn here, down a hall there and into the office of Jabo Waggoner. I'd never met Waggoner, but knew of him. Who could forget a name like Jabo? Technically, Waggoner was State Sen. Jabo Waggoner, R-Vestavia Hills. For giggles, reporters called him State Sen. Jabo Waggoner, R-HealthSouth, a play on his day job as Richard Scrushy's vice president for public relations. In any event, Waggoner was a conservative Republican from the Birmingham area who as I learned upon entering his suite maintains an impressive stock of spirits and mixers.

We found Suzanne seated, chatting away and drinking a glass of red wine. As her phone voice suggested, Suzanne was fun, and not one to take herself seriously. Among her duties was lobbying for passage of law enforcement-related bills important to the Attorney General's office. No such legislation was pending that night, so she'd come over for kicks. She offered me a glass of wine, and after a moment's self-debate, I accepted.

Suzanne wouldn't have cared if I'd asked for a Coke, but I opted for the wine. Dumb, but not done in conscious violation of any rule prohibiting drinking in the Statehouse. I'd never given the subject a thought, and if I had, Senator Waggoner's bar would have served as the final word on the matter. He should know the rules, right?

Senators came and went, many with drink in hand. Suzanne introduced me around. It was a Republican crowd, and I received much hearty praise for the stories on G.H. Construction and Honda. At some point Ted Hosp stuck his head in. He didn't ask for anyone in particular, and I had the distinct impression he'd heard I was there and came to verify.

A brief hello, something short of friendly, and Ted was off.

"Oh great," I thought. I hopped up and chased after Siegelman's lawyer. In the hallway outside Waggoner's office I gave some rushed and unnecessary explanation of how I came to be there. I couldn't gauge his reaction and returned, slightly troubled.

Ted, no doubt, was the source of the drinking in the Statehouse with Republicans charge made three months later in the letter to Bronson. In fact, two of the seven charges originated from what was for me a rare night out in Monkeytown.

I seldom left for Montgomery before 9 p.m., primarily for procrastination reasons but also because of a preference for night driving. Daytime glare makes me sleepy, not so cooler nights with less traffic. Strong coffee and loud, fast-paced rock'n'roll make falling asleep impossible even should I seek it. Often as not I was sorry I had to stop, and if lucky, was asleep in a cheap hotel by 1 a.m.

During the Siegelman years, 8 a.m. generally found me walking into a state agency or courthouse. From then until 5 p.m., I didn't stop, and then only because offices closed and people went home. Lunch often as not came from a machine — maybe a pimento cheese or chicken salad sandwich and a candy bar.

Most of these trips lasted one day. After being booted out of offices or courts at 5, I'd swing by the *Register's* Montgomery office, make some calls, do some computer searches, get back in my old station wagon and coffee-up for the night ride back to Mobile.

I was, as goes Montgomery, a saint. Couldn't have named a bartender in town. With rare exceptions, a teetotaling working machine.

As for the Republican aspect of the charge, had Suzanne been in the office of a Libertarian Party senator or a Green one that's where I'd have gone, not that Alabama has any of those.

After about an hour I left to go watch the senate, which, good to its reputation, provided fine entertainment. After the buzzer tolled on the session I returned to the party in Waggoner's office. Claire said Fine & Geddie, the state's premier lobbying firm, had rented Bud's for a post-session gathering open to all, and asked if I was interested.

Should I go to a party paid for by lobbyists? The needle leaned to yes. I justified it on grounds that I'd never attended such a function and supposed it could prove educational, since lobbyists and lobbying appeared frequently in my stories. That and I felt like going out.

My car was at the hotel and Claire offered me a ride. She dropped me off at Bud's and went across the street to Sinclair's. "You go in alone. I'm scared to even be seen with you," she said. Some already suspected her of being my source on the G.H. stories, and she didn't want to encourage such thinking.

I'm not sure what I expected, but more than I found. It was all guys, like a gathering of a fraternity to which I didn't belong. Bud's is a roomy bar, and against the far wall was a table with chicken fingers and other appetizers. In the near corner a mass of lobbyists and legislators drank and re-hashed the night's action. I recognized a few, but knew none of them, or in any event, not well.

I bought a drink – as in, paid for it myself -- and was relieved when Chris Pringle, a house member from Mobile and a year ahead of me in high school, walked in. We talked, and after awhile I walked across the street to Sinclair's. By 1:30, more tired and bored than "inebriated," I began thinking hotel and sleep. I asked people I didn't know or to whom I'd just been introduced if they were heading back downtown, and if so, could they give me a ride?

None were, and none offered to go out of their way. I returned to Bud's. The only people I knew were sitting at a table nursing drinks. I remember thinking: Should I? The brief run-in with Hosp – his caught-you look -- weighed in favor of yes. I felt it wouldn't be a bad idea, perception-wise, to make my night out a bipartisan affair. Lawyers are famous for ripping each other's heads off in court then meeting over drinks as if nothing happened. Might this sort of civility apply as well between a reporter and subjects of his political stories?

"Mind if I join you," I said, and Hamrick and Mabry motioned for me to sit down. Soon I wondered aloud if either was heading back downtown. Neither was.

I asked the bartender if he could call a taxi. I'd not anticipated going out and had spent what little money I had. The bartender said the taxi company didn't take credit cards. Was there a money machine nearby? No, there was not.

Damn.

I was staring at a 2 a.m. walk of three miles that would take me under an interstate and through some of the city's more crime-ridden neighborhoods. I had a full schedule the next day and the clock was ticking against my sleep allotment. Walking was out of the question.

Much as I tried, I could think of no other way. I approached Hamrick and Mabry and in a tone as apologetic as I could make it, asked if one of them could spot me money for a cab. Without a second thought Hamrick handed me a $20. I assured him that he would get it back in the morning and thanked him.

The cab delivered me to the hotel, and sleep. I might have slept longer were I not so cognizant of owing $20 to Siegelman's chief of staff. That slate needed wiping, fast. My first act post-breakfast was to retrieve cash from a money machine. I was in the waiting area outside Hamrick's office by 8 a.m., gave the receptionist a $20 and asked her to please make sure to give it to Paul Hamrick as soon as he arrived and, equally important, please tell him that it came from Eddie Curran.

Hamrick was out $20 for about six hours, and for most of that time, it's reasonable to assume, he was snoozing.

The night's activities returned three months later like a boomerang bound for my neck with the seven charges list sent to Mike Marshall and Howard Bronson; and again, in September, when the paper published a story about the allegations.

I made a cursory effort to research the supposed prohibition against drinking in the Statehouse and found a 1997 story by Robin DeMonia of the *Birmingham News*. She had reported finding empty bottles of Scotch, gin and Jack Daniels in a dumpster behind the Statehouse on the morning after the final night of that year's session.

Capitol Police Chief Cecil Humphrey told Robin that alcoholic beverages generally aren't allowed in state buildings, but that the legislature makes its own rules. State representative Ron Johnson told her that no such rules were posted, and acknowledged that some lawmakers were known to drink in their offices. "They're the members' offices. They're pretty much free to have in them what they want," he said.

My personal research on the final night of the 2001 session supported Robin's findings 100 percent. I was not, though, in a position to offer that in my defense or to suggest we consider the irony of this administration's making an issue of me or anyone else taking a cab home from a bar.

How could Don Siegelman, whose wife was almost killed by a drunk driver and who'd long advocated for increased punishment for drunk drivers, fault anyone for calling a taxi from a bar, even if it meant having to borrow money from one of his aides? He should have touted me as an icon of responsible drinking.

I wanted to ask, "Hey Gov, how'd your buddies Paul and Henry get home? Drive? And after drinking? Saw 'em drinking, Gov! Witnessed it myself. How'd they get home?"

This was all inner-monologue, and ignored the real reason I didn't drive home: I can't say with any certainty that I'd have called a cab had my car been available.

Our story in September about my seven transgressions concluded with comments by Keith Woods, an ethics professor at the Poynter Institute, a journalism graduate school in Florida.

Curran, said Woods, "left himself and his newspaper open for attack" by cursing at a governor's aide, drinking with a source and borrowing money from another.

"When we start to say those things are OK, the risk begins," he said.

Something short of fun it was to read those words in my hometown newspaper, to say nothing of the one that employed me.

Chapter 12
The Siegelman Tax

"Since Siegelman became governor in 1999, the state largely stopped seeking competitive proposals for computer services, industry sources maintain. That decision has increased the need for companies to turn to well-placed lobbyists to capture and keep contracts, said several computer firm executives."

-- From June 2001 story, "Is contract best deal the state could get?" about a $6.5 million a year contract with Quality Research Inc.

"I was in a meeting with Al Austin, and Al turned to me point-blank and said, 'I hate this, and it's crappy, but you guys, you're going to have to have a lobbyist if you're going to play with this administration.'"

-- Allen Spradling, an official with computer services company Advanced Systems Design, recalling a meeting with Austin, the chief of computer operations for the Department of Human Resources

In mid-March, before I knew there was a G.H. Construction, a man named Bob called from Atlanta, or so I supposed, since caller ID showed a 404 area code. But Bob, as I discovered months later, wasn't from Atlanta. He had bought a cell phone with a 404 number for the sole purpose of throwing me off if in the event I tried to discover his identity. Not only was Bob not from Georgia, but his name wasn't Bob. He started nameless, and without too much trouble, we christened him Bob.

He said he had read the Honda stories, done some discreet asking around, and was told I could be trusted. Even so, he was nervous. He had never done anything like this, but then again, he had never come across the likes of the Siegelman administration.

Bob proposed a meeting at Brookley Field, the old downtown area airport used for private as opposed to commercial flights. He and another man would fly in and tell me about corruption in the administration's awarding of tens of millions of dollars in what are called computer services contracts. And they'd back it up with records.

Companies in this business are essentially high tech staffing firms. They provide workers with varying specialties and titles like, "systems analyst." Their employees show up each morning and labor side by side with state workers, the main difference being the name on their paychecks. The workers don't come cheap, and the firms that provide them depend on public contracts, where the needs and contract sizes are greatest.

The Brookley Field meeting tickled my fancy for intrigue, but for reasons I can't recall, perhaps my immersion into G.H., it never happened. Bob, though, stayed in touch.

———

Bob's call initiated my least satisfying major endeavor of the Siegelman years. I put in as many hours on the stories as on G.H.; the subject matter was complex, involved an army of players, and was in its way without a resolution. On the plus side, our computer services stories -- along with those by the *Birmingham News* and by that paper on other technology contracts -- illustrated as no other two essential elements of Siegelman's philosophy of governance.

To the winner goes the spoils; and, the second, what prosecutors call "pay to play."

Companies wishing to do business with the state had two choices: Pay the equivalent of a Siegelman tax, or forget it.

———

In the mid-1990s the state's need for computer specialists increased dramatically, same as the rest of the world's. State agencies filled part of the void by hiring, the rest by outsourcing.

Such work qualifies as a profession service, so the bid law doesn't apply. That's not the same as saying there shouldn't be competition.

It's instructive to briefly compare the Siegelman approach to that of the previous governor.

To its credit, the James administration recognized that the state needed to establish a structured, competitive means to award these increasingly large contracts. State communications experts designed a request for proposals (RFP), and invited all comers.

Almost 40 companies responded. They were rated on cost, qualifications of their workers, and references from government and corporate clients. The finance department sent a memo to agencies granting them responsibility over the contracting, along with the results of the RFP. Firms sold themselves to agencies based on their rankings.

The process left little room for political influence because the agencies, not the governor or his finance director, chose the firms.

Enter, Siegelman.

With much ballyhoo the new governor largely stripped agencies and departments of their contracting authority. They were prohibited from entering into contracts for professional services, property leases or to make expenditures of more than $500 without Mabry's permission.

As noted earlier, Finance Director Henry Mabry's refusal to sign many such requests and his long delays on others had won him the sobriquet, "Dr. No." Siegelman bragged on his penny-pinching finance director, lauding him as a blockade against spending. But there was another consequence to the new methodology, as summarized in one of our stories:

If cutting costs was the primary purpose, the centralization of authority over all of state government's financial affairs had another result: With a Siegelman appointee overseeing virtually all state contracts and expenditures, the administration wielded enormous power over who received contracts and the terms of those contracts.

A little-recognized aspect of Mabry was that, when the governor flipped the switch, Dr. No turned into Dr. Yes.

Bob's first tip regarded the biggest boondoggle of all the computer services deals -- a series of $6.5 million per year contracts between the highway department and Quality Research, a Huntsville company that designing specialized software for the military.

In August 1999, Quality Research created a new division as a provider of computer workers. It did so to serve a contract it had arranged to get with the highway department, and before it had a Montgomery office or employees there. The firm had ponied up $10,000 to Siegelman's lottery foundation -- the required sum for computer services companies seeking contracts.

The industry contained a wrinkle that left companies susceptible to the administration's manipulations. The product they provided was workers, and the ultimate loyalty of those workers was to their paychecks. If Company A fell out of favor and couldn't find new jobs for its employees, those workers would often choose to remain at the state agency but as employees of Company B, which was in favor with the governor.

The Siegelman administration could and did force contractors to surrender their workers to better-connected competitors. Some firms were told: Fight it, and we'll cut you out entirely; don't fight it, and we'll let you keep some of the work.

Such was the case with a Montgomery company called Informs. During the James administration the highway department contracted with the University of Alabama to manage its computer services. The university sought bids, and Informs, as low-bidder, won the contract.

The key that opened the door for Quality Research was James H. "Jimmy" Rowell, a two-time acting finance director. After retiring in fall 1998 as the state's top technological services specialist, he had formed a one-man firm called

Enterprise Technologies. In early 1999 the Siegelman administration contracted with Enterprise to advise it on technology matters. At about the same time, Quality Research retained Rowell as a consultant and business finder.

He used his contacts with the governor and highway director Mack Roberts to line up the work for Quality Research's new division.

The story, as told by Bob and others, was that a second company, Camber Corp., also wanted the work, and it too had pull. The firm retained two lobbyists, including former state senator and Siegelman backer Fred Jones. The word was that the governor's office negotiated an arrangement whereby the contract would go to Quality Research as long as it agreed to use Camber as a subcontractor.

Instead of forcing the companies to compete and get the best price for taxpayers, the administration created a situation that by its very design generated massive overcharges.

These businesses make money on overhead and profit charged in addition to what they pay their employees. Overhead includes employee benefits and contract administration costs. Profit, is, well, profit.

Quality Research's invoices showed that Camber billed far more hours on its subcontract than did Quality Research. It seemed, best I could tell, that Quality Research added its overhead and profit atop not just its workers, but also Camber's.

Whatever the actual arrangement – and nobody would say -- Quality Research was charging the state overhead of 107 percent and profit of 14 percent, for a total of 121 percent.

Translated to dollars: For a worker making $60,000 a year, the state was paying almost $132,000.

Executives at other firms said such rates were outrageous and, far as they knew, unprecedented. They put overhead norms in the 20 to 30 percent range and profit at 10 percent.

———

In October 2000, Quality Research's contract came under attack from an unlikely source.

The administration had hired Montgomery lawyer Pat Harris to re-negotiate computer services contracts after Mabry determined that the state was spending too much for such work.

Harris is best known the assistant secretary of the state senate when it was in session. His selection by the Siegelman administration bore the marks of politics, as did many of his dealings with the computer firms. Harris did cut costs, but appeared to be receiving guidance from above.

Firms out of favor with the administration got whacked, those in favor, nicked. None came out better than Quality Research. With its bloated overhead, the firm seemed ripe for the knife, and initially, Harris felt that way as well. During a meeting he told the company it had to cut its rates by 10 percent.

The next week, Quality Research assigned its new Washington lobbyist to the problem.

Ray Cole was a top aide to U.S. Sen. Richard Shelby until leaving in 1999 for the political persuasion profession. The Siegelman administration immediately signed the 34-year-old Cole to a $125,000-a-year contract to lobby Congress for the highway department. The Alabama State Docks, at Siegelman's request, gave him a second contract, for $84,000 a year.

Like Rowell, Cole wore two hats – one that said, Quality Research, the other, "services paid for by Alabama taxpayers."

In an e-mail to a finance department official, Cole said Quality Research was only making a 10 percent profit and "couldn't work for free." What's more, Pat Harris had asked his clients some sensitive questions, including: "How did they get this contract? Who are their subcontractors and why did we choose them? What is the cost breakout on the contract?"

Good questions. Six months later I was dying to know the answers.

Cole wrote that he was "going to talk to Henry" about the situation and asked that the e-mail be forwarded to Mabry.

Since no one was saying, what was said by Cole and done by Mabry is open to conjecture. However, we were able to report the results.

Harris shaved the company's contract by 1.5 percent, far below the proposed 10 percent and the 14 percent average the administration claimed on other contracts.

Once again, Dr. No had evolved into Dr. Yes.

Cole declined to be interviewed, and the press office said Mabry was too busy. Harris said his handling of Quality Research was no different than as with other firms, that he made them cut as much as they could without harming service.

A separate finding shot holes though his story.

After getting the state work, Quality Research began seeking federal computer services contracts as well. The federal government awarded such work through competitive bidding, and firms had to publicly post their prices. That allowed us to report that Quality Research was billing the state "25 to 30 percent more than the firm charges the federal government for the same level of computer specialists."

I'd begun researching the story in March and made the first records request in early April. I sought the usual: correspondence, bids/proposals, and other records generated during the awarding of the contracts. Specifically requested were records pertaining to efforts by Cole and Rowell on behalf of Quality Research; for Fred Jones and Camber; and efforts by other companies seeking the work.

The administration eventually produced the Quality Research contract, its initial proposal, and to my considerable surprise, the Ray Cole e-mail described above. Other than that, very little, and nothing at all on Camber and Jones, the lobbyist.

Paul Bowlin told readers there were so few records because negotiations were "just verbal." And probably much of it was. Unfortunately, negotiations with lobbyists produce next to nothing in the way of documents and much in the way of closed mouths.

In late May – at a time when I was still pounding away on G.H. stories -- I pointed out in an e-mail to the press office that not one piece of paper mentioning Camber had been provided. If there was none, could the administration fill that vacuum by explaining the genesis of Camber's lucrative subcontract and the role played by lobbyist Fred Jones?

The press office's reply: "It is our understanding that Camber does technology work at ALDOT as a subcontractor of Quality Research. It is also our understanding that Fred Jones does work for Camber. Jones is a contributor to the governor."

It didn't serve our readers to accept this nebulous "our understanding" business. And what was the deal with pronouns over people? Who understood? Based on what?

And so I gave them another chance. Could they clarify?

"By clarify, I mean, say how you came to 'understand' the above, and state *who you are.*"

The clarification, in its entirety: "Administration officials do talk to Fred Jones and have worked with him over the years."

What administration officials? Talk to Jones about what? The Alabama-Auburn game? Old movies? They were in effect saying: "We know you know what happened, but we're not going to confirm it."

We had little choice but to fudge it, and did, reporting that "sources in the computer services industry" said Camber sought the contract and was given a major subcontract "as a sort of consolation prize."

As with so many of the stories, the piece was as much about their efforts to conceal as what was being concealed. We told readers about our efforts to determine the nature of Camber's arrangement and Jones' role in negotiating it and presented the vague responses verbatim.

––––

Six months later we reported that highway department auditors had found Quality Research's overhead excessive and demanded a refund of $73,512. This was a slap on the wrist, a fraction of its overcharges, but supported our June story, not that it had needed it.

The audit wasn't volunteered. I had continued reviewing the company's bills during visits to the comptroller, and one invoice showed a credit to the state with the explanation, "Retro-active invoice to correct Overhead Rate." I used that to wedge the audit from the highway department. By this stage the administration wasn't answering any of my questions. However, a quote by Siegelman during a December visit to Mobile was on point.

He took time from promoting an education initiative -- his purpose for the trip -- to let us have it. "If the *Mobile Register* ever bothered to check the facts and compared my record of negotiating contracts with other governors, you would see that the people of Alabama are getting a better financial deal under this administration than they are under, say, Fob James. But the facts don't bother the *Register*."

As it so happened, after the first Quality Research story I "bothered" to request the very type of information Siegelman was accused us of ignoring. Readers went directly from the governor's quote to this:

After the Register's story in June, the paper requested a comparison of the hourly rates, with overhead and profit included, between the Quality Research contract and the rates from the year before as charged by the university and Informs.

A chart provided by the highway department showed that in the 1999 fiscal year -- the last for the university team -- the state paid $75.60 an hour for project managers, which are usually the highest-paid positions. The next year, the state paid $100 an hour to Quality Research for the same position.

For a project manager, then, the difference in rates from one year to the next led to an increased cost of $200 a day, $1,000 a week and about $50,000 a year.

For the four other classifications of workers shown on the chart, the hourly rates were: $61.56 per hour in 1999, compared to Quality Research's $85 an hour; $59.40 an hour compared to $75 an hour for Quality Research; $70.20 an hour compared to Quality Research's $80; and $54 an hour for the university/Informs team, compared to $65 an hour billed the next year by Quality Research.

In some cases, the state was paying the higher rates for the services of the same people, since some of the Informs workers stayed at the highway department but simply began receiving their checks from Quality Research or Camber Corp., a company that had a subcontract with Quality Research to provide workers.

Again, for emphasis: The state was paying $50,000 more per year for the same work – even many cases, the same worker -- than during the James administration.

That's called the Siegelman Tax.

Chapter 13
FRICTION

"Our press office has spent late nights and weekends answering your questions, which are not related to any emergency. We have gone above and beyond the call of duty attempting to satisfy your requests, but only seem to have caused you greater frustration."
-- Portion of May 31, 2001, e-mail from Siegelman's press office.

"I apologize for any friction that has developed with what I acknowledge are frequently difficult and touchy questions. As I've told you before, I may ask tough questions, but I don't stick surprises in my stories. No sucker punches, as I've said, probably one too many times. The alternative would be to ask sweet questions, then stun you with the printed word."
-- From my response to the above e-mail.

On May 29, I learned that Siegelman was to be in Mobile the next day to make a business development announcement at the Alabama State Docks. I'd been writing about his administration for five months without speaking to him once. Even in the heyday of the Carrie Kurlander Openness Experiment, the person I most wanted to interview was off limits. Carrie would say something like, "That's our job, to answer questions on the governor's behalf."

Well, now he was coming my way. Tension had understandably developed in my relationship with his staff, but communications remained for the most part cordial. Open warfare was still two months away. I told Paul Cloos I wanted to go, he said sure, and the next day it was off to the Docks.

It was exceptionally bright out, which created problems. I had just undergone Lasik surgery, the chief side effect being temporary but acute post-surgical sensitivity to light. This is why, as a going away present, Lasik doctors give patients a pair of black, over-large sunglasses. More like goggles, really. Goofy as hell looking, but remove them outside on a sunny day and you're going to cry. Nothing you can do about it.

I pulled up to the loading dock chosen for the governor's appearance and first thing I saw was Siegelman, Carrie and Nick stepping out of a car. The latter could have passed for a Secret Service agent. He was slim, clean cut, wearing shades and the trademark Secret Service style earpiece. I want to say he was packing heat. Years later at trial, Hamrick lawyer Jeff Deen made snide references to Bailey's secret service dress code in an attempt to belittle him before jurors. Had I not gone to the Docks that day, I'd not have known where Deen was coming from, and don't think the jurors got it.

The three saw me and, figuratively speaking, wet their pants. Don't ask me how I know, I just do. Could smell the panic. Nick vanished. He didn't accompany Siegelman to the announcement, and unless he was prostrate in the back seat, wasn't in the car when it departed.

I arrived with a proposal identical to the one presented by Carrie when she walked over to me.

The deal: The governor will make his announcement with local leaders then take questions from the TV folks. I agreed not to muck up the dog and pony show by asking warehouse questions with the cameras rolling. In return, Siegelman pledged to grant me a solo interview.

Good to his word, as the television crews packed up, Siegelman ambled over, shook my hand and smiled. Though we'd met, it was always brief, a handshake and hello when he visited the newsroom for sessions with our editorial board. This was my first and only interview with him during the two years of my near full-time coverage of his administration. It would be almost five years later, at trial, before we spoke again.

Carrie joined the governor, as did a large, silent man hunched down and toting a long boom stick, crowned with a fuzz-covered microphone that hovered below whoever was talking. He wasn't introduced, and I joined Siegelman and Carrie in pretending he wasn't there. After a bit I couldn't help but notice he was struggling. The contraption was heavy, the sun strong and hot, not to mention bright. There was not a strip of shade on the expansive loading dock.

The governor began by telling me of our many shared friends and of their high opinion of me and my work. I replied with pleasantries, but the real conversation was in my head: "He's trying to charm you. Fight it. Don't forget what you're here for."

Then Siegelman said, "I'd like to look you in the eyes and tell you how much I appreciate what you've done for the state."

He was already looking me in the eyes, or in any event, where one would suspect them of being behind the Lasik goggles. So was he saying, in effect, "Could you please remove those funny glasses so we can make uninhibited eye-to-eye contact?" Since that's what he seemed to be saying, I couldn't very well refuse. I mumbled that I'd recently undergone Lasik surgery, thus the unusual shades, but removed them so I could deliver the requested mano-on-mano eye contact. The sunlight and its reflection off the white cement pierced my eyeballs like squirts from a lemon. It was all I could do to fight recoil. I squinted into Siegelman's eyes for as long as I could stand it, maybe 30 seconds.

With torture and banter behind us, I came out with the real stuff, starting with the warehouse and the involvement of his friends, Lanny and Blount. Siegelman surprised me by railing against the pair.

"I did not know until you called the office that Lanny Young and Bill Blount were involved in this project," Siegelman said. "As I told them, it breaks my heart.

It was extremely disappointing that so-called friends would seek to take advantage of the state in that way."

Blount and Young "knew better, somebody knew better," and he was "outraged and disappointed" to learn of their involvement. "It's embarrassing to me and embarrassing to my administration, and hurtful," Siegelman said, in a comment that, like the others, was presented in the next day's paper.

The governor bemoaned that the warehouse deal "hurts people's trust in government."

Then, with a conspiratorial nod, he said, "The full story is not over yet."

What did he mean by *that*? It was clearly intended to indicate that the real story was going to get worse, but surely he meant for others, not him. When I asked him to elaborate, he grinned and said something cryptic to the effect that in time I would understand.

Siegelman wasn't merely lying, he was acting. You didn't need to be Hercule Poirot to deduce that neither Lanny nor Blount could have secured a spot on the G.H. money train without his say so. To accept the governor's tale, one had to believe that Nick took off on a solo run. He assembled the warehouse team without running it by the boss. Then, not once in months of 10 hour days at Siegelman's side, had Man Friday make a peep about the involvement of Lanny and Blount.

It was illogical that Bailey would conceal their roles, since both Lanny and Blount were longtime friends and supporters of Siegelman.

But here was the governor, looking me straight in the goggles, declaring he had no idea that Lanny or Blount had the first thing to do with the warehouse project. This man who gloried in his reputation as a detail man and micromanager expected me to believe he knew next to nothing about a $21.5 million project that, among other things, would revamp the means used by the state to process its liquor operation.

Siegelman either knew I'd recognize this tale as malarkey or he was a victim of self-hypnosis, having convinced himself of his ability to persuade others without regard for their common sense or the absurdity of his claims. Here was the power of positive thinking taken to an extreme where fantasy trumped reality.

G.H. wasn't the only topic that day. I'd been trying for weeks to nail down the circumstances regarding to the highway department's contract with Quality Research and the Camber subcontract.

A year later I would have expected his answer to my question about Quality Research, but at this stage, some measure of respect remained.

"Who are they?" he asked, all wide-eyed innocence.

If I had been a hard-ass like one of those Washington D.C. reporters grilling the president or his spokesman, I would have told him in so many words to cut the nonsense, that I knew he knew about the company. Instead, I was polite if persistent, and tried to approach it from different angles. Carrie stepped in to say the governor had to go. Siegelman said he had more time, but the most I could get out of him was a sham pledge to find out about this Quality Research business.

From the Docks announcement to then we'd been in the blistering sun a good 45 minutes. With the exception of Siegelman, everyone, myself included as I scribbled down the great man's words, was sweating. It was in the 90s, steamy humid, and Siegelman looked like a man in an air-conditioned room.

He was different. Heat? Lying with his every word? No sweat. I left thinking he could convince a lie detector he was born on Pluto.

If I hadn't figured it out by then, I did that day. Driving back to the paper, I was thinking: This man deserves serious watching.

My primary editor on probably 95 percent of my Siegelman stories was Paul Cloos. I'd been assigned to Paul in 1994 when I moved from sports to news. Paul is from New York and a graduate of Boston College. He's a light-skinned red-head, slightly younger than I, and I owe much to him. He is extraordinary fair and vigilant for any hint of editorializing or evidence of bias within news stories.

My name was on the Siegelman stories, but he was my silent partner. For Paul, that often meant working well into the night and on Saturdays, though he usually did that anyway.

I soon learned that in news, and especially with investigative pieces, I had to attribute everything. In those early years Paul and I butted heads almost daily. I would be doing the loud talking with him sitting in his chair, looking up at me with a calmness I wanted to wipe away. I knew I was scoring if he reddened. But moving him from a position? That was another thing.

"If the sun is shining I have to attribute it to someone else!" I'd complain, to no effect. If a subject of a story was 500 pounds, then "heavyset" was as far as I could go in describing him to a reader.

It soon became apparent that I needed public records to support almost everything I reported. As a result I became a student of public records and the accepted expert on them within in the newsroom. I developed a near obsession with public records. A reporter could turn out three stories a day if all it required was quoting one or more people saying so-and-so is a crook, liar or idiot. I prefer spending more time on a story and laying out what that someone did and why. Quotes help, but if they're not supported by evidence they're just hot air transposed to print.

On one level investigative stories are written for an audience they'll never have. That's the lawyers who might represent your subjects should they choose to sue. I've had a number of stories "lawyered." This happens when editors fear the allegations within a story could lead to a lawsuit and they bring in the lawyers to review a story or series. It can be a painful, tedious process but I learned much from it.

The frequency of my clashes with Paul diminished over time, with me pre-lawyering, he making fewer changes, and the two of us often joking about how easy that one was compared to the old days.

A common length for a long news story 20 column inches. Many of my stories were three times that, sometimes more. Numerous studies – notably taken to heart by *USA Today* and the Gannett-owned papers -- tell us that readers don't have the attention span to digest 20 inches, must less 75. I don't doubt it. As a reader, I don't have all the time in the world either. But there is a place in newspapers for long stories. Many of my best read pieces and certainly those that delivered the greatest impact have been monsters.

It would be an exercise in masochism to research stories to the degree that I do knowing I'll have to wrap it up in 20 or 25 inches. After awhile I would choose the path of least resistance – easier stories. Somehow that seems like quitting.

As I was forever pointing out to my editors, the acts about which I reported invariably transpired within the context of a specialized type of business or contract governed by laws and norms that must be explained if a reader is to comprehend their violation. That was one of my excuses.

Perhaps the most unnerving part about writing long investigative pieces is worrying about them once they've been filed. Will the editors gut the story? Remove that lead I love? For these and other reasons, relationships between reporters and editors can be tense.

Paul was city editor during that period, and after he finished one of my stories and we worked through his questions it went up the next wrung, to managing editor Dewey English.

Among his other skills, Dewey is an exceptional line editor – great at finding the word that replaces and does a better job than the four-word phrase presented him. He cuts out extraneous words and phrases that, once removed, you realize didn't need to be there. Seeing Dewey's thin, precise fingers dance on a keyboard while editing is a thing of beauty. He is also a caring editor. He will listen to a reporter make his case for something he was going to cut or alter, and if you do a good job of making your case, he sticks with the way you wrote it or finds a middle ground that makes it better.

———

The final read belonged to the paper's editor, Mike Marshall. He only pulled one of my Siegelman stories, and the thing was convoluted, if a byproduct of the facts I was working with. Most importantly, Mike granted me the space to tell the stories and backed me up when the administration came after me.

And all of them – Paul, Dewey and Mike – trusted me enough to let me spend weeks or more following leads and hunches. Had I not been granted that trust and time, none of my Siegelman stories could have been reported.

———

After a May 10 cabinet meeting, Siegelman and Hamrick left, but others remained for what a memo reflects was a "post cabinet meeting."

Years later, in going through the Siegelman archives, I found a memo of a "post-cabinet meeting." It was dated May 10, 2001, at the height of the G.H. stories and the drubbing that entailed. The memo reflects that members of the cabinet hung around after Siegelman and Hamrick departed.

"The Chief of Staff seems to focus more on political issues and less on managing day to day operations," it read. "Perhaps there needs to be someone designated with a formal position in the chain of command with responsibility for managing the non-political day to day aspects of the operation."

Also remarked upon was the waning influence of Siegelman's old friend Jim Hayes, who was known to dislike Hamrick. "Others feel frustrated that they are not able to have a much closer management relationship with the Governor. Things worked better when Jim Hayes was more active as a conduit."

The memo was obviously provided to Siegelman, as it contains his scribbled comments – one to the effect that he was standing by Hamrick. "Paul is the Political Director," Siegelman wrote, nicely summing up the chief of staff's real job.

The memo concluded: "One comment was made that even though many of us feel like we are doing a good job, we do not feel that much a part of what (Siegelman) is doing."

———

In early June -- in keeping with his practice of announcing a reform on the heels of every scandal -- Siegelman signed an executive order. It directed "all cabinet members to require disclosure on any contracts of any interest by state employees, elected officials, appointed officials, lobbyists, or their family member."

"If there's no disclosure, there'll be no contract, no state money. Period," he declared with flourish.

He also announced that Nick Bailey was leaving ADECA for the newly created position of, "Confidential Assistant to the Governor."

———

Regarding Bailey's handling of the warehouse project, Siegelman said Nick was "taken advantage of ... I have full faith and trust in Nick Bailey."

In fact, no one was at fault. "Every once in a while, something may slip through," Siegelman said. "The system let us down."

Once more, for effect: It was *the system's fault.*

A week later, the system screwed up again.

The AP's Bill Poovey reported that state senator Roger Bedford had tried to strong-arm the Marion County Commission into using $3 million in state funds to buy land from developer/timber company owner Dennis "Blue" Harbor. It was a classic Alabama pork tale, though hardly the first starring the notorious northwest Alabama legislator.

Marion County was trying to build an industrial park to boost its sagging economy. And in Bedford, it had a friend famous for his ability to deliver state funds to his district. The problem this time was that Bedford delivered too much, and with strings attached. Bedford displayed his power over state finances and cozy relations with the administration by rounding up $3 million in state funds for the project. Of that, $2 million was in the form of a check from ADECA to the county. It wasn't sent to the county, but handed to Bedford by Bailey.

Bedford told the commissioners that if they wanted the check, they had to build the park on 600 acres owned by Harbor, his friend and political benefactor.

Problem was, the parcel was appraised at $1 million, and that was later deemed high. The county – fearing criminal repercussions -- reluctantly refused the money.

Bedford yanked the first $1 million, and after holding on to it for six months, returned the $2 million check to ADECA.

"I've never seen anything like this in my life," Bedford told the AP's Poovey. "All of a sudden the local officials bow up."

Bedford philosophy of governance is such that he couldn't fathom the mindset of public officials refusing to pay $3 million for land worth a fraction of it.

The *Birmingham News* jumped on the story, exposing a series of real estate and business transactions involving Harbor, Bedford and state representative Michael Millican, who'd also urged the county to buy Harbor's property.

The "Blue Harbor" story reverberated throughout the state, causing grief for Siegelman, and deservedly so. Harbor had contributed $7,000 to Siegelman's gubernatorial campaign; Siegelman had authorized the $2 million ADECA grant; and Bedford and Siegelman went too far back for Siegelman to plausibly distance himself from the state senator.

Not that he didn't try.

"I am not familiar with Blue Harbor. It sounds like a place where they make margaritas or something," he quipped at a press conference.

He blasted Bedford, went easy on Bailey, and declared that the "system is broken and it needs to be fixed."

And maybe the system did deserve some blame. Is there, after all, any other state that lets its legislators walk around for six months with $2 million checks?

———

Even after G.H. and the revelations about Hamrick's best pal Lanny, Siegelman had to be goaded into removing his chief of staff. The two shared a love of gamesmanship and Siegelman felt comfortable around Hamrick, whose ethical compass also pointed south.

On June 16 the governor announced a cabinet shake-up. Hamrick was out and Mack Roberts gone as highway director. Roberts had wanted out for months, ever since Siegelman publicly pinned the Honda no-bid debacle on him. Siegelman managed to be on an industry hunting trip in Europe when the announcements were made. Accompanying the governor was Bailey, his new, "confidential assistant."

The press office reported that Hamrick was leaving to run Siegelman's re-election campaign. That never happened. Instead, he went to work as a lobbyist for the Matrix Group, the mysterious and famously cutthroat political consultancy firm headed by Joe Perkins.

Siegelman replaced Lanny Young's best friend with 53-year-old Jim Buckalew, at the time the chief of staff for Montgomery Mayor Bobby Bright. From 1989 to 2000 Buckalew served as chief of staff for Bright predecessor, legendary Montgomery Mayor Emory Folmar. Though Folmar is as Republican as they come, Bright looked past that because of Buckalew's talents, and Siegelman did as well.

"I know that he will be sure that none of the nonsense that we have been reading about in the papers will be tolerated," Siegelman said of his new chief of staff.

Perhaps it's to Buckalew's credit – and if I may say so, the work by the *Register* and the *Birmingham News* – that most of that nonsense occurred before May 2001. My 2002 would match or exceed the year I had in 2001, but the bulk of those stories -- as well as many to come by Brett Blackledge and Kim Chandler at the *News* -- unearthed activities that preceded Buckalew's arrival.

I don't think it a leap to suggest that, were it not for the G.H. Construction stories, the nonsense would have continued unabated for the remainder of Siegelman's term and possibly into another four year term; Bailey and Hamrick would have stayed on; and the cost of the Siegelman method to Alabama taxpayers would have continued climbing, unabated.

Instead, the Siegelman administration, post May 2001, was by Alabama standards a pretty clean ship. My chief complaint is that the administration, as much as ever, continued to withhold records and lie and dissemble to cover-up activities from the dirty years.

Real men don't apologize when there's nothing to be sorry for. Real men don't feel compelled to explain themselves. And real men don't write long e-mails.

There are, however, exceptions.

From early May to late July, most of the quotes from the administration arrived by e-mail, without a name attached. Actual conversations with anyone authorized to be quoted ceased. Wasn't announced, just happened. Carrie wouldn't be in and didn't return calls, and for the most part I stopped trying. I was unofficially assigned to Rip, or he to me, and Rip wasn't permitted to be quoted.

William Reeves "Rip" Andrews is square jawed, trim, and on the short side. He's from Birmingham, or more specifically, Mountain Brook, the small, very Republican township that's home to many of that city's lawyers, doctors and business leaders. He came to Siegelman from Al Gore's presidential campaign. Gore's people thought enough of Rip to make him one of its lead writers of press releases and even granted him occasional quoting duties.

He was at the time a political toddler, fresh out of Georgetown. There he had led a movement that sought to reform student government.

During his D.C. years Rip met and became an acolyte of Clinton soldier Paul Begala. He instilled in Rip the importance of one attribute above all – loyalty. When the source of the stain on Monica's blue dress was revealed for what it was, Begala, like James Carville, didn't turn tail and give up on their man. He fought harder.

My armchair analysis is that Rip sold himself hard on Siegelman and also saw his work for Alabama's governor as a stepping stone to future assignments on the national stage. Quitting, going soft, agreeing with even one negative word about Siegelman – not options. Rip's future in politics depended on him sticking with his man, and did he.

When I met him he was slaving away, working 16 hour days. Work, like politics, is in his blood. In May 2007 he graduated first in his class from the University of Alabama law school. Rip is quite smart, but I'd rate his drive and work ethic above his brains.

Treatment of Rip in the pages to come won't be kind, but I admire his fight, and am certain he will go far.

—

Because of the complexity of the issues it was agreed that I would e-mail my questions to the press office. Problem was, they chose to respond in kind, and only that way. E-mail is a wonderful tool but shouldn't be used to entirely supplant verbal communications. For obvious reasons real quotes read like they come from human beings. Readers experience inflection, personality, opinion, honesty or, in its absence, deception.

The e-mail responses were maddening as much for their evasiveness as the literary voice, if that phrase can be applied. In one missive I told them their answers appeared drafted by HAL, the computer villain from Stanley Kubrick's, "2001: A Space Odyssey."

I'm certain lawyers drafted the responses. That's the only possible explanation for the impressively bland, non-committal and stubbornly uninformative answers.

After Honda I was always working on multiple stories, like a fisherman with five or six lines in the water. When a pole dipped hard, it's the one I grabbed. May, June and July found me seeking records and comment on G.H.; Mercedes; the

Quality Research computer services contract; legal fees paid to Siegelman after he became governor; and payments to the law firms of two state senators for work on state bond deals. All were valid lines of inquiry, all developed into stories.

Though usually concentrating on one story, for efficiency sake I had to be laying the groundwork for the next and the next. This entailed seeking records frequently well in advance of my ability to use them. And a good thing I was. Their serial violation of public records laws invariably meant lengthy battles for documents sought but not produced.

The limitations of the e-mail format contributed mightily to their length. Interviews are fluid. You can go into one without thinking of every question ahead of time. Responses determine the direction of the interview. That wasn't possible with the format dictated by the administration. To ensure thoroughness, I had to ask questions and include follow ups that depended on answers I could only guess at. If I started with a yes-no question and their answer was no, that led to one set of questions; if yes, another set of questions; and on and on, like a reverse playoff bracket.

These multi-page e-mails were no more fun to write than read. It was not unusual for me to finish and fire them off at 3 or 4 a.m., and then after a stressful day of writing and editing a story. By that hour carriers were tossing papers into front yards, the newsroom was empty, even the cleaning people had come and gone.

Not infrequently the e-mails were, well, less than professional. Grammar and punctuation suffered as well. This was a reflection not just on their author, but in his defense, his addled brain at the hour. One, to Carrie, ended thus: "On a personal note, don't think me a turd. Just doing my job, and I trust you and Rip recognize that … Eddie."

Memo to impressionable young reporters who might be reading this: Probably best to keep turds out of e-mails.

During these wee-hour episodes I occasionally fell prey to a silly need to assuage guilt I had no business feeling. I became a one man good cop bad cop. "For your info, I keep ethics forms on numerous public officials, including Steve Windom," began one conscience-easer.

I proceeded to tell them about a story on then-state senator Windom's sponsorship of several distinctly anti-consumer bills pertaining to the collection of overdue loans. His role on such matters was relevant because he was a partner in Sirote & Permutt, which had the largest loan collection operation of any firm in the state.

Another time I attached stories referenced in the guilt trip. "One thing: I imagine y'all think I'm beating up on the governor, looking at his finances. I can assure you I've looked at the private finances of lot of public officials, and spent a long, long time on Fob James' landfill, much more than have spent on this governor's finances, and focused almost entirely on stuff that occurred prior to him being governor."

Why, I told them I'd conducted extensive research into the sale of James' house after he became governor; and could "send you zillions more stories on (James') sons' businesses, including one with the state docks, favors from DOT, etc., that I wrote about."

Mostly, though, I bitched about their failure to answer questions and their inability to locate basic records that would be generated in the regular course of business. I said it was inconceivable the state would enter into a multi-million dollar contract (with Quality Research) without generating records.

They replied with a pledge to provide such records should they "come across" them. That ignited my inner smart-ass. I told them the phrase "come across" suggested that "the records themselves have to somehow exert themselves, such as by shinnying out of a file, to then fall in front of a walking person, and then to have been 'come across.'"

And from there, a series of yes-no questions, starting with: "Does the administration and the finance department have a filing system?"

If the answer was yes, they were asked if the files were "identified by subject matter, such as by tabs, so that they can be easily and efficiently identified, retrieved and produced?"

And lastly: "Does the administration often have difficulty locating its own files?"

"Of course the administration keeps files. We do our best to stay organized," came the reply.

The questions about their filing system – among a group of questions sent late on the day of my interview with Siegelman -- did not sit well. "Rather than answer each of your approximately 40 questions, we have decided to respond to your general areas of interest."

Then came out firing:

You had an exclusive interview with the governor yesterday that lasted nearly half an hour. You were able to interview Dr. Mabry on one of the busiest and most crucial days of this year's legislative session for more than three hours. You were able to interview Mack Roberts for more than three hours. You have had hours upon hours of unprecedented access to Ran Garver and Nick Bailey…

That unprecedented time and access is not, frankly, how this office treats other reporters from your paper or any other reporter. You broke the story on G.H. Construction, and frankly, did this administration and the state a real service. We thank you, but that does not mean we should give you more attention and greater consideration in the future when answering your questions or setting up interviews for you.

Naturally, this required a response. I wrote that they had "substituted answers to specific questions with anger at me for wasting too much of your time. I don't mind anger, I just wish it came with answers to my questions."

I told them it was their choice to "route most if not all remotely prickly questions (about business at state agencies) through the governor's press office" and that because of that, there was, "a small army of well-paid public information officers who aren't allowed to do their jobs."

And for good measure: "As for Nick Bailey, yes, he did spend three hours with me. Thank goodness I didn't believe a thing he said."

Siegelman read my e-mails. I know this because a year later, he told one of our Montgomery reporters, Bill Barrow, that my long-winded communiqués reminded him of the letters sent him from inmates seeking pardons. Bill admitted that he laughed when Siegelman made the comparison, and that the governor thought it funny too.

While it stung a bit -- for there was an element of truth in the comparison -- I also saw the humor. Because I associate humor with humanity, my estimation of him climbed. Not a lot, mind you, but in that one regard, yes.

Touché, governor.

Chapter 14
Siegelman's Big Score

"Sometime ago, I publicly announced that I personally would waive any compensation for my involvement in this litigation, but those who hold public office and who have refused to prosecute our state's claims against tobacco companies continue to suggest that this litigation is somehow designed for my own personal financial benefit. My withdrawal from this lawsuit should terminate these politically motivated criticisms."

-- Portion of October 1997 letter Siegelman sent to Montgomery County Circuit Judge Charles Price.

"Don has never been shy about asking for money, or about the degree of prestige his name carries with it."

-- Mobile lawyer Chris Peters, in explaining Siegelman's reason for demanding that Peters' law firm pay him a severance package in the neighborhood of $800,000.

On a Sunday night in June 1996, Todd Cunningham ran out of gas on Interstate 85 just east of Montgomery. Leaving his wife and two young sons in the car, the 30-year-old contractor took off with a plastic jug in hand. It was close to 9 p.m. and dark when Cunningham started walking down a service road to the nearest gas station.

Later that night, Howard Fitts, an inmate from the Montgomery Work Release Center, told prison officials that the blood on the van came from a deer he'd run over. His story didn't survive the subsequent discovery of Cunningham's body.

The next morning, Cunningham's parents returned home from comforting their daughter-in-law to find among their many phone messages one from Nick Bailey. He'd introduced himself as an aide to the lieutenant governor, left a number and asked the Cunninghams to call Siegelman.

"We were getting lots of calls of condolences, and it was one of the first ones," said Todd Cunningham's mother, Cheryl. "I really thought it was something more to do with the actual accident, and was thinking, 'OK, the state has some more information about what actually happened.'"

That afternoon or the next day, Cheryl's husband, J.C. Cunningham Jr., received a call from Siegelman.

"He said he would like to talk to us about our son's death and that the state owed us a lot of consideration," said Cunningham, a retired Montgomery police officer. "At that time I wasn't really interested in suing anybody and getting money. I was very hurt and very sad, and my interest was in comforting my wife and daughter-in-law. I wasn't even thinking about it. I had other things on my mind.

"I told him I'd have to think about it. It was before he was buried."

Cheryl Cunningham was so incensed she took notes of the message left by Bailey and Siegelman's subsequent efforts to recruit them as clients.

"I was furious that someone like that would use a death like that for profit. It was beyond hurt – I was furious," she said years later. Siegelman's calling so soon after her son's death and offering to sue the state he'd been elected to serve was "off the charts," she said.

Later, J.C. Cunningham received a short hand-written letter from Siegelman. The envelope bore the seal of Alabama, as did the stationary, which in all aspects but one appeared to be the official stationary of the lieutenant governor's office. The lone difference was the tiny print at the bottom, which stated, "Not printed at government expense."

"Last year I sued the State (Alabama Dept. Dept. of Agriculture) for the death of a state employee," Siegelman wrote, the parentheses his. "If I can be of any help to you in any way please do not hesitate to call."

Siegelman signed it and provided Cunningham with his private pager number.

When Cheryl Cunningham told her daughter-in-law's attorney about the letter, he asked for the date. He wanted to know, she said, because state bar association rules require lawyers to wait at least 31 days before sending solicitation letters to accident victims.

"We received his handwritten letter 32 days after the accident, and that just infuriated me," she said. "It was so devastating. I just looked at it and said some most un-ladylike comments, and I said it will be a cold day before I call him."

The state settled the case without ever being sued. Bill Gray, the legal advisor for then governor Fob James, told a reporter at the time that the state agreed to pay almost $1 million to Todd Cunningham's widow and children because the "facts in the case were very bad."

Siegelman's attempt to represent the Cunninghams isn't directly related to the *Register* stories that examined more than $1.3 million in legal fees paid to him while he was governor. The Cunningham case is, however, an indication of the sort of law Siegelman practiced, to the extent he practiced law at all.

He was an ambulance chaser. And when the chase produced a client, he handed it off to another lawyer. A real one.

———

Every summer since we've been married, my wife and children go to Bratislava, the capital of Slovakia, for about six weeks. I join them for about three of those weeks, and we stay with my dear mother-in-law Bobbi. During the 2001 trip I was, for the first week, working almost full-time finishing up stories. I didn't have a lap-top, and worked at various "internet cafes," writing, saving and sending stories on my AOL account, and editing back and forth with Paul the same way, and a colossal pain it was.

I was at a downtown spot called Internet@Tea on June 19 and checking the state wire to see what was going on back home. Within minutes I knew what I would be working on when I returned, and e-mailed Paul Cloos to tell him as much.

The tip to the stories that I believe spooked Siegelman more than any besides the warehouse series was an Associated Press piece by Phil Rawls. It began: "Gov. Don Siegelman, who hasn't practiced law in more than two years, makes far more from his old law firm than he does as governor."

Siegelman had disclosed on his ethics form that he was paid more than $250,000 in 2000 from the law firm that will be called here, for simplicity sake, Cherry Givens. The firm, which had offices in Dothan and Mobile, changed names many times as partners came and went. In 2000, for example, Cochran supplanted Cherry as the first name on the letterhead, when (since deceased) O.J. Simpson lawyer Johnnie Cochran either joined the firm or it joined his national firm. It was difficult to tell.

Rawls had obviously gone to the ethics commission to review the financial disclosures for 2000 that would have just come due. Each year, in late spring or early summer, local and state elected officials and non-federal government employees with salaries above $50,000 must report their outside income from the previous year by completing a "Statement of Economic Interest." Alongside sources of income are monetary ranges, starting at, "Less than $1,000," and maxing out at, "More than $250,000." Siegelman had checked that last box, listed the source as Cherry Givens, and scribbled a note reporting that the payment was "associated with prior years' service."

Carrie Kurlander – assuredly after getting it from the horse's mouth -- told Phil that Siegelman had "dissolved his agreement" with the firm to run for governor and "waived the right to legal fees on a case-by-case basis in return for a lump sum of money paid in three installments."

She said the first installment had been paid in 1999, his first year as governor. And from there, the story continued:

She said he has one more installment coming in 2001, and the installments are not all in the same amount. Kurlander said Siegelman had been working on 20 to 30 cases when he left the firm.

Former law partner Keith Givens said Siegelman, like other lawyers in the firm, handled plaintiff cases, such as wrongful death and consumer fraud.

"He was a good lawyer and made significant contributions to the firm," Givens said.

He said that most of the firm's cases are on a contingency fee basis, and financial settlements can sometimes take a long time.

I had and was familiar with Siegelman's ethics reports going back years, including the one for 1999, his first year as governor. It didn't include the first mention of Cherry Givens, which wasn't a surprise. He'd ended his association with the firm in 1997.

On that 1999 report Siegelman hand-wrote, "Legal (P/I case 1998)," and checked the income range, "$150,000 to $250,000." P/I obviously stood for personal injury. I assumed that 1998 indicated the year the lawsuit was settled, that the fee arrived in 1999, and that it was a referral fee, since everyone knew that Siegelman hadn't practiced law in the conventional sense.

I'd given little thought to the payment. While quite large, a referral fee of that size wasn't outside the realm of possibility in a serious injury or death case against a heavily insured defendant. A case would need to settle or otherwise be resolved for at in the neighborhood of $2 million for a referring lawyer to make that kind of money.

Now, it appeared that Siegelman, through Carrie, was giving an explanation that conflicted with the ethics report he'd filed the year before. The $150,000 to $250,000 was no longer payment for a single personal injury case. It had morphed into the first installment of a three-year "lump sum" deal with Cherry Givens.

Something was amiss there and merited attention, but that's not why I e-mailed Paul. The shocker was the apparently immense sum Cherry Givens agreed to pay Siegelman *after* he became governor.

When G.H. Construction and the no-bid work at Honda blew up, Siegelman blamed others. He removed top aides, suggesting that the mistakes were theirs, not his. But not even Bailey could be thrown under the bus on what became the legal fees scandal.

I believe our stories on Siegelman's payments from Cherry Givens made a convincing case of a crime graver and definitely more lucrative than any of his other activities, including those involving Lanny Young and Richard Scrushy.

Understanding why the AP story made the impression it did on me that day requires some familiarity with events years earlier.

In the early 1990s, the public relations tide started to turn against Big Tobacco. Decades of damning memos and scientific studies by the industry confirming awareness of the addictive, cancer-causing qualities of their product were leaked to the likes of "60 Minutes."

Still, the industry's legal scorecard remained unvarnished. Never had a cigarette-maker been forced to pay a dime to a smoker-plaintiff, despite countless attempts by some of the country's best trial lawyers. A turning point was the May 1994 congressional hearing when seven tobacco company executives stood with hands raised and took turns swearing under penalty of perjury that nicotine was "not addictive."

With that ludicrous declaration, the dour-faced executives from central casting departed D.C. with targets on their chests.

That spring, dozens of the country's top plaintiffs firms banded together to finance a legal blitzkrieg against Philip Morris, RJR Nabisco, Brown & Williamson and others. The Louisiana-based "Castano Group" chose as its weapon a nationwide class action against the industry seeking hundreds of billions of dollars. A federal appeals court rejected the mammoth case, and in 1997, Congress rebuffed a similar attempt by the Castano lawyers.

With Big Tobacco still vulnerable, some Mississippi attorneys devised a novel mode of attack. The group, led by powerhouse Pascagoula trial lawyer Dickie Scruggs, convinced Mississippi Attorney General Mike Moore to sue cigarette-makers. The theory was that the companies owed the state for money spent, such as through Medicaid, in treating indigent patients for smoking-related disease. "It was like choosing the right weapon in a war," Scruggs said later. "If you use the wrong weapon against a tank you're not going to blow it up."

Scruggs (now in prison for bribing a judge) suggested adding the South Carolina firm Ness Motley on the team. Partner Ron Motley was among the country's most feared trial lawyers, and like Scruggs, had made a fortune suing asbestos makers.

Mississippi brought its history-making lawsuit in May 1994. A smattering of other states followed, including Florida and Texas. The floodgates opened in 1996 as dozens of states filed similar suits, usually with Scruggs and/or Ness Motley leading the way and partnered with home-grown lawyers. Victory on this level – even a middling settlement – guaranteed fantastical riches for any attorney lucky enough to be included on his or her state's team.

Alabama, unlike its neighbor, was not to be among the 40 states to bring suits against cigarette-makers.

Republican Attorney General Jeff Sessions abhorred plaintiffs lawyers and the Democratic candidates they bankrolled. His contempt was if anything exceeded by Bill Pryor, his assistant and political son. Pryor, a member of the ultra-conservative Federalist Society, despised so-called "judicial activism," or anything that suggested using the courts, such as through lawsuits, to establish public policy and, as Pryor saw it, usurp the role of legislatures and Congress.

After Pryor succeeded Sessions, he became, in a sense, Moore's nemesis. As Moore flew about the country urging attorneys general to sue Big Tobacco, Pryor did the same, beseeching fence-sitting AGs to withstand the pressure to sue.

"Who do you sue next?" Pryor said. "Whiskey companies? Blue Bell ice cream? McDonald's because they sell fatty foods?"

There was no way Alabama could sue without the approval of the attorney general and governor, but that didn't stop the lieutenant governor from trying. Siegelman had historical and financial ties to plaintiffs' lawyers, and, loosely defined, was one himself. Crucially, he was, as a former attorney general, a past member of the National Association of Attorneys General, or NAAG. Siegelman maintained ties to the group and frequently attended its national gatherings, and the association was a chief proponent of suing cigarette-makers.

"Don Siegelman was involved with us in fighting this fight, it seems like throughout the whole thing," Arizona AG Grant Woods told me for a 1998 story examining Alabama's role in the tobacco wars. "I talked to him dozens and dozens of times. His main goal was to make sure Alabama didn't get left out of it."

(In 2007, Woods was to become one of the most vocal critics of the Siegelman prosecution with his accusations that the federal government went after Siegelman for political reasons. Woods helped gather the signatures of many of Siegelman's friends in the former attorneys general community on legal briefs and letters urging officials and courts to drop the charges against Siegelman.)

Memos unearthed years after the tobacco wars revealed that lieutenant governor Siegelman fought for Alabama with dollar signs in his eyes.

One, dated June 23, 1996, was from Siegelman to Jere Beasley; lawyer and State Sen. Michael Figures; long-time Siegelman friend Jack Drake of Birmingham; and Mobile attorney Chris Peters, from Cherry Givens. Siegelman reported that he had spoken with Dickie Scruggs and Ron Motley and signed up a group of "clients" to serve as plaintiffs in a private as opposed to state-sanctioned class action on behalf of Alabama taxpayers and against Big Tobacco.

Most of the plaintiffs were state employees with ties to Siegelman, including lead plaintiff Barbara Crozier.

The next week Drake sent a memo to the Crozier lawyers. It reported that most in the group had agreed to a proposal for dividing the "Alabama share" -- that being the total of any legal fees awarded should the case succeed, minus the money paid Scruggs' and Rice's firms. It was, after all, the out-of-staters who'd amassed the documents and legal arguments upon which the lawsuit was based.

"The proposal continues with a 10% across the board distribution to each component group, that is 10% to Siegelman, 10% to Cherry, Givens, 10% to Michael Figures, 10% to Jere Beasley and 10% to Cooper, Mitch (Drake's firm)," wrote Drake.

Siegelman was to receive an additional five percent for "bringing about the litigation group." Division of the remaining 45 percent of the "Alabama's share" was to be determined later, based on the amount of work by group members.

On Aug. 6, 1996, Siegelman held a press conference announcing the filing that day, in Montgomery County Circuit Court, of Crozier vs. American Tobacco Company.

News stories questioned the propriety of the lieutenant governor being paid should the lawsuit bear fruit. Siegelman said he was acting as a private lawyer and not in his public capacity. This was preposterous, since it was his elected position, not his legal acumen, that placed him in a position to pursue the tobacco cases.

Ethics Commission Director Jim Sumner allowed that Siegelman could accept fees as long as he refrained from mixing his work as a private lawyer with his duties as an elected official.

Two weeks after the group filed the Crozier case, Siegelman requested a meeting with Sessions. He hoped to talk the attorney general into joining the growing number of states who had sued tobacco makers. A memo of the meeting written by Bill Pryor reflects that fees were uppermost on the minds of the lieutenant governor and Jack Drake, who also attended.

Drake told Sessions that he, Siegelman and other members of the team expected a contingency fee of 25 percent. To clarify, if cigarette-makers agreed to pay Alabama $4 billion, Siegelman, Drake, et al., would split $1 billion; if $2 billion, they'd get $500 million, and so on.

"Siegelman said that we should downplay this issue ... by telling the public that the court would award the attorneys fee," wrote Pryor.

Pryor responded that "the public rightfully would want to know what amount the state's attorneys intended to request from the court."

Siegelman tried to appeal to baser instincts. He offered to "bring on board" Republican lawyers who would, naturally, share in the fees. He suggested Pryor's former firm -- the omnipresent Walston Wells Anderson & Bains, the home of Hamrick's brother-in-law Ellis Brazeal; and Capell & Howard, where Sessions' top assistant, deputy Attorney General Richard Allen, had been a partner.

"I told the lieutenant governor we were not interested in discussing anything like that," Pryor wrote.

Siegelman and Drake sought the meeting in part because they recognized that the Crozier class action was a pie in the sky proposition that would require "three to five trips to the Supreme Court of Alabama to create a new legal theory," Pryor wrote.

About that, they were correct. It went nowhere. The Crozier case will, however, figure into this convoluted tale, though not nearly as prominently as a second lawsuit.

———

The following spring, the Siegelman group tried an end-run around Pryor, who by then was attorney general, having replaced Sessions after the latter was elected to the U.S. Senate.

Their plan was to recruit two government-funded hospital systems – one affiliated with the University of Alabama at Birmingham (UAB), the other with the University of South Alabama (USA) -- and file lawsuits on their behalf. Both served substantial numbers of indigent patients. As with the state lawsuits, the hospitals would sue to recover sums spent treating tobacco-related illnesses in that population.

The attorneys would work on a contingency fee basis. If the universities didn't get any money from the tobacco companies then the lawyers wouldn't get paid;

but in the unlikely event that the cases succeeded, there would be big money for Siegelman and his lawyer teammates.

An angry Pryor declared that state-funded universities, like state agencies, couldn't initiate lawsuits without his approval. UAB backed off. South Alabama did not. In May 1997, the university filed its lawsuit suit in Mobile County Circuit Court. USA president Fred Whiddon and the university's board had defied the attorney general. Whiddon said Pryor would have to put him in jail to prevent him from pursuing the case. Siegelman declared that he didn't "expect Dr. Whiddon to back away from the tobacco industry or to give in to Bill Pryor."

Pryor came to Mobile to confront Whiddon and the board at its regular spring meeting. The anticipated fireworks didn't materialize. Whiddon and Pryor presented their positions and essentially agreed to let the courts decide. Soon after, the case vanished from the public eye. As corporate defendants often do, the tobacco companies "removed" the South Alabama lawsuit to federal court, arguing that was the proper jurisdiction. There, a judge agreed with Pryor, ruling that the university couldn't pursue the case without the AG's blessing.

Sayonara to the USA case, or so it seemed.

Two months after the board meeting, Big Tobacco blinked. Philip Morris et al., agreed to pay Mississippi about $4 billion, and separate and above that, some $1.4 billion in legal fees to 12 firms, the lion's share going to Scruggs' and Motley's firms.

There was no way Mississippi would be the only state to settle, and the parties began slowly moving toward what became the national Master Settlement.

On October 17, 1997, Siegelman filed motions withdrawing from the Crozier case before Montgomery County Circuit Judge Charles Price and a second South Alabama tobacco-related case in Mobile in which he'd also participated. In a letter entered into the record, Siegelman informed the court (see quote at top of chapter) that he would not accept fees from the Crozier case should it produce any. That same day he convened a press conference to announce the decision. He told reporters that "not one penny will be paid in legal fees to me from this case."

Also that day, Siegelman ended his association with Cherry, Givens. This hardly seemed a major sacrifice. The next spring, when he filed his ethics report for 1997, Siegelman reported revenues from the firm in the income range, "less than $10,000." He crossed that out and changed it to, "$10,000 to $50,000." This suggests that Siegelman's take that final year was insubstantial.

Within a week of repudiating claims on tobacco fees, Siegelman surprised no one by announcing his intent to run for governor in 1998.

Fast forward three years, to July 2000 and midway through Siegelman's second year as governor.

A young *Register* reporter, Jeb Schrenk, called the University of South Alabama to ask about a matter related to the university's hospitals. As Jeb remembers it, Gordon Moulton, Fred Whiddon's successor as university president, assumed Jeb had learned about a secret December 1999 settlement of the university's lawsuit against cigarette-makers. In truth, Jeb didn't know the first thing about it. But after Jeb's call, Moulton drafted a memo informing university trustees that it "was inevitable that this settlement would eventually be made public."

It was best to provide the facts to the paper and "continue our posture of openness with the news media," he wrote.

Moulton and other university officials took the unusual step of driving downtown to the newspaper to meet with the brass. During the meeting, they revealed that seven months before, the university had settled the long-forgotten 1997 lawsuit against Big Tobacco.

Under the terms of the deal, South Alabama was to receive $20 million over 10 years.

Twenty million? Why hadn't they told us? Told the world, for that matter.

That's what Jeb wondered. There's no such thing as a gift or grant to South Alabama that we don't hear about, whether it's them wanting a picture or a story, and for amounts nowhere near $20 million. What's more, the money was to help build the university medical school's much-ballyhooed cancer center. This was bragging time – pop the corks, call the press, and if the paper didn't put it on the front page, complain.

Instead, not a peep. For seven months. And maybe forever, had Moulton not mistook Jeb's question and assumed the reporter had learned about the settlement.

Before proceeding, a question. Some will know the answer, but even so, it bears asking for point-making purposes.

Who agreed to settle the South Alabama lawsuit and where was the $20 million to come from?

The tobacco companies, right? When parties settle lawsuits and the plaintiffs receive money, the defendants pay, right?

Scribble the answer on your hand or a scrap of paper or that little notepad in your brain. This is not optional. Do it.

———

So: Who agreed to pay $20 million to South Alabama, and where was that lofty sum coming from?

If you said the defendants – the tobacco companies – you would be wrong.

If you said the Siegelman administration chose to settle the lawsuit, with the $20 million coming from state coffers, you got it right.

As I knew from Jeb's and subsequent *Register* stories, including one I wrote, the $20 million settlement was orchestrated by the administration; it was kept a secret from the legislature and the public; and, the kicker, it contained a provision for South Alabama to route 14 percent of the settlement funds to the university's lawyers.

Fourteen percent of $20 million is $2.8 million.

The recipient of most of that $2.8 million was to be none other than Cherry Givens – one and the same as the firm that was now known to be paying in the neighborhood of $1 million to governor Siegelman.

That's why Phil Rawl's story rocked me that day in Bratislava.

It instantly registered as a potentially criminal act, a quid pro quo arrangement designed to funnel hundreds of thousands of dollars in state funds into the governor's pocket.

Siegelman, it appeared, had used his position as governor to assign public funds to a law firm that was in turn paying him. The wall between the quid and the quo -- the University of South Alabama – was for me rendered invisible by Jeb's story the previous summer outing the secret settlement.

Part of me couldn't wait to get back to Mobile, the sooner to commence a crash course on Siegelman's legal career, study the settlement, and shoot record requests to the administration.

Several things would need doing, among them the formation of a timeline. Especially important was the answer to the question: When did Siegelman negotiate and finalize his severance deal with Cherry Givens? Before the settlement with South Alabama? The same day as? After?

I knew the date of the USA settlement – Dec. 20, 1999. According to Carrie, Cherry Givens paid its first installment to Siegelman in 1999.

As will be seen, the first payment from Cherry Givens wasn't until 2000, but I had no way of knowing that at the time. As always, I had to rely on the latest information, ever mindful that if the source was Alabama's governor, facts were fungible and subject to change.

I knew the severance deal was negotiated after Siegelman's election. That placed it, at the earliest, more than a year after he ended his ties with the firm. That looked bad right there, but I wanted specific dates, not estimates.

When I returned I would want to request correspondence between the governor's office and the university regarding the negotiations leading to the $20 million settlement. Such correspondence would presumably indicate when the plan was hatched.

I would also want a copy of Siegelman's severance agreement with Cherry Givens. This was more problematic. It wasn't a public record, meaning I'd need to rely on Siegelman's nonexistent sense of public disclosure.

As a serial collector of ethics reports, I can say without reservation that I would have retrieved Siegelman's 2000 report first thing upon returning from vacation. The disclosure of more than $250,000 from Cherry Givens would have made the same impression whether I read it in the ethics commission lobby or on a computer screen in Bratislava. In other words, the legal fees stories would have been written regardless. But Siegelman's answers to Phil Rawl's questions as delivered by Carrie provided an invaluable starting point for my inquiries.

When pursuing certain types of stories, I visualize a room. Inside is the subject of inquiry. The room has at least two exits, one of which is forbidden. It represents guilt, whether of a potential crime or merely an egregious conflict of interest. All other doors represent innocence or, if not quite that, a lesser and more palatable degree of naughtiness. Metaphorically speaking, if the subject's only exit is the forbidden door, there's a story.

With the legal fees investigation I began with the thesis that the severance deal was in whole or part payback for Siegelman's use of the governor's office to arrange the $20 million settlement and the related $2.8 million fee.

For Siegelman, that was the forbidden door. Acknowledgement of a relationship between the USA settlement and the firm's payments to him was tantamount to confessing a criminal act.

I would need to test his explanation, as provided through Carrie to Phil Rawls, for Cherry Givens' decision to pay him in the neighborhood of $1 million at least two years after he cut ties with the firm.

To put it another way, I had to demonstrate that Siegelman didn't have an interest, referral or otherwise, in 20 to 30 cases still being litigated by Cherry Givens as of November 1998, when he was elected. If I refuted that tale, it would -- metaphorically speaking -- lock the door Siegelman claimed to have walked through when leaving the room.

The flipside was that if I found 20 cases, or even close to it, Siegelman's explanation gave him an acceptable out, no matter what I thought.

Had Siegelman been a hotshot lawyer, I might not have pursued the story. But he wasn't. He was a referral lawyer, nothing more.

In itself, there's nothing wrong with lawyers referring cases to other lawyers. Say an attorney has a long-time client seriously injured in a car accident, but the lawyer has little or no experience trying personal injury cases. If the lawyer were to pursue the case it might well be a disservice to the client. So to provide the client with better representation, the attorney refers the case to a lawyer who practices personal injury law.

Plaintiffs' lawyers work on a contingency fee basis, usually charging the 30 to 45 percent of the money collected for a client. When there's a referring lawyer, he or she gets a cut of that fee. Some lawyers, and generally it's the less talented ones, spend much of their time bird-dogging clients with strong personal injury or fraud cases, then referring them to lawyers more capable or willing to do the work.

In most respects, Siegelman was no more lawyer than astronaut. But he had a law degree and a license to practice. He was technically an attorney, and therefore, could reap referral fees.

But as previously noted, his ethics reports for period before he became governor suggested a modest income from the law, which for him was one and the same as referral fees.

Siegelman's 1994 report listed his employer as Cherry Givens, but didn't provide his income other than to report that it was more than $10,000. He also disclosed revenues from helping his wife sell cosmetic products by Utah-based Nu-Skin. Siegelman told a reporter at the time that he sold Nu-Skin only briefly, but continued to use it. "The products are wonderful," he said.

His association with Nu-Skin – a pyramid-style operation -- enhanced the Golden Flake element of Siegelman's reputation.

In 1995, his first year as lieutenant governor (a part-time position that paid an annual salary of $48,870) he again reported his employer as Cherry Givens, and disclosed income greater than $10,000 and less than $50,000.

The next year he reported income of between $50,000 and $150,000 from the firm. In 1997 – his last with Cherry Givens -- Siegelman, again, had checked the box , "$10,000 to $50,000." In 1998, a year that found him campaigning almost around the clock, Siegelman reported that he was self-employed – as in, not affiliated with any firm.

To summarize, Cherry Givens paid Siegelman less than $50,000 in 1997, and apparently zero in 1998. Then, presto, after becoming governor, the firm agreed to pay him nearly $1 million.

––––

Problem: How to test the 20 to 30 cases story?

Solution: Alacourt.

In addition to its primary value – allowing subscribers to plug in names and locate everything from lawsuits to criminal cases to traffic tickets – Alacourt has a mechanism for finding every case in which a lawyer made an appearance, and going back to the early 1990s. Punch in an attorney's name and you get his or her code. Punch the code and up comes every state court case, criminal, civil and otherwise, in which the lawyer participated.

If what Carrie said was true, Alacourt would show Siegelman with 20 to 30 cases still pending or resolved no later than late 1998. Presumably he'd have already been paid for cases completed prior to his becoming governor.

Alacourt came up, if not empty, damn close to it. The Siegelman name produced just a handful of cases in the 1990s. All had been resolved by the time he became governor, though I decided to research them anyway. For each I called the defense lawyers and, if I could locate them, the plaintiffs shown as being represented by Siegelman.

Though jumping ahead, here's how those findings were presented in our first story on Siegelman's legal fees:

For purposes of searching for cases that might still be active and generating fees, the Register focused on cases filed since 1995 in which Siegelman is listed as being one of the attorneys of record. That search showed two tobacco cases, including the USA suit, two wrongful-death cases, and a property dispute case in which Siegelman represented one of a host of defendants.

One of the wrongful-death cases, filed in Mobile County Circuit Court in 1996, was brought by Yolanda Roberts of Theodore, whose father died in an accident at the Alabama State Docks. She recalled that someone introduced someone, who in turn put her grandfather in touch with Siegelman.

She said she met Siegelman -- who was lieutenant governor at the time -- once. "He flew in, got there to the lawyer's office just in time, introduced us to Chris Peters, and told us that he (Peters) would be handling our case, and he had to rush out to fly to Birmingham," Roberts said.

Mobile attorney Jack Janecky, who defended the lawsuit, said he vaguely recalled seeing Siegelman's name on the case, but that's all. "I never saw him, I never heard from him," Janecky said. "Chris Peters did everything I remember. I never heard nor saw of Siegelman."

The case settled for $85,000 in 1997, according to Janecky and Roberts.

The only other non-tobacco plaintiff's case showing Siegelman's name and found on the state computer went to trial in Selma in 1997. The computer records show Siegelman among four plaintiff's lawyers with the Cherry, Givens firm who worked the lawsuit.

"I don't remember him having any involvement in the case. I don't know why he was on the pleadings, but I never saw him in court or in depositions," said Selma lawyer Rick Williams, who defended the lawsuit with his partner.

A jury returned a $100,000 verdict against Williams' client, but the Selma lawyer didn't believe that the Cherry, Givens firm has been paid. His client wasn't insured and, to his knowledge, hasn't been able to pay the judgment, Williams said.

I found one case – the one mentioned in the story by Yolanda Roberts -- that made money. Using the most generous scenario, Siegelman could have been paid a $15,000 referral fee from an $85,000 settlement, though $5,000 to $10,000 was more like it. And that payment would have presumably come in 1997, so it didn't qualify anyway.

The research indicated that Siegelman's clients – those folks he met briefly before handing them off to Cherry Givens – were themselves a political payoff, whether from unions, trial lawyers or others eager for his favor.

He was without the usual means of attracting clients. He had no track record, no ad in the paper, not so much as a shingle outside an office. He was a middle man, damaged people his chattel.

When I presented the Alacourt results to the governor's office as evidence that Siegelman hadn't been associated with anything close to 20 or 30 lawsuits I was in some small way bluffing. They could have diminished the impact of the research by noting that Alacourt isn't infallible, or claimed that most of Siegelman's cases were in federal court (though a search there didn't show anything either). Siegelman, through his press office, didn't say any such thing, nor did he provide with a list of cases to rebut my findings.

As I suspected, Alacourt presented a good snapshot of Siegelman's legal portfolio, and proved that the real bluffer was the governor.

Out of backwards bending fairness, I told readers that Alacourt has some limitations. "For example, it's possible that a county clerk could fail to put an attorney's name into the state computer, even though the pleadings might show the lawyer's involvement." Also noted was that referring lawyers are supposed to be listed as among the attorneys of record, but that's not always the case.

———

Separately, I reviewed Cherry Givens' partnership history, using secretary of state corporation and Mobile County Probate Court records. I wanted to make sure Siegelman had never been a partner in the firm. If so, it would support his position that he'd deserved a severance package of some size.

Partners, as the word suggests, are part-owners. They share in the expenses, such as for office rent and salaries and benefits for secretaries and paralegals. Siegelman, as confirmed later, bore no such costs at Cherry Givens, or anywhere else, for that matter.

Beginning in 1991 and lasting well after he lost the 2002 governor's race, the Alabama Sheriff's Association and its director, Bobby Timmons, provided Siegelman with a rent-free office and use of a secretary at its downtown Montgomery headquarters. The office served as his political headquarters and, to the extent he practiced law, his law office. He probably didn't even pay for paper clips. Timmons is a Siegelman crony from way back, and Siegelman was known to carry the association's water in the legislature – a violation of the ethics law if ever there was one, but so brazen as to seem normal, which perhaps it is on Goat Hill.

Because partners share costs and other responsibilities, they generally have a claim on a share of a firm's assets, including the potential value of unresolved lawsuits involving other lawyers. In most cases, a firm and exiting partner negotiate a severance package. Sometimes such negotiations get ugly, and the threat of litigation by a departing partner is a source of leverage for a partner on the way out. But the Siegelman name didn't appear once on Cherry Givens filings at probate court or the secretary of state going back to the firm's beginnings in the early 1990s. He had no such leverage.

Firm letterhead listed Siegelman as, "of counsel." That generally refers to a lawyer who isn't a partner but who has a loose affiliation with a firm. Of counsels are frequently semi-retired lawyers or those, like Siegelman, who don't practice full time. As an "of counsel," he didn't have a leg to stand on in demanding that the firm pay him a dime, much less the $800,000 to $1 million he received.

He wasn't and never had been a partner and hadn't contributed to the firm's overhead costs. What's more, if the firm felt obligated to open the bank for Siegelman, why not do it in October 1997, when he left? Why wait two years? This reasonable question was all the more relevant following the elimination of the 20 to 30 cases baloney.

For comparison purposes, I called John Lockett, an old friend of Siegelman's and a founding partner of what was for years called Cherry Givens Peters & Lockett. John was a major contributor to the firm, largely through his position as city attorney, an appointment that came from Mobile Mayor Mike Dow. That assignment produced considerable legal work for other lawyers in the firm in addition to John.

Lockett, widely respected as city attorney and now, as a Mobile County circuit judge, left Cherry Givens in June 1999, which he said was before Siegelman and the firm reached their agreement. For that reason and others John said he didn't know the details of Siegelman's severance package. Though he declined to put a dollar figure on his parting arrangement, Lockett said it was nowhere close to the sum Siegelman was reported to be getting. And John, it bears repeating, was a full-fledged partner of many years who shared in the firm's expenses and had a legitimate ownership claim to the firm's outstanding cases, including those involving tobacco. Yet Siegelman – the loosely associated "of counsel" – received far more than he.

The governor and Chris Peters could say that the $800,000 or so had nothing to do with the South Alabama settlement or other tobacco related litigation, but none of the other explanations for such a fee were bearing up under scrutiny.

———

After returning from Slovakia I resumed my inquiries on G.H. Construction, Mercedes and other previously plumbed matters, having decided to postpone the more explosive legal fee questions until concluding the research on Alacourt.

On July 9, I e-mailed Rip and Carrie, informing them that I'd read Phil Rawls' story and was looking into the governor's legal fees. I went straight to the chase, asking Siegelman to provide a copy of his severance contract with Cherry Givens. I wrote that the firm was a major beneficiary of the USA settlement that would not have happened were it not for Siegelman. I told them about the Alacourt findings and said it seemed unusual that Siegelman and firm waited so long to negotiate a severance deal.

I cited Siegelman's many public pledges to refuse payment from any tobacco lawsuits; wrote that it "would seem incumbent upon him to explain why he was to receive more than $250,000 this year (2001); and asked the governor to provide documentation of his arrangement." Also sought was the date that Siegelman and Cherry Givens signed the severance contract.

In another e-mail – again, actual conversations, per the unstated, unofficial rules, not permitted -- I reminded Carrie that she told Rawls that Cherry Givens was paying Siegelman in three installments, the first in 1999, the last in 2001. I told her that explanation seemed to contradict Siegelman's ethics filing for 1999, which reported a payment of between $150,000 and $250,000 from a single personal injury case, and with no reference to Cherry Givens.

"I'm hoping that the governor's responses can address this, and consider this another reason why a copy of that lump sum agreement would be so helpful in putting things in place. Let me know when I can expect something," I wrote.

How about never.

Had Carrie so responded it would have saved us both a lot of time, me from writing e-mails, her from reading them. The Rip Andrews incident, then only weeks away, merely made official the administration's pre-existing if unstated policy of refusing to provide meaningful responses to my questions and to withhold public records they deemed embarrassing.

The week before the story I sent an e-mail describing in detail what was coming Sunday and repeated my request for a copy of the severance contract. I tried to create guilt leverage by noting that Fob James had responded to questions about his finances by releasing his tax returns.

Thanks to the trusty computer in the comptroller's office, I'd learned that the administration had awarded Cherry Givens, and specifically Peters, a legal services contract with the Finance Department. By other means I found another contract, also arranged by the governor's office, for Peters to do work for the Alabama State Docks. Combined payments to that point came to about $160,000.

I reported those findings in the e-mail to Carrie and summarized campaign records showing that members of Cherry Givens contributed $65,000 to Siegelman's 1998 gubernatorial campaign and in 1999 pledged $90,000 to guarantee a loan to the lottery campaign (Not to be confused with the secret loan that involved HealthSouth and Scrushy. The loan guaranteed by Cherry Givens and others was properly disclosed, as was its repayment.)

All of the above, I told them, would be in the story.

"It is because of these relationships and questions that I feel the governor should be as forthcoming as possible about his finances as they relate to his legal career," I wrote.

Four days later they sent a response in the form of a press release, complete with bolded, underlined heading.

"Statement from the governor's press office in response to Eddie Curran's July 16 letter."

The governor has already disclosed more than is required by law.

The governor never received any money from the tobacco settlement. He will continue to voluntarily disclose any amounts he received from cases before he was governor on an annual basis as he has done since he has been governor.

Neither the date of the severance agreement was given, nor the amount paid as a result of it.

The statement ended with a diatribe excoriating Steve Windom, then me, for "asking the governor about a law firm he is no longer a member of." Its author opined that I should instead by quizzing Windom about his employment with his law firm of many years.

Instead of answering questions or turning over records they had tried to misdirect me, or in any event, readers, from the amount of and reason for Siegelman's legal fees and towards a powerless lieutenant governor who had not, as I believed Siegelman had, routed state funds in the neighborhood of $1 million into his own pocket.

———

We published two stories that Sunday, a mainbar on the front page and a shorter story inside that focused on the USA settlement. The mainbar began:

Since becoming governor, Don Siegelman has reported receiving at least $400,000 in income from a law firm he left in 1997, with more due this year. Thus far, however, he has declined to make public a copy of his contract with the firm.

As a result, it remains unclear why a firm would agree to pay a non-partner hundreds of thousands of dollars after he departed and why, if such an agreement were reached, payments would not begin until 1999.

Siegelman hasn't worked for the Dothan- and Mobile-based firm since 1997-- a year when the firm paid him between $10,000 and $50,000, according to his annual financial disclosures with the state Ethics Commission.

The Mobile Register sought the terms and date of the contract and other information about the governor's legal career and finances, because his actions taken as governor and possibly as lieutenant governor appear to have benefited the lawyers he once worked for.

At the time that Siegelman worked for the firm, it was known as Cherry, Givens, Peters & Lockett. In December 1999, Siegelman pledged $20 million in state funds over 10 years to settle an otherwise dormant tobacco lawsuit he and members of the Cherry, Givens firm had filed in Mobile in May 1997 on behalf of the University of South Alabama.

Essentially, the settlement authorized by Siegelman will provide $17.2 million for USA and $2.8 million for Siegelman's former firm, with some of that going to a separate, Birmingham-based firm, Whatley, Drake.

We reported that Siegelman "declined the *Register's* request that he identify any former cases in which he was associated or performed legal work and that generated the sort of money he's now being paid."

I provided Chris Peters and his Dothan partners with copies of the questions I'd sent to Siegelman, and requested responses, either by e-mail or interview. Keith Givens answered by fax that it was "not the practice of this law firm to disclose information about our clients or cases."

"To suggest that we turn information regarding these matters over to the press would not be appropriate. I'm sure you understand our position," Givens wrote.

I couldn't argue with Givens. It was Siegelman, not the firm, who had a public responsibility to clear the air.

There were, as often is the case with financial and political stories, complications, distractions of the type that allowed Siegelman to cloud the issue.

Of those, the most disingenuous was his claim that he'd taken a hands' off approach to the South Alabama settlement. "I refused to talk with the lawyers. I refused to talk to the university. I directed them to settle the case with the attorney general," he said after our first stories.

Siegelman had so washed his hands of the affair as to have Hosp sign the December 1999 settlement on his behalf, as if that made any difference.

Records unearthed later showed the governor ordered the settlement, and later, arranged special appropriations to route settlement funds to South Alabama. Each time the university received a payment it immediately sent a check for 14 percent of that total to Cherry Givens.

The second complication pertained to the purported legal basis for the $20 million deal.

While negotiating the national settlement, cigarette-makers insisted on a provision designed to prevent public entities – cities, counties, public hospital systems – from pursuing post-settlement lawsuits, and thus taking two bites out the apple. Should that occur, and succeed, any funds won by the local entity would be deducted from their state's share.

The federal judge in Mobile had seemingly killed off USA's lawsuit by ruling that the university couldn't sue the tobacco companies without the attorney general's approval. But in February 1999 – about a month after Siegelman was sworn in as governor -- the federal appeals court overturned that ruling. It didn't find that the university *could* go it alone, only that it was a matter for the state courts to decide. So the lawsuit was sent back to Mobile County Circuit Court.

For the university to proceed with the lawsuit, it still had to defeat Pryor in court to win permission to pursue the case.

The rationalization for the settlement, then, was that without it, the university would have pursued that fight against Pryor (not likely); won that battle (less likely); then pried tens or hundreds of millions of dollars from cigarette makers (not even slightly likely).

The administration and USA went to considerable lengths to win Pryor's blessing of the settlement.

After my first stories, Pryor told me the USA settlement was essentially a funding decision made by the executive branch, and no business of his office. Off the record, he said he was outraged to learn of Cherry Givens payments to Siegelman. Pryor did allow me to quote him saying that being lieutenant governor "obviously gave (Siegelman) prominence as an attorney that an ordinary attorney would not have had," in convincing USA to sue the tobacco companies and to retain him, Peters and Drake.

Pryor blessed the $20 million settlement after language was inserted stating that his office didn't "acknowledge the authority" of the university to sue the tobacco industry without his approval. Though a small matter to Pryor, for Siegelman, the attorney general's signature was akin to the Pope's blessing. It would become one of his primary defenses for the sanctity and general above-boardness of the settlement.

Because the tobacco companies were the defendants, they too had to sign off on the settlement. It doubtless didn't take much arm-twisting to convince them to do so. After all, they weren't paying the plaintiffs. The state of Alabama was!

––––

There was one more distraction, and it too bore the pain in my rear quality of complexity; of requiring research, explanation, and of course, additional length to the stories. Again, recriminations for not being a police reporter, with its corollary, easily comprehended and thus described elements like guns, bullets, wrecks, alive and dead. But no, I chose the world of bond issues, highway contracts and, here, something called Exhibit S.

As a term of the Master Settlement, the tobacco companies agreed to pay an estimated $12 billion in legal fees of the lawyers hired by the states to sue them. The states that sued submitted lists of the lawyers they retained and those lists were compiled as an attachment to the settlement called Exhibit S.

The states that didn't sue didn't submit such lists.

However, during negotiations over the Master Settlement the Ness Motley lawyers – major players in those talks – insisted that Alabama be permitted to submit designees for Exhibit S, with a provision that the sum due those lawyers be tiny. Relatively speaking, that is. From the perspective of most lawyers, Jack Drake, Chris Peters, et al, were about to share in the lottery. But in terms of the staggering sums awaiting lawyers from states that did sue, tiny's right.

The lawyers on Exhibit S were one and the same as those who'd brought the Crozier taxpayer lawsuit. They included Scruggs' firm and Ness Motley; and from Alabama, Jack Drake's firm, Cherry Givens, and Montgomery lawyer Bobby Segall – Siegelman's personal lawyer and the replacement for Jere Beasley, who had dropped out of the case.

It's my understanding – as in, I've never seen a record revealing it -- that about $7 million was paid to in 2000 to the lawyers on the Alabama list. Of that, the out-of-state heavy-hitters got half, with the Alabama lawyers sharing the rest, or an estimated $3.5 million.

Exhibit S shouldn't have muddied the waters because Siegelman publicly and officially removed himself from the Crozier case with his October 1997 letter to Judge Price and his emphatic statements to the press.

The Exhibit S distributions certainly didn't change these facts: That Siegelman promoted an unnecessary settlement projected to put $2.8 million in the hands of a law firm that subsequently paid him $800,000.

However, the Exhibit S/Crozier matter required telling and remained a distraction, especially, as will be seen later, when the ethics commission considered the Siegelman case.

———

The embarrassing alibi. You've heard them in countless movies and detective shows. "I couldn't have killed Drayton. I was in a hotel room in Santa Monica with my secretary. Must my wife find out?"

With his embarrassing alibi, Chris Peters acknowledged that Siegelman's story about having an interest in 20 to 30 cases wasn't true, so replaced it with another. I could hardly believe my ears – and couldn't contain my laughter – when the gravelly-voiced Peters presented the firm's justification for paying Siegelman by belittling him, essentially portraying Alabama's governor as a greedy, egotistical ambulance chaser.

His comments provided the lead to our next story, four days after the first. It began:

While breaking ties with his former firm, Gov. Don Siegelman argued he should be generously compensated for the wealth brought in by his name, Mobile attorney Chris Peters said.

"Don has never been shy about asking for money, or about the degree of prestige his name carries with it," Peters said, chuckling....

The firm's partners essentially agreed with Siegelman's argument that his name had contributed considerably to the firm's business, Peters said.

"When he won the election, we had to sit down with Don and take into consideration what he was leaving with us, and make a determination about what would be fair compensation," he said.

During his almost eight years with the firm, Siegelman's primary contribution came from generating personal injury cases, Peters said. He did this using his contacts within the same grass-roots groups that help in him politics, said the Mobile attorney. Those groups put Siegelman in contact with people who had been hurt, and he introduced those potential clients to the Cherry Givens firm, Peters said.

"As an originator of cases, Don was quite good, and we certainly appreciated it and he was well paid for originating those cases and there's nothing wrong with that," Peters said.

In his effort to clear the governor, the Mobile lawyer disrobed him.

As seemingly frank as Peters was on the subject of Siegelman's lawyering or lack of it, he said he couldn't remember even the general time period when Cherry Givens negotiated or signed the severance deal, and wasn't willing to refresh his memory with a short trip to his files. Peters and Siegelman knew I wanted to compare the date of the severance agreement with that of the USA settlement, and neither was going to help me do that.

I e-mailed Peters' description of Siegelman's legal talents to Carrie to give her boss the opportunity to respond. "Again, I think that if the governor is going to state that he actually practiced law, as opposed to acting as a rainmaker, then I think he would be able to provide some examples of his work. Like I explained, it would be real easy for a plaintiffs' lawyer to show work he's done, or point to a case (I'd go to whatever court if need be) that has evidence of him in a court or participating in the lawyering of a case."

Per the norm, the press office replied with a written statement.

"Before he became governor, Don Siegelman actively practiced law, both in and out of court. His legal experience, particularly as Alabama's attorney general, provided a unique perspective few attorneys have. The governor has never received any money from the tobacco settlement," the statement read, in its entirety.

We quoted Peters saying that Siegelman was neither a partner nor salaried associate but was paid on a per case basis for lawsuits he referred and that generated money. Siegelman, though, had demanded he be treated like a partner.

As Peters put it, the governor, "felt that he had a claim to an equity (shareholder) position, and he felt very strongly about that, and we felt that he had some kind of legitimate basis for that."

Demand or not, Siegelman had no legal standing for such a claim. Any such case would have been laughed out of court, and worse, brought political ruin on the governor.

Peters said Siegelman demanded more money than he received. Even so, the sum agreed upon was too large for Cherry Givens to pay in one year. The firm "had to have some time to pay him," Peters said.

The Mobile lawyer said Siegelman made a "major concession on his own volition" not to accept any money from the firm's work on tobacco lawsuits, even though Siegelman had done "actual lawyer work" on those cases.

What did he mean by "major concession?" Was Peters saying that Siegelman wasn't being paid for tobacco cases, but rather, in appreciation for not accepting tobacco money? And if so, what was the difference?

The conflicting explanations – the 20 to 30 cases, name value, a "major concession" -- had reached the point of absurdity, still without answering a simple question: Why was Cherry Givens paying the governor so much money?

———

On July 26, perennial Republican candidate and gadfly Jim Zeigler filed an ethics complaint against Siegelman that tracked our Sunday stories. That day, Siegelman told *Register* reporter Jeff Amy that he wouldn't be providing additional details about his finances. "I don't feel the need to do it," he said.

Siegelman said the severance package was based on his overall value to the firm, not on individual cases. "I argued my value was higher than they thought and we eventually settled on a number. It wasn't based on a case-by-case basis, so there's really not anything to reveal," he said, gutting for good and all time the 20 to 30 cases fairytale.

He repeated for something like the fifth time his October 1997 renouncement of fees from any tobacco cases. "Running for governor, it just wouldn't look right and it just wouldn't be right."

The ever-shifting story changed in another respect days later. Siegelman told the *Birmingham News* that Cherry Givens was paying him in two, not three, installments. He'd received about $400,000 in 2000 and was getting roughly the same that year (2001). That put the total at about $800,000, assuming – a large if – that this time he was telling the truth.

According to this revised version, the 1999 payment of between $150,000 and $250,000 was back to where he'd reported it on his ethics form – as a fee for a 1998 personal injury case, the payer someone other than Cherry Givens.

I didn't discover the surprising source and amount of that fee until August 2006, while reviewing exhibits after the trial. Siegelman's lawyers had introduced several bank statements from 1999 and 2000 to show jurors that Siegelman had plenty of money and thus, according to their argument, no need to ask Lanny Young for money, such as the $9,200 routed from Lanny to Nick to a check in Siegelman's wife's name.

Testimony was limited to the monthly balances, and the entire statements, while entered as exhibits, didn't become public until after trial. Among the attachments to Siegelman's June 1999 statement was a copy of a check.

It was for $319,474. The source: Jere Beasley's law firm, Beasley Allen.

I had to give Siegelman credit. For seven years he'd managed to conceal a $320,000 payment from the state's biggest plaintiffs firm made to him six months after he became governor.

First he'd reported under penalty of perjury on his ethics form to receiving a fee of between $150,000 and $250,000. He apparently couldn't bring himself to check the correct box – for income exceeding $250,000. After Phil Rawls called in June 2001, the personal injury case morphed into the first payment on a three-year installment plan from Cherry Givens. Now it was back to story one, give or take $70,000.

I called Beasley. He said Siegelman had referred a case involving a 16-year-old killed after being rear-ended by an 18-wheeler, and which was settled before trial.

One can only imagine how Siegelman got his hands on this can't lose cash-machine of a case. Certainly it wasn't because the teenager's parents heard the lieutenant governor was a terror in the courtroom.

My guess is that Siegelman lied to Carrie (Kurlander declined to be interviewed for this book), and she believed she was telling Phil Rawls the truth when reporting to him that Siegelman's 1999 payment was the first of three installments from Cherry Givens.

As a result of that story, the first time-line I made showed that Cherry Givens probably started paying Siegelman before finalization of the December 1999 USA settlement.

The revised timeline reflected that Cherry Givens didn't begin paying Siegelman until 2000 – definitely *after* the USA settlement. It also meant that firm and former "of counsel" waited at least 26 months after parting to enter into a severance agreement.

Why, after so much time, was Cherry Givens suddenly willing to pay Siegelman a sum approaching $1 million?

The answer – the only possible answer – was tobacco.

———

In three weeks I'd erased the 20 to 30 lawsuit explanation and for the first time, connected the South Alabama settlement with the governor's severance package. The research, stories and questions had forced Siegelman to move away from his initial, bogus explanations. He'd shown discipline by not succumbing to pressure and releasing his severance agreement. Far more irksome was the administration's failure to release what I suspected was a trove of correspondence on the USA settlement, all, in my mind, public record.

There was more to learn and report. I still knew precious little about the severance deal other than what had been revealed by people I didn't trust.

I wanted the terms, the date signed and by whom, the identity of the lawyer who'd helped Siegelman negotiate his severance contract with Cherry Givens -- wanted to know everything about the agreement. I wanted that baby in my hands.

It would all have to wait. Purgatory beckoned, and for this I had only myself to blame.

Chapter 15
The Phone Call

"Fuck you eight times."
-- *One of many obscenity-laced phrases shouted at Siegelman press aide Rip Andrews during July 30, 2001, phone call.*

"Mr. Andrews said Mr. Curran was excluded for being 'biased and unprofessional,' noting that Mr. Curran had yelled unprintable epithets at him in an argument. Mr. Curran later apologized in print for his language, saying it had been provoked when Mr. Andrews questioned his integrity. Mr. Andrews rejects this version of what happened."
-- *From Oct. 8, 2001, story in the New York Times bearing the headline, "Governors' Limits on Press Raise Concerns."*

Four days before the dumbest act of my career, Rip e-mailed to say he'd probably have most if not all of the records I'd requested on the South Alabama settlement, some bills on an unrelated matter, and asked when I planned to come up. Early the next week, I told him, and said I hoped to finish the story soon because of plans to take my son somewhere before school started. Where, I hadn't decided.

E-mailed Rip, "Do you and your son like to fish?"

"He really, really loves to, and I like to too, though I'm sort of a screw up at it. Wherever we go I was planning on doing some fishing. Got any ideas?"

"Yes, yes, yes!!" responded Rip. "Forever, my dad and I had been talking about going tarpon fishing. We finally, did it last weekend and it was fricin' amazing!"

Rip said he and his father caught two of the "best fighting fish in the world – they jump, dive, run at the boat, etc." They'd gone to Boca Grande, the famous Florida Gulf Coast tarpon fishing ground.

"If you are interested, let me know and I'll send you the name, # of our guide. He was awesome."

As the exchange reflects, after months of tough questions, Rip and I got along fine. Not all of our communications were so cheerful, but neither were we at each other's throats.

That weekend I e-mailed Rip to double-check the status of my records requests. I told him, again, that I was hoping to be shown "all the Finance Department's/ Governor's Office records, correspondence included, involving the negotiations leading up to the December 1999 settlement."

As of late Monday afternoon I didn't have an answer, so called him. This isn't verbatim, but is my best recollection of what was said:

Me: *Hey Rip. I'm driving up tonight and just wanted to check in and make sure y'all will have that stuff.*

Rip: *Well, we'll have some of it, but I'm not sure about the records on the South Alabama settlement.*

Me: *What do you mean? I've been asking for that for several weeks. This is ridiculous.*

Rip: *This is a game to you, isn't it, Eddie?*

Me: *What do you mean by that Rip?*

Rip: *I wonder if when you go to bed at night, if you lie there wondering if you're being used by Steve Windom.*

Me: *You fucking piece of rat-shit.*

I didn't time it, but five minutes became the official length. Like a bungee jump that seems to last longer than it is, three to four is more likely. But if you're really into it you can expel plenty of expletives in three minutes. There's no telling how many times I called Rip a "fuckinging piece of rat-shit." I suppose the phrase entered and locked into my subconscious because of the alliterative, monosyllabic similarities between Rip and rat.

My pent-up frustration from months of their lies and refusal to turn over public records, his subtly worded accusation that I was a pawn for Steve Windom and the implication (the bed-time imagery) that my conscience should be troubled kicked a switch. Rip's words registered as a grave insult. I should have told him as much in a stern but professional manner and hung up. Instead I damn near self-destructed. Not merely using profanity, but shouting it.

At some point I noticed city editor Dave Helms standing above me, ordering me to stop. But I couldn't. To bastardize Charlton Heston's famous don't touch my gun phrase, Dave was going to have to pry the telephone from my cold dead hands. Which is about what he did. As I came to my senses I realized that everyone in the newsroom was looking at me. They were in shock, and there was nothing I could say. It was over, and maybe I was too.

Within minutes of the tirade, I received the following e-mail:

Fuck you
Fuck you
Fuck you
Fuck you
Fuck you
Fuck you
Fuck you
Fuck you

It was from Joe Danborn, one of our many good young reporters and someone I considered a friend. It stunned me. It reflected extreme disappointment and more than that, anger. Had I been alone, I might have wept.

It wasn't until two years later, during a conversation with Bill Barrow, that I learned Joe was kidding. Bill was recalling how, in my tantrum, I'd said to Rip, "Fuck you eight times." Not the F-word eight times in a row – though possibly I'd done that as well -- but the phrase, "Fuck you eight times." This was news to me. At the time I saw just one explanation for Joe's e-mail – anger. I'd no recollection of, "Fuck you eight times." It's not in the repertoire. No clue where it came from. Like a drunk who forgets what happened the night before, I'd so lost control that I couldn't remember everything I said. "Fucking piece of rat-shit," I remembered, due I suppose to frequency of use.

While Joe was kidding, at least one of my co-workers didn't think it a joking matter. Jim Buckalew, Hamrick's replacement, wrote Bronson that I'd cursed at Rip "so loudly and for such a long time that one of your own reporters felt compelled to express his embarrassment the next time he called our office."

I'm fuzzy on what happened next. I remember walking into Mike's office and him shutting the door, which is never a good sign. I slumped into a chair, defeated. Other editors may have been there. I vaguely recall being told that I was this close to being fired, that if I ever did something like that again, I was gone, that I'd let the newsroom down, that the editors counted on my setting a good example for the younger reporters.

I told them what Rip said, but other than that, offered no defense because there was none.

Mike permitted me to go to Montgomery, but warned I was finished if I didn't behave. If Rip tried to goad me, I wasn't to respond. The warning was unnecessary. I was a lifeless blob, incapable of being provoked. The ferocity of the outburst had surged through me like an electric current. When the current switched off, I went limp. Stayed that way for days.

About once a year my temper detonates, though never like that at work. Targets have included two of my oldest friends, and it's always the same – I didn't see it coming, and for days, even weeks, I walk around in a cloud of shame and sadness.

———

I drove up to Montgomery that night, and the next morning, chose not to enter the press office, instead remaining in the reception area. Carrie and Rip killed me with kindness. Carrie pointed to wires protruding from a socket and made a crack about how ratty it looked. She could have pointed to a gorilla in a dress getting off the elevator. It wouldn't have mattered. My lone response was a nod.

They provided me with one record on the USA settlement, and not a bad one at that. It was a May 1999 letter from Chris Peters to Mabry that obliterated Siegelman's implausible claim of playing no part in the USA tobacco settlement.

The letter, attached to a copy of the proposed settlement, bore the heading, "Personal and Confidential." It was from Chris Peters to Henry Mabry.

The Mobile lawyer told the finance director that Siegelman had advised him that morning to be sure the proposed USA settlement "was in your hands as soon as possible."

Ted Hosp, said Carrie, had determined that everything else related to the deal was protected under attorney-client privilege. This was crap. The case was settled. It was no longer "pending litigation," to the extent it ever had been from the administration's perspective.

South Alabama hadn't sued the state, or vice versa. For that reason and more, records relating to an arrangement to spend $20 million in state taxpayer money should have been available for public review and it wasn't even a close call. But I was in no mood, and certainly no position, to complain. I took Hosp's decision as further proof that the USA deal was criminal and what's more, that Hosp knew it and participated in a cover-up.

Rip and Carrie showed me spending records on a contract that had caught my attention. I flipped through them, saw nothing of interest and handed them back. Captain Suspicious had come up empty. A little victory for the Siegelman team, a dash of salt in my wounds.

I ghost-walked out, never to return to the governor's wing of the Capitol while Siegelman remained its inhabitant.

———

Later that night, and this shouldn't surprise attentive readers, I sent a long e-mail to Carrie and cc'd it to Rip. I told her I'd "exploded on him;" had "basically lost it;" there was no excuse from my action; and I was ashamed and disappointed with myself.

Then—and sitting here, re-reading this gibberish, I'm embarrassed for myself – I took off on a long riff summarizing, not for the first time, my past stories on Fob James, my frustrations with their unwillingness to provide public records and saying no doubt more than they or anyone on earth cared to know about how and why Eddie does stories. And concluded:

I would advise Rip never again to make such a comment to a reporter, though I expect that most reporters, outraged though they would be, would show a lot more self restraint than I did.

For yours and Rip's information, I hope we can work in some fashion so that I can get the only thing I've ever wanted: Public records in a timely manner, and responses that address the questions I'm asking.

Once again, though, I sincerely apologize for my outburst. I am not only ashamed, but mad as hell at myself.

There were many things said about me during my coverage of the administration, most of which bothered me, if at all, only briefly. An exception was Rip's repeated denials of having said anything to incite me.

"Have been thinking about how to respond to this," answered Rip. "Basically, just want you to know that I do appreciate you sending this email to express your regret for what happened Monday night. I agree that what happened is regrettable. But, as I tried to make clear during our conversation, I didn't make any accusations. You're characterization of what I said to you Monday is way off-base. Most of it is made up."

Made up? I couldn't believe it, and wrote back asking him to "re-create, as close as you can, your word for word comments to me, seeing that you're claiming I made it up, and, I imagine, that you've probably said the same to Carrie as well."

Did I make up the part about you wondering about my thoughts as a lay down to bed? So you never uttered the words sleep and bed?

Did I make up the part about you wondering if I realized while lying in bed that I was being used by the Windom administration? Or did you never utter the name Windom?

What exactly did you say, Rip, and what did I make up? Now, Rip, as you know, feigned innocence or not, the going to sleep thing is a metaphor for someone's conscience, as in, guilty conscience.

Since you've accused me of making something up, though, please re-create what you contend you did say to me, or are you saying you didn't say anything at all?

He didn't respond. In late September, when we were compelled to write about my situation, Rip continued to deny my account of the call without offering his own.

In a press briefing called Wednesday to address the new records policy, Andrews denied making any remarks to Curran about the reporter being in league with Windom.

When Andrews was asked why Curran would invent such a story, Siegelman's chief of staff, Jim Buckalew, interjected: "Because Eddie's butt was on the line, that's the reason."

My first reaction was: Who does this Buckalew man, who I've never met, think he is talking about *my ass*?

Mike, as before, defended me. He told readers that my "professional integrity and temperament have never been questioned by sources before this episode."

"I am certain that Eddie's version of that conversation is dead-on accurate. Clearly, something angered Eddie."

Later, Rip told one of our new Montgomery reporters, Sallie Owen, that my recollection of the call was "wholly inaccurate."

Asked by Sallie if he'd mentioned Windom, Rip said, "I'm not going to claim to remember what the exchange was. You can't do that, that's why you tape record conversations."

Tape record calls to spokespersons when making inquiries about records? The notion was absurd. Had I done that, I could have proved Rip a liar. But considering the totality of the call, it's probably a good thing I didn't.

———

I wrote three stories in the week after the Rip incident, all of which I'd been working on for some time. One raised questions about the 1998 payments to Siegelman totaling $100,000 to $150,000 and which he'd reported on his ethics form as having come from six un-identified, "professional associations." I'd assumed he meant organizations like the sheriff's association that represent their members in the legislature.

After receiving my questions, Siegelman wrote Jim Sumner to amend his 1998 disclosure. He told the ethics director that he'd represented only one "professional association." That was the Alabama Sheriffs' Association, for which he told Sumner he, "proudly served as general counsel from 1991 until I was elected governor in 1998."

"The only compensation I received for my work ... was office space and secretarial support," he wrote.

General counsel? Lobbyist was more like it. And a free office and secretary is a considerable financial benefit, as any lawyer – especially solo practitioners – will tell you.

To clarify, the governor informed Sumner that the payments totaling between $100,000 and $150,000 were "intended to refer to my individual legal clients."

Replacing professional associations with legal clients created another quandary: Who were these clients? My guess, and it's only that, is that by professional associations, Siegelman meant law firms; and that six law firms gave him money, and by give, I mean give, as payback for his heavy lifting during the tort reform wars. A future chapter, "The $50,000 fee," may explain why I feel this way.

Another story reported legal fees on state bond issues totaling $137,500 paid to two small law firms, one headed by State Sen. Hank Sanders, the other by State Sen. Rodger Smitherman. This might have been a major story in another state, but not Alabama. It was a "par for the course" story on powerful state legislators bagging some state money. It was worth telling, not shouting about.

The third– and my last on the administration for two months – was a G.H. story. It reported that the company, or rather, someone acting in its capacity, had failed to take precautions to prevent erosion when clearing the wetlands-covered site. The state environmental agency was trying to fine the company and force it to clean up the mess but was having a hard time of it. No one, least of all Lanny, was even accepting mail for the now infamous company.

The next week, Mike Marshall told Jim Buckalew that he wouldn't be pulling me off covering the administration. Soon after, Siegelman's chief of staff reported back to Mike that there were serious additional issues regarding my behavior. His staff was compiling the evidence and anticipated presenting it to the paper in the coming weeks.

Mike told me not to worry, a directive I was emotionally incapable of following. He said it would be a good idea to hold off on Siegelman stories until this played out, which I thought reasonable.

Jerry and I took off for Florida. We followed Rip's suggestion, went to Boca Grande and splurged for a guide. We had a nice day on the water, but caught nothing. We did Disney World, fished off a few public piers, and took advantage of the Tampa Bay Devil Rays' woeful attendance to see a major league game in seats a few rows behind the dugout.

At the end of August, Rip was promoted to deputy press secretary. From that point on, Carrie shared quoting duties with Rip. She tended to take questions about legislation and the basic operations of government. He handled the scandal questions and delivered the broadsides against Windom and Riley, federal prosecutors and other bad people, such as myself.

Chapter 16

War

"Alabama Gov. Don Siegelman found himself going head-to-head with Mobile Register investigative reporter Eddie Curran, who brought to light records suggesting that Siegelman may have steered lucrative state contracts the way of his friends and relatives. After the series of stories began to undermine the governor's credibility, Siegelman retaliated by publicly denouncing the reporter's professionalism and tightening the reins around release of state records."

-- From Oct. 1, 2001, daily summary of news involving state governments throughout the country and distributed by State Net Capitol Journal.

"Late last month, Alabama's governor, Donald Siegelman, ordered all state agencies not to respond to inquiries from Eddie Curran, an investigative reporter for The Mobile Register. Shortly thereafter, the governor's staff announced that all news media requests for state records would be channeled through the governor's top legal aide."

-- Second paragraph in Oct. 8 New York Times story bearing the headline, "Governor's Limits on Press Raise Concerns."

On Aug. 17, Jim Buckalew sent the paper's publisher, Howard Bronson, the letter and attachment listing the seven charges against me. I immediately began building my defense, and updated Marshall on my progress.

"Eddie, again, this stuff from the Siegelman administration is pure baloney," he e-mailed back. "I know it to be pure baloney and we're just getting the straight skinny so we can show them what pure baloney it really is…. Howard (Bronson) is trying to get aholt of 'em now, so we can get back down to business. If you are feeling the tiniest qualm about our confidence in you, come see me quick, cuz you sure should not be."

His reassurance meant a great deal but didn't stop me from worrying. I asked accounting to pull my long-distance records from January through July to rebut count six: "Mr. Curran called Press Secretary Carrie Kurlander at her home on a Saturday night after 9:30 p.m., in a non-emergency situation."

I remembered two calls, both in early May, when I was writing G.H. stories almost daily. The first was on a weeknight. She'd had to go home early, gave me her number, and told me to call her at home, which I did. I remembered a Saturday night call, but was sure it hadn't been that late. I combed through pages of bills – I'd been making upwards of 250 long distance calls a month, with some 450 during a three-week period on the Honda stories. I'd been a dialing machine.

I found three calls -- the one on the week-night and another on a Saturday afternoon that lasted a matter of seconds, indicating we hadn't spoken. The third was on a Saturday night, but at 6:15, not after 9:30. I'd called five other numbers after reaching her, and several before. This was during a time when I was working seven days a week damn near around the clock, and no doubt bothering many people.

I didn't consider Carrie to have lied, just figured she was so sick of dealing with me that months later, during find-bad-stuff –about- Eddie time, the call seemed later than it had been. Still, citing the call as a reason for refusing to deal with me was laughable. No paper is without a list of the home numbers of public officials and spokespersons, and people in such positions are or should be accustomed to the occasional home call from reporters.

Marshall released me to resume coverage of the administration in late August. Soon thereafter I e-mailed Carrie seeking records for a follow-up on the computer services contract with Quality Research I'd written about in June.

Carrie responded, not to me, but to Paul Cloos. She informed him that "this matter" – an obvious reference to my situation – was "being discussed by the governor's chief of staff and your boss."

"Until that discussion is resolved, I will not be responding to this inquiry," she wrote.

I'd sought public records, not comment. Her response implied a blank refusal to give me records, as opposed to the past policy of pretending they didn't exist or couldn't be found.

Paul put his name on my next request, sent two days later, for the Mercedes records we'd been seeking for months.

As far as we were concerned, "this matter" was resolved. But the administration couldn't accept that their attempt to erase me from the pages of the *Register*, or in any event covering them, had failed. And they were not giving up.

On Sept. 2, the station wagon and I made our first trip to Montgomery in five weeks. The shopping list included records at the Finance Department and the Department of Public Safety – the agency that employs state troopers and oversees driver's licenses. I planned to review records pertaining to Public Safety's decision to transfer a computer services contract from a company called Advanced Systems Design (ASD) to one called Digital One Services.

I knew exactly what to ask for thanks to my anonymous source, the so-named, Bob. I specifically mentioned correspondence between Public Safety and Mabry reflecting the finance director's role in the decision to switch a major contract from ASD, which had won plaudits for its work, to Digital One, which at the time of its selection had zero employees.

I also e-mailed James Bryce, head of the Finance Department's technical operations, seeking other records involving ASD and similar companies. We spoke and scheduled an appointment for Wednesday.

So far, so good.

On Tuesday morning I went to Public Safety expecting to see the records I'd been told would be available. Doris Teague, a long-time spokeswoman for the agency, sheepishly told me that the agency's director, James Alexander, had ordered her not to give me the records. Why, she couldn't say.

I told her I'd pop out a second request, this time tacking on the public records law – something I didn't like doing unless I felt it necessary. Better, always, to keep things informal. Adding the law might be a good idea, she said.

That afternoon Bryce e-mailed to say he was busy and had to cancel the next day's appointment. I e-mailed back, offering to remain in Montgomery until the end of the week, but received no response.

At day's end I called Paul Cloos and told him that something unusual was going on.

The next day began with a visit to the finance department's Office of Debt Management, and Pat Haigler, who runs it. This small operation maintains records on state bond issues, including expenditures from the hundreds of millions of dollars raised each year through such deals. I didn't call ahead, which wasn't unusual for my relations with that office. Pat had to go somewhere, so it was agreed that I'd return in an hour to review records I hoped would answer my Mercedes questions.

Upon my return, Pat -- more serious than I'd ever seen her – said she'd been told by Mabry that all requests by me to view records were to be forwarded to the governor's legal office.

I returned to Public Safety, hoping the records law citation had brought them to their senses. It hadn't. As had Pat, Doris told me that under orders from Mabry, all records request from me were to be sent to the governor's legal office. I told her this was happening everywhere and that it was unbelievable. Doris, in a tough spot, acknowledged that she'd never been given an order like this, and said this particular policy applied to one reporter, me.

I called Paul and told him it was weirdo time in Montgomery, that people were refusing to give me records, and something had to be done.

––––

On Sept. 13, Buckalew drafted two memos. With the first, the chief of staff informed Marshall that in addition to refusing to take my questions, the administration wouldn't provide answers or comment to anyone "serving as Mr.

Curran's surrogate or representative." The directive applied to all state agencies under the governor's control.

Paul, for example, couldn't ask a question on my behalf to the highway department. We were directed to include the following statement in every story by me on the administration:

"Due to the bias and unprofessional behavior of this Mobile Register reporter, the Governor's Press Office does not respond to his requests. While we respect the Mobile Register, its other reporters and its editors, we regret the paper's decision to endorse Eddie Curran's unprofessional behavior. Among other inappropriate actions, Mr. Curran cursed a member of the governor's staff for almost five minutes, repeatedly calling him a 'fucking piece of rat shit.' Such behavior is inappropriate and unprofessional. We will not dignify it by continuing to communicate with this reporter."

Lastly, Buckalew stated that all requests for records by me to the administration or state agencies would be forwarded to Ted Hosp.

Buckalew's second memo went to heads of and public relations officers at state agencies. They were told to forward "all requests for public records that your agency receives from the media" to Hosp.

"Mr. Hosp will work with members of the media to ensure that any and all public records relevant to a specific request are provided in a timely manner," wrote Buckalew.

The administration had, on the surface, put into place a mechanism requiring that every records request from every reporter in Alabama and to almost every state agency be routed through the governor's lawyer. Then they kept it a secret from every newspaper but one – us.

They had failed to eliminate me with the seven charges, gone back to the drawing board, and devised a replacement strategy: Make it impossible for me to cover them.

Might the paper, faced with the prospect of a quote-less reporter and the demand that we reveal my use of "fucking piece of rat-shit," choose surrender, and remove me from the Siegelman scandal beat?

If that's what they expected, they were wrong. My people stood behind me. If the administration wanted a fight, they were about to get one. It was lawyer time.

———

Just sue 'em. Draft up a lawsuit, file it, kick their ass.

It ain't that simple. Not, in any event, if you've got lawyers who're serious about what they're doing, the case being contemplated is complex, and the target defendant is a lawyered-up governor.

I was humbled that Mike and Mr. Bronson and the folks at Newhouse found my situation serious enough to spend no telling how many thousands of dollars in legal fees challenging the administration and working on a lawsuit that, in the end, was never brought. And for that, thank goodness.

Almost being a plaintiff ate up much of my time for about seven weeks. Had I become one, my new job would have entailed preparing for depositions, mine and others. Just drafting a lawsuit of this magnitude required untold hours writing narratives of my dealings with the administration and many more gathering e-mails to and from Carrie, Rip and others. These had to be attaching to the narratives, by date and subject matter, like exhibits in a court filing.

Many days were spent at Ed Sledge's downtown Mobile law firm, McDowell, Knight, Roedder & Sledge, usually across a conference table from Ed's bright younger partner, Archie Reeves. Archie reviewed the mountains of records I provided, discussed them with me and fashioned several versions of a lawsuit. I was impressed throughout with the care and caution they brought to the task. Ed and Archie had no intention of suing the governor of Alabama if there was even a chance of losing.

While our efforts never produced a lawsuit, they gave Ed grist for several strongly worded letters laying out the administration's failure to produce records I'd been seeking for ages. I think the threat of a lawsuit and the weight of Ed's reputation on a younger lawyer like Ted helped us win the day. Or in any event, got me back into the reporting business. Not right off, but eventually.

————

I wasn't thrilled at being the subject of a story airing charges of drinking, using foul language and the rest, but accepted that we had no choice. We would be playing charades with readers to report in every story under my byline that the administration declined comment without giving their reason. We had to face it head on, and did, on Sept. 22. An unfortunate Jeb Schrenk drew the assignment.

The allegations discussed previously, including cussing out Rip and those arising from the night drinking in the Statehouse, won't be re-hashed here. All, though, were presented in the story.

One charge was similar to the allegation of me calling Carrie late on a Saturday night. It read: "After having the opportunity to interview members of the governor's staff for hours, Mr. Curran continued a pattern of harassment against certain staff members, including calling Nick Bailey once after midnight."

I have no idea what they meant by a "pattern of harassment," and doubt they did either, since if there was a specific example they'd have used it, such as with the Saturday night call to Carrie and "calling Nick Bailey once after midnight."

That, I did. I was frustrated at his refusal to answer questions on new revelations regarding the G.H. mess. I was working late one night and on a whim, and around midnight, called Bailey's home number and left a message on his machine. I was wrong to have called so late.

In re-reading the story for this book, I was alarmed to see we reported that, "Curran remembers no such late-night call to Bailey." I can only assume that, as the least serious charge, it received the least attention. For good cause I wasn't allowed to proof the story, but if so, I'd have caught that one. I don't see where we corrected the error, and can't recall why not but will accept fault. In any event, the story was wrong on that point.

The piece presented, for the first and only time, the entire statement the administration asked us to use in stories beneath my byline. Being a family paper, we omitted a few letters from the offending language, but, "fucking piece of rat shit," left little to the imagination.

"Eddie should not have lost his temper. He has apologized, I've apologized, so now it's time for everybody to get back to work," Marshall was quoted saying.

He called the administration's other allegations "distortions of reality, and most of them are of such trivial significance that I'm surprised they bothered raising them."

Most embarrassing was charge five: "Mr. Curran once commented to Mr. Hamrick about the breast sizes of women working in the Governor's Press Office."

I had to let Carrie and her staff know that I'd not said the first word about anyone's breasts. I wrote her an e-mail in which I confessed to having made "a sort of kidding comment to Paul (Hamrick) that he'd sure hired a good-looking staff, or something to that effect," and described it as, "one guy sort of needling another."

During the call, which would have been in or about March, I may have used the word, "babes," or something equally corny. I remembered it, primarily because of Hamrick's response. He hadn't laughed, instead responding tersely that Carrie hired the staff.

My comment was in some way a reflection of Fob James' media team, which was distinctly grey-haired and led by Alfred Sawyer, a bald, 55-ish Episcopalian minister.

"To the extent that you and your co-workers think I made a comment on anyone's anatomy, I would somehow hope to convey to them that I did not make any such comment," I wrote. "They seem like a nice group and I certainly meant no offense in describing them as attractive."

Months later, and to my considerable horror, Mike told me that Hamrick had accused me of using the word, "titties."

———

Four days later we published a story that kick-started a month-long battle between the administration and the state's leading newspapers. Jeff Amy's report revealed the contents of the second of Buckalew's two Sept. 13 memos, the one directing state agencies to forward media requests for records to Hosp.

Hosp told Amy he knew little about the policy and referred questions to Buckalew. Hosp, I heard later, hadn't sought and didn't want responsibility for reviewing every public records request from the media to every state agency, and who could blame him.

The story included portions of a letter sent the day before by Ed Sledge to Hosp and Buckalew in which Ed presented examples of long-delayed records requests and demanded that the records be "immediately provided." The policy of referring records requests to Hosp was "another example of foot-dragging by the administration."

"These are just a few of what appear to be many violations of the Alabama Open Records Act," wrote Ed. "The public has a right to know from the records of state government how our government is functioning. Currently, the state is violating both the letter and spirit of the Alabama Open Records Act."

Mike Marshall told readers the paper was "absolutely" considering a lawsuit against the administration; and called the policy a "clumsy attempt" to keep me from getting records.

The AP picked up Jeff's story and added one of their own, quoting top Republicans criticizing the policy.

The Alabama Republican Party, God bless 'em, issued a press release that could have been written by my mother. I was described as "an excellent investigative reporter" who "uncovered wrong-doing without partisanship."

"The Siegelman folks and Democratic leadership have been caught a number of times with their hands in the cookie jar," stated party chairman Marty Connors. "Now they are attempting to discredit the reporter who caught them. Everyone sees through that."

The *Birmingham News* quoted Siegelman saying there was no connection between the new policy and the situation with me. "That is a different matter. I have a policy against abusive language. That policy, in my mind, is disconnected from this one."

Ed Mullins, chairman of the University of Alabama's journalism department, told the *News* that the run everything through Hosp policy was probably unworkable and appeared "like it started as a vendetta against one reporter." Other stories quoted editors and political science professors throughout the state. None bought the claim that the new records policy was unrelated to the administration's fight with us.

Another story contained a troubling revelation. Hosp told Amy that he'd always examined "big files" or "whole files" prior to letting reporters see them. Since January 1999 he'd screened "in the neighborhood" of 25 to 50 such requests to remove material that shouldn't be released.

The notion of Siegelman's lawyer culling records prior to handing them over to reporters and failing to disclose that documents were removed was disturbing. "Embarrassing to the governor" is not a basis recognized in the law for withholding records, though I've little doubt the administration considered it so and acted accordingly.

As soon became clear, the administration had committed a blunder in what at its core was a battle against me and the *Register*. They'd recruited every major newspaper in the state to our team. The policy could impact them as well, so naturally, they raised hell too.

The governor, as well as his new policy, took a pounding in the state's editorial pages.

"Trying to put a good face on the Siegelman administration's new policy on public records requested by reporters is like trying to use make-up to turn Frankenstein into Brad Pitt," opined the *News*.

A *Montgomery Advertiser* editorial warned that funneling media records request through the governor's lawyer "could dam the flow of public information in a way that would seriously hamper the efforts of the state's news reporters to inform the public about the workings of state government."

———

In late September, I dashed off a memo to Paul, Dewey and Mike suggesting solutions to the stand-off and presenting my views of the people we were dealing with. With years of hindsight at my disposal, there's not much I'd change. Here's most of it:

Don Siegelman has been in politics since he was about three.

To Siegelman, losing the next election would almost be worse than death. It could prove the death knell of his political career, and he knows it. He is desperate to win, much as a man held underwater is desperate for air, and will do anything to get air.

Our stories have exposed activities by his administration that have greatly harmed his chances of being re-elected, and have given his opponents plenty of ammunition to attack him in ads and such when the campaign heats up. Also, some of his associates, and maybe even him, could be indicted because of our stories.

As a result of questions and public requests I now have outstanding, Siegelman and his advisors know that I/we are on the verge of publishing more such stories. There may be other deals and such that he is aware of, and that, if exposed, would damage him even more. He and his advisors, and my guess is those advisors now include at least one white collar criminal defense lawyer, have already made a decision: better to take our lumps for not providing information than to provide information and really get slammed.

The Siegelman administration, then, is willing to weather some real heat before it will surrender these records ... The administration, right now, is hunkered down, fully expecting, and scared of, the lawsuit that they think the Mobile Register is about to file against them. They rolled the dice by accusing me of drinking to incite non-drinker Howard Bronson, and failed. And without sounding arrogant, they're scared of me and scared of what they know I know.

I urged a return to writing stories. I reminded them of the success in May, when the combination of Ed Sledge's letter to Hosp and our story on their refusal to turn over the G.H. contracts led to the production of those documents.

I'm not saying that we use stories to wage a public relations war, or that we print propaganda, but simply that we take charge of this situation by doing what we do.

Well, if they won't give us records, we write a story on the subject anyway, making it very clear why we can't provide all the information we and the readers need to decide what happened here. Also, we make sure the administration knows that we're going to write the full story – making it two stories rather than one – when and if we do get the records. They might start deciding it's better to get their medicine in one lump rather than two, and to avoid the hit for refusing to turn over the records.

This strategy means that we will have to write a number of incomplete stories. That is not our fault, and we make that clear to the reader. If nothing else, these stories will make it clear that the Mobile Register is trying, and waging the good fight to give them the facts of how tax dollars are spent. The failure of the stories to provide all the facts will be clearly laid on Don Siegelman's doorstep. One after another after another. His failure to provide records, then, becomes its own scandal, and a recurring scandal, and in my mind, it damn well is a scandal.

It worked. On Oct. 7, I was freed to write my first story about the administration in more than two months. It bore the headline, "State withholds documents on Mercedes plant project," and began:

On April 3, the Mobile Register filed a public information request with the Alabama Department of Transportation and the Siegelman administration seeking records on an estimated $14.4 million construction project to prepare land for the expansion of Mercedes-Benz's Tuscaloosa County plant.

To date, not a single record or document has been provided in response to that request and subsequent related requests.

As a result, it remains unanswered how much the state has paid or will pay for ongoing Mercedes work, under what terms the work has been done and what negotiations or processes led to those arrangements.

The piece summarized previousl findings on EPM's no-bid work at Honda and the administration's decision to give the Mercedes job to the same company without taking bids. Readers were told that the paper began seeking the Mercedes records in February, well before we made a formal request in April.

We reported having asked many times for the state's contract with EPM for Mercedes; payment records to the company; and correspondence files involving the highway department, the governor's office, EPM and Mercedes. Readers were given an example of one of many e-mailed requests for the Mercedes records.

The story illustrated in a straightforward manner my efforts to obtain public records and them at their dodgy best, refusing to comply with the laws requiring production of those records.

———

On Oct. 8, the *New York Times* published a story about our fight with the Siegelman administration and a similar conflict between Minnesota Gov. Jesse Ventura and that state's media.

"Relationships between governors and the reporters who cover them are seldom smooth," began the piece by Felicity Barringer. "Shouting matches or official cold shoulders have been part of the landscape from Annapolis to Tallahassee to Sacramento. But in Alabama and Minnesota, chief executives have gone to unusual lengths to keep information from reporters or news organizations that have fallen from favor."

I was glad to see that it placed my outburst in the broader context of the sometimes combative relations between reporters and public officials, though I dare say my "shouting match" was on the extreme end of the scale. The editor of the *Cleveland Plain Dealer* told the *Times* that Siegelman's decision to funnel all media requests through his lawyer was "unheard of."

Rip handled quoting duties. He said the new policy was instituted to "facilitate the production of records;" and that the decision to have the governor's lawyer review all media requests was unrelated to our paper. After which, Barringer quoted *Huntsville Times* editor Joe Distelheim saying that the link between the policy and the *Register* was "unmistakable."

Had Rip been honest about his contribution to my outburst it might have diminished the administration's justification to cease answering my questions, but I never disputed their right to quit talking to me. Had another reporter exploded with equal ferocity at spokesperson for a local official, a similar ban might well have resulted.

———

Of the seven charges, one troubled me more than the others combined. It was the accusation that I conspired with Jim Zeigler in bringing his ethics complaint. File this one under, "No good deed goes unpunished."

The last straw was seeing this in the *Times* story:

"Aside from the outburst, Mr. Andrews said, Mr. Curran had shown bias by 'editing' an ethics complaint filed against Governor Siegelman by a political opponent. Seeking comment, Mr. Curran had faxed the governor's office a draft of the complaint, bearing two scrawled question marks and some highlighting. When the final complaint was filed, the governor's staff contended that Mr. Curran had edited it."

A charge like that in a newspaper as widely read as the *New York Times* posed a threat to my livelihood. The next day I wrote a letter to Carrie, Rip, Hosp, Siegelman, Jim Buckalew and Boots Gale, and which I ran by my editors before sending. It didn't contain a threat of litigation but perhaps implied as much. It must have worked, as the administration never again repeated the allegation.

I wrote that Andrews and Kurlander – for this was a last names sort of letter – had "made the Zeigler charges in their roles as spokespersons, and have on some occasions stated to Alabama reporters that I assisted Zeigler in writing the complaint."

"Last week, Andrews repeated these charges to a reporter for the *New York Times*. I like to think I could have cleared up these misconceptions on your part had one of you merely taken the time to call or write me. Because you continue to make these charges against me, and in such public forums, this seems like a good time to once again tell you my side of this affair, unsolicited though it is."

Exhibit one in my defense was, well, Jim Zeigler.

In 1974, at age 25, the former president of the University of Alabama Student Government Association ran for a spot on the Alabama Public Service Commission, and won. This marked him as a young star on the rise. Zeigler, though, was already on the cusp of his legendary losing streak. Halfway through his term, he ran for chairman of the PSC, and lost, as he did in his next race, for the Alabama Supreme Court. His record in statewide elections is now one and seven.

Zeigler's second claim to fame is as a serial filer of ethics complaints and taxpayer lawsuits – as Alabama's best known political gadfly. As likeable as he is eccentric, Citizen Jim struck first in 1983, when he brought an ethics complaint against attorney general Charlie Graddick and sued state auditor Jan Cook. He subsequently became the driving force behind the Taxpayer Defense Fund, which existed to file ethics complaints and taxpayer lawsuits.

Two days after our stories on Siegelman's legal fees, Zeigler faxed the paper a press release to my attention. Attached was a copy of a taxpayer lawsuit, Zeigler as plaintiff, demanding that Siegelman refund to the state the legal fees paid him by Cherry Givens. Zeigler declared his intent to file the lawsuit two days later. Paul and I agreed it was either a non-story or, at most, worthy of a graph or two in our next story. In keeping with my near obsessive full-disclosure practice with the administration, I e-mailed Carrie and Rip. I told them of Zeigler's plans and that we considered it a non-event.

Two days after that, Zeigler left me a voice mail saying he'd decided against suing Siegelman. He was about to drive to Montgomery to file an ethics complaint, a copy of which, he said, had just been faxed to the paper. Far as I can tell, neither citizen's lawsuits nor ethics complaints have much chance of bearing fruit, but given the choice, an ethics complaint is the smarter call. The administration later sought to link me to this decision that was made, far as I know, solely by the most prolific filer of ethics complaints and taxpayer lawsuits in state history.

An ethics complaint was more of a story than a citizen's lawsuit, but in large part because of who was filing it, we decided not to make a big deal of it, and to run it on an inside page. Regardless of the strength of a complaint, if brought by Zeigler it's subject to attack.

As always when reviewing documents, I read the complaint with pen in hand, circling this, underlining that, scribbling stars, making question marks and check marks, what have you. I do this to prevent having to hunt for the important bits when it comes time to write. I made markings on four of the six pages. Those on one page generated the bulk of the case against me.

As previously explained, Cherry Givens was receiving fees from South Alabama by way of the Siegelman-authorized state tobacco settlement; and, separately, from placement on Exhibit S of the national settlement. For the last one, we had reported that the firm was due an unknown share of the estimated $7 million fee to be split among a host of in and out of state law firms.

Page four of Zeigler's complaint contained an allegation that Siegelman used his public position to ensure Cherry Givens placement on Exhibit S; and stated that "the firm gained $2.8 million" form placement on Exhibit S.

Lower on the same page, Zeigler wrote that the firm "gained $2.8 million" from Siegelman's "manipulating the $20 million settlement for USA …"

As I explained in my letter to Siegelman, Carrie, Hosp and the others, I "noticed that Zeigler's complaint included the figure $2.8 million in two different places, and representing two different sums of tobacco related legal fees."

Upon seeing this, I circled each $2.8 million, connected them with a line, then scribbled two question marks. Back to the letter:

Though I think I'm pretty familiar with both the tobacco cases, I have never been told, nor seen it reported elsewhere, that any of the several firms slated to share in what has been estimated as a $7 million fee was to receive $2.8 million or, for that matter, any specific amount. It's an unknown, at least to me.

Did Zeigler get this from somewhere else? Or did he have it confused with the other $2.8 million. As I've probably stated to you on many previous occasions, I consider it my job not merely to present numbers, facts and comments as presented to me, but to do my best to make sure those numbers, fats and comments are indeed correct. The purpose being: Don't given the reader bad facts.

I needed comment from Zeigler and the governor's office. I figured Zeigler, driving to Montgomery, would be in cell phone dead zone (there were many of those in 2001), so put off calling him. As for Siegelman, how could he respond to an ethics complaint he hadn't seen?

I e-mailed Carrie, informing her that Zeigler had changed his mind on the lawsuit, was on his way to Montgomery to file an ethics complaint, and had faxed us a copy. "I'd be glad to fax you this complaint. In any event, would want to get some kind of comment."

She took me up on the offer, and I faxed her the evidence against me.

I waited a couple of hours to call Zeigler, though not long enough. Had I waited a few extra minutes, all this nonsense could have been avoided. When I reached him, he'd just parked his car outside the commission. I was nearing deadline and asked if he could answer a few questions while I had him on the phone.

My main question: Was the first $2.8 million, the one described coming from Exhibit S, correct? Was it possible he got that mixed up with the $2.8 million fee from the USA deal?

Jim said something like, "Oh, you're right. I'll have to change that."

His response immediately registered as trouble. I'd sent Carrie my marked-up copy, and now, prior to filing it, Zeigler was going to change it based on a question I'd asked.

He said he had a laptop and a portable printer and could fix the complaint right there in his car. I concluded by asking him to call me after he filed it, in the event the commission was closed or he got run over crossing the street. I didn't want to report an ethics complaint against the governor if one hadn't been filed.

Our story the next day quoted Zeigler calling his complaint the "first step in the impeachment of Don Siegelman."

Like the pea under the princess, Zeigler's decision to alter the complaint based on my question continued to trouble me. So – another grievous error – late that afternoon I dashed off an e-mail to Ted Hosp, explaining what happened and telling him I "didn't want you think I was conspiring with this guy to assist him on his ethics complaint. I can promise you that I did not."

It may be that my paranoia did me in, that they would not have noticed the changes and my markings had I not e-mailed Ted.

Jeb's story on the seven charges contained the allegation on the Zeigler matter and brief denial from us. Now, the public records battle between the paper and the administration was at a boil, and Rip and Carrie, when commenting to reporters, started pointing to the Zeigler allegation to sully me and the paper.

Zeigler, to my dismay, entered the fray again. He brought a citizen's lawsuit accusing the administration of violating the open records law by refusing to give us records. Of the suit, Carrie told the *Birmingham News*: "This is what we expect from a guy who conspired with the *Mobile Register* to write an ethics complaint against the governor. True to form, he's at it again."

A few days later, commenting for a story in our paper, Rip said, "I just think that it's unfortunate to see that the *Mobile Register* continues to sacrifice its credibility in creating these tabloid headlines in an attempt to cover up one simple fact, which is that one of its reporters edited an ethics complaint against the governor."

Because of the administration's focus on the Zeigler case, the editors decided to do another story, this time addressing only that charge, and in more detail. In his back and forth with the administration, Jeb learned of two new incriminating pieces of evidence, the first, as presented here in his story:

Andrews said an e-mail Curran sent Ted Hosp, Siegelman's legal adviser, also points to Curran's involvement.

After Zeigler filed the complaint, Curran sent the e-mail explaining that Zeigler amended his complaint. The change dealt with the $2.8 million figure. Curran said he sent the e-mail to assure the administration, which had already received the copy with Curran's notes, that he did not intend to help Zeigler.

Curran's e-mail references the $2.8 million figure and states Zeigler "called me back later after he filed it. ... He said he had his laptop and changed the thing."

Andrews said Curran's comment about the laptop is not consistent with the fact that the notes (corrections) Zeigler made were handwritten.

They were saying that the order of my sentences in my e-mail to Ted proved the conspiracy or in any event, supported it. I can only suppose that in my haste, the bit about changing the complaint on his laptop entered my brain after the part about him calling to report that he'd filed the complaint. The sole purpose of the second call was for Zeigler to confirm he'd filed the complaint. It lasted, maybe, five seconds. He didn't say anything about the manner in which he'd corrected the complaint, nor would it have crossed my mind to ask or care.

As it turned out, Zeigler changed the incorrect first "$2.8 million" by hand, not with computer and printer, as he'd told me he intended do and as I'd told Ted. Therefore, I'd lied.

Their theory failed to explain why my co-conspirator would call me after filing the complaint to report that he'd made the changes with computer and printer if he'd done so by hand. Nor did it suggest a motive for me to declare that Zeigler made the change with a printer if he hadn't, or why I'd be dumb enough to tell Ted the complaint he had in his hands was changed with a printer if I knew otherwise.

The whole thing was maddeningly stupid and convoluted.

In my letter after the *New York Times* article I told Team Siegelman that I "continue to be mystified as to the significance of the manner in which it was changed, be it by laptop/printer or handwriting."

For our story, Jeb called Zeigler and, I like to think, shattered this aspect of the conspiracy.

"Zeigler," wrote Jeb, "said he had planned to make the changes on his laptop and that's what he told Curran before filing the complaint. But after talking with

Curran, Zeigler said he realized his printer wouldn't work without a power source, so he made the changes by hand."

More problematic was another new clue. Someone in or associated with the administration, a sleuth of Holmesian powers of observation and deduction, had proved beyond a shadow of a doubt that I'd assisted Zeigler.

The sleuth, apparently with magnifying glass in hand, noticed something on the final page of Zeigler's complaint. At the top of the page, the typed word "four" was crossed out in the sentence: "I expect to call the following witnesses to prove the *four* ethics violations against Don Siegelman."

Above the crossed out "four" was a "five" – spelled out and handwritten.

The administration had at least two copies of the complaint, the "pre-edited" version I'd sent them with my scratchings; and a copy of the actual complaint, or in any event one of the copies taken to Montgomery for dispensation by Zeigler.

When Jeb called to say we'd be doing a story on the Zeigler-Me conspiracy, the Siegelman press office faxed him the goods: The last page from the marked-up copy I'd sent them and the same page from one of the other versions.

Jeb was told to examine the differences in the two fives. And they were different, though not, mind you, in appearance. It was obvious or should've been to anyone not legally blind that both came from the same hand. The discrepancy regarded the placement of the "five" over the crossed out four. One was about a half-centimeter to the left of that from the other complaint.

Thus, the charge: While Curran was editing the complaint he noticed that the four should have been a five, crossed out the four, and wrote a five above it. He alerted Zeigler to this error and Zeigler, in his own hand, changed the fours to fives on his other copies, including the one bound for the Ethics Commission.

Our story reporting the complaint hadn't mentioned the number of charges against Siegelman. It was an ethics complaint. Probably only Zeigler, as a lawyer, would break such a thing down to "charges." Four, five, two or ten, it didn't matter to me nor, it's my guess, to the ethics commission. Utterly irrelevant.

But I was, as I later acknowledged in my letter to the Siegelman gang, without ready explanation for this teeny-weeny disparity. "I knew immediately it wasn't my handwriting, and that it was obvious that the same person who crossed out one four and wrote five was the same person who did the same thing on the other copy. Otherwise, I admit, I was flummoxed. Why would the complaint faxed to me from him and which I subsequently faxed to you have slightly different markings?"

Jeb and I still laugh at what I did next. I grabbed a pen and started writing fives. "See, mine are in cursive! I don't print! Look!"

Paranoid that Jeb might think me trying to write them differently, I bolted to my desk and ransacked my notes looking for prior examples of my fives-manship, found something and showed it to him.

But Jeb, steeled as he rightly was against efforts by me to steer the story this way or that, stuck with his guns. He said he wasn't in a position to declare that the "fives" were in my handwriting or not.

Well then, I said, I'll find a damn handwriting expert. I called a lawyer in Mobile known for working on complicated litigation. Yes, he said, he occasionally used a hand-writing expert. The guy lives in Atlanta and charges thousands of dollars. I punted on the handwriting expert defense.

I saw no choice but to call Zeigler and ask him to solve the riddle, which he did. After printing out several copies of the complaint, he'd noticed that the five should be a four. He deciding it was a minor change, and fixed it by hand on each rather than re-printing all the complaints. In other words, the handwritten "editing" on that portion of the complaint occurred before Zeigler faxed the complaint to me.

I told Jeb, who turned out to be the real Sherlock Holmes.

"Do you still have your copy of the ethics complaint, the one that you faxed to the governor's office?" he asked.

Jeb explained that the five on my copy should be mimeographed, since it was copied by the fax machine. But all the other markings on my copy, including the telltale circles around two $2.8 millions, would be in my virgin blue ball-point ink.

There was a flipside. If the five on my copy was in virgin ink, I was toast. That would show I'd changed it myself. I knew I hadn't, but also knew I had to prove it. I raced to my desk. I was tossing papers about, not believing I couldn't find it and sure that Jeb would suppose I couldn't because I didn't want to. We eventually located the original in Mike Marshall's office.

"Sure enough," I later wrote Carrie, Hosp, et.al., "it showed my un-copied ballpoint markings, clearly in ballpoint ink, and showed that the crossed out four with the handwritten five was in mimeographed form, such as a copy from a fax machine. In other words, there was some hand-writing -- the crossed out four and the hand-written five -- when the complaint came to me that day."

I concluded with a self-righteous flourish:

I hope this explanation has satisfied your concerns about my so-called role in the filing of the Zeigler complaint.

In the future, prior to making public allegations against me, I would ask you to provide me with the opportunity to respond. As a reporter, I make every effort to get the responses of people I'm writing about. It may be, though, that the ethical rules that govern political public relations are different, and that from now on, I need to be aware of that.

––––

Four years later, while rummaging through the Siegelman archives, I came across a letter from Hosp to ethics director Jim Sumner. It was dated Aug. 1,

2001, two weeks before the administration's seven-sins letter to Bronson and seven weeks before our first story on their charges.

Ted laid out the Zeigler-Curran conspiracy for Sumner.

The governor's lawyer declared that since I'd "received, reviewed and edited the complaint, it further seems likely that this complaint should have been filed by Mr. Curran himself."

"As you know, it is a violation of the ethics laws to 'file a complaint for another person … in order to circumvent' the ethics laws."

And then, the knife:

In conclusion, based on the documents attached, I do not see any possible conclusion other than Mr. Curran actively participated in the filing of Mr. Zeigler's ethics complaint by editing that document to make it consistent with Mr. Curran's mistaken understanding of the facts…

I therefore request not only that Ziegler's politically motivated allegations be summarily dismissed, but that the Commission consider investigating the circumstances that led to the filing of the complaint, and that it take all appropriate actions against the responsible parties.

I'd known they'd tried to get me fired, but never could I have imagined them requesting an ethics investigation of me. A reporter investigated by the Alabama Ethics Commission? It was past bizarre.

Here was Ted Hosp, who far as I was concerned helped enable the whole scheme. He had signed the secret $20 million South Alabama settlement on Siegelman's behalf, as if doing so relieved Siegelman of responsibility for an arrangement to send $2.8 million in state money to the same firm that was at the same time negotiating with Siegelman to pay him almost $1 million.

If Ted didn't know in December 1999 about the whopping sum going to Siegelman from Cherry Givens, he did by the time he wrote the letter to Sumner. He knew it because of Phil Rawls story in June reporting Siegelman's ethics filings and because I'd written my stories the week before his letter.

Ted should have been turning in his boss to the ethics commission, if not the attorney general or U.S. Attorney. A second option: Resigning because he could no longer tolerate being a party to those activities and so many others.

Instead, he sought an ethics investigation of me.

Reading Hosp's letter years later in the quiet archives room, I thought to myself: "Ted, you can kiss my ass."

———

With one exception, the opinion pieces by the state's newspapers focused on the administration and its policy.

An Oct. 14 the *Birmingham News* published an op-ed by Carol Nunnelley, then its managing editor, and Mullins, the University of Alabama journalism department chairman. Osama bin Laden wasn't mentioned once in the story that bore the headline, "Will Sept. 11 also reshape journalism?" I was named or identified by my actions six times.

The piece opened with two famous examples of journalistic conflicts of interest. The first told of liberal columnist Walter Lippmann secretly drafting a 1945 speech for Sen. Arthur Vandenberg, then praising the speech in a column. The second recalled conservative columnist George Will helping Ronald Reagan prepare for one of the 1980 presidential debates.

Nunnelley and Mullins used the two examples to support their thesis that journalists are "adept at having their cake and eating it too."

"And now comes, September 11, 2001, the day that changed the world. Will it also be the day that changed American mass media institutions, the public's perception of them? Both?"

Twenty inches into the 55-inch piece they segued from their discussion about media conflicts of interest and the public's attitudes toward journalism post-9-11 right on to me.

The media's belated effort to reclaim support for the sound values of a free press is hardly a booming movement, however. And government that wants to operate in secret still can exploit public distrust and dislike.

It would be interesting to know, for example, whether the public comes down on the side of Governor Don Siegelman and his decision to require all reporters — and presumably the public — to clear their requests for many records through his staff lawyer. Or would they side with The Mobile Register reporter whose profane outburst contributed to adoption of the misguided policy in the first place?

The journalism community correctly sees the governor's decision as a threat to open government and possibly a violation of Alabama's open records laws. But the journalism community also should see reporter Eddie Curran's profanity toward the governor's press secretary — when denied records we believe he and every other Alabama citizen are entitled to — as unacceptable.

Any citizen who has been denied access to records or meetings can sympathize with reporter Curran's frustrations when denied what is rightfully his as a citizen. But Curran's behavior? There can be no sympathy for that.

Alabama's newspapers have excoriated the governor on his decision. They have let their own off the hook without even a wet-noodle lash. No wonder the public thinks we are more interested in serving our own interests than the public's.

Facing the war on terrorism, a new kind of war with an unseen enemy, journalism will need all the trust and confidence it can muster. Reporter boorishness, and a media culture that thinks it unimportant, will not win that trust. In fact, Curran's behavior is likely to have won sympathy for the governor's wrong-headed response.

I didn't – couldn't -- disagree with their condemnation of my behavior. I was unaware of being a source of sympathy, but if I was, hadn't asked to be nor should I have been.

If they wanted to opine on my outburst, have at it. It wouldn't have thrilled me, but I'd have accepted it as another consequence of my stupidity that day. I took issue, though, with their decision to place my cussing of Rip in a piece bemoaning the public's lack of faith in the media after the most horrific act of terrorism in American history.

To use me as the example – in fact, the only one -- in an epic length op-ed declaring that public trust in the media was "too low for a healthy democracy?"

I should have swallowed my anger and let it be, but that's not what I did. Instead – and perhaps you guessed it -- I e-mailed Nunnelley and Mullins. I explained what I believed to be the genesis of the administration's new records policy, told them my outburst was "unprofessional and inexcusable" and that I'd never said otherwise.

"I can promise you that I and my bosses and my family lashed me with many wet noodles," I wrote.

I was particularly incensed with Nunnelley, and suspected that her outrage was not unconnected to the praise our paper was receiving for busting open so many Siegelman scandals while the larger, better-funded paper she led was, at that stage, mostly missing in action.

At the end I dispensed with niceties and niceness. I told Nunnelley and Mullins they were "either naïve or imbeciles" to believe the administration was refusing to provide us records simply because I'd cussed out Rip; and said their decision to pair a criticism of my actions with what happened on Sept. 11, was "bizarre and distasteful."

"Let me finish with one comment: The readers I've been serving in Mobile for going on 13 years know my work far better than you, and I continue to receive their support."

And if I may say so, that last bit was the truth.

Mullins, who I would meet later and for whom I have great respect, called me, far as I could tell, to deflect my anger away from Nunnelley and onto him. I apologized for my tone at the end of the letter, though can't say I meant it.

Mike Marshall wrote a short letter to the editor that the *News* published. He pointed out that we had apologized to the administration well before the cussing incident became a public issue. "Stories under Eddie Curran's byline carry great weight with *Mobile Register* readers because Eddie has built a reputation for getting his facts straight. That's what credibility is about," he wrote.

Once again I'd bristled at the presentation of my actions in a newspaper article. The irony wasn't lost on me.

On Oct. 19, the administration waved the white flag. Buckalew dispensed a memo to agency heads directing them to cease funneling records request to Hosp. "It gets us back to where we should have been," Huntsville's Distelheim told Jeff Amy, who wrote our story.

Buckalew's memo cited portions of the public records law and notified agency officials that "one of Governor Siegelman's goals is to restore the public's trust in their government."

"An important part of fulfilling this goal is ensuring complete and prompt access to public records …. As you have in the past, requests for specific documents should be responded to immediately. Immediately will mean as soon as the document can be located," Buckalew wrote.

The directive distinguished between specific and non-specific requests, which for my purposes was significant. I rarely know a document exists until coming upon it. If I'm researching a construction project, I need to see the entire file. I've found meaningful information from handwritten notes jotted on the inside of file jackets.

When I ask for records, I want the entire file, and if that means 20 boxes full, so be it.

The administration initially showed signs of complying.

The next week I received a letter from Mabry saying the finance department was working to gather records I'd first sought in September, on the computer services contracts at Public Safety. His letter opened with the salutation, "Dear Mr. Curran," notable, I thought, because it implied an official if frosty acknowledgement that I both existed and had a right to public records.

The next day, ADECA's Childers sent me a similar "Mr. Curran" letter in response to a request to that agency. Both Mabry and Childers cited Buckalew's memo and said they were updating me on my requests "pursuant to that policy."

They were the first two letters of their kind, and the last.

But my problem never was with the administration's official records policy, whatever it was on this or that day. My problem was with the unofficial policy – the one that called for them to withhold records from me. With few exceptions -- and then only because of our persistence in refusing to take no for an answer -- that policy remained in place until the end.

———

I was sullied, but back on the job.

There was still one final matter of unresolved business -- their demand that my stories include the "fuckng piece of rat-shit" statement. After accepting that I was to be allowed to continue covering them, they softened it to: "Due to his unprofessional behavior and the slanted nature of his stories, we will not respond to his questions."

The editors nixed that. Instead, we used the following within the body of each story: "Gov. Siegelman's press office declined comment for this story. (See the editor's note at the end of this story.)"

Then, at the bottom: "Editor's note: The governor's office has a policy of refusing to comment to *Register* reporter Eddie Curran."

The editor's note developed into a signature of sorts. I couldn't count the number of times people told me what a kick they got from reading it.

I became, "the reporter Don Siegelman wouldn't talk to."

Chapter 17
Competition

"Two reporters worked from opposite ends of Alabama to whip up stories in a successful effort to take down former Governor Siegelman and to legitimize a highly political prosecution. In fact, they're good friends and former colleagues, and their strategy was apparently that the same story line emanating from two different papers makes for a convincing truth. I believe their work will one day provide a journalism school case study in journalistic hit jobs. Ultimate responsibility for this tragedy must, however, rest with the editors who approved and funded this exercise in journalistic terrorism."

-- Harper's web-columnist Scott Horton, referring to Brett Blackledge and I, in a July 2007 piece called, "There's No News in the B'ham News."

"Well boys, there's a new sheriff in town, and you boys are out of here."

-- Montgomery lawyer Pat Harris, hired by Siegelman administration to re-negotiate computer services contracts, in a meeting with officials from the company Advanced Systems Design.

Until the mid-1990s, and for decades preceding, we were frequently called, not the *Mobile Register*, but the "Mullet Wrapper." Our publisher, William "Bill" Hearin, was a wide, white-haired power-broker with a stubborn streak, and a will of steel.

To the fabulously wealthy Hearin, newspapering was a business. He not only did not demand good journalism, but might not have recognized it had he seen it. But if he did and it threatened ad sales, he would have discouraged it.

In his final years Hearin was permitted a downstairs office, and pleasured in hanging around even though he knew his replacements would have preferred him to spend his time anywhere else but there. We got along well, and I occasionally dropped in to say hello to the old man, chat, and pick his brain on matters Old Mobile.

During the Hearin reign we were the only game in town, newspapers ruled, and the paper made lots of money.

In 1992, the Newhouse family decided that its Mobile product needed improving. The Newhouses –technically, Advance Publications, the name of the family's media company -- picked a no-nonsense Louisianan, *Shreveport Times* publisher Howard Bronson, to turn the paper around. Bronson – a serious man who never fraternizes with the troops – chose as his editor a person who could not have been more different than he.

Stan Tiner was the former editor of the *Shreveport Journal*, Bronson's feisty, smaller competitor until its collapse. Tiner's six foot four and what might kindly be called big-boned. He's Bunyanesque in size, Barnumesque in personality. He is, as the hyperactive Michael Keaton character in "Night Shift" called himself, an "idea man." Story ideas spilled out of Tiner's brain like rain from a cloud.

Tiner was the perfect man for the job. He shook up a paper that needed shaking and rattled the community not a little as well. With his Sunday columns, he extolled himself, his family, and the changes the readers were seeing and could soon expect. When not selling and boasting, Tiner blistered public figures local, state and national. Before long, there wasn't anyone in town who didn't know who Stan Tiner was.

It wasn't all show. He brought in some new reporters, moved others around, hired a tough city editor, and let it be known that those who didn't produce might not remain. I was in sports, and like many others, didn't need pushing to work hard. Tiner, though, also expanded the paper's vision and sense of the possible. Suddenly you thought bigger than before.

One piece of Tiner advice stuck with me: He said he was not interested in knowing things that couldn't be put in the paper. This has its limits – there are always going to be off-the-record comments that can't be used or tips that can't be corroborated. But as a guiding philosophy, one could do worse.

Readers quickly noticed improvement, as did others in the business. The look of the paper -- eye-numbing before – was beautified dramatically, with a new masthead and design. Bronson and Tiner got the credit, and deserved much of it, but the silent heroes were the Newhouses. The company pumped money into the paper. Equipment was upgraded, travel budgets increased, and cash sunk into the ancient press.

The old *Press Register*, on Government Street a few blocks west of the Bankhead Tunnel, apparently has some architectural value but as a home for a modern newspaper its days were over. Visitors were forever saying they felt like they were walking into the past, with so many reporters, editors and clerks crammed into the stale old surroundings without a single window to the outside world. A common comment: "It's like that movie, 'The Front Page.'"

In June 2002 (by which time Tiner had moved on and been replaced by his top assistant, Mike Marshall), we moved into a $75 million building about a half-mile away, with much of the sum paying for a new press. I had feared missing the old place but needn't have. Our new digs were roomy, comfortable, and encased by huge windows. For the first year, every heavy rain drew crowds of reporters and editors to the windows. We'd stand there in awe, gaping at … rain.

We were a paper on the upswing. I'm not going to say we were better than the *Birmingham News*, but we were more daring and seat-of-the-pants, and because of it, an interesting, fun paper to read.

The *News* was the largest paper in the state, with more and better paid reporters. It had a far larger presence in Montgomery – five or so reporters to our two; and with Birmingham closer to Montgomery, it was easier for the *News* to send extra troops.

In terms of statewide reputation, my Siegelman stories were good for our paper and I like to think contributed to the rise in esteem that started in 1992. The political class certainly noticed. The talk in Montgomery was that we were kicking the bigger paper's butt.

The powers at the *News* also noticed. After the G.H. stories, the paper assigned two of its best reporters to the suddenly fruitful Siegelman scandal beat.

In late June, a month after our G.H. run, the *News* reported a $4.7 million competition free contract to a New York company called ACTV. The firm won the contract to give computer training to teachers after hiring Rick Dent, who'd been Siegelman's campaign spokesman and served the same role during the lottery campaign.

The deal was done immediately upon Siegelman becoming governor, yet another indication that the administration's second priority, beyond passage of the lottery, was rewarding friends (and when the lottery failed, number two jumped to one.)

Hamrick extolled ACTV's work and defended the practice of not seeking bids. But this was post G.H., the administration was getting hammered, and he presented it as just one more example of press negativity. "One lesson we've learned over the last six months is that no good deed goes unpunished," he groaned.

It's not a criticism of the piece to say that, in the long-run, its greatest impact was what it forebode for the administration, the public's right to know, and, well, me.

The story carried a double byline – Brett J. Blackledge and Kim Chandler – that was to become familiar to Birmingham readers and everyone else in Alabama who paid attention to state politics. Blackledge was the paper's top investigative reporter and Chandler one of its most aggressive statehouse reporters. Two days after the ACTV story the pair reported the first in a series of damning stories on State Sen. Roger Bedford, the Russellville Democrat and Siegelman ally.

Blackledge and Chandler churned out eight more stories by the end of July. The best-known told about another Dent client, Bessemer-based Trillion Digital Communications. The administration had awarded the firm a $790,000 contract without seeking bids or prices from anyone else. That was small fry compared to a second no-bid contract for $90 million. For that, Trillion was to build a computer infrastructure to deliver Internet services to all state schools for three years.

Trillion also retained Bedford, purportedly to serve as its lawyer. The *News* reported that Bedford and Dent joined Siegelman at a meeting of state school superintendents where Siegelman played chief salesman and introduced Trillion officials to the superintendents.

Hell-raising by outraged competitors had forced the administration to cancel the deal prior to the *News'* reporting on it, but the piece laid out Siegelman's efforts to award a $90 million contract without seeking bids or proposals.

That's called gubernatorial malpractice.

———

Chandler and Blackledge produced little in the way of investigative bombshells in August, September and October, but returned to form in early November with rat-a-tat blast of stories on a $15 million contract awarded by the Department of Public Safety to a little-known Pensacola company called SmartCOP Inc. The company was to develop a network to deliver crime data, traffic reports and such to computers in state troopers' cars in several counties. The contract was a stepping stone to a far more lucrative deal to provide the same technology and services statewide.

The *News* reported that Siegelman and Hamrick selected SmartCOP, as opposed to Public Safety, whose communications staff was rather more familiar with the technology than the governor and his chief of staff. At about the same time, Jefferson County was contracting for the same type services for its sheriff's department. The county sought bids but didn't receive one from SmartCOP. The story quoted the Jefferson County communications staff saying they had never heard of SmartCOP.

Hamrick could have told them plenty.

"Not only is this a unique company, it is the very best law enforcement technology software in the world…. There's nothing that compares to it," he told the *News*.

Hamrick's qualifications to make a worldwide ranking on police communications companies was nicely captured in the story, which went from his ridiculous statement to the revelation that the administration was unable to produce any materials from so much as one SmartCOP competitor.

SmartCOP became the greatest company on earth of its kind by hiring Montgomery lobbyist Johnny Crawford, whose PACs had donated almost $300,000 to Siegelman's gubernatorial campaign.

Siegelman told the *News* that Crawford was a "friend" and "contributor," but said the relationship "played no role in this project."

A later story reported that SmartCOP wasn't incorporated in Alabama when the contract was signed. Had the will to use the company remained, I don't think this oversight would have mattered. But Siegelman, pummeled into submission by no-bid contract headlines, used the technicality to end the firm's work for the state, and more importantly, put an end to those damn SmartCOP stories.

"That contract is over, it's finished, it's done with," he said, and indeed it was.

With Brett and Kim heavy on the beat I began my mornings by checking AL.Com, the web-site with links to the Mobile, Birmingham and Huntsville papers, and going straight to the *News'* site to see if they'd come up with something new. At that stage I was reading their work with interest but something short of concern.

They were working on their stories, me on mine, and we hadn't crossed paths. I wasn't accustomed to competition. We were a one-paper town and in the past, when working on investigative stories, whether local or state, I generally felt comfortable that I was the only reporter on the case.

What I didn't know was that, shortly after SmartCOP if not before, Brett and Kim began directing their efforts on a matter I'd been working on for months. For too long, as it turned out.

In mid-August, back when the war with the administration was heating, I'd resumed research into the computer services contracts, specifically, as mentioned earlier, some involving a Tallahassee company called Advanced Systems Design Inc., or ASD. The company had lost millions of dollars in state contracts; I hoped they would tell me why; called; and was directed to company vice president John Adams.

It wasn't two minutes in before I detected familiarity and awkwardness on the other end. Then, from both of us, laughter. John Adams and Bob – the "computer deep throat" who had called months before -- were one and the same. With that cat out of the bag, we could speak more freely.

ASD was embroiled in a lawsuit with Public Safety and a company called Digital One Services that had swooped in and taken its workers. The state had been compelled to produce the sort of records it routinely hid from me. John permitted me to indicate my familiarity with the documents in a request to Public Safety that signaled I knew what they had and would know if they withheld anything. This was the records request that sparked the administration's ill-fated decision to withhold public records from us.

I drove to Tallahassee and met with Adams and others at the company. We agreed to an arrangement identical to the one made with Keith Andrews for the Honda stories: I wouldn't quote them unless they gave me the go-ahead, which they ultimately did.

The ASD story as told me by Bob and others crystallized the Siegelman practice of forcing companies to pay-to-play. Siegelman fashioned a smaller version of the K-Street Project, the Republican blackmailing operation spearheaded by Tom DeLay. The K-Street Project compelled companies and interest groups to hire Republican lobbyists and donate to Republicans or face retribution in the halls of Congress. DeLay's project was, certainly in my mind, a criminal enterprise, as too the imposition of the Siegelman Tax.

ASD had opened its Montgomery office in 1993 with two employees and grew steadily, along with its reputation for providing top-notch workers to state agencies. In 1997, when the James administration conducted its request for proposals, ASD came out on top. In part as a result of that RFP, by the time Siegelman became governor, ASD provided some 70 workers to state government and had contracts totaling $9.2 million.

Its employees maintained the state government's e-mail system and computer infrastructure; provided similar services for the Department of Human Resources (DHR); and manned the state driver's license systems through a contract with public safety.

"We were not close to the James administration. We didn't know anybody. We weren't political," said Adams.

That changed after the inauguration. The company donated $1,000 to the lottery foundation and hired lobbyist Amy Herring, a Siegelman staffer when he was lieutenant governor. Allen Spradling, who managed ASD's Montgomery operation, told Herring about the contribution. She told him the company "should not make a contribution of that size."

Spradling believes Herring suggested ASD's next donation – for $10,000. "I guarantee you it was not a figure we came up with. Given our history, it was an unusually large contribution."

That sum was the going rate. In September, the month before the lottery vote, computer services providers Colsa and Tech Providers gave $10,000, the same sum Quality Research had already given. A company with substantial contracts at the Department of Human Resources gave $20,000.

With the Siegelman administration not seeking bids or proposals from companies but simply choosing them with no apparent criteria in mind, there was "a huge incentive for companies to make contributions to get work," said Spradling.

There was one mitigating factor. Montgomery legislator Alvin Holmes raised hell about many of the computer contracts when they came before the legislature's contract review committee. The committee can't kill contracts, but it can put a 45-day hold on them and generate negative headlines. By most accounts, when ASD's Adams appeared before the committee, he did not handle Holmes' harangues well. "He had me standing at a podium at a contract review meeting, and I wouldn't buckle down, and I think that was a mistake," said Adams.

By the time I came upon the story, ASD was down to 10 employees working for the state. Most interesting was how the administration filled the ASD void.

———

In October 1999, Lt. Col. C.E. Andrews wrote Henry Mabry to express his concern that Public Safety "had been contacted by Charlie Stephenson about replacing ASD personnel."

He might well have said, Charlie Who?

At the time, the 52-year old Stephenson had no company, no employees, no experience in the personnel services industry and by his own account didn't know how to use e-mail. He hadn't even incorporated the company, Digital One Services, that was to assume ASD's contracts and many of its employees.

Col. Andrews, along with Public Safety's director, pleaded with Mabry to be allowed to keep ASD or, failing that, for permission to use a "competitive environment" to select a new company. "I believe it to be to the department's advantage to have the ability to negotiate with other professional services providers in addition to Mr. Stephenson," Andrews wrote the finance director.

To which Dr. No responded, in a word, no.

Two years later, Stephenson and Digital One boasted more than $7 million in contracts with Public Safety and the Department of Human Resources. Far as I could tell, neither he nor the company donated the first dime to the lottery foundation or any candidates ever.

If the state's responses to my records requests can be trusted – a large if -- Stephenson never submitted a proposal or even a letter to the governor's office, the finance department or the agencies that awarded those contracts.

Stephenson refused to take my calls. Trying to get the first word out of anyone who had so much as ever seen or spoken to him was a waste of time. He was on one hand a sphinx, and on the other, as I put it in a subsequent feature on him, probably "the most prolific salesman ever of technological hardware and services to Alabama state government."

I ran his name through PACER and found gold – a deposition filed in a case against Stephenson by Nichols Research Corp., a Huntsville company for whom he had helped win millions of dollars in contracts going back almost 15 years, and with which he'd had a falling out.

For Nichols, Stephenson had sold the powerful, expensive computers used by the state supercomputer authority. He'd won a state prison phone contract for BellSouth, and perhaps his biggest coup, helped Alabama Power's Southern LINC subsidiary win a contract to provide radio cell phones and air time to state agencies.

"Southern LINC came to town, tried to get the business and was told, 'Thank you, but no thank you.' This information was relayed to me. They hired me to turn that around to get the GE Ericcson contracts canceled and to try to obtain the contract for them."

He succeeded, and per the terms of his contract, was granted exclusive marketing rights to all government entities in Alabama who piggybacked on the Southern LINC contract. He received a cut from the sale of each radio-cell phone sold as well as residuals for every call made on those phones.

In his rather expansive deposition, Stephenson extolled his talent for working in "those two areas, Finance and the governor's office."

When a new administration takes over, "it slows down the ability to get things done, but after a while, you get back up."

Asked if he also sold home computers to individuals, Stephenson cracked, "Not for $40 million, I didn't."

In a bill to Nichols Research seeking over $125,000 that the company was refusing to pay, Stephenson cited meetings with Mabry and Hamrick. In its way, this was rare – a public record with Hamrick's name on it. The chief of staff, more so than anyone at his level of government I have ever come across, excelled in keeping his name off of documents, or in any event, those that were released to the media.

Stephenson's power appeared to emanate from three relationships, the chief one being with Jimmy Rowell, the longtime state technology guru and member of the supercomputer authority. The others were with Dewayne Freeman, the long-time state senator, ADECA boss until his domestic incident, and since then, lobbyist; and University of South Alabama President Gordon Moulton, then chairman of the supercomputer authority.

When Nicholls stopped paying Stephenson for sales to the authority, Rowell and Moulton intervened with the company, and it resumed paying him. Both declined to answer questions about their relationship with the super salesman from Huntsville or explain the propriety of injecting themselves in a payment dispute between a company and its salesman.

Another story reported the alarm of Public Safety officials upon finding that Digital One was billing and being paid time-and-a-half for its workers. The state computer services contracts don't allow for overtime pay and agency officials, including its top lawyer, flagged the payments.

Their memos reflected concerns about fraud by Stephenson's company. In response to those concerns, the Siegelman administration transferred a politically appointed lawyer from another agency to Public Safety and he promptly authorized the overtime payments.

As a result, Digital One became the first and only such firm to be paid time-and-a-half on the outsourcing contracts.

Whatever Charlie Stephenson wanted, Charlie Stephenson got.

———

As of Nov. 25, I'd not written any of the stories described above. That morning I checked the *Birmingham News* link on Al.Com and read with horror a story about the computer services racket. It bore the headline, "Firms Flourish Under State's No-Bid Edict."

The story by Blackledge and Chandler summarized the Siegelman method – lobbyists and contributions replacing competition as contract selection criteria – and gave multiple examples.

Whereas I was focusing on ASD, the *News* made not the first mention of that company. Their story reported the ASD-like demise of the computer services arm of Nichols Research. For whatever reason that contract failed to attract my notice. The company had $7 million in contracts at the Department of Human Resources – a huge user of computer workers -- and was canned after it got upside down with Stephenson. The $7 million void was filled with $8.5 million in contracts awarded to three firms that played the game.

The *News* reported the hike in contracts enjoyed by a company called Tech Providers after it hired Joe Perkins and his "Matrix Group" lobbying and political consultancy firm.

I knew plenty about Perkins, including his work for Tech Providers. I'd been working about a month on a story on him and Matrix. That was my problem. I was working on too many stories and seeking every last drop of information before reporting them. As much as anything that's why I got beat.

Worst of all, Brett and Kim found Charlie Stephenson's lawsuit and deposition. They quoted liberally from it and reported Digital One's ascendance from non-entity to flourishing state contractor.

They had beaten me on something I had been proud to find and was eager not just to report, but be the first to report.

The pain was magnified exponentially when Mike Marshall elected to run the Associated Press write-through in our paper that, naturally, credited the *News*. I feared Mike would kill my story, but was spared that hell. Nevertheless, I took it as a message to get moving, and did. I worked non-stop, one night crashing at about 4 a.m. in a tiny corner room at the Malaga Inn, a famous old hotel a few blocks from the paper. I ate the cost. I knew if I went home my kids would wake me and I had to get some sleep.

Our story ran four days after Birmingham's. I thought it better but suppose they felt the same about theirs. In any event, our story was *longer,* and we had *more of them.*

From that point on I viewed the *News* and, more specifically, Brett and Kim, as competitors. If I was on a story, I was looking in the rear view and speeding up.

I wanted, in the age-old tradition of big city papers, to whip the competition. I'm sure the feeling was mutual.

––––

In summer 2007, someone pointed me to a column on the web-site of a magazine, *Harper's,* I'd always respected. The author, a Scott Horton, declared that the Mobile and Birmingham papers -- and by extension, myself, Blackledge, Chandler and our respective editors and publishers -- had teamed up to destroy Siegelman. The nail-in-the-coffin proof was that both papers were Newhouse publications.

Horton wouldn't merit a sentence here had he and Team Siegelman not succeeded in selling their loony conspiracy theories to leading voices in the national media and to congressional Democrats. To a considerable degree they convinced the national reporters who worked the story that Karl Rove was behind the Siegelman prosecution and that, consequently, the home-state press had it all wrong. The truth according to Horton was that Siegelman was a shining light of Democratic purity in a Republican hellhole called Alabama and was targeted for destruction by a cabal of Republican prosecutors and right-wing newspapers.

There were so many irrational elements to Horton's Newhouse conspiracy that it's difficult to know where to start. How about: What motive would the New York-based family have for destroying Don Siegelman? Which Newhouse? The bald matriarch Sy? And why did Carol Nunnelley, the editor of our co-conspirator paper, co-author a column torching me for my outburst at Rip?

For the record, I have never spoken to a Newhouse in my life, but have read two of their best known publications, the *New Yorker* and *Vanity Fair.* Both lean left.

The best thing I can say about the Newhouse approach to newspapering – and its high praise indeed -- is how little the organization gets involved in its properties. In any event, that was so when I was doing the Siegelman stories. The newspaper business has changed, and so too, perhaps, has Newhouse. But at the time, the company's philosophy was the opposite of the Gannett cookie-cutter approach, in which every paper must adhere to corporation-wide dictates on style, design and mediocrity. The Newhouses left their papers alone. But if a Newhouse or for that matter anyone were to direct me to report a story contrary to the evidence to fit a story line, I'd refuse, as, I'm sure, would my editors. I'm confident the same applies to the editors and reporters at the *Birmingham News.*

In accusing the *News* and *Register* of conspiring, Horton had it backwards, but I shall make use of his gibberish to get in a few words on the Alabama media; what it takes to produce investigative reporting; and the merits and perils of competition among reporters and papers.

There are two essential requirements for investigative reporting. The first is the willingness and wherewithal of management to support and finance it. A reporter must be freed from daily stories if he or she is to have time for the necessary digging and figuring out. Had my editors been dumping daily assignments on me, forget it. I was given the freedom to search for and develop my own stories, and since well before Siegelman became governor. Smaller papers have fewer reporters and are far less likely to have the luxury of freeing one up for an extended amount of time.

The main reason the Birmingham and Mobile papers generate most of the investigative reporting on state politics (at least during the period covered in this book) is size, and that's a function of circulation numbers. More money equals more resources.

Alabama's third largest paper, the *Montgomery Advertiser,* should lead the way in covering state government. Once a fine paper, the *Advertiser* was purchased by Gannett in 1995. Several good reporters fled, demoralized, the exodus particularly pronounced during the Siegelman years. In Ken Hare, the paper has an editorial writer with flair and an encyclopedic knowledge of state government. But as a contributor of investigative reporting, the *Advertiser* was, during the period covered in this book, largely AWOL. (However, recent developments suggest improvements at the *Advertiser.*)

The state's fourth-largest paper, the *Huntsville Times,* maintains a one-man Montgomery bureau. State coverage at the *Times* (also owned by Newhouse, but apparently not cc'd on the directory to crush Siegelman) focuses on legislation and matters that impact the paper's north Alabama readers. It generally relies on the Associated Press to cover broader state issues.

The AP has several excellent reporters in Montgomery, but they're swamped with the day to day developments and the must-have news. Bill Poovey frequently delivered major investigative pieces, though left in 2001 to work in the AP's Chattanooga bureau.

The final source of such reporting is Dana Beyerle, the one-man Montgomery bureau for the state's three *New York Times*-owned papers. But Dana, like the AP reporters, usually has his hands full covering issues important to the mid-size papers he serves.

To a considerable degree, then, in-depth investigative reporting on state government fell – or did during the period covered in this book -- to the Birmingham and Mobile papers. Either we did it, or it didn't get done.

The second, equally important component to producing investigative stories is having on staff one or more reporters who excel in it. Management can declare it's going to emphasize such reporting, but to consistently produce it a paper must have reporters with the particular obsessive-compulsive genetic defect and a dash of the killer instinct.

One is forever hearing tales of newsrooms riven with hostility, reporter rivalries, backstabbing and battles for assignments and placement of stories. A newsroom without some competitive tension is probably not going to generate many groundbreaking stories. At the same time, I feel blessed at having worked for so long in a newsroom where friendship and good cheer ruled. Many reporters have come and gone at the *Press Register,* usually arriving young and leaving to larger markets or other professions. With few exceptions, all have gotten along well, built lasting friendships and enjoyed a come-one come-all camaraderie as regards outside socializing.

It's my experience that rivalries tend to be generational, among reporters of similar age and who are inclined toward investigative reporting. For example, Brett Blackledge and me. He came to the paper in 1993 and we worked together from 1994, when I moved to news, until 1998, when he left for Birmingham.

In making his conspiracy charges, Horton wrote that Brett and I were "good friends and former colleagues." This is true, with a caveat. Brett and I got along well, in the newsroom and out, but there was an undercurrent of rivalry. Because investigative reporters don't have beats, they are forever poaching. They must do so gingerly and with respect for the reporter whose beat is being infringed upon. I poached a time or two on Brett's beat and while he never complained, I believe he was short of thrilled, for which I do not blame him.

We stayed in touch only sparingly after he left. He quickly became the *News'* lead investigative reporter, but story-wise, we didn't cross paths until 2001 when he and Kim moved into the Siegelman scandal beat. On the rare occasions we bumped into one another in Montgomery we were friendly, but by then we were on opposing teams and in direct competition. There were no hugs or hearty handshakes. With Kim Chandler the tension was minimal because at the time I really didn't know her.

The sense of a rivalry with Brett and Kim has long since dissipated. Post-Siegelman, Brett was to win a Pulitzer Prize for his remarkable work on the astonishingly polluted relationship between Alabama's renegade junior college system and the Democratic leadership in the state legislature. I've lost count of the people who have pleaded guilty or been found so in no small part due to Brett's reporting.

In 2008, Auburn's journalism program awarded him a prize and he honored me by asking that I introduce him. I opened by saying that during the time we'd competed on the Siegelman beat I'd wanted to kill him. The joke worked, winning laughs from Brett and the crowd, though it looks a little rough on paper.

———

I trust that readers don't believe that the *News* and *Press Register* conspired to whoop up on Siegelman. But there's another question worth considering: Does competition between reporters and news organizations breed an atmosphere in which politicians become hunted, as prey?

I can hear the politicians' response: "YES!"

And indeed, that can be the case.

When reading stories with an obvious investigative bent, ask yourself these questions:

Did the act or acts merit reporting?

Was the story well sourced, as best you can tell accurate, and were those reported on granted the opportunity to give their side?

Warning signs include too many petty stories, such as about politicians occasionally using government cars to pick up kids from school; or those based on accusations by enemies or "whistleblowers" but lacking supporting documentation and public record.

I can think of one or two pieces during the James' administration that I'd take back, but the Siegelman stories? Not one.

As someone who publicly clashed with the administration, I couldn't afford to report piddling stuff. To do so would feed their story line that we, and more specifically me, were out to get them. For the same reason the stories had to be air-tight. We had to assume they were giving them the fine-tooth treatment, hunting for errors that would require correcting and that could be used against me. My editors and I worked hard not to give them any such opportunities.

I believe I can say the same of the competition. I don't recall any stories by Kim and Brett that struck me as trivial. There was, after all, plenty of corruption and favoritism to go around, some of which went unreported simply because of its abundance.

In the second half of the Siegelman administration, competition between the Mobile and Birmingham papers contributed to the production of strong reporting that enlightened the public and saved tax dollars.

In the final analysis, the *News,* and specifically, Blackledge and Chandler, did me two great favors: With their entrance into the Siegelman scandal beat, I was no longer the lone ranger, and unlike me, neither of them cussed out a member of the administration. That made it harder for Siegelman to single me out in making his case as a victim of overzealous reporting.

And as will be seen, one of their stories led to my discovery of the secret second life of the lottery foundation and the half-million dollars routed to it by Richard Scrushy.

———

The most satisfying result of the exhausting work on the computer services contracts was a piece on Joe Perkins and his mysterious Matrix Group. It was less investigative than feature story, and began as follows:

MONTGOMERY -- On a resume published on the Internet, a former employee of the Montgomery-based political consulting firm the Matrix Group stated that his duties included "client security and counter-surveillance."

According to its Web site, the Matrix Group specializes in: "Communications - Governmental Affairs - Intelligence - Executive Security."

At the end of a creaky hallway in a redecorated downtown Montgomery train station resides what could be the closest thing Alabama politics has to a non-governmental secret agency.

Though the firm employs researchers, a lawyer and several people who lobby the Legislature, the Matrix Group is primarily associated with one man: its founder, 51-year-old Joseph W. "Joe" Perkins Jr.

In political circles, Perkins is regarded as one of Alabama's premier practitioners of "opposition research" -- the art of finding something potentially controversial about someone, usually a politician, then molding it into a message that can be put before the public.

My initial intent wasn't to write about Perkins, but about a contract of which he was a party. While researching his role in the computer services contracts I came across another contract awarded, naturally, without hint of competition.

The previous December Perkins incorporated a non-profit called the Keystone Foundation, just in time for the administration to award it a $200,000 contract to publish a report by the Siegelman-appointed Early Learning Commission.

Maybe it was a story, maybe not, but to make that determination I needed to research the circumstances of the foundation's selection and review its work product and bills. Had the administration's weeks-old pledge of public records openness remained intact, this would not have been a problem.

I knew enough about Perkins' proclivity for bare-knuckle political warfare to realize that digging into his business might provoke a response. There's no such thing as an investigative story that doesn't make me a little nervous – not for my physical well-being, but a natural concern about how people will respond to facing the sort of questions I must ask. With Perkins, there was a greater than usual psychological girding, a recognition that if he felt under siege, he might respond in kind.

The administration ran the Keystone Foundation contract through the Department of Human Resources. In early October I'd asked the agency to produce the basic records one expects to find for public contracts. Also requested was an explanation for the failure to run the contract through the legislature's contract review committee.

After a month of trying I had little to show for my efforts, chiefly because the bills were so slight on details.

On Nov. 2, I called Perkins and agreed to e-mail my questions. They were thorough but reasonable. For example: "Why should the state have to pay the foundation's rent? Doesn't the foundation have other purposes besides a contract for the state?"

Perkins called several veteran statehouse reporters, including Phil Rawls and Dana Beyerle, and asked them to come by. I learned about the meeting and found that Perkins told them about my plans to report on the foundation, so he summoned them to defend its work. What in the world he expected them to do about another reporter's story was beyond me, and them as well.

That was odd, but nothing compared to what happened next. A neighbor telephoned me at work and reported that, moments earlier, she'd received a call from a man identifying himself as Bob Franklin. He said he was conducting a national journalism survey and wondered if she'd participate.

"I said I would, and he started asking if I read the *Mobile Register* and if I was familiar with Eddie Curran. I said I was, and that you were my neighbor. Then he asked me if I knew that you had been caught drinking in the Alabama statehouse, and if I knew that you were a serious alcoholic. I told him that I certainly didn't know that to be true and that I didn't like where this was going, and ended it."

That night she showed me where she'd saved the caller ID. She'd determined that the "national journalism survey" was being conducted from a payphone in mid-town Mobile.

She was far as I know the lone neighbor reached by "Bob Franklin." I suspect he was looking for one hit, with the expectation it would be reported to me; that his intention wasn't to harm my reputation but to intimidate or piss off, perhaps with the hope of inciting another Rip-like tantrum. In truth I was less angry than bemused.

I drafted a memo for my editors, but didn't say a word to Perkins. This was mind-game time. Mentioning the call would be tantamount to accusing Perkins of ordering it. He would deny it and possibly scotch the story by arguing to my editors or our lawyers that any future reporting by me about him would be tainted by revenge. Investigating the Matrix meant getting sucked into it, but better to think like Perkins than get burned by him.

I don't know for certain that he was behind the call. Because of the timing and his reputation I suspect so. Possibly "Bob Franklin" knew I was working on the story, wanted me off and didn't tell Perkins, or there was another motive entirely.

The call was in any event an unusual example of hard-ball, and like none I'd ever experienced.

A month after Bailey's resignation his lawyer, George Beck, pres[...] prosecutors with a proffer letter laying out what Nick was prepared to [...]eral Despite the letter, Bailey's cooperation was to be a long time in coming. to.

He no longer worked for Siegelman, but he remained in the fold.

———

"Opponents want Siegelman judged by the company he keeps."

Below that November headline was an AP story by Phil Rawls forecasting the attack strategy to be employed by Siegelman's challengers in the 2002 election. "Gov. Don Siegelman's opponents are already making it clear they will build their campaigns around an old saying: A man is known by the company he keeps," wrote Rawls.

Riley compared Siegelman to "a teen-ager who was hired to cut the grass, but instead left the grass uncut and took the lawnmower." Windom accused the governor of "spending state money for crony contracts that should be helping our children."

Siegelman's opponents "have a successful pattern to follow," observed Rawls. "He used the same strategy himself in 1998, when he defeated Fob James with a campaign that repeatedly referred to the state Transportation Department as 'a cesspool of corruption.'"

Brad Moody, a political science professor at Auburn University at Montgomery, stuck in the knife. "Siegelman," said Moody, "is going to have to drink his own medicine."

Consider the pickings made available in '01 for Siegelman's opponents in '02:

- G.H. Construction and the active state and federal criminal investigation into all matters Lanny Young.

- The Honda-Mercedes no-bid reports.

- The odyssey of the $2 million check waived before Marion County officials by Siegelman ally Bedford and originating from Siegelman-controlled ADECA.

- The legal fee revelations and, by Jim Zeigler or not, the ethics probe into the relationship between the payments from Cherry Givens and the South Alabama settlement.

- The departures of Hamrick and Bailey, and the cabinet overhaul.

- The public records battle that boomeranged on the administration.

- The indictment in late October of Roland Vaughan on charges related to his secret, undisclosed part-ownership in the Ripley Street site that his architectural firm recommended for the two warehouses.

- The *Birmingham News'* entrance into the Siegelman scandal beat, and stories, like SmartCops, unearthed by Blackledge and Chandler.

- The stories on computer services contracts handed out to friends without a pretense of competition.

only did these scandals damage Siegelman politically in the obvious ways, they provided issues his opponents could use not merely to attack him, but develop their own identities to a public far more familiar with the incumbent. Siegelman tried to dig himself out from under the headlines by creating new ones presenting himself as an advocate of ethics reform.

Only about 50 of the 140 legislators turned up for the governor's speech preceding the special session he called in late summer 2001, about two months before Bailey's departure.

"This session ought to be dubbed the Don Siegelman rehabilitation session. His popularity had dipped below 30 percent," said one of them, Republican house member Mark Gaines from Birmingham.

Special sessions are generally called to address one or two pressing issues. The urgent matter that fall was to satisfy a federal mandate by redrawing congressional and state school board districts. Not sexy. So Siegelman loaded the session agenda with bills, many dealing with ethics and the bid laws.

Never was the fight between Siegelman and Windom to out-ethics one another more evident. From late August to mid-September, hardly a day went by without a story or editorial chronicling the duo's two-tracked effort to cleanse state government.

Windom held a press conference on Aug. 21 to introduce his package of ethics reform bills and to criticize Siegelman's. A few hours later, Siegelman gathered the media to tout his and disparage Windom's.

Siegelman captured additional headlines by signing an executive order requiring every state contract to be awarded through a competitive process. His reward?

"I think it will be viewed as basically political ... that he and his cronies have had their pork for four years," University of Alabama political science professor Bill Stewart told the AP. Stewart said the administration was trying to "appear to be Mr. Clean when they have taken full advantage of the spoils of office."

Headlines in the coming weeks included: "Ethics one-ups: Siegelman, Windom's fight could make voters victors"; "Siegelman requires ethics seminars for state officials"; "Ethics Utopia: If Siegelman and Windom keep going, we'll have it"; "Siegelman order: Pork stops here"; "Windom wants lobbyists to report all entertainment expenses"; "Siegelman proposes ethical makeover of state government"; and "Ethics placed atop agenda: Governor calls for cleanup as special session begins.

On Sept. 7 the pair squared off for another round of press conferences that again failed to produce signs that governor and lieutenant governor were rising above politics to work together for the common good. "The words of the governor say we need competitive bid reform, but his actions scream something else," said Windom. Countered Siegelman: "He's not willing to fight for higher standards. He's simply campaigning for higher office. He thinks he's cute. He thinks he's making me look bad. I think the people of Alabama are smarter than that."

In the end, two of Siegelman's proposals passed into law, if in scaled down form.

One required people and companies that provide professional services – including lawyers, engineering firms, computer consultants and construction managers like G.H. – to win placement on a state list verifying that they are qualified. Siegelman told reporters that if that law had been in place a year before, it's unlikely that G.H. Construction could have been awarded the warehouse construction management contract. In fact, it would not have made any difference.

The administration had chosen the Montgomery Downtown Redevelopment Authority to pay for and own the warehouses, and it was the authority, not the state, that technically hired Lanny's company. If there's a will to be crooked, there's almost always going to be a way. Still, the bill was an improvement.

The second law required agencies to give written explanations when awarding professional services contracts to companies charging 10 percent more than the lowest qualified competitors. It also required winners of contracts greater than $5,000 to name family members who work for state government.

Of most benefit, to my mind, was the requirement that contract recipients disclose the names of lobbyists or consultants hired to assist them win the state business. One hopes this has discouraged some companies from hiring consultant/lobbyists in the first place. The cost of paying such people is invariably passed to taxpayers, so maybe there's been some savings there.

Whatever his motivations, Siegelman had every right to trumpet the improvements. Windom even complemented him, though with something short of enthusiasm. "It's weak medicine, but weak medicine is better than no medicine at all," groused the lieutenant governor.

But in terms of public relations, Siegelman couldn't win. Stories about his reform proposals inevitably presented context -- that he was scandal-scarred and desperately seeking damage control. And these, mind you, were written by others, not me. I stayed away from analysis pieces that routinely included harsh comments from Windom, Riley, legislators and political scientists like Stewart and Moody.

Many were written by Phil, who can turn out a story in the time it takes me to type my byline and specializes in pieces that encapsulate issues with clear, easy to digest leads and supporting graphs.

———

During fall and early winter I continued to monitor court records and other sources for news of the departed but not forgotten G.H. Construction. One

...psulated the losses the state had eaten as a result of the administration's ...o give Lanny a project that he wasn't even to be allowed to do. The story ...al at about $410,000, that being roughly the amount the state had paid ...struction in early 2001.

...ncluded the hyper-inflated $161,566 in architectural services for one of ...ouses and paid to Nick Bailey friend Curtis Kirsch, and the land surveys done and, in CDG's case, not done. The land studies that were performed were useless, since the state wasn't going to buy the land. That included the $25,000 site recommendation study by Roland Vaughan's firm, it too down the drain.

There may have been additional costs – such as legal fees to help clean up the mess – but $410,000 was all I could prove.

Another story reported a pair of lawsuits against G.H. Construction for engineering and land clearing done prior to cancellation of the project. The company didn't respond to either, and the two plaintiffs won judgments totaling about $85,000.

Because of the cancellation of the bond deal, G.H. Construction remained the owner of the land. The bank foreclosed on the property, which was to have a bizarre, tortured life, with additional transfers and mortgages, but no warehouses or other structures.

In early December Siegelman visited Mobile's Davidson High to tout his education funding plans. Gathered for the occasion were about 35 students and the local media, including our education reporter, Rebecca Catalanello. Public officials hate it when reporters stray from the script and ask about tender issues unrelated to the day's message, and that's what Rebecca did.

Maybe it was because she worked for the *Register*, or Siegelman just wasn't in the mood for questions about un-bid contracts. In any event, something set him off, and Rebecca captured his rant on tape.

"If any of you saw the *Mobile Register* last Sunday – he was on the front page, they called him 'The Matrix Man,' If anybody opened the paper, you couldn't miss it," said Siegelman. "Joe Perkins worked in my campaign in 1986 – that was the last time I had any official or professional relationship with him. But if you read the *Mobile Register*, you would think that he is my bosom buddy. They have distorted the truth in article after article. And they don't care what the truth is."

After more of same, he concluded: "All I'm saying is, if the *Mobile Register* cared as much about the truth as it did about trying to nail somebody and make themselves look good, the public would be a whole lot better off. Next question."

After the crowd dispersed, Siegelman approached Rebecca and continued where he'd left off.

The paper had "made up their mind how they want to see me presented down in Mobile and thank God they're the only newspaper in the state that behaves this way....But the facts don't bother the *Register*. They don't care about the facts. They want to try to make politicians – and it goes back as part of their history. They think it's their birthright to make politicians look as bad as possible."

A few days later Mike Marshall sent Siegelman a letter to, as he put it, "clear up several misconceptions."

Marshall made particular note of Siegelman's complaints about our story reporting the role of Huntsville-based consultant Steve Raby in helping a client win one of the many computer services contracts awarded by the administration.

"In this case, you certainly have us confused with *The Birmingham News*," wrote Mike. "We have not written about Steve Raby. The *News* has. You said, 'Thank God they (the *Register*) are the only newspaper in the state that behaves this way.'

"Clearly, *The Birmingham News* 'behaves this way' as well," Mike wrote. He reminded Siegelman that the paper prints corrections on the front page and encouraged his staff to bring our errors to his attention.

"To the extent that our stories may not adequately present your administration's views on an issue, it is because you refuse to talk to our reporter and have ordered your staff not to talk to our reporter. I urge you to change this policy. If I can be of any further help in clearing up this confusion, please let me know," he concluded.

Bailey's resignation letter was among the records I came across in fall 2005 while rummaging through the state archives. The most unexpected find was a November 2001, letter to Siegelman from his physician, Dr. Gerald M. Pohost.

Pohost reminded Siegelman that he would soon be moving to California, then made suggestions to the governor based on a recent physical.

Siegelman was eating a diet heavy on "beef, sausage, bacon and cheese," drinking more than ten cups of coffee a day and, most alarming, had reported to Pohost that he was drinking heavily.

Paul and Dewey agreed with me that we shouldn't include the letter in the story I was writing about other findings in the archives. Given the private, sensitive nature of the letter, publication of its contents, especially under my byline, would have reinforced Siegelman's claims that we were out to get him.

Our decision not to report the letter is subject to second guessing. At the time I wrote the story, Siegelman was a candidate for governor. Should the public know that a candidate, by his own admission, drank substantial amounts of alcohol while serving as governor?

My sense is that we would have used it had Siegelman been known or widely rumored to have a drinking problem which he'd denied, publicly or in private to ɔur reporters or editors. But even in Rumor City, Ala., I'd never heard he drank too much, not so much as an old story about one occasion when Siegelman got sloppy drunk, and he'd been in the limelight for decades.

After finding the letter I made some casual inquiries and found nothing to suggest he was anything but a moderate drinker, if that. For Siegelman, heavy drinking might mean two beers four nights a week for a month, and that's normal or below it for many people. However much, it was above *his* norm.

In late 2001, Siegelman was feeling the stress, and like many people in such circumstances, was reaching for the old favorites – fatty foods, coffee, and drink.

It had been a crummy year for Alabama's governor, and 2002 would not bring relief.

Chapter 19
Landfill Lanny's Toxic Tax Cut

"We hear talk of kickbacks at the Capital."
-- Secretary of State Don Siegelman, during 1984 press conference in which he cited "hints and rumors of corruption and kickbacks" involving the operations at Emelle, the huge hazardous waste landfill owned by Waste Management.

"He (Siegelman) said, 'We'll get that revenue ruling you want but those bastards are going to pay for it."
-- Testimony of Lanny Young, who was paid $500,000 by Waste Management after the Department of Revenue issued a secret ruling slashing the taxes paid at Emelle.

When old-timers talk about the member of George Wallace's family who tried hardest to cash in on Wallace's power, it's always brother Gerald. Though colorful Gerald gets the attention, two quieter kin -- Wallace's daughter Bobbie Jo and her husband James Parsons – made the loudest noise at the bank. The Parsons almost certainly made more money from what my father calls "relative ability" than any gubernatorial relatives in Alabama history.

The Parsons owe their bounty to hazardous waste.

In 1974, the Environmental Protection Agency identified the area around the tiny Sumter County town of Emelle as among the most suitable sites in the country for a hazardous waste landfill. Emelle, with a population of maybe 100, is in central Alabama, near the Mississippi border. The EPA was drawn to the area for geological reasons. A chalky layer hundreds of feet thick provides what is said to be an impermeable barrier protecting groundwater from waste seepage.

Clients for hazardous waste landfills include plastics manufacturers, paint makers, chemical companies and other industries that generate waste too toxic for ordinary landfills. As might be expected, such waste poses a graver threat to the environment, is more heavily regulated, and costs substantially more to dispose.

Three years after the EPA report a group of Tennessee businessmen decided to make a go at Emelle. Among their first moves: Recruiting some home-grown relative ability.

The men invited James Parsons to become a partner and awarded Alabama's First Son-In-Law a 28-percent share -- more than anyone else in the company. The group incorporated Resource Industries of Alabama, bought a 300-acre tract near Emelle, and applied for the various permits needed before they could build such a facility.

Agencies like the Alabama Department of Public Health parted like the Red Sea, delivering the permits for the state's first and still only hazardous waste landfill. The company never built a landfill. Instead, it sold the land and permits to Chemical Waste Management. The company, a subsidiary of Waste Management (for clarity's sake that's how the company will be identified) agreed to pay Resource Industries 12 percent of the landfill's revenues for 20 years, then one percent a year until the landfill's closure. The Houston-based garbage giant bought an additional 2,400 acres and built the site.

Emelle generated more money than anyone could have imagined. In its heyday it accepted waste trucked in from more than 40 states, and was the most profitable hazardous waste landfill in the country.

The value of Parsons' relative ability was revealed in the 1990s when he and his partners sued Waste Management for fraud. From 1981 through 1995, Emelle generated some $1 billion in revenues. Of that, Waste Management paid Resource Industries $87 million. Based on his 28 percent share, Parsons banked about $24.3 million.

In the early 1990s, Parsons and his partners discovered that Waste Management had devised a scheme to hide revenues for the purpose of limiting the royalty payments. In 1996, a federal judge ordered the company to pay Resource Industries $91 million. Naturally, this further enriched George Wallace's daughter and son-in-law, by another $20 million plus.

To slightly restate a previously expressed truism, garbage isn't garbage, it's money, and the more toxic, the better.

In the 1980s, Alabama's secretary of state sought to boost his name recognition and advance his reputation as an ass-kicking man of the people by blasting away at Emelle. It didn't seem to matter that as the state's top elections officer, Siegelman had no role whatsoever in the regulation of landfills. He accused Waste Management of violating environmental laws and bribing lawmakers. Typically, he declined to identify the culprits, allowing him to appear to be going out on a limb without actually doing so.

During his 1986 campaign for attorney general he upped the ante.

"The first thing I will do is close that landfill," he pledged.

Siegelman was elected, Emelle stayed open.

Meanwhile, Gov. Guy Hunt developed an antipathy to the landfill he believed was taking too much toxic waste from other states. In 1992 the legislature passed a Hunt-backed bill that dramatically increased the per-ton taxes for such waste, up to $103 per ton for the most toxic substances.

In 1996 and 1997 Waste Management made a push to lower the taxes. In a series of letters, Montgomery lawyer Tom DeBray argued that since waste brought to the site was treated and rendered less toxic, it should be taxed at the post-treatment toxicity levels. The company wanted the state to slash the levy on the most common classification from $41.60 a ton to $11.60, the rate for its post-treatment toxicity.

DeBray made his case to Wade Hope, a Revenue Department lawyer responsible for overseeing the hazardous waste tax. In a letter, Hope told DeBray the department didn't have the authority to make the change. The legislature had passed the law defining the tax classifications, and "only the Legislature can alter the rate through a change in the statute," he wrote.

The company, despite donating generously to lawmakers and employing top lobbyist Johnny Crawford, hadn't been able to get it done in the legislature. After Siegelman's inauguration, Waste Management dropped Crawford. He was replaced by Austin-Young, the Lanny pairing with Claire Austin. Out as well was DeBray, the company's long-time Alabama lawyer. He was replaced by the ever-present Ellis Brazeal, attorney for Lanny and Paul Hamrick's brother-in-law.

Could the new team, with its near familial bonds with the Siegelman administration, accomplish what the old could not?

———

During my Lanny studies the previous spring I had talked to old source in the garbage business who I will call – because it's what he laughingly named himself – Deep Dump. He knew the industry upside down and backwards. He'd given me tips in the past and helped me understand the business.

Deep Dump didn't care for Lanny. Among other things, he said he had it from impeccable sources that Waste Management paid Lanny some extraordinary sum to win a huge tax break at Emelle. The company had been seeking the tax cut for years, with no luck. It hired Lanny and, boom, the Siegelman administration made it happen. Crooked as hell, he said.

Criminal or not, the deal satisfied the criteria for a story, but first I had to prove it.

One of Lanny's UCC loan records had seemed to confirm the tip. It showed that Waste Management had loaned Lanny $1 million in May 2000. The loan was collateralized by proceeds from what the loan record called a "consultant arrangement with Chemical Waste Management Inc."

Chemical Waste's only business in Alabama was at Emelle.

I'd reported the ChemWaste UCC in my June feature on Lanny. The story reported that the UCC didn't identify the purpose or financial terms of Young's consulting agreement; and that Waste Management refused to clarify. A spokesman acknowledged Young's services as a business development consultant for the company, but beyond that, nothing.

I called the Revenue Department and was handed off to the agency's lawyer, Susan Kennedy. I knew nothing of Kennedy at the time. In the coming year I was to

...earn considerably more about the politically connected attorney who prosecutors later designated an "unindicted co-conspirator" for her part in the tax change.

Kennedy confirmed that Waste Management won changes in state regulations affecting the Emelle landfill. The department, though, never heard from Young, she said. Lanny, who surprisingly took my call, told readers his work for Waste Management didn't involve hazardous waste issues. He said he'd had nothing to do with the tax cut.

After the feature on Lanny I asked the Revenue Department to let me review the "complete file with regard to regulatory changes made in the summer of 1999 that affected the Emelle landfill." I sought all correspondence pertaining to the change; "any financial impact analysis performed in relation to the changes (and) any indication that the governor's office was or was not consulted in relation to the changes."

Taxpayer records, whether for individuals or corporations, are, with few exceptions, private. My position was that the tax cut represented a change in the methods used by the state to tax hazardous waste, whether it applied to one company or 50. Such was the basis for my argument that the records should be public.

The department did not agree.

Several factors -- Deep Dump's reliability, the UCC connecting Lanny to Emelle and the fact that there had been a tax cut -- convinced me there was a story. But I'd hit a bunch of dead ends, was busy on other fronts, and, at least for the time being, closed the Emelle file.

By late December 2001, I'd been covering the administration for almost a year, not full-time but overtime. There was the amount and complexity of the stories, the competition from the *News,* and the emotionally draining battle following my verbal bombardment of Rip. I was whipped, with no strong stories in the hopper. Such was my frame of mind when I decided to make one final push on the Emelle story.

I hoped to determine Lanny's fee, but short of that, to confirm that Waste Management had hired him for the tax change. If I couldn't do that there was no story.

In late December and early January I traded phone calls and e-mails with Sarah Voss, the company's Houston-based spokesperson. She didn't take my questions as a personal affront – there was no, "How can you even ask such a thing of a company/politician as fine as (fill in the blank)?" The both of us realized that information decisions were made above her level. It was agreed that I would e-mail my questions, she would pass them up the ladder, then deliver the responses.

The Lanny-Chemical Waste UCC cited a role in the transaction by Ellis Brazeal's law firm, which confused me. Voss said Waste Management had retained

Walston Wells to work on the tax change and that the firm, with the company's blessing, had engaged Lanny as "an outside consultant."

With that, I had a story. The piece, which ran in early January, began:

In June 1999, a law firm for the company that operates Alabama's only hazardous waste landfill hired a friend and major supporter of Gov. Don Siegelman to help win a significant change in the way the state taxes such waste.

A Mobile Register review shows the change that Clayton L. "Lanny" Young was hired to help bring about has saved the company about $1 million in less than two years.

"It was for consulting on getting tax relief for this site, and it was contingent upon the success of the issue they had hired him to help with," Sarah Voss, a spokeswoman for Houston-based Waste Management Inc., said of the arrangement involving Young...

Voss said Young received one payment from the law firm "that was based on his achievement of the goals set when he was retained."

Readers were told that Waste Management declined to provide "copies of the contracts involving the company, the law firm and Young; identify the amount of the payment to him; or say whether Young had been due further payments."

By this stage Lanny was radioactive, and the relationship was not one Waste Management was keen on discussing.

The piece summarized previous reporting on Lanny, and reported two relevant contributions in 1999 to the lottery foundation – $10,000 from Brazeal's firm and the other, for $50,000, from Waste Management. That latter was to figure years later in the case against Siegelman.

Lanny wasn't to be found, but I had his old statement denying involvement in the tax changed, and used it.

Siegelman's old friend Jim Hayes was Revenue Commissioner when the change was made and had signed off on it. Hayes, who had since departed the administration, provided a second level of confirmation of Lanny's efforts on the tax change.

He said he had never heard of Lanny Young until Nick Bailey called to see if he had met with Young. Brazeal joined Young and did most of the talking, Hayes recalled.

"They laid out a case that the fees at Emelle were so high that the taxes for the state were dropping precipitously," said Hayes.

Brazeal and Young said that if the taxes were lowered, the site would do more business and that would generate increased collections for the state. Hayes agreed to consider the matter, and assigned a department lawyer to the situation.

Over the next couple of weeks Hayes received periodic calls from Young. He said he had no idea that Lanny was being paid on a contingency basis to get the change made, and was embarrassed and not a little disgusted to learn so when I told him.

If anything our story presented Waste Management's request -- that waste brought to Emelle should be taxed at post-treatment toxicity levels – as reasonable. But there's no shortage of companies, industries and interest groups with compelling arguments for new or altered laws, including tax changes. Generally they must present their case to the legislature, as difficult, unwieldy and polluted a process as that may be.

I wanted to show readers that it was different – and worse – for lobbyists to ply their trade at the Revenue Department, as opposed, say, to the highway department. Taxpayers, individual and corporate, often hire lawyers to engage the department in tax disputes, and there's nothing wrong with that. But lobbyists?

I called Jim Sizemore, a respected former revenue commissioner, who told readers that during his five years at the agency, lawyers routinely represented clients with tax disputes, accountants did as well, but never once could he recall a lobbyist doing so.

Subsequent records dispelled one of the primary justifications for the change: the prediction that lower taxes would make Emelle more competitive, generate more business, and produce greater revenues for the state. In the first four years after the change, the state took in more than $1 million less in revenues from Emelle than from the prior period.

———

Six months after the story, in late July 2002, the Dansby lawsuit – one of the two Lowndes County cases against Lanny and Waste Management brought by Susan Copeland and Doyle Fuller -- produced public records gold. Copeland, God bless her, had filed a portion of a transcript from a court hearing during which Lanny's fee for the Emelle change was divulged.

It was $500,000.

How many years, dear reader, did it or will it take you to make $500,000? How many hours might you put in before hitting the half-million dollar mark?

The fee was grotesquely excessive and decidedly story-worthy. The money originated in Houston, at Waste Management; was transferred to Walston Wells' account in Birmingham; and from there to Goat Hill, Ala., and into Lanny Young's bank account.

Walston Wells, while not a large firm, is prominent, very Republican respectable. The firm, it seemed clear, had acted as accessory, as launderer of Waste Management's dirty money. I suppose the firm looked the other way so it wouldn't have to see it that way. I felt this was serious enough to go above Brazeal to one of the name partners, Vernon Wells. He said I needed to talk to Ellis, since Waste Management was his client. I called Brazeal. He was polite but nervous. He declined comment, citing attorney-client concerns.

I called his client, or rather, Sarah Voss. I told her what I'd learned, and that I expected to shortly be in possession of the 1997 correspondence between Tom DeBray and the Revenue Department back in 1997. I e-mailed questions. The main parts are as follows:

That (1997) letter, I'm told, will state that the department determined that only the Legislature could make the change being sought by Chemical Waste. It appears that Chemical Waste then hired Ellis Brazeal and, along with him, Lanny Young, and they succeeded where DeBray had failed.

My questions:

To the ordinary reader, $500,000 will obviously seem like a very considerable sum. Could the company provide, with some degree of specificity, an explanation of what Lanny Young did to assist in this matter?

Were Young's personal and political connections with Gov. Don Siegelman and members of his administration, including former Chief of Staff Paul Hamrick, a factor in the decision to hire him?

Were administration officials involved in the decision, or was it handled completely within the Revenue Department?

Did anyone recommend to the company that it should hire Young and/or Ellis Brazeal?

How much has the company saved as a result of the change?

This story may or may not contain information from a transcript of a separate hearing in the Dansby case, in which it's stated that Young would have been paid $2 million by Waste Management if he succeeded in negotiating a lower tipping fee at the proposed Lowndes County landfill.

It may be, though, that this arrangement will be reported in a later story. In the event I include it in this story, I want to go ahead and ask my questions:

Does Waste Management regularly use consultants and/or companies to handle the permitting and political processes required for new landfills in a way that hides the company's role in such plans?

Does Waste Management consider it ethical to offer sums as high as $1 million or $2 million to such companies/consultants in return for their success in lowering tipping fees that Waste Management will later pay to host governments?

Has Waste Management or its subsidiaries been contacted by law enforcement authorities in connection with the investigation into Lanny Young and members or former members of the Siegelman administration? Has the company been served with subpoenas relating to this investigation?

Sarah, I guess I'm not giving away any secrets when I say I ask questions that I don't necessarily expect will be answered. However, as a general practice, I do like to let our readers know that we have asked questions, even when we have not received responses.

The company declined comment, beyond what it provided back in January. The story reported Lanny's fee, Waste Management's failed 1997 attempt to win the change, and summarized the salient points from the first story.

The AP picked it up and the *Birmingham News* published an editorial declaring that the "way the change came about, greased by Young's half-million-dollar efforts, smells as bad as any landfill."

I'd taken it as far as I could. I couldn't compel people to talk to me or produce records, but was proud of my efforts and hopeful that, in time, more would come out.

That time came in 2006, at Siegelman's trial.

Claire Austin testified that in spring 1999, Young rented a private room at the Vintage Year, an upscale Montgomery restaurant. The purpose was for Lanny and Claire to introduce their Waste Management clients to Alabama's new governor. Company officials Chuck Campagna and Tom Herrington came to Montgomery to dine with Siegelman, Hamrick and Bailey.

"In our business, it's all about who you know and what access you have. That's a pretty impressive dinner, when you have the governor come by for dinner," Austin told jurors.

Hardly a shocking revelation, but it's through such details that the curtain gets pulled back for ordinary folk.

Young testified that Waste Management first broached Emelle with him in late 1998 or early 1999, after which he discussed the matter with Bailey, Hamrick and Siegelman. Then, in late June 1999, the company put all its eggs in one basket and went for it.

On June 24, Brazeal filed a petition with the Revenue Department. He demanded a refund of more than $4 million in taxes he claimed his client should not have been compelled to pay. His client would sue if the state didn't return the money; or, a second option, cut the taxes on the most common classification of waste from $41.60 per ton to $11.60.

I believe the petition was filed to alarm Hayes, the commissioner, who was not a tax professional; and to provide political cover to the administration should this drastic cut in hazardous waste taxes be discovered. The administration could claim –as it subsequently did -- that Waste Management had the state against a wall.

Maybe the company would have sued, but there's a big difference between filing a lawsuit and winning one. If the case was so strong, the company should have sued for the refund and the tax cut.

Four days after threatening to sue, Waste Management entered into its secret arrangement with Lanny.

Trial exhibits and Young's testimony cleared up a few things.

For example: It hadn't made sense for a paid up contract to serve as collateral for the $1 million loan identified by the UCC. It only made sense if Lanny was due more money. And he was. He was to receive as much as $1.5 million more – or $2 million total – with the sum depending on the amount Waste Management saved as a result of the tax change.

Most interesting was another condition of the contract: From the day of its signing, Lanny had 30 days to get the tax reduced. If he couldn't deliver in a month, he didn't get paid.

———

Before our first story, Waste Management said it hired Walston Wells to seek the tax change; that the firm hired Lanny; and the company blessed it. The actual contract, dated June 29, 1999, showed otherwise, that the arrangement was between the company and Lanny, though, "all payments to Young shall be made through the trust account of Walston, Wells, Anderson & Bains." The firm was just the conduit for paying Lanny.

With 30 days to get the job done, Lanny moved fast.

The day after signing the contract he asked Bailey to set up the meeting with Jim Hayes, and Nick did as asked.

There was, however, a problem. Wade Hope, the department attorney who oversaw hazardous waste taxes, wasn't budging from his long-held position that only the legislature could alter the tax, and he said as much to Hayes. "I told him, 'Commissioner, this is the same thing that's come up before. We can't do that,'" Hope testified at trial.

The administration solved the Hope problem on July 5. That day Siegelman appointed Susan Kennedy, a friend of Hamrick's and Lanny's, as the department's new general counsel. She thus became the first political appointee to serve as the tax agency's top lawyer in state history. Longtime general counsel Ron Bowden, who supported Hope on the Emelle matter, was demoted.

(After the first Emelle story I wrote several pieces on the circumstances of Kennedy's departure from the Revenue Department. Prior to leaving in June 2001 she arranged millions of dollars in legal contracts for a law school friend, Pam Slate. While still with the department Kennedy formed a two-person law firm with Slate. The day after she left the tax agency she began billing on the contracts she'd helped direct to Slate. The firm Slate Kennedy LLC was paid $4.6 million by the Revenue Department from those contracts.)

———

In mid-July 1999, Hope, the department lawyer, was summoned to the commissioner's office for a meeting with Hayes and Kennedy. He restated his position on Emelle. Kennedy told Hope the matter was no longer his to decide. The ruling was going to be made at the commissioner's office level. She subsequently directed Hope to draft a cover letter to Brazeal informing him that the department had agreed to cut the taxes.

At trial, Bailey testified that Siegelman called Hayes and told him that the tax change was important to the administration. The day before the ruling, Lanny met Siegelman at the governor's office.

"He said we'll get that revenue ruling you want but those bastards are going to pay for it," Lanny testified at trial.

On that day the lottery vote was less than three months away. Siegelman was obsessed with its passage and was hitting up donors as never before. He told Lanny to tell the folks at Waste Management that he expected the company to donate $50,000 to the lottery foundation.

———

Soon after the meeting with Hope and Kennedy, Hayes, the Revenue chief, authorized the tax cut at Emelle.

Eleven days later, Waste Management wired $500,000 from Houston to the Walston Wells firm in Birmingham. That same day, Ellis Brazeal signed a Walston Wells check made out to Lanny Young for $500,000.

Three days later, Young gave some of it back, paying $50,000 to the firm.

At trial, prosecutor Steve Feaga asked Young why "Paul Hamrick's brother-in-law's law firm" paid him, and not the company.

"That is the method that Waste Management chose to use to get the money to me," Lanny answered.

———

Shortly after the tax change, Miller Matthews, an Atlanta-based Waste Management executive, asked Young to get him a copy of Siegelman's resume. Matthews wanted to familiarize himself with Siegelman before calling the governor. Lanny procured a resume from Siegelman and faxed it to Matthews.

On Sept. 7, Lanny escorted Chuck Campagna and another Waste Management official to the lottery foundation headquarters, a home near the mansion that was co-owned by Nick Bailey.

One of the Waste Management guys handed Siegelman a $50,000 check made out to the foundation. The politician who had years before railed at Waste Management for Emelle-related kickbacks accepted it.

———

On July 15, 1999, Siegelman presented Young with a framed picture of himself. On it was a handwritten note. The picture was introduced into evidence at trial. Lanny was asked to read the note to the jury, and did so.

It read: "Lanny, You are something. I really appreciate your friendship and look forward to us spending more time together. You are special, Don."

One supposes that Siegelman routinely gave friends and supporters autographed pictures of himself with nice notes. What made this keepsake an effective piece of evidence is that July 15 was the same day the Revenue Department issued the ruling slashing the taxes at Emelle.

Chapter 20
Selling a house, Siegelman style

"Political wags wink and suggest that Gov. Don Siegelman would be a natural as a real estate broker, considering a windfall of some $100,000 he appeared to receive when he sold his modest home in Montgomery. But the deal may not be a joking matter, if investigators probe the transaction as they examine his financial records. Details about Siegelman's sale of the property for $250,000, as reported by the Mobile Register, came on the heels of published reports that Siegelman's financial records were subpoenaed weeks ago."

-- *Bessie Ford, in her newsletter, Inside Alabama Politics, after the Register reported the 1999 purchase of Siegelman's home by Birmingham accountant Wray Pearce.*

"Please provide any and all appraisal information or other information you relied upon to induce J. Wray Pearce to purchase the house and former residence of Gov. Don Siegelman and his family for a price in excess of the fair market value."

-- *From June 2002 court filing by Pearce's lawyer seeking information and documents from Birmingham trial lawyer Lanny Vines, who was suing Pearce.*

The tip for the story that some of Siegelman's own people said cost him the election was a sentence in an Associated Press story.

On Jan. 12, 2002, the AP reported that Don and Lori Siegelman had weeks before bought a home in Birmingham to be close to the First Lady's mother. They'd paid $425,000, including $200,000 down. The governor's mansion was to remain the Siegelmans' residence and their children would continue to attend school in Montgomery.

There was no suggestion of impropriety in the piece – actually a re-write of a *Birmingham News* story – that we ran on an inside page. It ended with this sentence: "The Siegelmans sold their Montgomery home after he was elected governor, Kurlander said."

I made a note on the shopping list, under Montgomery County Probate Court, to review the deeds on the sale. By then I was suspicious of all things Siegelman, enough so that I was willing to waste 15 minutes on the unlikely event that the records of his house sale would suggest something odorous.

On the last day of January, during my second trip since reading the story, I found some time. I went to the probate courts records room, settled before one of the computers, and typed "Siegelman Don" on the grantor line. About a second later, I saw that the governor had deeded his home on June 4, 1999, to a J. Wray Pearce.

That put the sale at roughly five months after Siegelman became governor. I scribbled the deed number on one of the orange paper squares used in that office for this purpose, and handed it to a clerk. Moments later I was at the microfilm machine, reviewing the deed signed almost two years before by both Siegelmans.

The one-page deed showed that the Siegelmans sold their home to this Pearce fellow for $250,000. The price was reflected in a hand-written notation on the deed, and more importantly, on the probate court stamp, which showed that the buyer paid $250 in deed taxes, or $1 for every $1,000 paid up front by the buyer.

There was nothing indicating a loan or mortgage. This suggested that Mr. Pearce was a Mr. Money Pants.

I copied the deed and returned to the computer. I entered Pearce's name in the grantor line to see if he'd subsequently sold the home. He had. Five months later he'd deeded it to "Pearce Family Investments LLC, a Delaware Limited Liability Company."

Had that company since sold it?

No, according to the probate computer.

More scribbles on little orange sheets, and back to the microfilm. The deed reflected that Pearce sold it to Pearce Family Investments for the same $250,000 he'd paid the Siegelmans. A notice atop the document directed the county to send the property tax bill to Pearce, and gave a Birmingham address. This suggested that whoever Pearce was, he didn't live in Montgomery, much less in Siegelman's former home.

Might Wray Pearce, perhaps through his Delaware company, be in the business of investing in homes, such as to lease or fix up and sell? If so, the Siegelman house represented a branching out. According to the probate computer, neither Pearce nor his Delaware LLC owned, then or before, additional property in Montgomery County. That didn't rule out the possibility of dozens of rental properties elsewhere – something I later researched and determined to my satisfaction not to be the case.

I found it interesting that Pearce Family Investments was a Delaware company. The state is famous for its business-friendly laws, both in terms of taxation (low), and laws that help corporations conceal their owners. Unlike most states, Delaware corporation records aren't available on the Internet, or in any event, not then, and not for free.

I called the Delaware secretary of state's office to confirm that such an LLC existed, and was given a list of firms that do corporation searches. I had to fax a letter with copies of my driver's license and Visa card authorizing a charge of $25. For this I received same day delivery by fax of the one-page Certificate of Formation of Pearce Family Investments LLC. It was money well spent.

For my purposes the most interesting aspect of the document was its date. Pearce Family Investments was incorporated on the same day that, some 1,500 miles south, it paid Wray Pearce $250,000 for the Siegelman house. This suggested that Pearce Family Investments was formed solely to buy the governor's house. Why, I had no clue.

I stayed overnight in Montgomery and the next day, returned to the probate records room. I copied every deed related to the house, going back to 1978, when Siegelman bought it, including mortgages and cancellations of mortgages. In all, 45 pages, at a cost to the paper of $45.

At this stage, two things needed doing: Learn about Wray Pearce, and find out if that house was worth $250,000.

————

With search engines firing, the basics on Pearce took a few minutes. He was a founding partner in Pearce, Bevill, Leesburg, Moore PC, which I immediately recognized as Pearce Bevill, the Birmingham-based accounting firm where my sister Leslie worked some 10 years before. Black Sheep Edwin had discomfited father and brother with stories before, and now it looked like it might be Les's turn. Did my sister, a CPA-turned full-time mother of three, hope one day to return to the firm? And if so, might my continued burrowing kill such plans? Just one more thing to worry about.

Next was a Pearce-Siegelman connection. In December 2000, more than a year after the house sale, the governor appointed him to the three-person Alabama Securities Commission. That board oversees the agency that regulates the securities industry within the state. Its members serve without pay.

I sought opinions on the value of a seat on the commission and concluded that, as quid pro quos go, it didn't add up. I could see where Pearce's purchase of the home might have contributed to Siegelman's decision to appoint him, but was unable to find evidence that Pearce was burning for a spot on the commission in a way that, say, Bobby Lowder lives and breathes to be on the Auburn board of trustees or, for that matter, Scrushy and HealthSouth must have a seat on the CON board.

Might the administration have awarded accounting or auditing contracts to Pearce's firm? A dead end there, too. A comptroller's search revealed not a single payment during Siegelman's tenure.

I couldn't avoid reporting the appointment to the securities commission, but downplayed it in the story so as not to suggest a quid quo pro where I didn't believe one existed. In a two-sentence paragraph, we reported that Siegelman "had appointed Pearce to a non-paying position" on the commission and that Pearce Bevill hadn't received any state business from the administration.

By far the strongest element of the story was the case it made that Pearce – for reasons unknown – paid the Siegelmans far more than their home was worth.

————

Step one in determining the value of the house value was as obvious as it was easy. I went to the county tax assessor's office, provided a clerk with the address and asked for the appraised value of the home in 1999, the year it was sold. The appraisal of $125,450 was almost right at half the amount paid by Pearce.

I could have stopped there and started writing. For probably 95 percent of readers, the county appraisal would settle the issue. But I'd have known that a story based on a county appraisal was potentially flawed, likely to be unfair to the governor, and would, at least among those familiar with county tax appraisals, reflect badly on me.

County tax assessors are notorious for undervaluing property, the better to avoid disputes with citizens angry at their property tax bills. With school budgets becoming more pinched throughout Alabama, assessors are tightening up, though there's considerable variation among counties. I didn't know the first thing about the Montgomery County tax assessor's office, but even if it was regarded for its accuracy, that didn't mean this particular property was correctly valued.

The 1-1/2 story, 2,100 square-foot home with three bedrooms and two baths was built in 1935. Siegelman bought it in 1979, paying $36,000 to Marian Folmar, the mother of long-time Montgomery mayor Emory Folmar. I called Montgomery County Appraiser Tommie Miller, who as luck had it was familiar with the home and the county's valuation of it. This from the story:

"Value is in the eye of the beholder," said Miller, noting that former Montgomery mayor Emory Folmar's parents lived there before selling to Siegelman in 1979. "It may have some historical significance value, but as a residence only, $125,000 would be accurate, and $150,000 would be extreme."

In the weeks after finding the deeds I'd learned everything I could about the home. I walked around it, took pictures, talked to neighbors. One of the first things I noticed were the bulky air-conditioning units jutting from the windows, indicating a lack of central heat and air. A six-foot high fence erected years earlier by the Siegelmans, and in dreadful condition, prevented passers-bye from seeing the home.

Initially I had difficulty locating records for the home, only to find I had the wrong address. When the Folmars lived there, the home bore the address 1905 Norman Bridge Road, and indeed that is its location. Norman Bridge is a busy thoroughfare and somewhat ratty on that side of the road along that particular stretch. The home next to the Siegelmans was a small one-story with a dirt driveway. Some years before Siegelman changed his address to the more socially upscale Park Ave., which intersects Norman Bridge and runs alongside his property. A block down Park Street the neighborhood – or, in any event, the quality of the homes – vastly improves.

A real estate agent gave me printouts of recent listings in the area that included descriptions and pictures of the homes, the listing and the ultimate sales prices. The sales prices along Norman Bridge ranged from about $40,000 to $70,000, though most were smaller than Siegelman's.

More telling were the prices of the homes along a street a block east of their home. Most were listed or had sold in the $100,000 to $130,000 range, were far nicer than Siegelman's and roughly the same size. They had central heat and air, were well cared for and on a peaceful street with manicured lawns and shrubs. That research, and it was plenty, was summarized and presented thusly in the story: "A *Register* review of sales prices along Norman Bridge, and in the nicer neighborhood behind the Siegelman home, shows that homes as large or larger, and in far better condition, have sold for considerably less than $250,000 in the past several years."

The sales comparisons increased my comfort level in reporting that Pearce overpaid for the house. At this stage I had enough to make a case that he'd done that, but had an idea to take it one step further: Since Pearce had bought a house, but not a home, why not analyze the purchase for what it was, an investment? After all, didn't the name -- Pearce Family *Investments* – declare it so?

If the house was an obvious loser as an investment then something was up, especially considering Pearce's background. He was head of one of the state's largest accounting firms and a member of the state board that regulates the sales of stocks and bonds. He had no excuse for making an investment as sorry as I imagined this was. Then again, if I found he was enjoying a reasonable return on his investment, it would drill a hole in the story.

Readers were given the formula we used to analyze the home as an investment, and which came recommended by real estate professionals interviewed for the story. The first step was to determine the gross annual income – a simple enough calculation of 12 times monthly rent, minus expenses. The following are the estimated expenses as they were presented to readers:

- *Annual property taxes of $899 due for that property, according to county records. (Because it is not the owner's primary residence, a homestead exemption, which would lower the tax, does not apply.)*

- *Insurance of about $950 a year for such a home, experts said.*

- *About $780 (or) 10 percent of the rental income, for a property management firm, which Pearce uses. Another 10 percent, or $780, as a projected vacancy factor, given that investors must assume that their properties will not always be inhabited.*

- *A minimum of 40 cents per square foot for maintenance, about $840 a year.*

That maintenance figure is arguably on the low side, given the home's age and condition. One real estate professional noted that an owner would need to consider *setting aside at least $1,000 a year to paint an older wooden home every five to seven years. For the Register's analysis, that painting figure was not included.*

The total of these estimated expenses is about $4,250.

I had the equation and all the numbers but one. I needed the value of X – the monthly rent charged a tenant living in the house.

I considered calling the leasing agent, June Wilder. At the time, the house was vacant and her name and number were on a sign out front. I recognized her name from sales involving others in the administration, including some Nick Bailey transactions I'd been reviewing and was soon to write about. If I went straight to her I'd have to identify myself and my reason for calling. I doubted she'd tell me anything and figured she might call Siegelman, and at this early stage, I wanted to keep the house research a secret.

I decided instead to locate the former tenants. The city directory gave me a name and number, but when I called, no forwarding number was given. A neighbor said a couple had lived in the house but had moved some months earlier, he thought, to Charlotte. Information confirmed that and gave an address, but their number was unlisted.

I punched the address into a database that gave me others who lived on the street and, if available, their phone numbers. I picked a nearby address and called. I was about to ask a most unusual favor of someone who didn't know me, so I had to play it right. As soon as I heard a man's voice, I was off, polite as possible given the rate my words spilled out. I had to move fast, or so I thought, to enable his brain to compute that my odd request was in its way reasonable before he decided otherwise and hung up. It went something like this:

"Mr. Jones I'm a reporter with the *Mobile Register* it's a newspaper in Alabama and I have what I know is going to sound like a strange request but I'm doing this story that involves our governor and his former house and I think your new neighbors used to live in the house and I really need to talk to them but their number is unlisted but I got their address and that's how I got your number I was wondering and I know this sounds strange but I was wondering if you could walk over and give them my number and sort of explain why I called you and to ask them if it would be possible if they'd call me."

A breath, and then: "Is there any way you could do that for me? I know it's an unusual request."

Within minutes I was doing another sales job, this time to the former resident of what was officially known as the Folmar-Siegelman House. It didn't take much. He told me the rent right off, since it was my first question once I realized he was up for talking.

With X=$650, I knew immediately that Wray Pearce Family Investments LLC of Delaware was almost surely losing money on its lone holding.

Mark was 42, a nurse, and his wife a doctor who had been assigned to a Montgomery hospital for her residency. They'd moved into the house in September 1999, three months after Pearce bought it and nine months after the Siegelmans vacated it. They lived there for two years.

They'd moved out four months before I called. He was apparently itching for someone to ask him about his old Montgomery home – not because of its former owner, but because of its condition. I was willing to be that someone, and typed for everything I was worth.

Here are my notes as they hit the screen, with a few parenthetical phrases for clarity's sake:

"$650 ... 3 bedroom and two baths ... it was a dump. I mean sincerely. Well, there was no maintenance during time ... we couldn't close the windows ... had been painted (sealed slightly open) ... they didn't have central air, ... the last winter we stayed there ... heater was so inefficient, and house itself, windows wouldn't close, and hadn't been maintained, during winter we couldn't (get) it above 60 degrees ... (we used) wood in fireplace ... multiple space heaters .. (lived there) two years ... (from) September 1999 .. we were first people after the governor, the floors were uneven, put a ball in floor and it would roll to the other end ... cockroach infested ... carpeting rotten in hallway ... they wouldn't replace the carpet ... I would say $125,000 is really highly inflated unless think of making a museum out of it. I have absolutely nothing good to say about it, other than only 650 ... everything is real old, refrigerator about the only thing modern in the house ... the fence was in pathetic shape..."

What he gave me nailed down the story. With X = $650, I could report that Pearce's projected gross annual income was $7,800. The following is as we reported it:

Subtract the (estimated expenses of $4,250) from the gross income and the resulting figure suggests that Pearce should have been able to forecast income of about $3,550 a year. That translates to a rate of return of about 1.4 percent on a $250,000 investment.

If Pearce had taken out a conventional mortgage to pay for the home, such a return would not have been enough to cover the note.

A respected Mobile appraiser, who asked not to be identified because of the political nature of the story, said that as an investment, the numbers presented to him about the sale made no sense.

"This is not a rule of thumb, but let me put it like this: If you had $250,000 today, if you put it in treasury bonds, you would get a ballpark return of about 5 percent a year, or about $12,500," he said.

Treasury bonds are considered the safest of investments. Someone taking more of a risk - which would include buying property as an investment -- would expect to earn considerably more than the interest that otherwise would be made on government bonds, the appraiser said.

"If you had a house worth a quarter-million, I would think you would want $1,500 to $2,000 a month in rent," the appraiser said.

But it was also, well, sad. There was no way to hear the description of the house and not feel sorry for the Siegelmans, though such pity was probably unwarranted. It would have been in far better shape when the family lived there. Later, reporters who had visited the Siegelmans there told me it was comfortable, nicely decorated and in no way ratty. By the time Mark and his wife moved in it had been vacant for nine months, through a steamy Montgomery summer and with a landlord with no interest in keeping the place up. The cockroaches had moved in, the carpet steam-heated to rot.

The story I wrote contained more of Mark's description of the home than did the published version. Paul cut much of it, fearing that it might come off as insulting, and pointing out that we weren't fully identifying the source. Mark, and I thought this reasonable, asked that the story not give his last name because he feared being inserted into a potential political scandal in Alabama.

After interviewing Mark I drafted a letter for Paul to send Carrie. It notified her that we planned to publish a story on the house and summarized our findings. It concluded with the following questions, one originating from a rumor Mark passed on – that he'd heard several lawyers bought the house.

Could the governor describe the process by which he sold his home, including how Wray Pearce became a potential buyer?

Does the governor know if Mr. Pearce was buying the home on behalf of others? Does the governor feel the home was worth $250,000?

If it is/was not worth that much, does the governor know why someone would pay that much for the home?

Carrie asked Paul if the story was to appear under my byline, was told it would, and declined comment.

I found Pearce's e-mail on his firm's web-page and wrote to notify him that we planned to publish a story about his purchase of Siegelman's home. I presented my findings, asked him if my calculations were correct, and asked several questions, including: How did you become familiar with the home and decide to buy it?

Then I waited. That afternoon, having not heard back, I called his office, spoke to a secretary, and asked if she could tell Pearce that I'd e-mailed him some questions, and to please call or e-mail me. He did neither, so that night I called his home. The conversation was quite brief.

"I really don't have anything to say. I have zero comment," he shot back in a gruff, I-don't-give-a-crap-what-you-write tone that told me that he'd read the e-mail.

The story ran on Feb. 23. The Associated Press picked it up, summarized our findings, and called the administration for comment. Rip offered up a lesson from Economics 101. He said that a "house is worth what someone is willing to pay for it. That's how the market works."

The *Birmingham News* editorial page drilled Siegelman in a piece that credited us for breaking the story. It began:

Talk about a homeowner's dream . . .

You've been elected governor, a good job that comes with a house. You find you have one home too many -- that is, until someone comes along and agrees to buy your old house for double its appraised value.

Where do we sign up for a deal like this?

The editorial concluded by making a point that was to be repeated in many subsequent analyses of the deal:

A house sale like this may do more damage to Siegelman's credibility with voters than the multi-million dollar deals that most of us don't have any experience with.

Unfortunately for Siegelman, many of us know what it's like to sell a house. And it doesn't happen like this, except maybe in realty ads and dreams.

Other editorial pages, our own included, chimed in. Jim Zeigler, bless his heart, filed a complaint with the Ethics Commission, contending that the house deal was a payoff for Siegelman's subsequent appointment of Pearce to the Securities Commission. The AP reported the complaint, and we ran it on an inside page. For reasons that should be obvious, I didn't touch it.

After the story, Joe Perkins, aka Matrix Man, had one of his minions research the modest midtown Mobile house my wife and I bought in 1995; and provided the fruits of his labors to several reporters. We paid $82,000, and according to Matrix's crack researchers, it was appraised by the county at about $20,000 less. To the extent it's necessary to explain, we didn't know the sellers, got the best deal we could, actually move into in the home, and its value has more than doubled in the years since.

The house story generated considerable talk, but no tips worthy of a follow-up. I had presented a strong case that a prominent Birmingham accountant had made a gift of about $125,000 to Siegelman, but was unable to explain why.

It was a mystery lacking a final chapter. I didn't like it that way, but didn't see what I could do about it.

Months later, in early summer 2002, a Mobile lawyer told me he'd heard the "street talk" in Birmingham was that Pearce bought Siegelman's house on behalf of Lanny Vines. I didn't need to ask who that was. With the exception of Jere Beasley, Vines is probably the best known trial lawyer in the state (not the same as being the best, a distinction likely held by Mobile's Bobo Cunningham or one of his partners in the Cunningham Bounds firm).

Big verdicts in personal injury cases and gargantuan class action settlements are not the sole source of Vines' fame. Among the others are his annual Christmas cards, mailed since the early 1980s to every attorney in the state, every student at the University of Alabama law school, and many others as well. For years the expensive, fold-out cards showed a grinning, pompadoured and tuxedo-clad Vines with his wife, two daughters and two massive canines posing in front of a pink Rolls Royce. For background there was Vines' neo-Norman Manse in Birmingham's historic Redmont district, which straddles the crest of Red Mountain.

Legend has it that one of the cards -- I haven't seen it – shows one of the dogs in an excited state, sporting a pink-tipped erection.

After Vines' divorce, his wife then daughters ceased joining him in the Christmas pictures. Now it's just him and his car and his mansion.

Vines grew up poor, worked like a fiend, made tens of millions of dollars and reveled in spending it. He owned condominiums in the French Quarter, and regular attendees of his famous Sugar Bowl parties there included judges, politicians and other Alabama notables.

Vines has long been a major go-to guy for Democratic candidates, nationally as well as on the state level. He's donated hundreds of thousands of dollars to state campaigns, much of it going to Siegelman and plaintiffs-oriented candidates for the state Supreme Court. He contributed $102,000 to Siegelman's 1999 lottery campaign, making him the largest individual, non-corporate donor.

If the "street talk" was right and Vines was the real buyer, then Pearce was a "straw man."

Straw might not smell, but straw men do. They don't suggest deception, they spell it out in big bright letters in the sky. All I had, though, was a rumor. And if Vines had put up the money, I couldn't imagine how I was going to locate a public record verifying it.

My only option was a long shot – that he'd tell me. I called his home, left a message, and didn't hear back. Had I known with some certainty that Vines was the real buyer, I'd not have left a message or called from my work phone. He surely had caller ID and wouldn't pick up if it showed the call coming from the *Mobile Register*. My effort was lackluster, and ended there.

In September, having largely given up on the house story, I decided to poach on territory plumbed by Blackledge and Chandler. They'd done stories (as will be seen later), on state investments business awarded to Siegelman's stockbroker. My working theory – and I was not alone here – was that the broker, Trava Williams, and his firm, AFS Equities might be a source of dirty money to Siegelman and his aides, a secret mechanism, if you will, for businessmen to express their gratitude to the governor.

I figured the best way to advance the story was to locate Brett and Kim's source. PACER, the Internet site for the federal courts, showed a lawsuit by AFS against a former broker. I suspected the broker – who I'll refer to as James -- might be their source. Whether he was or not, I hoped he'd become mine.

I called James and found him to be a devoted enemy of AFS, Trava Williams in particular. He said he'd be glad to talk, but not on the phone. He lived near Birmingham, and said any time was good. We scheduled a morning meeting. That would give me time in the afternoon to go to Jefferson County Circuit Court and review several lawsuits then burning a hole in my shopping list. Among those was a lawsuit by Anthony Fant, the AFS co-owner and Siegelman donor, against Lanny.

The interview with James was illuminating but of limited value. He refused to let his name be used and nothing he showed me was public record. I beat a path north to Birmingham and soon was at the counter of the Jefferson County Circuit Clerk's office, asking one of the employees to pull the lawsuits on my list.

As she gathered the files I did what I usually do when waiting at circuit clerks' offices. I gravitated to the judicial system computer on the counter, and typed in names. These sessions are pure fishing – thinking of names I hadn't thought of in awhile and giving them a ride. Since I was in Jefferson County, I tried to think of Birmingham-area folk. Might EPM Constructors or one of its three member companies have been sued? And if so, might the lawsuit reveal previously undisclosed details about the no-bid Honda contract? I gave them a spin, saw nothing promising, and racked my brain for local names. And then I remembered the house story.

I typed "Pearce J," and to my astonishment saw, "Vines Lanny" in the column opposite Pearce. It was like yanking the arm on a slot machine and seeing three cherries lined up. I raised my hand to get the clerk's attention. "Could you add CV-02-963 to the list?"

Minutes later I was speed-reading Vines v. Pearce. It had been filed in February, about a week before publication of the house story. There is no way, when researching that story, that I hadn't performed the usual Alacourt search for Pearce-related lawsuits. But it would have been one of the first things done, and as such, before Vines filed his suit.

My failure to discover the case earlier was a blessing. Like fine wine, good lawsuits improve with age. It's often best to withhold reporting on a new lawsuit, but instead to sit back, monitor the filings, wait for the parties to kick up some dust, then dive in. If litigants smell a reporter monitoring their case, all can be lost.

To my disappointment, the complaint failed to mention Siegelman or his old Montgomery home. But the disappointment ended there. As civil disputes go, Vines v. Pearce was a very sexy piece of litigation. Siegelman or no, this was a story.

By his own account, Vines had hauled in a $30 million fee following the 1999 settlements of a group of class action lawsuits against finance companies. The first $15 million arrived in April 1999, with the second installment paid in early 2000. In total, Vines earned about $35.5 million in those two years.

Even by his standards, $30 million was a once-in-a-lifetime score, and it arrived during that period in our economic history that will forever be associated with Alan Greenspan's phrase, "irrational exuberance." Perhaps the fed chairman was thinking about Lanny Vines when he coined that one.

After the first installment, Vines, or so stated his lawsuit, asked his doctor to explain the Internet's application as a means of trading stocks. The patient liked what he heard. Vines wound down his law practice and in fall 1999 transformed the basement of his mansion into a stock trading floor. He hired two traders and spent some $200,000 on "sophisticated and professional trading equipment for his new securities trading business which was to begin on a regular and continuous basis in early 2000," as his lawsuit put it.

In mid January 2000, he deposited $25 million into a trading account with New York-based brokerage Donaldson Lufkin & Jenrette.

From the start, Vines engaged in the high-risk game of buying on margin. This entails borrowing from a brokerage firm, using the loan to buy stock from the firm, then applying that stock as collateral for the loan. When the value of the stock increases, the trader-gambler sells it, bags the profit and repays the loan.

But if the stock falls below a certain price, the brokerage firm can make what is known as a margin call. That's when it says, in effect, game over. The stock is sold at a loss, and the trader must repay the firm the money lost on the stock, plus interest on the loan.

A "gain/loss" chart filed as an exhibit showed that Vines made a quick kill of more than $1.5 million on his first two purchases, both of which he held for less than a week. For the ordinary guy, $1.5 million is the lottery. Quit the job, move to Tahiti. But for Vines, one imagines the quick score buttressing a belief that trading in the law for the stock market had been a brilliant call.

On Feb. 9, he bought $17.5 million in shares of America Online. A week later he sold the AOL for a loss of almost $2 million. In mid-March, Alabama's most flamboyant trial lawyer bought $7 million worth of Broadvision. Within a month, the value of those shares had plummeted to $3.3 million. Vines took a $4.2 million thrashing on Conexant; dropped $5.7 million on something called Rare Medium; and suffered a $4.2 million setback on the software company Red Hat.

It took him less than four months to lose what differing court records indicate was either $26.7 million or $31 million. Almost all of his trades were in the Internet/tech sector, the chief inspiration for Greenspan's "irrational exuberance" remark.

On April 14, 2000, Donaldson Lufkin & Jenrette blew the whistle. Game over. It was time for Mr. Vines to settle up.

His losses were such that he had to liquidate many of his assets, including an $820,000 condominium in Gulf Shores purchased the summer before. Vines reportedly threatened to sue the seller of the condo if it wouldn't buy it back from him. He did sue Donaldson Lufkin & Jenrette, but the case was dismissed.

Not only had his class action millions vanished, but – and this is where Pearce comes in – the IRS was sending scary letters.

Uncle Sam was demanding about $15 million in back taxes, penalties and interest on revenues from Vines' law practice, the bulk of that from his $30 million class action bonanza.

In his lawsuit, Vines claimed that Pearce neglected to advise him that tax law at the time would have allowed him to write off his trading losses against his legal fees. For Vines to receive the benefit of the write-off, he would have needed to notify the IRS by April 17, 2000, and hadn't done so. So here was Vines -- having won the legal lottery and kissed it away day-trading -- staring at a $15 million tax bill.

I reviewed the various exhibits and Pearce's response to the lawsuit, and perked up when I came across a filing by Pearce's lawyer, called "Interrogatories and Request for Production of Documents to Plaintiff." It is within such filings that litigants demand the sort of information that their opponents invariably prefer not to provide.

This was my last hope to verify the "street talk" that Vines, not Pearce, was the real owner of Siegelman's house. The requests were interesting, but by the time I flipped to page 18 of the 19 page document, I'd given up hope of finding a Siegelman connection. Then, midway through that page, the governor's name hit my eyes as if written in giant neon letters.

Discovery question 46 through 50 read as follows:

46. *"Please provide all notes, correspondence, and memorandums concerning negotiations to purchase Gov. Don Siegelman's residence in Montgomery.*

47. *Were any phone conversations recorded with Gov. Siegelman? If so, then please provide copies of same or transcripts?*

48. *Please provide each and every bit of money paid directly to Gov. Siegelman in the past five (5) years as legal fees, advances on fees, and/or for any other purpose.*

49. *Please provide all notes, letters, memorandums, documents, correspondence or documents of any type whatsoever concerning the purchase of Gov. Don Siegelman's house or the LLC that owned the house."*

And the kicker:

50. Please provide any and all appraisal information or other information you relied upon to induce J. Wray Pearce to purchase the house and former residence of Gov. Siegelman and his family for a price in excess of the fair market value.

Taped phone conversations with the governor? Additional payments unrelated to the house? In excess of fair market value? HO-LY COW. This was public records heaven.

I paper-clipped the entire file to indicate to the clerk which pages I wanted copied. I called Paul while waiting for the proof to carry back to Mobile, and we agreed to move fast. The *Birmingham News* was a few blocks away, this stuff had been sitting here for three months and for all I knew, they'd seen it and were working on a story that minute. And if not, this story was one tip or loose lip away. To save time I'd drive to Montgomery and write in our office there.

The story was much easier than the first. It was largely a matter of presenting Pearce's discovery requests identifying Vines' role in the purchase of Siegelman's house; summarizing the findings from the first story; and telling the reader about Vines' class action fee, how he lost it, and why he was suing Pearce. All of that was in the court file, so I had no need to hunt elsewhere.

I called Bob Girardeau, shown on the files as Pearce's attorney. He directed me to Mark White, a Birmingham criminal defense lawyer.

I e-mailed White about 10 questions, most asking him to expound on the discovery requests. Did Pearce have information that Vines or his law firm had made payments in the past five years to Don Siegelman? Had Pearce met with Don or Lori Siegelman during the sales process?

I concluded with a sales pitch and an offer to come to Birmingham to meet with White and his client:

"Mark, I always figure it doesn't hurt to ask, so I asked pretty much. I would argue that when our story runs, on Friday, that it will lead to interest by other media, including the high likelihood of follow-ups by me. I would argue that, if Mr. Pearce provided his side of the story sooner than later, then the focus would be on those who haven't spoken, and who the court filing indicates, may know more than he anyway. Obviously, that would be Lanny Vines and Gov. Siegelman."

I hadn't expected him to bite, and he didn't. He wrote back to say it would be inappropriate to comment because of the ongoing litigation.

The story, published on Sept. 27, 2000, started thusly:

The Birmingham accountant who bought Gov. Don Siegelman's former Montgomery home in 1999 for almost twice its appraised value suggests in a lawsuit that prominent trial lawyer and Siegelman supporter Lanny Vines orchestrated the deal.

In a response to a lawsuit brought against him by Vines, accountant J. Wray Pearce also seeks information from Vines about "every bit of money paid directly to Gov. Siegelman in the past five years as legal fees, advances on fees, and/ or for any other purpose."

The governor and his representatives have described the house sale as an arm's-length transaction, with the governor and his wife placing the property on the market, and a buyer coming along and paying the asking price.

The governor's press office declined to comment for this report. (See editor's note at the end of the story.)

Vines' lawyer, Gusty Yearout, filed a brief declaring that Pearce's demand for records pertaining to Siegelman were "immaterial, irrelevant, overly broad, unduly burdensome," and unlikely to lead to evidence that would be admissible at trial. He asked Jefferson County Circuit Judge Tom King Jr., to declare as off limits records related to Vines' law practice and all matters regarding Siegelman.

Vines didn't return my calls so I called Yearout. He told readers he knew little about the house sale, and said, far as he could tell, neither Vines nor Siegelman had done anything wrong.

The Associated Press picked it up, and in keeping with the drill, called Siegelman's people seeking comment on the disrobing of Vines as the real buyer. "Andrews said the governor did not feel he was paid one cent more than the house was worth," the wire reported.

Rip -- who by then had left the governor's office to become chief spokesman for Siegelman's 2002 re-election campaign --hadn't budged from his comment after our first story earlier in the year. Best I could tell he'd completely dodged the Vines' revelation.

The AP delved into territory I'd made a point of avoiding. Given the proximity to the election and wary of feeding the beast accusing me of trying to destroy Siegelman politically, I'd avoided all mention of Riley. The AP called him.

"Bob Riley, Siegelman's Republican opponent in the governor's race, said the *Register* story 'connects the dots on the sweetheart deal, and, as usual, the dots lead right from Don Siegelman to his political cronies,'" the news wire reported.

I checked Alacourt several times a day looking for new filings. In mid-October Pearce's lawyer filed something, the brief description of which on Alacourt looked promising. I called my sister Leslie. Could she drive to the courthouse, ask for the Vines-Pearce case, copy the new filings and fax them to me? And thus began her new, unremunerated career as my occasional runner in Birmingham.

Later that day the fax purred out several bits of gold. The most unusual document was a "register report" listing every transaction by the Lanny S. Vines Foundation in the final eight months of 1999, starting soon after he received the mega-fee. During that period Vines deposited $21.1 million into the foundation and spent or withdrew $19.9 million. There were substantial payments to other lawyers and firms and transfers in and out of his various accounts.

Among the personal expenditures: $76,171 for a Mercedes; $823,737 for the Gulf Shores condo; $19,400 to a plastic surgeon; $64,746 on international wines and $300,000 for antiques. That year's Christmas cards ran to $16,720. He also gave generously to political candidates and organizations ($5,000 to his friend Ralph Nader), and to charities, including $125,000 to the United Way.

Litigation is war, and I assumed that in June, as with the recent filing, that Girardeau was shooting for the opponent's soft underbelly. Lawyers do this all the time, which is why reporters, when seeking to learn as much as possible about a person or company, should always locate and read lawsuits by and against a subject of inquiry. One never knows what will be there.

We held the story for three weeks, in keeping with the paper's policy of not dropping bombs on candidates in the final days of a campaign. I had to sweat it out, fearing the *News'* would see the new filing and pounce.

The story, which ran on Nov. 11, 2002 – after the election, but before Siegelman conceded to Riley -- focused on one transaction: a Nov. 29, 1999, which ran on Nov. 11, focused on one transaction: a Nov. 29, 1999, payment by Vines' foundation of $260,000 to Wray Pearce. In return, Pearce transferred to Vines all the stock in Wray Pearce Family Investments LLC.

That payment, as we told readers, showed "conclusively that Pearce bought the governor's house for Vines and … that Vines later bought the home from Pearce."

In his court filings, Girardeau argued that the home sale was relevant to defending his client because it exemplified Vines' bad financial judgment. "What motivation did Vines have for buying the Siegelman home without the benefit of an appraisal to determine the market price?" wrote Girardeau, in a quote we used.

The AP picked up the story, and as always, the administration response was hapless. Mike Kanarick -- the spokesman since Carrie's departure to have a baby and Rip's to the campaign -- declined comment when asked if Siegelman knew Pearce was acting on Vines' behalf.

I continued to monitor the case after Siegelman left office, hoping the court would compel Vines' to turn over various records, especially the tapes or transcripts of phone conversations so enticingly mentioned by Pearce's lawyer. I'd have walked to Birmingham for those. But it wasn't to be. Judge King ordered most of the records sealed and issued a series of rulings favorable to Vines. Among them: a denial of Pearce's demand that Vines turn over his Siegelman-related records.

The parties reached a confidential settlement in February 2004. A source with ties to Vines who contacted me later said Pearce, or more likely his malpractice carrier, had to pay about $3 million to Vines. Maybe that's accurate, maybe not.

Soon after the story I received a call from an investigator with the ethics commission. He said he'd been assigned the house investigation and wanted to know if I had any ideas. The guy sounded about as enthused as a lazy kid assigned a homework project. I told him to read my stories and bid him farewell.

About a year later the FBI went to the commission, scooped up what materials it had on the house sale – which, given the talent there, probably consisted of my stories – and took over the investigation.

With Siegelman claiming the home was worth $250,000 and Vines saying the same, and with no connected act by Siegelman on Vines' behalf during the time period, there was, or so I assume, no evidence of an explicit quid pro quo agreement, or in any event, none dug up. Apparently it's legal to enrich a public official by using a straw man to secretly and vastly over-pay for his or her home.

I can't help but wonder if a case could have been made that Siegelman committed tax fraud by not claiming the extra $125,000 or so separate from the value of his home, as I assume he did not.

The question remains: Why had Vines wanted to give Siegelman so much money?

I believe that Vines was rewarding Siegelman for the latter's efforts as lieutenant governor in staving off tort reform. Siegelman helped give the likes of Vines a few more years of massive fees. The payback was the house and other favors, such as one to be explained in the next chapter.

Vines' historical value defense was probably bolstered by the marker in front of the home proclaiming it the Folmar-Siegelman House.

Soon after the first house story I researched a follow-up but never wrote it. It would have reported that in his first weeks as governor Siegelman had aide Howard McCullars approach the Alabama Historical Commission about placing marker outside the home. Commission rules, though, forbid erecting markers until after a person's death, as did the other obvious option -- the city of Montgomery's historical commission.

Someone had to be wearing his thinking cap to come up with a third and probably final option. Problem was, the Cahaba Trace Commission, which is devoted to preservation of historic sites in 11 Alabama counties, also has a must-be-dead clause, and for 20 years before being honored.

Folmar, unquestionably one of Montgomery's historical figures, was, like Siegelman, much alive, and besides, he'd never lived in the house. His parents bought it in 1955, after Folmar left the nest, which would seem to dilute the already dubious "historical value" argument.

The Cahaba Trace Commission -- which had never erected a marker in Montgomery -- agreed to pay the entire cost of the marker, as opposed to its usual 40 percent. The Folmar-Siegelman House sign was manufactured in Ohio and shipped to Montgomery in the fall of 1999.

It was erected by the governor's staff.

———

Wray Pearce Family Investments LLC of Delaware remained owner of the home until 2009, with Lanny Vines remaining owner of the LLC named for the accountant he sued. It's been vacant since the day Mark and his wife moved out in September 2000.

In November 2008, a contractor appearing on Vines' behalf sought permission from the city architectural board to demolish the place after another arm of the city condemned it. He said it would take $166,000 – or more than the house was worth – just to bring it up to code.

The board denied the request to raze the home located within the historic Old Cloverdale district. Old Cloverdale Association president Joe Petranka said the owner's treatment of the home amounted to neglect.

"We have people like this who buy homes in historic neighborhoods so they can just rot. This has got to stop," he said.

Six months later the local historical society found a buyer, and in the nick of time. The buyer stepped forward an hour before an expected Montgomery City Council vote to demolish the home.

The sales price: $10.

Chapter 21
The $50,000 Fee

"Lanny Vines has asked that I write you regarding the $50,000 fee advance he paid you in December of 1998 on the Tapscott and Michael cases. For tax purposes, Emond & Vines did not deduct this payment to you in 1998 as the amount was treated as an advance on your fees."

-- April 5, 2001 letter, from Wray Pearce to Siegelman and stamped "Personal and Confidential."

"There was a better chance that George Wallace was involved, and he's dead."

-- Birmingham lawyer John Galese, after being told that Lanny Vines paid Siegelman $50,000 for non-disclosed services relating to the lawsuit known by the name of its lead plaintiff, Gregory Tapscott.

Of the discovery questions posed by Wray Pearce's lawyer in October and seeking Siegelman-specific information, one had nothing to do with the sale of the governor's house.

Pearce was Lanny Vines' former accountant, so it seemed unlikely that his lawyer was flying blind when he asked Vines to disclose "every bit of money paid directly to Gov. Siegelman in the past five (5) years as legal fees, advances on fees, and/or for any other purpose."

As the October document dump showed, Girardeau and client were sitting on the answer. Among the records filed that day was a short letter written by Pearce and dated April 5, 2001, the start of which is above, the remainder here:

In 2000, the cases were settled and the fees previously advanced to you were earned. Emond & Vines treated the previous advance as a deduction on its 2000 income tax return.

If you previously reported this income on your 1998 income tax return, there is no problem. If you have not previously included this income on your return, this amount should be included on your 2000 income tax return.

The letter was all business, with no mention by Pearce of a personal or business relationship with Siegelman. There was no, "P.S. Love the house!"

By this time I knew enough about Siegelman's legal career to doubt that he'd performed actual work in the Tapscott and Michael cases. I assumed that a review of the lawsuits would reveal another barely-earned referral fee, with a political pal delivering a plaintiff to Siegelman, who handed him or her off to Vines, who later paid Siegelman $50,000 from the settlement. I envisioned something along the lines of, "Mr. Tapscott, I'm Don Siegelman, and this is Mr. Lanny Vines. He'll take care of you, might even make you a rich man. Would stick around but I have a plane to catch."

The story published on Nov. 16, 2002, established almost to the point of certainty that this time, Siegelman hadn't even done that. His involvement in the Tapscott/ Michael cases was, best I could determine, non-existent. The facts presented in that story and never refuted by Siegelman or Vines suggested one explanation: That Vines used the lawsuits as cover to give Siegelman $50,000 a month after Siegelman won the election and a month before he became governor.

Tapscott and Michael were related wannabe class actions filed in 1994 and 1996 and merged into one case, the Tapscott case, which was settled in 2000. The case involved finance contracts between car dealers and buyers. For my purposes, the actions of the defendants, fraudulent or otherwise, were irrelevant.

After reviewing the convoluted history of the case, I called and spoke to about a dozen people whose names appeared on the filings, including Gregory Tapscott, the lead plaintiff. Though the settlement was confidential, one of the defendants said the total amount paid by all the defendants -- a sum to be split by the named plaintiffs and their lawyers -- was about $100,000. Others also described the settlement as small, especially considering the amount of time put into the case by writing and arguing briefs. Tapscott said each class representative received $3,750 for his or her efforts.

Assuming a settlement of $100,000, then half the money paid by the defendants went to Siegelman, if indeed the Tapscott case was the source of the $50,000 Vines paid him.

Tapscott had no reservations about discussing his uneventful six-year turn as a lead plaintiff in a class action. A Birmingham lawyer had found Tapscott's name on a list of people who'd bought cars from Jim Burke Automotive. The attorney explained that to Tapscott that he may have been defrauded, and set up a meeting with a second lawyer, Robert Gorham.

Tapscott said Gorham asked him some questions then signed him up as a plaintiff in a lawsuit against the dealership.

"Sure don't," Tapscott said, when asked if he recalled any involvement by Siegelman. He never met Vines, either, but knew the Birmingham lawyer was in charge.

From filing to conclusion, what drama there was in the case transpired within highly technical legal briefs focusing on the convoluted laws that govern financing agreements used by car sellers. About all Tapscott did, he said, was keep a file of letters sent him from Vines' office.

I called Gorham, figuring he'd be the one person, outside of Vines, who might be able to tell me about Siegelman's involvement. Since most plaintiffs' lawyers supported Siegelman, I supposed he'd give the governor a fair shake and then some. Maybe something along the lines of, "Don was quite involved in drafting the many appeals briefs and was, truth be known, sort of the hidden workhorse on the case. I personally think he deserved at least $50,000, and probably a lot more."

But that wasn't what he said. Gorham told me, and our readers, that he wasn't aware of "any involvement by Siegelman in the case." However, he'd dropped out of the lawsuit early, and said it was possible the then lieutenant governor became involved later.

Because so many dealerships were sued, there were lots of defense attorneys. Of the many I spoke to, none recalled any involvement by Siegelman. One lawyer willing to go on the record, Birmingham attorney John Galese, described himself as having been very active in the Tapscott case.

"You've got to be kidding. That's incredible," he said upon hearing of Siegelman's fee, and the reason for it as explained in Pearce's letter.

"There was never a document or a pleading or a court appearance or a single spoken word of or concerning Siegelman in the case," he said. "Lanny Vines, a hot shot lawyer, needed Siegelman to assist him behind the scenes? It doesn't make sense at all."

For perspective, I called Gil Kendrick, a staff attorney with the Alabama Bar Association, and suggested the following: I'd give him the facts and read the accountant's letter, but not identify the parties. I'd make this arrangement clear to the readers, so no one could accuse Kendrick of basing his response on the identities of those involved. He said it was most unusual for a lawyer to pay a referral fee before a case was settled, in great part because the paying lawyer wouldn't know what sort of fee, if any, the case would generate.

And here, from the story:

"Where did the money come from? The attorney just came out of pocket to pay the lawyer?" Kendrick asked. "I don't know what is going on here."…

(Kendrick) explained that referrals begin when, "Client A comes to Lawyer A. Lawyer A says this is not really the kind of work I do. Let me refer it out to a lawyer who specializes in this kind of law." A client must agree to the decision to refer his case, Kendrick said.

All contingency fee contracts must be in writing, with the clients agreeing to the percentage-based fee arrangements, Kendrick said. Most plaintiffs' cases -- including the Tapscott and Michael cases -- involve contingency fees. In such arrangements, a client and his lawyer agree that the lawyer will be paid only if the case generates money. If lawyers come aboard in the middle of a case, the client must be told and must consent if the new lawyer is to share in the fees, Kendrick said.

Tapscott hadn't consented to paying Siegelman – he said he'd never been asked to – and I was unable to locate any evidence that Siegelman signed up any of the other plaintiffs.

The purpose of Pearce's April 2001 letter was to remind Siegelman to report the $50,000 on his 2000 tax return if he hadn't previously done so. I'd no way of knowing if Siegelman had reported the fee for tax purposes, since tax returns aren't public record. The best I could do for the reader was his 1998 filing with the Ethics Commission. That year, as noted in an earlier chapter, he'd checked a box on his 1998 report indicating he was paid a total of between $100,000 and $150,000 by six "professional associations."

After we asked what he meant by, "professional associations," Siegelman changed his report to reflect that he'd meant six "individual legal cases which were concluded in 1998." He had, of course, declined to identify those cases.

After learning that one of the six was in all probability the Tapscott case, my curiosity as to the other five only increased. Might some other well known lawyers have paid Siegelman, and if so, for doing what? The press office, per the drill, declined to respond to our questions, as did Vines.

The Associated Press, God bless 'em, picked it up, re-writing as it always did. The wire lead: "The firm of a prominent trial lawyer gave Gov.-elect Don Siegelman a $50,000 advance the year before the same attorney arranged the sale of Siegelman's home for twice its appraised value, the *Mobile Register* reported."

As always when AP picked up one of my stories, my chief interest was the administration's response. Which was: "Siegelman spokesman Mike Kanarick called the payment 'entirely appropriate' but declined further comment, citing ongoing litigation."

Entirely appropriate? For doing what? What "ongoing litigation?"

My initial response was laughter, but I was also frustrated. I wasn't going to all this trouble to make Siegelman's life difficult or to harm his political career or, to the extent newspapers stories can do this, put him in jail. These were little mysteries of the type I'm in the business of solving. I wanted the truth, exactly as things occurred and why.

For me, as always, the greater outrage wasn't what Siegelman did – in this case, letting a politically active trial lawyer give him $50,000 for apparently doing nothing.

It was his refusal to come clean about it, to solve the mystery, and in so doing, provide the public with the explanation it deserved.

Chapter 22
The Governor's Stockbroker

"Months after Gov. Don Siegelman took office in 1999, his administration helped his personal broker take over several state investment funds worth nearly $330 million."
-- Lead of Birmingham News story exposing pressure placed on state agencies to use a small Birmingham brokerage called AFS Equities.

"Gov. Don Siegelman and aide Nick Bailey invested in a Colorado company days before a friend announced publicly he wanted to acquire it ... meaning that Siegelman's and Bailey's purchases happened before the stock's price increase in the wake of the announcement."
-- From another Chandler/Blackledge story reporting apparent insider trading by Siegelman and Bailey.

On Feb. 6, the Al.Com competitor check showed a hit by Brett and Kim. The story and others to come on a Birmingham-based brokerage firm called AFS Equities (rumored to stand for, Another Fucking Stockbroker) were in my opinion their most valuable contributions to the Siegelman scandal beat.

I didn't know the first thing about AFS. That allowed me to read the story with interest. Had I been working on the story I would have approached it with sweat-dripping trepidation, fearful of each new sentence and the prospect of finding they had discovered some juicy nugget I'd thought my own.

For chutzpah and provincialism, it's hard to top a governor, or for that matter a small town mayor, bullying agencies under his control to *hire his personal stockbroker to invest public funds.*

Actually, Trava Williams – the AFS broker in question – didn't manage a dime of state money. The 31-year-old friend of Bailey and Siegelman was foisted on the respected, Alabama-based firm of Sterne Agee & Leach. At the time Siegelman became governor, Sterne Agee didn't have a single contract to manage state money. The firm approached the administration seeking to get a leg in and was told, or so it would appear, that it could, if it hired Williams.

Williams – who years later would help run Siegelman's legal defense fund – also managed investments for Bailey, Hamrick and Siegelman's usually bulging campaign fund.

Sterne Agee's won its largest contract right off the bat, when it was hired to manage and invest some $300 million of the $2 billion Alabama Trust Fund. Williams was identified in Sterne Agee's contract as its "marketing coordinator."

Both Williams and Sterne Agee declined comment for the *News's* story. Siegelman, performing his customary scandal-story vanishing act, handed off to Rip. "Neither the governor nor Henry Mabry nor any member of the administration that we know of did anything to help ensure that Trava Williams had any role in this project," said the denier in residence.

My wounds from being beaten on the computer stories remained fresh and my competitive juices were surging. This AFS stuff looked promisingly nefarious. I was working on about five other stories at the time, but wanted in.

—

An Al.Com competitor check on March 8 revealed news that I probably took worse than Siegelman. Blackledge-Chandler reported hard-ball tactics used by the governor's office to try to force a little-known agency called the Peace Officers' Annuity and Benefit Fund into ditching its long-time investment managers in favor of Sterne Agee.

On that very day I was wrapping up a Sunday spectacular on the same story, had been working on it for weeks, conducted a couple dozen interviews and perused untold stacks of documents. Once again, they'd beaten me, though I continued to outpace them in the category known as, "Length of Story."

Irrespective of the teller, it was a tale of David telling Goliath to kiss his ass.

The police officers annuity fund is a supplemental retirement fund for state law enforcement personnel and is, by state standards, tiny, with about $19 million in assets at the time. It has a director, a small clerical staff, and is overseen by a seven-member board of former law enforcement officers. For years the commission had used the same four firms to invest its money, and had a fifth contract with an actuarial company to provide annual, mandated audits of the fund's condition. "We used two companies on stocks and two on bonds, and that way, we have a little competition, and they do battle with each other," said retired trooper Douglas Nelson, the board chairman.

As with most state contracts, the fund's contracts were for one year. They concluded at the end of the fiscal year and were routinely renewed prior to Oct. 1, the start of the next. In August 1999, the legislature's contract review committee signed off on the fund's five contracts and sent them to the governor's office.

"With previous governors, our contracts have never been an issue, period," Nelson said. "The contracts weren't huge (each with fees of about $25,000 per year), there was nothing unusual about them, and they were with reputable firms, including Merrill Lynch and AmSouth Bank."

October 1st rolled around with the governor's office not having delivered the contracts with Siegelman's required signature. The four firms and the actuarial company agreed to proceed without them, since all assumed the situation would work itself out.

A few weeks later, Bailey called agency director John Hixon to ask that the commission consider a presentation by Trava Williams on behalf of Sterne Agee. The next month Hixon wrote to inform Bailey that the board would do so. He told Siegelman's right-hand-man that the $16,000 contract with the actuarial firm remained unsigned and that the required review of the fund had been suspended. "The release of this contract would be much appreciated," wrote Hixon.

Williams came before the commission and gave his spiel, after which the members voted to let Sterne Agee manage a portion of the fund, along with the others on board.

"Trava Williams said they weren't interested in a portion. They wanted it all," said Nelson.

The commission balked. Meanwhile, back at the governor's office, the contracts remained in the unsigned pile. Hixon wrote Siegelman, pleading for the governor to sign the contracts. Nine days later, Siegelman's office delivered the five contracts.

All were unsigned.

"It was a response," said Nelson, laughing. He characterized Siegelman's return of the contracts as "a message."

The day the governor's office returned the contracts, Hixon wrote a letter to Siegelman on behalf of the 4,000 retirees invested in the fund. He pleaded with the governor to sign the contracts. Siegelman was unmoved.

The commission discussed liquidating all its assets – regardless of whether it was the prudent financial move or not -- and placing them in index funds, which don't require management by a firm. "There was very much concern on the board," Nelson said.

In early January, Merrill Lynch secured Siegelman's signature on its contract as well as that of the actuarial firm. Why Merrill Lynch and not the others?

It had retained the Matrix Man.

Joe Perkins went to Siegelman's office and, pronto, got Alabama's New South governor to get off his pen.

By February, the three other contracts remained unsigned and the companies were, among other things, concerned about being paid. Another letter to Siegelman; another no response.

In March, word was leaked to Siegelman that the commission was considering holding a press conference to embarrass the governor for his efforts to force Trava Williams on the fund. The threat worked. Siegelman signed the contracts, but not in time to prevent the liquidation of stocks held by two of the firms, which had bailed out. "Basically, what this did is it caused us to change our strategy of investing," said Nelson.

Did Siegelman's toying with the fund lead to losses? Nelson said there was no way to know. He added that, if given the choice, he'd like to return to the fund's old way of doing business.

Can you see why, if you were a reporter, you would be motivated to write stories on these people? Did they or did they not deserve it?

Naturally, the administration declined to comment for my story, and by now Siegelman was probably wishing that Brett or Kim had cussed someone out. Rip told the *News* that since Siegelman ultimately signed the contracts and Sterne Agee didn't get the business, suggestions of favoritism were "completely absurd." He said the administration hadn't held up the contracts to help Williams and Sterne Agee. The delays were simply part of a larger backlog of contracts then under review, he said.

Several other small state funds managed to bust the backlog faster.

As the retired officers struggled to get a few Siegelman signatures, the Alabama Crime Victims Compensation Commission faced a similar quandary. The renewal of its contract with AmSouth was sent to the governor's office and been returned, also unsigned.

At its October meeting, a board member recommended that the commission hire Sterne Agee to assume management of the fund. The board voted to end its 15-year relationship with AmSouth and award the business to Sterne Agee and Trava Williams.

I reported as much in my annuity fund story, but several days later, Kim and Brett topped me with records I'd not found. They'd obtained an audiotape of the meeting. A board member, Doris Dease, had suggested splitting the business, keeping AmSouth but moving some of the money to Sterne Agee. And here, as the *News* reported it:

> *"I don't think the governor will sign that," board member Miriam Shehane said on an audio tape of the meeting.*
>
> *"I don't see why the governor has a problem," Dease responded. "We've been dealing with AmSouth for 15 years."*
>
> *Board member Benny Peoples then told the staffer running the recorder, "Turn the tape off."*

When the tape resumed, the board voted to ditch AmSouth and award all its business to Sterne Agee. The new contract swiftly busted through that backlog that was giving the annuity fund such fits.

Their story ran on March 15. I read it on Al.Com, perhaps at the same time Brett and Kim were reading my two offerings for the day. The first reported details of two more Sterne Agee/Trava contracts, both, again, with small funds. Brett and Kim's story had reported them as well. About the only thing I had that they didn't were some details of Williams' pay -- 30 percent of Sterne Agee's fees on one of the contracts and 40 percent on the other.

Those figures, when added to and others previously reported by the *News*, indicated that Siegelman's broker was making about $85,000 a year as Sterne Agee's very part-time "relationships manager."

The AFS stories revealed Nick as an arm-twister on the investment contracts. Unquestionably, Siegelman knew what was going on every step of the way, probably told Bailey how to play it. Still, Bailey – at the time the state "budget officer" -- performed the task too well. On the AFS deals, perhaps more than any other, the lackey label didn't fit. He was a real live player.

My second story that day also focused on Nick. The *News*' reported in its stories that Bailey and Williams were business partners, but without providing any detail. I jumped in and gave plenty of it, thanks to time well spent at Montgomery County Probate Court.

The story began:

At the same time he was helping Gov. Don Siegelman's personal stockbroker win state business, former top Siegelman aide Nick Bailey was involved with the broker in a series of real estate deals, according to deeds and state corporation records.

Bailey and Trava Williams -- primarily through two companies called the Provident Group Inc., and Greenday LLC -- have at times in the past three years owned three Montgomery properties, including the one-time home of the Alabama Democratic Party, and two homes, one of which was Bailey's residence for a time.

The best known of the properties was a circa-1920s home across the street from the Governor's Mansion. It had served as the lottery foundation headquarters, then by the state party. In 2002, it became home to Siegelman's fund-raising operation for his re-election, and was by then owned by the omnipresent Joe Perkins.

This was where Siegelman went to dial for dollars throughout his four years as governor.

The story reported details of the transactions, including several no-money down purchases, the entire sums coming from Colonial Bank mortgages. The bank -- with its many political ties to the administration -- apparently decided that Bailey, unlike John Doe and the rest of us, didn't have to put down any of his own cash before getting such loans.

In October 1999 – during the time Bailey and Siegelman were forcing agencies to use AFS -- the property near the mansion was mortgaged to the hilt, and then some. The probate records showed three mortgages totaling $208,000, all with Colonial. A year later Bailey and Williams sold it for $110,500 to a real estate agent. Two months later the final mortgages were recorded as being paid off.

The story also reported Bailey's failure to make the first mention of Greenday or the Provident Group on his ethics forms, despite several categories on the forms requiring disclosure of such interests.

I tossed in an interesting nugget from a newspaper database search. Two years before, the *Montgomery Advertiser* published a short piece on the property across from the mansion. It noted that zoning rules had forced the Democratic Party to move out, and reported that Bailey, as president of the Provident Group, was part-owner of the property.

Bailey demanded a correction. He said it was another Nick Bailey who owned the house. The *Advertiser,* chastened, printed a correction.

Soon after, the paper determined that it was right all along – that the owner of the house was indeed *the* Nick Bailey. So the *Advertiser* called him back. Bailey had a spokeswoman say his demand for a correction was based on a misunderstanding.

––––

A week after that round of stories, Brett and Kim upped it a notch, giving Siegelman a new title: Inside trader.

Though not a broker, Anthony Fant, the Birmingham businessman and Siegelman backer, was a part owner of AFS. Fant had some years before invested heavily in a Minnesota-based manufacturer of medical devices called HEI Inc., and was the company's chairman. In August 2000, he was secretly preparing a hostile takeover by HEI of a company called Colorado MEDtech.

Days before announcing the takeover attempt Fant personally bought some $9.5 million in Colorado MEDtech stock, using various means to disguise this. Williams made some of the purchases, and not just for Fant. Brett and Kim's story began:

Gov. Don Siegelman and aide Nick Bailey invested in a Colorado company days before a friend announced publicly he wanted to acquire it.

The stock purchases for Siegelman and Bailey were arranged in the summer of 2000 by Trava Williams, Siegelman's personal broker and Bailey's close friend, securities records show.

Months earlier, Bailey had helped Williams secure state contracts signed by Siegelman that allowed Williams to receive commission payments on state trust fund investments.

Siegelman invested $80,000 in Colorado MEDTech, his buying price at $8 per share. Fant's take-over offer, made days later, was at $12 a share. If things had gone as planned, Alabama's governor could have scored a quick $40,000.

The stock rose on news of HEI's takeover ploy, but not to $12. Siegelman held on to his shares, betting on the deal going through. But Colorado MEDtech rebuffed the takeover and the stock sunk below the $8 a share Siegelman paid for it. That created losses for him, Bailey, Williams, Fant and others who'd used Fant's inside scoop.

This allowed Siegelman's new lawyer, David Cromwell Johnson, to say his client had merely acted on a tip from his broker and lost money. "I don't think there was inside information. If there had been inside information, they would have sold it and made money, instead of keeping it and losing money."

From a legal if not a financial standpoint, Siegelman benefitted from the deal's collapse. Instead of facing possible criminal charges for insider trading, he merely had to deal with Another Fucking Scandal.

Chapter 23

The Canary Canard

"Johnson attempted to make his point by bringing along three canaries in a birdcage, along with a chart showing pictures of Tweety Bird from Looney Toons cartoons next to the names of Leura and Bill Canary. He said canaries sing just like Leura Canary sings to her husband and leaks information to the media. 'The difference between a canary and a parakeet is that a canary sings,' Johnson said. 'I think there is a leak in the grand jury.'"
-- *From March 25, 2002, AP story on press conference by Siegelman lawyer David Cromwell Johnson.*

"This will end because you can't sustain a lie forever."
-- *U.S. Attorney Leura Canary, in 2008 interview.*

The Siegelman investigation was to be characterized by fits and starts, long delays and changes in prosecutors, but it got out of the box pretty fast.

On Oct. 29, 2001, a state grand jury charged Roland Vaughan with a misdemeanor count of failing to disclose to the state his half-ownership in the land that his firm recommended for the warehouse site; and a felony theft charge that essentially accusing him of stealing the $25,000 that Sherlock Smith & Adams charged for the site study.

Not long after the indictment, Vaughan announced his resignation from the Montgomery architectural and engineering firm.

The indictment was a surprise to me. Five months before I'd asked Vaughan if he was in a partner with Andrew Nolin on the land deal. He had said he was not; we quoted him saying that; and I didn't learn otherwise until he was indicted.

Attorney General Bill Pryor said the case was "one piece of a much larger joint state and federal investigation that is ongoing."

Vaughan wasn't initially considered a suspect. After the investigation began he met several times with Bill Long, an investigator with the attorney general's office, to provide background information on the warehouse project. He did so willingly, without an attorney present. However, at no time during those meetings did he tell Long that he had become a half-owner of the land and made a neat profit upon its sale.

Long was to testify at Vaughan's trial that he was reviewing closing documents on the sale when he noticed a check to Vaughan for $48,434.

"I was just totally shocked," the investigator said.

He immediately called Vaughan, who told him had felt no responsibility to reveal his part-ownership in the land to Long or, at the time of the land sale, to the state. The attorney general's office saw it different, and prosecuted him.

Three months later, in early 2002, two lesser figures entered pleas.

Bryan Broderick pleaded guilty to a misdemeanor charge of giving false information to the state contractor's licensing board when applying for G.H. Construction's contractor's license. Broderick had over-stated both his qualifications and the firm's financial situation.

Lanny's front man was sentenced to a year's unsupervised probation and fined $750 in return for a promise to cooperate with the investigation. (Broderick did not testify at trial. I never once saw him.)

Also pleading to a misdemeanor was Richard Campbell, a Montgomery construction company owner. His real infraction was letting a friend talk him into doing something stupid. When applying for G.H. Construction's license, Broderick asked Campbell to vouch for an element of his work history that wasn't true. Campbell did so, and this was discovered during the investigation.

Campbell, reached for comment after his plea, gave a memorable quote. "I'm like the flea that was on the dog that was hit by the truck," he said.

He was sentenced to a year's unsupervised probation.

On Feb. 10, four days after their first story on Trava Williams and AFS Equities, Blackledge and Chandler reported that investigators had subpoenaed Siegelman's financial records, including his brokerage accounts.

The news was consequential. It meant that Alabama's governor was the subject of a criminal investigation.

Siegelman professed shock. He said he had no idea that his records had been subpoenaed until called by the Birmingham paper. Then he left the tough stuff to Rip.

"Republican Attorney General Bill Pryor, Republican U.S. Attorney Leura Canary and Republican gubernatorial candidate Steve Windom are engaging in a partisan witch hunt and character assassination of the governor by innuendo, rumors, lies and leaks from anonymous sources," Andrews said.

The next day found the governor in damage control mode. He took the unusual step of inviting members of the capitol press corps for one-on-one interviews in his office. During these sessions he professed his innocence and accused Pryor and Leura Canary of conspiring with Windom to torpedo his re-election campaign. He claimed that his GOP enemies passed on the information to the *Birmingham News* in violation of grand jury secrecy laws.

Siegelman's castigations of Pryor marked a stark about-face. Up until then the governor couldn't say enough good about the attorney general.

In the previous year, Pryor aced grumbling from fellow Republicans who believed him *too close* to Siegelman. He had supported the governor's Amendment One initiative and issued an attorney general's opinion on a Siegelman-backed education funding bill that angered some Republican lawmakers.

"Alabama has a history of nasty head-butts between its governors and attorneys general, but many Republicans say GOP Attorney General Bill Pryor and Democratic Gov. Don Siegelman have been dancing cheek to cheek," began a May 2001 *Birmingham News* story on their relationship.

"He's been closer to Siegelman than Reno was to Clinton. And nobody can figure it out," said Republican Baldwin County district attorney David Whetstone, of why he was considering running against Pryor.

"Most of (my decision to run) would be his extremely close association with the governor's political agenda," Whetstone said.

Then and later – including in the months after the opening of the G.H. investigation -- Siegelman defended the attorney general against the GOP grumblers.

"Bill Pryor is an incredibly talented, intellectually honest attorney general," Siegelman the News. "He calls them like he sees them. He's got a lot of courage, and he will stand up and fight when he believes he is right."

Flattery having gotten him nowhere, the governor and his minions unloaded on the attorney general.

During the one-on-one sessions, Siegelman told his reporter guests he hadn't hired a lawyer because he didn't need one. Three days later he announced that he had retained Birmingham lawyer David Cromwell Johnson to "expose those behind the leaks."

Cromwell Johnson was a legend, the wild-man of the Alabama white collar defense bar, known for his hard drinking and histrionics. His 2003 death at 60 denied me the pleasure of seeing him in action. Years earlier, while defending former Gov. Jim Folsom Jr., he called me out of the blue, blind drunk, to belittle the trial lawyering talents of then attorney general Jeff Sessions. He was laughing, and, as he made a point to say, it was all on the record.

Crazy like a fox, Cromwell Johnson specialized in creating spectacles that drew attention away from his high-profile clients and toward himself. He was, as they say in the newspaper business, good copy.

On his first day on the job he sent letters to Pryor and Leura Canary asking each to investigate leaks in their offices. They were, he said, to give polygraph tests to all members of their staffs. There was as much chance of Canary and Pryor submitting their employees to lie detector tests as there was of Cromwell Johnson taking one himself, and he knew it. It was a stunt, the sort of political theater that was to remain the core of Siegelman's defense, and long after Cromwell Johnson's death.

Naturally, he provided the polygraph demand letters to the press.

Cromwell Johnson accused prosecutors of tipping off Windom to the subpoenas, and said it was probably the Republican lieutenant governor who passed the information to *Birmingham News.*

"All we've done is compile newspaper clippings of the Siegelman administration's numerous ethical lapses. We might have to buy another file cabinet," said Windom spokesman Ragan Ingram, with the sort of wit that Rip was never able to bring to the task.

Though not at liberty to name names, Blackledge told me years later that his sources on those first subpoenas were Siegelman's fellow Democrats.

———

On a Monday in late March, Cromwell Johnson convened a press conference that was outlandish even by his standards. The federal courthouse in Montgomery served as backdrop for a scene constructed with the television cameras in mind. Many Alabamians who watched local news that night saw Siegelman's lawyer accompanied by three yellow canaries in a cage alongside a poster with a big Tweety Bird and the names Leura and Bill Canary.

A final visual aid – a box of "Windom's Canary Flakes" -- sat propped on the podium.

Though admitting he lacked proof, the master of ceremonies called the investigation a Windom-inspired witch-hunt designed to crush his client's re-election bid. He accused Leura Canary of feeding grand jury information to her husband, who then passed it on to the Windom and Riley campaigns.

"The difference between a canary and a parakeet is that a canary sings," Johnson proclaimed.

He called on Leura Canary to recuse herself from the Siegelman case because of what he called her husband's "documented financial ties with the direct political opponents of Governor Siegelman."

Bill Canary issued a written response accusing Cromwell Johnson of "legal terrorism" and demanding an immediate retraction. "Mr. Johnson and Mr. Siegelman are both experienced attorneys, and I find it repugnant and unethical for them to make such blatant accusations that are unfounded and untrue."

He should have saved his breath. Despite there being not one record or statement from a single witness not named Jill Simpson linking Bill Canary to the Siegelman case, it was, after her May 2007 affidavit, to become an article of faith that Bill Canary played a seminal role in employing the awesome power of the U.S. Justice system to destroy Alabama's Democratic superman.

Of the many mischaracterizations in the national coverage of the case after Jill Simpson's affidavit was the exaggeration of Canary's influence in Republican politics in Alabama. Anyone who got their news from *Time* or the *New York Times* or the likes of *Harper's* Scott Horton would've had every reason to conclude that Canary lorded over the state's GOP like a latter day Julius Caesar.

"Leura Canary, the U.S. Attorney whose office drove Siegelman's prosecution, is married to Bill Canary, Alabama's *most prominent political operative* and a longtime friend of Karl Rove's," declared *Time* reporter Adam Zagorin in his October 2007 story, "Selective Justice in Alabama?"

According to Scott Horton of *Harper's* magazine, Canary was a "legendary figure" in the state.

If it were possible to go back in time and conduct a poll in, say, January 2002, I doubt a half of one percent of Alabamians could have identified this legend among us.

Canary was described in a June 2007 story in the *Los Angeles Times* as a "Rove protégé" who helped lead the GOP effort to defeat (Siegelman) in 2002." This description proved infectious. The *New York Times* used it, and in a July 2007 letter to Attorney General Alberto Gonzales, House Judiciary Committee chairman John Conyers twice called Canary a "Rove protégé."

Before Rove won the sobriquet "Bush's brain," he was probably best known as a protégé of GOP master dirty trickster Lee Atwater. Those who labeled Canary a "Rove protégé," had to know they were insinuating to readers that he was a practitioner of black-bag political skullduggery.

I'm the farthest thing from a Bill Canary expert —I'd never heard of him until Cromwell Johnson's first press conference – but am not aware of even a rumor associating him with political shenanigans. Not, in any event, until Jill came along. And one supposes that if he had such a past, the old stories would have risen to the surface and appeared first in Scott Horton's columns, then in *Time*, the *New York Times,* and on "60 Minutes."

Post-Simpson, Siegelman and his acolytes made a game of exaggerating the Canary-Rove relationship. Canary was to learn that he was not merely a friend of Rove's, but his "best friend," and more.

One example was a December 2008 interview in which Siegelman described Leura Canary as "the wife of Rove's best friend and his former business partner."

In testimony given to the U.S. House Judiciary Committee in July 2009, Rove said he felt sure he must have been introduced to Leura Canary at some point, but had no specific recollection of ever having met her. That means he didn't even attend the Canary's wedding, such as to serve, best friend-like, as best man.

According to Bill Canary, Siegelman and many in the national media have "mischaracterized my relationship with (Rove) to serve their purposes."

"I was never a 'protégé' of his or for that matter a business partner as they claim. I know Karl but do not have a close relationship with him. I am definitely not his 'best' friend," Canary said.

Leura Canary was sworn in as U.S. Attorney on Sept. 6, 2001. That was four months *after* our warehouse stories and the start of the investigation. In case that's not clear enough: She was not U.S. Attorney when the decision was made to open an investigation into G.H. Construction.

She was, nominally at least, in charge of the Siegelman investigation from her appointment until May 2002, when she recused herself from the case.

Cromwell Johnson had to know his leak charges were a sham, but he was not out of line in seeking Leura Canary's recusal. Her husband, at least for a time, was a paid advisor for the Windom campaign. In a response to Johnson's request, Justice Department officials in Washington wrote that their analysis led them "to conclude that no actual conflict exists." However, the letter informed Siegelman's lawyer that Leura Canary had asked to be removed because "a reasonable person might question her impartiality were she to continue her current role in the investigation you describe."

Technically, at least, this was a victory for Siegelman, but one he and his lawyers chose to pretend they lost. The public relations benefits of linking Bill Canary to the investigation were simply too good to relinquish. More than seven years later, Team Siegelman continues to assert that Leura Canary was in charge of the investigation, and post-Jill Simpson, convinced leading national media voices and the Democrat-led House Judiciary Committee of the same.

What Siegelman and his lawyers and backers lacked in evidence they made up with in volume and repetition, working to death the old adage that if you say something enough, it becomes true.

———

Upon graduation from law school in 1981, Bill Canary's future wife, Leura Garrett, was hired as an assistant attorney general by Attorney General Charlie Graddick, who at the time was a Democrat. After the 1986 election she got a new boss – Don Siegelman.

"I never had any run-ins with him. He never did or said anything unkind to me until he got himself in trouble," she said.

She met her future husband in 1989, during a political exchange trip to the Soviet Union. At the time, Bill Canary worked in the administration of George H.W. Bush, as special assistant for intergovernmental affairs, working with cities and counties. The couple wed in 1990. She moved to Washington and took a job with the Justice Department. In the next four years she won accolades for her representation of law enforcement in federal cases involving constitutional law.

Bill Canary left the Bush administration in 1992 to become chief of staff to Republican National Committee chairman Richard Bond. Two years later, the New York native took a position with the Washington-based American Trucking Association, but, for his wife's sake, moved to and worked from Montgomery.

By then, the U.S. Attorney in Montgomery was Redding Pitt. He was a Democrat, a Clinton-appointee, and one of Siegelman's oldest personal and political friends. Pitt had worked with Leura Canary in the Siegelman-led attorney general's office and asked her to join his staff.

Pitt thought enough of Canary to make her chief of the office's Civil Division.

In the late 1990s her husband formed a Montgomery-based lobbying and political consulting firm. Clients included Bill Pryor, for the latter's 1998 campaign for attorney general; and Robert Aderholt, the Republican congressman from north Alabama.

Canary worked briefly on Windom's 2002 campaign for governor (when Windom was running against Bob Riley in the primary). That spring he returned to lead the American Trucking Association, though he did so from Montgomery.

Despite national media reports to the contrary, Bill Canary did not work on Bob Riley's 2002 campaign for governor. He, and a small army of others, would call with advice every now and then, but that was it. Riley, whether for his congressional races or his 2002 run for governor, was never a client of his consulting business, Canary said.

In 2003, Canary was made president of the powerful Business Council of Alabama, and remains in the position.

———

After George W. Bush defeated Al Gore, Pitt, like other Clinton-appointed U.S. Attorneys, resigned. Charles H. Nevin, a 25-year veteran of the office, became acting U.S. Attorney. He served that role until September 2001, when Leura Canary was confirmed as U.S. Attorney, and moved from running the civil side to running the entire office.

It was Nevin, not Canary, who was in charge on May 1, 2001, when Bill Pryor announced the joint state and federal investigation into G.H. Construction.

The decision to open an investigation into G.H. Construction and the warehouse project was no a source of controversy at the time. On the contrary. It would have been prosecutorial misconduct *not* to investigate the theft of at least $90,000 from the state by a straw company secretly owned by one of Siegelman's major supporters and a close associate of both Hamrick and Bailey.

As Siegelman and one supposes Cromwell Johnson knew, Bo Torbert, the former state Supreme Court chief justice appointed by Siegelman to review the warehouse project, had in his highly critical report cited "substantial questions as to the propriety" of payments to G.H. Construction.

Among those not complaining at the time was Siegelman. He was all outrage and disappointment, but at Lanny Young and Bill Blount, not prosecutors. He supported the probe. Publicly, anyway. Privately, one imagines him petrified, of prison and political doom.

The subsequent criminal investigation unearthed hundreds of thousands of dollars stolen from the state and payments by Young to Bailey, Hamrick and Siegelman. It would have been justified for that alone. These and other matters of record were not to be found in the national media's coverage of the case, which didn't begin until after Jill Simpson's affidavit.

To report those facts would have diluted the only reason for bringing the Siegelman story to a national audience – that he was a victim of a Republican-inspired political prosecution.

———

Non-existent leaks by prosecutors to Republican politicians and the Alabama press were to remain among the standard accusations by Siegelman and his lawyers and spokesmen for years come.

Some in the national press, instead of seeking to verify, simply reported what came out of Siegelman's mouth. For example, "60 Minutes."

On the night of February 24, 2008, CBS newsman Scott Pelley intoned: "Details of some of those investigations leaked to the press. And Siegelman lost his 2002 re-election campaign narrowly to Republican Bob Riley."

At that point, an October 2001 *Press Register* article written by myself and Jeff Amy was flashed on the screen. This obviously was intended to serve as evidence of the Pelley-described leaks. I wrote a letter to "60 Minutes," that pointed out errors in the piece, including the linkage of our story with leaks by prosecutors and, lastly, the presumed causal relationship between the alleged leaks to Siegelman's loss in the 2002 election.

I informed the "60 Minutes" folks that a careful read of the story shown to their viewers would show that our story cited the *Birmingham News* as the source of an investigation into Siegelman.

And then, in full huff:

"No proof whatsoever is offered to support what is stated as fact that the News or myself or anyone else received leaks from prosecutors. None. Because you have none. Prove me wrong.

"Also, and I could be wrong here as well, but I don't recall many grand jury type stories in 2002. There were dozens of stories on other matters, such as Siegelman's use of a straw man to sell his house for twice its value to Alabama trial lawyer Lanny Vines; the revelation of a $500,000 payment by Waste Management to his pal Lanny Young after Young secured a secret deal from Siegelman controlled revenue department slashing taxes at the company's massive west Alabama landfill; the many stories required to unearth the undisclosed 'campaign donations' (the Scrushy case) presented as routine by you; and many more instead.

"And that's just a partial list. Instead, contrary to any evidence or proof, you connected Siegelman's loss in the 2002 election to prosecutorial leaks for which you have no proof even occurred."

Of the more than 100 stories I wrote while Siegelman was governor, not one originated from leaked grand jury evidence or so much as an off the record tip from a prosecutor or investigator. Even in Mobile I don't have any go-to sources in the U.S. Attorney's office or the FBI, nor have I attempted to develop them. I pride myself on finding stories on my own. If the FBI is already on to something, anyone can report that.

With the exception of the grand jury that indicted Roland Vaughan, and which I certainly had no information on, there was no grand jury investigating Siegelman in 2001 or 2002.

The closest thing to collusion between myself and prosecutors and investigators was that they read my stories.

To play it safe and cover all bases, let me further add that neither Steve Windom nor Ragan Ingram nor anyone I know to be associated with Windom (or for that matter, any Republican official) was the source on a single Siegelman story under my byline. The same goes for Bob Riley, who I didn't know then and only barely know now. Ditto for Bill Canary, who I don't think I'd heard of at the time and who I've only spoken to in seeking comment for this book, and that was on the phone. I've never laid eyes on him.

———

The Canary canard always proved a hard sell to the Alabama press. This was in no small part due to our familiarity with those peddling it. But after Jill Simpson's affidavit and the stories in the *New York Times* and *Time,* husband and wife Canary got sucked into an echo chamber from which there was no escape. Because the myth required participation of so many others – including eventual prosecutors Louis Franklin and Steve Feaga – they, too, were to see their actions and motives twisted beyond recognition.

I met Leura Canary for the first time at the October 2005 announcement of the indictment against Siegelman and the others. She complemented me on my stories, and that was it. I believe she stopped by to watch the 2003 press conference announcing guilty pleas by Nick Bailey and Lanny Young, but am not certain.

Until 2008 or 2009, those were the only times I saw or spoke to her, telephone included. At no time during the investigation and trial and its aftermath did it even dawn on me to contact Leura Canary for information or updates on the Siegelman case. Had she or anyone been secretly doling out grand jury information to the media, I like to think I would have been on the list.

With the exception of the bleatings from Team Siegelman I never heard anyone, such as a fellow reporter, so much as hint at Leura Canary's involvement in the case or indicate that she (or her husband) had been a source on anything. She simply was not on the radar.

Had anyone taken the time to call, I'd have been glad to say as much.

———

Roland Vaughan went on trial in mid-March 2002, the spring of Siegelman's final year as governor.

He and his lawyers told jurors that he only became a partner with his friend Andrew Nolin to help the latter come up with the money necessary to buy the land for its ultimate use as a home to the state warehouses. They further claimed that the $25,000 site study by Sherlock Smith & Adams was completed before Vaughan decided to become a part-owner in the land.

Prosecutors stressed Vaughan's long-time participation with Nolin in trying to market the land. They presented testimony indicating that Vaughan was Nolin's partner before Sherlock Smith & Adams recommendation to build the warehouses at North Ripley instead of one of the two state-owned parcels.

Records were presented showing that Nolin's company, C&H Investments bought the land on Feb. 9, 2001, for $460,000; on the same day, sold it to G.H. Construction for $561,932; and that Vaughan and Nolin split the profit.

The plan, as previously described, was for G.H. Construction to be reimbursed upon sale of the bonds that were to fund the project. The bonds were never sold, but Nolin and Vaughan already had their money.

Unlike many white collar defendants, Vaughan testified. He told jurors he had been a top-ranked cadet at Virginia Military Institute, and would never take any act contrary to his high personal code of honor. "My honor has been challenged and I have lived my life as an honorable man, so my honor is on trial ... I did not steal and I would not steal. I am not guilty. I did not have a conflict of interest," he testified.

One of the more revealing snippets of testimony came from Nolin, who acknowledged that he had in the past referred to the site as, "The Swamp."

I had to stifle a snicker at that one. The Siegelman administration, per Roland Vaughan's recommendation, was going to build two warehouses at, "The Swamp."

The week-long trial ended with Vaughan being found guilty of the misdemeanor charge of failing to disclose his ownership in the land, but acquitted of the more serious felony theft charge.

The verdict all but assured he wouldn't serve time, but Vaughan saw it as a mark against his honor. From his comments, it seemed he'd been paying attention to the recent complaints by Siegelman and Cromwell Johnson. Vaughan asserted that he was targeted by Republicans because he had been mulling a run for Congress as a Democrat.

"This has been a vindictive political campaign by Mr. Pryor, and do not think Steve Windom's fingerprints are not all over this," he said, calling himself part of Pryor's "trophy hunt."

"At first I was going to be the little fish, and other people were going to be the big trophies," Vaughan said. "But when they didn't fall, I became the trophy."

Two months later, Montgomery County Circuit Judge Gene Reese sentenced Vaughan to a year's unsupervised probation; fined him $2,000; and ordered him to perform 40 hours of community service.

Prosecutors pleaded with Reese to give Vaughan jail time and, at the very least, make him repay his profit from the land sale – that last request unquestionably justified.

"He's shown no remorse; he's blamed it on other people; he's not accepted responsibility," said Attorney General George Martin, to no effect.

"I don't have any remorse for something I didn't do. I didn't have a conflict," Vaughan said after the hearing.

Vaughan had kept his land sale enrichment scheme to himself, or rather, himself and Andrew Nolin. I never heard anyone so much as suggest that Siegelman was aware of Vaughan's part-ownership in the warehouse land, and would be surprised if he knew about it.

The Vaughan prosecution was separate from the broader G.H. Construction case and caused no serious political damage to the governor that I could tell.

Siegelman's later complaints to the contrary, the Vaughan trial was, with one minor exception, the last real news on the investigatory front that year. In September, when the *Birmingham News* reported that federal agents had gone to Tuscaloosa's Worldwide Travel and carted away a load of records.

Soon after Siegelman became governor he ordered state agencies to purchase all their airline tickets through Worldwide, which was owned by a friend and supporter. After complaints, the order was rescinded, but the agency continued to receive most of the state's airline travel business. (Worldwide's owner adamantly denied wrongdoing and was never charged.)

Had the Siegelman-described Republican crew really wanted to ruin his career, prosecutors, whether ready to do so or not, would presumably have brought ordered to charge him before the November 2002 election, when he really was the state's most powerful Democrat. They didn't. Nor did they hold any press conferences or issue any statements saying the first thing about an investigation into Siegelman. I dare anyone, "60 Minutes" included, to find a story written near the election and reporting something that came from a grand jury.

By the time the prosecutors really got going, Siegelman was, to voters, donors and Democratic Party leaders, a scandal-plagued, headline hunting also-ran.

Chapter 24
The Foundation Phantom

"Governor Siegelman has pledged to fully disclose all contributions and expenditures related to his effort to pass an education lottery in Alabama. Today, we are calling on you, as the leader of the anti-lottery forces, to pledge that you and your allied groups will do the same."

-- Letter from Hamrick to Steve Windom, urging the lieutenant governor to ensure that the Christian Coalition and other groups opposing the lottery disclose all their donors.

"As a 501(c)(4), the Foundation may accept contributions without limitation from individuals as well as corporations. Neither the Foundation, nor an entity making donations to the Foundation, will be subject to federal or state disclosure requirements."

-- Portion of Feb. 15, 2000 memo from Ted Hosp to Siegelman, regarding the governor's plan to secretly reform the foundation and conceal its donations.

The first crumb on the long trail to Richard Scrushy fell on Friday, March 8, 2002. That afternoon a PAC associated with Sterne, Agee & Leach filed its annual report with the secretary of state showing its contributions and expenditures from the year before. Like other PAC's and candidate committees, Alabamians for Economic Development was supposed to have filed its report by Jan. 31. For whatever reason, the folks at Sterne Agee missed the deadline, and because of the PAC's obscurity, no one noticed.

Had Sterne Agee waited just one more business day – filing the report the following Monday rather than that Friday -- more than $730,000 in carefully concealed campaign donations from the likes of HealthSouth and Alfa would never have seen the light of day. The U.S. Treasury would not have received a nice chunk that I like to think our stories enabled the IRS to collect. Most important for this story, Richard Scrushy would not have become embroiled in the Siegelman investigation, to say nothing of being found guilty and sentenced to seven years in prison.

The series of stories that exposed the secret second life of Siegelman's lottery fundraising apparatus started with nothing. There was no tip, anonymous or otherwise, no street talk, and I had no idea where I was going until I got there. The administration fought, fabricated and delayed, and in the end capitulated, not because of us, but because of the case we made to our readers, to state election officials and to the Attorney General's Office that something was amiss.

It took almost five months to break Team Siegelman and squeeze out the truth. If they didn't hate me before the lottery stories, they damn sure did after them.

———

Without question, the *Birmingham News'* reports on AFS and Trava Williams begat the foundation stories. As previously described, I'd hopped on that bandwagon after reading Brett and Kim's first story on Siegelman's stockbroker.

On Saturday, March 9, Paul was editing the story on the police annuity fund that was to run the next day. I was at my desk, waiting for his questions. With nothing else to do, I decided to see if I could locate any Sterne Agee ties to Siegelman in addition to those involving Trava Williams. Maybe I'd find a detail worth plugging into the story, perhaps a contribution or two to a past Siegelman campaign.

I called up Merlin and punched in Sterne Agee and Siegelman. This produced a November 2000 story by Jeff Amy reporting donations to the campaign to pass Amendment One. Among them was a contribution from a PAC with the feel-good name, Alabamians for Economic Development (AED).

Jeff, like the good reporter he is, had looked up the PAC on the secretary of state web-site to see whose interests it served. As a result, he was able to inform readers that the donation was in reality a contribution from Sterne Agee. The other result was that 16 months later, I had the name of Sterne Agee's PAC.

Still on Merlin, I entered Siegelman and Alabamians for Economic Development. Up popped a run-of-the-mill donor story I'd written before the October 1999 lottery vote. I'd reported that Alabamians for Economic Development gave $30,000 to the lottery campaign, but unlike Jeff, hadn't gone the extra mile to determine the PAC's identity. But with my failings rectified by Jeff, I had the sort of detail – a substantial donation to Siegelman's lottery campaign – that strengthened the story. Turns out Siegelman had demanded more of Sterne Agee than that it hire his stock broker.

Might the PAC have made other Siegelman-related donations? Doubtful. Siegelman hadn't been on the ballot since 1998. But it would only take a minute and until Paul finished, all I had was time. I returned to the secretary of state web-site, called up the PAC's 2000 report, and found nothing of interest. I expected the same from the 2001 disclosure, but what's another 30 seconds?

Later I was to notice that the PAC's 2001 report was filed late Friday afternoon, less than 24 hours before I saw it. Had it not been there that Saturday – again, had Sterne Agee waited even one more business day to file – I would have never gone back to look for it. My interest in it was minimal. I would have assumed it hadn't made any donations in 2001, had no need to file a report, and for good and forever, been on my way. I would have never spotted that telltale crumb.

But it had filed a report, and when Adobe Acrobat completed its task, the 2001 expenditures page for Alabamians for Economic Development emerged on the screen. There were a total of two donations for the entire year. One -- for $1,250 to the state Democratic Party -- was of no interest. The second, for $13,500, made no sense.

The recipient was identified as, "First Commercial Bank Birmingham FBO (for benefit of) the Alabama Education Lottery Foundation." A note at the bottom of the page read: "Loan payment to First Commercial Bank pursuant to pre-existing 1999 commitment to make a contribution to, or pay, indebtedness of, Alabama Education Lottery Foundation."

The lottery foundation had closed up shop soon after the October 1999 referendum. Why, then, was Sterne Agee contributing to it in 2001? It made about as much sense as a donation to George Wallace.

Still on the secretary of state page, I punched in the lottery foundation's name to see if it had for some as-yet unreported reason continued to exist beyond 1999, and if so, filed reports for 2000 and 2001. It had not. The foundation's final filing, dated Feb. 29, 2000, was a one-page form called a Statement of Dissolution.

PACs and campaign committees must file these forms to notify the secretary of state that they have ceased operations. The dissolution form was signed by Mobile lawyer Richard Dorman, a long-time Siegelman friend and supporter who'd agreed to chair the three-person foundation board upon its formation in early 1999.

As a double-check I reviewed the foundation's year-end annual report for 1999, filed as required on Jan. 31, 2000. The summary page showed that the foundation ended the year with neither debts nor assets, or as the Associated Press put it in, the "foundation spent $5 million and closed out the year with a zero balance."

So why, in 2001, was Siegelman's dissolved and long-forgotten lottery foundation accepting a $13,500 donation?

I told Paul about this peculiar finding and asked if I could knock out a story Monday. He agreed it was strange and gave me the thumbs up. For the Sunday story on the police annuity fund, I reported Sterne Agee 1999 donation of $30,000 to the foundation, and added that it later "made an additional donation of $13,500." I was careful not to date the second contribution, lest a certain pair of readers in Birmingham notice its significance.

I knew that a story on the contribution would present more questions than answers, but felt it could be the start of something. On Monday I called Richard Dorman, told him about the donation, reminded him of the dissolution statement that he'd signed two years before, and asked if he knew why the foundation was receiving money in 2001. Richard said he'd closed his foundation file, placed it in storage, and couldn't comment without first reviewing those records.

Paul e-mailed Carrie. He took a clever approach, noting that while the administration didn't respond to questions for my stories, this was different.

"Since in the past the governor's office sought to keep comment on the lottery foundation a separate matter, we hoped that your office could direct us to someone who might comment on the matter."

The administration didn't see it that way, so we went with the usual no-comment. Paul's reasonable request for "someone who might comment" developed into a thematic and to my way of thinking comic underpinning of the stories. The challenge over the coming 4-1/2 months was trying to acquire records and explanations from an entity -- the lottery foundation -- that was without a physical address or a single human willing to accept responsibility for its actions, answer questions, and, most importantly, serve as a repository of its records.

The word "foundation" conjures an image of something solid and stable, but this one was gaseous, and manned by a phantom. That was the challenge to come – squeezing the truth out of a phantom.

The first story on the road to Scrushy ran under the headline, "Firm's PAC makes donation to now-dissolved lottery foundation," and began:

A political action committee associated with the brokerage firm Sterne, Agee & Leach reported donating $13,500 last year to the Alabama Education Lottery Foundation, the campaign fund used to pay for the failed 1999 campaign to pass a statewide lottery.

Records on file with the Alabama Secretary of State, however, show that the Alabama Education Lottery Foundation was dissolved in February 2000, making it unclear why such a donation would have been made in 2001. At the time it was closed out, it had no assets and no debts, records show. The lottery election was over, and there was no longer any reason to continue operating the foundation.

F. Eugene Woodham, a Sterne, Agee executive identified in state records as the chairman of the firm's PAC, declined Monday to answer a number of questions from the Register. Said Woodham, "I'm just not in a position to comment."

Woodham's response, both the tone of his voice and his words, told me there was something to this.

The date box on the PAC's filing was empty, so there was no way to determine when in 2001 the money was given. I brought the report to the attention of state elections specialist Vicki Balogh, and quoted her saying that disclosing the dates of contributions was "not optional."

The story was no bombshell, and ran on the bottom of Metro front. It didn't make the state wire, nor had I expected it to. The $13,500 donation was then and for some time to come an unexplained anomaly.

———

Later that week I called Chuck Grainger, the general counsel for the secretary of state's office. I explained my concern that the PAC failed to report the date of its donation and told him I thought it curious that the foundation appeared to have accepted funds well after its reported dissolution. I wanted the date as a second level of confirmation for this otherwise inexplicable contribution.

I asked Chuck for a favor: Could he contact Sterne Agee and ask the firm to amend its 2001 report, this time with the date of the donation. Chuck asked that I provide him with a written request, which I did. He forwarded my letter to Brenda Smith, a lawyer in the attorney general's office who frequently worked on election issues. On April 9, Smith sent Sterne Agee's Woodham a letter asking that Alabamians for Economic Development re-file its 2001 report, this time with the date.

"In addition," wrote Smith, "the expenditure to the Alabama Education Lottery Foundation appears to be in error, because the reports filed by the Education Foundation indicate that the political action committee was terminated as of Jan. 31, 2000."

With that in the oven and baking, I set about researching the foundation, reading old stories, looking up records, and writing e-mails, such as to Dorman asking him to retrieve his files from storage. There had been two board members in addition to Dorman. Both said they were unaware of any post-dissolution activities by the foundation. Dorman gave me the names of several people who worked as paid staffers on the lottery effort. They, too, claimed ignorance.

I knew Dorman from my days as a sportswriter, though his involvement in running, and later, from coverage of a monstrosity of a class action against Masonite that he spearheaded. The wiry, mustachioed bundle of energy was one the state's lead attorneys in the 2003 trial that produced a $11.9 billion verdict against ExxonMobil, later sliced to a slightly less towering $3.6 billion and ultimately obliterated to a fraction of that by the state supreme court.

I e-mailed Richard, saying I had little choice but to seek answers from him since he was, "the only chairperson the foundation ever had;" and that "an argument can certainly be made that you are responsible for, if not answering some of the questions I have, at least providing me with access to some records that I believe should be public."

"As a lawyer, I've never seen you show any quit, so I hope you understand why I'm continuing to seek these answers and records, and why I won't quit until I get one or the other. I hope you understand."

Much of the next two months was spent on an exhausting and not terrifically satisfying story about another non-profit, this one called the Alabama Water and Wastewater Institute. Lobbyist Fred Jones operated the institute, basically as a one-man operation. It received hundreds of thousands of dollars from three different state agencies, which meant I had to hunt down and review records from all three and interview boatloads of people. Jones was a Siegelman backer and had figured in one of the computer services contracts I'd written about.

He was a former state senator, a one-time aide to George Wallace, and was close to U.S. Sen. Richard Shelby. Each year Shelby routed federal funds to the legislature, which forwarded the money to the Department of Public Health in the form of a "pass through grant." Public Health had no choice but to pass the money to Jones whenever he sent one of his little letters asking for the money. When I first called Jones he said he was too busy lobbying. When the session ended, the excuse became a health condition so grave it rendered him "not able to deal with your harassment."

The story, really a big pain in the ass, ran on April 28, about the time things started to percolate on the foundation front. The next day, the Sterne Agee PAC filed its amended 2001 report. It didn't offer much new, but was a development just the same. The PAC reported contributing the $13,500 on Jan. 31, 2001. Attached was a letter from Alston Ray, Sterne Agee's lawyer, stating that his client hadn't known that the foundation had dissolved itself prior to the contribution.

The above information was reported in the second foundation story, published on May 7, almost two months after the first. It began:

A political action committee that donated $13,500 last year to the Alabama Education Lottery Foundation has provided more information about the gift, but questions remain about the contribution and the foundation's finances.

Chief among those questions regarding the foundation formed in early 1999 to fund Gov. Don Siegelman's political effort to win a statewide referendum on the lottery:

Why would the foundation -- more than a year after filing papers showing it had dissolved -- have accepted a donation in 2001?

Since the end of 1999, has the foundation received donations in addition to the $13,500 contribution made by Alabamians for Economic Development, a PAC formed by the Birmingham-based brokerage firm Sterne, Agee & Leach?

I tried to draw more information from Dorman and Ray, the Sterne Agee lawyer, both of whom probably wanted to shoot me between the eyes. I e-mailed Ray to ask why the PAC paid the bank directly. The normal procedure is for a contributor to donate to a recipient, be it a candidate, PAC or, in this case, foundation, for the recipient to disclose it as a contribution, and then, on the expenditures page, show the money going to the bank as a loan repayment. Sterne Agee's paying the bank implied that someone directed the company to do it that way.

The story included Ray's responses to questions I'd asked in trying to identify the foundation's lead actor. I wanted readers to appreciate the situation we faced in seeking to unmask this wacky phantom.

He (Ray) wrote that his client does not "believe it is appropriate to comment" about who, representing the foundation, contacted Sterne Agee about making the

January 2001 donation. Sterne Agee, he wrote, suggests "that any questions you may have regarding the foundation be directed to the appropriate foundation official."

When the Register then asked if Sterne Agee could identify an appropriate foundation official, Ray responded, "Our client is not aware of who you might contact at the foundation for information."

Also reported was Sterne Agee's refusal to furnish us with a copy of its check to the foundation. "The *Register* had asked it to do so -- though it is not required to do so by law -- in order to determine who endorsed the check," readers were told.

Siegelman – described as having been the "public face of the foundation" who "personally led the fund-raising efforts" – declined our invitation to clear up the matter of the $13,500 donation, so the story ended with the usual editor's note.

––––

A letter to the IRS laid the groundwork for victory.

Non-profits must file a type of tax return called a Form 990, and make them available for public inspection. Most 990s can be found on a web-site called Guidestar, but the foundation's return wasn't there. Public inspection was out of the question because there was no physical address, or in any event, not anymore. Dorman and the other officers said they hadn't a clue if a 990 was filed.

I had no choice but to take the slow route. Maybe they'd filed one, maybe not. Either way it would be a story.

I called Dan Boone, a Memphis-based IRS spokesman I'd been dealing with for years, and explained the situation. I faxed him a brief history of the foundation, both its names, its officers and addresses used by it. One was a P.O. Box which I recognized much later as the box used by the never-ending Siegelman campaign. The second was an apartment where one of the governor's many 25-ish staffers had resided. I went to the apartment and knocked on the door, more to say I tried than out of any expectation of locating a 990. I think the guy had already moved by then.

I e-mailed Dorman, and after the usual apologies, told him I was working on another story. "The way things stand, I'm going to have to report that, despite what I consider to be exhaustive inquiries, I can't locate a 990 or anyone who can state that there ever was a 990."

The final sub-head in the story read, "Did foundation file tax return," under which our 990 hunting efforts were reported, as follows:

For several weeks, the Register has tried but been unable to determine if the foundation ever filed or completed a Form 990. Neither Dorman, the two other foundation board members, nor the former foundation employees contacted by the paper could provide an indication if a Form 990 for 1999 -- and possibly other years -- had been completed.

The Register has made a public information request with the IRS seeking a copy of any tax returns filed by the foundation, such as for 1999, and perhaps 2000 and 2001.

I imagine this was when sweat beads began forming on the phantom's forehead. Withholding information from us and our readers was one thing, but screwing around with the IRS was another. To be told that the IRS had or would soon be receiving a request for all foundation 990s had to be unsettling.

Carrie declined to respond to our questions, but told Paul that the foundation's records would be provided "in the coming days."

The part about "in the coming days" didn't pan out. Two months and with a gun to their heads was more like it.

But the IRS angle paid off fast. Days later I took a call from the wild-man Cromwell Johnson, he giving me the lead on our third story:

The Alabama Lottery Foundation raised about $5 million to promote Gov. Don Siegelman's failed effort to win a 1999 lottery referendum but never filed a tax return as the law requires, an attorney for the governor said.

"It's a paperwork problem and a follow-through problem, and the truth is, Don knows nothing about this," Birmingham lawyer David Cromwell Johnson said.

Johnson – one of the state's top criminal defense lawyers, and Siegelman's choice to represent him during a state and federal criminal investigation into state contracts – said he's spearheading an effort to locate all the foundation's records.

The tax return or returns will be filed as soon as possible, Johnson said, and the return, and probably other foundation records, will be made available to the Mobile Register once that effort is complete.

Johnson said the governor and those he tapped to lead the lottery effort weren't aware of the failure to file a return until reading a story in Tuesday's Register.

Here again was Siegelman refusing to accept responsibility for his actions. Cromwell Johnson's claim that the governor "knows nothing about this" deserved a laugh track.

The Birmingham lawyer also introduced the defense that Siegelman continued to parrot up to and during his 2006 trial and still, despite mounds of evidence to the contrary: That he and others moved on to other things after the lottery defeat and simply failed to attend to some details, like the filing of a tax return.

Cromwell Johnson said he'd reviewed the foundation's records and found that its expenditures were made for legitimate purposes. "I feel like I've looked at it, and no money went into anybody's pocket," he said, implying a level of naughtiness we hadn't dared suggest in the stories.

The missing 990 put the story on the map. The AP picked it up and in a separate but simultaneous development, Siegelman announced his intent to again make passage of a lottery the focal point of his campaign. This meant that the campaign-trail addict would be raising the lottery issue at the same time I was doing my damndest to identify the secret givers to his first try.

————

Within a week my initial suspicion that Sterne Agee's $13,500 wasn't a solitary donation was confirmed. A Birmingham man with connections to Cromwell Johnson was given the task of opening a back-channel line of communication between the Siegelman camp, or in any event, Cromwell Johnson, and me. I believe Harold -- not his real name -- had a similar relationship with Brett and Kim that predated mine.

He wasn't to appear in stories or even obliquely referred to, as in, "according to a source with ties to the governor's legal team." He took his role, if not himself, seriously. Harold was a devoted Democrat and political junkie who realized that playing confrontational Siegelman defender wasn't going to fly. Besides, Rip was doing fine there.

Since he couldn't be quoted, Harold was free to blister and ridicule Siegelman and, as he often did, the campaign team. But he always presented the governor's actions in the context of politics as usual, and always on this side of criminal, even if just barely. Possibly he was also there to gauge what I (and Brett and Kim) knew and where I was going next, but I never suspected him of trying to deceive or trap me. In any event, I had nothing to hide. Before the schism I'd always let them know where I was headed, the better to draw out a response. If they got the same type info through Harold, so what.

We occasionally argued, usually by e-mail, with me taking exception to his laissez faire approach to corruption, and his conviction that prosecutors were, with few exceptions, fanatical, self-righteous weenies. Harold, for example, was an admirer of Edwin Edwards. One day we were carrying on when he wrote that if "government can't be efficient, it should at least be entertaining."

"Here we have mediocre services coupled with sanctimonious drivel. Give me Edwin Edwards for sheer entertainment value and Fritz Hollings for good sound bites coupled occasionally with sound policy."

"Everything is a surprise to us," Harold said during another exchange. "Remember that more than once we had to ask you for a copy of some document when we'd never seen it or even heard of it. The error of your premise is that there is, in fact, organization, coordination and sharing of information when people are supposed to be working for the same goal. In this instance, division of labor has been taken to radical extremes – to sum up, never underestimate our ignorance."

It was Harold, no doubt after consultation with Cromwell Johnson, who told me that the Alabama Democratic Party was an actor in this play. Party chairman Redding Pitt was prepared to disclose that role and was expecting my call, Harold said.

The Pitt-Siegelman friendship dated back to college. Pitt had worked for Siegelman when the latter was secretary of state, then followed him to the attorney general's office. I knew Redding from his days as the Clinton-appointed U.S. Attorney for Alabama's Montgomery-based Middle District. When Gore lost to Bush, he was out of a job, and Siegelman arranged his appointment as party chairman.

Thin and dark-haired, Pitt has mournful eyes, a deep voice and a weathered look. He frequently speaks in regretful tone, as if duty-bound to do things he preferred not to do. Despite his allegiance to Siegelman – especially pronounced since Siegelman was the party's nominee in a governor's race just months away – I felt then and still that Redding recognized he had an obligation to clarify the party's role in the lottery referendum, even if doing so created discomfort for him and his friend.

He told me that in the months leading up to the referendum, the party hierarchy had secretly agreed to provide the lottery campaign with a service known in the political world as GOTV, which, as Redding explained, doesn't have a thing to do with television advertisements.

"Get-out-the-vote is the ground campaign," he said, in a quote we used. "It involves phone banks, ground work identifying voters, campaign day efforts to turn out the vote, and taking people to the polls if they need a ride. It requires a lot of staff and it is an expensive undertaking that the party undertook in support of the lottery, which is entirely proper."

Pitt – and if he said it once he said it ten times – wasn't with the party at the time. But it was his understanding from things he'd only recently learned that the party had spent $700,000 to $1 million on GOTV services for the lottery vote, and that the foundation had pledged to repay the party.

Pitt was forced to make the embarrassing revelation that the party couldn't locate records reflecting how or even if the loan was repaid, though he believed it had been.

"That's from talking to our bookkeeper. She didn't have direct knowledge of how the loan was repaid. She said that was handled by other people at the party at the time," he said.

Like a PAC or candidate, political parties must disclose their contributions and expenditures to the secretary of state, so the party's failure to do so here, and for an amount in the $800,000 range, was not a good thing.

Our fourth story reported that the lottery effort cost some $700,000 to $1 million more than the $5 million disclosed by the foundation; that the state Democratic Party borrowed the money to fund that effort; and that it had no records reflecting the exact size of the loan or when and by whom it was repaid.

Siegelman, as it happened, was campaigning in Mobile as I was working on the story. Bill Barrow, who was covering the candidate, popped him with a live question about the foundation. In such circumstances it was all but impossible for Siegelman to invoke the anti-me rule. As ever, the governor did his level best to clarify matters. This from the story:

> *Siegelman, during a campaign stop Wednesday in Mobile at which he again promoted a lottery as a way for Alabama to fund education, said he couldn't say for sure if he knew about the arrangement during the lottery campaign. "I may have been aware of it, but what I was doing primarily was running around making speeches and encouraging people to vote for an education lottery," he said.*
>
> *"I'm not really sure on that," Siegelman said, when asked about fund-raising efforts to repay the Democratic Party. He directed an aide to find out more about the situation, and get back to the newspaper. The aide replied that he was working with the Register "to get them the information as fast as we can."*

The administration wasn't working fast or otherwise on any such thing. But here was Rip – the aforementioned aide that day – pledging assistance from the campaign, as opposed to the administration. That's not to say we believed him, but at least we had him saying so on record.

A week later Rip e-mailed an about face. "The campaign is a completely separate entity than the lottery foundation and is not the appropriate place from which comment about the lottery foundation should come," he wrote us and, more importantly, our readers.

Off the record, Rip told Paul that an unidentified someone was gathering the foundation records and that this person was going to ensure that everything was done right. This person, we were told, wouldn't be swayed by politics. However, it would probably be about a month before Mr. Trustworthy could complete the task, Rip said.

According to that timeline we could expect a full accounting by about June 20.

Separately, Pitt recommended that I call Giles Perkins, the party's top full-time employee during the period in question, and Jack Miller, the party chairman at the time. Perkins and Miller were partners in Miller, Hamilton, Snider & Odom, one of the more politically active firms in the state, and very close to Siegelman. Miller, for example, regularly let the Siegelmans use his place on the Virgin Islands during Christmas holidays, and Siegelman tossed a considerable bit of state business the firm's way.

Pitt made it quite clear that Miller (who died in 2009) and Perkins, not him, were running things during the lottery campaign and the year after.

I called Perkins. He said that the party established a separate account for the foundation's GOTV work, billed the foundation and that at some point, he felt sure, was paid. As for details, he had none. Miller, who seemed as surprised to hear my voice, barked out some bluster about the foundation deal happening too long ago for him to remember, and hung up.

"We keep loan records, it's just that this particular one, we have no records of," said Redding, in a quote that didn't engender confidence in the party's financial practices.

The next day's story quoted Pitt's promise to locate all pertinent records and file an amended disclosure with the secretary of state. It included the following "nut graphs," those one or two paragraphs we newspaper people use to summarize the gist of a story and/or convey to a reader why the issue being reported is important, or in any event, why we think so.

These graphs, probably fashioned by Paul Cloos, our nut-graph specialist, proved prophetic:

> *Given the amount of money involved and the questions that remain unanswered about the Democratic Party's role, there may be numerous lottery-related donations by lawyers, political action committees, businesses and individuals that remain undisclosed.*
>
> *In the past 18 months or so, news stories in the Register and other papers have reported that some of the companies that have received lucrative state contracts, often without facing competition, donated to the governor's campaign or the lottery effort.*

The *Montgomery Advertiser* and *Birmingham News* seized on the lottery loan mystery, each publishing editorials criticizing Siegelman's campaign promises for a lottery without first resolving questions about his last such effort. Concluded the *News*, "The governor should clear the air about the foundation's records, or other state authorities should step in to investigate whether the problems go deeper than sloppy bookkeeping. Moreover, the public should demand answers, particularly now that Siegelman has revived his push for a lottery."

———

As of May 17, I'd written five stories on the foundation. While no one with that phantom entity had made a peep, learning about the GOTV effort and the bank loans tipped the scales in my favor. When working on an investigative piece, the biggest hurdle is uncertainty: Is there a story here? As often happens, and should, continued doubt and failure to turn up corroborating evidence triggers a decision to quit and traipse down more promising trails.

But once I know a story's there, I will stay on it. And by this point, there was no question. Still, there seemed little I could do but wait for Mr. Trustworthy to gather the records and disclose them, to the secretary of state, the IRS in the form of 990s, and us. Trustworthy or not, this person was working for Siegelman and wasn't going to release the fruits of his labors until the boss gave the go-ahead. In other words, probably not until after the election.

———

The next week I drove to Montgomery to research other stories. Upon returning I found a package in my mail slot from, of all places, Ogden, Utah, the location, as the package revealed, of an IRS warehousing operation. A cover letter explained that I was being provided, per request, with a photocopy of the only 990 filed by the Alabama Education Foundation.

I was, to say the least, surprised. I'd forgotten about the request after Cromwell Johnson's emphatic statement that the foundation hadn't filed a tax return.

Unbeknownst to Siegelman's lawyer, someone had "followed through," though how well, or accurately, was subject to debate.

The amounts on the 990 didn't exactly jibe with the foundation's 1999 year-end report with the secretary of state. Instead of $5 million raised, $5 million spent and a balance of zero, the return showed $4.6 million coming in and most of it spent, with a final balance, as of July 31, 2000, of $3,043.

One section of 990s asks non-profits to disclose relationships with political organizations, a category that would clearly include the state Democratic Party. Specifically, non-profits are asked if during the reported period they had reimbursement arrangements with political organizations; loans or loan guarantees; or "sharing of facilities, equipment, mailing lists, other assets or paid employees."

Next to each, the foundation phantom checked the "no" box.

I wrote a draft e-mail for Paul to send Rip. It began by asking when we could expect the records promised us weeks before. It reminded Rip that some weeks before I'd filed a request with the IRS for the foundation's tax returns.

Then the strong medicine:

Eddie pretty much forgot about this after several people, including the governor's lawyer, told him there had not been a 990 filed. Also, Eddie had twice called David Kassouf, who records show was the accountant for the foundation, but Mr. Kassouf did not return Eddie's calls.

Eddie is reviewing (the 990) now for a follow-up story to run tomorrow or this weekend, but he's already noticed some things that he was hoping someone could explain. On page 5 of the return, where it asks: 'The books are in the care of,' the name given was Nick Bailey. Bailey, though not to our knowledge an officer of the foundation, signed the tax return on the foundation's behalf.

The e-mail did not state something along these lines: "Your boss is a coward for putting his loyal, in many ways naïve aide in harm's way by directing him to sign the 990 rather than doing so himself." Such was my reaction to seeing Bailey's name on the return.

The e-mail pointed to several items on the 990 that didn't jibe with the truth. Among them: the foundation's declaration to the IRS that it had no relationships with political organizations, such as the Alabama Democratic Party. And: "The

990 also states that the foundation has complied with the public disclosure requirements. This would seem debatable, given that the foundation officials and representatives told Eddie no such record existed."

Rip asked Paul to fax him the 990, thus allowing the foundation to maintain the pretext that it/him/they didn't know it/him/they had filed a tax return. Rip whined that he was sure our story on the 990 would put things in the worst possible light. When Paul passed this on, I was not sympathetic.

I called Cromwell Johnson to give him the opportunity to explain to our readers what he really meant when he said the foundation hadn't completed a 990. He didn't return my calls that day or the next, but through his secretary, asked me to fax him a copy, which I dutifully did. Me faxing the foundation two copies of its own 990. Here was irony.

The story as I initially wrote it focused on two components: That contrary to what we had been told by Siegelman's own lawyer, there was a 990; and more seriously, that it would appear that the foundation failed to disclose hundreds of thousands of dollars in donations and expenditures to the IRS.

As soon became evident, the greater value of the package from Utah was its impact on the administration.

I was finishing the story when, with no heads up, the Siegelman press office faxed us a batch of documents that confirmed the continued existence of the foundation, and more. After reading them I told Paul that the new records were the lead, not the tax return, and told him I was working at light speed to re-write the story.

He'd seen them before me, and agreed.

The revelations were such that I was astonished they'd turned them over. Someone deserved praise – Ted? Carrie? Boots Gale? Cromwell Johnson? Jim Buckalew? -- for insisting that the public records law required their disclosure. Though legal opinions, they involved a non-public entity, the foundation, but were in the possession of and had been sent to the governor's office. Thus, they were public records, though even I'll acknowledge it was a close call. I had been denied plenty of records that were not close calls, so seeing these was a shock.

I suppose that one or more of the above recognized that with our possession of a clearly falsified tax return we were about to expose possible law breaking, and the administration owed the public, if not the *Register*, a dose of disclosure. Either that or they mistakenly assumed that the legal opinions showed them being responsible, and cleansed them.

The memos showed that Siegelman had asked Hosp and Gale to devise a means of reincarnating the foundation in such a way that the public would never learn of its continued existence. To accomplish this, the pair sought counsel from a Maynard Cooper lawyer who specialized in tax-exempt organizations.

James Pool was a graduate of Yale Divinity School who'd subsequently chosen law, and I imagine the inclusion of his name in the stories caused him some pain. Far as I could tell Pool was given an impossible assignment and did the best he could.

The memos were in one direction – from Pool to administration officials and lawyers. But in giving his advice – and here I sensed self-preservation at play – Pool spelled out what had been communicated to him by Siegelman, Hosp and/or Gale, and based his recommendations within the context of that specific set of facts.

The first memo, to Siegelman and Gale, was dated Feb. 8, 2000. That was eight days after the foundation filed its 1999 year- end report with the secretary of state showing neither debts nor assets and a final balance of zero.

Pool explained that incorporation papers for the foundation described three purposes, all of which addressed a campaign to gain public support for a state lottery. He proposed losing all references to the lottery and recommended "that those purposes be broadened."

Only an ogre could complain about a non-profit formed to:

- *Inform the people of the State of Alabama of the benefits to be gained from improving the schools and education of the state.*

- *Conduct a public campaign to gain public support for the improvement of Alabama education and economic development.*

- *Perform all activities necessary to obtain the support of the people of the State of Alabama to seek practicable methods to improve Alabama.*

A question to consider: Why would a foundation seeking to do such wonderful things demand secrecy for itself and its donors?

An answer to consider: Because it never intended to seek "practicable methods to improve Alabama," whatever that meant.

Pool was asked to resolve two problems, one involving the size of corporate contributions to the new foundation and the other, keeping those donations hidden from the public. He told Siegelman that "concern has been expressed at various times" regarding Alabama's law prohibiting corporations from making campaign donations greater than $500. He discussed the Fair Campaign Practices Act and advised that the newly designed foundation could accept corporate contributions greater than $500 as long as it didn't participate in a political campaign.

"Therefore, it is *impermissible* for the Alabama Education Foundation to ever make expenditures related to a political campaign," Pool declared, the italics mine.

The second problem was broached under the heading, "Disclosure." Pool wrote that the foundation would not have to report its contributions or expenditures to the secretary of state as long as it avoided the same pitfall – that is, if it refrained from spending money to influence a proposition or election.

"One issue relates to whether an ongoing entity named 'The Alabama Education Foundation' would, in a year in which there is no referendum planned, attract any interest," he continued. Though interest isn't defined, it can be assumed that he was referring to the likelihood of poking around by the media. If the foundation didn't file reports with the secretary of state, then the money it raised couldn't be "used to support or reject a referendum," he warned.

The primary recipient of this very specific advice was a lawyer, a six-time candidate, a two-time secretary of state and former attorney general. No one in on earth had a greater claim to be an expert on Alabama's campaign laws than Don Siegelman. He shouldn't have needed a legal opinion, but got one anyway. So if he acted contrary to that opinion – as subsequent findings show he did and intended to do all along – ignorance of the law was out as an excuse.

Years later, and never more than after his June 2006 conviction, Siegelman and his supporters in the national media railed on prosecutors for bringing charges against him for crimes related to the acceptance of campaign contributions. In a letter to supporters, Siegelman wrote that if his verdict were to stand, the "traditional ways of financing a campaign or referendum could be turned into federal bribery charges on the whim of a federal prosecutor."

When he was accepting the money, he based the scheme to hide the donations by making a very different argument – that the funds were not campaign contributions.

Also among the items faxed that day were two records, both dated Feb. 29, 2000, both signed by Dorman in his position as foundation chairman. One -- the foundation's statement of dissolution -- I already had. The other was a document reincarnating the foundation killed off by Dorman with his first signature.

The "Articles of Amendment" to the foundation contained the three fuzzy, non-lottery purposes suggested by Pool. It was filed, not with the secretary of state, but at Montgomery County Probate Court, where it was unlikely to attract notice, and had not.

The trove also contained a Dec. 29, 2000, letter from Pool to Hosp. The date -- about a month before the deadline for filing year-end campaign disclosures for that year – suggested that someone remained nervous about the decision not to file a report with the secretary of state.

Hosp had asked Pool if a contribution to the foundation "in the following situation" was mandated by the campaign practices act.

Pool then restated the "situation" as described by the governor's lawyer: The foundation had amended its articles of incorporation, "thus ending its involvement with campaign related activities;" and since then, hadn't engaged in campaign-related activities "either through fund-raising or through election related expenditures."

Pool's recitation of the fantasy continued: "However, the Foundation has incurred a debt since (dissolving) for activities unrelated to any election purpose or any other purpose as described in the Act. An offer has been made to pay that debt, and you have asked whether such payment must be reported pursuant to the Act."

The problem was that foundation's debt *was* campaign related, and no amount of legal opining could make that go away. Hosp's use of the word "offer" – which implies something presented but not yet taken – was disingenuous. At the time he sought that opinion all the secret donations but one – the $13,500 from Sterne Agee – had been given to and cashed by the foundation, as opposed to merely offered. Even the debt to the party had been repaid. Hosp had to know he was presenting Pool with the impossible task of rendering legal an illegal act that had already occurred.

Pool offered what he called a "better argument" for the foundation's position that it needn't report its donations. Since the foundation hadn't participated in political activities since amending its articles, it was no longer "a political committee pursuant" to Alabama's campaign laws. And since only political committees must disclose their contributions and expenditures, it "appears that, based on these set of facts, contributions made to or on behalf of the Foundation should not be subjected to such reporting requirements."

If Pool's reading of campaign laws was correct, then you might as well throw the laws into a shredder. Based on this logic, a man could rob a bank, have his name changed, "give" the stolen money to his newly named self, and not be guilty of a crime. Pool responded to the impossible task by devising a shell game that described what Team Siegelman had already done.

The memos proved that the foundation had continued raising money and repaying a loan.

Separately, we knew and had reported that it incurred a debt $700,000-plus to the state Democratic Party, which it had in all likelihood repaid.

The foundation's debt to the party and its unidentified loan were obviously related, though I didn't have proof of it. The following graph hopefully helped readers connect the dots:

While the (memos) provided Friday don't describe the debt, or give its size, the apparent debt to the Democratic Party, as described by party officials, was clearly campaign related. According to state law, then, donations to repay such a debt would need to be disclosed to the Secretary of State's office.

For fairness if not accuracy's sake I added: "It may be, then, that the debt referred to by Pool is not the same as that owed to the Democratic Party." To which I'd have loved to add, "It may also be that if your aunt had ….."

Though trumped by the memos, the original lead still bore reporting. Near story's end readers were told that we'd received a copy of the foundation's tax return from the IRS and that its existence "contradicts statements made by the governor's lawyer that no such return was ever filed."

We reported that Nick Bailey signed the 990, was listed as the person responsible for maintaining the foundation's financial records, and that the "telephone number of the foundation, as listed on the return, is a phone number for the governor's office."

In the driest language possible, I wrote that both Siegelman's lawyer and his campaign had asked the *Register* to provide copies of the 990, and we'd done so. Readers were told that Team Siegelman still hadn't provided us with financial records of the foundation, despite our repeated requests and their earlier promises to do so.

After the story, "Harold" e-mailed to apologize for Cromwell Johnson's pronouncement that no 990 existed. He said Cromwell Johnson had told me what he'd been led to believe was the case, and I didn't doubt it. It wasn't hard to imagine Siegelman keeping his lawyers in the dark about such details.

Harold also complained that his and Cromwell Johnson's recommendations for dealing with my inquiries had "not been well received in certain predictable quarters."

"In fact, in no uncertain terms, we have been given to understand that, in fact, we have no understanding of dealing with the press, no sense of public perceptions of matters such as this, and that campaign professionals need neither help nor advice."

Shortly after the story I left for Slovakia to join Jana, Jerry and Eva. I was to be gone three weeks, or plenty of time, it would seem to a reasonable person, for the Democratic Party and the foundation's Mr. Trustworthy to compile their records, complete the required disclosure forms and – this time, accurately -- file them with the secretary of state and the IRS.

At this juncture, after two months and six stories, the name Richard Scrushy wasn't on my radar.

Chapter 25
A Scrushy surprise

"I have checked with several people here and none of them are familiar with the foundation. If I find out more, I'll let you know."
-- July 2002, e-mail from HealthSouth spokeswoman Kristi Gilmore after being asked if the company contributed to the foundation.

"The best we can come up with is that it was used with helping education in the state, and to pay off some debts of the lottery, and that it had to do with the governor's education initiatives. We donated money for the fund. Whatever it was used for is fine."
-- Scrushy, in interview two weeks later, after the foundation was forced to disclose more than $730,000 in donations, including a March 2000 contribution of $250,000 from HealthSouth. Scrushy said he couldn't recall who solicited the money on the foundation's behalf.

I returned from vacation in late June to find that neither the party nor the foundation had located the records promised by both nearly two months before. I don't think it's a stretch to suggest that, had I transferred to writing features for the Living Department, neither would have ever disclosed what they had long succeeded in hiding.

I immediately resumed my real avocation – writing, not stories, but letters and e-mails. Pitt said he was waiting on Colonial Bank to provide the party with its own bank records. Why this should have taken more than five minutes was beyond me. The party was a client of long-standing, it was seeking the record of a single transaction involving more than $700,000, and the bank's chief lawyer, Jack Miller, was Pitt's predecessor as party chairman.

Does the following sound so unreasonable?

"Jack, Redding here. We can't locate any records showing how that money y'all spent for Don on the lottery vote got repaid. We have to know so we can correct our report to the secretary of state, which as it stands, is wrong by, my guess, more than $700,000."

"Can't find it? Why, we need to fix that, Redding. Let me call Fred over at the bank. Heck, just stay on the line and we'll do a quick conference call. Won't take a sec."

Fiction, yes, but not fantasy.

Over at the foundation, the various unidentified minions were not burning the midnight oil either.

On July 1, the Siegelman campaign made another stop in Mobile, and as he had five weeks before, Bill Barrow used the occasion to ask Rip when we could expect to see the foundation records. "We're working on it," said Rip. Asked to provide a time frame, he gave a no-comment comment. "I can tell you that we're closer than the last time you asked," he said.

The next day I drafted an e-mail letter for Paul to send. It asked the administration to produce the foundation's campaign records. Team Siegelman was reminded that we knew the boss participated in the reincarnated foundation; that Nick Bailey signed the tax return; and that Ted served as its lawyer.

"Given those facts, and others, it is difficult to separate the activities of the foundation and the Governor's Office, and we believe the Governor's Office is the entity that should, under state law, respond to Open Records Act requests related to the foundation."

That and another letter, sent to Vicki Balogh at the secretary of state's office and Bill Pryor, were faxed on July 9. I cc'd the Balogh/Pryor letter to Hosp, Pitt, and Richard Dorman. Yes, guys, we're going to the top. We're tattling on you to the attorney general.

As in March when trying to learn more about Sterne Agee's filing, I asked the powers that be to intervene on behalf of proper public disclosure. The letter reviewed our findings up through our last story six weeks before; stated what Pitt said in mid-May about the party working to put its records in order; and how, going on two months later, this still hadn't been accomplished. Also summarized was the evidence supporting our position that both the party and the foundation had violated the state's campaign laws.

The letter concluded:

It remains unclear why both entities – the foundation and the Democratic Party – don't maintain accurate records of transactions that could involve in the neighborhood of $1 million, or, lacking such records, why they can't simply contact their banks and ask that they quickly produce those records.

I believe that a significant amount of money has been raised, probably from individuals, corporations and perhaps PACs, and that has never been disclosed. I hope you agree that the entities identified above should be required to provide these disclosures, and, given the time that has already expired, to be directed to do so promptly.

It worked. That afternoon, at ten 'til five, the Democratic Party filed a one-page amendment to its spring 2000 campaign report with the secretary of state. It revealed that on March 9, 2000, the party received a check for $730,789 from the foundation, which it immediately used to repay a loan from Colonial Bank. It had taken bank and party two months to locate this single, very large transaction. Attached was a brief letter from Pitt stating that the party didn't obtain the information from the bank until the day before. Vicki Balogh faxed me the goods in the morning and I went to work on the next day's story.

Was it a surprise that the party had borrowed hundreds of thousands of dollars to assist the foundation with the lottery campaign? No. We'd already reported it. Nor was it stunning news that the foundation was the source of the loan repayment. But with the filing, the foundation's debt to the party and proof of that debt's repayment was now part of the public record – official and incontrovertible. Most importantly, by its very nature – a filing with the secretary of state – the disclosure was a declaration by the party that the $730,789 payment by the lottery foundation was campaign related.

The filing rendered the ledger down at the secretary of state lopsided. Imagine a football statistician, post-game, counting passes caught by a team's receivers and those completed by its quarterback, and finding that the totals didn't match. He'd know something was missing, say, an additional completion by the quarterback. In football-speak, the records showed the party catching a $730,789 pass from the foundation but didn't show the foundation throwing any such pass.

That, minus the bit about passing and catching, was the case we made in again asking the administration to disclose the foundation's records. But this mule wasn't budging. Logic, the law, the right thing to do – none of that mattered, not with Siegelman in the midst of one of his quadrennial life or death struggles to remain in public office.

At trial, Grainger testified that he took copies of the party's amended disclosure to Hosp's office. "We've got a problem because they (the Democratic Party) have filed now,'" Grainger told governor's lawyer.

It didn't do any good. These people just flat out did not want to disclose the foundation's donors.

In addition to letters we had another form of leverage at our disposal, that being our raison d'être. That's French for writing a story about it. On July 14 we published the seventh foundation story since March, and the first in almost two months. It began:

Within weeks after declaring it had no money, no debt and no more reason to exist, the nonprofit foundation formed to fund the 1999 lottery campaign paid $730,789 to satisfy bank loans made to the Alabama Democratic Party, the party revealed this week.

The revelation, made in a letter from party chairman Redding Pitt to the Alabama Secretary of State's office, confirms Mobile Register reports that previous financial disclosures by the Democratic Party were incomplete.

The new disclosure also suggests that the Alabama Education Foundation -- formed by Gov. Don Siegelman to pay for the ultimately failed lottery campaign -- may have significantly under-reported its contributions and expenses to the Secretary of State.

Readers were told about the administration's previous, unfulfilled pledges to disclose the records. Also noted was our continued inability to locate a single human willing to accept responsibility for the foundation's actions. I took some pleasure in using the following Pitt quote, as it scratched our back: "When your paper pointed out the existence of these loans, and when we received the information, we reported it. Our commitment was to determine the donor, to amend our report, and for the present, that's as far as I'm able to go with it."

After the story I called Chuck Grainger, the secretary of state's lawyer, and offered to fax him various foundation-related records, including the Pool memos. With the party's disclosure, there was no longer any question that the foundation was in violation of the campaign reporting laws. It was equally clear that the phantom had no intention of coming clean just because some reporter in Mobile was asking him to.

On July 17, Grainger wrote a letter to Assistant Attorney General Richard Allen, with the subject heading, "Request of the *Mobile Press Register* concerning Alabama Education Foundation." He told Allen about the Democratic Party's report that the foundation gave it $730,749 in March 2000. "We have received no disclosure filings from either the Alabama Education Lottery Foundation or the Alabama Education Foundation since February 29, 2000 which would reconcile with the disclosure of the Alabama Democratic Party," Grainger informed Allen.

Allen responded by calling Ted Hosp, the lawyer for the governor and, or so it seemed, the Foundation Phantom too.

I imagined a distraught Siegelman calling the contributors and breaking the news that those donations that were never to see the light of day, well, he was being told that the damn things would have to be disclosed.

I could almost hear him add, "It's that damn reporter!"

Harold, recognizing it was going to come out sooner than later, said the foundation reports would show several sizable donations, but from reputable corporations. Yes, they should've been disclosed, but otherwise, there was nothing criminal in all of this. Sloppy and duplicitous, sure, but nothing prosecutable, far as he could tell. He gave me two names – HealthSouth and Alfa, and said he believed they were on the list.

Arch-conservative Alfa seemed the least likely because of its oil and water relationship with Siegelman and its fierce opposition to the lottery. I called and was told by a spokesperson that Alfa didn't donate to the foundation, nor would it have even considered doing so.

HealthSouth was more plausible. Despite its support of Fob James and right-leaning candidates nationally, Scrushy and company had enjoyed fine treatment from Siegelman, primarily through the latter's support for HealthSouth's planned $300 million "digital hospital," which Siegelman could have delayed to death had he chosen.

When I called HealthSouth the company was six weeks away from its duplicitous if still disastrous announcement that it was slashing revenue projections by $175 million due to changes in Medicare reimbursement levels. As subsequently developed, those revenues hadn't existed in the first place, and for reasons unrelated to Medicare.

I gave company spokeswoman Kristi Gilmore both of the foundation's names, with lottery and without, asked if HealthSouth had contributed to it, and suggested she research the years 2000 and 2001. She called back and left a message that my notes reflect was a no, but not definitively so. I e-mailed back and politely expressed what I sensed to be a lack of certainty in her response. This time I told her that it was possible that contributors donated the money indirectly, such as to First Commercial Bank or Colonial. "I heard what I can only call a rumor that HealthSouth was among the companies that donated to the foundation, in some form or another. But if you assure me this isn't so, then I'll trust that it didn't occur," I wrote.

Kristi responded, "I have checked with several people here and none of them are familiar with the foundation. If I find out more, I'll let you know."

I didn't consider that definitive, either. Had she checked with the janitor, or Richard Scrushy? But I didn't see how I could push it further without seeming rude, and besides, I didn't have it 100 percent that HealthSouth gave to the foundation. So I e-mailed back, "Thanks ton, Kristi. That's good enough for me."

—————

The charades ended on July 24. That morning Richard Allen called Hosp and told him that the attorney general's office, acting on a request from the secretary of state, had drafted a letter to the foundation asking it to comply with the law by disclosing its contributions and expenditures. To what address should he mail the letter, Allen asked. Hosp called back to say there was no need to send it, and shortly thereafter, the governor's office delivered a letter to Allen.

"Based on our discussion today, it is my understanding that the Secretary of State's Office has indicated to the Attorney General that the Alabama Education Foundation likely needs to file additional or amended reports under the Alabama Fair Campaign Practices Act," Hosp wrote. "As I mentioned to you when we spoke, based on conversations I have had over the last couple of weeks about this matter, it is my understanding that prior to today, the Foundation had decided to file additional reports."

Hosp's letter served as the basis for a story the next day reporting that the foundation had pledged to identify its donations by Monday. The piece quoted

Mike Marshall explaining that we'd sought help from the secretary of state and attorney general because we had been requesting the records for months and "our reporter has been stonewalled."

Two days later, on a Friday afternoon, I was wrapping up the story reporting Waste Management's $500,000 payment to Lanny after the Revenue Department slashed the taxes at Emelle. Much of the information in that piece showed up three years later in the Siegelman indictment, as did elements of another story in that Saturday's paper.

At quarter past five our fax machine churned out 45 pages of freshly minted foundation records sent from the office of Siegelman lawyer Bobby Segall. There were two 990s, for 1999 and 2000, and annual reports to the secretary of state for 1999, 2000 and 2001. I called home to deliver what had long since become the routine if not pain-free message that I'd be awhile and possibly longer.

Here, finally, were the identities of the donors concealed by the phantom for more than two years. Topping the list were two payments of $250,000, each of an amount more than twice as large as any of the more than 300 previously disclosed contributions. Donating that lofty sum were HealthSouth – a surprise given the company's recent denial – and Integrated Health Services Inc., a company I'd never heard of.

Integrated Health gave on Nov. 5, 1999. I had assumed all the secret money arrived after the foundation's February 2000 reincarnation, but the Integrated Health donation and two others on the same day showed that the phantom commenced his sneaky ways earlier than thought, and revealed that the original annual report for 1999 was a sham.

Google and Nexis told me that Integrated Health was a publicly-traded Maryland-based company that had operated about 400 nursing homes throughout the country, including one in Alabama. Most interesting was the company's fate: four days after the foundation contribution, the business press had reported the company's failure to make a $7.7 million interest payment due on a loan – a very bad sign indeed for a publicly traded company.

Three months later, Integrated Health filed for bankruptcy. Why would an upside down Maryland firm give $250,000 to a secret foundation run by Alabama's governor? Hmmm. I stuck that in my imaginary "Subjects Bearing Further Scrutiny" file, right next to Alfa Mutual Insurance, which was shown donating $100,000 in February 2000.

The other undisclosed contributors were: forest-products company Kimberly-Clark Corp., $25,000; steelmaker IPSCO, which had recently built a plant in Mobile, $25,000; Japanese electronics company Hitachi, $17,000; a Birmingham-based company called SCT Software & Resource Management Corp., $15,000; Oracle, which did business with the state and HealthSouth, $10,000; Tuscaloosa-based Bama Concrete Products, $12,500; Donald Leeburn, a long-time Siegelman benefactor and liquor distributor from Georgia, $10,000; and something called Skillsutor.com, which gave $5,000.

Last but not least was that little seedling. As we'd reported four months and nine stories earlier, Alabamians for Economic Development had given $13,500 in January 2001.

The final tally: 13 donations from 1999, 2000 and 2001, totaling $733,000.

Accompanying the reports was a letter from Segall to Pryor and Secretary of State Jim Bennett that purported to explain why the foundation was only now filing the reports. "Although I cannot state with certainty the reason for the failure to file these reports sooner, it appears that following defeat of the lottery in October 1999, those involved with the campaign gradually moved on to other pursuits, and inadequate attention was given to filing requirements associated with winding up the affairs of the foundation," wrote Segall, the erstwhile, "Mr. Trustworthy."

Here again was the old "everybody was busy and forgot" mantra presented months earlier by Cromwell Johnson. It was even less credible now. Segall couldn't present these excuses to Bennett and Pryor "with certainty" because as was obvious, his client the governor had paid enough attention after the lottery loss to raise more than $730,000; seek legal opinions designed to avoid disclosure; and take other measures to ensure that everything about the reborn foundation remained secret.

Segall signed the disclosures. This, he told Pryor and Bennett, was because the foundation ceased being a political committee soon after the referendum so it no longer had a chairman or treasurer to sign them. This contradicted the documents provided two months before by the governor's office, and which showed that the reincarnated foundation had both a chairman (Dorman) and a treasurer (a north Alabama sheriff and Siegelman backer). I supposed neither was willing to loan their John Hancocks to the cause, and Segall, whose service for Siegelman in this and other matters seemed to have no bounds, stood in for his client, aka, the Foundation Phantom.

For the record, Segall's letter did not state the following: "I signed it because we couldn't find Nick."

The governor's name didn't appear once in the new filings. Not anywhere. Plausible deniability, no matter how implausible, remained the name of his game.

The next morning's lead read: "Records produced late Friday by the Alabama Education Foundation, formed by Gov. Don Siegelman to promote a state lottery, reflect that previous reports by the foundation to the Alabama Secretary of State and the Internal Revenue Service were incorrect."

Incorrect? Fraudulent was more like it, but caution prohibited use of that word.

Because of the late hour, there was no way to even try to reach representatives of all the donors, but gave HealthSouth and Alfa a shot because of their prominence and the size of their contributions. I had no luck with the first, but was able to get Alfa spokesman Paul Till on the phone. I told him about the foundation's disclosure showing Alfa donating $100,000. He called higher-ups, then called me back. "Alfa Mutual Insurance has never given money to the Alabama Education Foundation for the lottery or any purpose," Till said, in a quote used in the story. "If such a report has been filed it is either an intentional or unintentional error and we would like for it to be corrected."

As little faith as I had in the foundation I could not imagine why Siegelman would falsely report a $100,000 donation from Alfa. Any fool could anticipate an angry denial from the company. On this occasion I placed my complete faith in the governor, but for the story, Alfa had the last word.

Near the end, and only because I was so fair-minded, I wrote, "What the disclosures don't reflect is who sought contributions for the foundation, or who managed its affairs after the defeat of the lottery."

I was back at the paper the next morning to work on a follow-up for Sunday. In going back over the disclosures, comparing the old with the new, I saw to my horror that I'd made a goof. The new 1999 filing contained all the donations that year, not just the three previously unreported ones, from Integrated Health, IPSCO and SCT Software. When racing through the reports the night before I'd seen two $100,000 contributions from the Alabama Education Association that for whatever reason registered in my brain as not being previously reported. I'd included them with the three other new 1999 donations, thus suggesting they'd been made in secret.

Now I saw that the donations from the state teachers union were properly disclosed on the foundation's original 1999 year-end report. When Paul came in I told him about my mistake and we reported the error prominently in the next day's story.

Because it was a weekend, reaching corporate donors was all but impossible. But one matter – the Alfa dispute -- demanded immediate attention. I had two big dogs – Alfa and the governor – in conflict on a substantial issue. Either Alfa gave $100,000 to the foundation or it didn't.

Company officials apparently remembered something in their sleep, because on Saturday morning, Alfa about-faced. "The bottom line is, we sent people this morning to our office in Montgomery, and after checking records, we verified that Alfa Mutual donated $100,000 to the Alabama Education Foundation," Till said, and I quoted.

Most importantly, for the first time I had someone saying what I'd always known had to be the case: That Siegelman solicited the unreported contributions.

"The governor personally came out and met with our president (Jerry Newby) to request the donation," Till said.

Siegelman had told Newby that the funds were to be used in some undefined manner to improve education in Alabama. "We oppose the lottery as much today as we opposed it then, and we are outraged that our donation apparently was diverted to pay off the debt of the lottery campaign," the Alfa spokesman said.

As it had many times in the past, and so graciously, the *Birmingham News* editorial page put things in a perspective that I was prohibited from doing in a straight news story. On Aug. 1 the paper published an editorial under the heading, "In denial." The piece ridiculed Alfa's claim that it had been "hoodwinked" by Siegelman into giving the $100,000, and was now "outraged" to discover that the donation was connected to the lottery vote.

"Alfa is hardly known for political naiveté. The powerful insurance/farmers organization is a masterful player in politics, one of the state's largest sources of campaign cash and one of its most formidable lobbies. Suffice to say, Alfa doesn't get surprised by much that occurs in the state capital. Yet the company claims this lottery contribution was an exception."

The piece credited the *Register*, stating, "It was because of this months-long reporting effort that Alfa's donation came to light."

I hoped to find, especially through Alfa and HealthSouth, if donors to the re-formed foundation had sought charitable deductions. The idea was suggested to me by the Pool memos, which in addition to exposing Siegelman's efforts to secretly re-form the foundation, taught me a few things about a type of non-profit – the 501(c)4 – with which I was largely unfamiliar. Contributions to the vastly more common 501(c)3s, such as the United Way and for that matter, most foundations, are tax deductible. You give, and at tax time, lower your bill to the government. With the federal corporate tax rate of about 35 percent, corporations can decrease their taxes by about one dollar for every three given to a 501(c)3.

The foundation, as I knew from the Pool memos, was a 501(c)4 in its first incarnation as well as its second. That's a classification for non-profits that engage in the political process, such as through issue advocacy. Well-known 501(c)4s include the American Association of Retired Persons (AARP) and the National Rifle Association (NRA). A 501(c)4 doesn't have to pay taxes on money it receives, but contributions to this type of non-profit – like campaign contributions – are not tax deductible for donors.

What I wondered – and this goes back to my suspicion of all things Siegelman – was whether he had, in making his spiel, told contributors they could take a charitable deduction. If so, this angle of inquiry might further solidify Siegelman's fund-raising role, such as with the sort of tax record thank you letters that non-profits routinely provide donors, and which I supposed might be signed by the governor.

Early the next week I asked Till if Alfa took a deduction on the $100,000; and if so, had the foundation provided the company with such a letter. By this point, Till was becoming feisty, taking the position I had no right to ask such questions. Because of what had transpired I felt the company owed me an extra level of truth. In an e-mail, I reminded Till that I'd asked him about this donation weeks before the foundation disclosures and was told that the company made no such donation; that on Friday night he'd again denied that the company contributed to the foundation; and on Saturday, when Alfa finally acknowledged the gift, he'd blasted Siegelman for deceiving Newby.

"Alfa made some fairly serious charges against the governor – it could well be construed as accusing him of criminal fraud. I've simply asked Alfa to back this up," I wrote, in pressing my case for a copy of the receipt donors get when they give $10, to say nothing of $100,000.

Alfa either was unable to dig up such a record, or did and just didn't give it to me. The company was under no obligation to give it to me, but it didn't hurt to ask.

———

I was making similar inquiries with HealthSouth. I assumed that Kristi Gilmore might be embarrassed, considering that two weeks before she'd told me the company hadn't contributed to the foundation. I didn't blame her. I assumed she'd asked someone who should know, and was lied to. Testiness did ensue, though, after Kristi told me that HealthSouth's no-donation answer had not been definitive. I couldn't let this have-our-cake-and-eat-it-too response go unchallenged.

I told her in an e-mail that I had ceased pressing for a definitive answer because I'd felt to do so would "be rude" and "reflect a lack of faith in your efforts and your word."

"Certainly I did everything that I could to ensure that you, and by extension, HealthSouth, knew exactly what I was asking. If you have any suggestions as to what I should have done differently, by all means, pass them on."

And proceeded to the matter at hand:

I have the following questions about this substantial donation:
Who authorized this donation for HealthSouth?
Who contacted the company on behalf of the foundation, seeking this donation?
Can HealthSouth provide any documentation, such as correspondence to or from the foundation, about this donation? If HealthSouth declines to provide such records, could you/the company state that it has the records, but has chosen not to provide them, or, other possibility, that it has never had any such records?
Did HealthSouth seek a tax-deduction as a result of this donation? If not, why not, since such a large gift would appear to have generated a nice-sized deduction?
For accounting and tax purposes, how did HealthSouth classify this expenditure?

The second to last question was borderline disingenuous. I knew why the company wasn't eligible for a deduction, but was hoping to draw them into telling me they'd taken a deduction if they had. And if so, under whose direction? Two days later, Kristi e-mailed a statement confirming that HealthSouth made the donation "with the understanding that it would be used to help with the education system in the state."

"There is no paperwork indicating who requested this funding for the Foundation. HealthSouth claimed a tax deduction for this charitable donation, believing that the Foundation was a 501(c)3. We at HealthSouth would be upset to learn that these funds were used for anything other than education."

The statement was mildly helpful, but not enough. The "no paperwork" bit was just a dodge. In my response I told them about Alfa's revelation that Siegelman had personally visited the company's chairman. "My guess is that something similar happened here: that the governor visited with or spoke with Mr. Scrushy and requested the donation…. Is that how it happened? And if so, could HealthSouth/Mr. Scrushy provide some details of the conversation/request."

I also asked when the company first contacted Siegelman about its wish for special legislation to let HealthSouth circumvent the CON board process (and the years of lawsuits that can entail) and begin construction of its so-called digital hospital. I wondered if the timing of that request coincided with the donation. Lastly, I wanted to know if HealthSouth was contemplating legal action. After all, Kristi Gilmore had said the company "would be upset" to learn that the funds were used in some way other than to benefit education and it was, after all, $250,000.

The next day Gilmore called to say that Scrushy wanted to speak with me. Well, that was an interesting development. Scrushy was a household name in Alabama and on Wall Street, but I'd never met him.

By then regulators and the business press were nicking away at his company. Questions were being raised about its accounting practices and a $25 million company loan to Scrushy. I had no interest in those matters, can't recall if I was even aware of them, and of course had no way of knowing that HealthSouth's share price was three weeks from a nose dive.

I was put through to a speakerphone and told that an assistant, Brooks Adams, was also participating in the call. I hoped Scrushy would confirm that Siegelman personally solicited the HealthSouth contribution. Alfa's Newby had placed Siegelman in his office. If the same occurred with HealthSouth, why not just say so? I figured Scrushy would. I was wrong.

Scrushy said that while he would have had to sign off on donation of such size, neither he nor anyone else at HealthSouth could remember who contacted the company on the foundation's behalf. I wasn't dumb enough to believe this, but was without evidence to contradict him. I had no way of knowing, for example, about the meetings between the pair in 1999 and 2000, during which the donations were discussed and checks passed hands.

Scrushy said the company assumed the foundation was a 501(c)3 and had taken a tax deduction. HealthSouth planned to contact the IRS, report the error and pay the government any money it had saved as a result of the deduction.

Contrary to the company's statement a day before, Scrushy said he wasn't troubled to learn that his company's $250,000 was used, not to promote education in the state, but to pay off the lottery's debt. "The best we can come up with is that it was used with helping education in the state, and to pay off some debts of the lottery, and that it had to do with the governor's education initiatives. We donated money for the fund. Whatever it was used for is fine," he said.

We parted with pleasantries. Later that afternoon, Adams called to report that he'd just received a call from Scrushy, who had remembered something. Scrushy, said Adams, seemed to recall that Elmer Harris, then still president of Alabama Power, had called to solicit the $250,000 donation to the foundation. Did Scrushy suppose I'd just accept this tale without checking it? If so, he was wrong. I called Harris and left a detailed message on his answering machine. I told him what Scrushy had said and asked if he could call me just to confirm this was the case.

Harris called back. I missed him, but he left the following message, which I transcribed verbatim: "During that period of time, I did not give any monies to the lottery foundation, nor did I solicit any monies for the lottery foundation."

Scrushy's recollection that Harris called him for the money and Harris's response were included in an Aug. 11 story that carried the headline, "Foundation a Taxing Issue for Alfa, HealthSouth."

The story examined the tax situation, which I thought significant though I may have been alone there. It also addressed Alfa's relationship with Siegelman at the time of its donation. The arch-conservative insurance company/farmer's association had been one of if not the top donor to Fob James' 1998 campaign, and was, as the story reported, "known to be on the governor's bad side."

News reports at the time told of a major legislative defeat suffered by Alfa after Siegelman personally became involved in the successful effort to pass a law requiring mandatory car insurance. The new law was seen as a major blow to Alfa, which along with its sister organization, the Alabama Farmers Federation, had long opposed mandatory insurance.

In late 1999, Siegelman allies in the Legislature were promising to push legislation that would eliminate a tax credit used by Alfa to cut the insurance premium taxes it pays the state by millions of dollars each year. The bill was filed, but never went anywhere.

Till did not respond to questions about Alfa's tenuous position with the governor at the time it gave the $100,000, and whether concerns about losing the premium tax exemption factored into the company's decision to give when Siegelman came asking.

The final subhead, "Mystery surrounds other $250,000 gift," described my findings or lack thereof regarding the Integrated Health donation. "In some ways, the company's $250,000 gift is the most peculiar of the 13 donations," I wrote, without knowing the half of it.

Integrated Health's failure to make a loan payment days after the donation was reported, as was its subsequent bankruptcy. A spokesman for what was left of the company confirmed that the donation had been made but said it was authorized by people no longer with the company. I located a former executive, Taylor Pickett, but he brushed me off. (Almost four years later, Pickett's testimony helped prosecutors convict Scrushy and Siegelman.)

My next best bet was the company's bankruptcy filing. Debtors must disclose expenditures made in the 12 months prior to seeking bankruptcy protection, including charitable and political contributions. Because of the size of the foundation donation and its date – three months before the bankruptcy -- I was certain it would show up. I hoped to find that a creditor challenged the contribution, and that the court record would solve this mystery.

As with most large corporate bankruptcies, Integrated Health had a web-site for creditors and claimants to get the latest information on the case. On it was a six-page list of the company's charitable and political donations in the year preceding its bankruptcy. Most were less than $100, but the foundation gift – which would have been by more than five times the largest on the list – wasn't there. I contacted two New York lawyers shown as representing the company's creditors. Neither recalled coming across a $250,000 check to the Alabama Education Foundation.

I called three state agencies – the Department of Public Health, the CON board, and the Medicaid Department – to see if either had any serious issues with the one Alabama nursing home operated by Integrated Health. "Representatives of all three agencies said they were unaware of any significant or unusual issues pending with them in 1999 and related to Integrated Health Services," readers were told.

Lastly, Nexis revealed a past relationship between HealthSouth and Integrated Health. Scrushy had been on the company's board in the mid-1990s, and in 1997, HealthSouth sold its nursing home business to the Maryland company for $1.2 billion. This was a coincidence worth asking about, and I did in an e-mail to HealthSouth's Gilmore that received no response. I elected not to report the link because Integrated Health did business in Alabama, the HealthSouth ties were severed years before, and I'd nothing concrete connecting the companies.

In early August someone – my recollection was that it was mailed anonymously – sent me a memo from Hosp to Siegelman and dated Feb. 15, 2000. That was two weeks after the foundation filed its 1999 annual report reporting a zero balance and no debts.

The memo served as the basis of a story that refuted, once and for all, Siegelman's professions of ignorance about the continued operations of the foundation. Here is the key portion of the story:

The memo, more than any other record previously produced, indicates that Siegelman was in charge of the quietly formed, post-1999 version of the foundation that had been created to fund the campaign to pass a state lottery.

In the memo, legal adviser Ted Hosp reported to Siegelman that, "as requested," changes had been made to the foundation's bylaws, and all reference to a lottery had been removed.... As a result of the changes, the foundation "may accept contributions without limitation from individuals as well as corporations."

"Neither the Foundation, nor an entity making the donation to the Foundation, will be subject to federal or state disclosure requirements," Hosp wrote.

A footnote at the bottom of the letter states that the Internal Revenue Service requires nonprofit organizations to file tax returns and make those returns public. On those returns, (Hosp told Siegelman that) "the organization is not required to disclose the names or addresses of any contributors."

One final story, in late August, reported that someone with the attorney general's office – Pryor himself, I heard – had gone to Alfa to question officials about the $100,000 contribution. It was the 13th story about the foundation in more than five months. Had the administration been forthcoming from the start, it might have been three stories over a week or two, instead of death by a thousand cuts. I was later criticized by Siegelman and his supporters for writing "more than 100" stories" about the administration.

This was their fault on two fronts: for being unethical and frequently crooked; then lying about it. Thus, lots of stories.

As Harold put it in one of his e-mails: "I have been urging a complete and accurate disclosure, since it is the piecemeal nature of releases and the various mistakes or omissions which fuel the appearance of impropriety and keep the story alive."

To which I replied, tooting my own horn: "Not to toot my own horn, but if they don't realize I don't buy bullshit and slink away by now, I just don't know that they ever will realize it."

I called all the donors, but to the extent I got anything, it was confirmation that, yes, we gave. A guy at Bama Concrete Products hung up on me, which piqued my interest. I requested highway department files related to the company and looked for payment disputes at the time of its donation, but nothing jumped out. Then again, a concrete company was likely to conduct state business as a sub-contractor, not directly with the state. I could have asked to review files on every project in which Bama Concrete supplied product, but they'd only donated $12,500, so I gave up that goose chase.

I was busy on other fronts. If someone with subpoena power wanted to take a run down the foundation trail, all the power. I'd given them a pretty good head start.

Chapter 26
Ethics, Alabama Style

"A portion of the $800,000 that Gov. Don Siegelman received from his former law firm compensated him for his role in tobacco litigation, but the payments were legal because he earned the money as a private lawyer, Siegelman's lawyer said."
-- Lead from July 2, 2002, Birmingham News story in which David Cromwell Johnson contradicted his client's explanation for his legal fees from the Cherry Givens firm.

"The Ethics Commission saw right through this charade and today the people of Alabama see it too. This was nothing but a baseless politically motivated Republican attack that has now been exposed completely."
-- Rip Andrews, in news release following the Alabama Ethics Commission's 3-1 vote clearing Siegelman of charge connecting his severance package from Cherry Givens with actions he'd taken as governor.

From October 1997 through our stories the previous summer, Siegelman never wavered: He would not, did not accept any fees from tobacco litigation. He stated so in court filings and multiple press releases and interviews. It was, then, a surprise when the voluble Cromwell Johnson told the *Birmingham News* just the opposite for a July 2 story.

The estimated $800,000 paid to Siegelman by the Cherry Givens firm *did* include money from tobacco litigation, just not the one involving the University of South Alabama settlement, he said. What's more, this would be acknowledged at the governor's impending hearing before the ethics commission.

Cromwell Johnson said the severance package with Cherry Givens rewarded Siegelman for his work on the Crozier case. Crozier, again, was the pie-in-the-sky taxpayer lawsuit brought by Siegelman, Jack Drake, Cherry Givens and national tobacco plaintiffs' lawyers Richard Scruggs and Ron Motley; and it was those lawyers who were tacked on Exhibit S of the Master Settlement between the states and Big Tobacco.

The Birmingham News' story recapped Siegelman's previous statements, including his pledge at a 1997 press conference that he would never accept as much as "one penny" from tobacco cases. When asked about this apparent contradiction, Siegelman, as was his usual practice, hid behind the investigation. "I want the Ethics Commission to be able to look at this knowing I have not made any public comment at all," he said.

Cromwell Johnson said he had given the commission details of payments to Siegelman made in 1999, 2000 and 2001 and records showing Siegelman as having worked on the Crozier case. He also gave the *News* affidavits he had submitted to the commission in Siegelman's defense.

One was by Samuel Cherry of Cherry Givens; the other, from Bill Pryor. In his, Cherry stated that the firm agreed with Siegelman's argument that he should be given an equity -- or part ownership -- share in the firm. He pledged that Siegelman "did not use his position as Governor to obtain any kind of contract for the law firm;" and said the money paid the governor was "entirely for work performed on behalf of the firm prior to (Siegelman's departure on) Oct. 17, 1997."

Neither Cherry nor anyone else explained why the firm waited three years to negotiate Siegelman's going-away bonanza.

In his affidavit, Pryor stated that the Alabama lawyers placed on Exhibit S were chosen by the Ron Motley-led trial lawyer group, the attorneys general and the tobacco companies who crafted the Master Settlement; and that putting them on the list to receive legal fees wouldn't reduce Alabama's payments from the national settlement.

Pryor provided the affidavit at the request of Siegelman's lawyers. He was only asked to address the narrow question of what he knew about placement of lawyers on Exhibit S.

The affidavit by Alabama's highest law enforcement officer was offered by Siegelman's lawyers as proof of their client's innocence. It was no such thing. Nothing in the affidavit, for example, addressed the South Alabama settlement, nor was Pryor asked about Siegelman's role in the Crozier case.

Had Pryor been asked I assume he would have said what he told me – that it was "irrefutable" that Siegelman would never have become involved in any tobacco litigation had he not been lieutenant governor. I presume, based on Pryor's response to learning of Siegelman's secret severance deal, that he would not have signed off on the $20 million South Alabama settlement had he known that Cherry Givens, a major beneficiary of the deal, was going to turn around and pay Siegelman in the neighborhood of $800,000.

That the ethics investigators never asked Pryor these questions – that they let the defense, through affidavits, provide their evidence -- is further proof of their incompetence. That, or their fear of getting to the truth.

———

Any doubt that Siegelman would skate on the legal fees case was erased in April, when the commission dropped its investigation of Dennis "Blue" Harbor, the friend, occasional business partner and backer of Roger Bedford and Siegelman.

I didn't think my estimation of the commission – the competence and backbone of its investigative and executive staff and its politically appointed commission – could sink any lower. The Blue Harbor case illustrated, not for the first or last time, that the commission, rather than policing corruption, enables it. It occasionally busts little fellas, but finds excuses to clear or avoid investigating powerful people. By doing so, it encourages rather than deters public corruption and should be abolished.

Based on his public title – member of the Marion County Water Authority –Harbor would seem to be one of those little fellas. He was anything but. He'd made a splash the previous summer when Bedford was revealed as having tried to force the Marion County Commission to pay $3 million for land owned by Harbor and valued at a fraction of that. He'd also donated $7,000 to Siegelman's 1998 gubernatorial campaign.

The ethics case against Harbor involved another matter, if most of the same players. As with almost every corrupt act exposed in Alabama, it was brought to the public's attention by print reporters.

Blackledge's August 2001 story made a strong case for a violation of a crucial and seemingly straightforward portion of the ethics law. It reads: "No member of any county or municipal agency, board, or commission shall vote or participate in any matter in which the member or family member of the member has any financial gain or interest."

In 1999, Harbor began pressing fellow members of the authority to fund a $945,000 water line extension along Marion County 25 – a route whose residents included Harbor. More importantly, the project would bring running water to his timber business and allow him to develop 200 lots on 255 acres he owned.

The purpose of such projects is to provide water to rural, frequently poor areas where residents get their water from wells and springs. Boards like the one on which Harbor sat seek Community Development Block Grants (CDBG), which are federal funds awarded through ADECA. CDBG grants are supposed to be competitive and blind to politics, but in the Siegelman administration, were anything but.

Until Harbor came along the Marion County 25 project was well on the back-burner. Authority members were focusing on a project to extend service along Alabama 19. Residents along the road had petitioned the board seeking water services; it was a cheaper project; and satisfied the program criteria to a far greater extent than the one pushed by Harbor.

Harbor won the day because, as he told the other members, Bedford could guarantee funding for Marion County 25, but no such assurances existed for the other project.

The smell factor was ratcheted up with the news that Bedford had sold Harbor much of the land to be improved by the water line, and done so just months before the funding went through.

Harbor didn't recuse himself from voting on the project and, amazingly, didn't tell authority members he stood to benefit from it.

Blackledge's story presented all the key elements of a serious ethics violation: An official using his influence to promote the spending of public funds in a way that would benefit him; failing to disclose the conflict; and voting for the project.

Huntsville lawyer Dean Johnson cited the story in filing an ethics complaint against Harbor. The commission, as is its normal practice, assigned the matter to one of its investigators.

Complaints determined to have merit are presented to the five-member commission. The commission's lawyer, Hugh Evans, serves as prosecutor, which must encourage defendants. Evans is one of those poor souls frequently seen not inside but outside office buildings, dragging for dear life on a cigarette. Nothing about him suggests a prosecutor with fire in his belly.

The commission's chief investigator, Charles Aldridge, got his first job with the state when then-attorney general Siegelman hired him in the late 1980s. (Aldridge was in charge of the Siegelman legal fees case).

It doesn't help that the commission operates under a weak law. It doesn't have subpoena power and can't compel witnesses to testify. Its hearings are held behind closed doors. As a result, there's no way to gauge the effectiveness of the staff or learn the first thing about evidence for and against a government official.

Defendants are present and represented by lawyers who can call witnesses, argue their client's case, and invariably dwarf Evans' skills and vigor.

After the hearing, the doors are opened. Commissioners cast their votes in public, though without comment. They don't determine guilt or innocence, but rather a finding of probable cause – much the same as a grand jury

If the commission finds probable cause, the case is forwarded to a local district attorney or the Alabama attorney general's office for potential prosecution. Many commission cases aren't pursued because prosecutors, especially those in the attorney general's office, have such low regard for the legal and investigative skills of the staff and the strength of the cases it does produce.

Defense lawyers love to say of grand juries that they will "indict a ham sandwich." One could say of the Alabama Ethics Commission that it would indict a ham sandwich, but not a steak.

The process is a crooked politician's dream, made all the more so by the staff's failures of talent and courage.

On April 2, commission investigator David Green wrote Dean Johnson, the complainant, to report that the Harbor case "has been closed after an initial inquiry."

Green informed Johnson that the commission staff found "no evidence that Mr. Harbor benefited from the Highway 25 water project *any more than any other member of the class of property owners along the highway.*"

Nothing could have been further from the truth. No other property owners along the road had holdings to compare to Harbor's home, his timber business and 200 undeveloped lots. To refresh, I re-read Brett's first story. It bolstered my impression that the Harbor decision could gut the state's ethics law. I made my case to Paul that we do an in-depth piece analyzing the decision. He agreed and I went to work.

I called some of the authority members and was surprised to learn that no one with the ethics commission had contacted them. No wonder the commission hadn't found any evidence that Harbor benefitted more than others – it hadn't looked!

The decision was so bad as to make me wonder if Melvin Cooper -- the commission's director from its inception in 1974 until his retirement in 1994 – would comment. Cooper said, as we reported, that he'd made it his policy never to criticize his successors in the various military and civilian positions he'd held. But the Harbor decision threatened the ethics law and for that reason, he would make an exception.

He said the commission staff had disregarded "the clear wording of the ethics law prohibiting public officials and employees from voting on matters in which they have a financial interest or they were not fully cognizant of the future effects of such a poor decision."

We quoted other experts saying much the same thing.

As its rationale for killing the case, the staff reached out to a 1985 state Supreme Court ruling pertaining to the innumerable Alabama legislators who hold jobs in public education. The court had been asked to decide if those lawmakers could vote on raises for teachers and educators if such votes would increase their own pay. It ruled that educator-legislators could cast such votes.

The Supreme Court concluded that the prohibition against voting on matters of "personal or private interest" was intended to prevent public officials from using their influence to help themselves either individually or *as a member of a small group.*

The ruling noted that courts in other states had decided that lawmakers could vote on matters in which they might benefit as long as the class of those benefiting was *substantial.* In the educator pay raise case, the size of the class that would benefit from the lawmaker votes was in the tens of thousands.

The story ended what had been a cordial relationship with Ethics Commission Director Jim Sumner. Until then, it wasn't unusual for him to see me in the lobby reviewing ethics reports and invite me into his office. But he was angry that friendly Eddie would scrutinize the commission and livid to learn that Cooper had commented on the case.

The Harbor decision that Sumner signed off on put him in a corner and he knew it. I simply wanted him to explain to our readers the potential impact of his actions on the ethics law. His bristling tone suggested he'd rather do anything but.

I asked him at what point a class became small enough so as to prohibit an official belonging to it from taking actions that would benefit the group. Sumner said there was no specific answer. It was possible, he said, that a class could contain very few people. "The more local the entity, the smaller those classes become," he said. "But our general rule is if a matter affects you in a particular way, you shouldn't vote on it."

In a state crawling with politicians blind to conflicts of interests, *shouldn't* is an invitation to steal.

Alabama's ethics sheriff tried to dodge a central question that I basically insisted he answer: Must a public official with a financial interest in a matter recuse himself or, lacking that, inform his fellow board members of the potential conflict?

Sumner said that while he recommended that public officials refrain from voting on projects that would benefit them financially, in many if not most cases, it's allowable for them to cast such votes.

He further said that officials don't necessarily have to reveal that they could benefit from a project, though out of caution and because it's the right thing to do, they should.

If it wasn't so pitiful it would've been funny.

I didn't believe for a moment that Green, the investigator, came up with the "member of the class" excuse.

I suspect that this novel pretext for giving Blue Harbor a pass came from outside the commission staff, that pressure was exerted and that Sumner, possibly out of fear of losing his job, caved in. But it matters not. Nothing can excuse the Harbor decision or Sumner from signing off on it.

The writing was on the wall. Siegelman had nothing to fear from this gang.

———

For reasons one supposes were due to Siegelman's status, the hearing on his complaint – unlike those of lesser persons – wasn't placed on the ethics commission's July agenda. Soon, though, news spread that the panel had cleared him.

Our story, by Bill Barrow and me, began:

Gov. Don Siegelman, faced with ethics scandals involving his administration and a tough re-election bid, scored an important victory Wednesday when the Alabama Ethics Commission ruled there is no evidence that he broke the law by receiving legal fees from a tobacco lawsuit settlement.

Siegelman campaign spokesman Rip Andrews said the 3-1 vote by the Ethics Commission exposed the case for what it always was -- a politically partisan Republican witch-hunt.

"Today, the Ethics Commission exonerated the governor completely, just like we knew it would. These were trumped up, groundless, false charges by a known Republican Party operative designed to hurt the governor politically and nothing else."

Jack Drake had left the room before the hearing. The Birmingham lawyer and Siegelman appointee had been shamelessly coy about whether he would recuse himself on a matter in which he had multiple, blatant conflicts, among them his participation in both tobacco cases.

Bobby Segall, not Cromwell Johnson, represented Siegelman. I thought this odd. Segall had participated in the Crozier case, and presumably shared in the fees.

In addition to being among the state Democratic Party's leading legal minds, Segall was Siegelman's long-time attorney in matters personal, political and when the time came, criminal as well.

Once seen, he is not forgotten. Segall's bushy white mustache covers his lips, and curls upward in finely primped tips. He wears his hair, equally bushy and white, shoulder length, and the whole of it, especially considering his city of his residence, suggests the last surviving Confederate general. In fact, Segall is famous in Alabama for his ferocious advocacy of civil rights and his work for the ACLU. He is also a past president of the Alabama Bar Association.

It's is my strongly held opinion that Segall crossed boundaries to serve as one of Siegelman's many enablers, and in so doing, did his state, his profession and his reputation a disservice.

Though I didn't know it then, years later I found a letter in the Siegelman archives indicating additional involvement by Segall in the Siegelman legal fees matter. The letter, dated May 29, 2000, was from Siegelman to Segall. The governor asked his long-time personal lawyer to "review a proposed dissolution agreement that I am drawing up with my former firm of Cherry, Givens, Peters Lockett and Diaz."

The date reflects that Cherry Givens didn't enter into the severance deal for at least 2½ years after Siegelman ended his association with the firm, and definitely after the USA settlement. In a normal court of law, Segall would have been barred from representing Siegelman, and possibly been called as a witness. But the ethics commission process is but a shadow of the normal judicial process. As a result, Segall was allowed to blow past his myriad conflicts and represent Siegelman.

Among those voting to clear Siegelman was Raymond Bell, a young lawyer who'd worked for Siegelman in the lieutenant governor's office, then the governor's office. He'd moved to Mobile and been appointed by Siegelman to the ethics commission. In a normal court of law, Bell would never have been able to sit in judgment of Siegelman, so substantial were his conflicts.

Sumner said he couldn't comment on the case because of the commission's secrecy provisions. However, he pointed to a 3-inch thick case file and described the investigation as an "exhaustive and thorough effort on the part of the commission, using months of staff time." Three-inches? Hell, I've got five files on the case, and none are that skinny.

As usual in such circumstances, Siegelman left the commenting to Rip. The spokesman repeated the boss's refrain that tobacco cases *were not* a factor in Cherry

Givens' decision to pay the governor $800,000, or whatever it was. "Someone" – an obvious reference to Cromwell Johnson – had been mistaken to say otherwise, Rip said.

"(Siegelman's) past statements are accurate. The governor negotiated his severance package based on what he thought was his value to the firm independent of any tobacco litigation," Andrews said.

We told readers that we'd asked Siegelman to make public the severance arrangement and to give the date when it was finalized and signed.

"I doubt there are any plans to release that settlement, but I can tell you that the statements he has made in the past (about it being unrelated to tobacco litigation) are accurate," said Rip.

A month later, Kim Chandler tried one last time, during a face-to-face interview with the governor. Siegelman told Kim that the money from Cherry Givens was "totally separate from any tobacco litigation whatsoever."

———

Will say it one last time: Of Siegelman's crimes, none equaled the Cherry Givens deal.

He said it had nothing to do with the South Alabama settlement, but that was a lie. There was, for example, the "Personal and Confidential" letter from Chris Peters to Henry Mabry attached to the proposed settlement. In it, Peters wrote that Siegelman had advised Peters to make sure that the USA settlement "was in (Mabry's) hands as soon as possible."

It was in any event ridiculous to suppose that someone other than Siegelman would, or could, authorize or even dream up a decision for the administration to commit $20 million in state funds to settle a dormant lawsuit in which the state wasn't a defendant. Again, the defendants, the tobacco companies, were not required to pay a dime.

When first asked about by the media about his payments from the firm, Siegelman said he was being paid for 20 to 30 unfinished cases. That was not true, as he acknowledged, if only after our research blew away that story.

The governor, the university, all involved kept a $20 million settlement between two government entities – the state and the University of South Alabama – a secret.

Siegelman and his lawyers gave multiple, conflicting accounts about the severance agreement, including incorrect disclosures on his ethics filings that were made under penalty of perjury.

I remain frustrated at never acquiring a copy of the severance agreement, but am not sure what more I could have done (and my efforts far exceeded those described in these pages.)

I know little of the decision not to include the legal fees matter in the Siegelman prosecution. Certainly any such case would have been complicated by the ethics commission's clearing Siegelman. Also problematic was the lack of anyone who rolled on and testified against the governor.

However, I'm of the opinion that prosecutors bringing white collar cases rely too heavily on flipping witnesses. I've come to that conclusion by covering civil trials.

There are differences in the burden required for a plaintiff to win a civil case and a prosecutor to convict a criminal defendant, but it's still about convincing a jury of wrongdoing.

The monster verdicts I've seen have one thing in common, and it's not a strong case or a defendant deserving of a big dollar whipping. The common denominator is defendant lying. Nothing pisses off a jury like being lied to. It may be that the lies are largely irrelevant to the central claims in the case. But when they're being told, you look at jurors and see doom for the defendant.

Had it been me, I'd have subpoenaed all of Cherry Givens records on Siegelman and its tobacco payments and brought every member of the firm before the grand jury to see if they'd stick with the public story under oath. I'd have called every administration official even remotely connected to the deal and the folks from the University of South Alabama as well.

Carrie Kurlander (and for that matter, Rip too) would have been subpoenaed and asked where she got the 20 to 30 cases explanation she gave Phil Rawls. While she was there, she would have been asked about what she reported to Siegelman, and what he said to her, before, during and after my meetings about G.H. Construction and the warehouses, with similar questions about his knowledge of a host of other matters.

I'd have shown the grand jury Siegelman's 1997 letters to the judges declaring his removal from the cases before them and his decision not to accept any fees; his ever-changing financial disclosures; and presented his wildly varying public statements about the severance package.

If, at trial, Siegelman and his lawyers based their legal fee defense on the ethics commission's clearing him, I would have grilled Sumner and his staff and revealed to all just how lame is the Alabama Ethics Commission.

I think the prosecutors – a wholly different set of lawyers at the end than the beginning -- were overwhelmed by the other material and did little ditch-digging on the legal fee matter, probably because the ethics commission had already been there.

A footnote: While Siegelman got his money up-front, it would appear his old mates took it on the chin.

As of July 2001, when we published our first story, the state had paid $2.85 million to the University of South Alabama. Of that, the school had forwarded about $400,000 to Cherry Givens.

In Siegelman's final two years the administration arranged for another $2.5 million in settlement funds to go to the university. Budgetary woes in Siegelman's final years contributed to lesser than projected payments and the payments stopped when Riley became governor. I like to think our stories spooked the administration, and saved state taxpayers millions of dollars.

At the end of the day, the state paid the university $4.49 million -- $15.5 million less than the promised $20 million. Of the $4.49 million, the university passed on $629,361 to Cherry Givens – less than a fourth of the amount the firm was projected to receive.

Though Siegelman was no longer governor in spring 2003, he still had to file an ethics report for 2002, his final full year in office. I could hardly believe my eyes when I pulled the report. He'd done it again. Our story on his disclosure began by telling readers that Siegelman had continued "a four-year streak of making more than $250,000 per year in legal fees while in public office."

This time it wasn't Cherry Givens, but Dickstein Shapiro Morin & Oshinsky, then the sixth-largest firm in Washington, D.C. Siegelman didn't describe the nature of his work nor when he'd done it, only that the payment was for "prior years' service."

Siegelman, of course, declined comment. A Dickstein Shapiro spokeswoman said Siegelman "served as co-counsel to us on various matters -- that is our relationship to him." I didn't expect the firm to reveal how much it paid Siegelman but was hoping for a when and a why. I got neither.

I did the usual searches and found that Dickstein Shapiro had donated $2,000 to Siegelman's 2002 campaign and been awarded one state contract for $50,000. Both details were included in the story, but not stressed.

We reported the above and I went to work trying to learn more. It appeared that Siegelman was asked by one of his contacts with the National Attorneys General Association to recruit some major Alabama agricultural companies and cooperatives to serve as plaintiffs. At the time, there was a mammoth class action against foreign vitamin-makers accused of fixing the prices of vitamins added to animal feed. Dickstein Shapiro was looking "opt-outs" -- that is, plaintiffs who break out of the class and pursue claims on their own in the hope of getting a better deal than that negotiated for the class.

I researched the hell out of the case, found some Alabama plaintiffs, including Birmingham-based poultry company Marshall Durbin. I called them but they refused to say up or down if Siegelman had contacted them on behalf of Dickstein Shapiro. I felt sure he had, but couldn't prove it.

Considering the dates of the case, this plaintiff recruiting almost surely occurred while Siegelman was governor. One presumes that the agribusinesses, when taking his calls, were quite cognizant that a governor can in many ways make life hard or easy for companies as regulated as the likes of chicken farms.

The research was for naught. I felt comfortable that I knew what happened, but couldn't prove it, and never wrote a follow-up.

———

If Siegelman was telling the truth when he said Cherry Givens paid him $800,000 – and it's unlikely he'd overstate it -- then he received, at a minimum, $1.37 million in legal fees while governor. This is all the more astonishing given that before becoming governor, he'd never made anywhere near such sums.

To put it in perspective, a survey by the bar association taken the year before Siegelman became governor found that only 12 percent of the Alabama's lawyers generated fees above $200,000 per year. Sixty-one percent earned less than $100,000.

The survey also looked at overhead, such as for rent, personnel and supplies. Twenty percent reported that overhead ate more than 50 percent of their income; for 33 percent it consumed between 41 and 50 percent; and 28 percent estimated overhead at between 31 and 40 percent of their revenues.

Siegelman – with his free office and secretary at the Alabama Sheriff's Association -- had no overhead.

At a minimum, he cleared an average of $342,000 per year in legal fees while serving as Alabama's governor. As a son, brother and friend of lawyers I can tell you that many attorneys who work 50 and 60-hour weeks have never cleared $342,000 in one year.

It had been quite a run for Alabama's First Lawyer.

Chapter 27
Siegelman v. Riley

"If the first question to you is a stupid, little ethics question?"
-- First line of a debate preparation sheet containing suggested responses to questions Siegelman could expect to be asked during his debates with Bob Riley.

"Mr. Siegelman went to sleep on election night thinking he had won. But overnight, Republican Baldwin County reported that a glitch had given Mr. Siegelman, a Democrat, about 6,000 extra votes. When they were subtracted, Republican Rob Riley won by roughly 3,000 votes. James Gundlach, a professor at Auburn University, crunched the numbers and concluded that Mr. Siegelman lost because of 'electronic ballot stuffing,' possibly by an operative who accessed the computers and 'edited' the results, though others dispute his analysis."
-- From, "A Tale of Three (Electronic Voting) Elections," a 2008 column by the New York Times' Adam Cohen.

Siegelman's re-election bid started smoothly enough, he corralling 76 percent of the vote in the June 2002 primary against combative, nutty and under-funded Agriculture Commissioner Charles Bishop. (Five years later, Bishop, then a Republican state senator, gave Alabama a black eye when he slugged Lowell Barron on the last day of the legislative session. The punch was captured by cameras and widely broadcast.)

The Republican primary appeared competitive going in. Fob James' son Tim was always a long-shot, but, at least until near the election, Windom and Bob Riley rated a toss-up. Windom had won a statewide election while Riley, as one of Alabama's seven congressmen, was little known outside his north Alabama district.

James and Windom dueled for Roy Moore's affections, each surmising that a blessing from Judge God would deliver his rural flock into the anointed one's camp. James – the one of Fob's three sons most like him in looks and temperament -- touted his wife's friendship with Moore's wife Kayla. Windom mailed fliers with a photo of the smiling candidate standing next to Moore. Riley, on the other hand, made little effort to connect himself to Moore, who in the end refrained from endorsing anyone.

Riley, then 58, seemed a genuine, decent man. He's a tall, personable fellow who made millions in the private sector – as poultry farmer, then owner of a car dealership and trucking company – before winning the first of his three terms in Congress. The various conservative Congressional scorecards graded him at or about 100, though he wasn't stridently right-wing, say, in the mold of a Jesse Helms or Rick Santorum.

Register cartoonist J.D. Crowe captured Riley's signature feature -- his full head of black hair, hair-sprayed or somehow naturally rigid, and to J.D.'s mind's eye, jutting forward like a runway on an aircraft carrier. He was often described as Reaganesque, an attribute his consultants happily co-opted with ads showing the candidate walking on his farm and riding a horse. The Republican money men liked Riley too, thus allowing him to flood the airwaves and erase his name recognition deficit.

In a rebuke to his father as well as himself, Tim James drew just 9 percent of the vote. But the stunner was Windom. Riley ate him alive, polling 73 percent to his 18 percent.

It was to be Siegelman vs. Riley, on Nov. 5.

In late March, shortly before the big push on the foundation stories, I received an anonymous, handwritten letter suggesting I check out payments to and work done at ADECA by a firm called Group One. The source said ADECA had paid the company about $800,000 to build and maintain its web-site, and that the company's performance was atrocious.

A few weeks later, I opened my e-mail to find a similar if more entertaining tip on Group One from someone identifying himself as Maxwell Smart. For younger readers, that's the comically inept spy played by Don Adams in the 1960s sitcom, "Get Smart."

"The contract states that Group One will redesign the (ADECA) web page for a cost of over $798,000. Web pages can be done for under $2,000! What is going on here? The company is not in the phone book."

By then I'd already made the first of what would be a good dozen requests for ADECA's Group One records, each necessitated by the obviously incomplete offerings made available when I arrived to review what were time and time again represented to me by Larry Childers -- the agency spokesman and my off and on nemesis – as the entirety of the Group One records.

Even early on, though, they couldn't withhold the contracts or the cover sheets submitted with them for the legislature's contract review committee. "Contractor selected by Governor's Office," was the surprisingly candid declaration on the cover sheet.

Had ADECA and the administration, given us the complete records when first sought, the story would have run in late spring. Instead, it was published Sept. 1, with the gubernatorial campaign heating up.

It began:

A company owned by two supporters of Gov. Don Siegelman received more than $760,000 to design and maintain the Web site for the Alabama Department *of Economic and Community Affairs, but the state wound up scrapping the work, records show.*

State employees in the Finance Department's technology division are rebuilding the Web site. For the work done to date, Finance will bill ADECA no more than $3,800, and the final cost is not likely to exceed $7,000, agency records indicate.

It's unclear why state officials will be able to do the work for so much less than what Montgomery-based Group One Inc. was paid.

It's also unclear, based on a review of ADECA files and other records provided to the Mobile Register:

- *Why Group One was picked.*

- *What the firm did for almost two years before being terminated in October.*

- *Why, after expressing dissatisfaction, state officials entered into a second, $399,000-per-year contract with the company.*

As with my other investigative stories at the time, we refrained from teeing the ball up and calling Riley and asking him to take a whack at it. But the Associated Press, in its re-write, used portions of a Riley press release that rehashed the story, with commentary. "This is another example of fraud, waste and abuse of the people's money by the Siegelman administration and a major reason why Alabama's government remains in financial crisis," declared candidate Riley.

Another ADECA story that fall, and work intensive as hell, reported that Dewayne Freeman, Siegelman's first appointee to head the agency, ordered agency employees to change their scoring on federally-funded grants for the poor, known as CBGB grants. This blatant violation of the federal regulations was done so that applicants that Freeman, Siegelman and others favored for political reasons received funding even if they didn't qualify.

A second Group One story reported that state employees had rebuilt and redesigned the web site at a grand cost of $4,000; that the rebuilt site went online in early October; and was yanked the next day.

ADECA -- to the bemused delight of those who knew why -- went a week without a Web site. When the site came back on-line, it was the faulty model designed by Group One.

The agency used the Group One site until the election, after which it was replaced, for good, by the state-designed $4,000 model that worked.

"Two state employees told the paper that an order came from ADECA management to use the old site until after the election," we reported. "The employees requested anonymity, saying they feared reprisal if they were identified."

A report by the state auditor supported our findings. When auditors asked Group One executives to produce internal records showing hours worked by its employees on the ADECA contract, they were told that the company hadn't maintained such records.

A report by the U.S. Department of Housing and Urban Development (commonly known as HUD) was more damning. Every dime of the contract had come from HUD, and after agency officials read our story, they demanded answers. The agency concluded that almost $800,000 in expenditures "could not be documented or explained by the ADECA staff."

In February 2003, we reported HUD's demand that ADECA refund $518,270 of the $761,500 paid to Group One. The feds ultimately gave the state a break by settling for a $140,196 repayment.

Years later, at trial, Nick Bailey testified to having received money from Group One co-owner Jim Lane. Bailey said Lane gave him about $90,000 in 1998 and 1999.

Bailey testified that Lane also gave him about $20,000 to supplement his campaign salary during Siegelman's 1998 run against Fob James. Bailey said Siegelman knew about the off-the-books campaign money but testified he didn't tell the boss about the $90,000.

As I've stated before and will again, I think here, as in other matters, Bailey was protecting Siegelman. For one thing, it made no sense for Lane to give Bailey $90,000 in 1998 and 1999, at a time when he was, in reality if not title, Siegelman's driver and errand doer. Bailey didn't become head of ADECA until 2000, to the extent he ever really was.

With the campaign heating up I received an unusual tip regarding the governor's brother. Siegelman, according to the source, had tried to sell the Bush White House on an Alabama-based entity that was to play some undefined role in preparing the country for disasters, including terrorist attacks, and was proposing that his brother Les run it. The Alabama National Guard was said to have some role in the plan as well.

The governor's office declined to comment and National Guard officials unconvincingly denied the existence of any such plan. Needless to say, no documents that fit my public records request were produced. The source said records pertaining to the deal were destroyed after I called seeking them. I even tried the White House, but a low-level Bush administration spokeswoman, sounding irritated that I would trouble her with actual questions, never called back.

I believed the tip, which came from within the National Guard, but hadn't been able to confirm it. Thus, no story.

Before leaving in January 2003, the Siegelman administration went to considerable measures to cull revealing documents before turning over all its records to the state archives, as the law requires. However, a few nuggets -- I suppose inadvertently slipped into the wrong files – survived. Among those I came across three years later when reviewing the Siegelman archives was a document confirming the Les Siegelman tip.

The document described something called the "National Domestic Preparedness University," which would purportedly generate a possible economic impact of $2.5 billion a year for the state.

Les Siegelman – whose business history suggests not one iota of experience in disaster preparedness or anything remotely like it – was shown as being co-chair of the project.

To my surprise, Siegelman responded to written questions we sent him about findings in the archives for a story that ran in early October 2005. He declared that the preparedness university "would have brought hundreds of jobs to Anniston, would have made Alabama the national center for Homeland Security training and response and just might have prevented a lot of the damage done to New Orleans from Katrina."

Siegelman reported that a "national blue ribbon delegation" traveled to Washington to present the proposal to Tom Ridge, then head of Homeland Security. He claimed that a Ridge aide told him that the university "was exactly what we need, but we may have some political hurdles to get over."

"Apparently, they were not able to 'get over' those political hurdle," wrote Siegelman.

Siegelman neglected to explain how or why his brother was selected to lead or in any event play a key role in what was, at least on paper, an important, highly technical and hugely expensive project to help spare America from the torments of terrorists and natural disasters.

I didn't make a second effort to seek such an explanation. It was hard to take the nepotism angle seriously, so farcical was Siegelman's pie-in-the-sky pitch for an Anniston-based National Domestic Preparedness University run by his brother.

———

Among the other finds in the archives was a pair of crib sheets prepared – my guess, by Rip -- to help Siegelman prepare for the 2002 debates against Riley. They could have doubled as a greatest hits package of our stories. Subject headings were in bold, followed by bulleted responses. For example:

The House?

- *I was paid exactly what the house was worth.*
- *My wife and I listed the house for what we thought it was worth.*
- *In my opinion I was not paid more than the house was worth."*

The one for the second debate opened with, "If the first question to you is a stupid, little ethics question?"

Siegelman was directed to answer the question, then say, "But I hope we can talk some tonight about what the people of Alabama care about. Schools, jobs."

Both sheets presented the well-practiced lies, such as this suggested retort under, "Lanny Vines?"

"I don't know what arrangements Mr. Pearce may have made as far as a partner is concerned," Siegelman was to say.

Other headings included: "Will you release your tax returns?"; "Severance package?"; "Lottery Foundation?"; and "Lanny Young and Chemwaste loopholes?"

The response to that last one ended with this amusing bit, the parenthetical phrase theirs: "But at least that company is still paying taxes. However, there are hundreds of huge, out of-state corporations that are paying NO taxes. (Diversion, smokescreen) Transition to corporate loopholes message."

Diversion? Smokescreen? The "corporate loopholes message?" This was a reminder for Siegelman to bang away on one of his new themes – he as defender of the little guy against what he'd taken to calling the "Enrons of Alabama."

On the stump he ceaselessly plugged his success recruiting industry while ignoring the tax breaks he used to lure those trophies to Alabama. With the next breath, he'd reach into the populist playbook and pledge to close the tax loopholes of corporations who "cook the books to avoid paying school taxes to the state."

He refused press requests that he identify a single "Alabama Enron." One suspects that had he done so, reporters could have located contributions from the corporate miscreant to Siegelman.

If asked during the debates if he expected to be indicted, he was to deny wrongdoing and say: "Republicans will sling ANY mud or sink to any level to win this election. They will do ANYTHING to win, anything except talk about the issues."

Other headings were: "Friends and aides been indicted?"; "No bid contracts?"; "GH?"; "Will you pledge to bid every single contract?"; "Contingency Fund"; and, "Did not receive any fee from tobacco but lawyer (Cromwell Johnson) said you did?"

Ethics was among the topics chosen for the first debate, on Aug. 5. Siegelman stuck to the script when asked about his ethical potholes, including no-bid contracts, legal fees, and as here, answering a question about the sale of his home from *Montgomery Advertiser* reporter Mike Cason.

"Well, Mike, let me say that my wife and I talked about what we wanted for the house and what we thought it was worth. I got an offer and we accepted it," he said, adding that this was "another issue being thrown out there by Republican Party operatives."

Both candidates delivered feisty performances in the first debate, with no shortage of the silly one-liners planted in debate scripts by consultants and campaign spokespersons. Siegelman called his opponent "Fob Riley" for opposing the lottery.

When Riley told Siegelman that some black lawmakers were switching to him because Siegelman ran "the most corrupt administration they have ever seen," the governor roared in retort: "Now I want you to look into that camera or either shut, either shut up or put up congressman!"

Riley was in the midst of putting up when moderator Tim Lennox, seeing too much fur flying, exclaimed, "Governor! Congressman! Governor Siegelman!"

Siegelman was considered to have given a rather shrill performance. Most analysts pointed to Riley as the winner if for no other reason than he held his own and showed voters that he was more than an empty cowboy hat. Most of those same people judged the second debate, in October, a tie.

Though I wasn't covering the campaign, I chipped in a story in late September that the Siegelman campaign was kind enough to tout with a press release under the headline: "MR (*Mobile Register*): Honest Bob Not So Honest About 50K Photos."

The piece reported that Riley failed to keep his promise to identify contributors who'd donated what for an Alabama fundraiser was a record-breaking $4.02 million take. That extravagant sum poured forth on July 15, when the president came to Birmingham for what was called the, "Salute to George W. Bush."

More than 2,800 people attended the $1,000-per-person event. A lesser number ponied up $25,000 for a VIP reception, and some of those managed another $25,000 – or $50,000 total -- to have their picture taken with the president.

The story began:

During last month's gubernatorial debate, Congressman Bob Riley bowed up and told Gov. Don Siegelman and a statewide television audience that his campaign would identify those who ponied up $50,000 apiece to have their picture taken with President Bush at a Birmingham fund-raiser.

"First, the governor says I need to release my records. Governor, they'll be coming out in a 45-day report. You'll be able to see them," the Republican challenger stated during the Aug. 5 debate.

But on Monday, when Riley's campaign released its 45-day report -- so-called because it comes about 45 days prior to the general election -- there were no $50,000 donations to be seen.

Riley spokesman David Azbell called the promise a "spur of the moment statement during the debate," made because Riley hadn't recalled that the fund-raiser was sponsored by the Republican Governor's Association, so the donations weren't made directly to his campaign. Because of my status as a non-person, we had Bill Barrow seek comment from Rip, who slugged away.

"I think that's just another lie in an increasing series of lies coming out of that campaign," Rip said. "He's a candidate of honesty who lies on the air."

Days later, Cason's column in the *Advertiser* bore the headline, "Campaign messages can come from strange places."

Wrote Cason: "In some cases, politicians want to shoot the messenger when the message is about them. When it's about the other guy, well, the messenger is just doing his or her job."

The *Advertiser* reporter remarked that there was nothing unusual about candidates using newspaper stories "to spread bad publicity about their opponents."

"What was odd about the Siegelman campaign using the story, though, was the source. It was written by Eddie Curran, investigative reporter for the *Mobile Register*. For about a year, the Siegelman administration has refused to talk to Curran, who has written lots of stories about no-bid contracts and other issues that raise questions about the administration."

It's my recollection that I called Mike to thank him for that one.

———

When the $50,000 donors were revealed, the most surprising name on the list was that of Colonial Bank chairman Bobby Lowder. Since the mid-1990s, Lowder had spent untold sums bank-rolling Siegelman and Democratic leaders in the state senate as part of his megalomaniacal pursuit to dominate Auburn University by controlling its board of trustees. Though governors appointed the schools trustees, they had to be confirmed by the senate.

When Fob James appointed two non-Lowderites to the board, the Siegelman-led senate blocked their appointments, all but shutting down the legislature. The mess provided Alabamians with an astonishing civics lesson – that in their state, almost nothing, state budges included, was as important as appointments to the Auburn board.

Lowder paid, and Siegelman, Lowell Barron and the rest of the Democratic leadership in the senate gave him whatever he wanted.

Siegelman's fealty to Lowder continued after he became governor, as he continued to appoint trustees whose primary qualifications seemed to be their personal and business connections to Lowder and Colonial Bank. He even appointed an Alabama graduate, his friend and backer Jack Miller, to the board. Miller was Colonial's lawyer.

If there's one Siegelman scandal getting short shrift in this book, it's his use of his public positions to help Lowder control Auburn. Thus the surprise in seeing Lowder among those donating $50,000 at the Bush fund-raiser. But the real shocker was Rip's statement on behalf of the Sicgelman campaign.

"Bob Riley is a bought and paid for puppet of Bobby Lowder," he said.

There was no way to read that and not feel that Rip, in the service of Siegelman, would say anything.

———

Almost every story analyzing the race broached Siegelman's ethics problems, as did a Phil Rawls' piece two months before the election, and which read in part:

By most measures, Siegelman ought to be in good shape. In the past four years, he spurred the largest school construction program in state history, replacing most of Alabama's portable classrooms. He pushed through the state's biggest rural road program ever, replacing hundreds of outdated bridges. And thousands of new auto industry jobs have come to Alabama as Honda, Hyundai and Mercedes announced new plants or expansions with Siegelman's encouragement.

But Siegelman has been damaged by an investigation of his finances and by allegations that friends have won sweetheart deals from the state.

Riley is focusing his campaign almost solely on Siegelman's ethics. With the slogan "honest change," he tells voters that the Siegelman administration is "sinking into a quicksand of corruption and fraud."

Polls taken in September and October showed the pair even, but as the election neared, Riley began pulling away. A poll published two days before the election suggested a comfortable Riley win, showed Siegelman's "negatives" higher than ever. Just 30 percent picked him as the more ethical of the two.

Siegelman's desperation in the late going was illustrated by three seamy affairs, the first during an address to the state Alabama Roadbuilders Association. According to multiple accounts, the governor's talk quickly evolved into a tirade against roadbuilders who'd donated to Riley through PACs.

"I know who you are!" Siegelman bellowed, to the discomfort and shock of those in the audience that included state and federal highway department officials. Though he didn't name names, the governor glared at a southwest Alabama roadbuilder known as a Riley backer. None of the half dozen or so people I spoke to were willing to go on the record so Siegelman's behavior that day went unreported.

A September trip to Alabama by Charlton Heston produced a second example of Siegelman's willingness to go to any lengths to win an election.

The Riley campaign and state Republicans had arranged for Heston to come to Alabama and join Riley for stops throughout the state. Six weeks earlier, the actor turned National Rifle Association bulldog announced he had Alzheimer's. It was obvious during his trip to Alabama that Heston was fading.

"You expected Moses to walk in, bearing tablets," said Azbell, the Riley spokesman. "What you got was this elderly man, obviously infirm, who kind of shuffled to the podium."

Heston had to read off cue cards, and even then, only spoke for a minute or two at each stop. On the day's last stop, in Hunstville, Heston told the crowd that he "enjoyed my trip across Texas today."

Heston did go to Texas, but the next day. Azbell said it was his understanding that the Lone Star trip was Heston's last such public appearance.

Soon after the visit, the Siegelman campaign announced that Heston, while in Alabama, had signed a letter endorsing Siegelman for governor. This seemed impossible, since the NRA almost never endorses Democrats, and because Heston had, after all, traveled the state with Riley and other Republicans.

Heston, it turned out, had flown into Mobile the night before with his public relations assistants. That evening, Siegelman and his wife came to Heston's hotel room. There, Heston signed the letter endorsing Siegelman.

The Riley campaign and state Republican officials accused Siegelman of taking advantage of Heston's near-senility. However, a spokesman for Heston said the former actor knew what he was doing. Republicans later alleged that Heston's P.R. people, working at the bequest of a Siegelman backer, arranged the hotel visit and endorsement.

Regardless of the how Siegelman managed it, his calling on the ailing Heston during the latter's trip to Alabama to support Riley and Republicans was a cheeky, immature bit of political gamesmanship.

The lowest act of the campaign came with an assist from Stan Pate, one of the more eccentric players in Alabama politics. Pate is a wealthy Tuscaloosa real estate developer who vaulted into the spotlight by flirting with running for governor as an arch-conservative, tax-fighting Republican. He's remained a player because he spends a lot of money being one.

He started off a Siegelman enemy, helping fund the anti-lottery campaign. Somewhere along the way, post-lottery, Pate and Siegelman patched things up, and in a big way. After Nick Bailey resigned from the administration in December 2001, Pate hired him to do God knows what, and at this writing, is still his employer.

In 2007, Pate was to have some unclear role in the Jill Simpson affair, meeting with the woman who did more than anyone to transform Siegelman into the nation's number one political prisoner.

Near campaign's end, Pate paid to produce a race-baiting ad showing a clip from a taped meeting between Riley and a group of black Republicans. The producer switched from color to bad quality black-and-white to achieve a seedy effect. A narrator said that Riley was "cutting back-room deals for African-American support;" and that controversial Birmingham attorney Donald Watkins, who is black, had endorsed Riley.

The *Birmingham News* reported the ad and Pate's role in producing and peddling it. Siegelman publicly if not at all convincingly denied knowing about it.

When TV stations refused to run the commercial, Pate tried to pawn it off on the Libertarian Party, along with a $100,000 donation so the party could buy air time. That effort also failed.

This might have been it had Paul Hamrick's boss, Joe Perkins, not gelled up a press release and distributed the ad to the media. The Matrix Man told the AP he had no connection with Pate, but publicized the ad because he thought it interesting.

Pate declined to respond when asked if he was working with the Siegelman campaign. He would only say that he financed the spot because he was tired of Riley's "hypocritical rhetoric about backroom deals."

It was Alabama politics at its duplicitous, racist worst, and played by a man who owed his every win to black voters.

"We can't do it without you," Siegelman told a mostly black crowd in Selma at the same time he was trying to scoop redneck votes away from Riley by showing his foe conferring with blacks.

Post-election analyses revealed that it was a heavy turnout by blacks that almost delivered a second term to Siegelman.

Never does the news room buzz as on election night. Every editor, clerk and reporter, regardless of beat or schedule, is at their stations, save those out following candidates. Pizza is delivered and engulfed. The atmosphere is fun, with folks joking and screaming the latest results across the newsroom and everyone settled in for a long night sure to end, at least for many of the reporters, at a downtown bar.

As the night progressed, the expected easy Riley win turned nail-biter. With half the state's precincts in, Siegelman held a tiny lead. Among those still out was heavily-Republican Baldwin County, where the early numbers showed a big Riley edge -- enough to give him the lead and, in all likelihood, the election.

Joe Danborn's assignment that night was to monitor the Baldwin County vote, precinct by precinct, so we could unofficially call races in our neighboring county by press-time.

At about 10:20 p.m., Danborn let out a cry. The Baldwin County Probate Court had just released the unofficial totals it provides to the media and candidates. Joe's precinct totals – and for that matter, the precinct by precinct totals on the probate court's web-site -- showed Riley with a shade over 31,000 votes, and Siegelman with 12,736.

Out of nowhere, Siegelman's total had shot up by 6,334 votes, to 19,070. After the numbers from the late-reporting counties came in, Siegelman led – meaning he'd been re-elected -- by a sliver of some 3,000 votes.

The Siegelman campaign knew something funny had happened in Baldwin County. It too had people on the ground, collecting precinct by precinct tallies. But Siegelman – as perhaps would many candidates in the same situation – didn't look the gift horse in the mouth. He raced out to declare victory.

"How sweet it is!" he yelled out to his backers.

"You have delivered a great victory for Alabama today," he said, and urged Riley to concede. "I would hope Mr. Riley would not prolong it and would not drag it out."

The Riley campaign, befuddled by the Baldwin change, declined Siegelman's invitation. Within an hour of Siegelman's victory speech, Baldwin County Probate Court Judge Adrian Johns reported the mistake.

Siegelman's phantom 6,370 votes evaporated. The pendulum swung back to Riley, making him the victor by 3,117 votes, or less than a quarter of a percent of the 1.3 million ballots cast. It was the closest gubernatorial election in Alabama history.

At 1:20 a.m., Riley's son Rob stood in for his dad by announcing to the Riley crowd that his father was claiming victory.

At a press conference the next morning Siegelman came out firing. "Votes were changed after midnight with nobody present," he charged.

We were about to have our own mini-Florida.

The many post-mortems established beyond question that a downloading error caused a computer to misread a data pack from the Magnolia Springs precinct, where Siegelman actually received 342 of the 1,294 votes cast. The data pack – a cartridge similar in appearance to an eight-track tape -- spit out the correct number at the precinct level. The problem occurred when it was taken to the sheriff's department with all the others. For reasons not entirely clear, when inserted into the computer there it produced the whacky numbers.

These weren't the official results, but numbers generated early for a summary sheet distributed to the media and representatives for the candidates. Siegelman wasn't the only benefactor. The same sheet showed an astonishing 13,935 *write-in votes* for a state senate race. The actual total was 235.

"That tells you right there that you've got fried numbers," said Mark Kelly, a representative for the company that provided the election systems used by the county.

Most felt that fault rested with county election officials, who should have double-checked the numbers before releasing them to the media. Some blamed the AP for reporting the numbers too soon, but considering the rush to get the results, it's not surprising that the wire service accepted the numbers provided by the county.

For the Siegelman side to be right, more than 50,000 people would have had to vote in Baldwin County. That's about 6,000 more than actually did.

Five years later the blunder became part of the fabric of claims by Siegelman, Democratic congressional leaders and many in the national media that pretty much everything bad that ever happened to Siegelman was due to "Republican operatives." This silliness, like so much else, occurred post-Jill Simpson – as in, after the Rainsville lawyer signed an affidavit accusing Karl Rove and others of engineering Siegelman's prosecution.

Before June 2007 – which is to say, before Jill Simpson's affidavit and her national debut in the pages of the *New York Times* and *Time* magazine -- Siegelman blamed Riley for his prosecution but never once mentioned Rove. After Simpson, he let Riley slide and spoke of nothing else but Rove. As Siegelman's story developed, he began assigning Rove a role in the Baldwin County snafu.

"Mark, I mention the vote stealing in every interview," he told Mark Crispin Miller, who runs the far-left blog, "News from the Underground," and is, egads, a professor of media studies at New York University.

"'60 Minutes' cut it out. Dan Abrams didn't want to go there either. I have told the story to the *Washington Post* and *L.A. Times*. The hook is Rove's fingerprints are found there too," said Siegelman.

You have to hand it to Team Siegelman – they sold the stolen election fantasy to the *New York Times* and plenty of others. A June 2007 editorial in the *Times* conjured hobgoblins in action by referring to Siegelman's 2002 defeat as being "marred by suspicious vote tabulations."

Three months after that editorial, Adam Cohen, the assistant editor of the *Times* editorial page, wrote an op-ed below the ominous headline, "The Strange Case of an Imprisoned Alabama Governor." Cohen told readers that Siegelman "appeared to have won by a razor thin margin" but that "a late night change in the tallies in Republican Baldwin County" gave Riley the win.

"Mr. Siegelman has charged that the votes were intentionally shifted by a Republican operative," wrote Cohen. "James Gundlach, an Auburn University professor, did a statistical analysis of the returns and found that the final numbers were clearly the result of intentional manipulation."

Cohen cited the Gundlach in another column as well.

Best I can tell, the theoretical spine upon which the Gundlach study rests is an assertion that computers don't make mistakes or, in any event, that they don't produce different results if operated in a consistent manner. That's an absurd notion, as anyone who has spent any time at all working on computers can attest.

With Gundlach having eliminated mechanical error, fraud – and thus, a stolen election – was the only remaining possibility, and the conclusion reached by his study.

Gundlach, incidentally, was a professor of anthropology and sociology, not computer science, and his politics are as left as Rush Limbaugh's are right.

What's amazing is that in many influential circles – including the editorial board of the *New York Times* -- it's now accepted as gospel that Siegelman beat Riley, that the election was stolen from him by Republican operatives, and that the Gundlach study *proves it.*

In 2008, the Democratic majority of the U.S. House Judiciary Committee climbed aboard when it unleashed its report on "selective prosecution" by the Bush Justice Department. The report mentioned the Baldwin County vote in making its case that Siegelman was prosecuted for political reasons. The report stated that the 2002 election was, "marred by serious allegations of vote tampering, focused on the as-yet-unexplained shift of several thousand votes" from Siegelman to Riley.

The committee was wrong on multiple counts, including that votes were shifted to Riley. Not even Siegelman said that.

――――

Siegelman's actions immediately following the election belie his claims of an election stolen by GOP operatives in Baldwin County. Nothing is more telling than his insistence upon a statewide recount. If all he needed was 3,117 votes, why not focus all his energies on the 6,370 "stolen" votes from that county?

The answer: Because they weren't stolen; they never existed; and he knew it.

Siegelman and his legal team knew that victory wasn't to be found by a recount in Baldwin County, but used the goof-up there as a stalking horse for their broader goal – a statewide recount. If they could pull that off, they just might be able to scrabble up enough Siegelman votes, void some of Riley's, and scrap their way to the magic number of 3,117.

"I cannot imagine a more fair way to resolve this situation," Siegelman said at a press conference the next morning, in urging a statewide recount.

"What Don Siegelman wants now is to get his hands on the ballots," responded Republican lawyer Matt Lembke, adding that Riley's team would not "stand by and let this unwarranted and dangerous recount occur."

Three days after the vote, and with election officials throughout the state seeking his guidance, Pryor issued an attorney general's opinion based on a 1953 law that prohibited breaking seals on election materials without a formal challenge. "You can't break the seal based on not liking the count," wrote Pryor.

To which Rip responded, "The bottom line is it's a Republican conspiracy at its worst."

Siegelman's alter ego, Golden Flake, erupted with novel grounds for a statewide recount: His voters were stupid.

"I would argue that most of Bob Riley's voters have taken a test where you have to fill out those things. I represent poor people, working class folks, mom-and-pop store owners. A lot of those people didn't necessarily know the right technique to vote an optical scan ballot."

――――

It was Siegelman's fellow Democrats who drove the stake into his recount dreams.

In 2000, Democrats throughout the country went to war for Al Gore. Alabama's Democratic leadership made no such effort on Siegelman's behalf. He sent a mass mailing to supporters asking for help in raising the $500,000 he estimated he'd need for the challenge. The response was underwhelming.

His only real hope was the legislature. State law provides a means for a candidate to challenge an election in legislature, which in theory -- it's never happened -- would consider evidence and decide the election. Montgomery lawyer Joe Espy, a Democratic Party go-to guy for such matters, was hired by Siegelman to lead his recount challenge. Espy said the governor was considering calling a special session in late November to turn the election over to the legislature.

On paper, Siegelman looked unbeatable. Democrats held 64 out of 105 seats in the House and boasted a 25-10 majority in the Senate.

But in public statements and private meetings, Democratic leaders told Siegelman to forget it.

"It would be totally divisive to come before the legislative body. To a man or woman, nobody was interested in having it before the legislature," said House Speaker Pro Tem Demetrius Newton, a black Democrat from Birmingham, after a meeting of Democratic house members.

Party leaders described it as a no-win situation: Support Siegelman and get accused of stealing the election; support Riley, and anger your base by risking the perception that you care more for Republicans then Democrats.

"I think it's over. You get beat, you go to the house," said Democratic House member Jeff Dolbare. "Stop moaning and groaning."

"Siegelman just never has had a great reserve of hard, hard relationships . . . that he could call on that would just tow the line for him, particularly in the legal arena," lobbyist Bob Geddie said after Siegelman folded. "(His) support in the Legislature had just about dwindled to a handful in the last couple of years."

Siegelman's final option was the Alabama Supreme Court, which he hoped would order recounts in all 67 Alabama counties. The court directed the Riley campaign to file its argument against the recount by Nov. 18, a Monday. Siegelman's lawyers were to file a response the next day, with the court to entertain oral arguments on Thursday.

Nobody seriously believed Siegelman had a chance. His legal arguments were shaky; eight of the nine justices were Republicans; and there was no evidence to suggest that a recount could erase Riley's 3,117 vote advantage.

The Riley team filed its brief early Monday. To the extent there was a response, it was a call that afternoon from Siegelman, congratulating Riley on his victory.

"The two men had a very amicable and friendly conversation," said former state Supreme Court Justice Terry Butts, who Riley had engaged to assist with the recount battle.

At 6 p.m., Siegelman, his wife at his side, publicly conceded. Though smiling and outwardly calm, his hands began to shake as he approached the end of his speech. The 56-year-old political lifer told the gathering he believed he would have won a recount, but, "for the good of the state of Alabama, for the good of our people, I am dropping my request for a recount."

"This decision has not been easy and it's been painful. It's been painful in part because I feel like I'm letting you down, letting you supporters down. But I truly believe it would hurt Alabama more to put us through this divisive process."

Siegelman was, with what even his harshest critics acknowledged, bowing out with class. He'd spent 20 of the previous 24 years in public office and surely recognized that only a miraculous comeback could return him to the highest perches of government and the only life he'd ever wanted.

In the newsroom reporters and editors gathered around the televisions. My chief recollection is of the camera panning Siegelman's disconsolate staff and finding Jasper Ward, Rip's friend from Georgetown. He was or had been crying, and I couldn't help thinking, "Why is a bright kid like you crying over his loss?"

It was another example of me failing to appreciate the something in Siegelman that others – many good people included – saw in him, and inspired them to follow.

There are of course two accounts of what occurred the day Siegelman conceded – the one described above, and the one introduced five years later, by Dana Jill Simpson.

Chapter 28
The KKK Took My Election Away

"I understood from what Rob told me that Terry Butts talked to Mr. Siegelman and some of his campaign people is what I understood. And in that conversation basically, Mr. Siegelman had been offered to go ahead and concede, that the pictures (from the Klan rally) would not come out and that they would not further prosecute him with the Justice Department."
-- Jill Simpson, during September 2007 testimony to lawyers for the U.S. House Judiciary Committee.

"I never heard that. I was never around any talk like that."
-- Response by Montgomery lawyer Joe Espy to Simpson's KKK story. Espy spearheaded the Siegelman campaign's legal bid to challenge the results of the 2002 election.

The prosecution of Don Siegelman was largely a state story until June 2007, when *Time* and the *New York Times* reported on the affidavit signed 10 days before by Jill Simpson.

In her now famous affidavit, the Rainsville, Ala., lawyer claimed to have participated in a November 2002 conference call in which Bill Canary revealed that Karl Rove directed the Justice Department to prosecute Siegelman; and, separately, that "his girls" were also on the job. "His girls" was a reference to Canary's wife Leura, the U.S. Attorney for the Montgomery-based middle district of Alabama; and Alice Martin, the top federal prosecutor for the Birmingham-based northern district.

Strangely, neither *Time* nor the *Times* nor any of the other major media who were to propel the Siegelman prosecution into a national scandal so much as mentioned the central element of Simpson's affidavit. The bulk of her sworn statement described a never-before-told and, if true, history-changing story about the end of Alabama's 2002 governor's race.

The following represents a best faith effort to tell that story. Doing so is complicated by matters in addition to the fact that it's not true. For example, Simpson's tale changed frequently, or rather, developed, like a young tree sprouting new branches, all shaped like curlicues.

It is convoluted as hell. I ask that you not blame the author.

Sources for Simpson's version are her affidavit; interviews she gave reporters; and, primarily, her September 2007 testimony to lawyers for the U.S. House Judiciary Committee.

According to Simpson and no one else but Simpson:

About a week after the election, and with the recount battle in high gear, Rob Riley called her seeking a favor. He'd received an alarming report that his dad's campaign signs were disappearing in the Scottsboro area. Could she find out who was behind this? (Simpson didn't explain why the Riley campaign would give a fraction of a damn that someone was uprooting a few signs *after* an election.)

Simpson sleuthed around and determined that the sign-stealer was Grady Edmiston, an area lawyer active in Democratic politics.

Independent of Simpson, the Riley campaign learned of additional Democratic shenanigans up that way (this, too, according to her and her only.) That weekend – on the second Saturday *after* the election – area rednecks were to don the garb and hold a Ku Klux Klan rally in front of the Scottsboro courthouse. Rumor was that an effort was to be made linking Bob Riley to the Klan, thus tarring him as a racist.

This spawned the Riley campaign's second request: Could she attend the rally and take pictures of the sign-stealer and which could be used to defend Riley?

Simpson accepted this assignment as well.

During her Judiciary Committee testimony, Simpson said Edmiston didn't see her at the rally so hadn't known she'd taken pictures of him taking pictures of Riley signs. She told the rabidly pro-Siegelman blog, "Locust Fork," that she parked several blocks from the courthouse. "And she even wore a disguise to keep the local press from recognizing her," wrote Glynn Wilson, Locust Fork's one-man band.

(There was in fact a KKK rally that night in Scottsboro and it was filmed by law enforcement. I haven't seen the video. Simpson doesn't appear, but it's my understanding that Edmiston does. He did not return calls seeking his version of the evening.)

Simpson neglected to call Rob Riley with the hot news that night or the following day, nor did Riley, bursting with curiosity, call her.

Instead, she waited until Monday, and then not the first thing. That morning she went to the Jackson County Courthouse and came upon Edmiston showing off pictures he'd taken of Riley signs planted at the Klan rally. "He allowed me to see the pictures and when I asked he gave me a couple of photos and told me that these pictures were on a web site," Simpson testified.

Upon leaving the courthouse, Simpson called Rob Riley at his Birmingham law office to report her findings.

———

By miles the strongest evidence supporting Simpson's story is her cell phone bill. It shows that she called Rob Riley's office that Monday at 10:52 a.m. The call lasted 11 minutes. Simpson asserts that the Riley told her the group was "waiting on her call."

According to Simpson, other members of the group were Bill Canary and Terry Butts, the former judge retained by Bob Riley to assist with the recount battle.

Simpson's audience listened as she described seeing Edmiston at the KKK rally, then seeing him again that morning at the courthouse. Rob Riley was "very concerned" about the potential negative impact of the photos on his father and "wanted to go to the press," she told the Judiciary Committee lawyers.

"But Canary didn't – my interpretation was he did not really think that they should go to the press; that they just needed to use it and let Terry (Butts) go see him and get Don to concede," she testified.

The experienced hands on the Riley campaign team decided that Butts should act as emissary. He was a former Democrat with longstanding ties to Siegelman. "Terry Butts said in the conversation that he believed that he would confront Don Siegelman regarding the (Riley) signs and get him to concede the election. He believed that Don would concede over that by the 10 o'clock news so as to avoid any embarrassment," testified Simpson.

According to Simpson – and again, only her -- someone from the Riley campaign hauled butt up to northwest Alabama, retrieved the pictures, and high-tailed it back for the hand-off to Butts. (No pictures, either taken by Simpson or Edmiston or having appeared on a web-site, were provided by Simpson in 2007 to substantiate her story. She explained that she took her photos with a disposable camera, which is what she gave the runner for the Riley campaign that day.)

——

During her congressional testimony Simpson added a significant element she neglected to include in her affidavit four months earlier or in media interviews since. She claimed that during that November 2002 conference call, Canary, Butts and Rob Riley discussed a second, even more powerful lure to encourage Siegelman to concede. They said they would arrange the end of the criminal investigation into Siegelman if he would drop out. This was in addition to making the KKK pics vanish and of much greater value to Siegelman.

According to Simpson, that afternoon, Rob Riley called her to report that Butts had met with Siegelman and his people and all had gone as planned (there is no record of this call.) Siegelman agreed to end his bid for a recount after Butts promised "that the (Klan) pictures would not come out and that they would not further prosecute him with the Justice Department."

"So it wasn't just an issue with the KKK rally; it was now an issue that all future prosecution would go away?" asked a Judiciary Committee lawyers during the 2007 questioning.

"Yes, that's right," replied Simpson.

Simpson reassured the skeptical congressional lawyers. Her memory of the day's events was sharp, she said, because it "caused Governor Siegelman to concede."

——

Among the many problems with Simpson's story is Canary. As in, he was not at Rob Riley's law office that day.

That's according to Canary and many who were there, including Rob Riley; Steve Windom; Butts; Riley campaign manager Toby Roth; and Matt Lembke, a Birmingham lawyer enlisted to lead the recount fight and direct the legal arguments.

Butts, Riley, and Lembke stated as much in affidavits provided to Congress following release of Simpson's testimony.

As previously noted, in the fall of 2002, Canary was president of the Washington-based American Trucking Association. He spent much of his time traveling and was that morning en route to Virginia. "Billy has told me and I believe it is true that he never came to my office and I doubt he ever visited our campaign office in Montgomery during 2002," Riley said.

During her congressional testimony Simpson was asked how she knew Canary was on the conference call. Had she been on a call with him before, and recognized his voice?

Simpson, or so it would appear, invented a new story on the fly: Canary, she said, had been on the phone a few days before when Rob Riley called to assign her to spy on the KKK rally. Thus, she knew his voice.

Those described as participating in the conference call refuted in the strongest term and not without sarcasm the entire KKK story. Best was Butts' comparison of Simpson's affidavit to the imaginings of "a drunk fiction writer;" and his statement that he didn't know "anyone who would give a good Southern 'damn' or a 'hoot in hell' about what the KKK thinks."

Butts also ridiculed the bone-headedness of a prank that would involve "placing of anyone's campaign signs at a Klan rally *after* an election."

(Butts was one of Richard Scrushy's lawyers in the Siegelman case. Scrushy, of course, stood to benefit from anything that helped Siegelman – for example, Simpson's affidavit, should anyone believe it. Shortly before Simpson's affidavit, Butts filed a motion with the court removing himself from the case.)

When Simpson burst on the scene in June 2007, I was working on this book and a few other things as well. I paid her and her stories little mind. I had never heard of Jill Simpson but – and this I suppose can be seen as something of a defense of the initial national stories – assumed there had been some sort of phone call. What kind of person would make something like that up?

My initial take was that the various folk described as being on the call indeed had been, but that Simpson took things out of context and wildly over-stated the import of what she'd heard.

Those identified by Simpson as participating in the call could be excused for not remembering. There are entire stories I've written five years ago that I can't recall. I assumed Bill Canary had made the "my girls" comment but in a joking manner. Something along the lines of, "Hey! I'll get 'My Girls' to crush ole'

Don!" Reporters are forever making silly statements like this in the newsroom, and for laughs only. This time, a long-forgotten crack among the guys had been misinterpreted intentionally or otherwise and Simpson was hanging it around Canary's neck.

In early 2008 I embarked on a story for a weekly publication called the *Montgomery Independent,* my purpose being to counter preposterous and vicious attacks on Mark Fuller, the judge who presided over the Siegelman trial. The stories were written by Scott Horton, published on the web-site of *Harper's* magazine, and reprinted by the *Independent.* I asked and was granted permission to present a different perspective. So began my crash course into the Jill Simpson follies, because as I soon discovered, one could not write about Horton and the charges made against Fuller and so many others without addressing Simpson. Her tales were the Rosetta Stone for Horton's tortured fantasies of Siegelman's send-off to the Gulag and Fuller's role in that drama.

In early February 2008 I called, for the first time ever, Rob Riley. He was friendly, if exasperated that Simpson's imaginings continued to be believed, and had taken a defeatist approach to discussing the matter. "It's like mud-wrasslin," he said. "Even if you win, you still come out with mud all over you."

Among the kernels of truth in Simpson's story is that she really does know Rob Riley. Like Siegelman 20 years before, he was, in 1987, the "Machine" candidate for president of the University of Alabama student government association. At the last minute, the opposition candidate withdrew. The replacement: Dana Jill Simpson.

Riley won and had little contact with her that year or after. He went to Yale law school, while she remained in Tuscaloosa for law school. In the mid-1990s Riley ran into Simpson at a northeast Alabama courthouse. His firm encourages referrals from other lawyers, so he gave Simpson his card and told her that if she ever came across a good case and needed help, to give him a call.

She sent him a few cases, so they had sporadic contact in the late 1990s. One was on behalf of a contractor seeking more money from FEMA, and involved a hearing in Washington.

The web-site DonSiegelman.Org, hatched after Siegelman went to prison in 2007, contains a hilariously flattering mini-bio of Jill Simpson. Among the claims within: That while on legal business she, "would often run into her old friend Rob Riley at the classy watering holes of D.C."

And then:

"When Rob Riley told her his dad had decided to run for governor, she agreed to help. At that time, she says, the Rileys had virtually no money to run a campaign for governor. So she put together a volunteer operation in North Alabama that could 'knock up signs' and such for virtually nothing. 'We beat Karl Rove and Bill Canary in the primary, with almost no money,' she says with a touch of glee in her voice."

Asked to comment, Rob Riley hardly knew where to start.

"If by 'classy watering hole' she means bar, I have never been in a bar in Washington D.C," he said. "In fact, I never bought any alcohol in any bar ever in my life. With the exception of sipping on some wine that someone else might serve at a special occasion, I don't drink alcohol. I don't go to bars, not in Alabama, not anywhere, nowhere, never."

It's true that Bill Canary did for a brief period serve as a paid advisor to Steve Windom's campaign (Bob Riley of course defeated Windom in the primary). Rove, though, did not participate in Alabama's 2002 Republican primary on anyone's behalf, nor does anyone other than Jill Simpson assert that he did. If the president's senior advisor had inserted himself into the Alabama governor's race it would have been, in addition to highly unusual, a major state news story.

"She has no clue who or what she is talking about," said Riley. "Jill was never in any strategy meetings, fundraising meetings, volunteer meetings, or anything else and did not do anything that would put her in the 'we' beat Windom category. She organized nothing."

Riley said the during the 2002 election his two-attorney Birmingham law office was converted into his father's de facto headquarters. There were about seven phones installed in the basement and about as many upstairs. It wasn't unusual to have 20 to 40 people crammed into his office. "This is where my father was on the night of the election, where the campaign was run, to be honest.

"We were in a legal battle, all our focus was on legal arguments before the Alabama Supreme Court. It was all big time legal theory. We had lawyers from D.C., from the National Republican Committee, studying Gore v. Bush. We weren't thinking maybe we can get him to concede because someone put up signs in Scottsboro at a KKK rally."

Riley doesn't entirely rule out the possibility that Simpson reached him on the phone and regaled him with some tale of a KKK rally. But if so, he doesn't remember it, nor would he have cause to, he said.

The second assertion of Simpson's affidavit – that Butts also presented Siegelman with an offer to make his prosecution go away – was refuted by the messenger. Butts declared in his affidavit that he "could not ethically approach another attorney's client (Siegelman), nor did I contact any of Governor Siegelman's 'campaign people.' Additionally, I would have no authority to prevent, stop or end any federal or state investigation/prosecution of anyone."

——

I propose the following scenario:

No one called Simpson asking her to scope out Scottsboro for missing Riley for Governor signs. She made it up.

She was neither asked to attend the KKK rally, nor did she go to it. She made that up, too.

Simpson did not learn about possibly the lamest dirty trick in Alabama political history until coming upon Edmiston at the courthouse that Monday morning, this being the one element of her testimony I believe. Spotting an opportunity to be a player, this woman with a small life but bigger than life dreams raced to call Rob Riley – her lone connection to the big time.

Lawyers -- even those whose offices haven't been converted into gubernatorial campaign headquarters -- rarely answer their own phones. I suppose that a secretary or campaign worker took the call. In all likelihood Simpson spent some and quite likely the entire 11 minutes on hold. Possibly someone located Riley and told him that a Jill Simpson was on the phone.

Considering the matters at hand and the identity of the caller, Riley would have probably directed his secretary to take a message. At most, he took the call and listened with half a mind as Simpson hyperventilated about a KKK rally in Scottsboro. If the latter, he probably said something kind to her, perhaps that he'd get back to her, hung up, moved on to the real issues at hand, and within five minutes to say nothing of five years, forgot it ever happened.

For the sake of argument, let's assume that you have considered Simpson's version, the denials by Rob Riley and others, and my theory, and are still sitting on the fence.

On, then, to the tiebreaker: The KKK pictures deal and the offer to end the investigation as remembered by Siegelman and his campaign and criminal defense lawyers.

———

Siegelman did of course concede the election that Monday. It can be assumed that considerable thought and debate preceded what had to be among the most painful decisions of his life. His fourth and long ploy for legislative intervention was denied and the odds of the Republican-dominated state Supreme Court seeing things his way were non-existent.

In June 2007, after *Time* and the *Times* bit on Canary's "his girls" quote and the Rove tale, the Alabama media had no choice but to report on Simpson's affidavit.

Unlike the *Times* and *Time*, numerous state reporters – including Bob Johnson with AP; several at the *Birmingham News*; and Dana Beyerle, the Montgomery bureau reporter for the three *New York Times*-owned Alabama papers -- took the trouble to examine the KKK tale.

The tenor of their stories reflected a degree of skepticism not to be found in the national reports, to say nothing of basic fact checking.

"Two of three Republicans who reportedly took part in a 2002 telephone conference call to plot against former Gov. Don Siegelman said Friday the phone call never took place and the third called reports of the conversation an 'outrageous allegation,'" began Bob Johnson's wire story the day after *Time* and the *Times* introduced Simpson to the world.

One of Bob's stories concluded with commentary from Bill Stewart, the long-time political science professor at the University of Alabama and a favorite go-to guy for reporters seeking pungent analysis on state politics. Stewart said it would be most improbable for a veteran politician like Siegelman to have conceded under the terms described by Simpson.

"I can't imagine someone dropping out for something like this," he said. "Those sorts of things happen in campaigns. It's not something to be proud of, but on the scale of things that have happened in Alabama campaigns, I don't find it to be very important."

The story also quoted participants in Siegelman's 2002 campaign saying they recalled nothing about the KKK deal. Rip Andrews told Bob he didn't remember any talk of a Klan rally, but said Simpson's story was possible since "the Republicans would do anything to get Siegelman to concede."

After Bob's story, Rip issued a strongly worded statement distancing himself from the piece. Rip declared that he believed "everything in that affidavit -- every paragraph, every sentence, every word" and said he respected Simpson's "courage and honesty."

Several weeks later Beyerle gave his readers the most thorough examination yet of the KKK farce. He interviewed Simpson, Butts, Rob Riley and, most importantly, Siegelman.

Of all people, Siegelman would know if he conceded the 2002 election for the reasons sworn to by Simpson. But he told Beyerle he dropped his recount challenge because he was facing "what Al Gore had just gone through – this painful experience in Florida and the U.S. Supreme Court."

Siegelman didn't recall the first thing about a KKK meeting but deployed his elasticity with the truth by declaring in the same interview that Jill Simpson was a "great American citizen" who had placed Karl Rove "at the scene of a crime."

Another AP story by Johnson remarked that "even the Siegelman camp discounts" the KKK pics deal.

Joe Espy and Bobby Segall, Siegelman's lawyers during the recount battle, rejected the KKK story with a certainty equal to that of Riley's people. "I never heard that. I was never around any talk like that," Espy told Johnson.

Siegelman conceded for a number of reasons, Espy said. He was worried about putting the state through a protracted, Gore-Bush type battle; didn't know where he'd get the money to pay for an ongoing legal challenge; and recognized that the final say belonged to the Republican-dominated Alabama Supreme Court.

In October 2007, following release of Simpson's congressional testimony, it was again left up to the Alabama media to provide a reality check on Simpson's new story – that in addition to making the KKK pictures vanish, Butts also pledged to make the joint state and federal criminal investigation into the Siegelman administration go away if Siegelman would concede.

Ever since it was first revealed in early 2002 that he was the subject of a criminal investigation, Siegelman had relentlessly accused Bob Riley and Bill and Leura Canary of targeting him for political reasons. The drumbeat intensified dramatically after his indictment.

Imagine for a moment that Jill Simpson's story is true, then consider Siegelman's response to being indicted, first in the Bobo case (2004), and later, in Montgomery. From three states away you could have heard his yelps at those double-dealing Repubs for going back on their promise to kill the investigation if he'd concede the 2002 election. Instead, not a peep.

"Siegelman, who conceded the narrow loss in November 2002 but continued to be investigated and prosecuted by the Justice Department, has never made any comment indicating such an offer was made," noted the AP's Johnson.

Walter Braswell, in 2002 a partner of David Cromwell Johnson's and an active participant in Siegelman's defense, told the *News* he'd never heard that the investigation was to evaporate upon Siegelman's concession of the election.

To summarize: Siegelman, his election lawyers and criminal attorneys – top-tier Democrats all -- said they had never heard of the KKK deal or the vanishing investigation offer.

———

The stories by state reporters vaporizing Simpson's tales about the two-pronged offer to make the KKK pictures and the investigation go away should have been the end of it. Those in the national media who had based stories on Simpson's allegations should have come back and informed their readers that her credibility was shattered and that her claims, against Canary, Rove, the Rileys and others should accordingly be reconsidered as almost certainly false.

That's not what happened.

The reporting by the Alabama media, to say nothing of the facts upon which it was based, was ignored by the *Times, Time,* CBS News, the Judiciary Committee, and many others as well.

Congressional Democrats and those in the national media who swallowed Simpson's story had become too invested in the fantasy placing Karl Rove "at the scene of the crime."

Chapter 29
Warming the Bench

"Nick has been a good friend of mine and my family. My thoughts and prayers are with him and his family during this difficult time."
-- Statement released by Siegelman after learning that Nick Bailey had pleaded guilty to accepting bribes and other crimes, and was cooperating in the investigation.

"It is unfortunate that Lanny Young didn't do things the right way. Lanny Young didn't."
-- Waste Management official Charles Campagna during 2002 meeting with state environmental officials who were criticizing the company for secretly using Lanny when trying to win business in Alabama.

The Siegelman administration cleared out of the Capitol on Friday, Jan. 17. That night three of the younger members returned. Though never publicly identified, they were viewed by security cameras erasing data and programs on more than half of the office's 50 computers.

When Riley's people arrived that Monday for their first full day, many found their computers useless, unable to perform routine tasks like sending e-mail. The new administration kept mum about the mess for weeks, until word of the night's activities leaked and the time and cost of repairing the damage – about two months and $75,000 to $100,000 -- became known.

"Our computers had a full frontal lobotomy," said Riley spokesman David Azbell.

Riley told the AP that his administration "wanted to look forward and not worry about what the last administration did," but that the damage to the computers proved both expensive and time consuming.

Riley's criticism of his predecessor was the exception, not the rule. There was a reticence, then and later, for the governor and his staff to comment on activities of the prior administration.

The favor was not reciprocated.

Each year, some $700,000 to $1 million is provided to the governor's office to pay for all manner of expenses, from legal bills to the staff's coffee vendor. Administrations are given considerable latitude when spending money from the fund. State law merely requires that it be used "for a public purpose at the governor's direction or discretion."

Unlike other state expenditures, the Comptroller Office doesn't maintain the supporting documents for those charges, though a print-out of the vendors and amounts is easily available. If you wish to review the supporting records, you ask the governor's office, and it provides them. That, in any event, is how it's supposed to work, and until Siegelman, always had.

In February 2002, Mike Cason, the *Montgomery Advertiser* reporter, submitted a list of 45 expenditures to Siegelman's press office and requested the supporting documentation. Cason requested records for travel-related expenditures by Siegelman and others; and credit card bills and receipts explaining charges to American Express cards issued to Siegelman, his wife, Bailey, and several others.

Some records were provided, but many, including the AMEX bills, were not.

Rip told Cason that the administration was of the position that some spending records were private. He and others, including Hosp, were unable to cite any case law supporting that position.

Rip said the withheld records pertained to the industry recruiting trips and that their disclosure could jeopardize future efforts. He assured Cason that there were no personal items charged to the cards, and that receipts and supporting documentation existed for all the purchases.

After Cason reported this, a *Birmingham News* editorial scolded Siegelman for disobeying one of his own post-G.H. ethics reform executive orders. In that particular Aug. 2001 order, Siegelman demanded that all state agencies generate annual reports of their grants, contracts and expenditures, and make the reports public. The order covered the governor's office and the contingency fund.

"This is just one more example of Don Siegelman saying one thing publicly and doing another thing privately," opined the *News*.

I'd been reviewing contingency fund expenditures since early in the James' administration and made good use of them. One such record submitted by an investment banker in high favor with Fob showed -- in combination with other records -- that the banker had double billed the state for travel and expenses on an industrial recruiting trip to Europe. Among other things, the state had paid twice for the same $13,000 round-ticket flight on the Concorde. I found that the banker, Frank Daniel, had incorporated an investments partnership with two of James' cabinet members and another man who later joined the cabinet.

The story blew a hole in the administration. Within a week of its publication, James' chief of staff, finance director and the head of the department of public safety were gone, and Daniel had done his final bond deal for the state.

A year later after Cason's story, Siegelman was out of office and the contingency fund records were in the safekeeping of the Riley administration. I was of the position that they merited a look see. I called the new governor's press office and asked if I could review the records. No problem, they said. It was all public.

It took five days and two trips to Montgomery to sift through a roomful of file cabinets bearing thousands upon thousands of pages of bills. On these days, from 8 a.m., until 5 p.m., I eyeballed tens of thousands of itemized expenses. I copied all the AMEX bills and much else besides. I couldn't feed the records into the copier, but had to do it page by page. Wore my ass out, to say nothing of my fingers, sentenced to hell by a thousand papercuts. Don't expect this will engender much pity, but I sure felt sorry for myself.

At this stage we were sensitive to the potential for claims that I, and the paper, should leave Siegelman alone. I justified the stories on the following grounds: He had refused the year before to divulge the records; he would surely be running for statewide office again; and above all, the expenditures were newsworthy.

The laws governing the contingency fund were explained in the first of several stories, which ran a month after Siegelman left office. Readers were told that state employees all the way up to governor provide receipts and other documentation explaining the expenditure of public funds. As anyone who's completed one knows, expense reimbursement forms are drudgery. But the law, as it should, demands them.

The state Examiners of Public Accounts audits the contingency fund every four years. These reports are notoriously picky. Four years before, the audit of the James' administration cited First Lady Bobbie James' use of her own money to buy silverware, furniture and other items for the mansion. She'd turned in the receipts and been reimbursed. According to the examiners, Mrs. James' actions cost taxpayers $72 – that being the amount in sales tax the state would have saved had the administration bought the items, since the state doesn't pay sales tax.

The examiners inability to determine the purpose of an out-of-state airline ticket was remarked upon in the audit and news stories on same, as was the James administration's failure to document the purpose for spending $945.56 on 21 hams.

Considering the reporting of these minor infractions, Siegelman could hardly claim he didn't know the rules governing the fund, or, having tortured them, complain at being called out for it.

One charge in particular impressed me for its gall.

Every year graduates of high schools and colleges receive letters seeking donations to their alumni funds. Most of us would like to give, or contribute more than we do, but our generosity is mitigated by financial realities. No such realities plagued Siegelman upon receipt of a letter (included in the files) seeking donations to the alumni association of Mobile's Murphy High School.

The governor contributed $500 to his old school. It came, not from his pocket, but from Alabama taxpayers. Here he was, using public funds to play big man on campus at donor time.

Among the multitude of other relatively small if equally dubious charges was $35 to renew his membership in the National Rifle Association; $336.35

for "Personal Power" audiotapes by tanned, tall and toothy motivational speaker Tony Robbins; $43.45 for a pair of shoes; payments to a tailor; and all manner of items purchased while flying, from Delta's Skymiles airline catalogue.

Among the larger outlays were:

- $6,251.35 in flight, hotel and assorted purchases in December 1999, when the Siegelman family and Nick Bailey flew to and stayed in Puerto Rico, then on to the Virgin Islands. There they spent the Christmas holidays at the vacation home of Siegelman friend Jack Miller. The Mobile lawyer was the state Democratic Party chairman and beneficiary, through his firm, of substantial amounts of state legal business awarded by Siegelman.

- $3,690 to fly Bailey and unidentified others on two charger airplane flights to Las Vegas.

- Thousands of dollars in unexplained purchases from vendors including Banana Republic, the Gap, Bloomingdales and Amazon.com.

- Thousands more in flight, hotel and expenses so Don and Lori Siegelman could attend three of the annual summer gatherings/junkets held by the Conference of Western Attorneys General, one in Custer, S.D.; another in Sun Valley, Idaho; and the last, in Monterey, Calif.

It's difficult to fathom how the Siegelmans presence at a conference of attorneys general from western states could benefit Alabama citizens, but the former Alabama Attorney General deemed it so, and used the contingency fund to pay for airline tickets, hotel bills, meals and the rest. Years later, Arizona's Grant Woods and many of Siegelman's friends in the ex-attorney general community came to Siegelman's aid with several heavily publicized letters and court filings accusing Republicans of prosecuting him for political reasons.

With a few exceptions, no itemized receipts or written explanations existed for trips and credit card charges by Siegelman, his wife, and Bailey. Within the files was a December 1999 memo from governor's office accountant Becca Crawford to state examiners, in which she wrote: "I cannot make any sense out of some of these receipts."

The first contingency fund story enraged Siegelman as perhaps no other before or after. Among other things, it reported undocumented trips and charges by the First Lady. The bills indicated, for example, that when in Birmingham, Lori Siegelman was a regular customer at Planet Smoothie, which sells fruity frozen energy drinks; that she used her state card at restaurants in Birmingham; and to buy various items including vitamins, books and artwork.

Also reported were a host of trips by Lori Siegelman, such as to Canada for a week; New Orleans; Monterey, Calif.; Albuquerque, N.M.; and Boston. The purpose of those trips, public or otherwise, was not to be found in the records, as the law requires.

We knew that the Siegelmans would refuse to answer questions from me, but recognized the sensitivity of reporting on his wife's spending. She had been, well, the First Lady, and first ladies frequently use their positions to advocate for pet causes or public projects. Still, spouses and children of governors should not be confused with those of presidents in terms of what taxpayers fund.

It was decided that Bill Barrow would contact Siegelman. He did, but Siegelman declined to take our questions.

I went beyond the call of duty by searching Merlin and Nexis for stories reporting trips, official or otherwise, and this allowed me to verify or reject the public purpose of some of the travel. I was under no obligation to present readers with what amounted to guesses for permissible reasons for charges by the Siegelmans and Bailey, but did so anyway, as here, in that first story:

Siegelman's decision not to comment to the Register makes it difficult to know for certain if any charges were made for personal expenses.

Some purchases, such as art or even books, could have been for the Governor's Mansion -- an allowable use of contingency funds, assuming the art or books remained at the mansion following the first family's departure.

Another example: In November 2001, the first lady charged $621.42 to Sleeping Bear Press, a publisher of children's books. Lori Siegelman's chief project as first lady involved the promotion of art for children, and she hosted several arts festivals for children from throughout the state.

The children's books could well have been associated with those festivals -- an expense that would be allowed from the contingency fund.

The AP picked up the story, with Kanarick telling the wire service that anyone "who attacks the integrity and fine character of the former First Lady has stooped to a new and unconscionable low."

That was to include the *Montgomery Advertiser,* which published an editorial that asked, "Was former first lady hunting for industry?"

After our paper editorialized on the spending, Siegelman wrote a long letter to *Register* publisher Howard Bronson complaining that I knew "or should have known" that his wife "personally paid for personal items and that all of Lori's travel was for a public purpose – namely, the advancement of arts education for Alabama's school children."

"Your reporter has shown a continuous reckless disregard for the truth."

Siegelman's criticisims were such that a story was deemed necessary. Barrow, assigned the piece, reported Siegelman's complaints and our responses to them. Readers were told that Siegelman had refused our request to explain the charges; and that I had sent multiple e-mails to the press staff of the new governor as well as the governor's office accountant seeking any additional records from the prior administration that might explain the bills.

Bill reported Siegelman's explanation for many of his wife's trips. Some were to meet other first ladies to help build houses for Habitat for Humanity, and certainly met the public purpose requirements. Others involved travel to conferences related to the arts – Lori Siegelman's chief interest -- and seemed to as well. Some – such as using state funds to travel with a friend to Chicago to watch the Alvin Ailey dance troupe – struck me as questionable.

I didn't relish Siegelman's attack on me for writing about his wife, but appreciated his vigorous and clearly heartfelt defense of her.

Though defending his wife, Siegelman refused Barrow's request that he explain other charges, such as those incurred by himself and Bailey.

A second story reported the first family's trip to Puerto Rico and the Virgin Islands and presented an overview of the American Express bills. The abuses presumably would have been worse, or in any event, more numerous, had someone not stepped in and put the kibosh on the cards midway through Siegelman's term.

———

Three days after our first story a Siegelman emissary delivered a $38,799 check to the state. A memo described it as a partial settlement of expenditures disallowed by the examiners.

In May, the examiners issued a report that supported our findings, and then some. Phil Harrod, who had audited the Guy Hunt administration and every governor's contingency fund since, told readers he'd never come across problems "of this magnitude."

Despite considerable time and effort, the examiners were at the end of the day unable to determine the public purpose of $483,935 spent on trips, meals, and truckloads of other items, many of which couldn't be identified by the available records and memory banks.

Harrod spoke to Siegelman once, in an exit interview. Of this meeting, readers were told:

In summarizing the $483,935 worth of trips, meals, and assorted items that the examiners could not issue an opinion on, Harrod wrote that Siegelman "represented to me that these disbursements were made for a public benefit and purpose."

Harrod determined, however, that "the lack of supporting records, travel authorizations, contracts and other written documentation limited my ability to determine whether public funds were spent in accordance with applicable state laws and regulations."'

Harrod, for example, was unable to determine the purpose, public or otherwise, of Bailey's trips to Las Vegas, or able to learn what Bailey and Lori Siegelman bought from airline catalogues.

"In a lot of cases, they didn't have an answer," he said. "Time had passed and they said they just did not know."

Soon after, the Riley administration began posting, on-line, all of its expenditures from the contingency fund as well as uses of state planes, which had been the subject of much reporting by others during the Siegelman years and, for that matter, many previous administrations. (See: Guy Hunt.)

———

After eight years dominating the state from his perches as lieutenant governor and governor, Siegelman returned to the private sector, if only on a very part-time basis. He incorporated Don Siegelman & Associates, called it a law firm, and for an office, used his old digs at the Alabama Sheriff's Association.

In November 2003, Phil Rawls profiled Siegelman the private citizen, with the latter declaring himself in high spirits, happy to be spending time with his family and away from the political grind. "Their Birmingham-area home looks out over the hills toward Sylacauga, and its big windows allow them to watch deer and fox wander through the yard," Phil wrote.

Some reporters told of receiving calls from Siegelman and not really knowing what to say. After all, he was no longer governor and the public wasn't exactly screaming for his input on the topics of the day, not that it stopped him from trying.

I cut way back on trips to and stories about Montgomery, though continued to report developments in the investigation.

———

I did our stories on the annual ethics filings, and, as I did with Fob James after he left office, included Siegelman's disclosures along with those by current officials like Riley and Lucy Baxley. (Siegelman had to file two reports after leaving office, the first in spring 2003 for the year 2002; and the last, in spring 2004, for 2003, since he was still governor for three weeks of that year.)

Additional details about his income appeared in another routine type story I often did, reporting payments by investment banking firms to so-called consultants. The national board that regulates firms that sell non-taxable bonds for government entities requires them to disclose non-employee "consultants." These are often former politicians who use their connections to lobby cities, counties and other governmental entities that sell bonds. Siegelman was hardly alone there. Former governor Jim Folsom Jr., and Steve Windom are among the many former officials who make easy money that way.

Siegelman, like Folsom, was associated with Raymond James & Associates. The firm paid him $35,802 in 2003 and about $130,000 in 2004.

On his report for 2003, Siegelman reported being paid between $25,000 and $50,000 from a source that was almost surely Raymond James and a payment in the same range from someone in the miscellaneous category. Most interesting was a third source of income -- between $50,000 to $100,000 from a company identified as being in the mining business.

It almost had to be Birmingham-based Drummond Company. A major coal supplier to Alabama Power, Drummond and its officers and owners had donated hundreds of thousands of dollars to Siegelman's campaigns and provided him with use of a company jet on campaign trips. He had rewarded that support with official action that benefitted Drummond directly and, when aiding Alabama Power, indirectly.

I called a Drummond spokesman. He sounded perplexed; said he was unaware of any payments to Siegelman; and promised to find out and call back. He didn't, nor did he return calls made to him over the next several days. Couldn't get company chairman Garry Neil Drummond on the phone, either. I believe the company would have denied paying Siegelman if it had not done so, and acknowledged the payment if the reason was unquestionably valid.

To be safe, I called the state's other major coal company, Jim Walter Resources, and got a convincing no. Rip, still assisting Siegelman with media relations matters, declined to identify the mining company or describe the services for which Siegelman was being remunerated.

During his first year in office, Bob Riley stunned many of his largest contributors by proposing a $1.2 billion tax increase. Landowners and the Alfa constituency, major backers of Riley against Siegelman, were livid, as was the tax-hating religious right.

The state's leading editorial voices – including the publishers and editorial writers of our paper and the *Birmingham News* – had long supported so-called progressive policies regarding local and state taxation, especially as pertains to property taxes. Alabamians pay among the lowest property taxes in the country, and rank near last -- or near first, depending on your position -- in per capita taxation.

Politicians, no doubt in part to curry favor with the editorial boards, frequently give lip service to reforms, but their support usually ends there. Raising property taxes? Necessary perhaps, but politically unrealistic and quite possibly suicidal. So what you got is barrels of ink spilt advocating – nay, demanding – these changes, but little else.

Then along comes Bob Riley – one and the same as the candidate who rode a horse in ads invoking Ronald Reagan. Within months, Reagan the tax-cutter metamorphosed into Don Quixote with a grand plan to hike taxes for the rich and cut them for the poor.

The $4,600 annual income threshold at which Alabama began taxing its citizens was the lowest in the country. Riley proposed increasing that four-fold, to $20,000. In sum, he wanted to raise taxes on his supporters and lower those for Siegelman's backers.

The Democrat-controlled legislature, knowing it was Riley's butt on the line, not theirs, gave the new governor what he wanted – a referendum, set for Sept. 9, with the fate of the tax increase up to the people.

A month before the vote, *Time* magazine ran a piece about Riley with the headline, "Alabama's Most Courageous Politician."

For Riley's referendum to stand a chance, it needed the backing of the state Democratic Party and its leaders, one of whom, still, was Siegelman. And the package seemed a natural fit for the party that purports to represent the lower and middle classes. One might have expected Democratic leaders to set aside party affiliation, join hands with Riley, and climb aboard bully pulpits throughout the state to sell like hell.

They did not.

The political philosophy of Alabama Democrats in the legislature can be summed up as follows: Do whatever it takes to maintain control of the legislature; support gambling and anything teacher's union leader Paul Hubbert wants; kill all legislation seeking to strengthen Alabama's laughably weak ethics laws; and ensure the defeat of efforts to ban PAC to PAC transfers. Concealing the identify of donors is the apparent if unofficial platform of state Democratic Party.

As *Time* put it, Alabama Democrats couldn't "decide whether to support the plan or stay on the sidelines, hoping Riley impales himself on the referendum."

Democratic leaders preferred Riley's humiliation to their party's principals and their constituents' best interests. On Sept. 9, voters ravaged Riley's referendum. Only 33 percent backed it. Three years later, during the 2006 campaign, Siegelman was to ridicule Riley's effort to reform Alabama's tax structure in the same breath that he, again, proposed a state lottery, which is to say, a tax on the poor.

Governing, a national publication that covers local and state government, named Riley one of its public officials of the year. Its piece on him bore the headline, "A Profile in Courage," and quoted Wayne Flynt, the esteemed Auburn University historian and tireless backer of constitutional and tax reform.

"No opportunistic politician concerned about his own reelection would have done this," said Flynt. "He's one of the few governors in recent generations to try to exercise leadership."

Less kind was a comment by Grover Norquist, the head of Americans for Tax Reform and unlike Bob Riley, a close confidante of Karl Rove. Said Norquist: "Every Republican governor who thinks of raising taxes next year will walk past Traitor's Gate and see Bob Riley's head on a pike."

―――

On June 23, 2003, the seemingly-dormant criminal investigation roared back to life. Prosecutors filed documents revealing that Lanny Young, Nick Bailey and

Curtis Kirsch had agreed to plead guilty to charges arising from the warehouse deal and other matters.

Young had begun cooperating way back in September 2001, though he was then and, to my way of thinking, forever reluctant to really pull the trigger on Hamrick or Waste Management. Lanny, though, had come to despise Siegelman. His greatest contribution to the prosecution was probably the information he provided about Bailey's role in the various schemes. Bailey was ultimately the more valuable witness in terms of making a case against Siegelman and, as it turned out, Richard Scrushy.

Nick had refused to cooperate in an investigation into his beloved former boss until the day before the plea deal was announced. The evidence against Bailey was powerful. Had he refused to roll on Siegelman and gambled at trial, he almost surely would have been found guilty. A sentence of 10 years would not have been out of the question.

With his plea, Bailey admitted to receiving more than $100,000 from Lanny and about $21,000 from Kirsch, with some of those payments in cash, and going back to 1996. Among other things, he acknowledged assisting Young in criminal matters relating to G.H. Construction; and to helping with the tax cut at Emelle for which Waste Management paid Young $500,000.

Lanny and Kirsch pleaded to essentially the same charges as Bailey, just going in the other direction, paying rather than receiving.

Kirsch, 69, short and roundish, seemed a kindly soul. Prosecutors were to give him a break. Citing his age, health problems and cooperation, they asked that the court that Kirsch be spared prison time, and he was.

Bailey admitted to arranging for Kirsch to be given a contract to design one of the warehouses – for ADECA -- and to helping conceal Kirsch's role by having him bill through another architect. Kirsch was paid about $160,000 -- extraordinarily high for the minimal services he provided. Bailey also admitted helping Kirsch, an old family friend, land work with the two other state agencies.

Lanny and Bailey also pleaded guilty to not paying taxes on their ill-gotten gains. The prosecution filing stated that Young did "corruptly give, offer, and agree to give things of value" to Bailey and "other agents of the State of Alabama."

However, those other agents were not identified.

Bailey's lawyer, George Beck, said his client "was not the instigator" of the warehouse project. "I think you'll find that people other than Mr. Bailey came up with that," he said, while declining to identify those other people.

The prosecution filing also introduced what was to be the motorcycle element of the case against Siegelman. The January 2000 transactions were briefly described, though the official who was the ultimate recipient of the $9,200 from Lanny was not named.

Records dug up by reporters soon made it clear that the $9,200 went to Siegelman, and neither the ex-governor nor his lawyers denied it.

The next day, Attorney General Bill Pryor and John Scott, a Justice Department lawyer from Washington, formally announced the pleas at a press conference. They offered little in the way of details, and declined to identify the recipient of the $9,200 or provide any other names.

I called Waste Management to get the company's take on the news that the man it paid $500,000 to win the tax cut had just pleaded guilty to bribing a top aide to Alabama's governor in return for the aide's help in delivering the tax change.

I did a short piece reporting a spokeswoman's statement that Waste Management had opened an internal investigation into the matter, but otherwise, wasn't issuing comment.

———

After the guilty pleas of Bailey and Lanny it was assumed that the investigation was at the boiling point. It wasn't.

Pryor, who had initiated the investigation, had by then largely handed off leadership of the case to federal prosecutors. Before her recusal, Leura Canary put an assistant U.S. Attorney, Julia Weller, in charge of the case.

Weller, though, had little if any experience in such cases. She sought and received assistance from the Public Integrity Section, a sub-agency of the Justice Department that focuses on public corruption cases; and Public Integrity assigned Scott to the Siegelman investigation.

Scott had kind words for my stories when in Montgomery, so I called him a few times to try to gauge the progress in the Siegelman case. He was friendly, but too careful to give me any actual information. During one call, about two months after his visit to Montgomery, Scott said the Siegelman investigation was probably headed for the back-burner. He said he'd been assigned to re-try the Olympics bribery case in Salt Lake City. It was going to take him months to prepare for the complicated case, and the trial itself would take months. Until it was over, he was not going to be able to give much if any attention to the Siegelman case.

It was, I believe, the last time I ever talked to Scott. He left the Justice Department not long after the Olympics bribery case – a total disaster for the government – and never returned to Alabama.

There was not to be any substantial news regarding the warehouse investigation until June 2004 – a solid year after the pleas by Bailey, Young and Kirsch.

Franklin and Feaga. **Siegelman prosecutors Steve Feaga, left, and Louis Franklin, relax a few weeks before the biggest trial of their lives.** *Photo by Eddie Curran*

Siegelman and Kilborn. **Siegelman and his lawyer, Vince Kilborn, were not ones to avoid the cameras and microphones during trial breaks and at the end of each day.** *Photo by Eddie Curran*

The Scrushys leave court. **Scrushy, flanked by his wife Leslie and a supporter, leaves court after another trying day.** *Photo courtesy of Kyle Whitmire*

First couple rides together. At trial, Siegelman's lawyers told jurors that his wife was scared of motorcycles. Along with other evidence, this 2001 picture of the pair about to ride in a rally seemed to refute Siegelman's claimed reason for selling the bike to Nick Bailey. *Copyright, The Birmingham News. All rights reserved. Photo by Phillip Barr*

Lanny to Nick to Siegelman. The motorcycle sale in 2001 from Siegelman to Nick Bailey was, in the end, a ruse to cover-up a series of checks written on the same day in January 2000. The first, not shown here, has Lanny Young using a personal check to purchase a $9,200 cashier's check. That check, at the top, was made out to Bailey, with Young shown as "remitter." Bailey then cut a check for the same amount to Lori Allen, the maiden name of Siegelman's wife. Siegelman deposited the check to avoid bouncing a large check he'd written days earlier, and which was the reason he asked Young for money.

Press Register cartoonist J.D. Crowe captures the surprise of the defendants, and skewers Scrushy for once again -- incredibly as it seems -- trying to play the race card. *Used courtesy of J.D. Crowe*

Katie Langer. Ever since the trial, Scrushy, Siegelman and their lawyers have been finding ways to attack juror Katie Langer for the sin of thinking them guilty. Here she's shown after graduating third in her law school class.
Photo courtesy of Katie Langer

U.S. District Judge Mark Fuller presided over the Siegelman trial with great care and fairness. He, like so many others, was to be publicly savaged by the defendants and their backers in the media.
Photo courtesy of Mark Fuller

BUSH LEAGUE JUSTICE
DID WHITE HOUSE PUSH JUSTICE DEPT.
TO PROSECUTE DEMOCRATIC GOVERNOR? MSNBC

Simpson blasts Rove. **The night after her taped interview with "60 Minutes,"
Jill Simpson went live with MSNBC's Dan Abrams and repeated her story
about Karl Rove assigning her to catch Siegelman having extramarital sex.
The network's long-time legal correspondent relentlessly baited Rove for
leading the prosecution charge against Siegelman.** *Photo courtesy of MSNBC*

Siegelman with his patron saint. **Scott Horton chats with Siegelman
after the Harper's writer gave his "Watchdogs or Lap Dogs" talk in
Huntsville, blasting the Mobile Register and Birmingham News and
praising Time, the New York Times, "60 Minutes," and himself.** *Eric
Schultz, photographer with the Huntsville Times, copyright April 23, 2008,
The Huntsville Times. All rights reserved. Reprinted with permission*

Press Register cartoonist J.D. Crowe envisions then-inmate Siegelman envisioning Rove, but "Bush's brain" doesn't look too worried. *Used courtesy of J.D. Crowe*

Rove in last days at White House. **Karl Rove and President Bush and Laura Bush on the South Lawn in August 2007, days after Rove announced his resignation. By this point Rove was the embroiled in various scandals, including one – ordering the Siegelman prosecution – for which he was innocent as a newborn.**

John Conyers, legendary Michigan Democrat and chairman of the U.S. House Judiciary Committee, was Siegelman's most powerful backer.

Siegelman, a ragged t-shirt atop a sweat shirt, returns home to Birmingham after being released from prison pending his appeal. *Copyright, The Birmingham News. All rights reserved. Photo by Jeff Roberts*

Celebrity victim signs autographs. **Siegelman chats with a fan at the 2008 Democratic Convention in Denver after rousing Colorado Democrats with a talk about his Rove-directed prosecution.** *Photo courtesy of J.D. Crowe*

Scott Pelley. **"60 Minutes" correspondent Scott Pelley presented an open and shut case that Karl Rove and leading Alabama Republicans, including Gov. Bob Riley, conspired to prosecute Siegelman for political reasons.**

May 2009 mug shot
of Scrushy at Shelby
County jail, where he
was brought from prison
in Texas to testify in a
shareholders lawsuit
seeking a $2.6 billion
judgment against him.
The shareholders won.

Eric Holder. **From the
moment he became U.S.
Attorney General, Eric
Holder has been the target
of an intense lobbying
effort by Siegelman and
supporters wanting
Holder to dismiss the
charges against the former
Alabama governor.**

The New York Times
nytimes.com

June 30, 2007

EDITORIAL

Questions About a Governor's Fall

It is extremely disturbing that Don Siegelman, the former governor of
Alabama, was hauled off to jail this week. There is reason to believe his
prosecution may have been a political hit, intended to take out the state's most
prominent Democrat, a serious charge that has not been adequately
investigated. The appeals court that hears his case should demand answers, as
should Congress.

The "political hit" editorial. **This June 2007 piece marked the first of three
editorials in which the New York Times applied the term "political
hit" to Siegelman's prosecution. The paper, incidentally, refused the
author's request to use pictures of editorial writer Adam Cohen or
Adam Nossiter, who wrote many of the *Times'* news stories.**

The first $250,000. **A common denominator of the coverage of the Siegelman
case in the *New York Times, Time* magazine, on "60 Minutes," and
others is that none reported the first thing about the first $250,000 check
Scrushy gave Siegelman. As jurors if not national readers knew, the check
to the lottery foundation from the almost-bankrupt Maryland company
was the farthest thing from an ordinary campaign contribution.**

Noel Hillman. Noel Hillman, the head of the Justice Department's Public Integrity Section during the Siegelman investigation, said Karl Rove had never called him for anything, much less to order the prosecution of Don Siegelman.

Nick Bailey, who testified against his former boss, during a trial break. *Photo courtesy of Kyle Whitmire*

There's no such thing as having too many J.D. Crowe cartoons in your book. This one requires no explanation. *Used courtesy of J.D. Crowe*

I'd Rather Have DON'S LOTTERY Than BOB & LUCY'S TAXES

Ruth Peters, REPUBLICAN
Hoover, Alabama

In his last desparate run for governor, in 2006, Siegelman,
as with his three previous tries, based his campaign on
a state lottery, as this bumper sticker shows.

*The enclosed email shows that the jurors in the recent trial of Governor Siegelman and
Richard Scrushy violated the Judges order by having communications and discussions
outside of the jury room. You should subpoena their records so you have the whole
picture.*

Truth and Justice

Truth and Justice. This note was attached to the first batch of purported
juror e-mails mailed to lawyers for Siegelman and Scrushy. If the person
or persons behind "Truth and Justice" are ever identified, they should be
prosecuted, locked up, and the key thrown away. The circle is my doing.

Q. Have you seen a doctor to help you with your symptoms? Some of the problems you
have mentioned are common for post jury stress or post traumatic shock syndrome

*"No, but I am going to that's for sure. I have talked to my wife's Pastor. He prayed and
talked with us, and told us to come and talk to you today so maybe something can be
done."*

A bogus affidavit. This is a portion of Charlie Stanford's first affidavit,
which was drafted and for the most part written, not in Stanford's
words, but by Birmingham pastor Charles Winston, a member
of Scrushy's Kingdom Builders religious organization.

Final days. **Siegelman awaits breakfast at his much beloved Walt's Diner in Montgomery. This shot was taken in early January 2003, two months after he lost to Bob Riley and with two weeks remaining in his only term as governor and, barring a miracle, a public career that spanned three decades.** *Copyright, The Press-Register. All rights reserved. Photo by Kiichiro Sato*

PART THREE:
USA v. Siegelman

Chapter 30
The Bobo Debacle

"I managed to get some additional funding put into the Fire College with the blessing of the administration .... It's not a one-time deal . . . So, I mean, y'all got a lot of – that's a lot of incentive. This governor is going to be governor for eight years."
-- *Dr. Phillip Bobo, who unbeknownst to him was being taped, offering what prosecutors called an $800,000 per year bribe to a competitor to drop out of the bidding for two multi-million dollar Medicaid contracts, with most of the bribe to be paid with state funds arranged by Siegelman.*

"He's indicted. He goes to trial. That's a pretty big deal to have your former governor on trial. Everybody's there. The government gives their opening argument. The judge says, 'I want to see you in chambers because this case, there's no case here.' ... The case is so lame that he throws it out."
-- *Former Arizona Attorney General Grant Woods, commenting on the Bobo case during the February 2008 piece by "60 Minutes," which made the case that top Republican officials engineered Siegelman's prosecution.*

In late May 2004, my brother-in-law Paul retrieved me from the Vienna airport for the hour drive to Bratislava and that year's vacation. My wife Jana and our children had preceded me by about a week and, as usual upon arrival, I looked up to see my wife and children waving and smiling from the small third-floor balcony of my mother-in-law's apartment. This time, my son Jerry yelled out the most astonishing news.

Don Siegelman, he said, had been indicted.

My first thought was amazement. I hadn't heard a thing about the investigation in ages. And suddenly he's indicted?

Paul Cloos had called and asked that I call him when I arrived. I did, and his news was as surprising as my son's. Yes, Siegelman had been indicted, but it didn't have the first thing to do with G.H. Construction, Lanny Young, the house sale, the tobacco fees, the lottery foundation or any of the other prime suspects. And the charges came out of the U.S. Attorney's Office in Birmingham, not Montgomery.

A federal grand jury had indicted Siegelman, Hamrick and Tuscaloosa doctor Phillip Bobo, accusing the trio of trying to rig bids for a pair of multi-million dollar Medicaid contracts.

The Bobo prosecution was a mess from start to finish. Think of a well-conceived bank robbery – an inside job – foiled by an honest man before the first dime could be stolen. Had matters proceeded as Bobo intended, the government may well have had a slam dunk case against Siegelman. But that's not what happened. As a result, the case against Siegelman was weak, the one against Hamrick, almost non-existent. And when the prosecutors drew U.S. District Judge U.W. Clemon, that was it.

I consider the decision to charge Siegelman and Hamrick in the Bobo matter to be the gravest prosecutorial error in the Siegelman drama.

The collapse of the case was later used to great public relations effect by Siegelman after his 2005 indictment in Montgomery. After Jill Simpson took the Siegelman case big time, the national media and the House Judiciary Committee made hay with the Bobo debacle, citing it as evidence that Siegelman was pursued for political reasons. Siegelman and his supporters presented the Montgomery prosecution as a second bite at the apple by Republican prosecutors hell-bent on destroying Alabama's Democratic golden boy.

The real story isn't that the U.S. Attorney's offices in Birmingham and Montgomery teamed up against Siegelman, but that they were often as not at odds with another.

The Bobo prosecution exemplified, neither for the first or last time, the lack of cooperation between the two offices. There never would have been a Bobo case, at least with Siegelman and Hamrick as defendants, were the decision left to the middle district prosecutors.

Failure though it was, the Bobo prosecution revealed acts that were corrupt and, at least in my opinion, criminal.

It also shined a light on possibly the worst federal trial judge in the country at the time, and more importantly, on the outlandishly corrupt Alabama Fire College.

The Bobo case involved attempts to rig the bids for Medicaid contracts to provide prenatal, delivery and post-birth care to indigent mothers and their babies. The state was divided into 13 districts, and thus, 13 contracts, with a total value of more than $100 million per year.

The prosecution focused on two of those contracts, one in the west Alabama district (District 4) that included Bobo's hometown of Tuscaloosa; the other, for the area (District 7) just south of Tuscaloosa. Evidence was presented indicating that Bobo sought to rig bids in other districts as well.

In October 1998, the James administration solicited bids, with the contracts to be awarded in December. After Siegelman defeated James in November, the governor-elect asked the outgoing administration to suspend the bids on the maternity contracts. James' people did so, with the bid openings delayed until Jan. 22, within days of Siegelman becoming governor. Prosecutors later cited the request to postpone the bids as the first act by the governor on Bobo's behalf. The bids were subsequently postponed for another month, and another, to March.

Phillip Bobo, then in his early 50s, was a well-known figure in Tuscaloosa, especially so because of his position as the sideline doctor for the University of Alabama football team. He was also majority owner in a company called Neighborhood Health Services. He'd donated $23,500 to Siegelman's gubernatorial campaign, and three of his partners in the company gave $5,000 apiece, for a total of $38,500.

When state Medicaid officials opened the bids in March, Neighborhood Health won several contracts, but was not the low-bidder for either districts 4 or 7. Another Tuscaloosa-based firm turned in lower bids for both. For simplicity sake, that company – which was associated with the University of Alabama hospital system -- will be called Capstone, the name of one of its partner firms.

After the bids were opened, Mabry took the extraordinary step of calling a top administrator at Medicaid. Dr. No offered to come to work over the weekend to sign letters awarding five of the 13 contracts to Bobo's company, including to one of the two Tuscaloosa-area districts seemingly won by Capstone.

"It was not the low bid and there was no indication it was a better bid over (Capstone)," the Medicaid administrator later testified.

Before she could voice those objections Mabry and Siegelman had signed the contract giving the Tuscaloosa district to Neighborhood Health.

Based on projected births, it was estimated that awarding the district to Bobo's company would cost taxpayers about $1.4 million more per year than if the contract were given to Capstone, the low-bidder.

Capstone officials screamed foul. The Siegelman administration responded that the state bid law didn't apply to the Medicaid contracts because they were professional service contracts. While there was some merit to this argument, competitive bids had been advertised. Even if they had not, Capstone was cheaper and, according to Medicaid officials, better qualified based on its greater physician network.

The administration – recognizing it was on thin ice – announced it would re-bid the Tuscaloosa area contract. It was at this point that the dirty business commenced in earnest.

Days later, Siegelman's most trusted emissary boarded a charter plane to Tuscaloosa paid for by Bobo.

Nick Bailey arrived at the doctor's home bearing confidential bid information. Dale Walley, the Medicaid director early in Siegelman's tenure, testified years later that his office had on that same day faxed the information to the governor's office, which sought it.

The documents delivered by Bailey to Bobo revealed information from Capstone's bids and disclosed the maximum costs above which the Medicaid agency would not award the contracts. Thus armed, Bobo knew how high he could go -- in other words, to what degree he could screw taxpayers.

But first he had to eliminate the competition.

The Alabama Fire College is a small school in Tuscaloosa that trains and certifies firefighters and emergency personnel. Organizationally, it is situated within Shelton State Community College, so is under the umbrella of the state's two-year college system.

The fire college had for years served a second, unofficial role as a mini-ADECA, thanks in no small part to William Langston, the school's permissive, exceedingly crooked director. Langston maintained wonderful relations with powerful Democratic legislators who liked to channel education money to the fire college, not to train firefighters, but to fund pork projects and, to give just one example, pay a lawmaker's gambling debts.

The best evidence in the Bobo case – and quite good at that -- were recordings of phone calls made by two doctors who served as administrators at Capstone.

In May and June 1999, Bobo made several calls to Marc Armstrong and John Maxwell -with an offer he supposed they couldn't refuse.

If Capstone would drop out of the bidding for district 4 and relinquish its district 7 contract, Bobo would arrange for the company to get a sham $550,000 a year contract with the fire college. Bobo's company would chip in another $250,000, bringing the total annual bribe to $800,000.

After the calls, Armstrong and Maxwell called Capstone's lawyer. The attorney – who so happened to be former Guy Hunt chief of staff John Grenier -- advised the pair to tape Bobo and anyone else calling funny about the contracts.

"Y'all give up (District) Seven and you give me two residents for each football game in the first aid station … I think Santa Claus just landed. . . . It ain't no strings attached other than what we talked about the other day," Bobo told one of the Capstone doctors and his running tape recorder.

Bobo told the Capstone doctors that the governor's office had pledged to route the money from the state education budget to the fire college for the purpose of paying Capstone.

During one call, Armstrong asked Bobo what would happen if the other administrators at Capstone refused to withdraw the District 4 bid on principle. "They can take that principle and stick it… We are talking about greenbacks," retorted Bobo.

Later, when the recordings became public, administration officials tried to portray Bobo as a big talker who was bluffing when he claimed he could arrange for $550,000 to be made available to Capstone. The evidence, however, indicated that Siegelman, Hamrick and others arranged for the state senate to place the money in the fire college budget. Indeed, that very amount arrived at the college in May.

Langston, the fire college director, was to testify that he was surprised to see the money in his school's budget, and assumed it was placed there for pork use by Phil Poole, the Democratic state senator from Tuscaloosa. Other testimony reflected that Langston knew the purpose of the funds.

Bobo also arranged for Siegelman and Hamrick to call Andrew Sorenson, then the president of the University of Alabama. Sorenson later testified that Siegelman called, spoke to him, then handed the phone off to Hamrick. During this brazen to say nothing of inappropriate call, Siegelman's chief of staff asked Sorenson to intervene in the battle for the district 4 contract.

Sorenson told them he would do so, but testified he did not. However, another university administrator did contact the Capstone doctors and urged them to pull out, suggesting that the Siegelman-Hamrick tag team call influenced somebody.

The Bobo case was unique in the Siegelman scandal canon in that it was revealed, not by a reporter, but a lawsuit.

In mid-June, with tapes in hand, Capstone sued the Medicaid agency. The strength of the lawsuit was quickly made apparent. Neighborhood Health withdrew its bid for the Tuscaloosa district and weeks later, the state stripped it of the four other contracts it had been awarded.

The next month Attorney General Bill Pryor ordered the seizure of records from the state Medicaid agency and empanelled a grand jury.

At Siegelman's trial, Claire Austin testified that the governor's office called her then lobbying partner Lanny twice. They told Lanny to tell her to call her friends at the attorney general's office and "get them off Nick's ass and quit investigating them."

Austin said she called an investigator she knew at the attorney general's office and reported the unusual request.

The problem for prosecutors in 1999 and forever more: Bobo's company never got the contracts and the fire college never sent the $550,000 to Capstone. Thus the foiled bank robbery metaphor.

———

The Bobo case vanished from the radar for almost two years. In late April 2001 – just as we were publishing our first G.H. Construction stories – Bobo was indicted for healthcare fraud.

The case went to trial in Tuscaloosa in early October and provided Rip with some of his first opportunities to bat off accusations made against the administration. Of testimony placing Bailey at Bobo's home with bid information in hand, Rip said: "That piece of information certainly sounds absurd and certainly sounds crazy."

Bobo's defense was that he was simply negotiating with competitors to improve services, and that he hoped Capstone could participate with his company in providing the maternity care.

On Oct. 11, 2001, the jury in the trial that would become known as Bobo One convicted the doctor. Federal judge Edwin Nelson sentenced Bobo to two years, but permitted him to remain free on bond, pending appeal.

In August 2003, the 11th U.S. Circuit Court of Appeals overturned Bobo's conviction on a technicality, finding that Nelson should have tossed the indictment because it failed to cite the particular statute in the health care laws Bobo was accused of breaking.

After that, the Bobo case – never considered one of the major Siegelman scandals – fell completely off the screen. The next I heard of it or so much as gave it a second thought was that day in Bratislava.

Siegelman immediately blamed Bob Riley for the indictment. He said it was, "Republican politics at its worst," and designed to derail his re-run for governor in 2006.

In one of his many mass e-mailings, Siegelman wrote: "Republican prosecutors know they can't break my spirit, but they just might break me financially. That's why I need your help to raise money for my legal defense fund … Please send a contribution in *the largest amount you can afford without hurting you or your family.*"

———

The prosecutors secured their fate by initiating a game of judge-shop roulette.

Karon Bowdre, the first judge assigned by the court's random selection system, stepped aside because her husband, a lawyer, had represented one of the companies that competed for the maternity contracts. Lynwood Smith, a Clinton appointee and one supposes a Democrat, was then assigned the case.

U.S. Attorney Alice Martin and Matt Hart, the lead prosecutor in the case, sought Smith's removal on the grounds that he was Bob Riley's second cousin and had once attended a party at a neighbor's home in honor of Riley. The prosecutors must have felt Smith would lean against them, but had to know they were playing with fire. U.W. Clemon was among the northern district judges who could get the case should Smith remove himself, as he did.

From there, each side took turns seeking recusal of judges, in each case for minor reasons. After the fourth judge recused, the defense hit pay-dirt.

U. W. Clemon was a former civil rights lawyer and two-term state senator when, in 1980, Jimmy Carter appointed him as Alabama's first black federal judge.

By the time Siegelman came before him, Clemon had developed a full-blown case of black robe fever. That's the phrase lawyers use to describe judges who've been around too long, treat attorneys with disdain, and think they can do pretty much anything they want. And one of the things Clemon liked to do was give prosecutors hell.

His record suggests either a pathological hatred for prosecutors or a special place in his heart for wealthy, lawyered-up white collar defendants. Many believe Clemon's hostility towards prosecutors dates to a federal criminal investigation of him.

In March 1996, the U.S. Attorney's Office in Los Angeles informed Clemon they it was considering charging him with fraud and other crimes related to $450,000 paid him by a Los Angeles-based program called the Institute for Successful Living. The Birmingham-based Clemon served as the chairman of this program designed to help poor children. He came to the position through his sister, Arnese, who did live in Los Angeles, and served as the administrator for the Institute of Successful Living.

In 1995, Arnese Clemon had pleaded guilty to bilking the Los Angeles school system of at least $780,000. She'd falsified records to show services provided to hundreds of children who'd never attended the institute.

California prosecutors believed the judge had profited from his sister's scheme and tried to help cover-up the fraud. Clemon told investigators he owned the buildings where the program was located and said the payments were for rent and loans. He was, however, unable to produce any documents, such as contracts or loan arrangements, to support his story.

For about a year, he removed himself from any cases involving the government, which meant all criminal cases.

At this juncture, Clemon appeared in serious trouble, but he had powerful friends. The influential Jefferson County Citizens Coalition, then led by Birmingham mayor Richard Arrington, hired several top dollar criminal defense lawyers to investigate the investigators. Not surprisingly, they concluded that Clemon committed no crimes and determined that the feds had overstepped the boundaries of investigatory decorum in pursuing Clemon.

The report, though, did concede that, "in retrospect ... the record-keeping (by Clemon) with regard to payments . . . was unfortunately sloppy."

Arrington delivered the report to Washington, giving it to "anybody I thought it would get their attention," he said later. That included members of Congress and officials in the Clinton Justice Department. Soon after Arrington's visit, California prosecutors announced that they'd dropped the Clemon probe.

Arrington's success at killing the Clemon case suggests the very sort of political interference in prosecutions that Siegelman, the *New York Times*, and the Judiciary Committee have claimed occurred within the Bush Justice Department.

Clemon was lucky he didn't get disrobed, disbarred and imprisoned. Instead of counting his blessings, he commenced on what was to become an unceasing vendetta against prosecutors who had nothing to do with his and his sister's troubles.

Clemon's attitude toward the government – and his lack of fitness to be a traffic court judge, to say nothing of a federal judge – was displayed as perhaps never before in a series of sentencing rulings involving the HealthSouth investor fraud case. Some 17 former executives of the company pleaded guilty to crimes related to the $2.6 billion accounting fraud and agreed to testify against Scrushy. A number of those executives, including ones most culpable in the fraud, drew Clemon as their sentencing judge.

In each case he refused to send them to prison, even after prosecutors appealed and the 11th Circuit ordered him to re-sentence the executives.

Birmingham News editorials blistered Clemon time and time again, including with a piece called, "A serious fraud, a comical sentence." This followed Clemon's refusal to sentence former HealthSouth financial officer Tadd McVay to prison.

He sentenced Mike Martin, Scrushy's second on command, to probation and house arrest. Prosecutors routinely seek leniency for cooperating witnesses, and had for Martin, but this was going too far. They appealed. The 11th Circuit ordered Clemon to try again. This time he sentenced Martin to a week in prison. The government appealed again, and this time the appeals court removed Clemon from the case – an act that would embarrass most judges. Scott Coogler, a real judge, then sentenced Martin to three years in prison.

Matt Hart was an assistant attorney general under Pryor when the Siegelman investigation began. In those early stages, more than any other prosecutor, state or federal, he led the way. Hart oversaw the state grand jury that indicted Roland Vaughan, and would have tried the case were it not for the war. He was in the reserves and was called up to fight in Afghanistan. Upon his return he accepted a position as an assistant U.S. Attorney in Birmingham.

I never met Hart, but spoke to him a number of times on the phone after he became a federal prosecutor. He had a high-testosterone edge, and believed Siegelman and Hamrick to be supremely corrupt.

Once he criticized prosecutors who, as he put it, only pursue cases they know they can win. I took it as a veiled criticism of the Montgomery team. He put himself in another category: Those who will pursue a defendant if they believe he committed a crime even if it's not a slam-dunk case.

Hart was frustrated that the middle district was taking too long to bring charges. I feel certain he would have dove into the Montgomery investigation if he'd had the jurisdictional authority to do so. But he didn't.

I think Hart's irritation with the slow pace in Montgomery and his aggressive nature trumped his better judgment; that he sold the Bobo case to Martin; then flew into it with his natural gusto.

In short, he – and Martin – screwed up.

In July, Hart filed what's called 404(b) evidence. That's evidence of crimes or acts not directly related to the charges against a defendant. Sometimes judges allow such evidence, sometimes not. Most of the matters in these filings have been addressed, such as the $25,000 BMW payment by Lanny for Hamrick.

However, the Siegelman 404(b) filing told about one unsavory if typical act that had not been previously revealed and was never used at any trial.

According to the filing, a Huntsville gun dealer had come to Montgomery to meet with Siegelman and seek his support on a gun-related issue pending before the legislature. Soon after, while on a trip to Huntsville, Siegelman dropped in on the dealer at his store. The governor asked for a gun, free of charge. The dealer gave him the gun. Then Siegelman asked for, and received, three more guns, with the total value of the four guns exceeding $2,000.

The governor then asked the poor guy to give him a collector's gun valued at between $15,000 and $20,000. The dealer promised Siegelman he'd have it delivered to Montgomery, but never did.

The gun story and the other elements of the 404(b) filings, while revealing, seemed to underscore the weakness of the Bobo case. One got the feeling that the prosecutors suspected their case needed extra juice, and sought to provide it by injecting acts by the defendants with no relevance to the Bobo bid-rigging scheme.

———

If the prosecutors came in hoping to see a new Clemon, they soon found otherwise. Among the matters to be considered in a pre-trial hearing in July were motions by prosecutors arguing that Bobby Segall was conflicted and shouldn't be permitted to represent Siegelman.

Among those testifying at the hearing was Amy Herring, the former Siegelman staffer turned lobbyist who'd been hired by Bobo to help him win the maternity contracts. She recalled a 1999 meeting with Segall, who was a board member and lawyer for another company that was seeking the Medicaid contracts. Herring made an offer: If the company, called Gift of Life, would drop out of the competition for the districts Bobo wanted, then Bobo would do the same for the Montgomery district, where Gift of Life historically provided the services.

According to Herring and another witness, Segall said he couldn't make such a decision on his own and doubted his client would go along with the proposal.

Segall testified that he recalled no such offer. One hopes that the then-future state bar association president didn't recall it because it never occurred. As an attorney, he had an obligation to report to law enforcement what was, if as described, a blatant attempt at bid-rigging.

Clemon ruled that Segall didn't have a conflict and permitted him to remain in the case. But it was Clemon's conduct during the hearing, more than his ruling, that caused a stir. The veteran judge repeatedly baited and interrupted the government lawyers. Incredibly, he sustained objections by defense lawyers that the defense lawyers had not even made. So this will be clear: A prosecutor would be questioning a witness, the defense lawyers would not have said a word, and Clemon would interject to sustain the non-existent objection.

The victim of many of these sustained non-objections was Stacy Ludwig, a Washington-based Justice Department lawyer assisting on the case. Clemon also blocked Ludwig from making objections for the record. When she tried, he accused her of being rude to him.

Here, one of those phantom objections as reported by the *Birmingham News:*

Ludwig told Clemon that she never heard an objection and was unsure what objection the judge was sustaining. A defense lawyer, Mark Calloway of North Carolina, then stood up behind her and Clemon said, "Well, you don't have eyes in the back of your head."

When Ludwig tried to object to Clemon's questioning of a prosecutor about what the government perceived as weaknesses in its case against Bobo, Clemon told a U.S. marshal to arrest her at the next court recess. He already had warned her about interrupting him, he said, and now he had enough. "Now sit down," he ordered Ludwig.

Speechless, Ludwig sat down. She later apologized to Clemon and wasn't arrested, but the prosecution left court that day knowing the case was doomed. The government filed a motion asking Clemon to remove himself, but he refused. Soon after, the judge essentially gutted the case by agreeing with the defense that Bobo be tried separately from Siegelman and Hamrick.

———

On Oct. 4, Clemon entertained pre-trial testimony from several witnesses, including Nick Bailey. Clemon ridiculed the evidence he heard, then went through the motions of letting the parties select a jury.

By doing that, he attached jeopardy to the charges against Siegelman and Hamrick. That's to say, if he threw out the case or it was dismissed after seating the jury, prosecutors couldn't re-try it.

After seating the jury, Clemon ruled that prosecutors couldn't preset evidence to support their theory of a conspiracy because it was too weak. That left Hart and Martin with no choice but to drop the case.

Say this for Hart and Martin: They did not quit. Though Siegelman was no longer a potential target, they continued to pursue Bobo.

As part of that effort they asked Clemon to remove himself from what was to be called Bobo Three. Clemon refused. The prosecutors, citing Clemon's outrageous performance during Bobo Two, appealed. The 11th Circuit, long-familiar with Clemon's antics, agreed and removed the judge from the case.

Bobo's lawyers liked Clemon so much they appealed to the U.S. Supreme Court to have him reinstated, but the court declined to consider the request.

Bobo was retried in July 2007, with much of the same testimony from the first trial, minus that of Armstrong, the Capstone doctor, who had died. After deliberating for eight days, the jury delivered bitter news to the prosecutors, acquitting Bobo on all charges.

Hart and Martin erred in going after Siegelman and especially Hamrick, but they had every right – actually, an obligation – to pursue Bobo, even at the end. If not for the intervention of honest people like Armstrong and Maxwell, there is every reason to believe that Bobo would have succeeded in his plan to defraud state government of some $2 million a year – the extra cost of his company's services over Capstone, plus the $550,000 per annum to be routed through the fire college.

Bobo dodged prison, but was forced to file bankruptcy. In that there was some justice.

The Bobo case was a black-eye for Martin, Hart, and their office, but also served as the launching point for perhaps the most successful corruption investigation in Alabama history, and one that, at this writing, continues.

A month before trial, FBI agents working under Hart and Martin arrived in Tuscaloosa bearing subpoenas and hauled off all manner of records from the fire college. Clemon criticized the government for engaging in a "fishing expedition." Maybe so. The raid didn't turn up any additional evidence for the Bobo case, but in other respects, the government hit a grand slam.

It was as if prosecutors made an incision to conduct a minor operation and found the body infested with rot. The raid unearthed evidence that helped expose a world of payoffs, favoritism and nepotism within the leadership of the two-year college system and deep into the Democrat-controlled state legislature.

Brett Blackledge was to devote the next two years to tracking leads that started at the fire college, the result being his much-deserved Pulitzer Prize for investigative reporting.

The raid produced records on a non-profit called the Alabama Fire College Foundation that was funded primarily with state education money. Among other outlays, more than $65,000 was found to have been paid to Democratic state representative, Bryan Melton, the lawmaker who needed money to pay gambling debts; and more than $200,000 to one of Langston's deputies at the fire college.

In July 2008 a jury found the Boss Hoggish Langston guilty of theft, conspiracy, money laundering and other crimes related to more than $1.7 million he'd sucked out of the fire college foundation and funneled to, among others, himself, his children and the children of Roy Johnson, at the time the chancellor of the state two-year college system.

Evidence indicated that Bobo aided Langston by arranging the transfer of funds from the fire college to the ultimate source of much of Langston's booty – a little-known fire college offshoot called the Alabama Poison Center.

Chapter 31
The Crusades

"It means that three years of investigation has gone down the tube. I think he's shot as a witness for the government."
-- *Siegelman lawyer Doug Jones, after the office of Birmingham-based U.S. Attorney Alice Martin indicted Lanny Young in June 2004 for bribing Cherokee County Probate Judge Phillip Jordan.*

"The crusades were over before this."
-- *Birmingham criminal defense lawyer Mark White, in August 2005, after accompanying a client to the Siegelman grand jury.*

Early 2004 found the Siegelman investigation once again in limbo. There had been no developments to speak of since the June 2003 pleas by Lanny, Nick and Curtis Kirsch.

Julia Weller, who had been assigned the case in 2001, left the U.S. Attorney's Office to have a child; and John Scott, the Justice Department prosecutor, spent the latter half of 2003 preparing for and prosecuting the Olympic bribery case in Salt Lake City. There would be later reports that Scott wasn't eager to return to the Siegelman case, that perhaps he didn't think it was strong enough, at least at that stage. In any event, Scott left the Justice Department after the Olympics case.

With Leura Canary having recused herself, the decision to pursue or drop the Siegelman investigation fell to Louis Franklin, the chief of the office's criminal division.

Franklin chose to move forward, and asked Assistant U.S. Attorney Steve Feaga to join him. The word on Feaga is that he has never lost a criminal case tried before a jury, and he's had some big ones.

Before pursuing a case of such magnitude, Franklin and Feaga sought and received the blessing of Noel Hillman, the chief of the Justice Department's Public Integrity Section, where Scott had served. Franklin and Feaga led the prosecution, but Hillman's office was involved throughout.

———

In making their case of a Republican conspiracy, Siegelman and his backers talk about Karl Rove, Bob Riley and the Canaries, but rarely about the actual prosecutors.

There's a reason for that.

Franklin is black and to the extent he has a party affiliation, it's as a Democrat. He worked in the U.S. Attorney Office in the early 1990s, then left to join a local law firm. He hated civil practice, and asked then-U.S. Attorney Redding Pitt for a job. Pitt hired Franklin, and he spent most of the 1990s prosecuting drug crimes.

In the months before the spring 2006 trial, with Siegelman publicly accusing the prosecution of serving the interests of Bob Riley, Franklin fielded calls from relatives wondering what was up. "(They were) saying, 'I didn't know you were a Republican,'" Franklin said, laughing.

And then, with anger in his voice, "The idea that this is political just pisses me off."

I don't know how Feaga votes, but his pedigree is strictly Democratic. He earned his prosecutorial stripes in the late 1980s, working for Jimmy Evans, the archly-Democratic district attorney for Montgomery. Under Evans, Feaga prosecuted several prominent cases, including a case against aides of Attorney General Charlie Graddick for employing wiretaps and illegally procured tax returns during the 1986 governor's race against Bill Baxley.

In 1990, when Evans was elected attorney general, he took Feaga with him. Feaga was the lead prosecutor in what was until the Siegelman case probably Alabama's most famous political prosecution – the 1993 trial that led to the removal from office of Republican governor Guy Hunt.

Alabama Republicans were and to a great extent remain apoplectic over the Hunt prosecution. Second in line for the blame, after Evans, was Feaga.

When Republican Jeff Sessions defeated Evans in the 1994 attorney general's race, Feaga found himself no longer welcome. So he approached the U.S. Attorney and asked for a job as a federal prosecutor.

Louis Franklin, Steve Feaga and Leura Canary – all were hired by Redding Pitt, the great Siegelman friend and, at the 2006 trial, one of his lawyers.

The renewal of the case under Franklin and Feaga wasn't announced, and as far as the media and public knew, nothing was going on with the Montgomery-based Siegelman investigation.

That changed on June 21, 2004. The *Birmingham News* reported that Nick Bailey spent five hours testifying before a special grand jury convened to investigate a wide range of matters involving the Siegelman administration.

Kim Chandler's story also reported that the year before – in 2003 – prosecutors involved in the Siegelman investigation had shared and received information from Birmingham prosecutors working on the Scrushy accounting fraud case.

At least 10 of the witnesses in the grand jury's first week had connections to the lottery foundation aspect of the investigation. They included the three Siegelman-appointed officers of the foundation; HealthSouth attorney Loree Skelton; and Jack Miller, the state Democratic Party Chairman at the time of the lottery referendum.

Later, Siegelman, Scrushy and their supporters claimed that by including Scrushy in the Siegelman case, prosecutors were trying to: A) take another bite at the apple after Scrushy beat the government on the HealthSouth fraud case; and B) harm Siegelman by giving jurors in the Montgomery case the chance to finally punish Scrushy.

Among the problems with these theories: The Montgomery-based investigation was zeroing in on the HealthSouth/Scrushy/foundation element of the case in 2003 and taking testimony from witnesses in 2004 – all well before Scrushy's June 2005 acquittal in Birmingham.

———

Reporting on the grand jury was an unusual exercise.

On the days it convened, Kim Chandler, Phil Rawls and I would go to the Frank M. Johnson Federal Courthouse in Montgomery and sign-in at security. A U.S. Marshal gives you a badge with an identification number that's written next to your name, as is your destination within the courthouse. It was the same for the grand jury witnesses, so Kim, Phil and I religiously checked the sign-in sheet for people headed to the grand jury.

The grand jury chamber is in the basement, as is the cafeteria which, to our good fortune, had a glass wall. We would sit jibber-jabbering over coffee until one of the witnesses came out of the grand jury room. They curled into the elevator; we scampered up the stairs.

Many of the witnesses we recognized, and once outside, gingerly approached to ask if they would tell us what they were asked about. Witnesses before grand juries are not bound by secrecy laws, so are free to talk if they choose.

For those witnesses we didn't know, we raced to check the sign-out sheet to get their number and match it with the sign-in names we'd scribbled down earlier.

Some spoke to us, others not, and quite a few blew by us like we weren't there. Of those who did talk, few went into detail about their testimony.

Frustrating as it often was, the exercise allowed us to report the matters being investigated. For example, one day Lanny Vines signed in. Though he only spoke briefly to us – to say he'd met with prosecutors but not testified before the grand jury – we were able to report that prosecutors were almost certainly reviewing the sale of Siegelman's house.

Neither Franklin nor Feaga nor anyone involved in the prosecution told me or I suppose the others the first thing about the testimony or evidence presented before the grand jury. But when we asked, Franklin would tell us when the grand jury would meet next, and I assume that the Justice Department rules permitted him to do so.

The grand jury didn't meet every week, nor every day on the weeks it did convene, but was busy during that first month. It heard testimony about the hazardous waste tax cut for Waste Management and lottery foundation when, once again, outside developments intervened.

———

Brian McKee was going away for a long time. The former director of Etowah County's solid waste authority, his wife and County Probate Judge Dwight Faulk had been found guilty of stealing about $1.4 million from the authority.

The Big Wheel case – so called because that was the name of the waste firm used to steal the money – was another example of the corrupting influences of the garbage business on local governments in Alabama.

Federal judge Myron Thompson sentenced McKee to almost eight years and his wife to 15 months. Both were about to begin their sentences when, on March 17, 2004, McKee – seeking leniency for his wife -- wrote Thompson to report that he "might have useful information about an investigation."

The "investigation" of which he spoke was the ongoing, much-publicized Lanny Young case, with McKee's information pertaining to Lanny's as yet unplumbed activities in nearby Cherokee County.

Among the criticisms of the investigation by Siegelman and his supporters – and for that matter, many neutral observers – was that it dragged on too long and was timed to kill his 2006 gubernatorial bid. Many of the circumstances that caused the delays, such John Scott's Olympic bribery assignment, have been addressed.

The final delay, of almost a year, was created by McKee's letter.

He was eventually put in touch with the Birmingham-based U.S. Attorney's Office and told investigators what he knew about Lanny and Phillip Jordan, the probate judge and Boss Hog of Cherokee County.

In mid-June 2004, the small-town rumor mill in Centre, Ala., was bursting with news that the FBI was in town asking questions and seeking landfill records. Jordan retained a lawyer and they approached the government with a promise of cooperation and hopes for leniency.

This occurred, give or take a few days, right when the middle district was finally firing up the Siegelman grand jury.

Jordan admitted accepting about $65,000 in return for using his influence to help Lanny win substantial concessions from the county that were designed to increase the profits for Waste Management at the, "Three Corners Landfill."

With Jordan's confession and copies of the checks – such as to a "Darrell Jordan" for "cattle" and "hay" -- the case moved at lightning speed. In late June investigators interviewed Paul Thomas, the DeKalb County judge who helped Jordan cash some of the Lanny checks. The next day Thomas fell – or jumped – to his death.

On June 30, the 42-year-old Jordan stunned the northeast Alabama political community by resigning the dual position of probate judge and county commission chairman. He was a fixture, having largely run the county for 16 years since first winning election at age 26.

The next day, on July 1, Alice Martin announced a nine-count indictment against Young. I read the indictment and didn't see any wiggle room for Lanny. They had him dead to rights.

He didn't see it that way. Lanny and his lawyer, Steve Glassroth, foamed with righteous indignation. The latter claimed that he had never in 25 years of practicing law seen a federal district charge a defendant who was in the midst of cooperating with prosecutors from another district. Lanny issued a statement declaring his innocence and his intent to "fight like hell" and beat the charges.

Glassroth made it clear that his client's plea deal in Montgomery, along with the promise of testifying against Siegelman and Hamrick, was now at risk. He accused Alice Martin and the office she led of betraying their fellow federal prosecutors in Montgomery.

"I think that this demonstrates a fundamental lack of camaraderie and cooperation between the districts," Glassroth said.

Three years later, Team Siegelman and Jill Simpson convinced some of the most influential voices in the national media that Siegelman was targeted by a band of Republican conspirators led by, among others, Bill Canary. The "his girls" quote attributed to Canary helped make the case of a coordinated effort by the U.S. Attorney's offices in Birmingham and Montgomery and spearheaded by Canary's "girls" – Alice Martin in Birmingham and Canary's wife Leura in Montgomery.

The real story isn't that the two U.S. Attorneys offices teamed up against Siegelman, but that they were often at odds. The Bobo case was a nightmare for the Montgomery prosecutors. So too the Cherokee County case. If Alice Martin and Justice Department officials in Washington were conspiring to ruin Siegelman – whether under orders from Bill Canary, Karl Rove or the Masons -- they would have foregone the lower-profile Cherokee County case and cleared the way for the grand jury in Montgomery. They did not.

In 2007, the most oft-quoted source in support of the political prosecution conspiracy aside from Jill Simpson and Siegelman was Doug Jones, Siegelman's lawyer in 2004.

In testimony before Congress and interviews with "60 Minutes" and other national media, Jones described a summer 2004 meeting with Franklin and Feaga in which he said the two prosecutors told him they didn't think much of their case against Siegelman at that point but that, "folks in Washington said, 'Take another look at everything.'"

(Franklin and Feaga have angrily disputed Jones' recollection of the meeting.)

It was during this same time frame that the Justice Department folks in Washington – who purportedly leaned on Franklin and Feaga to go after Siegelman – who blessed Alice Martin's decision to charge one of the two must-have witnesses in the Siegelman case. It was immediately clear to all that charging Lanny would harm and possibly destroy the middle district's case against Siegelman. Among those who saw it that was Doug Jones.

"It seems obvious to me that Lanny Young has been a critical component of the investigation going on in Montgomery," Siegelman's lawyer told the *Birmingham News* after Lanny was charged on the Cherokee County case. "What also seems obvious now is that Lanny Young has not been truthful with the government. He can't be relied on for anything."

Then Jones said: "It means that three years of investigation has gone down the tube. I think he's shot as a witness for the government."

The comments by Jones and Glassroth suggesting that Alice Martin's office was working at odds with the middle district prosecutors were so strong as to put Martin on the defensive.

"First of all, the investigation in the Middle District (Montgomery) is an entirely different matter," she said. "Mr. Young is cooperating in the Middle District but he did not choose to cooperate with the Northern District in our investigation, and as a result, this indictment was returned."

The Cherokee County case blindsided Franklin and Feaga. I'm sure they were given a heads-up prior to the indictment, but it was a serious blow to an investigation that was, after so much time, finally churning toward completion.

After Lanny's indictment the Montgomery grand jury continued to meet. By mid-August it had heard testimony from about 40 witnesses. Subjects of inquiry, in addition to Emelle and the lottery foundation, included AFS Equities, the stock brokerage awarded business by the administration; and the legal fees paid to Siegelman while he was governor

On Monday, Aug. 9, 2004, after presenting six witnesses to the panel, Franklin told Kim Chandler, Phil Rawls and me that the grand jury would meet that Friday for the final time. On that day, he and Feaga apparently believed they could resolve the Lanny problem.

They could not. Lanny told the middle district prosecutors that he would not testify while he remained a defendant in the northern district, and Franklin and Feaga needed Lanny.

The grand jury cancelled its planned Friday session, and didn't meet again for nine months.

Alice Martin's office erred badly by charging Hamrick and Siegelman in the Bobo case, but was thoroughly justified in prosecuting Phillip Jordan, Lanny and others for what occurred in Cherokee County. I don't see how Martin and her staff could have ignored such compelling evidence against a leading local official like Jordan, regardless of its impact on the larger Siegelman case.

I was surprised less by the charges than that the prosecutors in the middle district were surprised. At the risk of sounding arrogant, I had written several stories addressing Lanny's first big kill in Cherokee County and just assumed that his activities there were being investigated.

Every four or five months, from mid-2001 to 2004, I would call officials in Cherokee and Lowndes County and ask if the FBI had been there seeking landfill records. I spoke many times with the administrators for both counties – and once to Phillip Jordan -- and each time was told that, no, the FBI hadn't been by.

Lanny's M.O. was straightforward – he bribed people. Considering the incentives thrown before him by Waste Management, I was sure he had paid off someone in Cherokee County. Jordan – who virtually controlled the county and whose reputation was iffy – was the obvious suspect.

I went so far as to order the financial disclosures of Dean Buttram, at the time of Lanny's dealings the county's lawyer but by then a federal judge. I had heard that Buttram was friends of Siegelman which heightened my suspicions.

The middle district was swamped with so many complicated schemes that the investigators and prosecutors had missed the Cherokee County situation. Lanny, despite his cooperation pledge, elected not to volunteer that he'd made millions of dollars in large part by bribing the Cherokee County's top elected official.

Information provided by Jordan led to criminal charges against three others, including fellow Cherokee County commissioner Leonard Woodall. After being confronted about the landfill, Jordan spilled the beans on an unrelated matter, revealing that he and Woodall had accepted bribes from agents selling insurance to the county. The agents paid $16,500 to Jordan and a lesser sum to Woodall. As a result Jordan and Woodall's greed, Cherokee County paid more than $100,000 in extra premiums for its insurance.

Jordan wore a wire and recorded phone conversations with the insurance agents and lured them into talking about the bribes. Both were indicted and pleaded guilty, with one getting jail time, the other home-confinement. Woodall rolled the dice, went to trial and was found guilty.

As with most white collar defendants who lose at trial, Woodall's sentence far exceeded that of his co-conspirators who pleaded out. He was sentenced to more than three years. Phillip Jordan was rewarded for his assistance with a light sentence: Six months in prison followed by six months home confinement.

Most importantly, this slick, corrupt rural Alabama power-broker and his cronies were finished stealing from their constituents.

On top of all Young's problems – indicted for bribing Jordan, facing prison time for his Goat Hill plea – he added another. On Dec. 29, 2004, he was arrested for drunk driving in Boaz. It was his third DUI in three years, the last one earlier that same year, in Oklahoma, where the indicted but indomitable Lanny was working on, of all things, a landfill deal.

He spent two months in the Jackson County jail. Upon his release he turned in his driver's license, received treatment for alcohol abuse and submitted to electronic monitoring.

In March 2005, Lanny's determination to fight the Cherokee County charges dissipated, and at month's end, a court filing reflected that a deal was in the works.

On May 5, Young pleaded guilty to bribing Jordan. An arrangement between the middle and northern districts called for Lanny to resume cooperating with the middle district, and to be sentenced in that district.

Four days later the Siegelman grand jury convened for the first time since August. In the coming weeks it heard from witnesses related to G.H. Construction and the warehouse deal; the computer services and technology contracts awarded without hint of competition; state bond issues under Siegelman; and a highway striping product, called RainLine, used during the Siegelman administration.

On May 17, 2005, the grand jury issued a secret, sealed indictment against Siegelman and Scrushy on the lottery foundation charges. This was done because of statute of limitation concerns, and wasn't revealed until five months later, when the government announced its full case.

———

On the day the grand jury issued the secret indictment, Scrushy was five months into his epic six-month trial in Birmingham on charges that he directed the massive HealthSouth accounting scam. From 1996 to 2002 the company used accounting tricks and reported fake profits to overstate its income by some $2.6 billion.

The inflated picture of HealthSouth's financial health allowed Scrushy to bank $267 million in salary and bonuses during the period.

The company's unraveling began in August 2002, when it announced a $175 million reduction in earnings that it blamed, falsely, on changes in Medicare reimbursement rules. The following March, the FBI raided company headquarters, scooping up mountains of records. By then, a top officer had begun cooperating, worn a wire, and recorded some conversations with Scrushy.

Revelations of the fraud investigation sent the stock spiraling to a dime a share, meaning fortunes were lost, many in Birmingham. Thousands of HealthSouth employees were let go.

In October 2003 Scrushy was summoned to appear before Congress. He went, but declined to testify, citing his 5th Amendment privileges.

A month later, prosecutors announced Scrushy's indictment on more than 30 counts related to the HealthSouth scandal.

It didn't seem possible that the government could lose. More than a dozen company executives had pleaded guilty and pledged to cooperate. Among them were five men who had served as chief financial officer under Scrushy. All testified against him.

Alice Martin – whose tenure as U.S. Attorney was marked by spectacular successes (the junior college cases) and stunning failures – lost the biggest one of all by trying Scrushy in Birmingham. The government could have prosecuted him in New York, as was done with Bernie Ebbers, the former chairman of Jackson, Miss.-based WorldCom.

The jury selection methods used in the northern district worked in Scrushy's favor. In cases tried in federal court in Birmingham, the pool of potential jurors is limited to residents of Jefferson County.

Anticipating that his jury would be composed of at least as many blacks as whites, Scrushy and his public relations team spent millions of dollars reincarnating him as a black religious leader.

After the FBI raided HealthSouth, Scrushy left the white church in Vestavia Hills where he'd been a member for years. He began attending Guiding Light Church, a black church in the city with several thousand members. In the coming years Scrushy was to stand in the pulpit for sermons delivered there and at black churches throughout the Birmingham area.

Using his non-profit Richard M. Scrushy Foundation, Scrushy flooded those churches with largess. He gave $1.05 million to Guiding Light in 2003 alone. The next year the foundation contributed about $700,000 to black churches or affiliated organizations; about the same in 2005; and a whopping $1.9 million in 2006. The largest recipient that year – with $782,100 – was Project One, a program affiliated with Trinity Life Church. The church, where Scrushy also preached, received a separate contribution of $421,200.

During the trial an alternate juror was dismissed after a member of one of the black churches complained after Scrushy donated $5,000 to the church where the juror attended.

"We're just good people. We're givers," Scrushy told *Business Week* when asked about the donation.

Trinity Life pastor Scott Moore was among Scrushy's most visible supporters and a leader in what the media dubbed, "Amen Corner." This was a group of mostly black religious leaders and congregants who sat in the Scrushy section each day, Bibles in hand, and often joined the defendant for prayer outside court.

Another fixture was Bishop Lewis Jones of the World Outreach Ministries in Jacksonville, Fla. Jones. Scrushy's foundation gave $110,000 to his ministry. Jones lived with the Scrushys during the trial, was a regular at court, and was described by Scrushy as being his primary spiritual advisor.

Many of these religious leaders made frequent appearances on "Viewpoint" – a daily, half-hour "paid programming" show that began airing in March 2004, co-hosted by Scrushy and his wife Leslie. The morality and religion-centered show was taped at the Guiding Light Church and aired on a local cable television station purchased by Scrushy's son-in-law.

When the trial began, in January 2005, the station introduced a new show, "The Scrushy Trial with Nikki Preede." It ran twice daily, in the morning and night, and its primary commentator was a former member of Scrushy's legal team.

The Scrushy public relations machine didn't overlook "new media." A web-site devoted to Scrushy's many fine qualities noted that the HealthSouth founder was a son of Selma, a town described on the web-site as "the birthplace of the civil rights movement."

Scrushy's bid to court black religious leaders might not have been so transparent were it not for his history. HealthSouth under Scrushy – from its support staff up to its governing board -- was white as a country club.

"In all my visits to the executive suite at HealthSouth, I never saw a black person there, not among the executives, the doctors or the secretaries," said Paul Finebaum, the state's best known sports columnist and radio talk show host, and a former friend and business associate of Scrushy's.

Added Finebaum: "The first time I heard religion and Richard Scrushy mentioned in the same sentence was when I read about him going to Guiding Light Church."

Donald Watkins, one of Alabama's best known black lawyers and businessmen, was credited with devising the church and race strategy.

As Kyle Whitmire described it in the city's alternative paper, the *Birmingham Weekly*, Watkins began his closing argument by telling jurors about "growing up as a disenfranchised black boy in Montgomery and how jurors just like them in courts just like this one had allowed him to drink from the same water fountain as whites, go to the same schools, and eventually be able to defend someone like his friend 'Richard.'"

Among other factors in Scrushy's favor was the much-maligned performance of Judge Karon Bowdre. She'd been appointed to the bench two years before, and as she remarked to lawyers prior to trial, was "somewhat of a neophyte to criminal law." She acknowledged being "still on the upswing of that learning curve" and told the attorneys she would "rely on all of you to educate me about the legal issues that are involved."

Many who sat through the trial said Bowdre came to rely for guidance on the defense lawyers, especially Art Leach, the former Georgia prosecutor who was to lead Scrushy's defense in the Siegelman case.

Bowdre issued several rulings that hamstrung the prosecution, and along the way, belittled the government lawyers. Whitmire wrote in the *Birmingham Weekly* that Bowdre was "openly indignant toward the prosecution."

And then:

The stenographer's record won't reflect Bowdre's exasperated sighs and smarmy comments, but they were there. It is only natural to expect that the jury would follow her cues, even if her final instructions ordered them to disregard her take on the case … During the trial, Judge Bowdre allowed the defense to turn her courtroom into a passion play with Scrushy in the starring role … The latitude she allowed the defense was never reciprocated to the government.

One of Scrushy's lawyers, James "Jim" Parkman of Dothan, won over the jury with his folksy if at times outlandish performance. In his closing argument, Parkman called Bill Owens – the HealthSouth executive who'd taped Scrushy – a "big rat," and held up a large cartoon of a mouse eating cheese. He later wore a tie to court with a design similar to the cartoon.

Deliberations began on May 19, 2005, and covered 21 days over almost six weeks. On June 3, the jury sent Bowdre a note reporting it was deadlocked at 10-2, the majority for acquittal. The judge urged them to keep trying.

Victory for Scrushy was assured when one of two hold-outs against acquittal had to quit because of migraine attacks and was replaced by an alternate. Deliberations began anew, and the last remaining hold-out soon gave in to the majority's wishes.

One of the jokes after the June 28, 2005, verdict was that there were only 12 people in Alabama who believed Scrushy innocent, and all served on the jury.

Scrushy defined himself as much with his behavior after being charged as during his years of enriching himself by defrauding HealthSouth investors. There was his utter lack of contrition for those investors, then his shameless efforts to pollute the jury. Almost a year after the trial, the Scrushy legend was burnished by another unusual revelation.

Audry Lewis, a free-lancer for the *Birmingham Times*, a weekly well-read in the black community, admitted to being paid $11,000 for authoring pro-Scrushy articles published during the trial. The money was routed through a public relations firm owned by the son of the paper's publisher. Scrushy said he had no idea Lewis was paid and proclaimed himself angry to learn so. However, Scrushy acknowledged reading her articles prior to their publication, but only to assure their accuracy.

One pastor who received money from Scrushy later said it was for recruiting other black preachers to sit in the courtroom as part of the strategy to influence jurors.

It's impossible to know to what degree the race and religion ploy impacted the verdict. After all, there were five whites who also voted to acquit. Black defendants are convicted every day by black jurors.

In January 2009, black jurors in Birmingham voted to convict two well known members of the black community -- State Sen. E.B. McLain and the Rev. Samuel Pettagrue. The two were convicted of a scheme to funnel about $700,000 in state funds to a charity run by Pettagrue. The reverend kicked more than $300,000 back to McLain, and neither he nor Pettagrue could explain what the senator had done.

More than anything, Scrushy's race and religion strategy was a commentary on him and the people who cashed checks from him. He – and they – had no limits.

Anyone seeking to understand the Montgomery trial, especially the post-verdict attacks on jurors and the Jill Simpson affair, would do well to keep in mind Scrushy's tactics before and during his Birmingham trial.

———

The Montgomery grand jury met off and on throughout the summer and early fall of 2005. Some witnesses told of being asked about a state-funded road in Tuscaloosa County that benefitted a toll bridge owned by Jim Allen. Others reported testifying about legislation allowing liquor sales at the Talladega racetrack and passed in 1997, when Siegelman was lieutenant governor and ran the state senate.

Quipped Doug Jones, the Siegelman lawyer: "Fortunately, I don't think Don has had any pets or they would be subpoenaed, too."

Chapter 32
Indicted

"He's going to run again if he's breathing."
-- Joe Reed, vice chairman of the Alabama Democratic Party, when asked in January 2005 if he thought Siegelman would run for governor in 2006.

"When this case is tried there's going to be blood in the water, and the blood isn't going to be Don Siegelman's. It's going to be the U.S. Government's."
-- Vince Kilborn, after Siegelman hired him to be his lawyer.

In January 2005, Siegelman announced his intent to hold "listening posts" throughout the state.

"Of course I'm thinking about running," he said. "That's like asking a racehorse if he's thinking about making another race."

Lt. Gov. Lucy Baxley was the favorite of Democratic Party leaders and money-people, and the anticipated nominee. Siegelman, though, rarely mentioned her name, as if trying, magician-like, to make her vanish. Instead, he spewed bile on Riley, that architect of the stolen election and the continued investigation into him. It was part of his plan to hypnotize the electorate into assuming that a Siegelman-Riley re-match was a foregone conclusion.

He again touted himself as the only candidate backing a state lottery, and used that tired old proposal as a jumping off point to disparage Riley's failed effort to raise taxes.

A Siegelman backer bought several billboard ads with the slogan, "I'd rather have Don's Lottery than Bob & Lucy's Taxes." They were only a few because the campaign didn't have much money to work with. Even Siegelman's bread-and-butter donors in the trial lawyer community abandoned him, either giving to Baxley or sitting it out.

In mid-summer 2005, Siegelman started headline hunting in earnest, and with remarkable success. He charged down the populist trail, snagging free publicity with easier-said-than-done proposals as well as little things, like sending out fund-raising letters and making statements about how close he was to announcing plans to run.

With his title, ex-governor, and willingness to say anything, Siegelman is and one supposes always will be good copy. A dismayed Baxley harped at her foe's success in getting his name in the paper almost daily.

In July Siegelman scored headlines by calling for mandatory castration of sex offenders who target children. Then he upped it a notch: "If it was up to me, we would have the death penalty on the first offense," he said.

In early August Siegelman called a press conference accusing Riley of not doing enough to prevent the expansion of Indian gaming in Alabama. In the same breath, he said the state should permit the Indians to have full-blown casino gaming, in return for their paying substantial taxes.

Next up was a call for Riley to hold a special session and temporarily suspend the gas tax. At a press conference outside a Montgomery nursing home, he proposed ending the sales tax on food bought by seniors. He scored another story by suggesting that the state not collect sales taxes on the day after Thanksgiving. More attention came his way after he called for a series of gubernatorial debates to begin in November – a full year before the 2006 general election.

In early October, Siegelman's inner Golden Flake stepped off the plank with a bizarre comment about Baxley. He claimed that a recent poll showed voters had doubts about a woman being governor and, as such, in charge of the Alabama National Guard. The reason: Louisiana Gov. Kathleen Blanco's less than stellar response to the ravages of Hurricane Katrina.

"I want to make it clear those are not my feelings," Siegelman said. "I was reflecting on the results of a survey that was taken after the hurricane."

When reporters asked Siegelman to identify the poll, he declined. A leading state pollster said he was unaware of any such survey, the implication being that Siegelman just made it up.

Baxley called Siegelman's comments "insulting not only to women but to all Alabamians."

Siegelman's hyperactivity in early October was in all likelihood due to a sense that the hammer was about to fall. He told the *Tuscaloosa News* he expected to be indicted by prosecutors whose sole motive was to kill his candidacy. "They can kiss my ass, and you can quote me on that, too," he said.

In that interview and others, Siegelman extolled the candidacy of "Ten Commandments Judge" Roy Moore. Siegelman said that Moore was good for him because he would draw white evangelicals to the Republican primary, leading to "an amplified African-American vote" in the Democratic Primary.

Siegelman said blacks liked him, which would give him an edge over Baxley.

———

On Oct. 26, 2005, the government announced charges in the investigation begun more than four years earlier. I drove up to Montgomery and joined our state government reporters, Bill Barrow and Sallie Owen. Journalists from throughout the state, print and television, gathered in a room within the U.S. Attorney's Office. Among those standing before us were Franklin and Feaga, Alabama Attorney General Troy King and Noel Hillman, the Washington-based chief of the Justice Department's Public Integrity Section. Leura Canary was there, but in the peanut gallery.

Copies of the indictments were passed out. I was sucking it in, speed-reading but hyper-attentive and, as I soon noticed, breathing hard. Charged were Siegelman, Hamrick, Richard Scrushy and a fourth and totally unexpected defendant, Mack Roberts, the highway director during the first half of the Siegelman administration.

Franklin was kind enough to praise me before my peers, which is always nice. "It's much like a puzzle. It started with this one voice saying somebody needs to look into this G.H. Construction matter," he said. "G.H. Construction was the case or contract that started this investigation and led to the indictment you have now."

There were really three cases in one.

Siegelman and Scrushy and they alone were charged on two sides of the same coin for charges related to the two $250,000 checks to the lottery foundation.

Siegelman and Hamrick each faced obstruction of justice charges for repaying money given them by Lanny after the investigation began, the theory being that they were covering up bribes and thus obstructing a criminal investigation.

Together, the pair was charged with RICO (the Racketeer Influenced Criminal Organizations Act) violations pertaining to an alleged scheme that began in 1997, when Siegelman was lieutenant governor, and lasted well into his term as governor.

Those counts described an arrangement between Lanny Young on one hand and Siegelman, Hamrick and Nick Bailey on the other, whereby Young agreed to provide hundreds of thousands of dollars in cash, gifts and campaign donations, and in return, Siegelman and his two aides used their positions to enrich Lanny.

Examples of the acts on Lanny's behalf included the tax cut at Emelle, which allowed Young to make a quick $500,000; and secretly awarding him the G.H. Construction project.

Roberts, and Siegelman along with him, were charged with 16 counts of "honest services mail fraud," most involving the state's decision to use and spend some $42 million on the RainLine highway striping product. Both were accused of doing so to benefit toll bridge developer Jim Allen, who was selling RainLine.

Siegelman was also charged with trying to extort a $250,000 campaign donation from RainLine inventor Mac Macarto.

In all, Siegelman was charged with 29 counts, including racketeering, bribery, mail and wire fraud, extortion and obstruction of justice; Scrushy with two counts of bribery and one of mail fraud; Hamrick with eight counts of racketeering, wire and mail fraud, and obstruction of justice; and Roberts with 16 counts of mail fraud, none of which, incidentally, made much sense to me then or by the conclusion of the trial.

Siegelman released a statement calling the charges "absurd and false" and adding that he would be "proven totally innocent."

"A few obsessed government officials have spent millions of taxpayers' dollars in a pathetic attempt to control the election for governor because they don't trust the people of Alabama enough to let them make that decision on their own."

He also declared his intent to remain in the race for governor.

All four defendants announced their intentions to plead not guilty, as indeed they did at a subsequent arraignment hearing.

I will confess to some disappointment that neither the sale of Siegelman's house to Lanny Vines nor the $800,000 or so in legal fees paid him by Cherry Givens after the South Alabama settlement were in the indictment.

The purpose of corruption prosecutions is to punish crooked officials. I like them for another reason: What they reveal.

No matter how hard I try there almost always will be evidence beyond my reach. Bank records, for example, or public records secretly withheld. I can't subpoena records, nor can I make people talk to me if they just will not.

The fun part about the job is solving the mystery, and when I can't, I'm all for someone else jumping in there and delivering the denouement.

The only remaining avenue to get to the bottom of the house sale and the legal fees was through a criminal trial or a detailed plea agreement. Upon reaching the final page of the indictment, I knew that those two mysteries would never be truly solved.

Roy Moore and Siegelman appeared together in a story I did that fall. It was a routine piece reporting the financial disclosures of the four gubernatorial candidates. Siegelman had qualified for the race in early August, and like all other candidates for public office, state and local, was required to report his prior year's income with the state Ethics Commission.

In late November, when I went to the commission to review the candidate's filings, I found that one candidate – Siegelman – had failed to file a report.

He actually responded to an e-mail I sent asking about the oversight. "I will file an ethics update Monday. I wish it had a place to indicate how much money I have spent defending false charges."

The story led with the more interesting news that Roy Moore disclosed earning more than $250,000 in 2004 from speaking fees and sales of his book, "So Help Me God."

I also reminded readers about a promise made by Siegelman in May. He told the Associated Press that if he entered the governor's race he would release all his tax returns since the start of his political career, in 1978. He said he wanted to provide "total and complete transparency with regard to any income I have received in my personal life." The pledge allowed him to score public relations points without revealing anything.

When I asked in my e-mail why he hadn't released his returns as promised, Siegelman said he intended to, and when he did, would give them to the Associated

Press, not me. Despite subsequent reminders, by myself and other reporters, Siegelman never released his returns for even one year, much less his career.

The next week he belatedly filed his 2004 report. He disclosed being paid more than $250,000 for professional/consulting services on behalf of a client in the category, "miscellaneous."

————

The period between indictment and trial was marked by constant skirmishes between defendants and prosecution. Assigned to settle these matters – and preside over the trial – was U.S. District Judge Mark Fuller.

Fuller, then 47, had been the district attorney of Coffee and Pike counties when George W. Bush appointed him to the bench in 2002. He's serious, sandy-haired, nice looking man, and was to approach the trial with great care.

In late January, he set a May 1 trial date, making it possible, if it moved fast, for the trial to be completed before the June 6 primaries.

Three months before trial Siegelman was compelled for the second time to seek new counsel. Doug Jones, who stepped in after David Cromwell Johnson's death, was among the army of lawyers participating in a multi-defendant trial in Jefferson County involving allegations of fraud in the awarding of sewer construction contracts.

That case was going to trial in early April and jury selection for the Siegelman case was set for April 19. There was no way Jones could do both.

Siegelman's selection of a replacement was in many ways an inspired one, and totally unexpected. Vince Kilborn was a star of the Mobile trial bar, but as a plaintiffs' lawyer, not a criminal defense attorney. Though Kilborn has won many multi-million dollar verdicts, he's best known for his outlandish comments and wildman, motorcycle riding image. He has no qualms about trying a case in the press, which I suppose is one reason Siegelman hired him.

I had covered several of Kilborn's cases and knew him pretty well. His forte is demonizing his clients' opponents. He's not above grabbing hold of irrelevant fibs or miscues and twisting them into the gravest of sins against the "little guys" who hire him to fight for justice. As a seal of approval for justice done, he invariably asks jurors to award his little clients as many millions of dollars as they see fit.

When I called to report on his new assignment he gave a quote that was pure Vince. "When this case is tried there's going to be blood in the water, and the blood isn't going to be Don Siegelman's. It's going to be the U.S. Government's," he growled. "And after it's over, we're going to sue the government for damages."

Hamrick was in the same boat as Siegelman. His lawyer, Ron Wise of Montgomery, also had a client in the Jefferson County case and Hamrick, like Siegelman, looked south to Mobile. He chose Jeff Deen, who probably tries as many criminal cases, murder on down, as any lawyer in Mobile. He is prematurely gray and with a pair of the bluest eyes you will ever see. He's an amateur actor and can be a clown in court as well as on stage.

I knew and liked the Mobile lawyers and they were familiar with my work, so lines of communication were wide open.

Scrushy, too, added a Mobile lawyer, longtime white-collar criminal defense attorney Fred Helmsing. I knew Fred and his family, had on a number of occasions covered his cases, and was glad to have someone on the Scrushy team I could easily go to.

Scrushy's primary lawyer was Art Leach, a leader on the team that got Scrushy off in the HealthSouth accounting fraud case. Leach is imposingly sharp. You just know there is nothing getting past him, that he sees the implications of every word uttered by judge, lawyer or witness. I wonder, though, if his somewhat charmless intensity isn't better suited to his previous career, as prosecutor.

Scrushy had several other lawyers, including former Supreme Court Justice Terry Butts, but Leach was the boss, to the extent that anyone can be boss of an operation financed by Richard Scrushy.

In the months before trial Scrushy asked the court to dismiss the charges based on a claim that the middle district's method of choosing jurors and grand jurors produced an inadequate proportion of blacks when compared to the district's racial make-up. Scrushy, who is white as Casper, was piggy-backing on a then unresolved challenge by convicted Montgomery drug kingpin Leon Carmichael. Siegelman joined Scrushy in arguing that his constitutional rights were also infringed upon because the district's allegedly white-leading juror selection procedures.

Lawyers for Carmichael, who *is* black, based their appeal largely on an analysis by James Gundlach, a professor of anthropology and sociology at Auburn University. Siegelman and Scrushy made Gundlach their expert as well. This was the same James Gundlach who produced a report concluding that fraud was involved in the vote count changes in Baldwin County on the night of the 2002 election.

In an initial ruling on Scrushy and Siegelman's "Carmichael appeal," Charles Coody, the magistrate judge, wrote that Gundlach was "fond of making conclusions, to be perfectly blunt, I think he is unqualified to make."

Myron Thompson, the Democrat-appointed black federal judge who presided over the Carmichael trial and sentenced him to 40 years, rejected the drug kingpin's race-based jury appeal. Carmichael appealed to the 11th Circuit Court of Appeals, as did Siegelman and Scrushy.

Though it took several years for them to get to it, the 11th Circuit upheld the rulings by the Montgomery judges, thus ending the juror pool appeals by Carmichael, Siegelman and Scrushy.

On April 20, 2006, the prosecution and defense team struck a jury of 12, with six alternates. About 24 percent of those in the jury pool were black, with the ultimate jury of 12 broken down into seven blacks and five whites, reflecting that far more whites than blacks were struck.

So far so good for Scrushy, who once again was about to play the race card.

Said an upbeat Siegelman after the jury was picked: "The show is paid for. The tickets are free. Everyone is invited."

Chapter 33
Nick and Lanny, Under Siege

"Nick Bailey was the closest human being on the planet to this man (Siegelman), other than his wife and children."
-- Steve Feaga, during opening arguments.

"And we ain't finished with that son of a bitch."
-- Siegelman lawyer Vince Kilborn, after claiming that his partner David McDonald had "destroyed" Bailey during the first day of McDonald's two-day cross-examination of the former Siegelman aide.

On May 1, 2006, Alabama's political trial of the new century and the old as well began in Judge Mark Fuller's courtroom within the Frank M. Johnson Federal Courthouse. The state media was there en masse, as were friends and relatives of the four defendants and many who were just plain curious.

A relaxed Siegelman walked in after giving reporters another dose of the Canary canard.

"This is nothing more than a campaign tactic by Bob Riley's campaign manager, whose wife happens to be the U.S. Attorney," he said. "We are going to go on. We are excited about getting the trial over. This is the beginning of the end."

Louis Franklin was the first to address the jurors. He pledged that evidence would show that Siegelman "took the executive branch of state government and turned it into a criminal enterprise."

Kilborn told the 12 jurors and six alternates that he'd spent his life "suing big corporations" on behalf of "the little guy." Declaring himself nervous but appearing anything but, the Mobile lawyer said he and his partner David McDonald were "going to beat on the governor's witnesses."

He conceded that people close to Siegelman "lined their pockets" with bribes, to the considerable embarrassment of the former governor; and sought to soften the blow of testimony to come by describing his client as "a very aggressive fund-raiser," though one motivated by a desire to improve education and help the state.

Kilborn, Feaga and Hamrick lawyer Jeff Deen each told jurors that the case they were about to hear began with *Mobile Register* stories about G.H. Construction. Kilborn said the warehouse deal was a criminal enterprise from the start, but that Siegelman was uninvolved. Deen said the same on behalf of Hamrick.

Scrushy pulled a fast one on the first day, adding, at the last minute, a new member to his already large team of lawyers.

Tuskegee attorney Fred Gray Sr. was not among the attorneys introduced during jury selection and the prosecution objected to his participation in the case. Fuller, though troubled by the late addition, allowed him to remain.

Gray may be the most esteemed black lawyer in the state. A hero of the civil rights movement, he helped plan the Montgomery bus boycott and represented Rosa Parks in that history-making case; and was a close friend of and the primary lawyer for Dr. Martin Luther King Jr.

In his opening, the Tuskegee attorney described Scrushy's accomplishments in the business world and told jurors that Scrushy's charitable giving helps to "feed hungry children in Africa."

In an obvious reference to Rosa Parks and King, Gray likened Scrushy to the "kind of client I've represented in these courts for more than 50 years." Franklin objected, and Fuller sustained. Gray continued on, and with greater specificity. He compared this trial to the "the first case I filed in this court in 1955," after which he summoned Dr. King's name.

Franklin bolted out of his chair. "Objection. He's doing it again," he shouted, staring at Gray. "That's why he (Scrushy) hired you, so you could come here and say this to this jury."

Fuller pounded his gavel and called the lawyers to the bench. From then on – or in any event, until his closing argument -- Gray refrained from mentioning King and Parks.

As courtroom theater, Franklin's outburst worked, in no small part because he too is black. His anger was real, and considering that Gray had just compared Richard Scrushy to Martin Luther King, justified.

Another outburst, also in the first week, brought Franklin some embarrassment. Terry Butts was questioning a witness when he overheard Franklin mutter the word, "sleaze" from the prosecution table. "Did you just say that I'm a sleaze?" Butts demanded. "Tell the judge what you said."

Franklin approached Butts, and for a few hot seconds, the two stood face to face. Fuller called time-out, ushered the pair outside court, and when they returned, promised jurors they would not see any more of that from the lawyers, and indeed, they did not.

To the extent it was winnable, lawyers for Siegelman and Scrushy lost the case in the first week of trial with their over-lengthy, ill-conceived and dramatic failure to break Nick Bailey.

I felt there was a real chance that Bailey would collapse into a backtracking puddle of sweat and tears from the relentless, pitiless pounding promised by the defense lawyers, thus leaving prosecutors hobbling to the finish. Though Bailey could play enforcer for his boss, you could see a sensitive side in his eyes. He'd been devoted to Siegelman and his family for years and the old feelings had not dissipated. He teared up twice during Feaga's questioning, both times after being asked about Lori Siegelman.

The day before Bailey was to begin almost three days of cross examination, Kilborn boasted outside court that the witness would be "destroyed." I suppose Vince's tough talk was intended for Bailey's ears, to make him think, ruin his night's sleep and in every way soften him for the kill.

The next morning, to everyone's surprise, Kilborn ceded Bailey to David McDonald, his younger partner. It was a disaster. McDonald, though a friendly, engaging sort, suffered from too many years of watching Vince, saw in Kilborn his model, and given the biggest stage of his career, tried to surpass his master in bombast and scorn. They say of a good actor that you forget he is acting. With McDonald, you never forgot. Here's how I presented one aspect of his performance:

McDonald, Kilborn's younger law partner, spoke with supreme confidence and apparent good cheer throughout, often joking and flashing his teeth with broad smiles.

Seemingly every lawyer in the room, even those prosecutors he accused of misconduct, was "fine," as in, the "fine prosecuting team;" and Bailey's "fine lawyer, George Beck." U.S. District Judge Mark Fuller was "too young and too handsome," according to McDonald.

Joseph Fitzpatrick -- a prosecutor with the Alabama Attorney General's Office who like most of the lawyers in the room has not participated in the questioning -- was pointed at and described by McDonald as "the hero of the show."

No one knew quite how to respond, so there were plenty of blank faces. McDonald, though, was having too much fun to recognize the failure of his smarm attack.

He opened his questioning by smiling at Bailey and telling the witness that over the next two days they would get to know each other and become friends. Then, like a one man good cop-bad cop, McDonald began shouting at Bailey. During the ensuing hours of cross-examination he played the schoolyard bully, repeatedly peppering Bailey with insults. Here, as we reported it:

In a friendly tone, (McDonald) frequently addressed Bailey as Siegelman's "chauffeur," "business-card holder," and "gopher," at one time ending a question with the phrase, "...while fulfilling your important duties as gopher, business card holder and chauffeur."

To the extent McDonald's questioning elicited laughs or smiles from those in the court, they usually followed Bailey's retorts, sometimes issued with a grin.

"You forgot chauffeur," cracked Bailey, seconds after being addressed as a gopher and card-holder....

But at the end of a day's worth of often rambling, insult-filled questions from Siegelman lawyer David McDonald, Bailey appeared not "destroyed," as McDonald's partner Vince Kilborn III predicted, but emboldened.

Bailey's testimony ended dramatically, with McDonald rattling off a series of questions demanding that Bailey ... admit that he was lying about Siegelman and others to avoid a length prison sentence.

"If you think I'll sit here and lie about the people I care about to save my own ass, you don't know me well," Bailey shot back at McDonald.

It was just the sort of response the defendants didn't want – the witness, pushed to righteousness, declaring that he hated testifying against people he cared about.

Kilborn, who rarely gets mad at reporters, flashed in anger when asked outside court if McDonald had, as promised, destroyed Bailey. Kilborn snapped that indeed Bailey was destroyed. "And we ain't finished with that son of a bitch," he said.

McDonald resumed his assault the next day, to no greater effect. By the time Scrushy lawyer Art Leach got to him, Bailey was locked in a gear called "you can kiss my ass." Leach applied the same strategy as McDonald, if in a more direct, professional fashion. I thought I detected a glint of fear in Bailey's eyes when the former prosecutor approached the podium, but if so, he conquered it.

Leach, even more so than McDonald, repeated questions, changing a word or two but forever getting the same answer he hadn't liked the first time. For example, Leach asked Bailey if he had any documents supporting his testimony that Scrushy gave two $250,000 checks to Siegelman and that, in return, the governor appointed Scrushy to the CON board.

"The checks, Mr. Leach," answered Bailey, his derision the equal of the lawyer's. Then he added another: Siegelman's letter appointing Scrushy to the CON board.

This, from our story the next day:

Leach, appearing surprised by the answer, continued to ask the question, but with his directions to Bailey said that when responding, the checks and the appointment letter didn't count. It was like asking someone what they had for breakfast but telling them they couldn't mention the eggs. Prosecutor Steve Feaga objected, and Fuller sided with him.

Near the end of Leach's cross he let his frustration get the best of him. He accusingly asked Bailey if he was "on medication."

The question might have been appropriate had Bailey appeared dazed, disoriented or in some way not in control of his faculties. But the witness, especially considering how he held up under the sort of grilling that could turn many to mush, didn't strike anyone as crazy. Fuller jumped in before Bailey could answer. He ordered Leach to the bench for what looked like a whispered tongue lashing. The judge told the jury to disregard Leach's question, and Bailey never answered it.

Even as the defense lawyers belittled and ridiculed Bailey, they also sought to plant him as the administration Machiavelli, the one pulling the trigger on every bad act, from the motorcycle cover-up to the foundation's re-birth to G.H. Construction.

At closing, Feaga delivered the memorable line, "They couldn't decide if he was a chauffeur or a financial wizard mastermind."

Outside court – after all, he said nothing in court – Siegelman blamed Bailey for the re-birth of the foundation and its secret machinations. I was stunned, since we had reported years before and documents were presented in court leaving no doubt that Siegelman was in charge of re-born foundation and its fundraising.

Blaming Bailey for the foundation? There was no way to write as much as I had on Siegelman without occasionally asking myself if I was being too hard on him. And then he would say something like that, and I realized that no, I wasn't too hard on him. I was correct to have zeroed in on Siegelman halfway into his term and to have stayed on him.

————

My ability to cover the trial was briefly imperiled when Jeff Deen put me on Hamrick's witness list. Though exceptions can be made, witnesses are generally prohibited from watching a trial out of concern that hearing the testimony of others could impact their own. I called Jeff and he said that I was only to be called if Lanny denied some undeniable statement included in a story I'd written about him. It was both minor and unlikely, but he listed me out of an abundance of caution.

The editors had Ed Sledge write a brief arguing, among other things, that I was unlikely to be summoned and that even if so the matter upon which I would be asked to testify was insignificant. Ed spoke to Deen and the other defense teams and none objected to me covering the trial. Ed actually joined me in Montgomery for the pre-trial arguments, and Fuller ruled from the bench that I could attend and cover the trial. (I was never called as a witness.)

Phil Rawls, who was to cover the trial for AP, was listed as a witness for the prosecution. Phil had written a story in 1999 quoting Mack Roberts on a matter of substance in the case, and in fact, prosecutors did put Phil on. I supposed Phil could have received a waiver similar to mine, but he elected not to.

Our decision for me to cover the trial could be subject to second-guessing on journalistic grounds. The bottom line is that I knew the subject matter cold and was best suited to give our readers the insightful coverage they deserved. Had I been inclined to report in a slanted manner my editors would have edited it out and pulled me off the trial.

Our best defense was the stories. The paper gave me far more space to cover this complicated case than any other paper in the state. This gave me the freedom to provide context and detail for a story that needed it, and according to the editors, our readers ate it up. No one, such as a defendant or defense lawyer, complained about our coverage or sought corrections, and they were reading it.

Another issue was the frequency with which my name and our reporting came up during trial.

According to the trial index my name was invoked in questions, answers or opening and closing arguments some 70 times, including by seven witnesses. Much of this was done by the jocular Deen, who seemed to like tossing me out there for fun. To the extent those references had a place in the story we went with "the *Register*," or "a *Register* reporter." I wasn't going to have my byline atop a story that had my name in it as well.

Near the end of the prosecution's case Feaga pulled me aside and said he was strongly considering calling me as a witness. He wanted me to testify about my efforts, as described in the stories, discovering the second secret life of the foundation. Part of me wanted to set the record straight, to explain as only I could the obstacles placed in front of me by Siegelman and the administration.

But the arguments against trumped that wish. Chiefly, had I testified I would have forever been branded a "witness for the prosecution." I immediately called Paul Cloos and told him what was up. Bill Barrow raced over and finished out the day. Ed Sledge was summoned. He and Feaga spoke that night, with the latter agreeing not to call me.

The next morning I was back in court, reporting.

———

Feaga has a feisty but likeable and entirely unselfconscious courtroom presence. Whether intentionally or not, he seems to use his glasses as a prop. When questioning witnesses and speaking to a jury, they are either on the tip of his nose and threatening to fall off or in one of his wildly gesticulating hands, and a threat to take flight. His tie, often as not, is over his shoulder, where it's flown and stayed. He was the first to question Bailey, and introduced evidence that was harmful to the witness's credibility.

Had the prosecution not done so, the defense lawyers would have, so better to get it out there first under friendly questioning.

The information was terrifically interesting to me as it related to several stories I'd written about but which were not a part of the government's case. It also complicated my impression of Nick because it made quite clear that Nick also took care of Nick.

Feaga presented records showing that in the mid-1990s, when Lanny came on the scene, Bailey had debts, including more than $50,000 from a failed investment in cattle futures.

A series of 1995 letters to Bailey from Regions Bank reflected that interest payments on a $75,000 line of credit were, as one letter put it, "seriously past due."

Bailey testified to receiving a total of about $94,000 from Lanny, including $55,000 in 1996, when he was being hounded by the bank.

Of particular interest to me were payments to Bailey from Jim Lane and Keith "Tack" Mims.

Bailey admitted to accepting about $70,000 from Lane, the wealthy Montgomery businessman, former Siegelman supporter and part-owner of Group One, the hapless company paid almost $800,000 to develop and maintain ADECA's web-page.

After trial I did a winners and losers column and placed Lane in the winners column – there because he wasn't prosecuted.

Bailey said, unconvincingly, that he believed he had re-paid $30,000 to Lane. As previously described, Bailey said he didn't tell Siegelman about the money from Lane, with one exception. In 1998, when he left the lieutenant governor's office to serve on the campaign, as Siegelman's driver and assistant, Lane gave Bailey bout $20,000 to supplement his income.

Lanny also "supplemented" Bailey's income, with 11 payments to totaling $20,900.

Bailey told jurors that Siegelman knew about the campaign payments from Lane and Lanny; and that the boss was aware of similar campaign supplements from Lanny to Hamrick after the latter left the lieutenant governor's office to manage Siegelman's gubernatorial campaign.

None of the payments to his two campaign assistants were disclosed by the two-time former secretary of state Siegelman on his campaign reports, as required by the Alabama Fair Campaign Practices Act.

Lane's payments to Bailey were made in 1998 and 1999, before Bailey assumed the title of ADECA director. At the time he was in no position to help Lane, even assuming that, once he did become ADECA director, he actually had the authority to make such decisions without Siegelman's permission.

In any event, Group One was hired before Bailey moved to ADECA. I can't imagine why Lane would have given such sums to Bailey unless it was authorized or known by Siegelman, but, again, lack proof that Siegelman knew.

Bailey also admitted asking roadbuilder "Tack" Mims to give $50,000 to Trava Williams, Bailey's close friend and his partner in real estate ventures. Williams was the stockbroker for Siegelman, Bailey and others in the administration, as well as state agencies that were forced by Bailey and Siegelman to use his services.

Bailey said the money from Mims was injected into one of his and Williams' real estate deals. Mims was the "M" in EPM, the company awarded the $36 million no-bid contract for the Honda site work project. I'd written about Bailey's real estate partnership with Williams in 2002 and the Honda contract in 2001, but had no inkling of a link between the two until Bailey's testimony.

Lastly, Bailey admitted accepting four tickets to a Las Vegas show from dog-track owner Milton McGregor.

It was already known, from the 2003 plea agreement, that Curtis Kirsch – the architect overpaid to design one of the warehouses – gave Bailey about $19,000 in 1999.

When David McDonald crossed Bailey, he asked the witness to tally up the total from Young, Kirsch, Lane, Mims and Fant. It came to more than $280,000. Then McDonald went through each and asked Bailey if he had paid taxes on the money. Each time, the answer was no.

The evidence of Nick's willingness to take kickbacks and steal the public's money did not alter my opinion that Bailey shared everything with Siegelman and that he was, in some hard to define way, naïve, and certainly blind loyal to the great man he served.

The only reason people took directions from Bailey or responded to his requests, such as for money, was because it was accepted that he was asking on Siegelman's behalf. It might have been Nick on the phone, but the request or message was Siegelman's.

To believe that Bailey didn't tell Siegelman about the payments one must also believe that Bailey would deceive the man he served with total fealty; and who Bailey knew, as well as anyone, had no qualms about taking money from people who did business with the state.

––––

Bailey testified, most of it under cross-examination, for about three days. By the time he was handed over to Roberts' lawyers everyone, almost surely including the jurors, was tired of the endless, repetitive questioning.

Bill Baxley sensed the jurors' mood and with one line separated his client from Nick Bailey, Lanny Young, Richard Scrushy and so much of the case.

"On behalf of Mack Roberts, we don't see any need to question this witness," said Baxley, with typical flourish.

Siegelman, relaxed or pretending to be throughout the trial, had watched Bailey with clenched jaw.

"Nick is probably my single greatest disappointment," he told reporters.

Like other federal courthouses built since the Oklahoma City bombing, the Frank M. Johnson Federal Courthouse was designed with security in mind. It's an imposing granite semicircular building, with the entrance about 200 feet from the street. With many of the older courthouses, the steps lead to the street, which limits the ability of reporters to snag subjects for quotes. The broad expanse of cement created by the layout was perfect for reporters and worked out well for the Siegelman trial.

Near the street, courthouse personnel roped off an area for the television cameras. Those wishing to be interviewed – as Siegelman and his lawyers always did – merely had to walk over to the bundled microphones for instant publicity.

Scrushy, rather than his attorneys, did most of the talking for his side. Roberts, Hamrick and their teams laid low, which wasn't terribly difficult since Siegelman and Scrushy were the marquee names and camera hogs to boot.

I won't pretend that I wasn't apprehensive about being around Siegelman every day for weeks and girded myself against responding in kind if he insulted or berated me.

I needn't have worried. Siegelman was pleasant and friendly and didn't seem to take it personally when I asked tough questions outside court. He could be funny, often at his own expense, though my favorite example was a crack at mine. During jury deliberations, everyone raced to court for news that the jury was coming in. It was a false alarm – a question for the judge, not a verdict. I walked down the stairs and saw Siegelman as he exited the elevator. He approached me, and to my surprise, began praising the depth of my questions and reporting on the trial.

A marshal who busted me weeks before for interviewing Bill Baxley inside the courthouse – prohibited during this trial -- saw us and jumped on me again. I stammered that the governor had asked me a question, and Siegelman backed me up. When the marshal left, Siegelman laughed.

"Well, it's about time I got you in trouble," he said.

It was a nice touch, and another moment when I saw his good side.

In court as out Siegelman presented a natural and usually relaxed demeanor to jurors. He sat straight-backed, not just attentive, but bright-eyed and interested. He made regular eye contact with jurors and often smiled their way.

To the extent that a defendant can help himself by conveying a sense of humanity to jurors, be it with smiles like Siegelman or, as with Mack Roberts, a gentle if slightly bored serenity, Scrushy failed miserably.

It didn't help that he and his regiment of lawyers were seated at a table directly across from the jurors, their backs to the opposite wall, with Scrushy dead center. I wasn't always in the main courtroom, and even when there, could have missed it, but not once did I see Scrushy smile. If he made eye contact with jurors, it was fleeting.

The court was wired with the Internet, and many of the lawyers had laptops that allowed them to review documents scanned in as evidence. Scrushy was the only defendant with a laptop. He disappeared into it. His lawyers could be banging away at a witness, but their client was, or pretended to be, oblivious. Scrushy was in his own world, eyes searching the screen, his hand pressed on the mouse. I suppose he was reviewing court documents, but then again, maybe he was playing solitaire.

When jurors looked across the room they saw this man with a chalky complexion, hair black as the rims on his glasses, not a wrinkle in his expensive suits, obsessively working his laptop.

The armchair psychologist in me saw someone accustomed to commanding the attention of all in a room and controlling his environment. Here, Fuller was the boss, lawyers and witnesses did the talking, and protocol required Scrushy to remain silent. This made him intensely nervous, so he employed his laptop as escape mechanism.

Scrushy was the only defendant I never conversed with, the exception being the daily press gatherings. There was one awkward turn in the bathroom, when I walked in to find myself alone with him. To my surprise he said hello and used my name, and I replied in kind.

In court, the Scrushy contingent invariably included his wife Leslie, usually accompanied by several others and always by one or more black pastors.

Leslie Scrushy is, by any measure, attractive, a brunette with green eyes and smooth white skin, and always dressed to the nines. She was as personable as her husband was not. She appears genuine about her faith, if barmy.

During the trial the *Washington Post* published a remarkable feature story about her. She revealed that during the lead-up to her husband's fraud trial, the couple was awakened by a telephone call at exactly 2:51 a.m. The caller instructed Scrushy to fire high-powered Washington attorney Abbe Lowell and replace him with Jim Parkman, the hammy Dothan lawyer credited by many for getting Scrushy off.

The caller, said Mrs. Scrushy, was God.

Yes, He uses the telephone.

There was something else in the story about the timing of National Pancake Week and how that proved to Leslie Scrushy that God was on their side. The piece reported that each morning she anointed the Montgomery courtroom with prayer.

"Leslie is very prophetic, and I think God will show her things," her husband told the *Post*.

Lori Siegelman attended most days, usually with company. During Siegelman's last year as governor one was forever hearing rumors that they were about to split. She was famously strong-willed and spent much of her time in Birmingham. He was a workaholic governor and an indefatigable campaigner. There was also the criminal investigation. Even the strongest marriages would bend under those pressures.

The rumors were of such persistence that I'm inclined to think there were problems. If so, they were healed by the trial.

I had never seen them together until the trial and witnessed, not a pretense of closeness, but the real thing. She sat behind him most days, and once, carried away by a lawyer's argument, clapped. Fuller, didn't single her out, but angrily warned the crowd that future outbursts would lead to the culprit's removal from court by the marshals.

Outside the pair held hands and whispered to one another. She spoke little if at all to reporters and gave me more than a few looks that could kill, and I didn't begrudge her a one.

The most steadfast member of Siegelman crew was Kenneth Marshall, a paralyzed black veteran who watched the trial from his wheelchair, in the aisle and near the front of the court. A friendly, handsome man with a deep baritone, he was known as Maze – the nickname given him by Siegelman because he was "amazing."

Roberts generally had family members, regular folk who watched grimly on.

Hamrick's was the smallest supporting contingent, usually just his wife Tatiana, a thin, pretty blonde who rarely smiled, as one supposes might be expected of a woman whose husband was on the dock. Several jurors remarked after the trial that they were impressed by her stoic supportiveness.

Hamrick, 42 at the time, had two daughters, the oldest two. He fake-smiled through much of the testimony about him, as if to mock it. In other respects, he was the most nervous of the four. Breaks often found him outside, chain-smoking with his wife, the color drained from his face. In the latter stages of the trial reporters began to note that Hamrick appeared to be aging before our eyes.

"He's lost a lot of weight, his hair is turning gray and there's been a lot of strain on him and his family. It's been very hard on him," said Deen, in a quote I used.

I may have aged a bit myself. At the end of each day's session I raced to Cafe Louisa, a coffee bar in the Cloverdale section of town with an Internet connection. For two months it was my office. By the time I finished writing and answering questions from editors I was whipped.

The trial was the one stretch in my history of going to Montgomery when I went to bars somewhat regularly. I would eat at one of the Cloverdale restaurant/bars and often meet Bill Barrow at Bud's or one of the other Cloverdale spots, and frequently palled around with a couple of young, fun reporters from the *Advertiser*.

On May 16, court broke for lunch with Lanny in the batter's box.

"This afternoon, they're going to put their top card on the table, and it's a joker," said Siegelman.

The tension in the courtroom spiked when Young walked in, looking fit in a business suit and close-cropped hair. The jurors, at times, and with good cause, bored, were wide-eyed and eager to hear. The one exception was a young white male – an alternate, it turned out -- who dozed through most of the trial.

Lanny was probably the calmest person in the room. He said matter-of-factly that from 1994 through the 1998 governor's race he gave hundreds of thousands of dollars in money, goods and services to Siegelman's campaigns, some of it disclosed, some not.

"Nick Bailey would call and give me the name of the PAC for Governor Siegelman's campaign," said Young, explaining one manner of giving, after which the prosecution introduced records showing $85,000 in such checks, most in $5,000 increments.

He also testified to providing $127,000 worth of T-shirts, embroidered hats and wind-breakers for the 1998 campaign. That Lanny gave and gave simply wasn't in question.

He told of how, in September 1998, Hamrick called to tell him to expect a call from Jack Miller, the Siegelman friend and state Democratic Party chairman. Miller asked Lanny to donate $25,000 to the National Coalition for Black Voter Participation. The money was for a jeep that was to be given away as a prize in a competition to encourage voters to go to the polls. Lanny, as requested, contributed the $25,000.

This, like the campaign donations, wasn't particularly damning, but it served an important purpose – learning about and being able to report how Montgomery operates.

Most of Lanny's cash and gift-giving has been covered earlier, such as his testimony on the BMW for Hamrick.

Bank and investment firm records were introduced showing that Sterne, Agee & Leach wrote Hamrick in fall 2000 demanding $5,300 for his stock bet that went bad. Hamrick wrote a check to the firm, but it bounced. As the bank records showed, Lanny then wrote Hamrick a check for $6,000, which Hamrick used to pay off Sterne Agee.

There was one count against Hamrick and Hamrick alone, an of obstruction of justice charge. After the warehouse investigation began, Hamrick delivered a $3,000 check to Lanny. Hamrick told Lanny that they'd been partners on the stock bet, and the $3,000 was Hamrick's repayment of his half of the losses, since Lanny had paid the entire $6,000. This partner business, Lanny testified, was news to him.

That and other evidence showed that when covering his trail, Hamrick was a cheapskate. For example, he didn't re-pay the $25,000 for the BMW that he tried to characterize as a loan. Given the success of the government's obstruction of justice count against Siegelman, it's probably a good thing he didn't.

Jeff Deen could say what he wanted about Lanny's credibility, but with all the documentary evidence, it was easy to believe Lanny's testimony that when Hamrick asked for money, he delivered.

Jurors saw a number of checks from Lanny to Hamrick but more so, checks from Lanny for cash. Many were in the $5,000 range, some higher. Lanny testified that some of that money was given to Hamrick. At the end of the day, and including bills at bars and restaurants and strip clubs, there was no way to know how much Lanny gave Siegelman's top aide. I suspect neither of them could pin the figure down within $5,000.

Hamrick lawyer Jeff Deen didn't spend much time on the money and gifts, BMW included. He was wise not to. There was no grand defense for the slathering of favors to his client from a man who benefitted substantially from his relationship with the Siegelman administration.

Besides, Lanny could bite back, such as after Deen asked him about visits to the Platinum Club near Anniston. It was the state's only "full nude" strip bar, or as Deen called it, one of "those kinds of hoochie-koochie places."

"Yes, your client was with me on that, too," quipped Lanny.

Deen, rarely at a loss for words, hesitated, then discontinued the Platinum Club line of questioning, never to return to it.

The Mobile lawyer made the most of one thing he had – the friendship defense. If indeed Lanny ladled money on Hamrick, it was because they were best friends. Ethics, bribery and public corruption laws don't make exceptions for friends, but jurors might.

After the trial Deen said he and his co-counsel, Mobile attorney Michel Nicrosi, decided early to try the case in court and not in the media; and when in court, to avoid getting caught up in the verbal wars between the prosecutors and other defense lawyers. They laid low, and it worked.

I'd seen Young testify once before, during a civil trial, and he'd been unflappable. Even Kilborn wasn't claiming he was going to break Young. Instead, the Mobile lawyer insulted him. For example, he repeatedly asked Young about seeing women other than his wife.

The questions about Lanny's love life were mild compared to a line of questioning in which Kilborn – irresponsibly, I thought -- appeared to accuse Young of murder. As described earlier, DeKalb County Probate Judge Paul Thomas died in June 2004 from a fall off a cliff days after FBI agents questioned him about helping Cherokee County Probate Judge Phillip Jordan cash bribery checks from Young.

Kilborn asked Lanny what he knew about Thomas falling to his death "with a plate of table scraps in his hand."

Lanny coolly responded that he never had any dealings with Thomas. To a follow up question from Kilborn, he said he didn't feel responsible for the judge's death.

Lanny testified for about a day -- far less than Bailey. This was primarily because he had nothing to do with the HealthSouth case. As a result, Leach – who could spend hours cross examining a door-knob – let Lanny be.

During his roof-raising opening Fred Gray strayed from comparing Scrushy to civil rights icons by accusing the government of timing Siegelman's trial to ensure his electoral defeat.

"That's why we are here. Alabama politics 2-0-0-6," Gray memorably intoned.

In his opening argument Kilborn suggested that his client's fate should be decided not by the jurors, but by the citizens of Alabama. For this to happen, the jury must clear Siegelman and "leave it up to the voters," he said.

Prior to the trial's start Fuller told the lawyers he hoped to have the case wrapped up by the June 6 primary. It became clear early that wasn't going to happen, in no small part to the marathon cross-examinations by the Siegelman and

Scrushy teams and their endless objections during questioning by the prosecutors. Their job wasn't to win an election but save their clients.

Siegelman knew this, but that didn't stop him from accusing the government of stretching things out to ruin his gubernatorial bid.

The line separating Siegelman's campaign strategy from his defense was non-existent. The two were interdependent. As Siegelman said the week before the trial, in Ali-speak, "This case is about the race."

In one way Siegelman was in his element. Always a media magnet, he had only to walk to and from the courthouse to find reporters seeking quotes. Upon leaving court he would make a beeline for the cameras. One day he was answering questions from newspaper reporters who'd caught him before he made it to the TV area. When he spotted Kilborn holding court before the television folks, he laughingly bade us goodbye. "You know I'm always anxious to be there," he said, his sense of humor, as during most of the trial, intact.

Siegelman demagogued for all he was worth during his TV news performances. He would stride over to the cameras and start giving it to Riley, punctuating his broadsides by stabbing his finger east, toward the capitol. Television news, because it has little time to devote to each story, was the perfect forum for these harangues.

Absent was a single mention of Karl Rove. The fantasy of Rove as the puppeteer behind the Siegelman prosecution had yet to be invented. Jill Simpson's affidavit was still a year away, so Bill and Leura Canary and Bob Riley served as the villains in Siegelman's passion play.

At the close of each day, Siegelman morphed into Robo-Candidate, hitting the highway for gatherings in towns small and large in the evenings and going full bore on weekends. At these appearances he savaged Riley, ignored Baxley.

On the Friday morning before the election Fuller became aware of a new Siegelman television ad. The spot opened with Siegelman looking into the camera, shaking his fist, and repeating his shtick about Bill Canary ordering his wife to prosecute Siegelman as a means of helping Riley.

Every afternoon, before dismissing the jurors Fuller reminded them to avoid media reports on the trial. That day it was the first thing he said to the jury. He ordered them to avoid not just media reports but also "advertisements from any person about this trial."

Outside, Siegelman defended the ad's accuracy and claimed its sole purpose was to generate votes.

"Think of it this way: If he didn't say that, what would he say?" remarked Riley.

Siegelman also ran radio spots using Gray's declarations that the trial was about politics, not justice.

On the day before the election the defendant cheerfully predicted that 15 of the 18 jurors would vote for him the next day. "You can just look at them and tell," he said, adding that he'd developed a "warm relationship" with the panel.

Siegelman's brain had to know he didn't stand a chance against Baxley, but his heart was another matter. One of my enduring images of the former governor was seeing him late afternoon on election day, sitting on a bench outside the courthouse. He was on the phone, and from his body language and the strain on his face you just knew he was getting bad news.

His usual spark was gone and he looked old. My memory wants to put a cigarette in his mouth, but I'm not sure. The cynic in me gave him credit – yes, the campaign was part of his defense strategy, but he wanted to win, and the disappointment evident in his bearing suggested he actually thought he might.

In what was surely the final election of his career Siegelman polled 36 percent, and in a Democratic primary. Baxley coasted with 60 percent, with several lesser candidates splitting the rest.

A smallish crowd joined Siegelman that night in Birmingham. Reports described him as relaxed and in good humor despite the results. He said he planned to call Baxley the next day to congratulate her. Someone asked if he intended to do the same for Riley.

"I might call him a son of a bitch," he said.

By June 2006 Riley's recovery from the shellacking taken by his 2003 tax referendum was complete. The economy was strong and his administration largely scandal free, a real rarity in Alabama. Voters found him likeable and sensible, a sturdy presence at the helm. He crushed Roy Moore, 67 percent to 33 percent.

Baxley's candidacy, largely based on her likability, never took off. Riley, with a dominating advantage in funds, defeated her easily in November, 58 percent to 42 percent.

Siegelman's obsession with Riley didn't cease with his loss in the primary.

In late June, with the jury deliberating, he pulled a stunt that won him some of that free publicity he so craved and which he surely hoped would find its way to a juror. Siegelman wrote a letter advising Riley that contributions to his failed 2003 tax increase referendum campaign should be considered a "thing of value."

"Gov., I simply want you to know that I am well aware that your Amendment One tax increase proposal was structured identically to the lottery referendum," Siegelman wrote. "While you also raised funds for an issue that was important to you, I stand firm in my belief that you committed no crime."

This was Siegelman the school-yard smarty-pants. A Riley spokesman said the ex-governor should "end his sideshow theatrics and let the jury do its job."

Chapter 34
The Motorcycle

"No. This was a Honda. I'm a Harley man."
-- Lanny Young, when asked if he purchased or had any interest in buying the Honda motorcycle at the center of the obstruction of justice charge against Siegelman.

"When have you ever needed two lawyers to draft up an agreement to sell a car or a motorcycle?"
-- Louis Franklin, during closing arguments, ridiculing the October 2001 meeting attended by Siegelman, Bailey and their lawyers, in which Siegelman finalized the sale of the bike to Bailey.

After the Jill Simpson ruckus, when the *New York Times*, *Time*, "60 Minutes," Congress and the liberal blogdom planted Don Siegelman in Karl Rove's torture chamber, all of the above attacked the presumed shortcomings of the HealthSouth case.

Anyone who came to the story fresh would not have known that Siegelman was also found guilty of obstruction of justice or known the first thing about the Lanny Young/Waste Management elements of the prosecution. In the rare instances when the obstruction charge was mentioned, that was all it was – mentioned. Siegelman never talked about it during his innumerable interviews. Rove, yes, the cover-up verdict, no.

For my money the presentation of the "motorcycle" case was the most entertaining element of the trial, in part because I knew so little going in.

The bike's existence was introduced in June 2003, in documents filed with Lanny and Nick's plea agreements. But the circumstances surrounding the motorcycle were vague then and remained so even after opening arguments.

Had Lanny bought the bike for Siegelman? It just wasn't clear.

When asked about it during trial Louis Franklin would smile and say that all would be revealed in time. Like good storytellers, the government teased its audience, made them wonder, and in the end, satisfied them with a resolution that made sense of it all. They did this by weaving testimony with bank records, leaving no doubt as to what occurred.

The FBI and Attorney General investigators who worked the Siegelman case vacuumed every conceivable record pertaining to the motorcycle and located obscure witnesses whose testimony the defense could neither refute nor impugn. It's conceivable the government could have won a guilty verdict on the charge even without the testimony of Young and Bailey.

In late 2000, Siegelman, a longtime motorcycle rider, cast a longing eye on one of Honda's top of the line bikes, the Valkyrie. He discussed the bike with Honda executives involved in building the company's SUV plant in Talladega County. Honda offered to give him the bike.

Siegelman declined. The cynic in me says he ran it by somebody and was told in no uncertain terms that he couldn't accept it. But I don't know that, so Siegelman gets credit for rejecting a substantial freebie.

The dealer who sold the motorcycle testified that Honda told him to sell it to Siegelman at $2,500 below the retail price. He did, and the governor was fine with that.

With bank officials as witnesses, the prosecution introduced a series of checks. Blown up versions were placed on a screen for jurors to see. The first was from Siegelman to the Honda dealer for $12,173.35, and dated Dec. 7, 1999. That was to buy the motorcycle.

This left a $3,076 balance in Siegelman's checking account.

Siegelman paid his taxes quarterly, and on Jan. 18, cut a check to the IRS for $5,940. That check was also shown to jurors, to whom it was clear that if Siegelman didn't make a deposit soon the check would bounce.

Siegelman summoned Lanny. The governor, according to Lanny, said he needed $9,200. He told Young to "get with Nick and work out the details."

Three checks, all dated Jan. 20, all super-sized for jurors, left no doubt what happened next.

The first was from Young to his bank, to withdraw $9,200 in cash. As directed by Nick, Lanny used the money to purchase a cashier's check payable to, "Nick Bailey." Though a cashier's check, it still included Young's name, as "remitter."

Bailey cashed it, then wrote a personal check for the same $9,200 and gave it to Siegelman. It wasn't made payable to Siegelman, but rather, Lori Allen.

"That's the name the governor asked me to write the check to," Bailey testified.

Lori Allen is Mrs. Siegelman's maiden name.

In the final act of the day, Siegelman cashed the Lori Allen check and deposited the $9,200 into his checking account.

Five days later the IRS check came home to roost. Steve Feaga, voice to rooftop, asked the bank witness to tell "the ladies and gentlemen" of the jury what would have happened if Siegelman hadn't made the $9,200 deposit.

The witness answered that the IRS check and a smaller one for Siegelman's state taxes that came through about the same time "would have bounced."

In cross-examining the bank witness, David McDonald pointed to records showing that in January 2000 Siegelman had more than $600,000 in a stock account and could easily have sold shares to cover the IRS check.

McDonald was doing the best he could with the hand dealt him, but his point was inane. Selling shares is a pain and if there's another option, you take it. In any event, the records left no doubt that within one-day's time Lanny gave the same $9,200 that Siegelman deposited.

When McDonald sat, Feaga pounced.

My lead the next day read:

Federal prosecutor Steve Feaga startled a quiet court here Thursday by loudly asking whether former Gov. Don Siegelman "was so arrogant and so crooked and so tight that he would take $9,200 from someone else" to prevent a check from bouncing.

That "someone else," according to prosecutors, was convicted political consultant and landfill developer Lanny Young.

Feaga's Thursday afternoon broadside -- delivered in the form of a question to Compass Bank records custodian Mona George -- followed statements by Siegelman lawyer David McDonald that the governor didn't need the $9,200.

Feaga knew the witness was in no position to answer yea or nay, but it was an effective bit of legal theatrics that woke up a jury numbed by numbers.

———

To me the most disturbing performance of the trial occurred during McDonald's questioning of Bailey on the "Lori Allen" check. Kilborn's understudy began by describing the day in 1984 when a drunk driver plowed into the Siegelmans' car, almost killing Lori Siegelman, breaking most of the bones in her face and costing her an eye.

This, from our story:

McDonald, his voice rising like an actor in high drama, glared and pointed at Bailey, so much so that one had to remind oneself that it wasn't Bailey – known for years as being like a member of the Siegelman family -- in the other car that day.

McDonald berated the witness for testifying that Siegelman – who had "cradled" his bloodied wife "in his arms" – would dare allow his wife's name to be used in an illegal transaction.

Bailey was told "the absurdity" of his testimony, since it would suggest that Siegelman would do such a thing as use his wife's name in the commission of a crime.

Bailey, who appeared unsure how to respond, didn't, in part because there was no real question to respond to.

It was a moment McDonald had clearly practiced, the grand scene that was to grab jurors by the heartstrings and, once and for all, turn them against Bailey. But the lawyer could not extinguish the fact that it was Siegelman, not Bailey, who cashed the check in his wife's name. Then Siegelman blessed McDonald's histrionics to sully Bailey in an attempt to win sympathy with jurors. It was my impression, and perhaps that of the jurors, that it was Siegelman and his lawyers, not Bailey, who were exploiting his wife's tragedy.

By using Bailey as the middle-man in the $9,200 payment and the cover-up of that payment, Siegelman inserted his devoted, hero-worshipping aide into a criminal act, same as he did on so many other occasions. Then, when he got caught, he blamed Bailey.

If Bailey would ever talk to me, the central question would be a painful one to ask: Does he think Siegelman used him?

———

All politicians who find themselves under investigation should post a sign on their bathroom mirrors that reads, "It's the cover-up, stupid."

They should make it their mantra. But Siegelman, like many before him, just couldn't leave bad enough alone.

Sixteen months after the Lanny to Nick to Siegelman transactions, Bill Pryor announced the joint state and federal investigation into G.H. Construction and the warehouse deal. Siegelman immediately knew he had problems, specifically, Lanny Young problems. It didn't take a fortune teller to foresee that the FBI would be combing through Lanny's every financial transaction going back years, and probably Bailey's and Siegelman's as well.

The cashier's check from Young to Bailey would glow like a torch, as would the $9,200 Lori Allen check.

In the environment that prosecutors must cope with, the January 2000 payment probably wasn't on its own a prosecutable federal crime unless the government could show an explicit quid pro quo. But there was no testimony, such as from Lanny, that Siegelman pledged to deliver a specific act in return for the $9,200.

Instead of laying low, Siegelman delivered himself into the hands of prosecutors with what he did next.

———

Shortly after our first stories and Pryor's announcement of an investigation, Bailey called Young in a panic. He asked if Lanny remembered how he'd made out the $9,200 check. "(Nick) said, 'Because if it's on one of your personal accounts, you are going to have a motorcycle in your driveway tonight,'" Young testified.

The apparent initial plan was to make Lanny seem to have been part-owner of the motorcycle from the start. Instead, a decision was made to place Lanny in the lender's seat and Bailey in the Honda's seat.

On June 5, 2001, Bailey wrote a check to Young for $10,503.39. At the bottom was his handwritten notation, "repayment of loan with interest" – the "interest" being the portion in addition to the $9,200.

This, like the other checks, was blown up and shown to jurors.

Bailey and Lanny testified that the payment was made in consultation with Siegelman. If investigators asked, they were to say that the January 2000 check was a loan from Lanny to Nick, with this check the repayment of that loan.

Seeing the check at trial recalled my interview with Siegelman five years before, at the Alabama State Docks. After blistering Lanny and others over the warehouse deal, he'd said with wink and nod, "The full story is not over yet."

I knew he was trying to co-opt me, to bring me over to his side. Yes, bad things happened, and they'll come out, but as you will see, they won't involve me.

Nick's "loan repayment" check to Lanny was cut on June 5, 2001. That was five days after my interview with Siegelman at the docks.

———

What Siegelman did next was, to employ one of my father's favorite sayings, too clever by half.

In mid-October, Siegelman and Bailey met at the office of Siegelman's long-time friend and personal lawyer Bobby Segall. Joining them was George Beck, a highly regarded criminal lawyer who was to represent Bailey through his 2003 plea and the 2006 trial.

With the lawyers looking on, Siegelman wrote a check for $2,973.35 to Bailey. The check contained the notation, "balance on m/c" – m/c being motorcycle.

At the same meeting Siegelman signed a bill of sale deeding the motorcycle to his confidential assistant.

Feaga asked the bank official who introduced the check to add the two checks -- the $9,200 Lori Allen check from January 2000 and the one from Bailey to Siegelman and written in Segall's office. The total, $12,173.35, was the same amount to the penny that Siegelman paid for the bike in December 1999.

Siegelman and Bailey hoped that investigators would believe that Nick borrowed $9,200 from Lanny – with Siegelman unaware of the source – to buy approximately three-fourths of the motorcycle; then Nick waited almost two years to buy the final fourth.

Outside court Siegelman said Bailey expressed interest in the motorcycle, which is why he sold it to him.

Kilborn and McDonald told a similar story to jurors. They said the October 2001 payment simply finalized Bailey's purchase of the bike that began 21 months before, with the Lori Allen check. None of which explained, for example, why Nick, in buying 3/4ths of a motorcycle, wrote a check to Lori Allen, not Don Siegelman.

This theory took a whipping from some convincing testimony by Bailey. He told jurors that he didn't ride motorcycles, had no wish to own one, and that his purchase of the bike from Siegelman was a ruse to conceal the purpose of the $9,200 payment from Lanny.

Neither of the lawyers at the October 2001 motorcycle sale finalization meeting was called to testify. Bailey said that he and Siegelman kept their lawyers in the dark regarding the true purpose of the sale. The pair apparently wanted their attorneys along to grant a sheen of legitimacy to the transaction.

Neither Segall nor Beck strike me as folk who fall off turnip trucks, and I suppose they played the defense lawyer game of, "don't ask, don't tell."

Siegelman told reporters there was no special reason he and Bailey summoned their attorneys to finalize the sale of a motorcycle. "It certainly wasn't to cover anything up," he said.

Franklin mocked the Siegelman story line during his closing argument. He looked at the jurors and told them that "each and every one of you has bought a car in your lifetime."

"When have you ever needed two lawyers to draft up an agreement to sell a car or a motorcycle?"

An insurance agent testified that the Honda Valkyrie was insured "for the pleasure use" of a 55-year-old operator. Siegelman was 55 at the time, and made the premium payments. That changed in August 2001, when Bailey paid half of that month's premium.

Bailey made the insurance payment, he said, after Siegelman told him to, to make it appear that Bailey was part-owner all along. Bailey's insurance payment also was intended to reinforce the storyline placing him in the saddle and boogieing around on the thing.

The prosecution called several witnesses who trashed additional alternating defense story lines. One was that Siegelman sold the bike to Bailey to conceal his ownership of it from the First Lady; the other was that the governor sold it to Bailey to pacify his wife, because motorcycles frightened her.

A security guard at Scrushy's mansion on Lake Martin came armed with a log-in sheet showing that the Siegelmans arrived on a Saturday morning in September 2001 and spent the night with the Scrushys. The visit occurred one month before the motorcycle sales meeting at Bobby Segall's office.

The guard testified that the couple pulled up on a motorcycle driven by the governor. Feaga asked if Lori Siegelman appeared nervous. The guard replied that she was smiling and happy.

The guard's story came with a bonus for prosecutors, as it seemed to give the lottery foundation charges a nudge forward, revealing as it did the full healing of the old Siegelman-Scrushy breach.

Feaga also showed jurors a photo of Lori Siegelman seated behind her husband on a motorcycle. Both were wearing helmets and grins.

Lastly, the government called the manager of the Honda dealership. He testified that Siegelman returned about a week after buying the motorcycle, this time with the first lady. The manager said he fitted Lori Siegelman for a specialized motorcycle helmet, which Siegelman ordered.

Though not introduced at trial, a story in the *Birmingham News* further illustrates that it wasn't the prosecutors but Siegelman, Kilborn and McDonald who were using Lori Siegelman. The story, "First Couple Leads on Harley," was published in September 2001, the month before the motorcycle sale finalization meeting. Here's the start and a few key portions:

FLORENCE - Don Siegelman and his wife Lori looked more like weekend motorcycle warriors Saturday than the governor and first lady of Alabama. The first couple, riding a black-and-chrome Harley Davidson Road King motorcycle, led more than 80,000 motorcycle riders from Florence to Waterloo on the last leg of the annual 230-mile Trail of Tears Commemorative Motorcycle Ride.

... The governor was dressed in blue jeans, a light blue denim shirt, brown leather boots and a black half-shell helmet and sunglasses. Mrs. Siegelman, sitting behind him on the motorcycle, wore a red helmet, black leather boots, cream-colored jeans and a black long-sleeve Harley Davidson T-shirt that had orange and red flames down both sleeves.

The Siegelmans borrowed the Harley Davidson they used Saturday, but the governor noted he had a motorcycle in college and two years ago he bought a Honda motorcycle after Honda decided to locate a vehicle plant in the state...

"He's very good or I wouldn't ride with him," Mrs. Siegelman said of her husband's motorcycle skills.

The ultimate disposition of the Valkyrie was revealed six months after the Siegelman trial, during an unrelated trial in Huntsville involving the systematic corruption within Alabama's two-year college system. Winston Hayes, the owner of a software company called Access Group, had admitted to paying kickbacks to officials in the system in return for millions of dollars in contracts.

Hayes, whose company won substantial amounts of business from the Siegelman administration, testified that he'd contributed to Siegelman campaigns but had never made illegal payments to the governor. He had, though, done Siegelman an unusual favor.

In early 2002, Siegelman called and asked if he would buy a motorcycle from Nick Bailey. Hayes did as requested and was startled when Bailey provided him with the bike's title history. As Hayes told jurors, he saw "that Don Siegelman had been the previous owner."

In December 2000, a year after Siegelman bought the motorcycle, he set his sights on a 4-wheeler for his son. Once again, he called on Lanny. Per the norm, he used Bailey as middle-man.

Joseph Siegelman was pals with Young's son. During visits to the Young's home, Siegelman's son rode their 4-wheeler and wanted one. The Honda dealer who sold Siegelman the motorcycle testified that the governor returned the following December with his son to look at 4-wheelers. However, the dealer told Siegelman he couldn't sell an ATV to anyone under 16.

Days later, Bailey called Lanny to tell him that Siegelman wanted a 4-wheeler for Joseph and a trailer to haul it.

Among the documents shown to jurors was a price quote from another store showing that on Dec. 14, 2000, Lanny asked about a Polaris Magnum 4-wheeler and a trailer. At the top was the handwritten notation, "Governor Don Siegelman." That notation was made by Audie Ward, owner of Ward Motor Sales in Troy.

Ward testified to getting a call from Young and negotiating what he called a good price for the ATV and trailer that Young told him was for the governor. Ward never spoke to Siegelman, he said.

On Dec. 19, Siegelman sent Young a note thanking him for his "thoughtful gift," even though Lanny had yet to buy it.

A few days later Bailey called Lanny from Jack Miller's home in the Virgin Islands. The Siegelmans were spending Christmas there, accompanied by Nick.

Bailey told Young that Siegelman wanted the 4-wheeler to be at the mansion when they returned because he was taking his son hunting in south Alabama. The governor also needed Lanny to acquire a license tag for the trailer.

The ever-helpful Young went into action.

On Dec. 27, 2000, he paid $5,324 for the 4-wheeler and trailer and delivered them to the mansion. That same day he bought a tag at the county revenue office. He put the trailer in the name of Don Siegelman.

There was no separate obstruction charge involving the ATV, though the government put on evidence showing efforts were made to clean up the Lanny trail there as well.

In November 2001, the highway department was summoned to the mansion to retrieve a used, banged-up 4-wheeler and trailer that it neither needed nor wanted. For reasons clarified by hindsight, the resident of the mansion wanted them the hell out.

Records were jigged by someone unknown to reflect that the ATV and trailer were bought by the mansion. However, there were no payment records to back this up. The only payment records showed Lanny buying it, so Siegelman and his lawyers had to come up with something different at trial.

Jurors were told that the governor never asked for the 4-wheeler, that Lanny gave it entirely of his own accord, and that the gift surprised the governor.

It wasn't disputed, even by Siegelman, that late in his first year as governor he asked Lanny to pay for 1,000 coffee mugs the Siegelmans wanted to send to friends as Christmas presents. The first lady had selected a design. Siegelman asked Lanny to meet with his wife at the mansion, which he did.

The cost of printing and buying the mugs came to $13,453, which Lanny paid.

With Lanny on the stand, Feaga went for the irony angle, asking him to read the inscription on the mugs. "Thank you for helping Alabama believe in itself again," read Lanny.

Since they couldn't deny it or come up with a cover story transferring the onus to Lanny or Nick, Siegelman and his lawyers defended the mug deal with sarcasm and anger.

"Do you dare tell the jury that Lori Allen Siegelman was involved in a bribe for those mugs?" Kilborn barked at Lanny.

Young didn't skip a beat. "I would not say that, sir, but if you want to say that, that's fine."

Sarcasm was more effective. Outside court, Kilborn held up one of the mugs to the cameras. "This thing's so cheap, even the Chinese wouldn't put their name on it," he quipped. He belittled the mugs before jurors as well.

The prosecutors would have been better off stacking $13,000 in cash before the jurors, but as it was, they were stuck with a coffee cup.

Had the government provided scripts to Nick and Lanny, as the defense kept telling jurors was the case, then the pair could easily have connected the gifts to favors. For example, Lanny could have said, "Siegelman told me that if I gave him the $9,200, he would make sure I was picked to be the contractor on the warehouse project."

The prosecution did not allege nor was their evidence supporting specific quid pro quo arrangements connecting the gifts with official action. But the motorcycle, 4-wheeler and mugs did support the overarching case of an arrangement wherein Lanny was expected to give, and in return, get.

Chapter 35
Quid Pro Rico and the
Absolute Agreement

"We had an agreement – when Lanny asked us for something, we produced it and when we asked for something, Lanny produced it."

-- *Testimony by Nick Bailey regarding the conspiracy/RICO counts alleging a criminal conspiracy involving Hamrick, Siegelman, Bailey and Lanny Young.*

"It's the worst-drafted RICO I've ever seen. You find as much trash as you can, then you dump it in."

-- *G. Robert Blakey, Notre Dame law professor, expert on the Racketeer Influenced and Corrupt Organization Act (RICO) and a member of Siegelman's defense team, in quote given to the New York Times a year after the trial.*

What constitutes the bribing of a public official?

That seemingly simple question was at the heart of the Siegelman case and the post-verdict reporting and commentary on his conviction.

Siegelman and those who joined his army after Jill Simpson's affidavit relentlessly characterized the two $250,000 contributions at the heart of the HealthSouth case as routine campaign donations. From there, they asserted that Siegelman was prosecuted for acts no different than any other politician when raising campaign funds.

As Siegelman told the *New York Times* in a spring 2008 interview, if his conviction was upheld, then "every governor and every president and every contributor might as well turn themselves in, because it's going to be open season on them."

In consideration of the national controversy regarding the Siegelman case, the author deems that it will be instructive to explain the federal bribery statutes that were the basis of most of the guilty counts against Siegelman and Scrushy.

In March 2009, when the 11th Circuit Court of Appeals upheld the convictions of both men, it noted that the $500,000 helped Siegelman pay off a $730,000 loan to the lottery foundation for which he was a personal guarantor. As such, the two $250,000 checks satisfied the personal benefit standard, even though, as the judges stated, that standard wasn't necessary for conviction.

For the sake of argument, let's pretend there was no personal benefit – in other words, no loan guaranteed by Siegelman. Furthermore, imagine that the two contributions were properly reported to the secretary of state and the Internal

Revenue Service, as of course they were not. We will also suspend disbelief and ignore the long strange trip of the first $250,000 check, from Integrated Health in Maryland by way of UBS Securities in New York; down to Scrushy's office at HealthSouth; into Siegelman's hands in Montgomery; the long stay-over at Darren Cline's apartment; the check's return to Siegelman and, lastly, its deposit into a Birmingham bank.

Instead, let's analyze the half-million dollars handed Scrushy to Siegelman as their lawyers and Siegelman's supporters in the national media and the U.S. House Judiciary Committee presented it.

As best as I can tell, their position is that the giving and receiving of a campaign contribution *does not* constitute a crime; that for a public official to be guilty of bribery, he or she must *personally benefit*, such as from a bag of cash delivered underneath a table.

That is, thank goodness, not the case. Among other things, the Siegelman position presumes the non-existence of what are commonly called campaign finance laws.

To illustrate the fallacy of their position, here are two fictional examples of the giving of money to a politician. One is a crime, the other is not.

Example One: Bob, the owner of Bridge Engineering, Inc., visits Gov. John Doe and gives him a personal check for $1 million. Not a campaign donation, mind you, but money for the governor to spend as he pleases, such as to pay off gambling debts.

A month later, Gov. Doe orders his highway director to award a $15 million contract to Bridge Engineering, claiming he's heard great things about the firm.

A year later, federal investigators learn of the two transactions – the giving of the $1 million and the awarding of the $15 million contract. However, they are unable to disprove the claims by governor and businessman that during the pivotal meeting the pair discussed the weather and the upcoming Alabama-Auburn game.

Example Two: Sam, the owner of a small company that cuts grass along state highways, visits Governor Doe to seek his help regarding a dispute with the highway department. Sam tells the governor that the department is refusing to pay $3,000 in charges incurred when his company was asked to cut additional grass not included in his contract. He makes a strong case that his little business deserves the money. He is simply asking for the state to treat him fairly.

The governor tells Sam he will guarantee that his company gets its money, on one condition: That Sam contribute $250 to his re-election campaign. Soon thereafter, Sam sends the governor's campaign a $250 check. His company gets its $3,000 payment and the governor reports Sam's donation to the secretary of state.

Federal investigators find evidence indicating that the $3,000 payment to Sam's company was contingent upon his $250 campaign donation.

The first example is $1 million into the governor's pocket. The second is a $250 campaign contribution. Which is a violation of federal bribery statutes?

It's the $250 donation. Sam gave the contribution after being told he must in order to get his company's overtime money. Thus, the elements were there for a quid pro quo – Latin for "something for something" – and that is what is necessary to convict a public official of bribery.

That the $250 campaign donation led to a provable crime while the $1 million gift did not may violate our sense of the way things should be. But that's the way it is. Like it or not, those are the rules that prosecutors must abide by when seeking to bring bribery-based charges against public officials.

If anything, courts have in recent years made it harder to convict public officials of bribery. There was a time when example one would have constituted bribery, but a host of appellate court rulings, to the vexation of prosecutors, have placed a high hurdle on bribery or quid pro quo cases.

That's why Lanny Young's payment of $25,000 to Paul Hamrick so Siegelman's chief of staff could drive a new BMW did not on its own satisfy the standards for a bribery charge. There was no evidence linking the $25,000 to a specific act by Hamrick, and the government acknowledged as much.

That's why the payment – which so clearly entailed personal benefit – was not brought as an extortion (flipside of bribery) charge against Hamrick.

However, the prosecutors did claim – and prove to the jury's satisfaction – a quid pro quo between Scrushy and Siegelman on the two $250,000 checks to the lottery foundation.

The primary testimony from the important witnesses on the HealthSouth case has been presented throughout the book. Jurors, for example, heard from former executives with HealthSouth, the investment bank UBS and Maryland-based Integrated Healthcare. Each told about their roles in the hurried, convoluted and black-mail infested $250,000 donation from Integrated Health to the lottery foundation.

Much of that testimony – such as by UBS banker William McGahan – was powerful, as when McGahan recalled being told by HealthSouth's Mike Martin that he "was going to be fucked" if UBS didn't contribute $250,000 to the foundation.

Another strong prosecution witness was Darren Cline, the fundraising consultant hired to work on the lottery campaign. Among other things, Cline testified to his surprise at seeing the $250,000 check from Integrated Health and his instructions from Siegelman and Bailey to hold on to the check and not deposit it.

Charles Grainger was among the witnesses whose testimony demolished the story-line that the foundation's failure to report $740,000 in donations was an innocent oversight by those chosen by Siegelman to run the foundation. The secretary of state lawyer told jurors about the role our stories played in exposing the foundation; and how he and the attorney general's office had to force a recalcitrant Siegelman to disclose the donations, including the $500,000 involving Scrushy.

Aside from Bailey, the most important witness on the HealthSouth case was Loree Skelton. She was the HealthSouth lawyer who came to Montgomery in 1999 with Scrushy. She testified to waiting outside Siegelman's office with others, Bailey included, during the 30 minute meeting between Scrushy and Siegelman. State Sen. Jabo Waggoner also testified to being there and seeing Scrushy and Siegelman go into Siegelman's office and leave the rest of them waiting outside. While there was some question as to the date of this meeting – a red herring the defense built its defense on exploiting -- there was no doubt that the meeting occurred.

Skelton seemed to remain in thrall of Scrushy, and it may be that her testimony was that much more creditable because of it. She frequently meandered and backtracked, and to general questions – such as if she had witnessed a crime – said she had not. But boiled down to its main points, Skelton's testimony was very damaging to Scrushy and, by extension, Siegelman.

She told jurors how important it was to Scrushy for HealthSouth to be on the governor's good side; to have a position on the state Certificate of Need board; and to stay abreast of everything that board did. For example, she testified that one of her stock assignments was to research the backgrounds of all appointees to the CON board and to find out why governors appointed them. She was also tasked with reviewing all applications for hospital expansion and major equipment purchases that the board exists to review and approve or deny, not just in the Birmingham area, but throughout the state.

Perhaps most importantly, Skelton was in charge of political affairs on the state level for the company. As such, she was involved in decisions about contributions, such as which legislators and gubernatorial candidates HealthSouth would support, and how much the company would give them.

Skelton told jurors that she had never known HealthSouth to make a donation as large as $250,000. Particularly damning was the revelation that she wasn't consulted or even told about the $250,000 from Integrated Health or the second $250,000 from the company. She said she didn't learn about either until more than two years after they were made, and then not until I called HealthSouth in July 2002 asking if it had donated to the lottery foundation.

Scrushy's decision to conceal the $500,000 from Skelton "speaks volumes," Louis Franklin said after her testimony.

Scrushy, who appeared to recognize the harm done, told reporters that Skelton "was not the keeper of the checkbook – she would not have known about a lot of things."

But a number of government witnesses on the "HealthSouth case" fizzled. I think Scrushy had an improper if not illegal sway over the CON board and its processes, but the prosecution couldn't prove it. One problem was that neither the board's top employee nor any one on the board wanted to admit that Scrushy had more influence than any other members.

In any event, much time and tedious testimony was spent in a failed effort to turn Scrushy into the magical wizard who controlled the board.

In December 2005, two months after release of the indictment, the grand jury met one last time and added two final charges against Scrushy and Siegelman. Both regarded payments made by HealthSouth to Tim Adams, a young nurse from Blountsville, Ala., and like Scrushy, a Siegelman appointee to the CON board.

The Adams case hinged almost entirely on Skelton's testimony.

Adams didn't testify – wasn't called by the prosecution or defendants -- but the worst actor in the Adams portion of the case was Adams. The evidence and testimony showed that once on the board, he came to HealthSouth with hands open. Skelton called him "a pest." She testified he "was constantly asking for things, to go to events with Mr. Scrushy, hunting, air shows."

From the start he sought and was granted rides to CON board meetings with Scrushy on HealthSouth's helicopter. Skelton testified that she warned Scrushy about Adams, telling him that the helicopter trips could raise the appearance of a conflict. Scrushy, though, told her to keep Adams happy. When Adams asked Skelton for a job, she went back to Scrushy and told him that hiring Adams would violate CON board rules.

Scrushy, though, insisted that she take care of Adams. Scrushy didn't want to anger the nurse, who could create problems by casting votes contrary to HealthSouth's best interests.

Adams turned down Skelton's first offer – a job as a scrub nurse. He told her that he'd started a side business as a consultant writing proposals for, of all things, CON board applications. She hired him, at $8,000, to write a CON application for a mobile PET scanner HealthSouth was seeking. His work was so sorry it had to be re-done by company staff.

Adams was represented as having been appointed by Siegelman because he was the governor's friend. He obviously had no business on any government board. Not only was he essentially blackmailing a fellow board member and major healthcare company, but he was selling his services as a writer of applications to the very board on which he sat.

Several months after being paid $8,000, Adams called Skelton to inform her that he was out of state and would miss the July 2002 CON board meeting. But HealthSouth needed him there. Without Adams there wouldn't be a quorum. That would delay a vote on the company's request for permission to build a 38-bed hospital in Phenix City.

Adams said he would go, but for a price. He asked for more money and Skelton agreed to pay him an additional $3,000 for his sorry consulting work.

Good to his word, Adams attended the meeting, created a quorum, and voted for the project, which passed.

Under cross-examination by defense lawyers Skelton said she didn't apprise Scrushy of the details of her decision to hire Adams as a consultant, and said Scrushy wasn't involved in payment decisions.

As the prosecution did with other witnesses who, face-to-face with defendants and their lawyers backed off their stronger grand jury testimony, Franklin took a harsh tack when the defense handed back the witness.

Franklin gave Skelton a transcript of the testimony she'd given the grand jury and demanded that she read it. Skelton, upon being ordered by Franklin to review it, acknowledged telling the grand jury that Scrushy gave her a "major directive" to keep Adams happy; and that she stopped giving Scrushy the details of the Adams' arrangements because she realized it "wouldn't do any good."

Franklin turned potential disaster into victory with his aggressive re-cross of the reluctant witness.

In one of my stories I observed that the, "Adams' element of the case against Scrushy doesn't appear to involve Siegelman." I note this to support my position that my coverage was fair to Siegelman.

In March 2009, the 11th Circuit threw out two of seven charges against Siegelman. They were the two pertaining to Adams. The same charges, though, were upheld for Scrushy. I thought it a wise decision by the court, and an indication of just how thorough can be appellate review.

One problem Franklin and Feaga faced is that by the time they assumed control over the investigation – in early 2004 – many of the acts they probably would have liked to prosecute were no longer on the table for statute of limitations reasons. They solved this problem – as well as the obstacles presented by the high standard of proof for quid pro quo arrangements – by charging Siegelman and Hamrick with violations of the RICO statute.

RICO allows the government to claw back acts taken within the previous 10 years if those acts are deemed to be part of an alleged criminal conspiracy.

This set of laws, initially designed to tackle organized crime – as in, the mafia – was passed by Congress in 1970. In the late 1980s prosecutors began applying RICO to prosecutions of people with no connection to the Costa Nostra. Among the first non-mafia RICO defendants was investment banker Michael Milken, who was charged with RICO violations pertaining to insider trading and other charges.

The RICO counts against Siegelman and Hamrick alleged that those two and Bailey had what Bailey testified was an "absolute agreement" with Lanny Young.

Lanny, according to the prosecution, had an arrangement whereby he asked for and received an array of favors in return for payments, gifts and campaign contributions to the three public officials who were taking care of him.

A major problem for the government was the lack of a meeting at which such an agreement was formalized. Had the prosecutors been coaching Bailey and Young as the defense lawyers never tired of claiming, one assumes that the government and its two star witnesses could easily have concocted a place and time for an "absolute agreement" meeting and delivered some choice quotes.

"We each pricked a finger, and sealed the deal in blood."

Something like that.

About as close as the government came was testimony by Lanny regarding a comment to him by Siegelman before the 1998 election. "If I get to be governor, there are things I can do for you, things I can do for your company," Siegelman said, according to Lanny.

When Feaga asked Lanny why Hamrick helped him, Young said, "If I had money he would have access for money, if I had no money he would have no access to money."

What the prosecution lacked in evidence proving a sharply defined arrangement it made up for – or so I felt – with mounds of evidence supporting the fruits of such an agreement for all four parties.

The evidence was overwhelming that Lanny gave cash and valuable gifts to each of the three public officials – Siegelman, Bailey and Hamrick -- and that they used their public positions to help enrich Lanny.

One of the more telling moments came during a grumpy turn on the stand by Bill Blount. As described in an earlier chapter, the investment banker took a call in 2000 from Siegelman while dining at a Montgomery restaurant. The governor – delegating like an honest to goodness RICO-style mafia kingpin -- told Blount to expect a call from Hamrick.

Hamrick, as promised, called Blount right after Siegelman hung up. The governor's chief of staff explained his friend Lanny's grim financial situation and asked –on behalf of Siegelman as well as him – for Blount to help.

Blount promptly arranged for $2 million in loans to Lanny. That included his signing on as a guarantor for the largest loan, for $1.4 million.

Some fair-minded trial observers may not agree, but I believe that the prosecution made a convincing case that, stated or not, there existed something along the lines of an "absolute agreement" between the "inner circle," and that the arrangement resulted in criminal acts by all four men.

However, some of the alleged "sub-acts" within the RICO counts made little sense. For example, the defendants were accused of in some way effectuating a fax of Siegelman's resume from Lanny in Montgomery to a Waste Management official in Atlanta. The waste executive asked for the resume because he wanted to know more about Alabama's governor before meeting him.

To me and I suppose jurors as well, the faxing of a resume did not meet the criteria of a crime. Worse, the prosecutors never explained why the jury should find it so. My sense is that the inclusion of the fax and some other odd "sub-acts" within the overall RICO charges worked against the government. The jury, after all, was asked to find guilt of the entire charge, not just part of it.

As or more problematic were the charges pertaining to the tax cut at Emelle.

Franklin and Feaga spent considerable time and effort making what was unquestionably a rock-solid case that without the Governor's Men, Lanny could never have achieved the tax break at Emelle that allowed him to make a fast half-million bucks. And yet, having done so, they failed to connect that powerful evidence and testimony to the actual charges. Perhaps that was because the actual charges were, well, goofy.

Specifically, Hamrick and Siegelman were charged with the same three counts of "honest services mail fraud." Each count stated that the defendants were guilty of placing or causing the following to be put in the U.S. mail: "Hazardous Waste Fee Report mailed from a facility in Emelle, AL, to the Alabama Department of Revenue in Montgomery, AL."

The charges were the same but for the dates on which the three annual reports were mailed from Waste Management's operation in Emelle to the state tax agency in Montgomery.

I was exceedingly familiar with the Emelle matter, having studied the hell out of it and written the stories exposing it. I witnessed the effective presentation of the Emelle case, especially against Siegelman. Despite that, I didn't understand the actual charges or their relevance to what was proven.

I doubt Siegelman or Hamrick knew what a Hazardous Waste Fee Report was until they read that they participated in some fashion with sending or causing such reports to be mailed. There was, for example, no evidence presented at trial showing or even suggesting that Hamrick or Siegelman had ever seen the reports.

These same honest services mail fraud counts – as with the mailing of Siegelman's resume -- were among the acts included in the RICO counts. All were, at best, tangentially related to actions the prosecution did prove. The problem, again, wasn't with the evidence, but the charges themselves.

––––

Two "absolute agreement" witnesses in particular helped break the monotony that developed over six weeks of testimony. One was Lanny's former pilot; the other, his former secretary.

I had tried years before to interview the pilot, John Sanzo, after seeing on Alacourt that he'd sued Lanny for failing to pay him. Sanzo refused to speak to me, so his testimony was a revalation.

He produced a chart showing flights in which Siegelman, Hamrick and Bailey were listed as the lead passenger. Siegelman was lead passenger on 47 flights. That didn't mean he was the only one on the flight, only that he was designated lead passenger. Hamrick was so designated on seven flights and Bailey on two, for a total cost of $46,584.

Not shown were the number of times when Lanny was the lead passenger, and when others – primarily Hamrick – would have been on board.

The Sanzo flights occurred between 1996 and 1998, and all or in any event most of those in which Siegelman was shown as lead passenger were properly disclosed on the governor's campaign forms.

Sanzo's raciest testimony came in response to questions about a flight to Anniston to retrieve Hamrick. He said the Siegelman aide pulled up to the airport in a limousine, accompanied by two women. Hamrick had been partying at the Platinum Club, the Anniston strip bar.

Lanny had previously testified to paying for limousines to cart Hamrick to the club. After Sanzo's strip club testimony, Hamrick knew reporters would be coming his way, and handled it well. He was, he said, single at the time and, yes, had on occasion patronized the Platinum Club.

"I guess they (prosecutors) keep bringing it up because it makes me look bad," he said.

The testimony of Beth Crain, Lanny's secretary, was entertaining primarily for the build-up preceding it. Hamrick lawyer Jeff Deen pleaded with Fuller to let him ask Crain if Lanny had paid for her to have breast enhancement surgery. The judge refused to let him go there. But the debate was such that it was impossible not to look at Crain's chest when she walked into court – and that's not just me talking. Reporters and trial regulars, female as well as male, said the same.

A year or so before, Crain sent me a rambling, rage-fueled e-mail with as many exclamation points as words. It bore the title, "You and Corrupt Journalism." She called me, among other things a *"TWO FACED, SELFISH AND NOT TO MENTION JUDAS REPORTER!!!!!!!!!"*

And elsewhere: *"Do you have ANY INTEGRITY?------------PLEASE REMEMBER!,------ YOU HAVE MANY.MANY SKELETONS IN YOUR PAST!!!!!!!!!!!!!!!!!"*

I didn't hold it against her. She was loyal to Lanny, my reporting had negatively impacted his life, and she hated me for it.

Crain testified that Hamrick frequently called the office, she passed him through to Lanny, and those calls often led to requests from Young that she go to the bank and withdraw cash. At least once he told her the money was for Hamrick.

Prosecutor J.B. Perrine led Crain through an appointment book she kept for Young. It listed numerous meetings with Siegelman. One, in July 1999, was the day before the Revenue Department slashed the hazardous waste taxes at Emelle.

Crain testified that she had on many occasions accompanied Lanny, Hamrick and others for drinks and food at Bud's and Sinclair's, and couldn't recall a single time when Hamrick paid. It was always Lanny.

There were also tickets to athletic events, all on Lanny, and for Siegelman as well as Hamrick. Crain told jurors she sat next to Siegelman in the presidential suite at Talladega Superspeedway during one of the races there; and recalled a 1999 trip by Lanny and Siegelman to New York for that year's Winston Cup awards ceremony at the Waldorf Historia, it too paid for by Lanny.

While in New York with Siegelman, Lanny called Crain and read a press release he'd fashioned. She transcribed it and sent it to the governor's press office. The release, issued by the governor's office, told the people of Alabama that Siegelman was the first governor ever invited to NASCAR's premier awards ceremony. Siegelman was quoted extolling driver Dale Jarrett. The release, it being ghost-written by Lanny, reported that the governor was accompanied at this great event by Alabama businessman Lanny Young.

After Crain's testimony, Siegelman told reporters that he attended the NASCAR awards ceremony to help recruit business to the state. He said he couldn't remember if Lanny paid for the trip.

That same day Siegelman told reporters that he met only once with Lanny during his tenure as governor, that being the occasion when he asked Young to help the First Lady design and order the Christmas gift mugs.

———

A number of witnesses, like Washington-based Waste Management lobbyist Lisa Kardell, gave testimony that wasn't intended on its own describe a crime but rather to support the "absolute agreement" case. Kardell told of meeting Hamrick in Washington D.C., with Siegelman's chief of staff telling her that, "Lanny Young was doing a great job for Waste Management in Alabama and (Waste Management) would regret letting him go."

At the time the company was in the midst of cancelling some lobbying contracts and Kardell saw Hamrick's comment as a veiled threat that there might be consequences in Alabama if Waste Management ceased using Lanny. It concerned her enough that she told the company's vice president for government affairs.

Kardell also testified about a letter from Siegelman to a Waste Management executive that was shown to jurors. At the bottom was a hand-written note. "Lanny Young is doing a good job for you in Alabama," it read.

Kardell said it was unusual for Waste Management to receive letters from governors, especially with handwritten notes praising lobbyists.

Phillip Jordan, the corrupt former probate judge of Cherokee County, testified to conversations with Siegelman and Hamrick about the county's landfill. He said Siegelman called about the time the county commission was considering changes to the landfill contract that would expanded the area from which Waste Management could accept garbage and reduce the fees it paid the county. Waste

Management had secretly promised to pay Lanny $3 million if he the commission made the two changes.

"We have a mutual friend involved in a project up there and anything you can do would be appreciated," Siegelman told Jordan.

During the same time frame, Jordan ran into Hamrick at the Alabama Sheriff's Association office in Montgomery, and the Siegelman aide motioned him into a small office.

"He told me if we could help Lanny with some changes, there would be some good things for Cherokee County," Jordan testified.

Jordan told Hamrick he anticipated those "changes" happening.

The landfill contract was amended, after which Waste Management wired $1 million to Lanny, and a couple of months later, another $2 million.

Later, Jordan called Hamrick after Lanny ceased making his promised bribe payments. "I told (Hamrick) our friend Lanny Young had some unfinished business in Cherokee County and I asked him about 'lighting a fire under Lanny,'" Jordan testified.

Lanny made some of those payments, though not immediately after the call. Jordan acknowledged that in those conversations neither he, Siegelman nor Hamrick specifically mentioned bribes or even what it was that Siegelman and Hamrick wanted Jordan to do for Lanny.

Had the discussions been more specific it would have been worse for Siegelman and Hamrick. On the other hand, the lack of specificity suggests that there was no need to spell things out since each of the parties well knew what Lanny needed from Jordan and what Jordan expected in return.

Other "absolute agreement" evidence indicated that Bill Blount paid Lanny $35,000 after Lanny contacted Hamrick on Blount's behalf and helped Blount's firm win placement on a state-related bond issue.

On Jan. 10, 2001, Siegelman signed off on a recommendation from Henry Mabry that the state build warehouses for ADECA and the liquor board.

Siegelman has stuck with his story that he never asked Mabry or anyone else who was going to build the warehouses, where the money was to come from, or for that matter, asked any questions at all about the $20 million-plus warehouse project. On this one, we were to believe that the detail man just wasn't interested.

Young testified to having told Hamrick about the warehouses, but on this point, Hamrick came out rosy. Hamrick suggested holding a press conference to announce the two warehouses. To me, this indicated that at least at this early stage Hamrick was not aware of all the rotten details. If so, it's unlikely he would have recommended putting the deal out there for all to see with a press conference. As it was, wiser heads nixed Hamrick's idea.

Young also testified that he talked to Siegelman about the project, but there was no documentation supporting that. So try as they might, the government couldn't prove beyond a shadow of a doubt that Siegelman knew his administration hired Lanny and G.H. Construction to build the warehouses.

Siegelman claimed he didn't learn about Lanny's role until I called asking about it.

I don't believe the point was made at trial but my first calls were in late March or early April 2001. At no time in the next four weeks – during which there was no question Siegelman knew about Lanny's involvement -- did he move to cancel the project or remove Lanny from it. The theft of at least $90,000 through the bogus CDG bill was revealed during the second of my three meetings with administration officials. That didn't prompt Siegelman to fire Lanny and G.H. Construction or to halt the bond sale, which was a go until I sent his press office a letter spelling out exactly what I intended to report. Only then was the bond sale – and with it, the project -- killed.

To accept Siegelman's story, one must believe that Bailey, Bill Blount, Roland Vaughan, Henry Mabry and many others as well concealed Lanny's involvement in the warehouse project from The Boss.

I don't buy it, not for a second, but there was no compelling evidence presented to jurors proving otherwise.

Chapter 36
Siegelman 17, Government 0

"And (Siegelman) said, 'Well, you're a businessman and for you to operate you've got to have money. You've got to have cash coming in, you've got to have money ... Then he said, 'But think about it like this. I'm a businessman, too ... but my business is being the governor and running for governor ... He says, 'I have to have money to operate too."
-- Forrest "Mac" Marcato, inventor of the highway striping product RainLine, recalling a September 2002 call during which the governor asked Marcato to donate $250,000 to his campaign.

"A check in the amount of $36,300 from a contractor in Huntsville, AL, to RainLine Corporation in Montgomery, AL."
-- One of 16 similar and oddly-crafted charges accusing Roberts and Siegelman of honest services mail fraud, none of which resonated with jurors.

Among the few factually accurate arguments employed post-Jill Simpson to bolster the "political prosecution" theory was the number of counts on which the government failed to secure conviction. Siegelman was, as the Judiciary Committee noted in its 2008 report on selective prosecution, acquitted on 25 of the 32 charges (and post-appeal, the score fell to five guilty, 27 not guilty.)

The tally would not have been so lopsided but for the government's decision to prosecute former transportation director Mack Roberts -- and Siegelman along with him -- in the highway department or "RainLine" portion of the trial. There wasn't anything nefarious in the decision. It just wasn't very smart.

The government made a strong case that the extraordinary sum of $84 million was, if not wasted, spent for the wrong reasons and could have been used to far more effect elsewhere. But there were a host of problems with the "highway department" case, among them a failure – as with the Emelle charges -- to connect the evidence to the counts that prosecutors asked jurors to find guilt on.

To the prosecutions credit, the highway department evidence pulled back the curtain on seedy political practices in this hugely important state agency and the easy wealth that comes to those simply for having friends in high places. It was another slice of Alabama government under Don Siegelman.

―――

Jim Allen's rags to toll bridge builder story began in his garage, where he made cabinets. He created a thriving business then developed a technology to make them faster. He parlayed the process into great wealth with the sale of his company in 1988, at age 32.

In the early 1990s, anticipating Montgomery's growth, Allen developed an upscale residential community called Emerald Mountain. It was two miles from Montgomery as the crow flies but a half-hour journey by car because of the Tallapoosa River.

His first toll bridge, the Emerald Mountain Parkway, was built to enhance his development by shortening the drive, and opened in 1994.

Officials in Millbrook, a Montgomery-area town, asked Allen to build a bridge over the Alabama River. He agreed and advanced full-bore into the toll-bridge business. He hired Roberts to oversee construction of that bridge and future endeavors.

In the late 1990s, Tuscaloosa County leaders sought Allen's help with their transportation needs. His third bridge, a $17 million span over the Black Warrior River, opened in October 1998.

Toll bridges, to state the obvious, succeed or fail based on the number of drivers that use them. They invariably require the assistance of local governments, such as to encourage drivers to use to the bridges and, when necessary, build roads to them.

––––

The bulk of the highway department case radiated from two meetings, one in October 1998, the second in January 1999.

The first occurred weeks before the 1998 election, when Siegelman entertained Allen and Roberts at supporter Anthony Fant's Birmingham antique store. At the time, Allen desparately needed the state to build a road to his new bridge in Tuscaloosa. He simply could not afford to be on the wrong side of the governor, whoever it was.

Allen, as described in an earlier chapter, told jurors that Siegelman berated him for donating to Fob James, yelling: "You have not helped me one bit in this campaign, and I'm going to remember it."

Siegelman demanded that Allen donate $100,000, but Allen pleaded penury. Siegelman, according to Allen, said: "Will you give me $40,000, and if you give me $40,000, I will let you pick the next highway director."

Allen said he could. After the meeting he had Roberts monitor the polls. When it became clear that Siegelman would win the election, Allen – as directed by the Siegelman campaign – cut nine checks of $4,444 apiece to political action committees run by lobbyist Johnny Crawford.

The day before the election Allen and Roberts delivered the checks to Siegelman. This required Siegelman to give the checks to Crawford, who -- after washing them in his PAC money-laundering operation – contributed the same amount to the

Siegelman's campaign, thus concealing Allen as the source of the money. (This being a perfect example of the need for a law banning PAC-to-PAC transfers, but no such law will ever pass as long as Democrats control the state senate.)

After the election Siegelman appointed Allen to his highway department transition team. But even Allen didn't claim he told Siegelman to hire Roberts. Rather, Siegelman called him, told him he planned to appoint Roberts and asked for – and received -- Allen's blessing.

Outside court Siegelman ridiculed the idea that he'd let anyone, much less a "jerk" like Allen name the highway director in return for campaign contributions. I think he would, but it would take a helluva lot more than $40,000.

The second pivotal meeting was between Roberts and Allen in early January 1999, shortly before Roberts left Allen's employ to become highway director. Allen gave Roberts a check for $71,000, which was $110,000 minus taxes and other deductions. This allowed Roberts' lawyer David McKnight to crack in closing that if one believed the government's theory, then Allen's payment to Roberts was "the first bribe in the history of America they paid taxes on."

Allen also let Roberts keep his company car, and later, took a small loss by buying Roberts's house.

During the meeting or thereabouts, Allen told Roberts that he was getting into a second business, marketing a paint-striping product called RainLine. He also informed the soon-to-be-highway director that Burke-Kleinpeter, a Louisiana-based engineering firm, had engaged him to help win contracts with the department.

Allen testified that Roberts told him he would try to make sure the state used RainLine; and said he felt comfortable that Roberts would look out for his new bridge in Tuscaloosa.

Two months after becoming governor Siegelman joined Roberts and Tuscaloosa officials in announcing a $12 million project to build a road connecting a state highway to Allen's new bridge over the Black Warrior River.

Republican leaders, among them Steve Windom, howled that the road was a "payoff" to State Sen. Phil Poole. The Democrat from Tuscaloosa County was the final fence sitter in the vitally important battle over control of the state senate. By joining his fellow Democrats, Poole ended that battle, and with it, Windom's hopes of running the senate.

A week later, Phil Rawls added a new angle. The veteran AP reporter wrote a story raising the specter of a conflict of interest on the part of Siegelman's highway director. Phil reported that Roberts – who'd approved the new road -- had only months before ceased working for Jim Allen.

Phil noted that the road hadn't been in the state's five-year plan. This meant it leapt untold other projects, all of which, to the backers in their communities, were equally as vital as was the Tuscaloosa road to that area's leaders. Roberts, in a moment of frankness he had to regret, told Rawls that Allen's $17 million bridge was "losing a lot of money each month."

"It's not doing half what it needs to do for the cash flow," he said.

The quote reflected that the new highway director was acutely aware of and concerned about the financial situation of what was, after all, a businessman's investment, taken with risk and no promise of success. It was not the taxpayers' responsibility to ensure that Allen's bridge survived, much less profited.

That quote was the reason the prosecution called Rawls as a witness – to testify to its accuracy.

Soon after Phil's story, Roberts officially removed himself from all decisions regarding the Tuscaloosa project. However, trial testimony revealed that he unofficially remained involved, and made several key decisions to push it forward.

The most astounding testimony on the road to Allen's toll bridge regarded its cost.

The announced total of $12 million? Not even close.

The final bill came to $42 million. Highway officials testified that it was by far the most expensive county road project paid for entirely with state funds in Alabama history.

Projects of that size are invariably paid for with 80 percent federal funds and 20 percent state dollars. However, the federal government wasn't participating in the Mitt Lary project. The state could have sought federal assistance, but that would have taken time, perhaps years, and with the bridge bleeding money, that wasn't an option for Allen, Roberts, and the Siegelman administration.

But as with almost every aspect of the highway department case, there were mitigating factors. Among them was the fuss, entirely unrelated to Roberts, that Siegelman authorized the road to buy off Poole and assure that Democrats maintained control of the senate. Separately, jurors learned that Tuscaloosa area officials were pleading for the road.

Though I never heard anyone suggest this defense, I felt there was a possibility that Roberts wanted the road because he was *emotionally* vested in Allen's toll bridge. He'd overseen construction of it and wanted to see it succeed. Forget personal benefit – it was his baby.

That charitable view didn't apply to three lucrative side-ventures of Allen's that didn't commence until Roberts' appointment and which came to an end soon after Roberts' July 2001 resignation. The clear implication was that Allen's value to companies seeking business with the highway department derived entirely from his relationship with his former employee.

New client Burke-Kleinpeter put Allen on a $35,000 per month retainer. That comes to a staggering $420,000 per year. Another engineering firm, TTL, also hired Allen to win contracts with the highway department.

Jurors learned that the Roberts-led department awarded highway design work to both firms, with Burke-Kleinpeter reeling in contracts worth $12 million.

During Roberts' 2-1/2 years, the two engineering firms paid Allen a total of about $1.5 million. When prosecutors asked Allen what he did to earn such a sum, he answered, in effect, nothing at all.

In July 2001, I was fresh off G.H. Construction and chasing a handful of stories when a roadbuilder called with a tip. He said that immediately after Siegelman become governor the highway department started using a specialized type of highway striping called RainLine. Jimmy Butts, the director under Fob, had refused to use it because it was so expensive.

The source said Allen had started a side-business marketing RainLine and was making a mint from Roberts' decision to use it. The tip was made all the more interesting because, as he told me, Roberts worked for Allen's toll-bridge company before becoming highway director.

It sounded like a story, so I e-mailed Carrie, Rip, and Paul Bowlin at the highway department. I ended up talking to Bowlin. "I think we have used that product to some extent. I'm not sure to what extent – it's possible that's one of several products we use," he said.

Bowlin said it with something short of conviction, but I didn't press him. I like to think that if I hadn't been so busy on other matters that I'd have requested the records. But that would have been an insult – essentially me telling Bowlin I didn't believe him, and I'd given him plenty of those in the preceding months and guess I just wasn't up to doing it again that day.

Had I insisted on reviewing the RainLine records, we could have reported that in since Siegelman became governor the state had spent tens of millions of dollars on this unique striping product; and connected Allen's financial interest in RainLine to his former employee's decision to use it. But I didn't push it, and as a consequence, there was no such story, by me or anyone else.

It would be four years before I heard the name RainLine again. On May 15, 2005, the grand jury entertained a parade of highway department officials. Several acknowledged being asked about RainLine. Another visitor to the grand jury was a lanky, 6-foot-5 man with blinking blue eyes and an aw-shucks air that suggested the countrified absent-minded inventor that he was.

Forrest "Mac" Marcato developed RainLine in the early 1990s while trying to produce a stripe that would show better during night rains. Normal striping contains tiny glass beads. Car lights reflect off the beads and back to drivers, enabling them to see the lights at night. But during heavy rains, water covers the striping, diminishes its reflective properties, and with it, the visible boundaries of the highway.

RainLine is both a product and a means of applying it. The paint is thicker and suffused with more glass beads. The application process requires a machine, invented by Marcato, that slices tiny ridges into the asphalt. These ridges raise the striping so the beads face the light and reflect back even during heavy rains.

The grooves provide a second safety benefit. When drivers stray, the lines produce a zing noise (not to be confused with the much deeper grooves placed outside highway stripes and which make a car vibrate). The combination of the product and the specialized, time consuming application process means RainLine cost more than three times normal striping.

Allen, who became aware of the product through his bridges, entered into a marketing contract with Marcato to sell RainLine to states. Just as my source told me years before, after becoming director Roberts ordered the department to commence using RainLine on new highways and re-surfacing projects. A highway official testified that the state spent $42 million on RainLine in the roughly 2-1/2 years it was used. That was about $30 million more than would have been spent had regular striping been used.

Of that $42 million, Marcato's company paid Allen $2.8 million.

After Roberts left the highway department, Marcato ended his relationship with Allen. Soon after, the state cut way back on RainLine.

———

Allen testified under an immunity agreement. If he told the truth he wouldn't be prosecuted. Also, he agreed to repay the state $840,000 of his RainLine profits.

The toll bridge developer seemed a decent guy, and most embarrassed to be in the middle of the Siegelman circus. He testified that his efforts selling RainLine were largely limited to hiring lobbyist Crum Foshee, a renowned figure on Goat Hill. With his slit eyes and tanned, tight-skinned face, the former state senator looks like an assassin. Then Foshee smiles, answers a question with a quip and assassin transforms into wizened Leprechaun.

Allen paid Foshee $50 for every ton of RainLine used by the state. Foshee later sought to double that to $100 per ton. During the 2-1/2 years Roberts ran the department Allen paid Foshee about $800,000 for selling RainLine. Other evidence showed that during the same period, Foshee disgorged roughly the same amount on gambling losses and expenses at Mississippi casinos.

If anything, there were more mitigating factors in the RainLine case than those involving the road to Allen's bridge.

Other department officials thought RainLine a good product and the federal highway administration authorized its use, meaning it bore 80 percent of the costs. So while Roberts pushed it, he didn't have to fight for it.

The product's fate was eventually doomed by a University of Alabama study concluding that fatalities were not noticeably reduced on highways where it was used and a determination that the money would be better spent elsewhere.

Another problem: If Roberts could do everything on his own, why did Allen hire Foshee and pay him a big chunk of his RainLine earnings? This was apparently because Foshee was tight with Ray Bass, the legendary three-time former highway director and, during the last years of his career, the department's chief engineer.

Foshee had raised money for Siegelman. I have to believe Siegelman knew of and approved of the arrangement with Foshee but no evidence was presented indicating that.

In any event, Foshee's involvement in RainLine muddied the waters for a jury being asked to find guilt beyond a reasonable doubt against Roberts and Siegelman on the RainLine counts.

―――

The 17th and final "highway department" count was an extortion charge against Siegelman alone that arose from the RainLine investigation. While being interviewed by the FBI, Marcato told agents about a phone call he received two months before the 2002 election.

Marcato believed the caller to be a friend prone to phone pranks but soon realized that it indeed was Alabama's governor on the other end.

Siegelman, almost surely bluffing, told Marcato that he was about to "go into some big important meeting about RainLine," the inventor testified. Then the governor began the spiel at the top of the chapter, ending with a request for Marcato to "send me $250,000."

And then, as Marcato told jurors: "And I said, Sir, you must don't know me. You must have me confused with somebody else,' I said, 'because I ain't got that kind of money.' He said, 'Oh, I do know you too.' He said, 'I know you well and you could pay it.'"

Marcato insisted that he could not. Siegelman lowered his demand to $100,000 and got the same response. Finally Siegelman said, "Just send me what you can."

Marcato, reeling from the call, immediately told his wife, who also testified. "I was awe-struck," Nancy Marcato told jurors. "(Mac) said, 'I think (Siegelman is) trying to shake me down. I think this could make a difference in what happens to our business.'"

Marcato didn't contribute to Siegelman, but gave instead to Riley. He later met with Riley, but the new governor left the RainLine decision up to his new highway director, who completely ceased using it.

On cross examination Kilborn played Marcato just right. He recognized that the Siegelman call upset Marcato but that the inventor was long over it. Marcato, though, remained incensed at the University of Alabama study that threatened future use of RainLine not just in Alabama but everywhere. The study – a side detail in the government's case -- was an obsession for Marcato, and a major reason his testimony proved a disaster for prosecutors.

Kilborn ditched his usual two-fisted attack for a soft-spoken, gentle and at times humorous approach to the witness. The Mobile attorney talked about RainLine as if it were the greatest thing since asphalt, once snarling that regular striping was "junk."

Marcato eased up on the Siegelman "extortion" call and followed Kilborn where the lawyer wanted him to go – that is, showering criticism on Allen, the pivotal witness in the 16 other counts that comprised the highway department case.

That put Siegelman in something of a pickle. He couldn't go before the cameras and call Marcato a jerk or liar after Kilborn turned the inventor into a friendly witness. Instead, Siegelman called Marcato "a dear kind soul" unaccustomed to politics. He said he could understand how a political innocent like Marcato could have been thrown by his request for a quarter-million dollars.

Siegelman told reporters he couldn't recall if he'd told Marcato he was heading into an important meeting about RainLine. However, if he had, he certainly didn't intend it as a threat, and blasted prosecutors for accusing him of such a thing.

Siegelman also defended the state's use of RainLine by pointing to the 1984 accident that almost killed his wife, though that wreck would not have been prevented by any striping product.

The government made an air-tight case that Roberts used his public position to enrich Jim Allen. Not so that Allen enriched Roberts in return.

Yes, Allen's company paid Roberts $110,000 shortly before Roberts became director. But the impact of this payment was diluted by the revelation that years before, Allen promised pay Roberts a $1 million bonus if he stuck around long enough to build four bridges. The Tuscaloosa span was Roberts' second, and he was leaving. As a result, the $110,000 seemed less pay-off than reasonable reward for work well done. That taxes were deducted certainly didn't hurt Roberts' defense.

Roberts' team was to put on two witnesses who damaged one of the government's central charges – that Siegelman appointed Roberts because of Allen's donation.

State Sen. Lowell Barron testified that he had to badger Siegelman to appoint Roberts as highway director. It's difficult to believe anything that flows from Barron's mouth but it did appear that he and other senators favored Roberts.

Barron damaged the Allen-picked-Roberts storyline. The next witness, state Rep. Richard Lindsey, destroyed it. Lindsey testified that 100 out of 105 members of the state house signed a petition urging Siegelman to appoint Roberts.

For Siegelman, two interests had intersected. By appointing Roberts he made his fellow Democrats in the legislature happy and left Allen thinking he'd had a say in choosing the highway director. The government – which seemed taken aback by the testimony from Barron and Lindsey -- would have been better off alleging that Siegelman made Allen believe he could anoint the next director for $40,000. The prosecutors misread the strength of their evidence in believing that Siegelman appointed Roberts to satisfy Allen.

Again, Franklin, Feaga and their team should not have charged Roberts. They should have called him as a witness to support Allen's version of Siegelman's outrageous demand that day in the antique store, as I believe Roberts would have done.

That would have made a strong extortion charge – better, by far, than the one on the Marcato call. If the government wanted to include the highway department elements into the case they should have boiled it down to the one extortion charge involving the antique store shake-down; one charge on RainLine; one on the Tuscaloosa road; and drafted those last two counts in a manner that clearly connected the narrative presented jurors to the charges.

Instead, the 16 non-extortion counts – like those involving the tax mailings from Emelle and the faxed resume to Waste Management – didn't seem to describe crimes at all. The first three, regarding the toll bridge road, recited three letters, one for each count. In each the sender was the highway department and the recipient the Tuscaloosa County Commission. The letters, identical but for the date and amounts, merely notified the commission that the state was allocating more funds for the road. There was no logical way for jurors to find guilt on one count and not all three, and vice versa.

It was the same with the 13 RainLine counts –guilt on all or none, since they, too, were for all practical purposes, identical.

Each listed a check sent on a certain date from one of several highway contractors to Marcato's company. These checks were the ultimate source of the money paid to Allen by Marcato's company. That's because the state didn't pay RainLine. Instead, it put the product in its specifications for road projects and the contractors bought the product from RainLine.

One big problem: None of the contractors were implicated or even called as witnesses, and the recipient of the checks – Marcato's company – wasn't accused of wrongdoing either.

The government was asking jurors to find guilt on charges each many steps away from the schemes laid out in testimony and evidence. Then, to make it worse, prosccutors failed to adequately explain the connection between the evidence against Roberts and Siegelman and the 16 letters and checks.

One juror told me later that the panel was confused by it all.

The charges were even shakier against Siegelman than against Roberts. The government was asking the jury to find him guilty of the 16 charges based almost entirely on his shakedown of Allen and the resulting appointment of Roberts. There was little evidence tying Siegelman to the decisions to use RainLine or build the Tuscaloosa road, though he likely had a say in both. About the best evidence the government produced there was testimony by Allen regarding a meeting at the governor's office about a month after Siegelman's inauguration.

Allen, invited over by Hamrick, played a short video extolling the benefits of RainLine. Siegelman concluded the meeting by telling Allen that he "planned to use it."

The highway department case was such that not for one moment, from opening arguments to verdict, did I think the jury would find Roberts and Siegelman guilty. The jury rejected all 13 on the RainLine counts as well as the three related to the Tuscaloosa road project.

The 17th charge against Siegelman, regarding the call to Marcato, was voted down as well, rendering, for all time, and to Siegelman's great public relations benefit, a final tally of 27 counts not guilty to five for guilt.

Despite its failings, the highway department case paid a subtle dividend for the government.

For jurors to find guilt on the HealthSouth charges, they had to believe that Siegelman was not merely an aggressive fundraiser, but a menacing one. The first-hand accounts from the witnesses – Allen's story of the 1998 meeting in the antique store, Marcato's regarding Siegelman's call – made it easy to believe that Siegelman had it in him to threaten Richard Scrushy if the latter didn't come up with $500,000.

On the day of our story reporting Marcato's testimony about Siegelman's call, a south Alabama roadbuilder rang me. He was laughing.

"They could have witnesses circling the courthouse with stories like that about Siegelman," he said.

Chapter 37
Sudden Death Overtime

"Guilty."
-- Judge Fuller's clerk, reading the verdict on count three against Siegelman, after saying, "not guilty" on the first two counts.

"God is as good today as he was a year ago."
-- Leslie Scrushy, referring to her husband's acquittal in the HealthSouth fraud case a year and a day before the verdict in the Siegelman trial.

The prosecution rested at mid-morning on Thursday, June 8 after calling as its 65th and final witness the owner of the dealership that sold Siegelman the motorcycle.

Fuller sent the jurors home for the day. The next morning the defendants began presenting their cases.

Roberts' team went first. Bill Baxley and David McKnight raced through nine witnesses in four hours, setting a speed record for the trial. Most were character witnesses.

None of the other defendants put on character witnesses. To do so would have opened those witnesses to cross-examination for "character" based questions and even prosecution rebuttal character witnesses. I don't think either of the three wanted to go there.

Scrushy's lawyers kicked off Monday. Three members of the CON board testified that Scrushy hadn't controlled the board.

A retired HealthSouth pilot introduced flight records for July 14, 1999 – the day prosecutors contended that Scrushy flew to Montgomery to meet with Siegelman. The records showed the passengers as Jabo Waggoner and Eric Hanson, and the pilot said Scrushy was always listed as lead passenger when he flew. Under cross-examination, the pilot acknowledged that the records didn't absolutely prove that Scrushy wasn't on the flight and certainly didn't prove he wasn't in Montgomery that day, having traveled by other means.

Retired Alabama Power chairman Elmer Harris testified to the political realities of fund-raising. He also said he'd asked Scrushy to join the CON board, which was absurd. The last thing Scrushy needed was Elmer Harris telling him that it might be nice for HealthSouth to be representation on the CON board. Scrushy had been on the board during the previous three administrations.

Harris also said he spoke to Scrushy in 2000 about helping Siegelman retire the foundation debt. Assuming this to be true – and I suggest otherwise -- it would have been at the very least six months after the first $250,000 contribution from UBS by way of Integrated Health. Also, other records and testimony showed Scrushy had committed to donate the second $250,000 in 1999.

I missed Monday's session, but had I known Harris would testify and what he would say, I'd have been there. I was quite surprised to hear what he told jurors because I knew better. In August 2002, in one of our final foundation stories, I'd quoted Harris after Scrushy told me that Siegelman hadn't asked him to donate to the foundation. This was as we reported it then:

Scrushy said he would have had to have signed off on the donation, but that neither he nor anyone at HealthSouth could recall with any certainty who solicited the money on behalf of the foundation.

Scrushy said he seemed to remember that Elmer Harris, at the time the president of Alabama Power Co., had asked him to make the donation.

Not so, said Harris.

"During that period of time, I did not give any moneys to the lottery foundation, nor did I solicit any moneys for the lottery foundation," said the recently retired executive and longtime political power broker.

I'd called Harris, got his voice mail, relayed what Scrushy said, and asked him to call me back. He did. I missed his call but he left a message. The quote above was exactly as he said it. Assuming I was inclined to make up quotes, it would be professional suicide to falsify a quote from the likes of Elmer Harris, who could be counted on to see the story and is on a first name basis with our publisher. No one, least of all Harris, asked for a correction.

I was disappointed when I heard that prosecutors didn't grill Harris until the end of his days on Alabama Power's political activities during his tenure. I – as well as many other reporters – had written numerous stories in the 1990s on the company's seemingly illegal methods of supporting public officials and their friends. I'd have loved to have Harris under oath for a few questions.

————

Scrushy's lawyers handed off to Hamrick's team at mid-afternoon on Monday. Deen called two witnesses. Both were essentially custodians of records that purported to support Hamrick's claim that he wasn't in Washington, D.C., for the 1998 National Governor's Conference.

The records -- which only proved he didn't seek government reimbursement for such a trip and wasn't listed by the association as attending -- were intended to refute the testimony of Lisa Kardell. She was the Waste Management lobbyist who testified to seeing Hamrick at the conference and being warned that the garbage company's interests in Alabama would suffer if it severed its relationship with Lanny.

Hamrick's lawyers wrapped up soon enough for Siegelman's defense to at least get started before day's end. No one expected Kilborn to call Siegelman but surely he would summon witnesses to try to rebut the array of charges against his client. So it was that the gallery issued a collective gasp when the Mobile lawyer stood to call his first witness and instead said, "Governor Siegelman rests, your honor."

The four defense teams had taken less than two days. None of the defendants testified and none offered up a witness of the type the prosecution wanted – someone they could rip into on cross-examination.

In every way, the defendants had played defense.

Outside, standing before his beloved cameras, Kilborn growled that he "didn't want to give any credibility whatsoever to this rattle-trap, junked-up case."

"It took them six weeks to build a pile of garbage -- took us two days to disassemble it."

The drama was down to its final acts – closing arguments, then on to the jury.

Feaga kicked it off, reminding jurors of a prediction he made in his opening statement that the defendants wouldn't put on a case but would instead, "attack our witnesses."

"These are people we have plucked from their lives," Feaga said.

He reminded jurors that G.H. Construction was exposed in late April 2001, but that Bailey remained in Siegelman's employ (with the new title, "confidential assistant to the governor") for another six months.

"Ask (Siegelman) why he didn't fire him?" Feaga said.

He angrily told jurors he resented the defense lawyers' attacks on the prosecutors and investigators and asked the jury to hold the defendants accountable for those attacks. This request apparently didn't trouble the defense attorneys, several of whom ratcheted up their criticisms of the government in their closing statements.

The harshest censure erupted from an unlikely source. Bill Baxley's partner, David McKnight, had done a competent job of cross examining some witnesses but made little impression. He struck me as serious if perhaps on the dull side. That changed about five seconds into his closing.

McKnight started mad and progressed from there to temple-throbbing rage. "Shame on them for doing that to Mr. Roberts in this case," he all but shouted at the prosecutors table.

McKnight wasn't acting. He really was incensed at the prosecutors for charging his client.

So fierce was his closing that I felt sorry for the prosecutors. Later, Feaga said McKnight went way too far. I didn't say so, but didn't share his feelings. From McKnight's perspective, the government had gravely impacted Roberts' life, harming his reputation and finances.

As I've stated elsewhere, I think the government erred in charging Roberts. But I don't think for a moment that Franklin and Feaga and their fellow prosecutors charged Roberts for any other reason than they believed him guilty of the crimes charged and thus deserving of prosecution.

Far less effective was a bit of stock theater from Art Leach, as presented here in our story:

> *Swinging his pointed finger at the prosecution table with what could have been a roundhouse right, Leach lashed out at FBI agents Jim Murray and Keith Baker for failing to be "conscientious investigators."*
>
> *Leach asked jurors to remember the famous Abscam case from the 1980s, in which FBI agents dressed as Arab sheiks in a sting operation.*
>
> *Jurors in that case knew there was guilt, because they could see the guilty parties stuffing cash into their pockets, Leach said.*
>
> *Had Murray and Baker done their jobs, they would have provided jurors in this case with evidence of equal strength.*

I wondered if I was the only one imagining Murray and Baker duded up like sheiks and trying to sucker Siegelman into some hidden-camera contract for kickback action.

———

Like the fine actor he is, Kilborn showed considerable range in speaking for Siegelman. There was the usual snarling ridicule of the government, but pathos as well. His voice cracking, Kilborn told jurors that Siegelman "has a good heart."

"He has tried to help the people of Alabama. He is a good man, a good husband and a good father."

Siegelman was "human" and had "made mistakes," the biggest being that he allowed people to get close to him who were dishonest and who took advantage of their positions.

This was an obvious reference to Bailey. Kilborn piled it on Siegelman's loyal aide, telling the jury that some people have close friends, even spouses, who fool them for years.

His most effective moment was aided by a prop – a chart showing how much money Young made compared to what the government alleged Siegelman received in return. Kilborn, pointing to it, said it looked like Lanny "got $8 million for the landfill, $500,000 (for Emelle) and Don Siegelman got 3/4ths of a motorcycle, a 4-wheeler, and some mugs."

It was an excellent line, even if it did overlook several hundred thousand dollars in donations, disclosed and not, the almost 50 flights on Lanny's plane and assorted other favors, like the trip to New York for the NASCAR awards.

For Hamrick, Deen's primary objective was to diminish the importance of the $25,000 BMW down-payment. The Mobile lawyer invoked the friend defense, and relied heavily on the court rulings requiring a specific quid pro quo arrangement to prove a crime.

He told jurors that a gift to a public official was only a crime if made in return for specific public action. Deen said -- correctly -- that the government had not proved a direct connection to any one act by Hamrick in return for the BMW and the slew of other favors and cash showered on Siegelman's chief of staff by Lanny.

"Getting something from a friend is not against the law," said Deen.

Like everyone else, Deen directed the jurors away from his guy and toward the fall guy. "When anything is going screwy in this case, Nick is there," he said.

My name came up several times in closings, including by the government, but the reference by the clowning Deen was my favorite. He called me a "sly dog."

After Leach presented the factual arguments for Scrushy he ceded the stage to Gray. The famed civil rights lawyer spoke of the federal government with "all those resources" stacked against "my little client." That was laughable. What came next wasn't. I was sitting next to Eileen Jones, the black Montgomery television reporter. She was more appalled than I was by what followed.

I decided the best way to present it was straight up, without a trace of anything that might be taken for commentary. The next day's story began:

Jurors now deliberating the fate of former Gov. Don Siegelman, ex-HealthSouth Corp. Chairman Richard Scrushy and two others can "make Dr. (Martin Luther) King's dream come true by returning a verdict of not guilty" against Scrushy, famed civil rights lawyer Fred Gray said here Thursday.

Gray's rousing closing argument opened with a Psalm, then segued into a recitation of some of Gray's best known civil rights cases, including his representation of King in the 1960s and, later, the case against the federal government on behalf of black victims of the Tuskegee syphilis study.

As Gray spoke, another member of the Scrushy legal team quietly put up a poster-board of King's, "I have a dream," speech.

With his voice rising to a crescendo, Gray gave the final words from the defendants in this now seven-weeks-long public corruption trial. He implored federal jurors to "fulfill Dr. King's dream and fulfill that old song!"

"Free at last! Free at last! Thank God Almighty we're Free at last!" Gray sang out.

If this can be said in Gray's defense, he did exactly what he was hired to do. Seeing Gray after the verdict I sensed that he wasn't going to lose any sleep over his client's loss. It was a gig, and it had paid well.

The last word belonged to the government, or specifically, to Louis Franklin. "I know you think I'm going to get into his (Gray) civil rights preaching, but

I'm not," he began, referring to his outburst during Gray's opening argument six weeks before.

Franklin didn't mention it again. He told the mostly blue collar jury that "what you ought to remember about this case" is that "if you don't donate, you don't participate."

"If you are poor, you don't count. You've got to be Richard Scrushy to get to see the governor."

If it wasn't clear before Leach's presentation that Scrushy was laying most of his cards on the date disparity in Bailey's testimony it assuredly was after. Leach stressed that the Integrated Health check was dated July 19. As such, it would have been impossible for Bailey to have seen it on July 14, when he'd initially told investigators that was when Siegelman showed it to him. Leach insisted that the jury find Scrushy not guilty for that reason alone.

Franklin coolly reminded jurors that there had had been a second meeting between Scrushy and Siegelman two weeks later. The important part was that the meetings were held; the $250,000 was received after the intense pressure put on UBS and Integrated Health; and the check was delivered by Scrushy to Siegelman. Because Bailey at first thought he saw the check after one meeting when he saw it after another was irrelevant, Franklin said.

He methodically went through the evidence and matched McKnight in passion if not fury. The best gauge of Franklin's performance was the shell-shocked expressions on the faces of the defendants and their lawyers when he finished.

After closing arguments the six alternates were excused, revealing which of the 12 would decide the case. The breakdown was seven blacks and five whites, with the same ratio of women to men. They began deliberating that afternoon. Their first job was to elect a foreperson. Though he didn't ask for it, the job went to 47-year-old Sam Hendrix, who in real life was the development officer for Auburn University's College of Veterinary Medicine.

Deliberations were a nice break from the stressful days of trial and writing and editing until well into the evening. One simply had to remain within quick driving distance of the courthouse, whether for a verdict or as happened several times, when jurors sent Fuller a question, as they did the first morning. The jury asked the judge if the two $250,000 donations to the foundation constituted a "thing of value" for Siegelman.

The prosecutors pleaded with Fuller to simply recite the law, which made it clear that, yes, even if viewed as straightforward campaign contributions, the donations constituted a thing of value. Instead, the judge told jurors it was up to them to decide. It was one of two substantial directives that angered prosecutors, prompting them to file briefs asking Fuller to reconsider.

Later, the defendants and their backers sought to re-write history and portray Fuller as part of the alleged anti-Siegelman conspiracy, but during deliberations, it was the defendants and their lawyers, not the prosecutors, who were smiling at his rulings. If anything, it seemed he was erring on the side of the caution. If his rulings leaned in any direction, it was toward the defense. One supposes that the last thing Fuller wanted at this late stage was to make a reversible error that would allow a defendant, if found guilty, to win a new trial based on an error by him.

The jurors broke for the weekend and didn't make a peep that Monday. Though the election was lost and over, Siegelman maintained his routine. Each day he and Kilborn came to the courthouse in time for the TV stations from Montgomery, Birmingham and Huntsville to get live shots for their midday news programs, then returned to talk some more for the evening newscasts.

On Thursday, day six, jurors informed Fuller that they had been unable to reach a unanimous verdict on even one of the total of 62 counts against the defendants. The judge issued an "Allen charge," also known as a "dynamite charge." It's a formal set of instructions judges can give to deadlocked juries urging them to re-examine their opinions and, if at all possible, reach a verdict.

The following Tuesday -- day nine – Hendrix, the foreman, sent Fuller a note laced with frustration. He revealed that one or more jurors had expressed what he called "blanket reasonable doubt" on all the charges from the start, had become "lackadaisical" and was refusing to participate in deliberations.

Kilborn was outraged. He told Fuller that the foreman was "arrogant" for criticizing other jurors. The judge took the rare step of suggesting to the jury that it consider choosing a new foreperson. Here was another ruling at a crucial juncture that appeared to benefit the defendants.

When the jurors retired to the deliberating room they took Fuller's suggestion. The panel voted 11-0 to keep Hendrix, who abstained from the vote.

Fuller, outside earshot of the jurors, told the parties he would only declare a mistrial as a "last resort," but acknowledged that it was becoming a real possibility. A mistrial meant a do-over, at great expense for all. The glum-faced prosecutors pledged to re-try the case should it come to that.

The defense, though, did not want a mistrial, and urged Fuller to give the jury more time.

"We like this jury. We're not going to get a better jury. We might get a worse jury," Professor Blakey told the judge.

Blakey's statement reflected that, just two days before the verdict, Siegelman and his lawyers felt good about their situation and Fuller's directives to the jury.

After the hearing Scrushy strode over to the cameras. Stationed behind him were his wife, their two young daughters and four black pastors.

"A large group of pastors and bishops are here today," Scrushy announced. He told the audience for that night's news shows that the pastors were praying "that those (jurors) who are not there (for acquittal) will get there."

"It's in the right hands," said Scrushy. "I've handed this over to my spiritual father."

The next morning jurors sent out another note, and per the drill, the usual suspects raced to the courthouse.

This time Hendrix reported that the jury remained deadlocked and was discussing, not the charges, but whether it was worthwhile to continue deliberating. He told Fuller that the jurors should know by mid-afternoon if was worth it to keep trying.

Everyone remained close by, expecting another summons and this time, news that the jury had given up. The afternoon groaned by, with much watch-checking. At 4:30 court officials revealed that the jurors had gone home. This was read by all as a sign that the jury had decided to keep trying.

The next day, shortly before lunch, the jury reached a verdict on all counts. After deciding the final charge, the group burst into applause.

Word spread like wildfire that there was a verdict. By the anointed moment the courtroom was full, mostly with supporters for the defendants. Certainly for those of us who'd lived the trial, it was a momentous occasion when all stood to watch the 12 stone-faced jurors file into the courtroom and take their seats.

You could have fueled a moon rocket with the nervous energy.

Our story the next day began:

When the judge's clerk received the jury's verdict here Thursday, most in the packed courtroom knew that the findings on the first two counts against the first defendant –– former Gov. Don Siegelman -- could determine the trial's outcome.

The defendants were nervous, their lawyers were nervous, and so too was the prosecution team. Everyone was nervous, and everyone was ordered silent.

There were to be no outbursts, warned a stern U.S. District Judge Mark Fuller.

Those first two counts accused the 60-year-old Mobile native of conspiracy. Findings of guilt in either one would guarantee guilty verdicts on many of the charges to come, as those other charges were components of the conspiracy case.

"Not guilty," said the clerk, to count one.

And for the second conspiracy count, not guilty as well.

But when she read the verdict on Count 3, which accused Siegelman of receiving a bribe from HealthSouth Corp. Chairman Richard Scrushy, the tone in the room, the trial and Siegelman's reaction changed.

"Guilty."

The clerk would sound the word six more times with regard to the 32 counts against Siegelman.

For about 10 minutes -- or until the clerk finished reading six guilty verdicts against Scrushy and not guilty findings on all charges against co-defendants Paul Hamrick and Mack Roberts -- Siegelman seemed to freeze in the listening position, head jutting forward, face reddened with intensity, but with no discernible expression.

"I was shocked. Absolutely shocked," Siegelman later told reporters.

The jury found Siegelman guilty on all six counts regarding the HealthSouth aspect of the case. The other guilty finding was on the second of two obstruction of justice counts pertaining to the bogus motorcycle sale.

Scrushy had to know that the verdicts against Siegelman on the HealthSouth charges foretold bad news, and indeed, they did. He shook his head in disgust when the clerk made it official, stating "Guilty" on all six counts against him.

Many thought Hamrick had much to fear because of the BMW. When the clerk read the verdict on the last count against him – not guilty, like the five before – Siegelman's former chief of staff nodded at the jurors, as if to say thanks, and looked back at his wife.

Roberts, so serene throughout, gave a slight smile when the clerk confirmed what trial watchers had witnessed – the total failure of the highway department portion of the government's case.

Fuller permitted Siegelman and Scrushy to remain free, requiring minimal bonds of $25,000 apiece.

Because of the short notice Lori Siegelman was spared the verdicts and aftermath. Siegelman called her upon learning the jury had a verdict but she didn't arrive in time. He called her back to give her the news and she returned to Birmingham.

During the investigation and trial and in the years since Siegelman has blamed his troubles on all manner of hobgoblins. He has shown a disregard for the truth and the problems caused to the many people he and his lawyers and supporters have falsely accused of conspiring against him. But in the immediate aftermath of the verdict, he displayed real grace. Standing before the larger than usual phalanx of reporters and TV cameras, Siegelman said he hated it for his family and expressed confidence of victory on appeal. When someone asked if the verdict marked the end of his political career, he chuckled and said, "This certainly didn't enhance it in any way."

About 100 feet away Scrushy held a different kind of court. This man so accustomed to having his way had just seen 12 peons find him guilty of six felony charges and very likely send him off to prison. In a strong, angry voice he declared proof of his innocence. "Many people don't know this, but I took a lie detector test and passed," he said.

As reporters scribbled down Scrushy's every utterance, a cherry-faced Terry Butts burst in out of nowhere and howled that the verdict was "the worst miscarriage of justice since Sherman burned Atlanta."

Here was a first and maybe a last: A fabulously wealthy white defendant whose attorneys illustrated his plight first by summoning images of blacks oppressed during the civil rights movement, then with the torment of slave-holders pillaged in the waning days of the Civil War.

Can you say: Only in Alabama?

The verdict came a year and a day after Scrushy's acquittal in HealthSouth fraud case. This near anniversary was on Leslie Scrushy's mind when she relieved the man upstairs of culpability in the jury's findings. "God is as good today as he was a year ago," she said, and seemed to mean it.

After blowing off some more steam Scrushy grabbed his wife's hand and marched off, followed by reporters and television cameras. I asked loudly if he thought his strategy of injecting race into the case had backfired. "I've said all I'm going to say," he said, and kept going.

Outside court Hamrick's relief gave way to self-righteous anger. To hear him he was an innocent victim, and blamed prosecutors for tormenting him and sticking him with mounds of legal fees.

I thought he should have been thanking his lucky stars. I don't think Hamrick believes he did anything wrong. Like Siegelman, he seems to operate under the assumption that the phrase "just politics" provides coverage for all manner of unethical, illegal behavior. To my way of thinking, he deserved prison time for the BMW alone.

With its verdict, the jury rejected a major element of the prosecution's case – that alleging an "absolute agreement" between Siegelman, Hamrick, Bailey and Lanny. It hadn't gone for the RainLine portion either. But all in all, especially considering the length of the jury's deliberations, it was a major victory for the prosecution. This from our story:

Still, there were smiles and *expressions of relief on the faces of the team of lawyers* and *investigators that for the past two months has been castigated in court* and *out, primarily by lawyers for Siegelman* and *Scrushy and their clients.*

The prosecution was berated – particularly by Siegelman lawyers Vince Kilborn III and David McDonald – as incompetent, politically inspired and guilty of various types of misconduct.

As it happened, the two defendants who leveled those accusations were the ones found guilty.

With a legal pad full of notes and quotes I raced, per the norm, to Café Louisa. I was half-way through when Bill Barrow called to give me the astounding news that seven jurors had just walked into Buds and wanted to meet me, due I suppose to the frequency with which my name came up during trial. I was however secondary to Sinclair's and Buds. The jurors had heard so much about the two political hot-spots they just had to see them.

I was working at warp speed anyway, and once finished, scurried down to Buds. The fun was in being able to talk to these people you'd been looking at for two months but never spoken to or so much as heard their voices. There was much laughter, group pictures and some talking about the case. Several jurors remarked that they were impressed with all of the attorneys, prosecution and defense. One juror elicited giggles from the others with an impersonation of McDonald, who apparently was the source of some inside juror joking, though they were impressed by his lawyering as well.

The night was for them, myself and so many others, cathartic, regardless of the verdict.

Everyone was plain ass-whipped.

At some fairly late hour I left for hotel and bed. On the way to my car I saw Hamrick, his wife and some of his Matrix Group co-workers on the porch of Otey's, another bar on the Cloverdale strip. They had seen me and I figured it wouldn't hurt to walk up and say hello.

When I approached, everything was fine, if slightly frosty on their part, until Hamrick's wife asked if I considered the prosecutors to be "honorable people."

I wasn't going to lie and said that, yes, I did consider them to be honorable. Hamrick told me I should leave, and I did.

When news of Scrushy's conviction reached HealthSouth's Birmingham headquarters, employees erupted in celebration.

"Oh yeah, there were people swimming in the fountain," one of Scrushy's former employees told TV reporter Alan Collins.

Scrushy, apprised of their reaction, said his former underlings were "drinking the poison of hate and jealousy." He promised to pray for them. Also on his prayer list were the jurors who voted against him and the prosecutors who lied about him. He blamed the outcome on several "Siegelman haters" on the jury who convinced the others to find guilt where there was none.

Hindsight has given me an appreciation for the jury's verdict. To a great degree the jurors found guilt where the evidence matched the charges, and when it didn't, they acquitted. I think a better resolution would have been guilt on both rather than just one of the obstruction charges against Siegelman and not guilty for him on the two "Tim Adams" charges.

The HealthSouth case was built not merely on the word of Nick Bailey, but on the testimony of many people who played small but crucial roles in the acts charged. As important, the government showed jurors all manner of checks and documents in support of that testimony.

The investigators – Jack Brennan and Bill Long with the attorney general's office, and the Jim Murray and Keith Baker with the FBI -- did a meticulous job of investigating the HealthSouth case and the prosecutors presented it convincingly. The same can be said for the obstruction of justice charges involving the motorcycle transaction, and, really, everything related to the G.H. Construction portion of the case.

The jury correctly rejected the RainLine/highway department case. It was right to, if for no other reason than the charges failed to match the evidence, the exception being the Marcato extortion count, and that charge was polluted by Marcato's wavering testimony.

The Emelle-related "honest services wire fraud" charges were probably doomed by the way they were drafted. I believe the government could have won verdicts on the Emelle case, at least against Siegelman. But to do so, it had to give jurors charges that matched the evidence. Prosecutors made a convincing case that Siegelman sought and effected the change for the reasons they alleged, but blew it by charging him with counts that described tonnage and tax reports at Emelle that he likely never saw nor was aware of.

I believe the government proved the RICO/absolute arrangement counts pertaining to Lanny Young, more so against Siegelman than Hamrick. But elements of those counts were problematic. Considering the requirement for guilt – a unanimous finding by 12 individual jurors – the acquittals there were hardly a shock.

But for the expected appeals, the case was over. Finally.

Only it wasn't. Not by a long shot.

Chapter 38
Target: Jurors

"The enclosed e-mail shows that the jurors in the recent trial of Governor Siegelman and Richard Scrushy violated the Judges order by having communications and discussions outside the jury room. You should subpoena their records so you have the whole picture."

-- Message on cover sheet of anonymously mailed letter sent to Richard Scrushy, his lawyers, and Siegelman's lawyers. Signed, "Truth and Justice," it contained the first of what would be seven e-mails, all purportedly written by jurors to each other during trial.

"When the first one came out I was almost physically sick reading the thing. My initial reaction was seeing the capitalized K and knowing that wasn't my (e-mail) address. My second thought was that someone had hacked into my computer."

-- Katie Langer, one of the jurors shown as sending and receiving the e-mails.

In early September, a person who shall be referred to as the "e-mail bandit" sent a letter to Scrushy, Terry Butts, and Vince Kilborn. It was, like four later ones, postmarked Montgomery, without a return address, and in all ways anonymous. A cover page contained the message atop this page.

Within was a copy of what appeared to be a brief e-mail from juror Katie Langer to jury foreman Sam Hendrix and dated May 29, 2006, which was about the trial's half-point.

It read: *"…need to talk!.....!?"*

Also included were copies of three pages from Langer's *MySpace* page, none with any relevance to the trial or other jurors, and easily accessed by anyone with a computer. They showed Langer chatting back and forth with her brother and two members of her ski team (and were confirmed by Langer as real.)

Ten days later, the bandit sent the defense lawyers another e-mail, also purportedly from Langer to Hendrix and also dated May 29.

It read: *"I agree some of the kounts r confusing 2 our friends. Check text. (jurors) 30/38 still off trac."*

Two more were mailed on Sept. 21, both showing send dates of June 25, which was during deliberations and days before the verdict.

The first, supposedly from juror Shiranda Lyles to Langer, read: *"penalty 2 severe ... still unclear on couple of counts against pastor & gov."*

The second has Langer responding: *"... stay focused ... remember what judge said ... have plans for 4th ... right?"*

A fifth, sent to the usual suspects in early October, was also dated June 25. It shows Langer telling Lyles: *"proud of u...other 6 kounts most important....c.u.n. am (see you in the morning) ..Katie*

On June 28, 2007, almost a year to the day after the guilty verdict, Mark Fuller sentenced Siegelman and Scrushy, giving both about seven years.

Most white collar defendants are allowed to remain free on bail pending appeal. Not Siegelman and Scrushy. Fuller ordered them straight to jail. And immediately, found himself portrayed as a vengeful, Siegelman-hating Republican hit-man.

Fuller didn't explain why he sent them straight to jail without passing Go, he just took his lumps. The judge hasn't shared his thoughts with me, but I think I know why he did it.

It was the jurors -- what the defendants and their lawyers put them through after the trial.

First, the curious case of Juror #5; and second, the curiouser case of the "juror e-mails."

The first acts in the "juror misconduct" saga were news interviews granted by jurors Langer and Hendrix in the weeks after the verdict. By speaking frankly about their experiences, the two put X's on their chests. They also provided certain imaginative, unscrupulous souls with the fodder they used to inform the affidavits and e-mails given to lawyers for Scrushy and Siegelman.

Because there was no line separating the legal and public relations strategies of the two defense teams, Hendrix and Langer were to be savaged not just in court documents but in news stories quoting Siegelman and his say-anything lawyers.

During trial, Hendrix -- mid-sized, middle-aged, and bespectacled -- seemed a serious, conscientious man, an impression he made on his fellow jurors. They voted him foreman without considering anyone else and without him seeking the job.

Having never been one, Hendrix had little idea what it meant to be a foreman, so after being chosen he went on the Internet to research the duties of a foreman. He didn't think there was anything wrong with this, for he revealed it to his fellow jurors and, after trial, to *Montgomery Advertiser* reporter Bob Lowry, an old friend of his. He learned, as he told Lowry, that a foreman's job is to "guide the process, not take sides, but make sure everybody around the table has a chance to be heard."

Katie Langer, 26 at the time, was a gymnastics teacher and soon-to-be first-year law student. Like Hendrix, she was noticeably attentive throughout the trial and, also like him, made the mistake of answering calls from reporters after the verdict. This wasn't her fault or the reporters. There was no way to foresee how certain people would twist her and Hendrix's innocuous revelations.

The defendants latched on to Langer's statement to a Montgomery television station that she'd seen a headline or perhaps part of a story on the *Montgomery Advertiser's* web-site while looking for something else. Separately, she told the *Montgomery Advertiser* that she called the prosecutors after the trial to ask questions about the process, in part because of her plans to attend law school.

Both Hendrix and Langer told interviewers they found the evidence in the Scrushy portion of the case overwhelming. I think the defendants and their lawyers took this personally and that revenge, among other motives, factored into their post-trial activities.

The third juror victim, though in a different way, was Charlie Stanford, or, "Juror 5," as he was known in court records.

Stanford was among the 200 or so middle-Alabamians summoned to Montgomery in April 2006 for possible duty as jurors in the Siegelman trial. He's a 60-ish truck driver from Ozark, a small town 85 miles southeast of Montgomery, near Dothan. If he can read, it's just barely, as was revealed during two hearings called by Fuller, one in October, the other in November, and both related to the defendants' juror misconduct allegations.

A defense lawyer who participated in the case told me later that Stanford wrote on his jury questionnaire that, "All politicians are crooks." Such an attitude would seem to have made him an obvious candidate for striking by the defendants, but they kept him on.

The reason: In every other way he satisfied the criteria established by the defense lawyers and their jury consultants as the perfect juror for the case. For one thing, he was black. Siegelman always fared extraordinarily well with black voters and Scrushy would again be turning reality on its head by using race as part of his defense. For reasons I can't quite figure, the defendants favored working class jurors, the less education the better.

During the trial Stanford sat on the top row. A short, thick man, he looked like he could lift 400 pounds over his head without a second thought. He smiled often and frequently chuckled at Kilborn's jokes. If one juror fit the description happy-go-lucky, it was Stanford.

On August 8, 2006, Juror 5 was minding his business at home in Ozark. Unbeknownst to him, he'd come into the cross-hairs of people seeking to win a new trial for the two men who, according to other jurors, he'd believed guilty from the start of deliberations to the finish.

A week before, Stephen Hudson, the pastor of the Greater Sardis Baptist Church in Ozark, attended an annual leadership conference of black pastors in Selma. Also participating was the Rev. Charles Winston of the New Mt. Moriah Missionary Baptist Church in Birmingham. God knows why – and it wasn't at all clear from the subsequent testimony before Fuller – but the topic of conversation between the two preachers turned to the spiritual needs of one of Hudson's parishioners.

Not Charlie Stanford, for he didn't go to church, but his wife, Alice.

Hudson – if one is to trust his testimony – told Winston that Alice Stanford was troubled by her husband's behavior since serving as a juror on the Siegelman-Scrushy trial. A week after hearing this tale of woe, the Birmingham pastor made the three hour drive to Ozark.

At the first hearing, Winston testified that he went to Ozark after being directed to by his wife, Birmingham lawyer Debra Winston. She told her husband to interview and get an affidavit from Juror 5. Evidence was to reveal that Debra Winston was the moving force in the couple's decision to inject themselves into a matter with no apparent connection to either of them.

Testimony revealed that Alice Stanford and Hudson, the Ozark minister, had to nag and plead with Juror 5 to get him to leave his house and go to the church. Charlie Stanford showed "real hostility" about the demand that he go down to the church, Charles Winston testified. "When he came in it was as if he was forced and I think it was his wife forcing him," the Birmingham pastor told Fuller.

With the reluctant juror finally where they wanted him – in pastor Hudson's office at Greater Sardis – the production of three affidavits commenced. One was by Hudson, the others by Alice and Charlie Stanford.

In hers, at least as Charles Winston typed it, Alice Stanford stated that her husband "had become distant and isolated since the trial ended … things were not handled right during this trial, from Internet communications among the jury to pressure and intimidation from the judge ... He has been greatly distressed and unhappy by the outcome. He told me that he was led to believe that no one would serve time in jail…"

In his, pastor Hudson affied that he recommended to Mrs. Stanford that she *"seek further legal help to promote healing for her husband."* (italics mine.)

Fuller found it troubling that both of Juror 5's affidavits (there was, as will be seen, a second) were done in question and answer format. The first affidavit shows Charles Winston, the questioner on the first one, telling Stanford that some of the "problems you have mentioned are common with post-jury stress syndrome or post-traumatic shock syndrome."

If the affidavit is to be believed, Charlie Stanford told Winston that if he "had it to do all over again, I would not vote guilty."

He said he and some of the other jurors talked about the possible sentences, and believed that neither defendant would go to jail. "I thought maybe they would pay a fine because of who they were. Now I am unhappy that they didn't tell us right and the governor and Scrushy might go to jail for years."

In terms of usefulness for Siegelman and Scrushy, the meat of the affidavit came in the following Stanford "answer."

He stated that he was "confused between all the evidence and other Internet stuff and information that some of the jurors brought in and was talking about. I don't think they should have done that…I don't know who brought it (Internet stuff) for sure. They were pulling stuff out of files and some were talking about having Internet information and talking about that too. So we considered everything that everybody brought and pulled out of the file."

I doubt Rev. Winston was aware of Rule 47.1, but his wife was, as were the lawyers who were to make use of the affidavits.

The rule, which applies to all cases tried in Alabama's middle district (and many other districts as well), forbids attorneys, parties in a case or "anyone acting for them or on their behalf" from contacting jurors in writing or in person "in an attempt to determine the basis for any verdict rendered or to secure other information concerning the deliberations of the jury or any members thereof."

If parties wish to interview jurors after a verdict they must seek permission from the trial judge and make a damn strong case. No such permission was sought before the first affidavit from Stanford or the second.

———

When Rev. Winston returned to Birmingham he gave the affidavits to his wife. On Aug. 18, a Friday, she left messages with Scrushy lawyer Terry Butts and, on the Siegelman side, with Vince Kilborn and David McDonald. Butts didn't call back, but the next day, Kilborn did. According to McDonald and Kilborn, Mrs. Winston said she had a matter of interest, but declined to identify it.

"We had no clue what she had or even why she wanted to talk to us," Kilborn said.

Mobile to Birmingham is about a five-hour drive, the next day was a Sunday, and according to Kilborn, Debra Winston hadn't given him or McDonald even a vague idea as to why she wanted to talk to them.

The next day found the pair in her Birmingham law office, critiquing Juror 5's affidavit. They told her that it focused too much on Stanford's mental state. And there was another problem. Stanford, his wife and Hudson had signed the affidavits in Ozark, but they weren't notarized until the next day, in Birmingham. As legal documents that could be used to win a new trial they were probably useless.

After the meeting Debra Winston told her husband she was going to Ozark, this time to "do it and do it right." Her husband testified that during after the Sunday meeting his wife told him she had "committed" to David McDonald that she would get him an improved affidavit.

On Sept. 1, Debra and Charles Winston drove to Ozark as part of the continued spiritual legal counseling for the juror who wasn't seeking it. Hudson, the Ozark pastor, called Alice Stanford and told her that Winston and his wife were on their way and had to see her husband. Hudson told Alice Stanford that the Winstons needed the affidavits "for some legal case."

So once again, Charlie Stanford was roused from his home and hauled down to the pastor's office at Greater Sardis. This time, Debra Winston handled the duties, and with a notary present.

She went straight to the chase, making no pretense of trying to provide spiritual legal counseling. With her first questions she asked Juror 5 if there were any "documents, newspapers, information from the Internet, etc., discussed in the jury room to consider making a verdict in this case?"

"If yes, what was brought into the jury room, by whom, and did this information sway your decision to vote?"

If the affidavit is to be trusted, Stanford answered yes, but gave little in the way of detail. The second affidavit, but for being correctly notarized, was probably less useful to the defendants than the first.

Debra Winston tried to fax the affidavit from the church office in Ozark but couldn't get it to go through. She and her husband proceeded on to Atlanta, for a wedding. On the way, Debra Winston called McDonald to tell him she was going to fax him the second affidavit; and did, the next day, from a Staples location in Atlanta.

The most telling features of Juror 5s affidavits are the way they mirror the comments by Sam Hendrix and Katie Langer in their media interviews. For example, in the first affidavit, Stanford complained that he was confused between the evidence and "Internet stuff and information that some of the jurors brought in and was talking about."

I think it more likely that Winston told Stanford about the Internet material rather than the other way around. If so, the pastor learned about the "Internet material" from seeing Langer's interview and reading the stories about Hendrix's experience on the Siegelman jury. Both are unlikely. Winston lives in Birmingham. Langer's interview was given to station in Montgomery, while the stories about Hendrix were in the Montgomery and Auburn papers. The only other alternative (again, assuming the theory that Winston told Stanford about the Internet material) is that someone who read the Hendrix story and saw Langer on TV briefed Winston before he traveled to Ozark for the first affidavit.

In his *Advertiser* interview, Hendrix said that late in the deliberations, Fuller told jurors he had a lifetime appointment as a federal judge, then added that he did not "expect this to be a lifetime appointment for you."

In another interview, with the tiny *Auburn Villager*, Hendrix said Fuller was "always gentle, kind, encouraging and approving, as if we could just walk away!"

I asked Debra Winston if her husband knew Richard Scrushy? She said he did, but that she'd never seen Scrushy at their church. Nor had Scrushy donated money to their church.

"I mean everybody knows him," she said, in one of her quotes I used in a story. "He (her husband) knows him; there may have been some meetings some years ago and my husband is involved in many church activities."

———

Fuller ordered a hearing, not to investigate juror misconduct, but attorney misconduct. The narrow purpose of the inquiry was to determine if the defense lawyers or anyone on their behalf had violated Rule 47.1 through the post-trial contact with Juror 5. The judge informed the parties that he would subpoena witnesses and handle all the questioning.

Summoned for the Oct. 31 hearing were the two notaries; Charles and Debra Winston; Charlie and Alice Stanford; and Hudson, the Ozark minister.

Charles Winston's testimony was the most revelatory. He acknowledged that Stanford had to be coerced into coming to the church and giving an affidavit. That alone obliterated the cover story – that an anguished, post-jury-stress-syndrome-suffering Stanford just had to get things off his chest and went seeking legal spiritual help or some such malarkey.

The Birmingham pastor, a large man of about 60, said he typed his questions and what he "understood (Stanford's) answers to be." Then he read the finished product to Stanford.

Juror 5 didn't like what he heard, Winston acknowledged to Fuller.

"He basically said, 'This is not me. It doesn't sound like me … Man, I don't talk like that.'"

Winston's testimony eliminated the affidavit's gravest accusation – that being Stanford's supposed assertion that some jurors brought Internet material into the courthouse, pulled it out of files, and considered it along with the evidence presented at trial.

When Winston read that part back to Stanford, the juror told him it was "not accurate" because he wasn't sure any of his fellow jurors brought anything from the Internet.

Winston admitted that he didn't change the affidavit to address Stanford's concerns. And why not? It was late at night. So he printed it, and Juror 5 "agreed to sign it anyway," the pastor testified.

By this point in the hearing reporters were whispering to one another and looking at the defendants and their lawyers for signs of panic. There was no longer any question that there had been a Birmingham-based push to get a juror way down in Ozark to say things that could be used to help Richard Scrushy and Don Siegelman win a new trial.

I was surprised when Fuller acknowledged the elephant in the room by asking Charles Winston straight out if he knew Scrushy, who of course was there, watching the farce.

Winston said he'd met Scrushy within the past two years; had seen him preach; and had attended several meetings of Kingdom Builders, the "international ministry" founded by Scrushy after the FBI raided HealthSouth headquarters. Winston told the judge he was a member of Kingdom Builders.

Fuller asked if Scrushy had donated to his church, and Winston said he had not. The judge asked all seven witnesses if Scrushy or anyone connected to him paid them for their roles in the affidavits, and all said no.

A week after the hearing the *Birmingham News* published a story about a photo showing Scrushy standing with about 25 black pastors. Winston is in the front row, one minister between him and Scrushy. The picture was apparently taken in January 2006, four months before the start of the Siegelman-Scrushy trial, and published in the October 2006 issue of *Divine Favor Gospel Magazine*.

In a subsequent order Fuller wrote that it was "clear" that Charles and Debra Winston "had connections to Richard M. Scrushy prior to August of 2006." This was code for: I know you directed this charade, Scrushy, I just can't prove it.

I didn't believe every word out of Charles Winston's mouth, but on most counts found him candid. He'd made an open and shut case for a Rule 47.1 violation, at the very least by himself and his wife.

His wife's testimony was another story. The 55-year-old Birmingham lawyer was polite and composed, calling Fuller, "Sir." But her testimony was an insult to the court. I think she knew that no one believed a word she said, and it didn't seem to trouble her.

She told Fuller she decided to do the second affidavit after becoming "aware that Juror #5 wanted to meet with me."

That, like other statements, contradicted the testimony that preceded her, including by her husband. Juror 5 wasn't aware of her existence, to say nothing of asking her to come to Ozark for spiritual legal guidance.

She testified that neither Kilborn nor McDonald encouraged her to re-interview Stanford. "I don't think Mr. McDonald or Mr. Kilborn even knew I was preparing a second (affidavit)," she said.

Kilborn backed her up on this point after the hearing. "I had no idea she was going back to do a second one," he told reporters.

Fuller asked Mrs. Winston if she was familiar with rule 47.1. "Yes I am," she said. As if he hadn't heard, Fuller said, "Let me read it for you," and did.

She stuck with her guns. She said she didn't believe her visit to Ozark, her interview of Juror 5 and her contacts with Kilborn and McDonald before and after the second affidavit constituted a violation of the rule prohibiting post-trial contact with jurors.

For the Winstons story to be true, one had to accept that pastor and attorney took it upon themselves to invade the life and privacy of a man who lived three hours away; put words in his mouth; provide the fruits of their labors to Siegelman's lawyers; and did so voluntarily, without remuneration for their efforts or expenses.

Fuller, seething by the end of Debra Winston's testimony, was gentle with the final witness. He knew Charlie Stanford was a reluctant player in this drama. To one early question, a sheepish Stanford admitted before all that he couldn't "read that well."

It was sad watching this poor black man looking out at all us fine-dressed white folk admitting such a thing. I felt like I was witnessing a stunning failure of the educational system, and blamed the shame he felt on the win-at-all-costs defendants and their lawyers who'd dragged him back to Montgomery and put him in that chair.

Of his two affidavits, Stanford told Fuller that he thought the Winstons were going to "turn it into you all."

In other words, to the court, not lawyers for Siegelman and Scrushy.

With the witnesses finished, Fuller asked some questions of the lawyers, though not under oath. He zeroed in on the fax Debra Winston sent to McDonald from Atlanta. Fuller demanded to know why neither McDonald nor the Winstons had provided the court with the cover sheet to that fax. "The fax machine didn't eat it," said Fuller. "What happened to the original?"

McDonald told Fuller he'd lost it. Fuller's countenance suggested he didn't believe the Mobile attorney. He obviously suspected that the cover sheet might have contained an incriminating note from Debra Winston revealing a larger role in the second affidavit by McDonald or Kilborn than they were letting on. That Fuller would think that reflected just how low in his estimation Kilborn and McDonald had sunk.

After the hearing, Kilborn sold the Winstons down the river, but not the fruits of their actions. He said it was "irrelevant" if the pair violated Rule 47.1, as long as the lawyers for Siegelman and Scrushy didn't do so.

"The affidavits can still be used as evidence," he said.

Kilborn also distanced himself from the fax sent by Debra Winston to his law partner.

"I don't know anything about that Atlanta fax," he said.

———

Two years later, in one his many stories on the Siegelman case, *New York Times* reporter Adam Nossiter paraphrased from Stanford's affidavit, reporting, among other things, that some jurors "said that they felt pressured by the judge to reach a decision in order to go home and some jury members read about the case on the Internet during the trial."

Presented with the story, as support for the above declaration, was an Internet link to Stanford's first affidavit. This was the one that, as Stanford and Charles Winston testified, constituted Winston's words, not Stanford's, and that the juror signed just to get it over with. The affidavit was presented to *Times'* readers as evidence of juror misconduct.

Ignore for a moment that any half-brain with scissors, ruler, copier and basic computer know-how could fabricate an e-mail from Lincoln to Lee. That still didn't explain this: If the e-mails were bogus, how did their creator know the names and e-mail addresses of jurors? During jury selection and through trial, the names of the jurors were withheld from everyone, the defense teams and prosecutors included.

The answer was quick in coming. After reaching the verdict and before departing the jurors passed around two sheets of paper. Each wrote down his or her contact information, including, for those who had them, e-mail addresses. The marshals made copies and passed them out to the jurors. Every juror left the courthouse that day with such a list.

Langer gave me a copy. It showed her e-mail address as Katie.langer@blank. com. The k is upper case, but that's because handwritten Ks often appear upper case whether they are or not. Langer's "K" on the juror contact sheet certainly did. Though an e-mail sent to her using a capital K would reach her, e-mails sent from her always show a small k, as would the same printed off a computer.

A real Katie Langer e-mail tag looks like: katie.langer@blank.com. "I instantaneously noticed that the K was capitalized and my e-mail address is all lower case," she said.

Before seeing the e-mails, and the capital Ks, she'd feared that someone had hacked into her computer and created the e-mails, she said.

All seven e-mails (there were to be two more sent in December) reflect that they were printed from Langer's "inbox," even those she purportedly sent. Two were shown as being sent on May 29, the remaining five on June 25. All show that, at the time they were printed, there were 14 e-mails in Langer's in-box. This suggests that during that period Langer regularly maintained exactly 14 e-mails in her in-box or that the person who did the cutting and pasting failed to change the in-box number on the pattern he was using.

At the top and bottom of all the e-mails are the basic directives – "Reply," "Reply All," "Forward," "Delete," and "Report as Spam." On the top of both of the e-mails sent in the third batch, on Sept. 21, the phrase "Report as Spam," instead reads, "Report as Seem." The bottom on both is correct, showing, "Report as Spam."

There were issues with the content as well. Langer, Hendrix and Rase said that none of the jurors referred to each other by numbers. "I still don't know my fellow juror's numbers. We called each other by name. We didn't talk about numbers," Hendrix said.

Nor did anyone refer to Scrushy as, "the pastor," Langer said. "I don't even know if I knew in trial he was a pastor. I think he was just HealthSouth. I don't remember them ever referring to him in trial ever as a pastor."

A footnote in the Siegelman-Scrushy motion attempted to address that, declaring that Scrushy "is the Pastor of Grace and Purpose Church in Birmingham, Alabama." While Scrushy is a household name in Alabama, Grace and Purpose Church -- to the extent there is such a thing -- is not.

One of the first e-mails shows Langer and Hendrix discussing issues that would have occurred during deliberations. Two jurors, according to the e-mail, were "still of trac." The missive was dated May 29. That was weeks before the start of deliberations, and at a time when the jurors were under strict orders not to discuss the case among themselves.

I have no doubt the e-mails were fabricated. But to what end?

I think the long-shot first hope was that Fuller would accept them at face value, see them as inflammatory, and grant Siegelman and Scrushy a new trial.

Second choice: That Fuller would order the seizure of the jurors' computers and subpoena the records of their Internet providers. The offending e-mails wouldn't be found because they didn't exist, but maybe, just maybe, a scouring of Langer's and Hendrix's computer records would reveal something as bad or worse, such as one or both jurors regularly reading news articles on the trial or researching the backgrounds of Siegelman and Scrushy.

If the bandit didn't succeed, nothing was lost, as long as he didn't get caught. And there was much to be gained in the all-important public relations arena.

From June 2007 on, that being when the national media first reported Jill Simpson's allegations, Team Siegelman relentlessly cited the juror e-mails as additional evidence of the wrongs committed against him. For Hendrix and Langer the e-mails created a presumption of guilt that remains in the minds of many.

I don't believe that the trial teams of either defendant participated in the creation of the e-mails, and that was the beauty of the scheme. Kilborn, McDonald, Leach -- all had to suspect shenanigans. But they didn't know this as fact and made it their business not to look in that direction.

The e-mail bandit knew this particular group of lawyers, provided with the goods and the demands of their clients, would run hard, keep their blinders on, and rip into the jurors.

Soon after the hearing, Fuller called a second one, this time issuing subpoenas to all 12 jurors. He implied that he hadn't believed much of the testimony in the first hearing, especially Debra Winston's, who he essentially accused of perjury and violating Rule 47.1.

The purpose of the second hearing was to investigate one issue: Whether "extraneous" information, such as from the Internet or newspapers, was brought into the jury room or otherwise considered by jurors; and if so, did the material have a substantive impact on the jury's decision.

As with the first hearing, Fuller and only he would ask questions.

I think summoning the jurors back to Montgomery sickened Fuller, but he saw no choice. If he didn't, Siegelman and Scrushy would cite his failure to do so in their appeal, and maybe, just maybe, the 11th Circuit Court of Appeals would see it their way order him to conduct a hearing or investigation anyway.

The government wasn't happy. Feaga warned that in the future jurors could come to believe "they are going to be subjected to investigations" by "the very criminals that they convicted."

Nor were the jurors thrilled. Hendrix said the defendants had taken his free acknowledgement to a reporter that he'd researched the duties of a foreman and "turned it into the most horrendous thing that ever happened."

"None of us deserves this. We're just a bunch of regular people. We gave these guys a fair trial," he said. "That's what we were asked to do. Gracious knows, this was something you just can't prepare for. It was an incredible experience and it took a toll on us all. None of us knew this was coming. All of a sudden I go to my mailbox (and found a jury summons) and I'm locked up for two months."

Lawyers for Siegelman and Scrushy were encouraged by Fuller's decision to summon the jurors, though disappointed that the judge hadn't ordered the seizure of their computers and subpoenaed their e-mail and cell-phone records. They wanted him to set a new national standard post-trial invasion of a juror's privacy. I think Siegelman, Scrushy and their lawyers would have been thrilled by an order to subject Hendrix and Langer to interrogation by water-boarding.

Judges, especially when faced with unusual requests like those made to Fuller, seek direction in the law and the precedent-setting rulings of higher courts. While there were no prior rulings on point with the defendants' requests here (in part because of the relative newness of e-mail), the broader issue of post-verdict inquiries into juries and jurors has received considerable attention.

To the extent that courts permit such investigations, it's for one purpose: To determine the type and seriousness of extraneous influences on a jury. These include threats against or bribes paid to jurors; prejudicial contacts between jurors and outside parties; and – the one that applied here – exposure to prejudicial information not admitted into evidence. This can include media reports or independent investigations by a juror, such as by researching a defendant.

Post-verdict probes into allegations of juror misconduct are not to be entered into willy-nilly. In fact, the very opposite.

In layman's terms, would you want to serve on a jury argued by the likes of Vince Kilborn and Art Leach knowing that if you found their clients guilty they could seize your computers and personal communications records, possibly publicize them in court records, and stick you on the witness stand, all because of unauthenticated, anonymously sent e-mails and juror affidavits as polluted as those bearing Stanford's name?

That's how the courts see it too, and have for years.

In a 1979 ruling, the U.S. Supreme Court declared that some probes into juror misconduct would lead to new trials. But the court questioned whether the jury system "could survive such efforts to perfect it." And in stronger language, stated that "our very system of justice would be jeopardized" if courts were to fail to protect the finality of verdicts and the rights of jurors who reached them. Were the courts to allow it, jurors could expect "a barrage of post-verdict scrutiny" from dissatisfied parties, the court stated.

During the trial and juror misconduct hearings my primary go-to legal expert was John Carroll, the dean of Cumberland Law School and a former federal magistrate. He told our readers that e-mails were simply an electronic version of the sort of communication between jurors that, while prohibited, is not uncommon. As an example, he cited two jurors walking to the court parking lot and talking about another juror's position.

"(Courts) assume that jurors talk outside the jury room sometimes, even though they're not supposed to," Carroll said. "You could search long and heard before you find defendants getting a new trial because jurors were discussing the case outside the deliberation room."

On Nov. 17, the jurors returned to the courthouse for a reunion none sought or wanted, this time as witnesses.

Fuller opened by telling the defense teams that everyone summoned for jury duty is sent a package of instructions which includes a link to the court's web-site. The opening page of the court's site contains a link called, "Juror Instructions," within which is a brief guide for forepersons. Because it was such a high profile case, a link to the Siegelman indictment was on the court's home page before and during the trial.

He reminded the parties how frequently and carefully he had counseled the jury against talking about the case outside court and reading or watching media reports. He reminded them that during the trial he'd told jurors to report to him if they learned that a fellow juror was introducing outside evidence into deliberations. No juror ever contacted him to make such a complaint.

Katie Langer testified that soon after deliberations began she downloaded a copy of the indictment from the court's web-site because she'd found it difficult to find time to read it during deliberations. Langer made no effort to conceal this. She told her fellow jurors about it at the time, she testified.

Initially, Fuller had provided the jury with just one copy of the indictment. Hendrix later righted that by asking the judge to give a copy to each juror.

After deliberations started, Hendrix also downloaded a copy of the indictment from the court web-site. He made organizational notes on his and brought it into the jury room the first couple of days. He told his fellow jurors that he'd done it, and also disclosed having looked up the duties of a foreman.

In their testimony, the other jurors confirmed this. None said they were alarmed then or later by those revelations.

"I admired the way he handled it (being a foreman)," said Juror 30, a middle-aged black man with a no-nonsense demeanor.

Fuller didn't directly ask the jurors if they sent or received e-mails during the trial. Instead, he asked questions that covered the content of the e-mails. For example, he asked each if they had discussed the possible sentences facing the defendants. One of the e-mails – shown as being from Lyles to Langer -- stated, "penalty 2 severe."

Also, Stanford's second affidavit has him saying that "several of us jurors" talked about the likely punishment and none felt the defendants would serve time.

All 12, Stanford included, testified that no one ever discussed the sentences faced by the defendants were they to be found guilty.

Hendrix, Langer and Juror 22 testified to incidental exposure to media reports. Hendrix subscribes to two newspapers, and occasionally saw headlines atop trial stories. Juror 22 said she inadvertently heard some TV reports, but hit the mute button as soon as they came on. Langer said that she'd heard there was a story in the *Advertiser* reporting that the law school at Faulkner University in Montgomery had been accredited. (Such a story ran on June 17.) She was hoping to attend the law school in the fall (she did) and went on the Internet to see the story. While looking for it, she saw the headline/link to a story on the trial. She testified she wanted to read it but did not.

Stanford, appearing somewhat less than certain, said Langer brought a "foreman's book" into the jury room. The purported author of the two affidavits had it backwards. There was no foreman's book, but rather, a copy of the indictment, and it was Hendrix, not Langer, who brought that.

At hearing's end, Art Leach pleaded with Fuller to "bring (Stanford) back and walk him through his affidavit" because the juror from Ozark "was struggling to understand the questions."

Feaga popped out of his seat and told Fuller that the defendants were "just not happy with what they heard."

The judge declined to bring Stanford back for what would have been a third turn in the witness chair.

Leach breached hypocrisy with a post-hearing motion seeking access to Stanford's pre-trial records. He hoped to use them to make the argument that

Stanford wasn't qualified to be a juror because of an inability to read. The motion implied that Scrushy would seek a new trial based on this after-the-fact finding that an unqualified juror served on the panel.

Franklin ridiculed the request, saying that the defendants knew Juror 5 didn't have much education and that was "why they wanted him on the jury in the first place."

Within days of the hearing, Fuller ruled that the hearing revealed "credible evidence" that Hendrix and Langer considered outside evidence during the trial and ordered the parties to file briefs, after which he would rule.

What sounded like and was touted by the defendants as a major victory was anything but. In his order, Fuller remarked that the extent of the "credible evidence" was Hendrix's researching the duties of a foreman and the downloading of the indictment by Hendrix and Langer. It was most unlikely that those minor infractions would lead to the granting of a new trial.

In writing for Siegelman, McDonald introduced a new animal. He wrote that the jury didn't consist of 12 equals, but "two 'super jurors' and 10 'ordinary' jurors who deferred to the two who possessed more information than the others."

In addition to being bizarre, it was an insult to the 10 jurors and a commentary on the defendant's own jury-picking strategy of keeping the panel's education level as low as possible. Now they were complaining that the jurors they had largely chosen were too "ordinary" and manipulated by "super jurors."

On Dec. 13, Fuller ruled. He wrote that he had no trouble concluding that the amount of outside influences on jurors was insufficient to require a new trial.

As for the demand that the juror's computers and records be seized, the judge stated that the defendants "provided no legal precedent for such an unusual and intrusive investigation of jurors."

"In this Court's view, its role is to follow the law, rather than create it."

Given the intense media coverage it was not surprising that a few jurors had some mild and incidental exposure to trial reports. None sought it, and all were "conscientiously forthcoming" in acknowledging that exposure.

Fuller left no doubt as to his belief that the e-mails were fakes. To cover himself for appellate reasons, he addressed the implications of the e-mails if they were real. He concluded that the missives showed, at most, some discussion between jurors prior to deliberations, and during deliberations, brief comments about the possible penalties for the defendants.

Even if authentic, the e-mails didn't reflect any outside influences on the jurors, and thus, were not "in this Court's view grounds for granting a new trial."

The judge concluded the order, as he had the trial, by praising the jurors.

When Charlie Stanford's first affidavit came up short, the Winstons and those whose interests they served tried again. The pattern repeated itself with the e-mails.

A week after Fuller's ruling, the e-mail bandit struck one final time. He (or she) mailed a pair of new ones to the defense lawyers and, this time, the media as well. Both were purportedly from Langer to Hendrix and shown as being sent late on the night of June 25, 2006, which was four days before the verdict.

The first read:

> *....judge really helping w/jurors...*
> *still having difficulties with (juror) #30*
> *...any ideas???*
> *keep pushing on ur side*
> *did not understand ur thoughts on statute*
> *but received links.*
> *Katie*

And the second:

> *I can't see anything we miss'd. u?*
> *articles u sent outstanding! gov & pastor up s---t creek.*
> *good thing no one likes them anyway.*
> *all public officials r scum; especially this 1.*
> *Pastor is really a piece of work*
> *...they missed before, but we won't*
> *...also, keep working on (juror) 30*
> *will update u on other meeting.*
> *Katie*

Lawyers for Siegelman and Scrushy naturally filed motions, again asking Fuller to seize the jurors' computers and communications records. Kilborn said that Siegelman and Scrushy would be "guaranteed a new trial if these e-mails are authenticated."

The last two e-mails were, in addition to being longer and cruder, suspiciously on-point, as if crafted to address the very shortcomings Fuller found in the prior e-mails when assuming for the sake of argument that they were genuine.

This time the bandit had Langer and Hendrix sending each other articles and Internet links; Fuller "helping" jurors reach a guilty verdict; and Langer displaying alarming prejudice against public officials and extreme bias against Scrushy, with her reference to jurors in the first HealthSouth trial as having "missed" getting Scrushy.

Langer said she was sickened when she first saw them, and said she could understand how the public, seeing these e-mails, might think badly of her. "It has defamed my character. It portrays me in a way that is not true," she said.

The self-described Air Force brat said she has always respected public officials and, as a relative newcomer to Alabama, knew little about Siegelman or Scrushy before the trial.

The tailoring of the e-mails to address the conclusions in Fuller's order suggests that their creator was familiar with the judge's positions as presented in his order and savvy enough to address these concerns in the new e-mails. In other words, that bandit was probably a lawyer or assisted by one.

Fuller rejected the new motions. He'd had enough and assumed correctly that the 11th Circuit would see it that way too.

———

Almost two years later, in July 2008, the Justice Department notified the defense lawyers that there had been an investigation into the e-mails.

It was disclosed that the last two e-mails were also sent to Langer's supervisor and four of Hendrix's co-workers. The co-workers reported receipt of the e-mails to Langer and Hendrix, who, separate of each another, contacted the U.S. Marshals to complain. The marshals passed it on to Louis Franklin, who turned the matter over to postal inspectors.

The postal inspectors interviewed Langer, Hendrix and their co-workers, as well as a fellow employee of Hendrix's who monitored his e-mail during the two month trial to make sure Hendrix didn't miss anything. The co-worker said he never saw any e-mails from the Katie Langer address. The inspectors also printed out test e-mails to and from Langer's e-mail account and compared them to the anonymously sent e-mails.

The postal inspectors concluded that the e-mails were frauds. They submitted the envelopes and e-mail sheets to forensic testing, and described the results as inconclusive. The investigation was closed in September 2007, without a determination as to who had sent them.

Midway through the probe the U.S. Marshals Office informed Fuller about the matter, and the determination, already made by then, that the e-mails were fakes.

In July 2008, the Justice Department wrote the defense lawyers to apprise them of the results of the postal inspectors report, and gave them the report.

Incredibly, the news stories reporting the postal inspectors' findings and the incredibly spiteful act against the two jurors focused, not on the victims or the determination that the e-mails were frauds, but on the squeaky wheels. Team Siegelman, with Artur Davis playing point man, did a brilliant job of turning lemons into lemonade. The Alabama congressman handed the media copies of the Justice

Department letter to the defendants and accused Fuller and Franklin of misconduct in failing to disclose the probe to Siegelman, Scrushy, and their attorneys.

Franklin responded that the postal inspectors were investigating complaints of juror harassment and that neither he nor Fuller had any oversight over the probe, and that the e-mail investigation was done as a matter of court security, not as part of the case.

Probably the report should have been provided to them sooner, but what had they lost by not seeing it?

The defendants argued that the postal inspectors didn't go far enough in their investigation. I didn't think they did either, though not in the direction sought by the defense teams. If the inspectors had really wanted to crack some eggs they should have gone to see the Winstons and Juror 5, asked about the juror contact list that had the juror e-mail addresses, and climbed the ladder from there.

PART FOUR:
The Hoax that Suckered Some of the Top Names in Journalism

—————⟫•❀•⟪—————

Chapter 39
The Dishonest Broker

"There is extensive evidence that the prosecution of former Governor Don Siegelman was directed or promoted by Washington officials, likely including former White House Deputy Chief of Staff and Advisor to the President Karl Rove, and that political considerations influenced the decision to bring charges."

-- From introduction to April 2008 majority report by the House Judiciary Committee on "selective prosecution" by the Bush Justice Department. Scott Horton was quoted in the report and cited 15 times in the footnotes, more than any other source.

"For a few weeks now, I have been pointing out the similarity of the Alabama Newhouse papers (especially the B'ham News and Mobile Press Register) to the Soviet press of the pre-Gorbachev age. They are the golden voice of the Alabama GOP, presenting the world in politically flavored terms, start to finish. But yesterday, the coverage took a turn into territory that tops anything I ever remember in the Soviet press. Now the 'Bama mainstream papers are moving into decidedly North Korean territory."

-- Scott Horton, in his July 31 column on the web-site of the venerable Harper's magazine.

On April 22, 2008, a Huntsville-based group calling itself North Alabamians for Media Reform hosted, "An Evening with Scott Horton."

The subject of the evening's talk was, "Watchdogs or Lap Dogs?: Politics and the Alabama Press."

The speaker was a bespectacled, slightly tubby and ever so rumpled man who looked more like a journalist or professor – his new professions – than his old, an attorney at an elite New York law firm.

Siegelman was there, having recently been released from prison pending his appeal, by order of the 11th Circuit. So too Jill Simpson, who, though overweight, radiated star power. Maybe it was her bright red hair or her odd confidence, or that she was still glowing from her appearance two months before on, "60 Minutes."

The 200-plus crowd delivered standing ovations to Siegelman and Horton and gave Simpson a pleasant welcome.

Professor-like, Horton began by placing the failings of the Alabama media on the Siegelman case in historical context. He spoke of the blistering meted out by the state's newspapers, circa 1880, to progressive Alabama Supreme Court Chief Justice Thomas Minott Peters. The judge was far ahead of his time in advocating racial equality. His reward? A reputation shattering attack at the hands of the prosecutors and Alabama newspapers.

"And the national media took notice, and the national publication that stood most in the forefront in covering it was a periodical in New York called *Harper's* magazine," said Horton.

To state the obvious: Peters is Siegelman; the likes of myself, Brett Blackledge and Kim Chandler and our editors are racist journalists; and Horton is the courageous national reporter setting things right.

Example two was the Civil Rights movement. The state media remained largely silent as blacks were beaten and discriminated against, and it took the national media to tell the world what was really happening in Alabama. And who could argue with that?

With historical precedent established, Horton came to the meat of the program – the state media's coverage of Siegelman.

He said that once again developments in Alabama "were being catapulted into the national headlines, and I think the consensus emerged quickly amongst the national media, that the major Alabama papers, just as during the civil rights period, were not particularly reliable and they (the national media) needed to do their own work and reporting out in Alabama."

"I'm convinced that the local press fell down in its responsibility to properly report the Siegelman case and at this point, the national media is stepping in," he said.

Horton had reason to feel good about himself that night. He had in the previous year helped choreograph a propaganda campaign that transformed Siegelman from convicted criminal to a nationally-recognized victim of a White House-led Republican conspiracy.

He accomplished this by writing more than 130 on-line columns about the Siegelman case for *Harper's* and articles for the well-regarded *American Lawyer* magazine; waxing eloquent on national radio and television news talk shows; and, crucially, serving as the behind-the-scenes source for those in the national media and Congress who sang the song to a wider audience.

As I believe will be established in this final section, Horton fabricated meetings that never occurred, deals that didn't happen, comments never made. He was forever enlightening subjects of his derision by placing them, actor like, in dramas that occurred only in his imagination.

Initially I couldn't bear to read him, but later came to tolerate if not enjoy Horton. Reading him is like watching a documentary on one of those polygamy sects, fascinating and disgusting at the same time. His ability to cram multiple lies into a single sentence is awe-inspiring, and sentence after sentence, the fibs whizzing past like race-cars at Talladega, so fast you don't have time to grasp one before hitting the next, and the next. For example, he wrote that the Siegelman prosecutors "spent roughly $30 million in taxpayer's money to take down the state's most prominent Democrat at the direction of Karl Rove …"

Where he came up with $30 million is beyond me. Perhaps from Siegelman, who priced his prosecution at $40 million, apparently confusing himself with Clinton and the Whitewater probe. The state's most prominent Democrat? Not in 2005 he wasn't. Prosecuted at the direction of Karl Rove? Only if you believed Jill Simpson.

During the Clinton administration, the rhetoric and commentary about Clinton and his wife, even from responsible voices, was routinely vicious, indecent, even sadistic. Horton is the equal of the ugliest of the Clintons' critics, a Rush Limbaugh of the left. He doesn't dislike, he despises; he doesn't use sarcasm, but ridicule.

Frequent target Louis Franklin was referred to, among other things, as, "Leura Canary's sock puppet." Mark Fuller was a crook who traded rulings on the Siegelman case for government contracts. The judge was also derided as stupid, with one of his briefs called, "farcical, the sort of thing that any judge would be ashamed to allow see the light of day."

Horton seethed after the *Montgomery Advertiser* dared publish a pleasant feature on Leura (Garrett) Canary. He answered with a column comparing Canary to her "uncle" Si Garrett, the corrupt attorney general alleged to have played a part in the notorious 1954 murder of Phenix City reformer Albert Patterson.

"Would you expect anything different from Si Garrett's niece? It must be in her DNA," he wrote.

Among the errors in the piece – and they abound, each amplifying innuendo -- was that the long-dead Garrett wasn't Canary's uncle. He was from a different branch of family, something like her 10th cousin.

Blackledge's Pulitzer Prize notwithstanding, Horton wrote that in "most states a reporter like Mr. Blackledge would not venture very far… But in 'Bama, where they take their Kool-aid unalloyed, he's the real thing."

(In 2008, the Associated Press hired Blackledge to cover national intelligence issues, and he moved to Washington.)

Horton swamps his prose with literary reference. Cicero, Victor Hugo, Shakespeare and regional classics like Robert Penn Warren's "All the King's Men," and Harper Lee's "To Kill a Mockingbird," all used to add solemnity and weight to the crimes of participants in the plot. Because he spent time as a human rights lawyer in Russia, that country's writers make appearances. Comparisons between the Soviet Union and Alabama are frequent, usually in his obsessive lacerations of the Alabama press.

Horton started writing for *Harper's* within a month or two of leaving the prestigious New York-based international law firm, Patterson, Belknap, Webb & Tyler, where he was a partner. According to an on-line biography, he founded that firm's practice in parts of Russia and the former Soviet Union and also advised leaders in the region.

Horton's erudition and intellectual heft are not in question. He is fond of posting on, "No Comment," excerpts of, for example, German, Spanish, and French artists and philosophers, and in their original tongue.

The crowd in Huntsville that night took great delight in his matter-of-fact statement that coverage of the Siegelman case in the Alabama media was, "off the charts ... worse than most of the cases I've studied in the former Soviet Union."

In his world there is no middle ground, only saints and devils. His favored literary metaphor for the anti-Siegelman forces is Javert, the obsessive inspector from Victor Hugo's *Les Miserables*. Horton's Javert encompassed Rove, the Bush Justice Department, the Rileys, the Canarys, and, perhaps especially, Louis Franklin.

The Javert conceit appeared regularly in Horton's columns and in titles of his pieces, such as, "Javert's Wailings Grow Louder," and "More Responses to Javert," and "Javert's Amazing Pirouettes."

"Javert is a part of a culture of moral collapse and decrepitude ... This culture has nothing to do with justice and truth," Horton explained. "It is indeed the enemy of truth and justice. Its natural matrix is fetid and dark, it operates with innuendo and falsehood writ large, drawing heavily on the reputation of ancient and once noble institutions through which its rot swiftly spreads."

Swirling within this fetid matrix was the repugnant Alabama media, chiefly the *Birmingham News* and the *Press Register*, which as Horton never tired of pointing out, are "sister" papers, both owned by Newhouse-owned Advance Publication.

In his brain, that's no coincidence. In fact, we "co-ventured the prosecution," probably after being bribed, and should be subjected to a federal criminal investigation.

This from a March 2008 column, "A Brain Dead Press":

The bottom line is that these papers have an amazingly warm and cozy relationship with the current political powers-that-be in the state. I have no idea what they get out of this relationship, but on matters such as this I am far too cynical to think that they'd engage in such reputation-damaging factual contortions without very strong incentives.

The big offenders, as I have chronicled repeatedly, are the Birmingham News and the Mobile Press-Register. If a special prosecutor is appointed to examine the gross irregularities surrounding the Siegelman case—and calls for that step mount with each passing day—then the inexplicably cozy relationship between the two papers in Birmingham and Mobile and the politically directed prosecutors who pushed the case against Siegelman should be right near the top of the matters investigated."

Horton will be a regular presence in the final section of this book. I recognize that by making him so I risk appearing vengeful, as Javert writing about Javert. In fact I was far more troubled by what he wrote about others, especially the judge, jurors and prosecutors. Agree with them or not, they were honorable people doing their jobs. He treated them like dogs.

But that's not the reason Horton will figure prominently here. Rather, it's his relevance.

In part through his tireless advocacy of Jill Simpson and her story, this arrogant, nasty man – Javert if ever -- influenced the coverage of the Siegelman case by major national media and appears to have all but dictated the findings on the case by the Democrat majority of the U.S. House Judiciary Committee.

That is the central scandal of this last section. It's about a con, pulled off by Horton, Simpson and others, and leading his own charge, Don Siegelman.

Chapter 40
Dana Jill

"She's been smeared as 'crazy' and as a 'disgruntled contract bidder.' And something nastier: after her intention to speak became known, Simpson's house was burned to the ground, and her car was driven off the road and totaled. Clearly, there are some very powerful people in Alabama who feel threatened. Her case starts to sound like a chapter out of John Grisham's book The Pelican Brief. However, those who have dismissed Simpson are in for a very rude surprise. Her affidavit stands up on every point, and there is substantial evidence which will corroborate its details.

-- Scott Horton, defending Simpson in a column on the web-site of Harper's magazine.

"She's a complete lunatic. I've never met this woman. This woman was not involved in any campaign in which I was involved. I have yet to find anybody who knows her."

-- Karl Rove, in April 2008 interview with GQ magazine.

Early in the spring of 2007, the Muhammad Ali of Alabama fund-raising used e-mail, newspaper advertisements and personal requests to generate a different kind of support – letters to Judge Fuller.

"The letter just needs to be from the heart and tell the judge how I have made a positive impact on your life, or the life of someone you know or how I made a positive difference for the people of Alabama," went one such directive.

The letter came to the attention of John Ehinger, an editorial writer for the *Huntsville Times,* who used it for column fodder. "Say what you will about former Gov. Don Siegelman -- and there are many things you could say -- but that dude never gives up. I mean never," Ehinger began. "Convicted last year of corruption charges in federal court, Siegelman has gone to his grass roots. He's writing letters to friends, former associates and anyone else who might give him a good reference. No, he's not looking for a job. He's looking to stay out of jail."

Among other things, Siegelman told recipients that he'd once stopped on Interstate 59 to help a "sweet elderly lady" change her tire.

Siegelman's efforts to produce letters to Fuller and money for his legal fees could not have been more public. Privately, he had something else cooking. With sentencing closing in, Siegelman spotted opportunity in a scandal percolating in Washington.

U.S. Attorneys lead the 93 offices of federal lawyers who prosecute federal crimes and represent the government in civil matters. They are political appointees. That is to say, they serve "at the pleasure of the president." When a president from one party replaces a president from another, U.S. Attorneys throughout the country tender their resignations and wait to be replaced by the new president's appointees. Almost without fail, each state's senators select U.S. Attorneys, then pass their names on to the president who does the actual appointing.

U.S. Attorneys should not be political appointees. They should be selected from within the Justice Department, having earned those positions based on merit and seniority. But that's not how it is. As a result, it's not unusual for U.S. Attorneys to be political hacks. Competent or not, they must bear the burden of being viewed through the prism of affiliation with a political party. For most cases, such as those involving drugs, this isn't a problem. But in public corruption cases, a U.S. Attorney's political affiliation, if different than the defendant, can be counted on to become an issue regardless of the circumstances.

In late 2006, the Bush administration fired 8 of those 93 U.S. Attorneys. Each had served roughly five years. Concerns about the firings blossomed into uproar after it was reported that Republican Senator Pete Domenici of New Mexico had called U.S. Attorney David Iglesias at home to ask if a prominent Democrat then under investigation would be indicted before the November elections. Iglesias replied that there would be no indictments prior to the election.

Domenici hung up on him. That was bad enough. But then the aging senator lobbied the White House and the Justice Department to remove Iglesias, and indeed, that's what happened.

There were questionable circumstances in the firing of some of the others, though none rivaled the Iglesias case.

———

Because Republicans controlled both houses of Congress, the Bush administration received little in the way of congressional scrutiny. That changed in January 2007, when Democrats gained control of Congress.

The subjects demanding scrutiny seemed endless. What of the vast and deliberate underestimations of the projected cost of the Iraq war? What of the influence of oil companies on reports by federal agencies on global warming? How about the Cheney-led use of 9-11 as an excuse to keep all manner of government activities secret, most with no relation to national security?

Instead, the Democrats – clowns they so often are – aimed much of their ire and energies at a scandal that barely deserved the name. Of the eight fired U.S. Attorneys, one bore clear marks of impropriety and most of what was needed to know about Iglesias's firing had already been admitted to by Domenici.

Nothing illustrates the scantiness of the investigation into the politicization of the Bush Justice Department quite like the extraordinary impact upon it by a larger-than-life Southern character with a mile-wide inventive streak.

By blowing the whistle on Karl Rove, Bill Canary and so many other powerful people, Jill Simpson risked her considerable standing in the state Republican Party organization, a thriving law practice, even her life.

That's the story Siegelman, Scott Horton and other promoters of this farcical episode sold to great swaths of the public through their supplicants in the national media. What's most remarkable about this portrait of Simpson is not that it's an exaggeration of the truth but that it's a sham from start to finish.

None of it is true.

Hilly, rural northeast Alabama is one of few remaining non-black Democrat pockets in the state. The region was particularly hard hit by the Depression and folks there remain grateful for New Deal programs that helped put people to work and left a lasting mark on the area. As a result, the county Republican organizations that try and mostly fail to dent the area's Democratic power structure are close-knit. Everybody knows each other, and volunteers are always welcome.

Jill Simpson has never been an officer in the party organizations of Jackson County (where she works) or neighboring DeKalb County (where she lives), nor has she ever attended their meetings nor volunteered in any capacity.

And it wasn't because she was working at a level above the locals. State party officials, as they repeatedly tried to tell the national media, had never heard of Simpson. They gave it one final go after Simpson's February 2008 appearance on "60 Minutes." Mike Hubbard, the chairman of the Alabama Republican Party, issued a statement declaring that party staff had done "an exhaustive search" of party records going back several years and could "not find not one instance of Dana Jill Simpson volunteering or working on behalf of the Alabama Republican Party."

"Nor can we find anyone within the Republican Party leadership in Alabama who has ever so much as heard of Dana Jill Simpson until she made her first wave of accusations last summer in an affidavit originally released only to the *New York Times* (also to *Time*)."

You could almost hear the folks at the *New York Times* and CBS saying to themselves, "Well, they would deny it, wouldn't they?"

In fact, the only confirmed service by Simpson for any candidate was volunteer work for Roy Moore's gubernatorial campaign *against* Bob Riley in the 2006 Republican primary. And the "Ten Commandments Judge" is only nominally a Republican.

Jill Simpson's most striking physical characteristics are her height – she's 5-7 -- and her bright green eyes. She struck a colorful figure at the University of Alabama, where she ran for student government president and in her later years worked as a bartender. She remained in Tuscaloosa for law school, graduating in 1989.

But for a brief spell after law school, she's practiced alone.

Simpson's been married twice, both times in the early 1990s, each union lasting about a year. I believe that one of those marriages produced a son, that she later had another son with a boyfriend, and in 2004, adopted a daughter.

Financially and professionally, Simpson entered 2007 at a low point. She was, by her own account, broke.

She'd been hit with at least nine tax liens, state and federal, in the years preceding her career as a great American whistleblower. In 2006 – and file this in the "it's a small world" category – she hired Lanny Young-lawyer Steve Glassroth to represent her in a dispute with the IRS. Two years later she sued Glassroth, claiming he'd failed to adequately represent her, leading to a $150,000 judgment against her by the IRS.

By 2007 she'd moved in with her mother and out of a $640,000 home on Lake Guntersville. She'd entered into a lease purchase agreement with the owners but neglected to make her payments, compelling them to sue, seeking more than $130,000. Her law practice – she specializes in divorce law – was in a state of disrepair.

Simpson also has experience in traffic court -- as a defendant.

From 2000 to 2006 she saw more than her share of blue lights in the rearview, having been ticketed eight times for speeding, three times at 90 mph or plus. Among those was a December 2004 adventure when police stopped her flying 102 in a 40 mph speed zone.

Early 2007 found Simpson and a boyfriend in the midst of a lawsuit against doctors, a hospital, and other medical professionals she blamed for the December 2003 death of her unborn child. Simpson had arrived at the hospital believing the child stillborn, and indeed it was. By August 2009, with most of the defendants having been dismissed by the court, Simpson dropped the case.

At the risk of sounding callous, Simpson's loss of a child is the kindest explanation I can come up with to explain her actions. A close second is a pathological need for attention that demanded more and wilder tales to maintain her presence at center stage of a national political and legal drama she helped create.

Her sense for the dramatic cannot be underestimated.

Among the many reasons Simpson gave for swearing out an affidavit was her fear of getting knocked off. "I think she wanted to get it on record, more than anything else," her lawyer, Priscilla Duncan, told a reporter. "She's had had a couple of scares, which you're aware of."

Scott Horton was less circumspect. The *Harper's* columnist reported that Simpson's house was "burned to the ground" and her car "driven off the road and totaled" after "powerful people in Alabama" discovered her intent to reveal all.

The home, actually Simpson's mother's, was not "burned to the ground." It suffered smoke damage to two rooms. The carport, though, was destroyed. The fire, which fire officials assigned to an electrical surge, occurred on Feb. 21, 2007.

This was more than three months before anyone outside of the Siegelman-Scrushy legal/public relations machine had the first inkling that someone named Dana Jill Simpson planned to unleash her fantasies upon the world.

Four months after the fire, and after *Time* and the *New York Times* catapulted her into the national spotlight, Simpson called Rainsville Fire Chief Ronnie Helton to suggest that someone might have torched her mom's home. She was, though, unable to provide any evidence to support the claim. "There hasn't been anything suspicious I'm aware of," Helton said almost a year later.

He noted that the state Fire Marshalls office, which investigates arson cases, hadn't opened or been asked to open a probe of the fire.

Ten days after trying to burn her alive, the GOP goons tried again. According to a police report of the incident, a car driven by Mark Roden of Rainbow City, Ala., veered into Simpson's lane. She swerved, ran off the road, and slammed into a parked car.

Roden's motive?

Simpson, according to Duncan, was on her way back from a meeting in Birmingham with, of all people, Richard Scrushy.

From there we are led to infer that the Repubs knew about the meeting and assigned Roden to kill, maim or, at the least, scare Simpson, lest she reveal what she knew about Karl Rove's role in Siegelman's prosecution.

Simpson, Duncan, Horton and the left-wing bloggers who took up her cause should be horse-whipped for implying that Roden attempted to murder her on behalf of the Republican Party. If Simpson and Duncan believed there was even a possibility it was true they should have sued Roden. Then they could have deposed him, subpoenaed his telephone and financial records, and followed the trail, plumbers-like, straight to Rove and the White House.

If Simpson and Horton are correct in their suspicions, then the GOP needs to do something, and fast, about its Deep South death squad operation. Roden violated a cardinal rule of death squad members: Never stick around after a failed murder attempt to check on the victim. He did that, then, even dumber, waited for police so he could give them his name.

If there's a movie — and nothing would surprise me at this point — expect sinister replications of the fire and the wreck, with the Hollywood beauty who plays Jill coming within inches of losing her life.

———

Simpson would never have received her due as a great American citizen if not for two associations, one with Rob Riley, the other with Mark Bollinger.

Bollinger is nothing if not likable. He's a gregarious bullshitter, a Yellow Dog Democrat, and like everyone else in the world, a purported hater of corruption.

He was an assistant to Jimmy Evans in the attorney general's office in the early 1990s, and, when I met him in the mid-1990s, was working for the Alabama Bureau of Investigation.

Back in the '90s it was not unusual for Bollinger to call me dishing semi-scoop or rumor on this or that politician. At some point he left Montgomery and moved home to northeast Alabama. After that, his calls and e-mails became less frequent.

My intro to Bollinger was Priscilla Duncan, one and the same as Simpson's lawyer.

Priscilla was a former reporter who'd gone to work in the attorney general's office. She knew everybody and was in a real sense a mother figure to young reporters inclined toward digging up stuff. She was one of my first and closest friends in Montgomery and I spent many a night talking and mostly listening to tales about state politics as told by Priscilla, her late husband Don, and whatever guests happened to drop in. Several times I stayed over, spending the night in their guest room.

Don had worked for Siegelman and detested him. So, for that matter, did Priscilla. One night he retrieved a long box containing letters, old articles and fund-raising records on Siegelman. He'd pull something out, and with disgust, tell the story behind it. It gives me no pleasure to write that in her representation of Simpson, my old friend Priscilla became an energetic promoter and participant in the lunacy that poured from her client's mouth.

The origins of Jill Simpson's involvement in the Siegelman case are difficult to pin down because most of what is known comes from her mouth, primarily her September 2007 testimony to Judiciary Committee lawyers and some documents and e-mails from the period. It would appear that in January or early February 2007 she and Bollinger had a discussion about Siegelman and Riley, and the next thing, Bollinger's on the phone with Siegelman.

At some point during that period Simpson had a 45-minute telephone conversation with Siegelman, during which the former governor asked her to memorialize her story in affidavit form. She reached out to the other defendant as well, calling Scrushy lawyer Leach in early February to regale him with the KKK tale and possibly the one involving Rove as well.

She was initially reluctant to file an affidavit. According to Simpson, she embarked on an investigation of Mark Fuller's finances in the hope that Scrushy and Siegelman could use that information to have the judge removed from the case and, hopefully, win a new trial. She testified to the Judiciary Committee lawyers that she preferred this route to filing an affidavit.

In 1989, more than a dozen years before his appointment to the bench, Fuller purchased a large share of two related companies, both long-standing clients of his and his father and their Dothan law firm. The chief source of income for one, called Doss Aviation, is government contracts, primarily with the Air Force, such as for fueling and pilot training.

After being appointed to the federal bench Fuller ceased participating in the governance of the Doss companies, though continued receiving dividends. These he disclosed on the annual financial reports federal judges must complete.

Simpson was to testify to the Judiciary Committee lawyers that after researching Fuller's disclosures that she "realized that we had a problem with a federal judge." She said she "gave them the judge" after which they (Siegelman, Scrushy and their lawyers) "went full speed" on seeking Fuller's removal.

Simpson had help. Siegelman arranged for Birmingham lawyer and political researcher/operative John Aaron to assist her. The year before, Aaron had filed a freedom of information act request on Siegelman's behalf seeking records pertaining to Leura Canary's 2002 recusal. On Feb. 12, he sent Simpson a fax bearing the subject heading, "Political Campaign." Soon thereafter, Simpson and Aaron commenced researching Fuller's finances. As part of that research, Bollinger ordered Fuller's credit report – an act of questionable legality.

On Feb. 15 Simpson wrote Leach reporting information from secretary of state filings pertaining to the Doss companies. From her breathless presentation of these basic, vanilla corporate filings you'd have thought she caught Fuller running heroin for the Gambino family. "I hope that these documents assist you in getting a new trial for Mr. Scrushy and the old trial completely thrown out," she wrote the Scrushy lawyer.

Simpson testified that she met twice with "Scrushy's bunch."

"I said, 'Y'all go after the judge. Y'all don't have to do an affidavit from me.'"

She said she spoke twice to Siegelman, the first time being the 45-minute phone call, and the second, during a call from the former governor while he was visiting Bollinger.

Scrushy didn't depend entirely on Simpson's research. Separately, his lawyers retained a private investigator to conduct a similar review of Fuller's finances.

The Alabama media, especially the *Birmingham News*, reported Simpson's pre-affidavit associations with Siegelman, Scrushy and their lawyers after those connections were revealed in October 2007, following release of her testimony to the Judiciary Committee lawyers.

The national media – most notably "60 Minutes," the *New York Times* and *Time* – failed to note Simpson's connections to and work for the defendants with so much as a single summary sentence. Anything that even might damage the credibility of the only source that connected Karl Rove to Don Siegelman was omitted.

Without Jill, there was nothing, no story, no Karl Rove playing the Wizard of Oz with the Justice Department. Jill had to remain pristine.

Fuller's investment in the Doss companies was cited by Scrushy as the basis for a motion filed in April 2007 seeking his recusal from the case, and, thus, a new trial. Among the motion's many faults was its timeliness, or lack of it, the trial being long over by the time Scrushy's lawyers sought his removal.

Simpson later testified that Scrushy's people sent her the recusal motion for fact checking. She said she wasn't paid for what – if true -- can thus be called pro bono work for the still magnificently wealthy Richard Scrushy.

The recusal motion was initially filed under seal. Siegelman – one supposes wishing not to anger Fuller with sentencing approaching -- professed not to know the basis for the Scrushy team's recusal demand. In hindsight, it appears that he was fibbing.

In the motion, Scrushy's lawyers argued that Fuller had a conflict because Doss Aviation had Air Force contracts and Steve Feaga, as a Judge Advocate General (JAG) in the Air Force Reserve, could impact Doss's business. As such, Fuller was financially beholden to Feaga.

Feaga said he had nothing to do with awarding or reviewing contracts and called the motion frivolous.

Fuller dismissed it. In his ruling he stated there were no doubts about his impartiality at trial and wrote that the motion contained "rank speculation."

After stories reporting Scrushy's recusal demand, Siegelman's friend Bollinger sent an e-mail to myself, Brett Blackledge and others informing us that Fuller was, "a longtime GOP operative and friend of Rove (who) was deeply involved in the transport of cocaine and other contraband during the Iran-Contra days of the 1980s."

Bollinger's source was a web-site run by John Caylor, whose stock in trade is concocting conspiracy theories connecting, say, the "Dixie Mafia" with Al-Qaeda and George and Jeb Bush (that being the conspiracy on his page as I write this.)

After Fuller refused to retroactively recuse himself from the case, it was back to Plan A: Jill's affidavit.

First, Bollinger swore out an affidavit, stating what he said Simpson told him, and gave it to Siegelman. This appears to have had some role in prompting Simpson to come around. Once decided, she asked Aaron, the Siegelman operative, to assist her. Aaron drafted an affidavit on her behalf but she didn't like it and wrote her own.

Simpson's affidavit, as previously detailed, described the events leading up to and during the November 2002 conference call with Rob Riley and his father's campaign lawyers. Most of the affidavit – and the pretext given by Simpson for talking to the group in the first place – regarded the reporting of her success in uncovering the Democrats' Ku Klux Klan pictures plan to embarrass Bob Riley.

In her Judiciary Committee testimony, Simpson said that Rob Riley was only partially pacified by the plan to end the 2002 election by showing Siegelman the Klan pictures. Sure, Siegelman might concede, but what about 2006, worried Riley the younger.

His fears -- which he presented to the group and Simpson up in Rainsville – prompted the bombshell responses by Bill Canary that *Time*, the *New York Times* and others used to transform the Siegelman prosecution into a national scandal.

First, bombshell one – the famous "his girls" quote, from Simpson's recollection of the colloquy as told to the Judiciary Committee lawyers:

Rob Riley: *"I want Don Siegelman not to run.... I don't want to face – we don't want to face Don in running again in the future ...Siegelman's just like a cockroach, he'll never die, what are we going to do?"*
Canary: *"Rob, don't worry. My girls are getting him, will take care of him. (But) let's get this election contest behind us."*
Simpson (*interjecting, according to her testimony*): *"Who's 'his girls?'"*
Canary: *"Leura's my wife, Jill. She works for the middle district and Alice Martin works for the northern district."*

That wasn't enough to mollify Bob Riley's son. He simply could not stop fretting about the colossus Siegelman. Canary – like a calming father figure – told Riley the younger "not to worry."

And then, with words he never uttered, Bill Canary delivered the biggest bombshell of them all.

Canary said – or so says Jill Simpson – that he'd "already got it taken care of with Karl."

Canary told the group, as paraphrased by Simpson, that: "Karl had spoken to the Justice Department and the Justice Department was already pursuing Don Siegelman."

———

Three weeks before Simpson signed her affidavit, the *New York Times* published a little-noticed but prophetic story bearing the headline, "Some ask if U.S. Attorney Dismissals Point to Pattern of Investigating Democrats." The piece reported complaints by several Democratic defendants claiming to have been targeted for political reasons. Among the examples given was the Siegelman case.

The appearance of such a story so soon before the eruption of the "selective prosecution" scandal suggests that someone was already planting seeds with the paper.

———

Simpson, as she was to testify, chose to sign and have her affidavit notarized in Georgia because she feared that powerful forces in Alabama might bring trumped up perjury charges against her. On May 21, she called Bollinger and he met her at the office of a lawyer friend in Rising Fawn, Ga. During the drive there she called Richard Scrushy to give him the excellent news that it was a thumbs up all around.

Were there high-fives and hurrahs that Jill had come through? Probably we will never know. However, a chain of possession was decided upon.

"So your understanding is that you gave the affidavit to Mark Bollinger, who in turn would give it to John Aaron, who would then in turn give it to Richard Scrushy?" a Judiciary Committee lawyer asked her months later.

"And also to Don Siegelman," Simpson responded.

Can't forget him!

———

Before June 2007, no one – not even Siegelman -- had connected Karl Rove to his case.

Until Jill Simpson's affidavit, it was Riley Riley Riley, and the state media had long ceased listening to that song.

After Jill, everything changed. The show went big time. Forget Bob Riley, and for that matter, the Alabama media.

The new story was Karl Rove, and he was far bigger than us.

It was time for the likes of *Time* magazine, the *New York Times*, *Harper's* and CBS News to bring a fresh set of eyes to the case.

Chapter 41
Hook Line and Sinker

"The prosecution may have been a political hit. A Republican lawyer, Dana Jill Simpson, has said in a sworn statement that she heard Bill Canary, a Republican operative and Karl Rove protégé, say that his 'girls' – his wife, the United States attorney in Montgomery, and Alice Martin, the United States attorney in Birmingham – would 'take care' of Mr. Siegelman. Mr. Canary also said, according to Ms. Simpson, that Mr. Rove was involved."

-- From "Selective Prosecution," an Aug. 6, 2007, editorial in the New York Times, and one of three times the paper's editorial staff applied the phrase "political hit" to the Siegelman case.

"I was trying to get the tail to wag the dog. Actually, I should have been speaking to the national media the whole time, because I think the national media would have gotten the message earlier and maybe someone like Jill Simpson would have stepped forward earlier."

-- Siegelman, at April 2008 program in Huntsville featuring Scott Horton.

As Jill Simpson's Karl Rove fable spread and people asked my opinion, I called upon the fictional town made famous by Andy, Barney and Goober. My Mayberry metaphor goes something like this:

I work for the local paper. Several years back I wrote a load of stories which if I may say so proved that our mayor, his driver/budget officer and a host of dubious others were selling our little town for a song and dance. The feds read the stories, conducted their own investigation, brought charges against the by-then ex-mayor, the case went to trial and a jury of local folk found him guilty.

Then one of our more illustrious citizens filed an affidavit – sworn, as no one tired of saying, under *penalty of perjury*. Well, not really filed it. Gave it to a couple of big national newspapers. Guess you'd call it a notarized press release, if there is such a beast.

This fine character – by the way, in cahoots with the ex-mayor and his lawyers and friends -- claimed in this "affidavit" that the *senior advisor for the President of the United States* had it in for the former mayor of Mayberry.

Why the hell this Washington big-shot was supposed to care about Mayberry's ex-mayor I never could figure. Probably because he didn't.

But Ernest T. Bass swore he did. And if that wasn't enough, Otis backed him up 100 percent.

And those big-time national newspapers believed it!
And get this: So did Congress! The U.S. Congress!

You're Don Siegelman or one of his minions and you've got Jill Simpson's affidavit in hand. Now, how to convince responsible news organizations to report that the White House ordered the prosecution of Alabama's former governor when all you have is an unfiled affidavit by a person no one has ever heard of?

First, grow a big set of *cojones*.

Second, don't take it to the *Press-Register*, the *Birmingham News* or anyone in-state with the AP. We knew the territory and we certainly did not know Dana Jill Simpson. An un-filed affidavit handed to any of the above and making allegations that momentous would have faced scrutiny, and, after laughs, a flight into the garbage can.

Neither *Time* nor the *New York Times* revealed to their readers how they came to possess the affidavit. I think it fair to assume that Team Siegelman gave it to the above along with a spiel that convinced muddle-headed editors and reporters that it was true and bore reporting.

Still, Simpson needed credibility enhancement. For this the team turned to a pair of sham titles – "Republican operative" and "Republican lawyer."

In the media, as in everyday conversation, lawyers are not referred to by party affiliation unless they're known for performing legal work for their respective parties, such as during election disputes. A Nexis review of the phrases "Democratic lawyer" and "Republican lawyer" reflects that it's the same at the *New York Times*. Ben Ginsburg, that red-headed guy who was everywhere in Florida trying to prevent Gore from getting votes? He's a Republican lawyer. In Alabama, it would be accurate to call Bobby Segall a Democratic lawyer, so frequent is his service on party matters.

But Jill Simpson? She'd never represented the GOP on any matter, and barring a major run on talent, never will. Still, the *Times*, and others, were forever identifying her as a "Republican lawyer."

It would be impossible to overstate the importance of the pejorative "operative" in the post-trial coverage of the Siegelman case. Its primary uses were to tar Bill Canary as a Republican spy, and, if this makes sense, lend credibility to Simpson. In an effort to bestow *irony*, the word will from here on be dressed up in *italics*.

In addition to conferring a stature she lacked, the labels planted Simpson in the right party, for if a Republican squealed on other Republicans, why, the stories simply had to be true.

There is one more label frequently attached to Simpson that must be addressed as well. That would be "whistleblower."

A whistleblower is someone who, at some risk, exposes corruption. Then again, sometimes it's just a dingbat whistling Dixie.

———

June 1, 2007, was a bellwether day in the life of Don Siegelman. And for that matter, for Jill Simpson, Karl Rove, Bob and Rob Riley, Bill and Leura Canary, the prosecutors, defense lawyers, the Judiciary Committee's probe into the Justice Department, really everyone associated with the case. On that day two of the most respected names in American journalism stamped their imprimatur on Simpson's tale. When reporters and editors at *Time* and the *New York Times* determine something's news, others usually follow, and indeed they did.

"Rove Named in Alabama Controversy," was the headline perched above *Time's* story, which began:

"In the rough and tumble of Alabama politics, the scramble for power is often a blood sport. At the moment, the state's former Democratic governor, Don Siegelman, stands convicted of bribery and conspiracy charges and faces a sentence of up to 30 years in prison. Siegelman has long claimed that his prosecution was driven by politically motivated, Republican-appointed U.S. attorneys. Now Karl Rove, the President's top political strategist, has been implicated in the controversy. A longtime Republican lawyer in Alabama swears she heard a top G.O.P. operative in the state say that Rove 'had spoken with the Department of Justice' about 'pursuing' Siegelman, with help from two of Alabama's U.S. attorneys."

The *New York Times* effort carried the headline, "Ex-governor Says Affidavit Shows Politics in Bribe Case."

The *Times* nailed the decisive role played by Simpson's affidavit in elevating Siegelman from the ranks of convicted felon to political martyr. The story reported that Siegelman's defenders had been trying to connect his situation to the U.S. Attorneys firing scandal but to date had "produced no firm evidence of political interference."

"Now they have an affidavit from a lawyer who says she heard a top Republican *operative* (Bill Canary) in Alabama boast in 2002 that the United States attorneys in Alabama would 'take care' of Mr. Siegelman."

Only a newspaper getting its clock wound by Team Siegelman could call Jill Simpson's affidavit "firm evidence" of anything but an unhinged mind. But the bit about no one paying attention to Siegelman's martyr madness until her affidavit was smack on.

Time and the *Times* reported Bill Canary's fictional "his girls" quote, but the main attraction for both was Simpson's claim to have heard Canary say that "Karl" was on the job.

Adam Zagorin -- who was to write four extraordinarily misleading stories on Siegelman for *Time* -- reported that Simpson "confirmed" to him that the Karl in her affidavit was Rove.

Not once since the commencement of the investigation – a period that spanned Siegelman's indictment, the trial, and the year since the verdict -- had the name Siegelman appeared in a *New York Times'* editorial or opinion piece.

In the two years following Jill Simpson's affidavit, the *Times* opined about the case or referred to it in 15 editorials. All were heartily pro-Siegelman, and, when his name appeared, sharply anti-Rove. In addition, Adam Cohen, the top assistant to opinion page chief Andrew Rosenthal, wrote three columns on the case, all stridently pro-Siegelman. The *Times* declined to say who authored the 15 editorials, but it's not a leap to suggest Cohen.

In the late 1980s the Harvard law graduate spent a year in Montgomery, practicing civil rights law with the Southern Poverty Law Center.

The Simpson affidavit ignited a similar flurry of activity on the news side. With two minor exceptions -- brief stories in 2004 and 2005 when Siegelman was indicted in the Bobo case then the Montgomery case – the paper never assigned one of its staff reporters to the Siegelman story. The few pieces it ran were from the AP wire or by a stringer.

Post-Jill, the paper published 24 stories under the bylines of at least 10 different *Times'* reporters. Many were devoted entirely to Siegelman's situation, others primarily to him, and in some cases, his plight was noted in connection with other, supposedly similar matters.

Some observations on those 24 articles and 18 opinion pieces:

- There is not a single mention of the KKK pictures for election concession fable that was the centerpiece of Simpson's affidavit and which was refuted by everyone involved, including Siegelman and the lawyers who represented him during the 2002 election challenge.

- There is no mention of the similarly repudiated deal for Siegelman to concede the election in return for a Republican pledge to end the investigation.

- Never were *Times* readers told that Simpson was in contact with Siegelman, Scrushy and their representatives and legal teams in the months before she filed her affidavit; that she researched the trial judge's finances on behalf of both defendants; or that she helped proof Scrushy's recusal motion.

- Throughout, the *Times* characterized the $500,000 as a routine campaign donation. Not once in 40-plus opinion and news stories were readers told that the donations were concealed from the secretary of state and IRS until more than two years later, and that they were only disclosed under pressure from the attorney general's office.

- Not once did the paper present even a summary sentence indicating any degree of irregularity in the first $250,000that donation. The names of the real donors – Maryland-based Integrated Health by way of New York-based UBS – are not to be found in any of the 41 pieces.

- Not until December 2008 did the *Times* provide the first detail of the obstruction of justice charge regarding the $9,200 check from Lanny Young to Bailey to Lori Allen and the bogus motorcycle sale deal devised to make the payment appear legitimate. And then it couldn't be avoided. That story was reporting on the oral arguments before the 11th Circuit Court of Appeals, during which much was said about the cover-up charge. Still, it was breezily dismissed in the story and misreported. The name Lanny Young did not appear in any of the 41 pieces, nor did G.H. Construction.

- The *Times*, editorial and news sides, neglected to mention even once that Siegelman and Scrushy declined to testify at trial. Nor were the paper's readers ever told that Siegelman, after first saying he would testify before the Judiciary Committee, reneged on that promise. Siegelman's testimony avoidance is noteworthy because the paper – editorial and news side – spilt much ink on Rove's refusal to testify before the Judiciary Committee. And that was a decision by the White House, made largely for reasons related to legal precedent, not concerns about involvement by Rove in the Siegelman case.

- The bylines of at least 10 different *Times'* reporters appeared atop the stories, indicating that the coverage was to a considerable degree editor driven.

I might add that I *love* the *New York Times.* I visit its web-site a dozen times a day. It's my top source for national, international, business and cultural news, though I will confess my general aversion to editorials applies to that paper as all others.

(In mid-September 2009, I e-mailed the above-described summary along with two separate lists of questions, one to Adam Cohen and *Times'* editorial page editor Andrew Rosenthal, the other to news side, or more specifically, managing editor Jill Abramson, another editor, and seven of the reporters whose bylines appeared on the stories. In early October a *Times'* spokeswoman said the paper would not be responding to my questions and had no comment on its coverage of and opining about the Siegelman case. In the letter to editorial I asked Cohen if he knew Siegelman or any of the former' governor's associates; and if any friends from his time in Montgomery influenced "the *Times* editorials, or provide the *Times*, and thus its readers, with inaccurate information.")

Never in his 35-year public career has Don Siegelman done more to deserve the "Golden Flake" tag than after Simpson's affidavit. In their challenging manner, his broadsides against Rove recalled Muhammad Ali's pre-fight taunting of Joe Frazier. Ali, though, was kidding.

In going after Rove the Alabama quote machine milked forensic metaphors.

A week after the first stories, Siegelman said Simpson had placed Rove "at the scene of the crime, plotting for my political destruction."

And later: "Karl Rove had his hand on the gun that shot me."

"There's no question that Karl Rove's fingerprints are all over this case, from the inception," he told Times report Adam Nossiter for a June 2007 story and the first of the reporter's 10 stories on or relating to the Siegelman case.

"His fingerprints are smeared all over the case," Siegelman told Nossiter the following March, in what the paper touted as Siegelman's first interview upon his release from prison on an appeal bond.

Nossiter, based in the paper's New Orleans bureau, was a former *Anniston Star* reporter. Nossiter, possibly due to the fawning nature of his stories, got quotes from Siegelman when other papers could not.

In an appearance on Dan Abrams MSNBC show after his release, Siegelman took after Rove as never before, summoning the ghost of O.J.'s bloody gloves. "Karl Rove's fingerprints are all over this case. And you know, if you ask me, do we have the knife with his fingerprints on it? No, but we've got the glove and the glove fits."

And to the *Washington Post*: "We don't have the knife with Karl Rove's fingerprints all over it, but we've got the glove, and the glove fits."

According to Simpson, Karl Rove directed the Justice Department to crush Siegelman as a favor to Bill Canary and Bob Riley. After the national media latched on to the Rove component of Simpson's story, Siegelman began to assign additional, more personal motives for Rove's siccing the feds on him. Rove wasn't tormenting him as a favor for Canary or Riley, but because he bore an obsessive hatred for the former Alabama governor. Since this was neither rational nor something Siegelman had mentioned before, it demanded that he conjure a mythic Rove vs. Him grudge.

Rove and members of Siegelman's audience were to discover that Rove began hating Siegelman during the tort reform wars of the mid-1990s, when Rove helped Alabama's business lobby elect Republican judges to the state Supreme Court. Siegelman offered no proof of this ill-will, just claims that time had not healed it. If anything, Rove's animus had festered with time.

Siegelman's daughter Dana parroted another of her father's claims in an interview with Abrams. "My Dad was the first Governor to endorse Al Gore for the presidency," she said. "He spoke at the Democratic national meeting in Boston and said some things that scared the Republican Party into thinking that my Dad was also looking to run on a national scale. Well, Karl Rove is the guy to see if you want to stop somebody in the Democratic Party."

To clarify: Years later, Rove was still steamed that the *Democratic* governor from Alabama had endorsed the *Democratic* presidential candidate from Tennessee in an election won by Bush; and, furthermore, the White House feared that Alabama's once but no longer Democratic golden boy was *going national* if someone didn't stop him. In, "Karl Rove Destroyed My Life," a December 2008 story to Tina Brown's *The Daily Beast*, Siegelman repeated the Gore silliness, then enlarged upon the "going national theme."

Siegelman managed to make running for the presidency sound like a walk in the park.

Siegelman said that if not for the "bad press generated by these (Rove-generated) investigations," he would have won re-election as governor in 2002 then "hit the primary states."

"I had all these friends around the country -- so I thought I could gin up a campaign not for me but against George W. Bush, against his war, against his economic policies, and against his education policies."

Among the problems with that theory is that – even assuming those were his plans -- he didn't tell anybody. Siegelman seemed to be saying that Rove instigated the investigation to pre-empt a presidential run that Rove could not have been aware was coming (nor concerned him had he known.)

Some of Siegelman's statements, especially those made to left-wing bloggers, were simply funny.

Two personal favorites:

"Rove has been up to no good since he was a teenager."

And, "I think Rove is probably the most devious and evil political operative who has been trained to come on to the political scene in certainly the last 50 years. I can't think of *anybody in the annals of history* who could even rival this man's *pernicious thoughts*."

(Hitler, Herod, Pol Pot? Nicolae Ceauşescu?)

If Rove's fingerprints were so evident, why hadn't Siegelman noticed them before?

When that question was later posed by the otherwise fawning "Ring of Fire" radio host Robert F. Kennedy Jr., Siegelman responded that he'd always "suspected from the circumstantial evidence that Karl Rove was deeply involved in my prosecution."

"I mean, it was just so obvious that it was easy for me to put two and two together and connect those dots."

The same theme, as fleshed out later, to MSNBC's Abrams: "All of the roads lead to Rove. All of the dots, and when you connect the dots, they lead to Karl Rove. This case could be the *Mapquest* that sets Congress on a journey that will take them to Karl Rove if they will start to look at it."

One of those dots was the 2002 election. Siegelman told all who would listen that in the wee hours of that November night five years prior the omnipresent, omniscient Rove ordered his underlings to make Siegelman's votes in Baldwin County vanish, thus throwing the election to Riley.

Siegelman's ability to make things up on the fly merits some sort of praise. To MSNBC's Rachel Maddow, who replaced Abrams, Siegelman said that Bill Canary was not merely a friend of Rove, but that the two were best friends. He told Maddow that the investigation was "kicked into high gear in 2001 by Karl Rove's best friend's wife ... so we suspected almost immediately that Karl Rove was involved."

In another instance, apropos of any factual basis, he said the government spent $40 million prosecuting him, suggesting that he had himself confused with Bill Clinton, and Louis Franklin with Ken Starr.

———

On the afternoon of Jill Simpson's debut in *Time* and *Times*, she and Siegelman appeared for the first time in a column written by the man who was to become patron saint for the both of them.

"Some months ago one of my Alabama relations mentioned that she had been tracking the prosecution of Governor Don Siegelman, a Democrat. 'There's something awfully fishy about this whole prosecution. It just doesn't smell right. It smells like politics,'" wrote Horton.

"Don Siegelman is scheduled to be sentenced on June 26, and as his hearing approaches, the stench surrounding the whole case is beginning to rise and engulf the U.S. attorney's office."

He was right. The stench from the bullshit offensive Horton was helping manufacture was causing problems for the prosecutors.

———

In June and again in July the U.S. Attorney's Office issued lengthy press releases in a futile attempt to counter the Simpson tsunami. Each, my ego noted, cited my role in the start of the investigation, as here: "Federal and state agents began tracking leads first developed by investigative reporter Eddie Curran, leads that eventually led to criminal charges against local architect William Curtis Kirsch, Clayton 'Lanny' Young, and Nick Bailey, an aide to the former Governor."

The flipside was that I was presented by many in the Siegelman camp as for all practical purposes working inside the U.S. Attorney's Office.

Both press releases attempted to get certain national reporters to accept the fact that the investigation began before Leura Canary's appointment as U.S. Attorney. Franklin declared in the strongest language he could summon that Canary hadn't participated in the case after her spring 2002 recusal. He and Feaga, not Canary or Justice Department officials in Washington, made the decision to prosecute Siegelman. This he repeated time and time again in news releases and interviews.

"I get deeply offended when Siegelman says I didn't control this case. If he wants to put this on anybody, it should be me. I made the decision," Franklin told the *New York Times* for the paper's first Simpson story.

Franklin and Feaga were to make this and similar points over and over, to no discernible effect. Because, really and truly, where's the story in low-level guys like Franklin and Feaga deciding to prosecute Siegelman? Well, there isn't one. So Franklin and Feaga, like the Rileys, Canarys, Rove and others, got the well-they-would-say-that treatment from *Time*, the *New York Times*, "60 Minutes" and others.

Franklin had to refute two contradictory fables. Simpson, after all, didn't write one "political hit" script, but two, both erupting from Bill Canary's mouth. The first – the "his girls" scenario – had Leura Canary and Alice Martin pulling the trigger on the gun that shot Siegelman. Canary Canard Two placed the bloody knife in Rove's gloved hand.

On their own, neither the "his girls" story nor the Rove's tale deserves the time of day. However, because America's best newspaper, its top news magazine, its most honored investigative television show and the U.S. Congress swallowed them both hook line and sinker, it seems we have no choice.

———

For Simpson's version to be true, Franklin and Feaga and in all likelihood the entire prosecution team, clerical as well as investigative (FBI, etc.), had to be complicit in the cover-up to conceal the role of Oz, be he Karl, Leura, or Karl/Leura. But more than liars, the stories birthed by Simpson demanded that the above be remarkable actors. Franklin, Feaga, fellow Siegelman prosecutors J.B. Perrine and Richard Pilger and the rest of the government's team gave it their all. I dare anyone who watched that trial – Siegelman and his lawyers included – to say the prosecutors didn't believe in their case and didn't fight like hell to win it.

The "his girls" scenario was awarded decent play in the early post-Simpson stories. Over time, its importance diminished. And why, one wonders, was that?

Because from a national media perspective, Karl Rove is a Great White Shark. The Canarys are tadpoles. And who wants to write stories about tadpoles?

———

A week after Simpson's national media debut, the *Birmingham News* published a story suggesting a possible motive on the part of Mark Bollinger and Simpson to go after Bob Riley. The story, by Kim Chandler and the paper's Washington correspondent, Mary Orndorff, reported that a company owned by Bollinger had in the summer of 2006 sought and failed to win what became a $7.1 million contract to dispose of old tires stockpiled in Attalla, Ala.

After losing, Bollinger and his friend Jill called the Riley administration to complain. The story began:

The two people alleging that former Gov. Don Siegelman's prosecution was tainted by politics are tied to a company that did not win a state contract from Gov. Bob Riley's administration last year.

Former Riley Chief of Staff Toby Roth said he believed the lost contract could have been a factor when the two people signed statements accusing Riley's advocates of engineering the case against Siegelman, a Democratic rival.

"I think it certainly raises suspicions about their accusations," Roth said. "This has got a sour grapes aspect to it."

Bollinger and Simpson didn't – couldn't – dispute that the winner had submitted a lower bid than Bollinger's company. After the bid openings, Simpson wrote Riley urging him not to sign the contract based on what she described as negative information about the winner.

Though the governor's office was not the awarding entity, Bollinger called Riley's office several times and was quite aggressive in pushing for his company, Roth told the *News*. Bollinger said he remembered one call. He said Simpson's affidavit regarding the Siegelman prosecution and his involvement in that matter were unrelated to his company's failure to be win the contract.

Upon reading the story, Horton went ape. The next day, he and *Harper's* came to Simpson's rescue with something called, "Abramoff and Justice in the Heart of Dixie." He didn't dispute the facts in the Birmingham story. That wasn't an option, they being solidly reported. Instead, he veered off into one of Siegelman's favorite red-herring fantasies, one linking Bob Riley and scandal-plagued Republican lobbyist Jack Abramoff in a massive criminal conspiracy against him.

"As in the Sherlock Holmes tale of 'Silver Blaze' the really fascinating thing about the *Birmingham News* story consists of the facts which are strangely missing," wrote Horton.

"Might Toby Roth have some particular exposure or interest in the affidavit other than simply shilling for his old boss? … How about the fact that Governor Riley's son features smack dead-center in the allegations. That's a fact. It's not mentioned … Might there be any relationship between Toby Roth and Karl Rove? That would be another highly relevant entanglement, wouldn't it?"

From there it gets even harder to follow, which may be intentional. Horton knows most of his readers are like-minded and flying blind wherever he'll take them, and on this day, he guided them deep into a GOP hellhole he called the "Abramoff database."

"Now going back through the Abramoff database and looking at the names lined up against Siegelman in this affair is a curious exercise indeed. There's a hit every few seconds," wrote *Harper's* resident Abramoff database expert.

Some "hits" were familiar, but others, to me anyway, were not. Among them: Michael Scanlon, Tom DeLay, Dan Gans, the Alexander Strategy Group, Twinkle Andress, Dax Swatek, Bill Canary, Pat McWhorter, "Channel One," Ralph Reed, the Mississippi Band of Choctaw Indians, Nell Rogers, the Porch Creek Indians, John Ashcroft, John McCain, Alabama Attorney General Troy King, and the United States Interior Department.

And the common denominator, the link connecting, say, John McCain, something called Channel One, Nell Rogers and the rest?

"Indeed, looking at this list of names, it suddenly occurred to me: I've seen them many times before: they're all names that have appeared in connection with the Abramoff investigation – widely considered the 'mother lode' of modern political scandals. Indeed, it dawns on me suddenly that this story and the Abramoff story intersect, and the point of intersection is Toby Roth."

Shazam!

Chandler and Orndorff were chastised as "remarkable incurious and lazy" for not wading into the "Abramoff database" when reporting on a contract sought by Mark Bollinger with no connection to Jack Abramoff, the Interior Department or even Ralph Reed.

"The real story is that the deeper one delves into this, the more convincing the Simpson affidavit becomes," concluded Horton.

The real story is that Scott Horton is mad as a hatter; that his deranged world view is writ large on everything he writes and says; and – by far the most amazing part -- that journalists at places like CBS News, *Time*, the *New York Times*, and MSNBC cribbed off his cheat sheet!

And get this: So did Congress! The U.S. Congress!

Chapter 42
The Man in the Iron Mask

"I don't particularly like the idea of being the Nelson Mandela of Alabama politics, but if it is, so be it. I'll be writing my letters like Dr. King from ... jail."

-- Siegelman comparing himself to the two civil rights icons in a television interview seven months before his sentencing.

"Rejecting defense arguments that an appeal was likely to be successful, he (Fuller) denied their appeal bond and banged the gavel. Immediately, federal marshals escorted the two men from the room and into federal custody. Scrushy made a motion, like blowing a kiss, to his wife. And then they were gone."

--- Kyle Whitmire, who covered the Siegelman trial for the Birmingham Weekly and as a stringer for the New York Times, the above as he described the end of Siegelman and Scrushy's sentencing hearing for his Weekly readers.

Mark Fullers' sentencing responsibilities were divided into two parts – the first, to set guidelines to help determine punishment; and second, to render that punishment.

As is the practice in federal cases, probation officials applied various criteria to determine recommended guidelines. Siegelman wound up in the 10 to 15 year range; Scrushy between eight to 10 years. Prosecutors and defendants filed briefs asking Fuller to deviate from the guidelines – the government wanting him to go higher, the defendants lower, all the way to nothing.

Franklin and Feaga urged the judge to put Siegelman away for 30 years and sought 25 for Scrushy.

"These defendants have basically thumbed their nose at the criminal justice system," said Franklin in explaining the harsh requests.

"I think it's completely incorrect. I think it's actually absurd," responded Scrushy lawyer Art Leach.

Seeking 30 years was in my opinion one of the prosecution's two gravest errors, the other being inclusion of RainLine and Mack Roberts in the case. The worst mistake – charging Siegelman and Hamrick in the Bobo case – was the fault of the Birmingham prosecutors.

As nasty as were relations at trial, at least then prosecutors and defense lawyers had to see each other every day and maintain some sense of decorum. But since the verdict the gloves had come completely off. With the juror e-mails and the Jill Simpson nonsense the defendants and their lawyers had revealed themselves as willing to say and promulgate anything. But in asking for 30 years, Franklin and Feaga showed a lack of restraint that was to cause them problems. They could have made the same points and saved themselves considerable grief by taking a big breath, backing off, and seeking half that amount.

They also asked Fuller to fine Siegelman and Scrushy millions of dollars, much of it for damages that weren't clearly proved at trial.

The defendants' requests for no jail time were equally ludicrous but to be expected.

In fact, Fuller was to agree with the three arguments presented by prosecutors in urging a higher sentence for Siegelman. They were: That his actions damaged the public's faith in Alabama's state government; that the judge could consider charges for which the jury did not find Siegelman guilty if he felt prosecutors proved wrongdoing; and that with his words and actions post-verdict, the former governor displayed a refusal to accept responsibility for his crimes.

The sentencing, held during the final week of July, lasted three days. I missed it because of our annual trip to Slovakia. "It was more charged than any other sentencing I've ever seen. They were still trying to fight this thing to the very end," said Whitmire, the *Birmingham Weekly* writer.

Fuller frequently ripped into lawyers on both sides, chiefly for raising arguments already considered at trial and with no relevance to the sentencing.

Siegelman witnesses included civil rights leader Rev. Fred Shuttlesworth; his long-time lawyer and fixer, Bobby Segall; and Helen Vance, the widow of Robert Vance, the federal judge assassinated by a mail bomber, and for whom Siegelman worked in the 1970s.

The Jill Simpson issue raised its head, if barely. Susan James – a Montgomery lawyer hired to assist Siegelman with sentencing – said she was sure Fuller was familiar with the recent allegations that Karl Rove, Bob Riley and others targeted Siegelman for political reasons. Ms. James – most ill-advisedly, I think -- told Fuller that the case before him that day had received worldwide attention since Simpson's affidavit. She asked the judge to consider the possibility of prosecutorial shenanigans when issuing sentence.

Assistant U.S. Attorney J.B. Perrine countered that Siegelman's relentless presentation of himself as a victim of a government conspiracy evinced his "willingness to engage in propaganda to heap disrespect on this system."

On this count – accepting responsibility – Siegelman wasn't exactly helping himself with his extracurricular activities. Prosecutors played clips of, "Wrath of Injustice," a documentary produced by Scrushy's public relations team. Siegelman appeared on the video and lashed out at Republicans for using the Justice Department to torpedo his 2006 gubernatorial bid.

With their most senseless argument, Siegelman's lawyers told Fuller that their client faced peril in prison. Inmates with long memories might rough-up or even kill Siegelman because he'd been such a hard-ass as Alabama's attorney general in the late 1980s. The image of a federal prison system teaming with people seeking revenge on the lawman Siegelman does not convince.

Robert Blakey turned in a performance that struck most as more college lecture than legal argument. The Notre Dame law professor went on for almost two hours, compelling Fuller to urge him to move on.

"I've never seen anything like it at a sentencing hearing, but it was a history of the justice system going back Constantine, Leviticus, the Egyptians, Mesopotamia, John Locke, Thomas Jefferson, and it went on and on," said Whitmire. "I think Fuller listened to it but I don't think it did anyone any good in sentencing."

Blakey took several shots at the prosecutors, once likening them to "jackals who want to feed on carcasses."

The professor gave it to the prosecutors in the pages of the *Times* as well. His statements – he was quoted three times in reporter Adam Nossiter's story on the sentencing hearing – added muscle to the paper's portrayal of Siegelman as political victim. For example, Blakey called the HealthSouth aspect of the case "a joke."

"A guy walks in, gives a contribution, and gets an appointment? Until Congress reforms this, this is the system we live under. They are criminalizing this contribution," Blakey said.

Nossiter wrote that Blakey "derided the prosecutors' racketeering case against Mr. Siegelman."

"It's the worst-drafted RICO I've ever seen. You find as much trash as you can, then you dump it in," Blakey said, at story's end.

Nossiter, who worked in the paper's New Orleans' bureau, was to write 10 stories about or relating to Siegelman, far more than any *Times* reporter.

In his sentencing hearing story Nossiter gave Blakey's bona fides – Notre Dame law professor with a career at the Justice Department dating back to 1960 – but neglected one thing. He failed to disclose that Blakey was *Siegelman's lawyer.* As a result, readers were left to infer that Blakey was an impartial expert who had analyzed the case and thought it a pile of rubbish.

Imagine quoting Louis Franklin praising the case, describing him as a veteran federal prosecutor, but leaving out the part about him being the prosecutor in the Siegelman case. Such an omission assuredly would not have been allowed by my editors, nor would I do such a thing.

Scrushy based his case for probation almost entirely on testimonials regarding his devotion to God and his check-writing exploits to religious charities. Typical of his witnesses was Bernard Omukubah, who operates an Africa-based ministry called Kingdom Builders. He said Scrushy had given the organization at least $10,000 a month for several years, allowing it to help more than 3,000 orphans. "I don't know what I would do without Richard Scrushy. He has received the call of God on his life," said Omukubah, one of the many black pastors who comprised the "Amen Corner" at Scrushy's Birmingham trial.

As with each such witness, prosecutors pointed out during cross-examination of Omukubah that Scrushy's largesse didn't commence until after he ran afoul of the law.

Midway through the third day Fuller issued his ruling on the guidelines. For Scrushy, he adopted the probation office's recommendation of 8-10 years. For Siegelman, the judge increased the range, to 15 to 20 years. "I am convinced the conduct Gov. Siegelman engaged in damaged the public's confidence in the government of this state," Fuller said in explaining his decision.

But as the judge reminded the defendants, he was under no obligation to comply with those ranges.

With that, sentencing moved to its end stage -- last words from the defendants and lawyers.

Art Leach – and this stunned me when I read it – told Fuller that "without question Richard Scrushy is the greatest man I have met in my life." Meeting and serving as Scrushy's lawyer had "deepened my relationship with God," said the Georgia bulldog.

Scrushy followed his lawyer. The chairman of God Inc., told Fuller that "we" had 1,000 churches, and reminded the court of the good works he'd financed in Africa and elsewhere. Scrushy described himself as a simple pastor with no interest in money, and asked that he be allowed to remain free and continue his ministry. "I believe God has called me as an end-time soldier," he said.

At this point I don't think Scrushy would have surprised anyone had he begun speaking in tongues.

There are some Scrushy watchers who believe he believes his own rhetoric – that he is in fact sincere about his Christianity and his role as an "end-time soldier." Maybe so. He is, in any event, sane enough to recognize that many think he turned to religion and flooded black churches with money as a criminal defense strategy.

"It hurts to hear someone say you turned to God because you got in trouble," he told Fuller.

Siegelman, emotional where Scrushy was not, paused several times to wipe away tears. "I never intended to do anything that approached a crime," he said, voice wavering. "I'm not a perfect person, but I'm a good person. I've made mistakes. I've done some stupid things, but I believe in the people of this state. All I wanted to do was make the state a better place."

He spoke of his blue-collar parents "working so that my brother and I could have a better life than they had," and of holding his wife in his arms in the moments after the wreck that nearly killed her. Siegelman said he had "never been motivated by greed or power;" and said that the Montgomery home his family lived in for many years didn't even have central heat and air.

After almost three days of squabbling and largely meaningless testimony, it was time for the only part that mattered.

"There is no question in this court's mind that you have done many great things for the state," Fuller told Siegelman.

The judge said his task was unpleasant. "You and I both took an oath to uphold the law. You have violated that oath."

Then he issued sentence: Seven years and four months for Siegelman; six years and 10 months for Scrushy.

For both, he'd given sentences below the guidelines set by probation officials and those he'd established earlier in day.

It was what Fuller did next that blew everyone away.

He denied the requests by defense lawyers for their clients to remain free on bond, and which are routinely granted for white collar defendants pending appeal. He ordered the pair taken into custody and cracked his gavel. Marshals moved quickly, leading Siegelman and Scrushy away. Leslie Scrushy's sobbing was the only sound to be heard in the hushed courtroom.

The crowd filed quietly into the hall. Lori Siegelman was accompanied by the governor's brother Les. She was "obviously out of it ... all of Scrushy's people were crying," said Whitmire. Once outside, Leslie Scrushy gathered herself and started "giving orders like a general" to the Scrushy clan. "She was much more composed than Lori."

Franklin noted that Siegelman and Scrushy had remained free far longer than most defendants. "They had a year to get their affairs in order. They were allowed to travel all over the country. Most people don't get that," he said.

Fuller, who'd presided with such fairness over the trial, was soon to find himself enjoined with the likes of Rove, the Rileys, the Canarys and so many others as a participant in the well-oiled GOP conspiracy to bury Siegelman.

————

Seven months later, former Arizona attorney general Grant Woods told, "60 Minutes" and a national audience that Fuller "had (Siegelman) manacled around his legs like we do with crazed killers. And whisked off to prison just like that. Now what does that tell you? That tells you that this was personal. You would not do that to a former governor."

Neither Siegelman nor Scrushy were placed under restraint in the courtroom or anywhere else where the public could see them. As with all federal prisoners they were taken down by elevator to a holding cell in the courthouse. Siegelman and Scrushy were allowed to meet with their attorneys before being put into the holding cell. That night they were driven to a federal prison in Atlanta, where they shared a cell for about two weeks. Prior to and during transport both were placed in handcuffs and leg irons.

"Every prisoner we transport we have in handcuffs and leg irons. That's Marshall Service procedures. We didn't treat them any different than any other prisoners we have," said Jesse Seroyer, the U.S. Marshal in Montgomery.

Seroyer is an old Siegelman friend. He worked under Siegelman when the latter was attorney general, and Siegelman appointed Seroyer as the office's chief investigator.

The law does not, nor should, make an exception whereby former governors or CEOs are to be treated differently – and better – than other prisoners.

In the weeks after sentencing the public was treated to frequent reports of the indignities heaped upon Siegelman, with Scrushy receiving far less attention. Siegelman, his lawyers and supporters were apparently shocked that, upon being taken into custody, the former governor wasn't driven by limousine to a Hilton.

Siegelman lawyer David McDonald reported that in Atlanta, Siegelman and Scrushy were held in their cell for 23 hours a day. The ex-governor was losing weight because the food was so bad. "He was wearing orange pants, blue slippers and kind of a faded blue khaki type shirt. He pulled it off. He still looked dignified," said McDonald. "The conditions would be bad enough for a career criminal. It seems like overkill for someone like the governor."

Better conditions awaited, with Siegelman departing Atlanta first. During transport to his ultimate destination – Oakdale, La. – it was reported, as if this were just awful, that he was fed bologna sandwiches. This common if inelegant lunch meat is eaten by one supposes millions of non-incarcerated Americans every day.

"Heaven forbid that they treat a convicted felon like a convicted felon if his name is Siegelman or Scrushy," Franklin told a reporter who sought comment on the travails of the two men.

Oakdale is a minimum security facility with neither gun towers nor fences. It's about 470 miles from Birmingham and is the prison home of another former governor, Edwin Edwards, the charming scoundrel from Louisiana. During his stay there, Siegelman maintained his disciplined exercise regime and reported being treated respectfully.

Scrushy remained in Atlanta a few more days, after which he was transported to a low-security prison in Beaumont, Tex.

———

In the two months since Simpson's affidavit Team Siegelman had made some headway with its frantic efforts to persuade the House Judiciary Committee to take up his case. But in terms of public relations, nothing could top going to jail.

A *New York Times* editorial published two days after Siegelman was whisked away marked the first of three times for *Times'* opiners to apply the phrase "political hit" to Siegelman's prosecution. But in making their case for what the paper called, "selective prosecution," the nation's most influential editorial page betrayed the weakness of its argument.

"The most arresting evidence that Mr. Siegelman may have been railroaded is a sworn statement by a Republican lawyer, Dana Jill Simpson," the *Times* declared. The fabricated "his girls" quote attributed to Bill Canary was trotted out, as was the gibberish about Canary informing those on the 2002 phone call that he'd received assurances from "Karl" regarding Siegelman's fate.

The editorial – a rant based on fiction – concluded thus:

The idea of federal prosecutors putting someone in jail for partisan gain is shocking. But the United States attorneys scandal has made clear that the Bush Justice Department acts in shocking ways. Congress, though, should not wait. It should insist that Mr. Canary and everyone on the 2002 call, as well as Mrs. Canary and Mr. Rove, testify about the Siegelman prosecution. In standing by Attorney General Alberto Gonzales throughout the attorneys scandal, the Bush administration has made clear that it does not care about the integrity of the Justice Department. By investigating Mr. Siegelman's case, Congress can show that it does.

Readers of the piece included Artur Davis, the Democratic congressman from Alabama and a member of the Judiciary Committee. The next week Davis jumped on the Siegelman bandwagon, joining others in asking committee chairman John Conyers to include the Siegelman matter in the committee's ongoing probe of the Bush Justice Department.

"I think The *New York Times* editorial influenced the committee and that is certainly the indication I get from talking to committee staff," Davis said.

———

The final nudge came on July 13, when a petition signed by 44 former attorneys general was delivered to Conyers and the Judiciary Committee. The group asked the committee to add the Siegelman case to its investigation into the U.S. Attorneys firings scandal. As with the *Times* editorial staff, the AGs cited Jill Simpson's affidavit in justifying their call for action.

The petition received widespread coverage and helped sell the perception to the national public that the Bush administration had targeted this poor Siegelman guy from Alabama. Much was said about the "unprecedented" nature of all these former attorney generals – even some Republicans! – going to bat for Siegelman. The reality is that there never would have been a petition if Siegelman were not himself a former AG. Many who signed the petition were his friend.

Spearheading the group were former New York Attorney General Robert Abrams a Democrat, and Woods, the Arizonan. Both were Siegelman pals from way back.

Three weeks before, Abrams was in Montgomery, having been summoned by Siegelman to be one of his character witnesses at the sentencing hearing. Abrams testified that he befriended Siegelman when both were attorney generals. The

Siegelmans once spent Thanksgiving with his family; Abrams came to Montgomery to see Siegelman sworn in as governor; and Lori Siegelman sometimes stayed with the Abrams when in New York. He spoke warmly and convincingly of Siegelman's attributes as a friend and honorable man. But of the actual case against Siegelman, Abrams knew next to nothing.

Abrams had met Siegelman through the National Association of Attorneys General, or NAAG. Attorneys general from throughout the country "get to know each other quite well" at the association's meetings and annual conferences, he testified.

NAAG is well-known as a networking organization for former attorney generals seeking to win lucrative work in class actions and the like. Siegelman had continued attending its functions well after ceasing to be Alabama's attorney general. At least three times as governor, he used state funds to pay for him and his wife to fly and stay at resorts selected for the annual conferences of the attorney generals from western states, a related organization.

It's not uncommon at all for NAAG alumni to put their names on petitions. In 1997, Siegelman joined 22 other former AGs in signing a petition in support of a consumer-related issue. Thirteen of those signed the Siegelman petition 10 years later.

Woods, a Siegelman friend from way back, was to become the most outspoken and visible member of the group. In the late 1990s, I'd quoted the Arizonan praising Siegelman for participating in the legal battle against Big Tobacco at a time when Alabama attorney generals Jeff Sessions, then Bill Pryor, declined to do so. With few exceptions -- for example, a story in the *Los Angeles Times* -- Woods' old ties to Siegelman went undisclosed in national reports.

Woods, Abrams and the AGs group was to generate headlines for their man on at least three more occasions. They eventually pumped their numbers to 91 signees, for a 2009 brief supporting Siegelman's appeal to the U.S. Supreme Court.

On July 17, John Conyers announced that the Judiciary Committee had broadened its investigation into the politicization of the Bush Justice Department to include allegations that Democrats office-holders were "selectively prosecuted" for because of their party affiliation. In a letter to Attorney General Gonzales, the long-time Michigan congressman presented the greatest hits from Simpson's affidavit and cited the petition from the former attorneys general.

Conyers' letter sparked another round of national stories just days after the ex-Attorney's General petition did the same. In a letter from prison, Siegelman told the Associated Press that he was, "encouraged by the Congressional inquiry and upcoming investigation which should prove the political involvement and establish this Alabama case as the 'Watergate of 2008.'" He later upped it a notch, pledging that an investigation of his prosecution would reveal Rove's role and "make Watergate look like child's play."

Only someone as deluded by self-importance as Siegelman could compare his case to the crimes committed during Watergate and the resignation of a U.S. president.

———

In late August Nick Bailey appeared before Fuller to ask the judge to reconsider the 18-month sentence meted out a year before. Bailey, with backing from Franklin and Feaga, asked Fuller to give him home-confinement rather than prison. Feaga recalled the days of cross-examination endured by Bailey at trial. "He stuck to his guns. He told the truth," said Feaga.

Bailey testified truthfully on those elements that sunk Siegelman and Scrushy, but withheld far more than he gave. That's my position and I'm sticking with it. Had Bailey revealed all, Siegelman would have been past helping from the likes of Simpson, Horton and his colleagues in the fraternity of former state attorneys general.

Bailey, in so many ways Siegelman's victim, was at the end of the day an adult with a college education. It would have been an injustice for him not to serve time for his role in the warehouse debacle and so much more. Fuller rejected the leniency pleas. Fuller told those gathered that Bailey deserved to go to prison for the "depth and breadth" of his crimes, and ordered him to report three weeks later.

Bailey, by then 38, departed the courthouse wiping away tears. "I'm disappointed, but I'm prepared to deal with what I've got to deal with," he told awaiting reporters.

———

After returning from Slovakia I sent an e-mail to several of the reporters who'd covered the Siegelman trial. In it, I gave my unsolicited defense of Fuller surprising act at sentencing. It was hastily written and rough. Here's most of it:

Why did Fuller toss them straight into the pokey? He didn't say why, so we don't know, really. But I think we know, or in any event, I think I do... Have never had a conversation with Fuller, know next to nothing about his background, but after that crazy two months none of us will ever forget, I left respecting one person above all – him.

I wondered, as I imagine you did, if Fuller would take into consideration the words/deeds/court filings of the defendants and their attorneys after the verdict in rendering his sentence. My understanding is that the degree of acceptance of crimes ... can and in fact is supposed to be considered at sentencing. So I think their post-verdict actions were fair game, if you will.

I believe – no, I know – that the juror e-mails were bogus. Should this ever be fully investigated, proved in court, the person/persons behind this will, I believe, face substantial punishment. If Scrushy was even aware of it, I think he can pretty well count on spending the remainder of his days in prison.

Fuller, as you recall, heaped praise on the jurors at the end of this case. After that point, and before as well, he took quite seriously his role as their protector. He continues to serve that role. That role – and the protection of future jurors – compelled him to act at sentencing.

Whether it will be proved in court, the evidence of the bogusness of the e-mails mounted, and the acts taken to get poor pitiful Juror Charlie to file those affidavits was in my mind, and certainly in Fuller's, despicable. In his order, he basically accused that Birmingham pastor's wife (Debra Winston) of perjury.

Fuller gave them all the rope they wanted, and they kept pulling for more. Self-discipline is not my strength, and I think this gives me special insight into that problem. These guys – the two defendants, their lawyers – completely lost control of themselves, couldn't stop themselves… The creation of the e-mails and the use of them to attack jurors so viciously even as there was no proof that these anonymously sent pieces of paper were real – this, more than anything was … why the defendants were hauled off.

I don't believe Siegelman was behind it, involved at all, aware, etc., but especially as the evidence of the dubiousness of the circumstances dribbled forth, he/his lawyers still ran with the bullshit when they should have faced the facts and backed off. They heaped abuse on the jurors, on Katie Langer and Sam Hendrix, as if they were criminals. They did this in court, before television cameras, before anyone who would listen to them.

Had they been smart – showed just a reasonable degree of restraint -- they would have declared to Fuller, the court and the cameras outside that while they disagreed profoundly with the verdict, they are deeply disturbed by the attacks on the jurors and wish to disassociate their client from those attacks. Instead they did the opposite…

Judges have many responsibilities, among them, and near the top, is ensuring respect for the process. When Fuller sent those two straight to jail, that is what he was doing – protecting the process. It was a message to Siegelman, Scrushy, their lawyers, and any future defendants before him. You messed my jury, published – remember this? -- the "My Space" page of a juror! It was completely irrelevant, its sole purpose being to embarrass her (Katie Langer), to punish her. Fuller's response was stunning, yes, but inappropriate? Unprovoked? Unfair?

Sending them straight to jail and banging that gavel -- it was the final – the only -- dramatic stroke by a judge who had with abundant self-discipline avoided using this case to promote himself, to make it about him, to preside with anything approaching flair.

In the immediate aftermath of the sentencing Horton devoted some two dozen columns to Siegelman. In posts such as, "Lieutenant Gustl Visits Alabama" and "Rove Whistles Dixie," he blew blitzkrieg-like through all the usual suspects, launching verbal fusillades at Rove, Franklin, Feaga, the Canarys, the Rileys, and all manner of other conspirators.

Added to the group and singled out for special treatment was Fuller – the subject of seven columns after sentencing. Not surprisingly, the stories presented a picture of a wholly corrupt judge working hand in glove with the Rileys and Rove, Fuller a new-found cog in the conspiracy.

The New York-based writer obviously had Alabama compatriots digging up everything they could find on Fuller. He dressed up the product, dark, fetid and writ large with falsehood, innuendo, Javert-like, and *Harper's* gave it the good housekeeping seal of approval.

The state media was never far from Horton's mind. "It's hard to think of a place where the press is quite so blighted as Alabama. Albania perhaps? Zimbabwe? To be clear, Alabama's press isn't *that bad* …," he wrote, and in the next paragraph, praised the *New York Times, Time* and the *Los Angeles Times* for writing stories more to his liking.

Kafka, George Washington, Thomas More, Charles I, Andrey Vyshinsky, Thomas Paine, Voltaire, and Emile Zola were summoned to place the Siegelman sentencing in perspective, though Victor Hugo remained Horton's go-to guy. Les Miserables's pathological cop showed up for, "Javert's Wailings," "Javert in Alabama," and "Javert in Alabama, continued," often as a stand-in for Louis Franklin.

"On the surface (Javert/Franklin) is a prosecutor, but deep down inside he remains in fact, a criminal… (is) one of the most reprehensible characters in all of literature. … The spirit of Javert is alive and abroad in America today. In fact, he lives in Montgomery, Alabama."

Siegelman also merited literary context on a grand scale. For him, Horton summoned another Frenchman, Alexandre Dumas.

"The man in the iron mask truly existed, in the reign of Louis XIV," wrote Horton. "He was guarded in isolation under the most hideous circumstances, in remote and tightly confined prisons with double doors. As he was transferred from places of captivity, an iron mask was placed over his head so he could not be seen or heard."

In late July, Horton and Harper's published an exclusive: A press release from Jill Simpson. She declared that she was not about to let Canary and Franklin "deter me from testifying before Congress." The prosecutors – for defending themselves against her allegations -- had violated "ethical rules governing" prosecutors.

"I will quote my grandfather, who told me as a young girl that only, 'a hit dog hollers,'" wrote Simpson. "I knew when I decided to get involved in this matter that the Riley people would come after me but I am a strong person and I will continue to tell the truth … I will once again state, I am looking forward to raise my hand to God under oath and to testify to these matters recently revealed."

On this she was true to her word. And oh the stories she was to tell.

Chapter 43
Creative Perjury

"Oh, by the way, your dress is ugly."
-- Simpson, to Republican lawyer Caroline Lynch, after Lynch pressed her to explain some of her stories about the Siegelman case during Simpson's testimony before Judiciary Committee lawyers.

"Simpson's allegations match the facts we upturned in our investigative series on Judge Fuller this summer."
-- Horton, in October 2007 column on Harper's web-site, following release of the transcript of Simpson's testimony.

Faulty memories, fuzzy impressions, all manner of factors can cause a person to give testimony that is false but short of perjury. Jill Simpson has no such excuses.

The testimony she gave congressional lawyers on Sept. 14, 2007, was willfully false, told with flair and impugned the reputations of innocent people. Declaring that she committed perjury is not only too easy, but fails to get to the bottom of this mess. I will argue that she was coached, that one or more persons gave her a series of stories and talking points. Each was intended to buttress the case that the Siegelman prosecution was, as the New York *Times* never tired of calling it, a "political hit."

Simpson was the patsy, a weak, goofy character susceptible to flattery, melodrama and the lure of fame. Such a dingbat as to almost be blameless.

Two lawyers accompanied Simpson that day to the Rayburn House building. They were Mark Bollinger's pal Priscilla Duncan from Montgomery and Washington attorney Joseph Sandler. The latter was the general counsel for the Democratic National Committee and one of the party's premier lawyers on consequential election and political issues. A conservative estimate of his hourly rate is $500.

Assigned to question Simpson were Sam Broderick-Sokol, the majority counsel for the Judiciary Committee; and, on behalf of the Republicans, Caroline Lynch.

Simpson was administered the oath and told it would be "a crime to make any materially false, fictitious or fraudulent statement or representation in such an authorized investigation."

She spent most of the next four hours committing perjury, primarily of the fictitious variety.

Some elements of Simpson's testimony have been dealt with at length. They include her accounts of Siegelman's decision to concede the 2002 election (the laughable KKK photos deal and the equally preposterous GOP pledge to make the criminal investigation vanish.) While her accounts on the above represent overwhelming evidence of perjury, the following will address additional components of her testimony.

They are her sworn statements regarding:

- Rob Riley's alleged familiarity with Mark Fuller and the judge's part-ownership of Doss Aviation.

- Judge Fuller's alleged grudge against Siegelman.

- Rob Riley's alleged foreknowledge that Fuller would be assigned to preside over the Siegelman case.

- The decision to prosecute Scrushy along with Siegelman.

- A 2003 poll in the *Mobile Press Register.*

- The relationship between the Rileys and Rove, and Rove's alleged directive to the Justice Department that it prosecute Don Siegelman.

In the months preceding her testimony Horton wrote about the above matters in his columns and applied these manufactured grievances and motives to support the central conspiracy of a GOP plot to remove Siegelman from the political landscape by shuttling him to an American gulag. In columns written after the release of her transcript Horton cited Simpson's testimony as proving or reinforcing the concoctions presented in those earlier columns.

Simpson ascribed her knowledge on each of the above subjects to statements she claimed Rob Riley made to her on two occasions. The first was during what she called a client-related meeting in 2002; the second on a supposed social visit to his law office in early 2005 which, for clarity's sake, will be referred to here as the, "baby picture meeting."

It is conceivable if barely so that Simpson perjured herself without the assistance or knowledge of another. Either that or she read Horton's "No Comment" columns religiously, analyzed them rigorously, and choreographed her testimony to advance conspiracies introduced in his pieces.

The only other alternative – that she testified truthfully – is not viable.

Here, the case for perjury:

Count One: Rob Riley's familiarity with Mark Fuller's finances.

In 2002, Simpson represented a company that had performed storm clean-up and filed a claim with FEMA seeking more money. She called Rob Riley and sought his assistance. Riley agreed to help and retained Stewart Hall, a college friend who'd become a Washington lobbyist. That much is not in dispute.

Simpson mentioned the FEMA case when asked during Judiciary Committee lawyers asked why she researched the judge's finances for Siegelman and Scrushy.

She testified that during a 2002 meeting with Riley and Hall, both men, apropos of nothing, started talking about Mark Fuller. This was before Fuller's appointment to the bench and years before his assignment to the Siegelman case.

Simpson remarked that she didn't know Mark Fuller and – or so she testified -- Riley and Hall corrected her. She'd known Fuller in Tuscaloosa but must have forgotten him, they said. Riley and Hall then "proceeded to tell me that Fuller has all these contracts, but his contracts are not the same type of contracts" as those of her FEMA client, she said.

"They were amazed that my clients could get these (large cleanup contracts) whereas Fuller was getting large contracts, but he was doing more what I consider to be maintenance on aircraft and fuel contracts, aviation kind of stuff which was not anything I was familiar with. It really sounded kind of like an oil job or doing government contracting."

It's unclear why a Washington lobbyist and an experienced lawyer would be "amazed" that one type of company could win one type of contract and a different type of company could win a different kind of contract, but that was Simpson's testimony.

The second meeting between Simpson and Rob Riley was even more fruitful that the first. It produced most of the testimony she gave regarding Judge Fuller and other subjects as well. Simpson, who had recently adopted a child, said she drove to Birmingham in early 2005 to shop for baby clothes. While there she dropped by Riley's law office to show him pictures of her new baby (thus, the "baby pictures meeting.")

Simpson testified that the topic quickly turned to Rob Riley's favorite subject.

"OK, in that conversation in early 2005, Rob started talking about Mark Fuller. And I'm like, where have I heard that name? Because I'd heard it before. And (Rob) tells me, he says that Mark was going to be the judge (on the Siegelman case.)

"He said, 'Oh, you know him.' I'm like, 'No I don't.' He said, 'I think you do.'"

"I said, 'Is he that guy y'all said before (during the 2002 meeting with Stewart Hall) that does them aviation contracts?'"

"And that's when he proceeded to say, 'Yeah, he has a company called Doss Aviation.'

"I said, 'Is he still doing that since he became a judge?'"

"And he said, 'Oh yeah,' and he proceeds to start telling me about the company."

Rob Riley learned about the above and other claims after the release of Simpson's testimony transcript. He went on the Internet and found that Fuller was a third-year law student when he arrived in Tuscaloosa as a freshman.

"Ms. Simpson stated in her testimony that she understood that Judge Fuller was in 'college' at Alabama with Stewart and me," Riley said. "It is my understanding based on an Internet search that Judge Fuller graduated from college at the University of Alabama in 1982. I began college at the University of Alabama in 1984."

"I had a lot on my plate. I wasn't hanging out with any law students."

Riley said he didn't know Fuller at Alabama and still doesn't. He said the first he'd heard of the companies Doss was from Simpson's testimony. Nor should one expect any different. Fuller is older than Rob Riley and from a different part of the state. Doss, to put it mildly, is not a household name in Alabama.

"To my knowledge I have never spoken to Mark Fuller, ever, about anything," said the governor's son. "I hate to say that and have been at an event with 1,000 or so people and have someone say I met Mark Fuller, but to my knowledge, I've never met him."

Stewart Hall, the lobbyist, recalled meeting Simpson, twice, both times briefly, when she came to Washington for matters related to the FEMA dispute. On neither occasion did he have a discussion with her that remotely resembled what she testified to.

"I didn't know there was a Mark Fuller until the Siegelman sentencing. I don't know the guy, never met the guy. I don't know this Doss guy either," said Hall, who chuckled when told Doss was a company, not a guy.

"It's a complete unadulterated joke," he said of Simpson's ever-changing tales. Hall's voice took a harder edge when he said he didn't "feel like being part of baseless conspiracy theories."

Among the documents Simpson provided to the Judiciary Committee lawyers was an e-mail from Rob Riley about the FEMA claim that referred to "Karl."

"It was not uncommon for him to talk to Karl Rove and Stewart Hall about that because he would make reference to it," Simpson testified.

There was, however, another Karl in the mix – Karl Dix, an Atlanta lawyer who specializes in FEMA claims, who was also hired to assist Simpson's client and who, like the other Karl, also spells his name with K.

"The memo to Karl? Well, heck, that was for the lawyer in Georgia helping us with the appeal!" Riley said, his voice rising in astonishment as is often did when talking about Simpson.

And then revealed how much "Karl Rove" helped with the FEMA claim.

"We got zero!" Riley said, laughing.

If Rob Riley and Hall are telling the truth, then Jill Simpson learned about Fuller's perfectly legal and fully disclosed part-ownership in the Doss companies from someone other than the governor's son.

And if that's the case, the only remaining conclusion is that she committed perjury.

Count Two: Fuller's 'grudge' against Siegelman.

This example regards a dispute between Fuller and his successor as district attorney for Coffee and Pike counties. It produced the most oft-quoted line from Simpson's testimony – that Rob Riley told Simpson that Fuller told him he "would hang Don Siegelman."

Late in his tenure as district attorney Fuller nearly doubled the salary of his chief investigator for a one-year period. After Fuller's appointment to the bench, Siegelman, in keeping with the duties of his office, appointed a successor district attorney to complete Fuller's term. The replacement, Gary McAliley, was not Fuller's fast friend.

The new D.A. conducted an audit of Fuller's office and concluded that Fuller raised the investigator's salary in part to increase the man's retirement benefits. It's a sign of Scott Horton's twisted genius that he was able to convert a little-known, long-forgotten southeast Alabama dispute between the former district attorney and his successor into A) a reason that Fuller should have recused himself from the Siegelman trial; and B) a motive for Fuller to want to "hang" Siegelman.

It's almost inconceivable that Horton, up in New York, found this Fuller factoid or was otherwise already familiar with it, such as by possessing an encyclopedic knowledge of every aspect of the judge's past. I apologize to readers for not being able to say conclusively who fed this and other information to Horton, along with the angles for him to spin the data into the vast conspiracy storyline.

Horton's summer series excoriating Fuller included a piece called, "Judge Fuller: A Siegelman Grudge Match." He wrote that Fuller blamed Siegelman for the audit because the governor had appointed McAliley. He took it a step further in a subsequent column, declaring that it was inappropriate for Fuller to preside over the trial because of his "clash with the Siegelman administration over the 'salary spiking' case in Coffee County."

District attorneys are not members of a governor's administration nor considered as such by anyone I've ever met. Only someone of Horton's deeply-rooted dishonesty could place the district attorney of Coffee County within the Siegelman administration.

If Simpson was testifying truthfully, then Rob Riley was indeed far gone with his Fuller obsession. Per Simpson, the governor's son made it his business to know everything about Fuller. What's more, Riley was such a compelling storyteller that two years later Simpson was able to testify to the Fuller minutia with exacting clarity.

"(Rob) made a statement that Fuller would hang Don Siegelman," she said. "He told me about a backlogging case, which is what you call the salary spike. He called it the 'backlogging.'"

Simpson told the congressional lawyers she'd "never heard the term 'backlogging'" so "had to ask Rob what backlogging was."

Riley (baby pictures meeting) laid it all out for her, allowing her to do the same, thusly, for the Judiciary Committee lawyers:

"Evidently from what I understand, Fuller had an employee when he was at the DA's job ... And he had two employees, a secretary and an investigator. And during his term of being DA, somehow that investigator wasn't making your typical salary, and he (Fuller) kicked it up. And Rob got to telling me that there was an audit done, a couple of audits, I think, and that Fuller just hated Don Siegelman and thought he was responsible for these audits on those salaried employees and that there was something involving a backlogging because they go back to figure your retirement and there was something kind of backlogging deal. But I didn't understand it at the time ...

"He said that Don Siegelman had caused Fuller to get audited. That's what Fuller thought. He (Fuller) hated him (Siegelman) for that."

The day after public release of the transcript, Horton pulled the "hang Don Siegelman" quote from Simpson's testimony and reminded his readers that he had "previously documented Judge Fuller's grudge against Siegelman." To prove it, he gave readers a link to what he called "the complete background" on the issue. The link led readers to the "Judge Fuller: A Siegelman Grudge Match" column.

———

Rob Riley said he never told Simpson the first thing about the Coffee County district attorney dispute, in part because he didn't know the first thing about it. "I have no knowledge of any ownership in any business or alleged grudges Ms. Simpson says Judge Fuller holds against Mr. Siegelman, and I never discussed such with Ms. Simpson," he said.

The fantasy of Mark Fuller telling Rob Riley or anyone else that he "would hang Don Siegelman" appeared in stories published by *Time*, the *New York Times* and others, and was repeated on four different Dan Abrams shows. The Judiciary Committee Democrats footnoted Simpson's testimony to support its finding that Fuller was "a judge who Mr. Riley stated could be trusted to 'hang Don Siegelman.'"

From Scott Horton to Jill Simpson to the top names in the national media and, lastly, into a congressional report. Fiction to fact, Tinkers to Evers to Chance-like.

Count Three: Riley's foreknowledge that Fuller would be assigned to preside over the Siegelman case.

Among the mini-conspiracies conceived by Horton to support the primary conspiracy was his assertion that the Justice Department engaged in "amazing and blatant judge-shopping" by bringing the Siegelman case in Montgomery.

"In fact, moving the case out of the district in which it was initiated so as to evade the control of the federal judge (Clemon) to whom it was assigned was the first clear-cut sign of prosecutorial misconduct in the history of the Siegelman prosecution," he wrote in mid-July.

Horton's unique to say nothing of wildly erroneous interpretation was that the Bobo case and warehouse investigation were linked. They were investigated by prosecutors and agents from the districts in which the cases were brought -- the Birmingham-based Northern District for the Bobo case and for the "G.H." case, the Middle District. It would have been bizarre and maybe not even possible for Franklin to take the Montgomery case to Birmingham.

Assuming for the moment that Horton is correct – that the G.H. case was an extension or related to the Bobo case -- Clemon wouldn't have been the judge. After the judge's outrageous conduct in the second Bobo trial, the 11th Circuit Court of Appeals removed him from presiding over the continuing prosecution of the Tuscaloosa doctor.

Horton's "judge shopping" charges didn't end there.

In his first story on Fuller, he wrote that a "well-placed Alabama GOP source who wishes to remain anonymous" had told him that "senior figures in the Alabama GOP appear to have known from the start that this case was going to be handled by a man they counted a friend, namely, George W. Bush–appointee Mark Fuller."

Six weeks after that column, Simpson testified that state Republicans knew well ahead of time that the grudge-holding Fuller would get the Siegelman case. She knew this because Rob Riley told her so during the 2005 baby picture meeting.

After release of Simpson's transcript, Horton wrote:

"In her Congressional testimony, Republican attorney Jill Simpson charges that senior G.O.P. *operatives* had hand-picked Judge Mark Fuller as the judge who would handle the Siegelman case because they knew he was a loyal Republican who bore a deep grudge against Siegelman."

And concluded: "Simpson's allegations *match the facts we upturned in our investigative* series on Judge Fuller this summer."

The House Judiciary Committee completed the circle. The Democratic majority's April 2008 report on selective prosecution cited Simpson's testimony as the source for its assertion that Rob Riley "also said the case would be in the Middle District of Alabama and would be heard by Chief Judge Mark Fuller..."

That someone so dishonest and wrong on so many points could have an impact on the Judiciary Committee and, it would seem as well, the coverage by the likes of *Time*, the *New York Times*, CBS, and MSNBC jars the mind. I know – I know! – I've made the point before. And will again. Just because it happened doesn't mean it's any less incomprehensible.

Count Four: The government's decision to prosecute Scrushy along with Siegelman.

In one of his post-sentencing Fuller columns, Horton wrote that inclusion of "Richard Scrushy, the notorious CEO of HealthSouth" into the Siegelman case was "clearly calculated for dramatic effect ..."

Alabamians were "seething over the botched prosecution" in Birmingham and there was "a broad public demand for Scrushy's head," Horton wrote, and then: "Given this situation, the linkage between Scrushy and Siegelman was weak and highly prejudicial to Siegelman. The judge should have investigated whether prosecutors were attempting to capitalize on public anger against Scrushy to 'get' Siegelman -- but I can find no evidence at all that Fuller examined this possibility."

Six weeks after that column, Simpson gave testimony that, once again, confirmed that Horton as right on target.

She testified that Rob Riley told her (baby picture meeting) that "they had come up with an idea to prosecute Don with Richard Scrushy ... because nobody likes Richard Scrushy, and (Riley) thought that that would assure a conviction for Don Siegelman."

The governor's son said "they" had "figured a way to do it," she testified.

Riley's statement that day in 2005 produced another opening for Curious Jill. She was always asking, was Simpson. Hey, Rob, what is backlogging? she'd wondered. And, to Bill Canary during the 2002 conference call, she'd asked who he meant by "his girls," after which Canary hung himself with the words he never spoke. And, she'd wondered aloud to Rob Riley (baby pictures): Has Fuller, since becoming a judge, continued to be involved with the Doss companies?

This time Simpson's curiosity was piqued by Riley's statement that "they" had conceived a plan to throw Scrushy into the Siegelman case.

"... and I basically asked him, 'What way are you – how are they going to do that?' And (Riley) proceeded to lay out to me the lottery issue," she told the Judiciary Committee lawyers.

It's a good thing she asked and Riley answered, since it helped the Judiciary Committee get to the truth. This from the April 2008 "selective prosecution" report: "Mr. Riley's comments about plans to have Mr. Scrushy and Mr. Siegelman tried jointly have also drawn notice from *commentators* ..."

The footnote to that statement was a blog posting from the Huffington Post. Such is the nature of what passes for Congressional evidence these days.

Count Five: A 2003 poll in the *Mobile Press Register*.

Every Sunday for years, the *Mobile Register* published a poll, usually on a topic in the news. Not infrequently, ideas ran short and our pollsters were asked to query citizens on an arguably meaningless subject. So it was for the poll published Nov. 16, 2003, a year after the 2002 gubernatorial election and three years before the next one.

Two months earlier voters had crushed Riley's proposed billion dollar tax increase. He'd received national acclaim for trying to reform Alabama's tax code but angered many voters, especially his fellow Republicans. It was for such reasons that his popularity was at an ebb.

According to the poll, at that moment in time, Roy Moore held a 17 point lead over Riley among likely Republican candidates in 2006. Were there to be a repeat of 2002, Siegelman could expect about 46 percent of the vote to 38 percent for Riley, with the remainder undecided.

In 2007, this insignificant, long-forgotten poll found itself playing a critical role in the conspiracy. It served as the must-have motive the prompted Karl Rove, Bob Riley, the Justice Department and others to employ extreme and illegal methods to take out Siegelman. The poll established that a Siegelman candidacy in 2006 was simply too grave a threat to trust to the electorate. The Democratic behemoth had to be – must be – vanquished. That, in any event, became the story.

The poll's relevance to the Siegelman prosecution was first reported in Horton's columns. *Time* and others whose idea of research was reading what Team Siegelman gave them followed.

In one of his July 2007 columns, Horton wrote that the 2003 poll "set off alarm bells" and "was cause for a number of meetings and discussions about how to deal with the 'Siegelman problem.'" He wrote that unidentified "sources within the Alabama GOP" told him about the poll and the response to it within the Riley camp.

"Before long, I believe, a solution to that problem manifested itself in the form of an indictment," Horton wrote.

The 2003 poll was published almost two years before the charges were brought in Montgomery and six months before the Bobo indictment. Riley's fortunes improved dramatically from November 2003 onward, as shown by subsequent polls that Horton, *Time,* the House Judiciary Committee and others ignored.

A May 2004 survey by the polling arm of the state teachers' association and taken before the Bobo indictment showed Riley leading Siegelman 50 percent to 37 percent. The same poll showed Lt. Gov. Baxley topping Riley, by two points, indicating that she was the only Democrat with a chance of beating the Republican incumbent. If it wasn't already the case, the poll all but assured that when donation time came, the Democratic power structure would back Baxley, not Siegelman.

The Associated Press reported on the poll so it would have been available, from a simple Nexis search, to Horton, *Time,* the Judiciary Committee or anyone else with the slightest interest in being thorough.

A two-minute *Nexis* search of polls pitting Siegelman against Riley would have also turned up three other polls, all with far greater time relevance to Siegelman's actual chances of defeating Baxley or Riley.

In late January 2005 – after the dismissal of the Bobo case and well before the Montgomery indictment – the *Register* published two polls. Both were carried on the wire by the AP. The first had Riley beating Siegelman 46 percent to 34 percent.

The next week's survey was limited to likely Democratic voters. It showed the cheerful, responsible, much-liked Baxley pounding Siegelman 45 to 31 percent. The state's top-ranked Democratic official had a sky-high favorability rating of 70 percent. Her negative rating, of 7 percent, was so low as to seem like a typo. Siegelman's negatives were in the 40 percent range, and that according to self-described Democrats.

"(Baxley) comes into this with very little baggage … It's hard to imagine what kind of strategy Siegelman could be thinking of as far as attacking her," our pollster, Keith Nicholls, said of the Democrat liked, if not supported, even by most Republicans.

In early October 2005, a Register poll -- the last taken before Siegelman's indictment – showed Riley crushing Siegelman 46 percent to 31 percent.

Translation: Siegelman, pre-indictment, was political toast. The notion that he had to be indicted to secure Riley's and the GOP's hold on the governors' office is a joke.

I don't think it unreasonable to propose that if these later polls showed Siegelman advantages then they, not the grey-haired 2003 poll, would have been cited by Horton, *Time*, et. al.

Now, the relevance of the 2003 poll to the claim being made here that Jill Simpson committed perjury.

She told the Judiciary Committee lawyers that she and Rob Riley also discussed the 2006 election. They talked about Lucy Baxley's "weaknesses and how we could hit her, you know, with what we could run with on that."

With Baxley thus dismissed, Riley told Simpson that Siegelman "was the biggest threat that we had … and also we talked about a little fact that Don had – there had been a poll done somewhere in 2003. And based on communications I had with Rob … Don had decided to run (in 2006)…"

With that testimony, Simpson displayed familiarity both with the ancient Mobile poll and its place in making the case for what Horton, two months before, called the "Siegelman problem."

Only there was no Siegelman problem. It was a con conceived by Horton and his Alabama sources to manufacture a motive that never existed. Only those without an understanding of the Alabama political situation – such as dupes with certain national media outlets – could have believed and then promoted the nonsense.

By now, the pattern should be familiar enough so that you already know what *Harper's* on-line star did next. In one of his columns after release of Simpson's transcript he wrote: "At the moment when, according to Simpson's testimony,

Rove was being approached and encouraged to make the prosecution of Siegelman happen, a poll in … the *Mobile Press-Register* was showing Siegelman defeating Riley in a rematch."

One person not buying the Siegelman as Democratic Goliath story was David Prather, the editorial page editor with the *Huntsville Times*. In a column dismissing the burgeoning national conspiracy, Prather wrote at that point in Siegelman's career he "wasn't worth Rove's trouble."

And then:

The Don had bet the ranch on the education lottery that anti-gambling folks detested and people who believe in tax fairness had to hold their nose to support. When that failed, the rest of Siegelman's administration was without a map, and degenerated into cronyism and lethargy. Can you name another governor who named his driver to head a state agency?

Siegelman's career was on the skids, but the idea that someone is being persecuted strikes a chord in the public heart, and Siegelman and Scrushy know how to raise questions, innuendoes and uncertainty better than most.

Horton went apoplectic. The ink wasn't dry on Prather's column before Horton told Harper's readers that the Huntsville writer was a "Kool-Aid Drinker" whose column "perfectly demonstrates the mental integrity of his paper."

The *Huntsville Times*, like the Mobile and Birmingham papers, is owned by the Newhouses. Up until then it had escaped Horton's fury, one assumes because it did little investigative reporting or editorializing on the Siegelman case. But after Prather's column, Horton tossed the *Times* in with its sorry sister papers. He wrote that big hitters in the national media were forever shaking their heads at the "very sorry landscape of the Alabama print media … The worst species are the Newhouse papers which control the market, of which Prather's paper is one."

He completed the thrashing by diagnosing Prather with something called, "Tolstoy syndrome."

To show just how wrong Prather was, Horton again brandished the 2003 poll in declaring as fact that Siegelman had remained the state's Democratic colossus. Though *New York Times* did not cite the poll in its editorials or news coverage, the same notion of Siegelman as the great threat to Riley was embedded in the paper's opining and news stories.

The 2003 poll entered the public record when the House Judiciary Committee cited it to establish the required motive-related case that Siegelman was at the time of his indictment a "major political force" in Alabama.

Count Six: The relationship between the Rileys and Rove, and the latter's directive to the Justice Department that it eliminate the threat that was Don Siegelman.

Horton's fabrication of a White House-issued directive to ruin Siegelman naturally required someone at the Justice Department, for not even he could claim that Rove investigated the case himself. The natural link was the Public Integrity Section, the group of lawyers within Justice that focuses on public corruption cases.

Public Integrity's role in the Siegelman case had been widely reported on since 2003, and section chief Noel Hillman came to Montgomery when Siegelman's indictment was announced. Horton simply connected fantasy (Rove's role in the case) with reality (the involvement of Hillman and Public Integrity) to create conspiracy.

In a July column, "Noel Hillman and the Siegelman Case," Horton stated as fact the Simpson-generated wives' tale that, "Leura Canary's husband, William Canary" was "actively engaged in efforts to take down Governor Siegelman." From there, to the next dot: That Bill Canary "bragged about bringing Rove into the effort to 'get' Siegelman, and how Rove had involved the Justice Department in the process."

Horton's source for Canary's bragging was an unidentified and in all likelihood imaginary, "Republican lawyer working on the Riley campaign."

Having established Rove's participation with Simpson and the unidentified Republican lawyer, Horton next drew a line from Rove to Hillman, or as he described the latter, a "loyal Bushie."

And then, uncharacteristically, humility.

"Now we still don't know all the specifics of Karl Rove's manipulation of matters in the Department of Justice. We do know that he was feverishly involved … It seems reasonably clear that one of Rove's key levers at Justice throughout this period was the Public Integrity Section (PIN)."

Here, Horton is admitting that he lacks proof connecting Rove to Hillman.

If he was worried for the lack of it, he needn't have been. Help was on the way.

Two months after that column Simpson testified that Rob Riley had complained to her (baby pictures) about Alice Martin's "having messed up" the Bobo case. With the Bobo rap beaten, Siegelman was "definitely running" again, Riley told her.

"And then he proceeds to tell me that Bill Canary and Bob Riley had had a conversation with Karl Rove again and that they had *this time* gone over and seen whoever was the head of the department of — he called it PIS, which I don't think that is the correct acronym, but that's what he called it. And I had to say, 'What is that?' And he said, 'That is the Public Integrity Section…And I read in the paper since they call it PIN, but he called it PIS."

Simpson's use of PIS instead of PIN was an endearing touch. Just like it might have gone down *had it really happened.*

She appears to be saying that Bob Riley and Bill Canary met with Rove, then joined Bush's senior advisor in a visit to the Justice Department. There, they met with the head of "PIS," who pledged to "allocate whatever resources" were necessary to prosecute Siegelman.

With that testimony – under oath, mind you – Simpson had done it. She'd made the final connection – from the Rileys and Rove to the Justice Department.

After release of Simpson's transcript Horton wrote two columns that employed her testimony to solidify the Rove-Justice Department link. They were called: "Karl Rove linked to Siegelman Prosecution," and, "The Noel Hillman connection."

Though Simpson either hadn't been able to recall Hillman's name or pretended not. After all, it wouldn't be realistic for her to remember *everything*. But of course Noel Hillman was head of Public Integrity at the time. No one needed her to fill in that blank. Hillman had led the public corruption unit from 2002 to 2006, to considerable praise from the press and Democrats.

"Let's plug in a bit more information," wrote Horton, filling in the void for Simpson. "The head of Public Integrity during this period is named Noel Hillman. He's a New Jersey politico, and came to Justice as Michael Chertoff's sidekick."

In the other column he congratulated himself for being right all along.

"As noted in the past, all available evidence so far had already pointed to Noel Hillman as the principal *vehicle* through which Karl Rove *tasked* and pursued the Siegelman case. And now we have a *Republican attorney* testifying under oath about the Rove-Hillman links in relation to the Siegelman case."

The italics are mine, the lies and innuendo his, and, in keeping with the pattern, the Judiciary Committee's as well. Simpson's testimony was the footnoted source for this segment from the April 2008 majority report on selective prosecution by the Bush Justice Department:

> *Most significantly, Ms. Simpson described a conversation in early 2005 in which Governor Riley's son Rob, a colleague and friend of Ms. Simpson, told her that his father and Mr. Canary had again spoken to Karl Rove who had in turn communicated with the head of the Department's Public Integrity Section about bringing a second indictment against Don Siegelman since the first case in Birmingham had been dismissed. According to Ms. Simpson, Mr. Riley also told her that Mr. Rove had asked the Department to mobilize additional resources to assist in the prosecution.*

Though the report didn't identify him by name, Hillman, as the head of Public Integrity, was, or so it would appear, implicated by the Judiciary Committee as a key player in the scheme to destroy Siegelman.

In early 2006, about five months before the Siegelman trial, I called the Justice to request an interview with Hillman. I was thinking of doing a feature on him and the Public Integrity Section. This small sub-section of Justice was I assumed little known to our readers – I'd never heard of it before the Siegelman case – and Hillman was receiving much praise, including from Democrats, for Public Integrity's aggressive prosecution of public corruption, especially for its work on the Abramoff case.

Hillman seemed distracted, something less than thrilled to talk to a reporter, or in any event one from Mobile. He was polite enough, but I could see I wasn't going to get a story out of his yes-no and one-sentence responses.

This was pre-Simpson and thus, pre-Rove. Siegelman was of course still telling anyone who would listen that Bob Riley was behind his prosecution. It was a ludicrous claim but deserved a response from Hillman, so I asked.

He paused. "I'm – this just shows my ignorance – but is he the current governor?"

That was all the answer I needed but informed Hillman that, yes, Bob Riley was Alabama's current governor.

More than two years later, I called Hillman again, this time to ask about the accusations made by Simpson, Horton and others. By then he was a federal judge in New Jersey, and I was surprised when he took my call.

"Yeah I am mad," he said. "Horton and others have slandered and libeled me and the good people at (Public Integrity)... When this case started I did not know and did not care what party Siegelman called home.

"I've never spoken with, met with, communicated in any way with, Karl Rove or anyone I knew to be acting on his behalf. The notion that he would call a career section chief who himself reports to a career deputy assistant attorney general (Jack Keeney) about a pending case is absurd and everyone at DOJ thinks it's the biggest joke ever."

He expressed incredulity at the level of hearsay that's been allowed to fuel the fantasy that Karl Rove directed Public Integrity to prosecute Siegelman. "She (Simpson) said he (Rob Riley) says my father (Bob Riley) says that someone else said that they said that Karl Rove talked to Public Integrity – it's at least four layers of hearsay and there's a reason why courts don't allow hearsay as evidence. And everybody along the line has denied it.

"I've been sitting here scratching my head and wondering why this isn't clearly unreliable," Hillman said. "No one who asserts these things has ever bothered to call me and ask."

Leura Canary made no effort to influence the Public Integrity Section's decisions on the case, nor did she seek to have any input, he said. "The single biggest force pushing the case was Louis Franklin, with Feaga to a lesser degree."

Scott Horton, said Hillman, "literally makes stuff up."

Simpson had testified for an entire day, concluding at about 4:30 p.m. If one accepted her testimony at face value, she'd done much to advance the case that Siegelman was the victim of a political hit. She'd established motive for Bob Riley and the Republicans to seek the prosecution of Siegelman; a motive for Fuller to "hang" the former governor; and most critically, she'd sealed the Riley-Canary-Rove-Hillman nexus.

Her next appearance, or so it seemed, was coming soon, before the entire Judiciary Committee. This time it would be in public, for all to see.

———

Author's Note: As is probably clear, I think Simpson was coached, probably by Scott Horton, who she referred to, at least on occasion, as "Professor Horton."

In October 2009 I e-mailed questions to Horton and Simpson regarding, among other things, Simpson's testimony. I asked Horton: "Did you coach and/or assist Jill Simpson in the preparation of her September 2007 testimony?"

Neither he nor Simpson replied to my questions. I don't think they like me, so their failure to answer shouldn't be seen as proof of my suspicions.

Chapter 44
Dumb and Dumber

"The fact that those charges were never looked at will only heighten suspicions that the Siegelman prosecution was a case of selective justice and that in the Bush administration, enforcing the law has been a partisan pursuit."
-- Conclusion of Time *magazine story examining allegations by Lanny Young that he'd made questionable donations to Bill Pryor and Jeff Sessions as well as Siegelman.*

"When it gets to the point where says he believes that the governor of Alabama went to Washington, met with the Justice Department, convinced them to put the resources into a conspiracy to get Don Siegelman, that is so farfetched, that is so totally wrong that I'm disappointed that someone like Artur Davis could possibly believe that."
-- Alabama Gov. Bob Riley, after Davis statement before the Judiciary Committee that he believed Jill Simpson's story.

In early October, Team Siegelman closed a major sale to *Time* magazine.

"Selective Justice in Alabama?" asked the headline above a long piece by Adam Zagorin, who'd written the magazine's first story, on Jill Simpson's affidavit. The story, promoted on *Time's* cover, was to be cited from then on by Siegelman and Democrats on the Judiciary Committee as air-tight evidence of, well, selective prosecution in Alabama.

The headline was something short of original. Two months before, the *New York Times* introduced the mantra to come with its editorial that first used the phrase "political hit," called Bill Canary Karl Rove's protégé, and recited the accusations to date from Jill Simpson. The headline on that one was, simply, "Selective Prosecution." The people at *Time* people just added, "in Alabama."

The gist of the magazine's story: That the same prosecutors who investigated Lanny Young's payments to Siegelman ignored compelling evidence of potential criminal actions by Bill Pryor and Jeff Sessions, who, like Siegelman, also received campaign contributions from Lanny.

In an "unusual exercise of prosecutorial discretion, nearly all the payments and donations went uninvestigated," opined Zagorin.

This failure to investigate the Pryor-Sessions contributions was later disputed by a prosecutor who worked on the case in its early stages. In any event, one hopes that little time was wasted on the matter.

More than halfway into the story Zagorin acknowledged, albeit briefly, a rather compelling reason why prosecutors exploring corruption in the Siegelman administration didn't race off to open a new probe into Pryor, by then a federal appeals judge, and Sessions, a United States senator.

"Certainly in Young's statements about Sessions and Pryor, he did not allege a quid pro quo for his money laundering of their campaigns," Zagorin conceded, if with a final, unsupported dig about "money laundering."

Imagine the strength of cases accusing Pryor and Sessions of accepting campaign donations from Young and friends of Young at a time when Lanny wasn't known as crooked, and without any evidence of a single act by Pryor or Sessions on his behalf. The idea is laughable, yet *Time* presented the failure to investigate these non-crimes in making its case for "selective prosecution in Alabama."

The investigation into Young, G.H. Construction and the administration began two days after our story proving *theft* from the state of Alabama. Campaign donations became a part of the G.H. case, but were never the primary element and certainly not the originating factor.

Several lines from the *Time* piece jumped off the page and bopped me in the head, none more than this one: "But what Young had to say about Sessions, Pryor and other high profile Alabama Republicans was even more remarkable for the simple fact that much of it had never before come to light." To which Zagorin added that Young "openly offered details (to the FBI) about what he said were donations totaling between $12,000 and $15,000 to Pryor's campaign for state attorney general" from him and associates who he says he reimbursed.

The only thing remarkable was Zagorin's statement. Of our many G.H. stories in May 2001, one was about, and only about, donations *Time* claimed had "never before come to light."

That story, "Pryor Got Boost from Young," reported the amounts and types of donations to Pryor's 1998 campaign from Lanny and his landfill partners, Joey Tillman and Randy Baker, and made the connections between the three. Readers were told that Young provided travel valued at $365 to the Pryor campaign; that Tillman gave travel valued at $1,534 and donated $4,303 in advertising; and that Baker provided the campaign with travel services valued at $6,055.

I was able to report the donations in the above-described detail because they'd been *meticulously disclosed by the Pryor campaign* to the secretary of state's office and in a timely fashion. They were not a secret when Zagorin wrote about them nor had they ever been.

During the 1998 campaign Pryor had asked Richard Allen, his top assistant, to review his donations. Allen's task was to flag contributions from anyone under investigation by the attorney general's office so they could be returned. When I interviewed Allen for the 2001 story he said that when the donations were made, G.H. Construction was two years from being formed. Young was just another successful businessman, much like donors in most campaigns who provide large contributions or help candidates with travel.

Even if Pryor were so inclined, there would have been no motive to conceal donations made in 1997 and 1998 from Young or his partners.

According to *Time*, Lanny told the FBI he'd had others donate thousands of dollars to Sessions then reimbursed them in violation of federal election laws. However, none of those individuals named by Lanny showed up on Session's reports.

All Zagorin found was a single $1,000 donation from Lanny. It was possible, he wrote, that Young never made some of the donations he'd reported to the FBI and was "merely boasting." That was fair of Zagorin to acknowledge, but to keep the crime alive the reporter ventured deep into the land of ifs and maybes.

"But it would also mean that (Young) had lied to federal agents, which is a felony, and Young was never charged with that crime. If he had lied, that would also have diminished Young's credibility as a key government witness against Siegelman."

Diminish Young's credibility?

Had Zagorin been remotely familiar with the case he'd have known that Young had lied often to investigators and prosecutors, primarily to protect Hamrick and, I'm sure, Waste Management. As required, the government turned over to defense lawyers the interview reports and the like revealing Lanny's original stories, and at trial, defense lawyers battered him with those lies.

The Lanny Young presented to jurors – by prosecutors as well as defense lawyers -- was a serial briber, a thief, and a fellow with a loose attachment to the truth. That's why almost every payment or favor testified to by Young was supported with records or testimony from others.

There was no need for prosecutors to add perjury as a new charge to a witness who was already pleading guilty to far worse. Yet Zagorin suggested that the failure to charge Young with perjury was a prejudicial act, and as such, additional proof of "selective prosecution" in Alabama.

Our 2001 story reported that Pryor's connection to Lanny was Claire Austin. Claire, too, was the connection to Sessions, having worked for him before she worked for Pryor.

By the time the FBI started talking to Lanny he'd split with Claire and suspected, correctly, that she was my source on the warehouse deal. For this he despised her, and I believe that in his interviews with the FBI he was doing everything in his power to drag her down with him, such as by attempting to dirty up Pryor and Sessions.

The "selective prosecution" story – the second of four by Zagorin on the Siegelman case -- managed to encapsulate many of the elements of the story line promoted by Horton and Team Siegelman. There was, for example, the contextual placement of Siegelman as the ever-striving underdog Democrat valiantly challenging the GOP power structure. Alabama was "as red a state as the clay in its earth." From this red earth hell Siegelman "emerged as one of the few Democratic stars."

Prosecutors brought charges against the little battler "just as he was preparing to run for governor again;" and the trial overlapped with the Democratic primary "in which Siegelman had initially been a heavy favorite." Cited to support this fable was – perhaps you guessed it -- the 2003 poll cherished by Horton. Either Zagorin didn't do his own research and took what Team Siegelman handed him or he was familiar with the later polls and chose to conceal them from his readers.

In the Judiciary Committee hearing later that month, Artur Davis pointed to "Selective Justice in Alabama?" in accusing the Bush Justice Department was guilty of selective prosecution. The committee's April 2008 report – "Allegations of Selective Prosecution in Our Federal Criminal Justice System" – made hay with the *Time* story, referring to it frequently and citing it in four footnotes.

With Zagorin's story, the pattern had repeated itself: Team Siegelman made the pitch; one or more prominent national publications bought the goods; Horton and others touted the story as fact; and everything became official with the handoff to the Judiciary Committee.

"Of course, readers of *No Comment* are familiar with much of the Lanny Young accusations," Horton wrote in, "Justice in the Cradle of the Confederacy," a column published on the heels of *Time's* selective prosecution. The disclosures "that Adam Zagorin recently made" showed that Young had provided prosecutors with "whopping evidence" against Sessions and Pryor," Horton wrote.

Less than a week later Zagorin's wrote another story. "Rove Linked to Alabama Case," was published on *Time's* web-page, not in the magazine. It informed readers that *Time* had "obtained a copy of Simpson's 143-page sworn statement." Either Zagorin didn't read the transcript, read it and believed Simpson, or chose to conceal from readers her obvious falsehoods and fantasies.

He and *Time* reported that the "Republican lawyer" had "provided new details in a lengthy sworn statement" to the Judiciary Committee. The story presented some of the greatest hits from her testimony, foremost being Judge Fuller's plan to "hang Don Siegelman."

Zagorin's stabs at fairness were limited to the requisite denials from the Republican villains. Nowhere does one find the credibility- impugning statements from the horse's mouth. Nothing about Simpson researching Fuller's finances, ordering a credit report on the judge or working with the defendants and their people on the recusal motion and her affidavit. Zero on the remarkable advances in her descriptions of upper level Justice Department and White House involvement since the May affidavit. And of course no mention of Simpson's debunked stories that Siegelman conceded the 2002 election after the Riley campaign pledged to deep-six the KKK pictures and put the kibosh on the kibosh the investigation.

(Author note: Neither Zagorin or *Time* responded to questions I sent them about their Siegelman coverage.)

The *New York Times* story on Simpson's transcript opened by reporting that the "son of Alabama's current Republican governor" had "boasted" that Fuller would "hang Don Siegelman" for "partisan reasons."

The story by Philip Shenon was the shortest piece in the paper's growing library of Siegelman stories and fairer than those written by his fellow *Times*-man, Adam Nossiter. It didn't hang Simpson with her own words but gave sufficient space to the denials from some of those she'd slandered. The story's brevity suggests that the *Times*, having invested so much in Simpson's credibility, decided the less said the better.

Unlike *Time* and the *Times*, the leads in the *Birmingham News* and by the AP's Bob Johnson about Simpson's testimony raised questions about her veracity, as opposed to just tossing out her fantastical but headline grabbing declarations of GOP chicanery.

Both stories focused on Simpson's new tale that Siegelman conceded the 2002 election after Terry Butts promised him, on behalf of the Riley campaign, that the criminal investigation would be dropped if he would concede the election. Bob's report quoted Butts' emphatic denial of the Simpson's story and gave Rob Riley – Simpson's "source" in all things – ample space to rebut her version.

"If it had happened, we'd have heard about it before now from Don Siegelman," Riley said of Simpson's new explanation for Siegelman's ending his recount fight.

Johnson, who knew the history and the players far better than anyone at *Time* or the *Times*, noted that Siegelman had never once mentioned the promise to kill the investigation offer during the five years since it was made, and, if so, obviously reneged upon.

The Birmingham story, by Blackledge, Chandler and Mary Orndorff, also addressed at length this new reason for the end of the 2002 election. Both the AP and the *News* presented portions of Simpson's testimony on Fuller, including the judge's intention to "hang" Siegelman. But the Alabama reporters gave Rob Riley and Butts space not simply to deny having told Simpson this, but to provide context to their denials.

"Jill's allegations continue to change every time she gives new testimony," said the governor's son. "They've now gone from not only being untrue, but to being absurd and ridiculous."

The *News* published portions of the transcript, including those where Lynch, the Republican lawyer, asked Simpson why she never reported these horrific tales of political, judicial and prosecutorial misconduct to the state bar.

———

The protection of the whistleblower charade reached a new heights of absurdity after the stories by the Associated Press and *Birmingham News*.

John Conyers, the Judiciary Committee chairman, wrote Simpson to apologize and assailed Republican congressmen for releasing the transcript to

Alabama reporters. The letter apparently was intended to be private, as it was disseminated to the media. Simpson, who could teach melodrama to soap opera actresses, bemoaned that release of the transcript allowed her to be "attacked by surprise" by Riley supporters. This from the surprise attacker who'd filed an affidavit with *Time* and the *New York Times* accusing the Rileys, Canarys and an army of others of planning Siegelman's demise.

A Republican on the committee, Lamar Smith of Texas, shot back that, yes, the transcript was provided to Alabama reporters – but only after Democrats first gave it to *Time* magazine. "Any accusation of a 'leak' of the transcript after it was in the public domain and in the hands of *Time* is disingenuous and without merit," said Smith.

Horton was livid. Jill Simpson – that oh-so-fragile lone link to Rove, to everything – was facing scrutiny. The drama queen was the king on the chessboard. Lose her, lose the game. Horton could not permit that to happen.

He wrote that a Judiciary Committee staffer on the GOP side (not identified, probably fictional) told him that Republicans on the committee were going to "use the time-honored technique" of leaking the transcripts to a reporter "who can be trusted to get out message across."

"That is, not a real reporter, but a partisan attack animal," wrote the pot of the kettle.

"I wondered for a second just who the G.O.P.'s attack dog would be. But in fact, it didn't take much effort, since it's been clear for many months exactly who in the press could be counted upon to present Republican Party propaganda in the guise of a news story. And then, in a matter of only a few hours, the story appeared, just where I knew it would, in the pages of the *Birmingham News*."

It would seem from his response that Horton hoped Simpson's transcript would *never be released,* or in any event, not to anyone other than himself, *Time,* the *New York Times,* and other trustworthy national media outlets. Giving it to *Time* was fine. But the *Birmingham News*?

Horton accused the *News* of launching "a major sustained assault on the credibility of Jill Simpson." An alternative take is that the Alabama reporters were simply fact-testing uncorroborated stories based on hearsay and told years after the fact by a previously unknown witness who was implicating, among others, the White House, the Justice Department, Alabama's governor, and a federal judge in a criminal conspiracy to imprison Don Siegelman.

In this way their work was routine. Only when compared to the performance by the *New York Times* and *Time* does the work by the Alabama reporters appear outstanding.

Horton helped manufacture then foment a second front in his war against the Newhouse GOP mouthpieces. Not only did the national media "get it," but so did several smaller voices of reason in Alabama. The editorial pages of the *Decatur Daily*, *Anniston Star* and *Tuscaloosa News*, and especially the first two, were tireless promoters of Siegelman's cause and Simpson's story.

It appeared that Horton and Team Siegelman provided the smaller Alabama papers with the talking points, they sang his song in editorials, and he turned around and applauded their courage and insight in his, "No Comment" columns.

"Independent papers around the state, led by the *Anniston Star*, the *Decatur News*, the *Tuscaloosa News* and others, have adopted an appropriate attitude towards Javert, which can be summarized with one word: skepticism," he wrote in, "More Responses to Javert."

The Anniston paper published at least two of Horton's columns; and one of the paper's columnists mimicked the *Harper's* writer by also applying the "Javert" metaphor to Siegelman's prosecution.

In early September 2007, the *Times'* Adam Nossiter reported that in Alabama "a small war of editorial boards has erupted since Mr. Siegelman" was sentenced to prison.

"Newspapers in the state's smaller cities have repeatedly raised questions about the former governor's treatment," Nossiter wrote, with "raised questions" code for doing their job, the implication being that the larger papers were failing to do the same, post-Jill.

Horton provided examples of this "skepticism" toward "Javert," from the smaller Alabama papers that he had developed relationships with. My favorite was a sample from the "Locust Fork Journal," a far-left Alabama-based blog. Glynn Wilson, Locust Fork's one-man band and a Siegelman devotee, was riffing on the failings of the larger Alabama media and swerved off the subject to slap Louis Franklin.

"Well, not all of us at the Locust Fork News and Journal, the Anniston Star, the Decatur Daily, etc. are 'out of state,'" wrote Wilson. "In fact, we are right here in the neighborhood, and watched Mr. Franklin botch his first attempt at convicting Richard Scrushy in Birmingham. He was about as lame a lawyer as I've seen in my 27 years of covering trials."

If Wilson did attend the first Scrushy trial, he must not know what Franklin looks like.

Franklin did not participate in any way, shape or form in that trial. He couldn't have botched that trial if he'd wanted to.

It was one thing for a blogger as loose with the facts as Glynn Wilson to get something that wrong, but another for a publication of *Harper's* supposed credibility to pass it on to its readers, web-site or not.

Horton concluded, "More Responses to Javert," with a gaze into the crystal ball: "I'm told that several more editorials are in the works from every corner of the state, and Javert isn't going to like any of them. Stand by for more later."

And he was right. But how did Scott Horton know that the editorial boards of several small Alabama papers planned to publish editorials consistent with his viewpoint?

————

That fall I received a call from a scheduler for, "To the Point," a nationally syndicated, Los Angeles-based public radio program hosted by Warren Olney. Could I participate by telephone on Olney's show, along with Scott Horton?

Olney was a partisan (left of center), but a friend who listened to him assured me he was fair. I told his scheduler that the Siegelman case, especially the Scrushy aspect, was complex and could not be easily summarized, but said I would do it. I should not have.

The program was to be introduced by a reporter with the well-known and somewhat well-regarded *Talking Points Memo* web publication (which prior to this experience and their reporting on the Siegelman case, I occasionally read.) I was told that the TPM reporter would present a down the middle summary of the matter. She did not.

Horton was damn near the glibbest dude on the planet, his assertions as boldly made as they were fanciful. Olney was with him 100 percent. My attempts to explain the intricacies of the Scrushy case – the role played by Integrated Health and UBS, the concealment of both $250,000 contributions, etc. – were bulky and not at all what Olney wanted to hear.

My wife listened later on Olney's web-site and said I did fine. I chose not to. I thought I'd stunk. I had felt like the sacrificial liberal on a Bill O'Reilly-led panel discussing Hillary.

————

Blogging by the Talking Points Memo and lesser lights played some hard to define but undeniably important role in this saga (though he might say otherwise, I consider Horton to be an Internet columnist, not a blogger.) Siegelman was to give dozens of interviews to bloggers, and his statements suggest that the former governor would make an excellent blogger.

In 2008 and 2009 Siegelman was a speaker at Netroots Nation, the national conference of liberal bloggers, and has become a hero of sorts to that community.

The general public hears more about blogs than actually reads them. This is a good thing. Blogging requires a computer, opinions and lots of free time. Talent, sanity and accuracy are optional. But the blogs do have influence. People in politics and journalism are far more likely to read blogs than the average person, which gives them an opinion-forming power that far exceeds their readership.

Most political bloggers are extremist – far left or way to the right, and in either direction, polemical rather than factual.

During the Clinton scandals one often heard of the Free Republic (the Freepers), a blog community of the radical right. And scary. The two extremes are equally barmy and loose with the facts, but the liberal bloggers seem safer, less physically threatening in their rhetoric.

Among the members of that group is Larisa Alexandrovna, purveyor of the site, "Raw Story," and a contributor to the well-known Huffington Post. Many blogs seek and receive comments, and some of those posted on Alexandropova's site and elsewhere were priceless. One gave a link to Mobile County Probate Court and urged folks to research the mortgage on my home, apparently for evidence that Republicans financed my house. My favorite was an anonymous post seeking to connect my reporting to Bill Pryor through, of all people, my father.

"Maybe Jerry Curran is a member of the Federalist Society (like Pryor) and was another member of Rove's political machine. Eddie's father and Pryor's father look to be about the same age, were they classmates?"

(My father, while generally conservative, probably doesn't know the first thing about the Federalist Society. I can't type the suggestion that he's a "member of Rove's political machine" without laughing. I don't know how old Bill Pryor's father is or if my father knows him. I've never heard his name mentioned by my father, and can say with certainty that I couldn't pick out Bill Pryor's father in a crowd of two.)

One Alabama blogger who merits mention is Roger Schuler, aka "The Legal Schnauzer."

The Schnauzer is a tireless and fawning promoter of Siegelman, Horton, Jill Simpson, and all manner of conspiracies, many directed at him. As best I can tell, he started his blog after losing a lawsuit having to do with his house, then a legal malpractice case against the lawyers who represented him, and somehow he located Bob Riley's fingerprints on his two tiny, obscure lawsuits.

The Siegelman case has been very good to him. Many of Schuler's columns have been picked up by national-level political blogs, with quite a few seeing light of day on the Daily Kos, which is among the country's top liberal web-sites.

In May 2008, the University of Birmingham at Alabama fired Shuler from his long-time post in the university's publications department. The reason: He was spending several hours a day on the Internet researching for his blog.

Schuler countered that he wasn't researching for his blog, but rather, that his job required him to keep up with state news. He wrote that UAB fired him because, "my blog dealt critically with the Bush Justice Department, particularly its handling of the Don Siegelman case in Alabama, and that made someone in our state's GOP hierarchy uncomfortable."

He has blamed, among others, Karl Rove, for having a hand in his firing.

Those who came to his rescue, blog-wise anyway, were "Raw Story" and Schnauzer's hero, Scott Horton.

In a piece on *Harper's* web-site called, "The Argus-eyed University," Horton gave what he called a "George Orwell Honorable Mention" to UAB for firing Shuler. Horton noted that one of Shuler's sins -- in addition to "angering Riley's political cronies" – was spending too much time at work reading Horton's columns.

An old friend who I hadn't seen in years told me he'd Googled my name and the first thing that popped up was Schnauzer letting me have it over my Siegelman stories. At some point later, I called Schuler and found him to be friendly, not defensive or angry, but I also detected a sadness. When we said our goodbyes things seemed cool, but he continued blasting me, and I couldn't bring myself to care.

Horton deserves contempt, the Schnauzer, only pity. He's a misguided soul with a computer, a web-site, and some steam to blow off.

On Oct. 23, the Judiciary Committee convened to hear testimony on the selective prosecution scandal. What would've been a remarkably entertaining affair was robbed of its magic by the absence of one person who linked Siegelman to Rove and so much else as well.

The Democrats decided not to summon their star witness.

West Virginia Republican Randy Forbes accused the majority of failing to call Jill Simpson because "her credibility was shredded beyond repair." Alabama congressman Artur Davis snapped back that Simpson's phone records showed she'd called Rob Riley's law office that day in 2002.

The hearing marked Davis's coming out party. He'd had his finger in the wind since Simpson's affidavit, and the wind had picked up.

"Politics influenced this case," he declared, directing his comments to Lori Siegelman and her children, Dana and Joseph, all of whom were seated in the front row (Siegelman, at this point, was still in prison.) "That's the irresistible conclusion based on the facts. Washington politics. Karl Rove politics. And finally, the politics that says if I can't beat your ideas, if I can't have confidence that I can beat you at the ballot box, maybe I can do it the old-fashioned way and just destroy you and destroy your reputation."

Without Simpson, the closest thing to a star turn on the Siegelman story was provided by Doug Jones. The former Siegelman lawyer gave his version of the disputed 2004 meeting with Franklin and Feaga, and said there was no question but that the Public Integrity Section was intimately involved in what he called the invigorated Siegelman probe.

The other main witness was former Republican attorney general Richard Thornburgh, who claimed politics was also at the root of the prosecution of his client, Alleghany County (Pa.) coroner Cyril Wecht, who is a Democrat.

With Jones and Thornburgh, the committee had put on two white collar criminal defense attorneys saying that their clients were innocent and prosecuted for political reasons. This is what white collar criminal lawyers say, almost without fail, when defending public officials. It was enough, though, for the *New York Times* editorial staff. In "Tilting the Scales of Justice," *Times'* opiners pointed to the hearing to apply, for the third time, the "political hit" phrase to Siegelman's prosecution.

———

In making its case that Bush Justice Department engaged in a pattern and practice to target Democrats, the Judiciary Committee achieved just the opposite, not that anyone seemed to notice. Consider that the Siegelman case was the most egregious example of this pervasive effort during the entirety of the Bush presidency. That's according to the to the majority's own findings.

The two other signature outrages proving the slam dunk case against the Justice Department were the prosecution of a state procurement officer in Wisconsin (Georgia Thompson), and the one against Thornburgh's client (Wecht). A third, involving Mississippi trial lawyer Paul Minor, was also to gain some traction with Horton, Schnauzer, the *Times'* editorial page, and the Judiciary Committee.

For the sake of argument, let's assume that Thompson, Wecht and Minor are all shining examples of rectitude and were nailed without cause by overzealous federal prosecutors. The fact remains that John Conyers and his committee assembled this national scandal with cases brought against a defeated washed-up former governor, a civil servant in Wisconsin, a Mississippi trial lawyer, and the coroner of a county in Pennsylvania.

Compare that slugger's line-up to some of the Republicans prosecuted or under investigation by the same Justice Department.

In 2003, federal prosecutors indicted recent former Illinois governor and Republican powerhouse George Ryan, primarily for activities that occurred years before, when he was secretary of state. Ryan, in my mind over-prosecuted, was found guilty at trial and sentenced to more than six years in prison.

In 2004, Connecticut Gov. John Rowland, a Republican, resigned as the Bush Justice Department probed accusations that he used his office to help a contractor and a jet company in return for vacations, free construction work and other favors. He pleaded guilty and served 10 months in prison – an indication, among other things, that those who plead serve far less time than those who go to trial and lose (as did Ryan and Siegelman.)

The resignation of Tom DeLay, arguably the most powerful man in Congress, was in considerable part triggered by the Justice Department's investigation into

Republican super-lobbyist Jack Abramoff. Two White House officials, Ohio congressman Bob Ney and a host of other Republicans were found guilty or pleaded guilty as a result of the Abramoff scandal. Chief among those was Abramoff.

In 2005, Duke Cunningham, eight-term Republican congressman from California, pleaded guilty to federal charges related to his acceptance of $2.4 million in bribes from a defense contractor who Cunningham helped win almost $90 million in federal contracts.

In 2006, national-level fundraiser Tom Noe pleaded guilty to violating federal campaign laws in a case that shook the Ohio Republican party and spread embarrassment to Washington. Politicians including President Bush had benefitted from Noe's largesse. Noe was also convicted of embezzlement and sentenced to more than 15 years in prison on another matter.

In February 2008, the Justice Department charged Rick Renzi, a Republican congressman from Arizona, with extortion, money laundering and other crimes related to a scheme in which he collected hundreds of thousands of dollars after using his position on the House Natural Resources Committee to push land deals for a business partner.

Later that year, the Bush Justice Department charged Alaska's Ted Stevens -- the longest-serving Republican senator in U.S. history -- with seven felony counts related to hundreds of thousands of dollars in gifts and services received from an oil services contractor and not disclosed by Stevens. The indictment came four months before he was to face a re-election challenge from Mark Begich, the popular Democratic mayor of Anchorage, and with the new Democrat majority in the Senate slim and frail.

In late October a jury found Stevens guilty on all seven charges. A week later, he lost to Begich in an election so close that there is no question but that he would've won if the Justice Department had not prosecuted him.

(The Justice Department, admitting to apparent legal ethics failings by prosecutors on the Stevens case, later sought and was granted dismissal of the Stevens' charges. Siegelman, as will be seen tried and continues to try to mimic Stevens' complaints against prosecutors in an effort to have his case overturned.)

Most if not all the above-described cases involved or were spearheaded by the Public Integrity Section during Noel Hillman's tenure.

If that all-star squad were prosecuted during a Democratic administration one supposes that Republicans would howl politics. Such complaints are common. What's remarkable – no, inconceivable – is that so many believe Siegelman was targeted for destruction by the White House when the lone source connecting Karl Rove to Don Siegelman is the human laugh track, Jill Simpson.

This reasonable defense of the Bush Justice Department was raised, far as I know, in only one newspaper, and a prominent national one at that.

"Prosecutors note that the Justice Department has targeted more than a dozen high-profile Republicans in Congress and the executive branch in public corruption prosecutions during the Bush administration, including former California lawmaker Randall 'Duke' Cunningham and disgraced lobbyist Jack Abramoff, a Rove ally," reported Carrie Johnson of the *Washington Post* in an April 2008 story on the Siegelman-Simpson-Rove imbroglio.

The *Post* is the only paper in the country that compares with the *Times* in terms of covering national politics, and for that matter, the world at large. The *Post's* reporting on the Siegelman scandal could not have been more different than that of its New York competitor.

The paper never once editorialized on the Siegelman case. There were several pieces on news side, all reasonable, and mostly reporting basic developments in the post-Simpson era. The *Post's* one major treatment of the case was the above-mentioned story by Johnson, the paper's Justice Department reporter. It was the fairest and, well, most skeptical story on the farce not penned by an Alabama reporter (a close second being those by Ben Evans, a Washington-based Associated Press reporter.)

Johnson interviewed Siegelman. He gave her a Rove bloody glove and fingerprints quote. Rather than presenting the comment as if it were wisdom from a sage on a mountaintop (see *New York Times*/Adam Nossiter), Johnson played reporter and asked Siegelman to support his wild words with facts. That led to her reporting that Siegelman was unable to provide any "specific evidence tying his fate to White House political interference."

In what read like a swipe at the *Times*, *Time* and "60 Minutes," Johnson remarked that the former governor "has not petitioned the court to hear his allegations of political tampering, choosing instead *to make them on television programs and in newspapers and magazines.*"

With another obvious point rendered astute by the failure of anyone else to make it, the *Post* story remarked that in pressing his case with the Judiciary Committee, Siegelman was "seizing on a theme that is *newly popular with politically connected defendants*: turning the tables on a Justice Department vulnerable to accusations of interference because of missteps last year under" under former Attorney General Alberto Gonzales."

In its 20-plus news stories, the best the *Times* did in granting Rove's lawyer an opportunity to dispute his client's role in the Siegelman conspiracy was this, from one of Nossiter's stories: "There's absolutely, positively, no truth to any of the allegations and literally no evidence for any of it," Mr. Luskin said.

Base covered, barely. No explanation, just the denial. Then, back to storyline: Siegelman got screwed.

Compare the limited presentation of Luskin in Nossiter's story to that by the *Post's* Johnson:

Rove's lawyer, Robert D. Luskin, said that Rove "does not recall" ever meeting Simpson and "simply never had a conversation about targeting Siegelman. He didn't talk to anybody in the White House about it. He didn't talk to anybody in the Justice Department about it. . . . He had no role whatsoever in seeking the indictment."

And later: "Rove denies the assertions and derides the evidence offered by his accusers as vague and scanty. Federal prosecutors respond that they will argue in the courtroom, not in the court of public opinion."

Unlike the *Times*, the *Post* gave considerable space to the denials of those accused of participating in the Jill Simpson-generated conspiracy. But the story's real strength was context, as above, when mentioning some of the powerful Republicans prosecuted by the Bush Justice Department. Another example: The perspective brought to Doug Jones' claim that Franklin and Feaga wanted to drop the Siegelman investigation (a claim denied by the Montgomery prosecutors) but that they were told by the Justice Department to keep trying by conducting a "top-down" review of the case.

While Jones was careful not to connect that alleged order to Karl Rove, it was used by others as evidence of the Rovian dictate to Justice to press the Siegelman case. Johnson followed Jones' claim it with real word context, the gist of which was, "So what?"

Former prosecutors say there is a less sinister explanation for those events. Public corruption cases involving lawyers from the Justice Department routinely undergo a review by career prosecutors in Washington, in which evidence and legal theories are tested. It is not unusual, the lawyers said, for investigators to seek additional or different evidence after such a meeting, to bolster the case before they seek an indictment.

The *Washington Post's* story was a rare event indeed: A report in the mainstream national media by someone who wasn't frothing at the mouth to connect Rove to the Siegelman case.

———

After the Judiciary Committee hearing Brett Blackledge called Bob Riley and found an angry man ready to talk. It was the first time the governor had spoken at length about the case, despite eating Siegelman's rants for years. He professed profound disappointment and anger at Artur Davis, with whom he'd always gotten along. He accused the congressman of tossing truth and principal aside to solidify his position with hard core Democrats back home.

Riley said he'd refrained from commenting on Jill Simpson's 2002 election phone call fable because he thought it "the most ridiculous assertion" he'd ever heard and assumed others would see it the same way, especially after she tossed Rove into the mix. Simpson's stories had become outrageous "to the point of exaggeration that is becoming silly and absurd," said Alabama's governor.

Naturally, Horton couldn't let Riley-Blackledge get away with this crime against Jill. Two days after the story, he assailed the "highly contrived interview" between "two of the principal actors behind the scenes in the Siegelman drama, Governor Bob Riley and Brett Blackledge," or as Brett was referred to on second reference, Riley's "faithful bootlicker."

As he so often did, Horton called upon one of the greats to establish the timeless magnitude of that day's crimes against justice and journalism. "Riley doth Protest Too Much," began:

> *Hamlet: Madam, how like you this play?*
> *Queen Gertrude: The lady protests too much, methinks.*
> *Hamlet: O, but she'll keep her word.*
> *– William Shakespeare, "Hamlet, Prince of Denmark."*

> *Deep in the heart of Shakespeare's longest work lies a play-within-a-play which provides the code by which the entire work can be deciphered. At Elsinore castle, Hamlet works with a troupe of actors in a production of, "The Murder of Gonzago," which Hamlet later calls his "mousetrap." The play is a vehicle to do what social convention forbids, namely, explore the guilt of the king for high crimes.*

Only someone both bright and barking mad could compare Bob Riley to Hamlet.

Reaganesque? Yes.

But Hamletesque?

Bob Riley, tortured soul and tragic figure? Is he talking about the same Bob Riley who is governor of Alabama?

The thesis of this particular column, one might say the thesis of Horton's entire Siegelman oeuvre, was that Riley/Hamlet recognized he could never win a second term as Alabama's king as long as Siegelman prowled the political landscape. Thus Riley's enlistment of Rove, the Canaries, Fuller, the Justice Department, Franklin, Feaga, the FBI agents and others, and the assignment he gave them to take Siegelman out.

Or, as described by the man leading the U.S. House Judiciary Committee around by the nose:

> *The timing was keyed to the election process, with the intention of rescuing Bob Riley. And it achieved its purpose perfectly. Riley owes his re-election and second term to the indictment and prosecution of Don Siegelman. His political operatives not*

only followed this with the greatest care and attention, they were deeply engaged in it at every point. They exploited the culture that Karl Rove introduced to the Justice Department, namely its use and direction as a political instrument to accomplish the objectives of the Republican Party. And they exploited the Alabama G.O.P.'s key asset in Washington: Karl Rove.

"There's a reason for worry," concluded Horton. "Riley knows that the unraveling has begun. And his interview with the *Birmingham News* is the dead give-away."

After reading the Jill Simpson-based gibberish in the likes of *Time* and the *New York Times*, Riley finally defended himself. And to Horton, this was a "dead give-away."

You could not win with the guy. Remain quiet, and it was because you were guilty. Speak up for yourself, and get "doth protest too much" thrown in your face.

There was only one way to deal with Horton.

Chapter 45
Me v. Horton

"If just two percent of what Horton reports is true, he qualifies as one of the greatest investigative reporters of this or any other age, Gilded included. I intend to argue that two percent is at least twice Horton's average, and that, furthermore, his editors at Harper's know it."
-- *Me, in February 2008 story in the Montgomery Independent.*

"Just imagine. I have written 160,000 words about the Siegelman case. I am fairly certain there are some serious mistakes in there. But Eddie writes 7,000 words and finds zip, nadda. Quite a show."
-- *One of Horton's comments inserted into that article by Independent publisher Bob Martin.*

Throughout this book I've presented what occurred chronologically, not as it happened, but as I discovered it. Not so with this last section on the Free Siegelman movement. The research didn't commence until February 2008, well after Simpson's affidavit, her testimony, and so much of the reporting and opining by Horton, *Time*, the *New York Times* and others.

I wasn't unfamiliar with the subject, just hadn't dug into it. Was trying to finish the book, after which I intended to bone up on the Simpson nonsense and give it maybe a chapter. This plan changed after the mailman delivered, in late January, that week's *Montgomery Independent*.

Within was a column by Scott Horton that accused Mark Fuller of issuing rulings against Siegelman in return for the Air Force's award of a 10 year contract worth up to $18.1 million a year to a Colorado-based company called Doss Aviation. This was the company researched a year before by Jill Simpson, and used by Scrushy in his failed, belated motion seeking Fuller's removal from the case.

Horton's column, originally published on *Harper's* web-site, described what if true would rank as one of the more unusual criminal quid pro quos in American political history. Participants in this enormous scam included a federal judge, Alabama's governor, officials high and low in the U.S. Air Force, and by necessity, the White House.

The *Independent* is a weekly published by Bob Martin, at the time one of my oldest friends in Montgomery. During the Siegelman years Bob despised

Siegelman and routinely pulled my stories off the web and ran them in the *Independent*. This was fine with me, as it meant more people read them. In return, he gave me a free subscription.

After Siegelman conceded the 2002 election, Martin wrote the following in his weekly column: "Bob Riley didn't win the governor's race. Don Siegelman lost it, and he lost it primarily because of a newspaper reporter named Eddie Curran of *The Mobile Register*. Curran ferreted out the obnoxious greed of the Siegelman administration. He didn't get all of it, but he got enough to cost the governor re-election..."

Accurate assessment or not, it reflected both Bob's admiration for my work and his feelings toward Siegelman.

The *Independent* is well-read in Montgomery in part because of its coverage and commentary on state politics and I knew that Bob's decision to publish Horton's column had to cause Fuller great discomfort.

Bob later accused me of using him to attack Horton in his pages, and he was right. Bob had published vile garbage about honest people. That needed correcting, and if it required using him, so be it.

A few months before, Bob had begun re-printing some of Horton's pieces on the Siegelman case and writing columns that mirrored Horton's positions. He was trumpeting Jill Simpson's fantasies in prose as self-righteous as Horton's, gobbledygook about core American values being trampled upon and such.

Bob had long ago allowed the *Independent* to become a forum for his close friend, dog-track owner Milton McGregor. Anyone – judge, governor or lesser politician – who dared take a public act deemed detrimental to McGregor's gambling interests got it between the eyes in Bob's columns. McGregor is a major supporter of Democratic politicians, because in Alabama, taxing the poor through gambling is not only consistent with Democratic principles, but is among the state party's only objectives.

Bob Riley opposes gambling. Therefore, Milton McGregor detests Bob Riley. Consequently, so does Martin and his paper.

Equally revered by Bob is blowhard Montgomery attorney Tommy Gallion. McGregor and his dog tracks are and have for ages been major clients of Gallion and Haskell Slaughter, of which Gallion is a partner. Gallion despises Riley for the twin crimes of opposing gambling and ending Gallion's gravy train of legal work at the state insurance department.

The silver-maned publicity hound is the rare Alabama "source" indentified in Horton's articles, glowingly and as a bastion of Republicanism. Only people from out-of-state like Horton take Tommy seriously when he says he's a Republican or for that matter says much of anything. After years of making headlines with his mouth, Gallion is, one hopes, finally reaching the Chicken Little phase of his career.

In the summer of 2007 Gallion became a magnet to an unlikely assemblage of people whose lone apparent connection was a zealous, irrational hatred of Riley. For example, Jill Simpson.

That July, Gallion became, in some fashion, another of Simpson's lawyers. He noted in a memo later made public that his representation of Simpson pertained to what he called her courageous decision to "tell the truth concerning the Siegelman-Scrushy prosecution and other related political matters."

Into this party mix add another "Republican" -- Stan Pate, the Riley-hating, Siegelman-supporting, Nick Bailey-employing, tax-hating Tuscaloosa developer. Gallion's memo stated that Simpson and Pate met at his law office and shared information which it was hoped would "benefit all parties." How so, the memo did not say. Nor was it explained why Gallion would care, much less have a professional interest in, the fates of Siegelman and Scrushy – neither of whom he was known to represent.

Bob and Horton attempted in their writings to portray yet another of Gallion's clients – Montgomery insurance scoundrel John Goff – into a Siegelman-like victim of Alabama's conniving Republican governor and the prosecutors who served his every whim. I thought it odd that a New York-based writer for *Harper's* would write about a relatively unknown Montgomery character like John Goff, but Horton indeed did so, as, with great passion, did his faithful Alabama acolyte, the Legal Schnauzer.

(In February 2009, a federal jury in Montgomery convicted Goff on 23 criminal counts related to charges that his insurance company collected $4 million in worker's compensation premiums from customers but failed to pass the money on to insurers; and that he used the money to pay himself a $1 million a year salary and buy a private plane, a beach house and other extravagances. Federal judge Myron Thompson sentenced him to 12 years in prison.)

Tommy Gallion, Jill Simpson, Scott Horton, John Goff, Milton McGregor. These were Bob Martin's people.

The story that lifted me out of my seat was published in the *Independent* on Jan. 21, 2008. Martin presented it under the double headlines: "Siegelman's judge's firm got $18 million contract;" and, sub-head, "The same day he denied Siegelman's appeal bond."

Horton's column began:

"The story out of the Frank M. Johnson Federal Courthouse in Montgomery never seems to change. It is a chronicle of abusive conduct by a federal judge who treats his judicial duties with the same level of contempt he retains for the concept of justice itself. His name is Mark Everett Fuller, and according to the sworn account of a Republican operative (Simpson) testifying before Congress, he was handpicked to manage a courtroom drama to destroy Governor Don Siegelman, and to send him off to prison, post-haste. And that's exactly what he did."

The Judiciary Committee's back-door man told his readers that Fuller "sits in a shadow which has grown progressively more sinister as time passes." He derided a Fuller-authored motion as "farcical, the sort of thing that any judge would be ashamed to allow see the light of day." As if that wasn't enough, Horton piled on some more, saying Fuller's brief reflected the work of, "a third-rate legal mind."

Horton and Martin knew Fuller couldn't defend himself. He was a federal judge and the case remained active. He'd presided over the trial with distinction and fairness. If someone wished to question or criticize his rulings, that was one thing. But accusing him of selling rulings for Air Force contracts?

Horton was operating without boundaries or scruples, and my old friend Bob Martin had lost his.

Somebody had to throw himself in front of this runaway bullshit train. I knew the best man for the job, and it was me.

I had to approach Bob gingerly, to express my opinion of what he and Horton had written without offending. I told him in an e-mail that I thought the *Independent's* treatment of Fuller "most unfair," and asked if he would permit me to write, without pay, an article addressing the accusations against Fuller. "I anticipate that the *Independent* will continue publishing Horton and probably opining against Fuller. I simply would like to present your readers with one article providing another perspective."

Bob answered right back, said he'd love to have it.

Typically, the story took me far longer than I'd anticipated, and was much longer as well, requiring two installments, both long as hell.

It's the rare Horton paragraph that doesn't contain multiple errors and lies in support of his malicious attacks. These paragraphs required deconstructing, and that, among other things, took time.

I was already somewhat familiar with Horton, and had read a few of his columns, but not until my self-assigned work for the *Independent* did I carefully read the stories by *Time*, the *New York Times*, and others; Simpson's affidavit and her congressional testimony; and, by far the most time consuming, Horton's output on the Siegelman case. I was blown away by what to my mind was and remains, an alarming case of multi-level journalistic fraud. And this was before the "60 Minutes" report and the Judiciary Committee's April 2008, Horton-flavored report on "selective prosecution."

It was while doing that research that I realized my already over-long book on Siegelman was going to get longer.

The most enjoyable part of the *Independent* assignment was the writing. Gone were the constraints that prohibited me from tossing off one-liners, from having fun with the writing. I could work at the *Mobile Register* for 60 years and never get to write: "Of criticisms of Horton's writing, a deficiency of confidence is not among them. He makes his cases like a good poker player with a bad hand. He bluffs."

And a favorite, for its linkage to a man Horton assuredly hates: "Like the obviously embittered, multi-divorced radio host Rush Limbaugh, Horton crosses all lines of civil discourse in his personal attacks. In Horton's case, that group includes anyone he associates with the imprisonment of Don Siegelman -- or as Horton calls him, America's number one political prisoner."

The first installment was published on Feb. 21, 2008. In it, I disclosed that I was on an unpaid sabbatical from the *Register* to write a book about the Siegelman scandals. "If anyone should declare I have a conflict in writing this piece, let them. I contacted Bob and asked that I be able to write this, for free, because I am disturbed and disappointed to see that the Independent had begun running Horton's columns. However, I applaud Bob for allowing me an opportunity to correct the record, if even only a fraction of it."

I wrote that the purpose of the two-part series was to present a rebuttal of the Horton column accusing Mark Fuller of trading rulings for Air Force contracts. This, from that first installment:

(Horton's) article is laden with factual error, innuendo and a level of sourcing that would not be permitted in the lowest rank of newspapers. That it was published under the Internet masthead of Harper's -- the second oldest magazine in the country -- can only be seen as an indictment of that publication...

It is among my hopes that upon finishing this article you will see a different Mark Fuller than has been presented in Horton's pieces, including those published in the Independent.

Perhaps most importantly, I hope that you hold Scott Horton in contempt for the bully, liar, phony and pompous ass that he is.

I had to support such bold statements, and did.

There was no way to address all of Horton's fabrications, but I plucked out a few good ones. A particularly illustrative example of the Horton methodology involved two different accounts he gave for a trip Bob Riley made to Washington the previous June.

As it happened, Riley's trip coincided with Siegelman's sentencing.

Horton's first account of Riley's trip was published on the afternoon of July 28, published later in the day that Fuller sentenced Siegelman and sent him straight to prison. The headline on *Harper's* web-page was, "Siegelman sentenced; Riley Rushes to Washington."

The thrust of the column was, as Horton put it, "the plot involving Karl Rove to 'take care' of Siegelman." He wrote that "sources in the Cullman County GOP" told him that Riley had been "summoned urgently to Washington."

Followed by:

Riley told disappointed organizers of the Cullman function that he will meet with Bush Administration officials to discuss damage control relating to the Siegelman case.

"The sentence will come down today, and they're very concerned about all the questions about the role Karl Rove played in this prosecution," the source said.

If Horton was telling the truth, then:

- He had at least two secret sources within the GOP organization of a small rural north Alabama county, which is pretty amazing for a New York liberal.

- Fuller told Karl Rove and Bob Riley ahead of time that he planned to sentence Siegelman straight to prison.

- Riley blabbed this stunning news to the spy-infested Cullman County Republican leadership.

Either all of the above are true or, Jill Simpson-like, Horton made the whole thing up.

That was Version One of Riley's trip to Washington.

Version Two appeared in the column written seven months later and published in the *Independent*. This time, no mention was made of the emergency summons from Rove to prepare for the feared Siegelman sentencing fall-out. Instead, Riley's trip was used in service of Horton's quid pro quo assertion that Fuller ordered Siegelman straight to prison in return for the decision by the United States Air Force to award the big contract to Doss Aviation. Wrote Horton:

"Now let's recall that the day after sentencing of Siegelman, Governor Bob Riley suddenly canceled his plans to speak to fellow Republicans in Cullman County, and rushed off to Washington.

"(Riley) said he was meeting with the Air Force in order to promote the interests of some Alabama companies seeking contracts. True enough. And of the Alabama companies then pushing aggressively for an extremely lucrative multimillion dollar Air Force contract was named Doss Aviation."

———

During the weeks I worked on the story I sent several e-mails to Horton and his editors at *Harper's*. In one I noted the two separate purposes for the trip as reported by Horton; and asked "what evidence does Horton proffer to support his allegation that Riley, while in Washington or at any time in his life, lobbied for Doss?"

As with most conspiracy theories, there was one kernel of truth. Riley had indeed gone to Washington and he did meet with Air Force officials. His trip – and its purpose – was reported at the time in the Alabama press.

Then, and still, Alabama was engaged in a nationally-publicized battle over one of the largest Air Force contracts ever, worth up to $35 billion. A partnership of Northrop Grumman and France-based EADS was competing against Boeing and would, if it won the contract, build the giant mid-air refueling planes in Mobile.

Doss Aviation, again, is in Colorado. It was Horton's story that Riley canceled the Cullman County function to race to Washington to *lobby for Doss Aviation;* and that Alabama's governor did so to reward Fuller for nailing Siegelman. No mention was made of Riley's real purpose – to urge Air Force decision-makers to pick the Northrop Grumman-EADS team

I used a portion of one of my e-mails to Horton and his editors in the *Independent,* and do so again here:

Now, I realize that according to Harper's, Bob Riley is the devil incarnate and a pathological liar. Nevertheless, I felt it would be worthwhile to say nothing of fair to contact the governor's press office to seek clarification on this matter.

Of the 'sources in the Cullman County GOP' (who told Horton that Riley told them he was summoned by Rove to Washington), Riley spokesman Jeff Emerson said, "Whoever said that, if anyone indeed did, totally made it up"

"Riley did not meet with Karl Rove to discuss anything, much less damage control," Emerson said. He also provided me with Riley's schedule on that trip which I will be glad to forward it to you should you request it.

Emerson also said the following: "Governor Riley said that until Doss Aviation was mentioned in connection with the Siegelman trial, he had never even heard of Doss Aviation."

Neither *Harper's* nor Horton responded when asked to explain either one of the writer's two different explanations for Riley's Washington trip.

In the column run by the *Independent,* Horton wrote:

And shortly after that sentencing (of Siegelman) came down and Governor Riley made his push for fellow Alabamians seeking Air Force contracts, the Bush Administration took an important decision. On October 4, this story appeared on the HT Media wire:

RANDOLPH AIR FORCE BASE, Texas, Oct. 4 — The U.S. Air Force has awarded an $18.1 million contract to Doss Aviation Inc., Colorado Springs, Colo., for flight screening for USAF pilot candidates.

In fact, the contract – the result of a highly competitive bidding process that lasted three years -- was awarded almost two years before. It was simply finalized in October 2007. Horton knew this. He'd written about the pilot training contract in a column published two months before that press release in an August 2007 attack piece called, "The Pork Barrel World of Mark Fuller." In that column he quoted from Scrushy's recusal motion, the one for which Jill Simpson provided research. That motion, and Horton's column, gave the amount of the contract and when it was awarded – in February 2006, or 20 months before Fuller sentenced Siegelman.

Horton knowingly misrepresented Bob Riley's trip to Washington. He then misrepresented the timing of the award of the contract to Doss. Then he connected the two lies to make his ferociously declared quid pro quo accusation against Mark Fuller, Bob Riley, Karl Rove, Air Force contracting officials and everyone else who by necessity would have to be in on such a deal. All were smeared in the service of burnishing the Siegelman as victim storyline.

When I called the president of Doss Aviation, he told me that "60 Minutes" had also called. One can only wonder where the CBS news-hounds got hot Doss tip. I like to think they wasted a lot of time chasing down that and other sham leads sold them by Horton and Team Siegelman.

For the first time ever I called Mark Fuller. He was polite and acknowledged that he'd read the articles about him by Horton, but said he couldn't discuss them or anything related to the case. However, he suggested I contact his former law partner, Joe Cassady, which I did.

Cassady said he'd practiced law with Fuller's father for more than 30 years. When Mark Fuller graduated from law school he joined their small Enterprise firm. Fullers' father had represented Doss for years and when Mark Fuller joined the firm, Doss became a client of his as well.

He explained that some time ago Doss split into two companies. One, based in Dothan, makes fire-retardant clothing for emergency personnel. The other, Doss Aviation, provides pilot training, fueling and other aviation-related services. Their only connection is some common ownership.

In 1989, Doss's owners decided to sell. Mark Fuller encouraged Cassady and others to join him in buying a substantial share of the company. They did so, and the investment turned out well. Upon being appointed to the federal bench Fuller resigned from Doss's board. He sold shares to decrease his ownership, and ceased having anything to do with its operations, Cassady and others said.

As required of federal judges, Fuller has publicly disclosed his outside income, including hundreds of thousands of dollars a year from the Doss companies. His position as a shareholder was no secret during his confirmation process before the U.S. Senate. Neither Democrats nor Republicans made an issue of his part-ownership in this small, uncontroversial company.

Until federal judges are prohibited from having investments and receiving outside income -- be it from real estate, private companies, mutual funds or what have you – there is nothing remotely unethical about Fuller retaining shares in Doss. Nor, for that matter, did it present any conflict that would have required him to remove himself from the Siegelman trial.

———

While I was working on the story, *Harper's* – not its web-site, but the magazine -- published an article by Horton called, "Vote Machine: How Republicans hacked the Justice Department." It was promoted on the magazine's cover, and on the flap that *Harper's* has historically used to tout the major pieces within.

I scanned it until I came across Horton's presentation of the Siegelman case. It was immediately apparent that he and *Harper's* didn't limit their fact-retardant ways to the web-site.

In one four-sentence stretch, Horton listed what he called "several problems" with the prosecution's case. First, he told readers that Richard Scrushy had backed Bob Riley, not Siegelman, in the 1998 election. Problem: Bob Riley wasn't a candidate for governor in 1998. Fob James was Siegelman's Republican opponent.

Two sentences later, Horton wrote: "And finally, according to his own uncontradicted testimony, Scrushy didn't even want the appointment."

In an e-mail I informed Horton and his editors that Richard Scrushy didn't testify at trial, so he "didn't give uncontradicted testimony about anything." I also told them that there *was* testimony that it was very important to Scrushy for HealthSouth to have representation on the CON board.

That's just a sampling of the errors. There were plenty of others, and that's just on the Siegelman portion of the piece.

Blogs are usually one-person operations, and as such, are notoriously error-laden. However, I'd supposed that Horton's work for *Harper's* – whether called a blog or on-line column -- would have higher standards, or in any event, some standards. This seems a fair assumption, especially if, as we are told, that the Internet is the future. Will once-heralded publications like *Harper's* routinely publish error-laden columns and as a defense, say, "It's just the Internet?"

I addressed the issue in one of my e-mails to Horton and his editors:

I can say that my story, while not yet complete, will address Horton's (and by extension, Harper's) almost complete failure to identify sources cited for making some very amazing statements.

Prior to becoming familiar with Mr. Horton's work, I would have assumed that a magazine of Harper's reputation and historical significance would not allow anyone, be it in the magazine or under its masthead on a web-page, to publish serious allegations that are neither sourced nor corroborated by public record. Failing to adequately source does have the benefit of making it difficult to refute statements made by people who, I suspect in some cases, don't even exist...

I would like to be able to provide readers the answer to a few general questions, including:

Does Harper's have different standards for fact-checking and editing for stories in its magazine that it does for stories and under its masthead on the Internet page?

If so, why?

Does Harper's even edit Horton's copy?

Horton responded with a short e-mail saying that there were different standards for on-line columns than the magazine. Other major magazines operated in similar fashion, he said.

One can only hope that these other magazines keep a tighter rein on their Scott Hortons.

———

Well before I turned in the first piece, Bob realized that I was going to be critical of Horton. He suggested that I not write about Horton, whose columns, Bob said, were, after all, just "speculation mixed with fact." I responded that it was not possible to address Horton's accusations against Fuller without writing about Horton.

I sent the first installment, waited for questions from him, received none. When it came out, I saw that Bob had added a most unusual editor's note. He wrote that his own research had "corroborated" much of Horton's reporting. I held my tongue. I still had the second installment to sneak in there. And all in all, I couldn't complain. He'd given me tons of space and hadn't changed a word – in this way, my dream editor.

Thanks to the Internet the first installment won some notoriety in the loony-left blogosphere. On her, "Raw Story" blog, the deliciously melodramatic Larisa Alexandrovna breathlessly reported an advance warning that she and Horton were to be "swift-boated" by the "corrupt politicians of Alabama and their paid shills in the Alabama press."

"Scott Horton, it seems, will be the first victim. I just got word from folks in Alabama that the article on him just went out in the print version of the *Montgomery Independent* and authored by Eddie Curran (who it is suggested has an interesting relationship with Jeff Sessions)."

I hesitate to even speculate as to what she meant by, "an interesting relationship with Jeff Sessions," other than to deny it to my last breath and demand strict proof thereof.

Horton, said this hilarious woman, "will need your backing."

"I can only assume I am next in line," she wrote wishfully.

If you're among those who believe everything written in a "congressional report," consider this: One of Alexandrovna's "Raw Story" blog posts was footnoted as evidence in the Judiciary Committee's April 2008 selective prosecution report.

That's a true fact.

I shot Bob the second installment the following Tuesday morning, and waited. Nervously. And there's nothing unusual in that. It's part of being a reporter, especially for long, complicated pieces. You file a story, and wait. I've been through it a million times. But this time it was different. Bob had caught hell from certain circles for publishing part one. Part two ended with something that I almost didn't include for fear that Bob would kill the whole thing.

Shortly after embarking on the Horton project I began, like others in Alabama, to wonder what the deal was with this New York writer for *Harper's* and Don Siegelman. There was a rumor, widely circulated but unconfirmed, that Horton was related to a Birmingham lawyer, William Horton, who had two connections to the Siegelman case.

William Horton was the former long-time general counsel at HealthSouth. He'd been the rare HealthSouth official to serve as a defense witness in the accounting fraud trial in Birmingham. Upon leaving HealthSouth, William Horton went to work for the Haskell Slaughter firm which, through Tommy Gallion, had assumed some murky role in the representation of Jill Simpson.

No one, myself included, seemed able to confirm a relationship between the two Hortons. I finally took the direct approach, as described here. I gave this final part the subhead, "A Horton conflict?"

First I noted the above connections, and then:

Scott Horton didn't reply (to my questions) so I e-mailed William Horton to ask if he was related to Scott Horton. He replied that Scott is his second cousin.

"At the risk of telling you more than you want to know, we are not in close or frequent contact (Christmas cards are about it), and indeed, I wasn't aware of his activity for Harper's until this past fall and had assumed he was still practicing law. Shows you what I know, I guess," he wrote.

I take William Horton at his word. But I note the relation, as I did in the following portion of an e-mail to Horton and his editors, for this reason: "I wonder how Scott Horton would treat such a coincidence were it to be found in relation to the prosecution of Don Siegelman?"

I imagined Bob apoplectic. Here I was, not just exposing Saint Scott for the fraud he was, but noting, even if only in passing, that Horton's cousin was a partner of his much beloved Tommy Gallion.

This was an especially long piece. Did Bob have questions? Could he shoot me the story so I could give it a final proof, with any changes?

I e-mailed, called, left messages. Nothing.

Late Wednesday, which for the *Independent* was past the last minute, Bob sent an e-mail.

"Eddie, why do I get this feeling in my gut that I'm being used?" he asked. He informed me that the piece was so critical of Horton that he'd sent it to him for a rebuttal.

I had, as Bob knew, gone overboard in seeking comment from Horton and *Harper's*. Horton had every opportunity to respond and for the most elected not to. I asked why he was giving Horton this opportunity when he'd never done so for "Horton's victims -- people attacked like vermin."

Bob said he'd send me the story prior to publication. He did not. When I saw it in print, I knew why. He'd inserted Horton's quotes within the story, and in all caps. Bob also stuck in small editor's notes throughout. As a result, readers went back and forth from three different writers: Me, Bob and Horton. It was bizarre.

Horton's responses were sarcastic as ever but absent his signature arrogance and flair. After the part reporting his relationship with William Horton, readers saw this:

"I REALLY HAVE TO THANK EDDIE FOR TRACKING DOWN MY LONG LOST SECOND COUSIN, WHO I HAVEN'T SEEN OR SPOKEN WITH IN A DECADE OR MORE … BUT SINCE EDDIE HAS WORKED OUT MY ENTIRE GENEOLOGICAL CHART, I'D LOVE TO KNOW ALL THE OTHER RELATIVES I HAVE IN ALABAMA I LOST TRACK OF. MAYBE WE CAN HAVE A BBQ."

Elsewhere he explained that web-logs (blogs) such as his were "spontaneous and usually unedited."

Particularly revealing were his comments regarding those prized Cullman County GOP sources. He touted himself as being the, "FIRST SOURCE ANYWHERE TO NOTE THAT RILEY HAD SUDDENLY CANCELLED HIS LONG-SCHEDULED SPEECH TO CULLMAN REPUBLICANS IN ORDER TO TRAVEL TO WASHINGTON."

Not just the first to report it, but the last. Who cared? Had the sorry Alabama media fallen down again in failing to report that a chat by the governor to a county GOP organization was cancelled?

Horton wrote that he came upon the scoop while interviewing a source who "TOLD ME THE EVENT HAD BEEN CANCELLED BECAUSE SOMETHING URGENT HAD COME UP THAT RILEY WAS GOING TO WASHINGTON."

"THE UN-NAMED SOURCE QUOTED WAS AN UNHAPPY ORGANIZER WHO RELAYED THE INFORMATION TO ME. FRANKLY

I NEVER THOUGHT THIS WAS MUCH MORE THAN SPECULATION. WHO WOULD THINK HE WOULD HAVE ACTUAL INSIDE KNOWLEDGE? AT BEST THIS WAS SCUTTLEBUT. BUT IT SURE DOES SEEM TO HAVE EDDIE RILED UP."

When he wrote the columns, Horton didn't represent the information from his multiple GOP sources in Cullman County as "speculation" or "scuttlebutt." Assuming he was telling the truth this time – and my money says he didn't have one much less two Cullman County sources – Horton was admitting to using speculative scuttlebutt from an "unhappy organizer" to accuse a federal judge, Alabama's governor and so many others of engaging in this convoluted criminal conspiracy.

Horton cloaked his twisted fantasies in journalism and sullied good people. Worse, *Harper's* let him. When I showed the magazine's brain trust what he'd done – not just in his "blogs" but in the magazine – they neither stopped him nor made any effort to correct the record.

Then the Democrats on the Judiciary Committee let Horton either ghost-write or dictate the focus of their "selective prosecution" report, and for evidence, used 15 columns of his spontaneously written scuttlebutt.

The following December 2008 Horton authored the cover story for the magazine, and now holds the title, Contributing Editor. Bob Martin continues to republish Horton's columns in the *Independent*.

Chapter 46
'60 Minutes' kicks Rove's ass

"The people were standing up saying, 'You got screwed!' And I said, 'Well, 'You know, I think there were a lot of y'all that got screwed.' And then one guy stood up and said, 'No, I was guilty; you got screwed.'"
-- Siegelman, describing the reaction of his fellow inmates to the Feb. 24, 2008, "60 Minutes" segment on his case.

"Full disclosure: I have been repeatedly interviewed for the program's Siegelman coverage."
-- Scott Horton, on his contributions to the "60 Minutes" report.

By December 2007, the loony left blogosphere was in a lather over a piece that "60 Minutes" was said to have been working on for months. It would, the likes of Larissa Alexandrovna and Schnauzer promised, destroy the cabal summed up by Horton as "Javert." Because of the program's stature and viewership the report came to be seen as the Holy Grail of the movement to free Siegelman and crush his tormentors.

Horton had mentioned it several times in his columns. In mid-October, four months before its airing, he'd been able to report the angle that "60 Minutes" would take – that Siegelman's conviction had been "procured through judicially sanctioned rumor-mongering."

"And that farce is being exposed, not by the press in Alabama, but by *Time* magazine, the *New York Times*, the *Los Angeles Times* and CBS News… It's what *Time*, CBS News and journalists with a number of national newspapers are doing right now."

Chuckled Horton in a subsequent column: "Heaven forbid that people actually read the *Time* magazine articles, the *New York Times* stories, the *coming segment* on '60 Minutes' or that blasted blog at Harper's!"

On Dec. 13, Dan Abrams began what became a long-running diatribe on the Siegelman case in the, "Bush League Justice" segment of his nightly show on MSNBC. His guests for that first piece – called, "Alabama Outrage" -- were Horton and Artur Davis.

Abrams was a welcome addition to the team, but he wasn't "60 Minutes." In one of her "Raw Story" blogs, Larissa fretted that MSNBC's attention to the case "may have CBS thinking they had been scooped and considering dropping the story."

"*60 Minutes,* of course, is not only on a major network, it is also known for going into depth on stories like this and is reportedly in possession of some revelations not previously known about the back story that could be devastating for those who seemed determined to eliminate Siegelman from the Alabama political scene," she wrote.

As those on the Siegelman watch soon learned, every Thursday afternoon "60 Minutes" posts on its web-site the three stories selected for that Sunday's line-up. Of the three, one is chosen as the lead and receives heavier promotion. By late January, it had become a ritual of sorts to check the site. It seemed that each week the bloggers would say it's coming, it's coming, only to have their hopes dashed on Thursday.

In mid-February Bob Martin reported, on his column in the *Independent*, that the segment was on its way and would broach, among other things, the juror e-mails.

I decided (again) to breach protocol and call "60 Minutes." Wasn't going to say a thing about Karl Rove or Jill Simpson or the Canarys or Rileys or anyone else. Just the jurors. I was no longer reporting on the case but writing a book that would present a point of view consistent with that which I planned to tell "60 Minutes." The jurors had been through enough. I saw it, correctly or not, as a sort of humanitarian mission, similar to the one on Fuller's behalf.

I called Debbie Shaw at the U.S. Attorney's Office on the assumption that they'd been contacted by, "60 Minutes." Debbie was the chief administrative assistant for the criminal division and for all practical purposes, a member of the Siegelman trial team. If "60 Minutes," had called, she would know, and probably have a name and number. She did, and gave me the name and number of David Gelber, a reporter and producer for "60 Minutes."

I called Gelber and was in the midst of introducing myself when he snapped, "I know who you are. You're the guy who had a temper tantrum." I acknowledged that, yes, I had lost my temper (this obviously being the Rip incident.) Though taken aback, I started to tell Gelber my purpose for calling. I didn't get far. "Where did you get my number?" he demanded. I knew the honest answer would only reinforce his apparent perception of me as one of the enemy, but didn't want to lie and told him I got it from the U.S. Attorney's Office.

Moments later he put me on a speaker phone with another member of the Siegelman story team. The first thing he says, in an accusatory manner, if I thought Siegelman guilty. It's my recollection that I didn't give a yes or no to his litmus test of decency in journalism but tried to provide a more thorough recitation of the facts than the run of the mill campaign contribution tale spun by the defendants and their supporters. The guy said they'd call back if they wanted more from me. They must not have, as they did not call back. Because of their tone and stature – national-level media with "60 Minutes" – I felt belittled, like a teeny-tiny person, and for a few days at that.

On Wednesday, Feb. 20, *Harper's* web-site delivered a scoop.

"I am advised by CBS News that their long-awaited feature dealing with the trial of former Alabama Governor Don E. Siegelman will air on the next 60 Minutes program, on Sunday, February 24," Horton wrote. "I am told by people who have seen it that this is one of the best pieces of domestic exposé journalism the '60 Minutes' team has put together in the last several years."

The next day, the folks at "60 Minutes" made an honest man of Horton. Sure enough the Siegelman piece was airing Sunday and, what's more, it was the segment tapped for heavy promotion. I read the web-site story preview with a mixture of awe and repulsion.

It began:

A Republican operative in Alabama says Karl Rove asked her to try to prove the state's Democratic governor was unfaithful to his wife in an effort to thwart the highly successful politician's re-election.

Rove's attempt to smear Don Siegelman was part of a Republican campaign to ruin him that finally succeeded in imprisoning him, says the operative, Jill Simpson.

Simpson spoke to Pelley because, she says, Siegelman's seven-year sentence for bribery bothers her. She recalls what Rove, then President Bush's senior political adviser, asked her to do at a 2001 meeting in this exchange from Sunday's report.

"Karl Rove asked you to take pictures of Siegelman?" asks Pelley.

"Yes," replies Simpson.

"In a compromising, sexual position with one of his aides," clarifies Pelley.

"Yes, if I could," says Simpson.

I was moved, yet again, to violate protocol. I called Gelber, got his answering machine, and told him he and his people were fools to run such a piece. Shouldn't have, did.

The Associated Press had little choice but to report Simpson's claim, less because she'd appeared to implicate Karl Rove in remarkably brazen dirty trick than because her fantastic tale had presumably been vetted by one of the most respected names in American journalism.

The story was written by Ben Evans, a Washington-based AP reporter who wrote most of the wire service's national stories on the Siegelman-Simpson matter. His work was notable for its fair, one might even say skeptical coverage of the Simpson-Rove-Siegelman imbroglio. Evans wrote high up in the piece that Simpson had never mentioned Rove's astonishing request "in spite of testifying to congressional lawyers last year, submitting a sworn affidavit and speaking extensively with reporters."

The next day, a defender stepped forward. Evans, wrote the defender, was "dead wrong" in reporting that Simpson hadn't told others about Rove's intelligence assignment to tail Siegelman. "I interviewed Simpson in July and she recounted this to me; and I believe she recounted it to two other reporters as well, one with another major national publication, but I'll let them speak for themselves."

The defender was, of course, Scott Horton.

———

The futility of almost a year's worth of denials by Louis Franklin, the Canarys, the Rileys, and so many others was crystallized that Sunday night. The first words out of Scott Pelley's mouth forecast what was to come. "Is Don Siegelman in prison because he's a criminal or because he belonged to the wrong political party in Alabama?"

And from there, it was straight to the build-up. Viewers in places like Idaho and Nebraska learned that Siegelman was "the most successful Democrat in a Republican state;" that after he became governor, "many believed he was headed to a career in national politics;" that he'd proposed a lottery to improve education and challenged Republicans "to come up with a better idea."

"60 Minutes" neglected to mention, even in a single summary sentence, that the Siegelman administration was awash in scandal. The Don Siegelman presented to the country that night was a squeaky clean reformer, if anything, a victim – not just of Republicans, but of Nick Bailey. "Unknown to Siegelman, Bailey had been extorting money from Alabama businessmen," intoned Pelley.

There were three on-camera interviews – with Simpson, Grant Woods, and Doug Jones. The first was a nutcase; the second an old friend of Siegelman's who'd not attended a day of the trial; and the third, one of Siegelman's criminal defense lawyers.

Jones repeated the disputed account of Feaga and Franklin telling him that main Justice had ordered a top down review of the case. Though Jones didn't mention Rove, his story – when told alongside Simpson's -- supported the thrust of the piece, which was that Rove had directed the Justice Department to go after Siegelman.

Jones also told Pelley that Bailey's testimony changed after this "top down" review.

Jones: "Mr. Bailey had indicated that there had been a meeting with Governor Siegelman and Mr. Scrushy, a private meeting in the Governor's office, just the two of them. And then, as soon as Mr. Scrushy left, the governor walked out with a $250,000 check that he said Scrushy have given him for the lottery foundation."

Pelley: "Had the check in his hand right then and there?"

Jones: "Had the check in his hand right then."

Pelley: "That Scrushy had just handed to him, according to Bailey's testimony?" Pelley asks.

Jones: "That's right, showed it to Mr. Bailey. And Nick asked him, 'Well, what does he want for it?' And Governor Siegelman allegedly said, 'A seat on the CON Board.' Nick asked him, 'Can we do that?' And he said, 'I think so.'"

After portions of interviews with Woods and Simpson, the newsman returned to Jones. He said that prosecutors "zeroed in on that vivid story" Bailey told about seeing Siegelman with the $250,000 check after the first meeting with Scrushy. "Trouble was, Bailey was wrong about the check, and Siegelman's lawyer says prosecutors knew it," said Pelley.

Jones: *"They got a copy of the check. And the check was cut days after that meeting. There was no way possible for Siegelman to have walked out of that meeting with a check in his hand."*
Pelley: *"That would seem like a problem with the prosecution's case."*
Jones: *"It was a huge problem especially when you've got a guy who's credibility was going to be the lynch pin of that case. It was a huge problem."*

The government had provided defense lawyers with Bailey's initial recollections of seeing the check after that first meeting. Lawyers for the defendants, especially Art Leach on Scrushy's behalf, hung their hat on the date discrepancy, putting Bailey through hours of scorching testimony on that very point.

Had Jones attended the trial, he might have known and been able to inform the national audience that the jury heard all about the change in Bailey's testimony. From their verdict, it would appear that jurors recognized that, in testimony given several years after the Scrushy meetings, Bailey mistook something said after the first one with something said after the second one. Obviously Bailey hadn't intended to say that Siegelman made the remark *before* getting the check. Evidence and testimony was overwhelming showing that Scrushy met with Siegelman before the first check was generated; that Siegelman subsequently received from Scrushy the $250,000 check from Integrated Health; and that shortly thereafter, Scrushy went from persona non grata to vice-chairman of the CON board.

"60 Minutes" – like the *New York Times*, *Time* and so many others -- neglected to report so much as the first detail regarding the byzantine origins and travels of the first $250,000 check. Nor did CBS notify viewers that Siegelman used the money to pay off a loan he'd personally guaranteed; and that he'd failed to disclose the check and another of the same size to the secretary of state, the IRS and the public for more than two years; and then, only after being ordered to do so by the attorney general's office.

Viewers had no way of knowing that Siegelman and Scrushy both went to considerable lengths to conceal two $250,000 donations. The decisions by Scrushy and Siegelman not to testify also went unreported. Anything that even might have weighed in favor of guilt was omitted.

Woods was of course introduced as being among the attorneys general who'd asked Congress to investigate the Siegelman case. His old friendship with Siegelman wasn't disclosed. Viewers were left to assume that Woods – an Arizonan who hadn't held office in almost 20 years – just took it upon himself to lead the charge for Don Siegelman.

"I personally believe that what happened here is that they targeted Don Siegelman because they *could not beat him fair and square,*" Woods told Pelley.

Woods' assertion begged for the most obvious of follow-up questions: But wasn't Siegelman defeated, "fair and square," in the 2002 election?

Pelley didn't ask it. Had CBS pointed out this simple truth it would have diluted if not eliminated the supposed motive for the Riley-Canary-Rove conspiracy. If Siegelman had been and obviously could be defeated fair and square, then the answer to the question – "Is Don Siegelman in prison because he's a criminal or because he belonged to the wrong political party in Alabama?" – was no. And where was the story in that?

There is much truth to the adage that the media should "comfort the afflicted and afflict the comfortable," but no one – not even financially comfortable Republicans – should bear affliction without cause. The show troubled me, but imagine what it must have been like to be Rob Riley or Bill and Leura Canary (or Karl Rove!), to name just a few of the victims of CBS's journalism that evening.

The outrage committed against Rob Riley to say nothing of his father began with Pelley declaring that Siegelman had been vindicated in the Bobo case and was "focused on winning the 2006 election."

"And that's when Jill Simpson says she heard the Justice Department was going to try again. She says she heard it from a former classmate and work associate Rob Riley, the son of the new Republican governor," said the CBS newsman, as a segue back to the Simpson interview:

Simpson: *"Rob said that they had gotten wind that Don was going to run again."*
Pelley: *"And Rob Riley said what about that?"*
Simpson: *"They just couldn't have that happen."*
Pelley: *(paraphrased) How were they going to prevent that from happening?*
Simpson: *"Well, they had to re-indict him, is what Rob said."*
(Interview segment ends, back to Pelley looking at the camera): "Simpson told this same story, under oath, to Congressional investigators in a closed session."

Viewers who trusted "60 Minutes" based on decades of award-winning journalism had no reason to doubt the conclusions presented them. They had no way of knowing how much the show's producers elected to conceal. One supposes that most of the audience believed – and were appropriately outraged – to learn that a posse led by Karl Rove in Washington and the Rileys and Canarys down in Montgomery had been able to apply the awesome power of the Justice Department to destroy the only Democrat left standing in Alabama.

Several months before the show, Rob Riley provided "60 Minutes" with detailed, fact-based refutations of Simpson's many "under oath" tales (the KKK deal, etc.) and also gave CBS newsmen the affidavits by himself, Terry Butts and others.

At this point in the show it was time for Pelley to present that side of the story. And he did.

"Rob Riley told '60 Minutes' he never talked to Jill Simpson about this."

That was it. Base covered.

———

The report concluded with Pelley faux struggling to comprehend what he was hearing from Grant Woods. "Help me understand something," he said. "You're blaming the *Republican* administration for this prosecution. You're saying it was a political prosecution. You are a *Republican*. How do I reconcile that?"

To which I answered: Woods is a criminal defense lawyer in Arizona, you bonehead, not a Republican congressman about to cross the likes of Tom DeLay on a key Congressional vote or a Sunni walking gun drawn into a Shiite neighborhood. Republicans aren't going to *kill him* and few will even care, especially in Arizona.

The camera panned instead to Woods for the closing shot.

"We're Americans first. And you got to call it as you see it. And you got to stand up for what's right in this country."

It was over. From Karl Rove assigning Dana Simpson to do a black bag number on Don Siegelman to Grant Woods risking all for America.

It would be a cold day in hell before I trusted "60 Minutes" with anything more than a celebrity interview.

———

That night, Siegelman's 70-odd mates in his prison area voted to watch something else. The ex-governor loaded up on canned fish from the commissary and used the treats to sway his cellmates. "Don said they had the mackerel and salmon as hors d'oeuvres as they watched it," his brother Les reported.

Had Siegelman been incarcerated in north Alabama, canned salmon would not have helped. Just as the Siegelman segment was about to air, a technical glitch knocked out the signal at WHNT, the CBS affiliate in Huntsville. For about the first 10 minutes, viewers saw black.

Horton beat everyone to the story.

"In a stunning move of censorship, the transmission was blocked across the northern third of Alabama by CBS affiliate WHNT," he wrote in a "No Comment" posted that very night.

On the same post he reported another scoop, and one the *New York Times* would live to regret. The program was hardly over and Horton – either a lightning-fast researcher or the beneficiary of a crack team of Alabama-knowledgeable folks at his beck and call – reported that WHNT was owned by Oak Hill Capital Partners. "Oak Hill Partners represents interests of the Bass family, which contribute heavily to the Republican Party," he wrote.

Horton provided e-mail and telephone contacts to Oak Hill and encouraged viewers who were "displeased about the channel's decision to censor the broadcast" to complain. He added with no basis in fact that WHNT was "noteworthy for its hostility to Siegelman and support for his Republican adversary."

The same column cheered "60 Minutes" and ripped into the AP's Ben Evans for a story he filed that night. Horton complained that Evans's report was "carefully set out to mirror the attack line put out by the Alabama G.O.P., but using the wire service's own voice."

The *Harper's* columnist also took a bow, noting that the program "for which I was repeatedly interviewed" came through "on its promise to deliver several additional bombshells."

The *New York Times* would publish two stories and an editorial on the Huntsville blackout. Because it was in Alabama, Adam Cohen and the *Times* editorial staff simply had to make a connection to the civil rights struggle. "In 1955, when WLBT-TV, the NBC affiliate in Jackson, Miss., did not want to run a network report about racial desegregation, it famously hung up the sign: 'Sorry, Cable Trouble,'" the piece began.

Revolting, if you think about it, comparing Don Siegelman's situation to what blacks went through during the civil rights movement, though Siegelman was forever doing the same himself.

Days later Horton appeared on Dan Abrams show and told viewers that the Bass brothers were involved in one of President Bush's failed oil ventures; that they were big contributors to Bush; and that they were "of course" tight with Karl Rove. "I mean, they're very, very close to Bush, of course," Horton told the MSNBC newsman.

The man from *Harper's* repeated his accusation that the Huntsville station was, "known for its hostility to Gov. Siegelman, no doubt about that." This time he sourced the claim, telling Abrams he'd been told that by unidentified "CBS people in New York."

WHNT station manager Stan Pylant talked himself purple trying to explain the malfunction. In large part because of local interest – not just the Siegelman angle, but because Simpson is from the area – the station had heavily promoted the show and had nothing to gain and everything to lose by not showing it. And when the blackout occurred, station staff worked feverishly to get it back on. WHNT re-broadcast the Siegelman segment twice in the coming days. "The receiver failed at the worst possible time, and there's nothing I can do to make some people believe it," Pylant said.

Sen. John Kerry wrote a letter to the Federal Communications Commission seeking an investigation to determine if the blackout was "an act of censorship." Alabama Democratic Chairman Joe Turnham did the same. MSNBC's Keith Olbermann named the Huntsville station winner of his nightly "Worst Person" award. Needless to say, Horton's apostles in blogger-land went ape.

The *New York Times* – which either took its news from Horton or shared the same nutty Alabama sources -- must have wished it had left the story alone. In its first story, the nation's paper of record reported that WHNT was owned by Oak Hill Capital Partners, "which is managed by Robert M. Bass, one of a group of wealthy brothers who have all been major contributors to George W. Bush." That was innuendo aplenty for smart readers to figure out that Republican big-dogs had sabotaged the Siegelman segment.

The story, by a *Times'* entertainment reporter, was otherwise reasonable, though the very fact that the *New York Times* would report on the black-out was commentary enough on the position of the paper's news operation regarding the Siegelman case.

My sense was that the writer was assigned the piece after a Kool-Aid drinker at the paper provided his editors with the arcane connection between the Bass brothers and the Huntsville station.

The next day, the *Times'* opining side published its overheated editorial raising the specter of the Civil Rights movement. The paper declared that the blacked out "60 Minutes" report "presented new evidence that the charges against Mr. Siegelman may have been concocted by politically motivated Republican prosecutors -- and orchestrated by Karl Rove."

And a few paragraphs down, stated without comment but, as with the news story, innuendo aplenty: "WHNT is owned by Oak Hill Capital Partners, a private equity firm whose lead investor is one of the Bass brothers of Texas. The brothers are former business partners of George W. Bush and generous contributors to Republican causes."

Now, the punch-line: The "Bass brother" who owns most of Oak Hill and thus WHNT is the liberal brother, Robert Bass, who'd long ago broken with his right-wing brothers. In the preceding 10 years, Robert Bass had donated more than $1 million to *Democratic* causes compared to $4,000 to Republicans.

When Bass read the fairytales in the New York *Times* linking him to a Republican conspiracy to prevent viewers from watching the Don Siegelman show, he got *pissed off.*

Bass's home-town paper, the *Fort Worth Star-Telegram*, had some fun at the *Times'* expense, reporting that the "press shy" Fort Worth billionaire "took exception recently to an article in *The New York Times* that inaccurately linked him to President Bush" through political donations .

"But as most North Texas political watchers know, Robert Bass split from his brothers, giving largely to Democrats. Now *The Times* knows it, too."

Chastened, the *Times* published two corrections, one for the news story and a second for the editorial.

"For those keeping score, that's Robert Bass 2, *The New York Times* 0," chortled the *Star-Telegram*.

(WHNT sent the FCC its technical records and other documentation. As of October 2009, or 19 months since the broadcast, the FCC hasn't taken any action against WHNT, nor is any expected.)

———

In a second story on the "60 Minutes" piece, the AP's Ben Evans again gave the other side ample space to fight back. He quoted Rove's lawyer, Robert Luskin, saying that CBS owed his client an apology for "circulating (Simpson's) false and foolish story." His story ended with tragic news for Republicans everywhere. Jill Simpson's lawyer, Priscilla Duncan, said her client was leaving the Republican Party because "she's just so disgusted with their reaction" to the "60 Minutes" story.

The work by Pelley, Gelber and the others exceeded the expectations even of the bloggers. "If you care about justice in Alabama, and beyond, today has been like the Monday after the Super Bowl," wrote Schnauzer. Then he named winners of what he called the "Schnauzer Awards."

Grant Woods won MVP; Jill Simpson MCP (Most Courageous Person); and producers Gelber and Joel Bach shared BTG (Best Tour Guides). My personal favorite was MVB -- Most Valuable Behind-the-Scenes Source. And the envelope please ....

Scott Horton!

———

I had a powerful need to (again) transgress protocol and convey my scorn to Pelley and the show's producers – Gelber, Bach, and Jeff Fager, as well as Rich Kaplan, the president of CBS News.

But how?

The "60 Minutes" web-site provided an e-mail address for viewers to contact the show but I imagined that it received thousands of responses and supposed that one from me would vanish into the ether like the rest. Then it hit me: Write a letter and send it to the all-in-one viewer e-mail address. This would allow me to report to my real audience that, yes indeed, it was a "letter to '60 Minutes.'"

I gathered e-mail addresses of the real audience -- dozens of friends, journalists, people involved in the case including prosecutors and defense lawyers, Jill Simpson and her crowd – everyone I could think of who even might have an interest. These folks would naturally need an explanation for this odd, "Letter to '60 Minutes."

I knocked out a brief introduction informing recipients of the purpose of the effort. I wrote that "no one, such as through guilt by association, should assume another on the list is my friend, source or co-conspirator"; and told them to "feel free to disseminate, delete, ignore, etc., as you please."

"Also – can't seem to locate Karl R's e-mail so hoping someone, say, one of the Rileys, can pass this on to him. And if you get Karl, can you ask him to pass this on to Jill. And if he says he doesn't have her e-mail, say, 'Knock if off, Karl, give it up dude.' And then please pass it on to me. Thanks."

Cheeky? Yes.

A good career move? Doubtful.

The actual letter opened with the subject heading: "Substantial factual errors regarding the 'vivid story' and virtually every other major assertion made in Sunday's piece on Don Siegelman, as well as questions regarding journalistic integrity and work ethic by 60 Minutes staff in the preparation and presentation of the piece."

The best part of the letter – and damn fine work if I say so – was that devoted to Simpson. Here it is, in its entirety:

Dana Jill Simpson: *I assume you are aware of her constantly expanding and evolving stories. That you even put her on television after reviewing these ever-evolving tales is incredible. Furthermore, you absolutely had to know of her association with the Siegelman and Scrushy legal teams that began, at the latest, in February of last year. Among other things, she has testified to doing what would appear to be an illegal credit check report on the judge who presided over the case.*

We reporters in Alabama, no doubt because we're dumb rednecks or being paid off by Republicans, have from the beginning seen Simpson for what she is: a very lonely person with a very – and this is your word – vivid imagination.

It would appear – or at least, CBS made it appear – that this particular Rove claim (there have already been several by her relating to her allegations that Rove was involved in the Siegelman prosecution) was new. This was suggested by Scott Pelley's surprise, which I trust was not feigned.

As anyone who has ever worked in a newsroom knows, it is almost a daily occurrence for someone to come by or call and spin the most amazing stories. A few, a very few, are true. A decent reporter can usually tell the difference in about a minute.

The crazy ones are treated politely and ushered out the door as soon as possible. Considering her past stories -- none corroborated by a single human being -- 60 Minutes should never have interviewed her in the first place. However, after that mistake, once she started on the Rove tale, Pelley, the producers, the janitor, someone, should have pulled the switch.

This leads me to ask the following questions of the journalists at CBS:

After Simpson delivered these explosive and entirely uncorroborated accusations (again, all of her stories are uncorroborated) did "60 Minute" ask Simpson where she followed Siegelman, as in what cities and on what dates?

Having done so, did 60 Minutes conduct a simple Nexis search of stories during that period? After all, Siegelman's trips and actions were covered almost daily by the press, especially the AP.

And also asked her:

Who funded this top-secret mission? She does not live anywhere near Montgomery and one assumes that while carrying out this top-secret assignment she incurred hotel, travel, and meal bills. Did you ask her if she had any records of these bills? Is there anyone alive who can corroborate this?

Did you ask her: How was a big redhead like you able to follow Alabama's governor for months without being seen by the governor or his security?

Did you follow him by car? Hide in the bushes? Hover above in a helicopter?

You claim that this was not the first 'intelligence' assignment given you by Rove. What were the others?

You said you met him working on past campaigns. Which campaigns and can you provide us with a single person who also worked on these campaigns who can confirm that you worked on them and that, furthermore, you met Rove while doing so?

Pelley, with a wink and a nod, noted that Rove worked in some Alabama campaigns. This is widely known. They were judicial races in the mid-1990s. I was in Alabama at the same time and, remarkably, never ran into Rove. I doubt Simpson did either though. However, if we are to trust your broadcast, you made no effort to check this out. You simply tossed it out that Rove had been in Alabama, as if our state is the size of Mayberry.

I'm not sure what would be worse, for CBS not to have asked such questions or to have asked them but not shown or reported that it did so to the audience, and given her responses and the results of your verification.

Instead of actually doing some legwork to support such a serious to say nothing of unlikely claim on national TV, the network simply covered its ass with the old, obviously expected denial from Rove.

Is that characterization of your journalism correct or incorrect?

There is no question, such as with the Swift Boat campaign against Kerry, that Rove has done some exceedingly distasteful things. However – if I may opine – that would not be sufficient reason for 60 Minutes to put on Dana Jill Simpson stories without subjecting them through a level of verification that any decent reporter could do in an afternoon.

One of the vital links in the conspiracy built by Jill was of course Bill Canary. He connected Bob Riley to both Leura Canary and Rove. Without Bill Canary the conspiracy couldn't exist, not, in any event, without a serious re-write.

"60 Minutes" presented Canary front and center. Considering the program story-line, this wasn't surprising. What was surprising was Pelley's statement that the Siegelman prosecution was "handled by the office of U.S. Attorney Leura Canary, *whose husband Bill Canary had run the campaign of Siegelman's opponent, Gov. Riley.*"

Not even the *New York Times* awarded him that job. Toby Roth was Riley's campaign manager. As previously noted, Canary was in 2002 the president of the American Trucking Association. He was among a multitude of people who occasionally called the Riley campaign with advice and suggestions. Wasn't paid a dime. Had no position. Ran nothing.

But according to CBS News, Bill Canary *ran* Bob Riley's 2002 gubernatorial campaign.

"What documentation do you have supporting that Canary ran Bob Riley's campaign?" I asked in the letter. "If you don't have any such evidence, why not?"

Canary was also forced to eat, yet again, the "his girls" quote manufactured by Simpson.

I called Alabama's GOP superman, introduced myself, and found him, not feisty, but somber. He was he said fearful of saying too much in part because of his wife's position. "Apparently the national media seems to want to listen to her (Simpson's) version of the facts and no one else's," he said resignedly.

Canary provided me a two-paragraph statement he'd given "60 Minutes," in which he'd told the CBS team that he'd "never tried to influence any government official to prosecute Don Siegelman ... (had) never spoken to Karl Rove about whether to prosecute Don Siegelman .. (and) have no recollection of ever meeting Ms. Simpson or of ever speaking with her on the telephone."

He told the CBS reporters that "several newspaper reporters in Alabama who are intimately familiar with the Siegelman saga have written stories detailing serious discrepancies and contradictions in Ms. Simpson's various claims."

"Any fair and unbiased review of this matter would give full attention and consideration to these accounts," he concluded.

It is not only routine but often necessary for reporters to condense statements and press releases. However, given the time accorded by "60 Minutes" to the allegations against Canary and the seriousness of the charges, it would not have too much to ask for Pelley to have spent 20 seconds reading Canary's first paragraph containing his denials in his own words.

That's not what happened. This is:

"Bill Canary denies the conversation ever happened. He told '60 Minutes' he never tried to influence any government official in the case. His wife Leura Canary and Alice

Martin are top federal prosecutors in the state. Both were appointed by President Bush, and their offices investigated Siegelman. Details of some of those investigations leaked to the press ..."

"60 Minutes" had used Canary's denial to segue innuendo back at him, suggesting him as a source of the non-existent grand jury leaks.

A week later, Pulitzer Prize winning columnist Cynthia Tucker added insult to injury in her widely syndicated column. Tucker – and in her defense, she was basing most of her information on respected news sources – wrote that Canary had "run political *campaigns* for Mr. Siegelman's chief rival, current GOP Gov. Bob Riley."

The echo chamber had turned the truth – no campaigns – to one campaign, and then, who knows, two, three, four?

I concluded the letter to Pelley and crew by noting that a national audience wasn't told "even in a single summary sentence, that the Siegelman administration was beset by numerous serious scandals and that it was those, not leaks, that led to his electoral downfall ... The Don Siegelman you presented was a squeaky clean victim of Republicans."

I shot it off in several batches. Within seconds, boldness surrendered to anxiety and creeping doom. I'd screwed up. Again. Made a damn ass of myself.

Come back e-mail! Come back!

———

I waited, impatiently, for the bomb to drop. Most of all I feared a dud. If you're going to do something that crazy, any response beats silence. And within a few hours, the thing started moving. Though I hadn't sent it to the Alabama Republican Party – the thought didn't cross my mind – others did and the party forwarded it to some 60,000 people on its e-mail list. Power Line – an apparently well-known right-wing blog – used portions of the letter. Matt Murphy, a Birmingham radio talk show host, invited me on his show, by telephone. Murphy, like probably 90 percent of political talk show hosts, is conservative. On this issue, I was singing their song, and they mine.

The most startling call came from FOX News. The network flew in a three-person crew from Atlanta. They came to my home, were quite friendly, and I spent some 30 minutes on camera explaining the letter. Their last request was for me to take a "glory walk." And what, I asked, was that?

The "glory walk," they explained, is the shot one often sees on TV news, especially on reports about whistleblower types, with the subject just walking, thinking pensively, that sort of thing. I picked up our dog Bud, the hope being he would make it on national TV. I walked down the sidewalk in front of our house, toward the camera, grinning as opposed to pensive.

The glory walk did not make it on FOX. In fact, almost nothing did. The piece, about a minute or two long, was a major disappointment. Priscilla Duncan was quoted at greater length than I, extolling Jill Simpson's credibility. I was on for maybe 5 seconds, and best I can recall, the quote used wasn't particularly pungent and I looked fat. Worst of all, the report didn't take "60 Minutes" to task or so much as seek a response from the network. That is what I'd believed to be the purpose of the piece. I wanted answers from "60 Minutes" to my questions. Still do.

It was a waste of my time, and worse, I made an ass of myself sending e-mails to folks telling them I was going to be on national news, the recollection of which makes me cringe.

The response from the usual suspects was muted. I like to think the letter, and especially the Simpson portion, knocked the wind out of their sails. Horton didn't utter a peep, though Raw Story's Larissa took up the cause, pounding Rove, defending Simpson and "60 Minutes," and taking shots at me.

———

The night after the "60 Minutes" report, Dan Abrams welcomed the same trio – Doug Jones, Grant Woods and Simpson – to his show. To Simpson, Abrams read a release from the Alabama Republican Party, which he presented as "an attack" on Simpson.

The release stated that it was "becoming apparent that Dana Jill Simpson will fabricate any claim in order to extend her 15 minutes in the public spotlight." It repeated the party's earlier declarations that it had searched its records and was unable to locate a single occasion when Jill Simpson worked or volunteered for the Republican Party.

"Well, that is absolutely a lie," Simpson shot back. "That has been said by Mike Hubbard who is now the chairman of the Alabama Republican Party. But Mr. Hubbard is going to have a real problem because he's got to explain how I was talking on the telephone to the party headquarters in 2006, and also talking to the Riley campaign in 2002. And further he is going to have to also explain how I have records showing I was talking to (Rove) in Washington and also in Virginia about the campaign back in 2002."

Having never seen them, I can't say for sure, but my guess is that Simpson's phone bills show dozens if not hundreds of calls *from her* to lots of important people and offices, possibly including the CIA and the Kremlin. I'd be surprised if they show her receiving such calls, but if so, imagine they're return calls from people called by the Rainsville busy-body.

Simpson elaborated on her story for Abrams, claiming to have met with Karl Rove three times. Probably she told the same story to "60 Minutes" but Pelley and team realized that was just too far-fetched and left it on the cutting floor. Here, the juicy bits:

Abrams: *"There is no doubt in your mind that you met with Karl Rove and that he said to you, 'Spy on Gov. Siegelman, get pictures, try and show that he was cheating on his wife'?*

Simpson: *"That's exactly what the man asked me to do."*

Abrams: *"How many times did you meet with him?"*

Simpson: *"I met with Karl Rove probably three times, approximately and additionally, I also talked to him multiple times."*

Simpson told the MSNBC newsman that she'd given the story to others in the media but "they just did not use it because nobody wanted to go into the fact that I had been following Don Siegelman trying to get pictures of him cheating on his wife."

According to Simpson – and that's a dangerous start to any sentence – she also reported it to Judiciary Committee investigators, but they "preferred" she not bring up the story during her testimony.

On April 2, *GQ* magazine published an interview with Rove on its web-site. When the interviewer broached the Simpson allegations, Rove said on the record what so many were saying off.

"She's a complete lunatic. I've never met this woman. This woman was not involved in any campaign in which I was involved. I have yet to find anybody who knows her," said Rove.

Then how did this happen, the interviewer asked.

"Because CBS is a shoddy operation. They said, 'Hey, if we can say "Karl Rove-Siegelman," that'll be good for ratings. Let's hype it. We'll put out a news release on Thursday and then promo the hell out of it on Friday, Saturday, and Sunday.

"And Scott Pelley—the question is, did Scott Pelley say to this woman, 'You say you met with him. Where? And you say that he gave you other assignments earlier. When did he begin giving you assignments, and what campaigns did you work with him in? What evidence? I mean, this woman, she said she met with him: Okay, you met with him—where? Did you fly to Washington?' Now she says that she talked to me on the phone and she's got phone records. Of calls to Washington and Virginia. But what's Virginia? I don't live in Virginia. And it's 2001. What is in Virginia? It's not the Bush headquarters; that was in Austin, Texas. What is in Virginia? So—but look, she's a loon."

In many ways Rove's response mirrored my letter, and I suspect he read it. But the questions, regardless of who was doing the asking, were just so obvious. That's what made Pelley's failure to ask them – or if otherwise, the decision not to report they'd been asked -- so astounding.

The only explanation for that failure is that "60 Minutes" wanted to shield viewers from what the show's producers had to know: That their source on the amazing Rove story was a nincompoop.

The AP's Ben Evans used the "complete lunatic" and "shoddy operation" quotes in the lead of a national wire story reporting Rove's statements to *GQ*. Evans was, far as I'm aware, the only reporter to call "60 Minutes" for a response to Rove's charge, or in any event, to get one. A CBS spokesperson said the network stood by its story.

Despite its explosiveness, Simpson's imaginary assignment to catch Siegelman in flagrante was to have a short shelf-life. In that way it came to resemble her KKK photos story and most of her other tales – all too ridiculous for any but her hardiest sponsors, like Horton, to support.

How bad was it?

It was sooo bad ... drum roll please ... that not even the *New York Times'* editorial staff touched it!

Despite her "60 Minutes" performance, Simpson continued to be relied upon by the House Judiciary Committee and like-minded souls in the national media as the sole source connecting Rove to the Siegelman case. She was simply too necessary to discard.

———

In the week after my letter to "60 Minutes" I received two e-mails authored by the woman upon whose credibility CBS News, the Judiciary Committee Democrats, the *New York Times* editorial page and so many others had banked their own.

One was from Simpson to "Professor Horton" and David Gelber at "60 Minutes," and forwarded by Mark Bollinger to about a dozen people, myself included, for reasons I can't begin to explain. It bore the subject heading: "FW: 247Gay.com -- McCain Declares He is a 'Natural Born Citizen.'"

Keep in mind that the author of this e-mail was (according to her!) Karl Rove's go-to gal for high-level intelligence operations in Alabama and the *only reason* the national media and the Judiciary Committee dove headfirst into the Siegelman case.

Wrote Simpson (verbatim):

"McCains arguement that he is a natural citzen is captured here but his analysis is flawed Professor Horton because as you have seen in Barry Goldwaters case Arizona was recognized as terrritory of United States but the panama canal was unincorporated and not recognized this is a constitutional question of the highest order as republicans on the inside always knew when Mr McCain was running againnst Mr Bush. McCain

was hoping I am sure that no one would catch this but this issue has exploded all over the internet. I think it is a very interesting constitutional question what is a natural born citizen.

The other missive was from Simpson to me and cc'd to John Aaron, the Birmingham lawyer and Siegelman *operative* who'd assisted Simpson the year before with her affidavit and research into Fuller's finances.

"Just so you know I was blond when I followed Mr. Siegelman my suggestion take a look at the pictures and quit running your mouth when you don't know what your talking about. Have a great day Jerk."

Attached to the e-mail were two pictures, one of her with several boys at the Tennessee Aquarium, the other at a park. In both, she is a blonde. To the extent they proved anything, it was that at some point in her life – and I'll take her word that it was 2001 – Jill Simpson's hair was not blinding red but quite blond.

"OK. Next time I will say you were blond," I responded.

And from there, asked if she could provide documents or some form of corroboration to support the story told Pelley.

"My problem is that you've provided zero evidence, that I'm aware of, that you followed anyone or ever spoke to Karl Rove … I'm sorry but until you do that I cannot believe what you are saying. Nothing personal. Just need proof."

She didn't respond. My attempt to goad Simpson into giving me more silly string to hang with her didn't pan out.

———

In September 2009, I sent CBS and "60 Minutes" a series of questions about the Jill Simpson/Siegelman report. The final question: "Does CBS News and '60 Minutes,' stand by the Siegelman piece, including the decision to present such damning claims by Jill Simpson about Karl Rove as well as others? Another way of putting it: Does CBS News and '60 Minutes' regret airing the piece."

CBS spokesman Kevin Tedesco responded two days later with the following e-mail. "Eddie: We stand by our story and have no interest in participating in your book."

Chapter 47
Rappin' on Rove

"Karl Rove is like a double-headed rattle-snake. You are going to have to back him into the corner before you get before you get anything out of him. And just like an infected wound, the wound that has been created in this country by the subversion of our constitutional rights, the abuse of power, the use of the Department of Justice as a political weapon, this wound also has to be cleaned before the American people can feel safe about their democracy again."

-- Siegelman, during March 5, 2009, interview with MSNBC's "The Rachel Maddow Show."

"The only reason that my case is different, that I've gotten any attention, is because of a lifelong Republican named Dana Jill Simpson, who couldn't sleep at night and came forward to place Rove at the scene of the crime. When I got out of prison, I happened to be at a public meeting that she was also at. I just shook her hand and thanked her. I told her that she was an American hero."

-- Siegelman, in an October 2008 interview with GQ magazine.

On the afternoon of March 27, 2007, Vince Kilborn called the prison in Oakdale, La., with astonishing news for inmate Siegelman. Earlier in the day, a three-judge panel of the 11th Circuit Court of Appeals issued a ruling for Siegelman and against the prosecutors and, essentially, against Fuller as well.

The court found that Siegelman's appeal raised "substantial questions of law" that could lead to a reversal of his conviction. The 11th Circuit ordered the former Alabama governor released pending his appeal.

"It took him a minute or two to let it sink in," Kilborn said. "'I think he was pretty much stupefied."

Because of the lateness of the day, Siegelman had to spend one more night at Oakdale. Late the next morning, his wife and daughter picked him up for the eight-hour drive back to Birmingham. Reporters and TV crews assembled at a parking lot near Siegelman's home. He arrived at about 10 p.m. Pictures showed the 62-year-old former governor sun-burned, thin but fit, and weary. He wore sweatpants and a ripped T-shirt over a ratty looking sweatshirt.

Siegelman spoke briefly, and declined to take questions.

He told the gathering that nine months before, he was "handcuffed and shackled and brought to the basement of the federal courthouse in Montgomery and then put in a Chevy sedan and taken to the federal penitentiary in Atlanta."

When in prison, he began each day thanking God for his many blessings. "When I heard the news the 11th Circuit had granted my motion, I thanked God once more," he said.

I was, like almost everyone, surprised at the news. Because honesty is the attempted policy here, I will acknowledge that my first thoughts were for the crew at the U.S. Attorney's Office, and Fuller as well. All had been assailed, at times savagely, for participation in the conspiracy that wasn't. I called Debbie Shaw, the chief administrative assistant for the criminal division. She sounded crushed. Debbie cared for her guys and recognized, correctly, that the ruling would be misinterpreted by many as verification of all the bad things said about the office. Certainly it would be trumpeted as such by Siegelman, the *New York Times*, "60 Minutes," and others.

Jill Simpson was right all along. Siegelman was not only innocent, but the target of a political hit job orchestrated at the highest levels of the United States government.

The *Times*, again signaling the high value it put on the Siegelman case, ran its own story, as opposed to the wire report. Adam Nossiter stressed the national political implications of Siegelman's release, writing that Siegelman's prosecution "has been cited by Democrats here (Alabama) and in Washington as Exhibit A in their contention that politics has influenced decisions by the Justice Department."

He and his editors betrayed their lack of knowledge of Alabama politics by declaring that Siegelman's conviction, "sharply polarized the political climate in the state." Accusations that Rove may have played a role in Siegelman's prosecution "have only increased the tensions."

That was melodramatic claptrap. Yes, Siegelman had a tight band of rabid supporters, but I think most Alabama Democrats felt that when it came to Siegelman, it was always about him, not the overall well-being of the party. One needed to look no further than the 2002 recount battle. Democratic lawmakers told Siegelman he would come out a loser if he asked them to decide the election. As lobbyist Bob Geddie put it then, Siegelman "just never has had a great reserve of hard, hard relationships . . . (his) support in the Legislature had just about dwindled to a handful in the last couple of years."

The likes of the *New York Times* and "60 Minutes" were getting their lessons in Alabama politics from Siegelman and his supporters. In that skewed version, the state party still revolved around the former governor.

———

Siegelman exited prison with a bead on his imaginary tormentor.

On the drive back to Birmingham he called two journalists. One was Adam Nossiter, the other, Abrams. That night, the MSNBC pundit told guests Artur

Davis and Scott Horton that he was "amazed in my conversation with Governor Siegelman, only hours after leaving prison, how quickly he brought up Karl Rove."

Abrams concluded by telling viewers that Siegelman "had agreed to come on the program tonight; I know he wanted to, unfortunately his PR team is now calling the shots…They're out trying to cut deals with the media for access. Most importantly, we certainly hope to have the governor on in the future."

Nossiter's second story in two days bore the headline, "Freed Ex-Governor of Alabama Talks of Abuse of Power." He and his editors apparently viewed it as a big scoop, as they informed readers the paper was the beneficiary of Siegelman's "first post-prison interview."

Nossiter noted, as had Abrams, that the former Alabama governor "repeatedly cited Karl Rove."

"His fingerprints are smeared all over the case," said Siegelman.

In the paragraph following that quote, Nossiter wrote that Siegelman was speaking "in measured tones after spending nine months in prison." The phrase suggests thoughtful deliberation and factual accuracy. It was more measured tones in the next paragraph.

"When Attorney General Gonzales and Karl Rove left office in a blur, they left the truth buried in their documents," Siegelman said. "It's going to be my quest to encourage Congress to ensure that Karl Rove either testifies, or takes the Fifth."

Karl Rove's fingerprints, Karl Rove taking the Fifth, Karl Rove this and Karl Rove that. Siegelman was free, but he was not speaking in measured tones.

Siegelman told Nossiter that if his conviction were upheld, then "every governor and every president and every contributor might as well turn themselves in, because it's going to be open season on them." He could safely say that to the *Times*, knowing that neither Nossiter nor his editors would point out to readers the many ways in which the two $250,000 contributions were anything but ordinary.

The story repeated Jill Simpson's claim that Rove ordered Justice to go after Siegelman. One would have thought that her credibility was by then irreparably shattered from her performance on "60 Minutes." And indeed it was. But she remained the lone link connecting Rove to Siegelman's prosecution. For the folks at the *Times*, editorial and news side, this was an inconvenient truth they chose to ignore.

———

A year before Siegelman's release, and with sentencing still months away, Richard Scrushy took his wife, five of his children and their nanny to Disney World. His probation officer approved the trip to Orlando and from there to Palm Beach, so Scrushy could look at some property.

Scrushy, though, was less than candid regarding his itinerary and the purpose of his trip. He didn't say the first thing about boarding his yacht or going to Miami, both of which he did. He later claimed that after arriving in Palm Beach he received a call from Donald Watkins, the lawyer who helped devise the Scrushy as black man strategy for the Birmingham trial, and who had moved to Miami.

The FBI discovered that before leaving Birmingham, Scrushy wired $2,000 to the captain of the *Chez Soiree*, his 92-foot yacht. Along with the money were directions to wax the floors, gas up, stock it with food and prepare for travel. After four days at Walt Disney World, the Scrushys drove to Palm Beach and the awaiting *Chez Soiree*. They spent two days in-transit to Miami by way of the Intracoastal Waterway.

During the trip a source contacted the FBI to report that Scrushy was aboard the yacht and might be fleeing. Tamara Martin, another of his probation officers, reached Scrushy by cell phone. She elected not to ask him if he was still in Orlando for fear of alerting him. He neglected to reveal that he was on his yacht, instead implying that he was still at Disney World.

Scrushy did meet with Watkins, and the family returned to Birmingham aboard the lawyer's plane.

Franklin and Feaga filed a motion asking that Scrushy's bond be revoked and that he be jailed. Scrushy, who didn't testify in the HealthSouth fraud trial or the Siegelman case, actually took the stand at the bond revocation hearing. He acknowledged that he intended to travel to Miami by ocean, not the Intracoastal Waterway, but was prohibited by rough weather. He said it was his understanding that he had permission to travel throughout south Florida, Miami was in south Florida, and it didn't matter how he got there.

Feaga argued that were it not for the weather, Scrushy might have motored out into the Caribbean and fled. I think it unlikely that Scrushy intended to make a run for it, but he had violated the conditions of his probation and not been forthcoming about his travel.

Magistrate Judge Charles Coody told Scrushy he had been "coy" with his probation officers and reminded him that he was a convicted felon. He ordered Scrushy to wear an electronic monitoring device during out-of-state travel; to get court permission prior to traveling by private, non-commercial means; and to provide detailed itineraries of travel plans to his probation officers.

Those were rather mild restrictions. However, a far greater punishment awaited.

The following fall, when denying Siegelman and Scrushy's requests to be freed on bond, Fuller added an additional reason for blocking Scrushy's release. He ruled that Scrushy had failed to convince the court that he wasn't a flight risk – the basis of that finding being Scrushy's flaunting of the terms of his probation by boarding his yacht and going to Miami.

Two months before the 11th Circuit freed Siegelman, another panel of the same court nixed Scrushy's request to be released pending appeal. The appellate judges upheld Fuller's finding that Scrushy's yacht trip showed he couldn't be trusted not to flee. As such – for Scrushy, though not Siegelman – the larger issue of a likelihood of success on appeal was moot. So when Siegelman won release on those grounds, Scrushy stayed put.

Over the next year Scrushy was to secure ridicule, but not freedom, by offering to put most of what remained of his fortune up as bond if the 11th Circuit would release. When that failed, he tried again. Ten friends offered their houses as collateral for a bond if only the court would grant Scrushy his freedom. These attempts at rich man's justice were disregarded by the court.

Ultimately, Scrushy may be the lucky one. By remaining in prison during the year and a half or so Siegelman has remained free, he presumably will leave that much sooner should Siegelman return , as I believe will happen.

———

Nine days after Siegelman's release, "60 Minutes," ran a brief portion of what one assumes was a far longer interview with the former governor. "An update now on the story that we called, 'The Prosecution of Governor Siegelman," began Scott Pelley. "A federal court has released former Alabama Governor Don Siegelman from prison six weeks after our story."

CBS transcripts called the second report, "The Prosecution of Don Siegelman; Don Siegelman released from prison after '60 Minutes' airs story."

Translation: The judges on the 11th Circuit ordered Siegelman to be freed on bond after watching Jill Simpson et al., on "60 Minutes."

"What we need is Karl Rove to get himself over to the Judiciary Committee and put his hand on a Bible and take an oath and give testimony," Siegelman declared. "And he can either tell the truth or take the Fifth. Either one will satisfy me."

The next night Siegelman's PR team cleared him for what Dan Abrams promoted as Siegelman's "first live interview" since leaving prison. The host opened with the familiar hosannas – Siegelman being "a rare breed, a Democratic governor in a red state" and a victim of, "Bush League Justice."

Siegelman thanked Abrams profusely for "stepping out" and urged the MSNBC host to "continue this fight until we find out who hijacked the Department of Justice."

Then Siegelman delivered his ghost of O.J.'s bloody gloves comparison to illustrate his plight, ending with, "We've got the glove and the glove fits."

The Rove's fingerprints-bloody glove quote was the first of 25 times that Siegelman mentioned Rove on the show, pronouns included. Usually it was Karl Rove, as opposed to merely Rove. He frequently flushed out Rove twice, even three times in an answer, often within catchy, practiced, campaign-like slogans. For example: "Saying that Karl Rove is not involved in my prosecution is like saying George Bush is not involved in the war in Iraq."

For a moment it appeared that Abrams was going to actually challenge Siegelman's story. "You're not hinging all this on Dana Jill Simpson, because there are people who have questioned how she could be at certain meetings, where she was at the time," he said.

Siegelman, apparently surprised that Abrams was actually behaving like a journalist, offered several vague reasons to support the Rove against him storyline. There was, he said, the "totality of Rove's involvement in Alabama politics." He told Abrams that investigators and U.S. Attorneys and lawyers with the Justice Department were "violating laws with impunity" in bringing charges against him; and that there was "no logical conclusion" other than that someone higher up was "offering them protection."

Then Abrams dropped a bombshell. He told Siegelman that he had e-mailed Rove's lawyer, Robert Luskin, to ask again if Rove would testify before the Judiciary Committee. Luskin's response: Yes, his client would be testifying about the Siegelman case.

Bush's brain had called his bluff. Abrams asked Siegelman if he was surprised.

Siegelman said he didn't believe it would happen, but if so, he would welcome it. What he said next was telling.

"We also need to call those people in Alabama with political connections to Karl Rove," he told Abrams. "Those people who ought to be brought before Congress and they, too, should be asked to swear under oath their relationships with Karl Rove and whether he influenced their decision to move forward with this case. *That ought to be done before Karl Rove is called to testify.*"

From the moment he'd left prison Siegelman had been publicly taunting Rove, repeatedly demanding that Rove go before the committee.

Now it appeared he was about to get his way. He should have been exultant. He wasn't.

Siegelman's suggestion that others testify first answered what I think is a reasonable question: Was his Rove fixation a sign of sanity slipping, or a cynical ploy?

Insanity is not suggested as a joke or insult. I think anyone who followed Siegelman over the years and especially since the trial could fairly wonder if he wasn't losing it. His answer to Abrams told otherwise. He could still do the math, and fast. Siegelman immediately recognized that every major American media outlet would be there to report on Rove testifying before Congress. Siegelman knew that with such an appearance, the super-confident Rove would transform Jill Simpson from whistleblower to kook and him from political victim to crybaby conspiracy theorist.

He knew it because he knew as much as anyone that Karl Rove had nothing to do with his prosecution, that the whole thing was a hoax. So as soon as Siegelman got what he said he wanted he started tossing out roadblocks to prevent it.

Near interview's end Abrams asked Siegelman if he was "ready to go to Capitol Hill and testify."

Siegelman pledged to "go to Capitol Hill and give them whatever information I can."

Did he say he would testify?

No.

Was Don Siegelman insane?

Not at all.

Slick?

As ever.

A Golden Flake?

"Dan, thank you so much for what you have done for America," he said in bidding the host goodbye.

———

After Luskin's statement to Abrams it appeared that Rove would finally testify on the Siegelman matter. Luskin soon after announced that his words had been misconstrued. More likely his proposal was rejected by the Bush administration. In any event, the White House, Ruskin said, continued to assert executive privilege in objecting to Rove testifying on any matter before the Judiciary Committee.

At the time, the White House was also citing executive privilege in refusing to allow former long-time White House counsel Harriett Miers and former White House Chief of Staff Joshua Bolton testify on the U.S. Attorney firings.

Rove acknowledged having what he described as minimal involvement in the removals and/or recommendations for replacements of some of the eight fired U.S. Attorneys. He offered to answer questions from Judiciary Committee investigators, but only on the Siegelman case, and without a transcript. Conyers and his committee rejected that offer.

The committee subpoenaed Rove on May 22, 2008, demanding that he appear at a July 10 hearing to testify about the U.S. Attorney firings and the Siegelman case. He didn't show. Instead, he provided a written statement to the committee. It read:

"I have never communicated, either directly or indirectly, with Justice Department or Alabama officials about the investigation, indictment, potential prosecution, prosecution, conviction or sentencing of Governor Siegelman, or about any other matter related to this case, nor have I asked any other individual to communicate about these matters on my behalf."

Attached was a list of exhibits and statements intended to refute the Siegelman allegation. Rove wrote that the committee "should require Siegelman to substantiate his allegations about my 'involvement' in his prosecution -- something he has failed to do in either media interviews or court filings."

Later that month, the Judiciary Committee, voting along party lines, voted to hold Rove in contempt for failing to appear at a hearing for which he'd been subpoenaed. However, it required the full House, not just a committee, for a contempt vote to have force, and that never happened.

Siegelman relentlessly pressed the Rove angle for fund-raising and public-relations purposes. In mass e-mailings he asked supporters to donate money to his legal defense fund. The fight, he liked to say, wasn't just about him. It was about America.

The letters urged supporters to go to the web-site, ContemptForRove.com. Those who did were routed to DonSiegelman.Org, the site devoted to raising money and publicity for his cause.

"Since I wrote you last week, we have seen an outpouring of support from our online community in my effort to raise the $30,000 I need to pay legal expenses for my appeal on December 9th," began one such letter. "But, with less than one week left, I still need your help to reach that goal. Please donate what you can today – so I can have the resources I need to keep fighting back and to hold Karl Rove accountable!"

Siegelman was implying that he had to pay his lawyers *before* the appeals hearing or they wouldn't show up to represent him. This, of course, was hogwash.

The "Muhammad Ali of Fundraising," as Vince Kilborn memorably tagged him at trial, told supporters that his legal defense fund could accept contributions "of any size from any source."

Rove put the letter on his own web-site, Rove.Com, under the heading, "Personal Responsibility: Who Needs It When You Can Blame Karl Rove?"

———

DonSiegelman.Org is the internet home of the Free Siegelman movement, and is an excellent source for the myriad conspiracies and red-herrings thrown against the wall by Team Siegelman. If even a few stick, he wins.

The site is frequently updated to include the latest pro-Siegelman media reports; the most recent letters from Judiciary Committee chairman John Conyers to the Justice Department all but demanding that they kibosh the Siegelman/ Scrushy case; the latest splash made by the Grant Woods and Robert Abrams-led attorneys general group; and, nipping at everyone's feet, new investigative bombshells from the Legal Schnauzer.

The "60 Minutes" segment continues to hold front and center on the site's home-page, and probably will as long as DonSiegelman.Org endures.

There are no shortage of suggestions for those wishing to help, whether by contributing money, or writing congressmen, judges and, the main target, Holder.

Obama's attorney general could almost be excused for killing the Siegelman case just to end the assault on his letter-box.

DonSiegelman.Org provides supporters with a suggested "sample letter" to the attorney general. It begins: "I have personally witnessed the political prosecution of the finest man that Alabama has ever or will ever produce, Governor Don Siegelman."

A section called, "Players," is worth a look. Those listed under, "White House," are Rove, former Attorney General Alberto Gonzales and Noel Hillman, the former head of the Justice Department's Public Integrity Section. Sticking Hillman under "White House" is another in the endless series of demonstrably false innuendo generators to be found in Siegelman's world and on DonSiegelman.Org.

Those identified as "GOP *Operatives*" include: Bob Riley, Bill Canary, Rob Riley, Terry Butts, U.S. Sen. Jeff Sessions and Alabama congressman Terry Everett. No explanation is given for the inclusion of a governor, a U.S. senator and a congressman as *operatives*. I don't think even Jill Simpson claimed that Sessions or Everett had anything to do with Siegelman's prosecution.

Grant Woods and Artur Davis share billing with Simpson under, "Heroes." Simpson, as previously chronicled, is hailed as a "modern day Joan of Arc -- a rare true believer in truth, justice and the 'American way.'"

I got good play under, "Journalists," and was paired with Horton, whose columns and comments are peppered throughout DonSiegelman.Org.

"Two journalists who have taken an interest in the Siegelman case counter point each other's points of view. Each has different professional and journalistic standards. One is credited with instigating the Siegelman case, the other with encouraging a second look at the Siegelman case and the political system that produced it."

The site's authors seem to try to connect me to the 2002 "stolen election." Under my picture it states, "Eddie Curran, a writer for the *Mobile Press Register* in Baldwin County, Alabama." A summary of my role in the Siegelman drama takes it farther: "Eddie Curran is employed by the *Mobile Register* which serves the counties of Baldwin and Mobile. Baldwin County is the location of the computer glitch that altered the vote count resulting in Riley 'winning' the office of Governor of Alabama."

On April 17, 2008, the Democratic majority of the House Judiciary Committee released its report, "Allegations of Selective Prosecution in Our Federal Criminal Justice System," with Siegelman getting top billing. The report, as discussed earlier, was a compendium of the accusations against everyone but the janitor at the Middle District courthouse, one piled on the other to support the conclusion that there was "extensive evidence" that Washington officials, "likely including Karl Rove," directed the prosecution of Siegelman.

Jill Simpson was footnoted eight times; op-eds by *New York Times'* editorial writer Adam Cohen seven; and lawyers for Siegelman and Scrushy a total of 18 times. Stories by the *Times'* Adam Nossiter and *Time* magazine's Adam Zagorin made multiple appearances, as did the "60 Minutes" Siegelman segment.

No individual source was footnoted as much as Horton, whose writings were cited in support of 15 claims or statements in the report. He's referred to twice in the body of the report, first taking a dig at then-U.S. Attorney General Michael Mukasey. During a talk in San Francisco, Mukasey said that politics had no role in the prosecution of public corruption cases, and that he'd seen no evidence of that during his time in the department. And then, from the report: "One commentator responded, 'My reaction and apparently the reaction of much of Mukasey's audience in San Francisco, was the same: 'Wake up and open your eyes.'"

A footnote below identified the commentator as Horton. The remark had no evidentiary value whatsoever, and seemed only to serve an apparently obsessive bitterness Horton felt toward Mukasey, with whom he'd practiced in a large New York firm prior to his leaving in early 2007.

I can't imagine that the Judiciary Committee staff could have plucked out that irrelevant comment from a Scott Horton column on its own.

A few pages on, this: "In addition, a leading commenter on the matter has criticized an aggressive and ongoing prosecution effort by Alabama U.S. Attorney Alice Martin against a number of state Democratic officeholders and has linked these cases to the Siegelman matter."

The footnote revealed the "leading commentator" as Horton.

During a political event in Mobile, in 2008, I asked Artur Davis why Horton had become such an influence on the committee. The Alabama congressman said Horton had "certainly … captured the fact that the Department of Justice doesn't have a stellar record. Scott Horton has written a lot of articles. Some I agree with, some I don't."

My main reason for attending the event was to ask Davis one question: Did Horton write or contribute to the writing of the committee's report?

The Alabama congressman said he didn't know, as authorship of the report was done at the staff level.

In an October 2009 e-mail to Horton, I asked if he contributed "in any way to the report, whether by writing, proofing, editing, suggesting what should be in there?" And: "Have you been paid by the Judiciary Committee for any services provided to the committee?"

He didn't respond. I later e-mailed a letter to the Judiciary Committee staff seeking responses to questions and public records. I asked if the committee had "made or authorized" any payments to Horton; if so, for how much and what services; and asked to be provided copies of any bills that may have been submitted by him for payment.

I presented Horton's footnote count and the "leading commentator" business and asked if the man from *Harper's* wrote or contributed in any fashion to the report. I also asked why the committee "would seek information from Scott Horton on the Siegelman case?"

Horton never attended a day of trial and didn't write the first word about the case until Jill Simpson's affidavit, and, voila, he's the national expert on the case, appearing on Dan Abrams show and others, consulted, apparently, by "60 Minutes," and treated by the Judiciary Committee as the font of wisdom on the matter.

I talked to the committee spokesman, who said he would get back with me. I made several efforts to reach him, but ultimately gave up. I was without any leverage to make him do his job, and he or his bosses decided not to answer the questions from the guy in, of all places, Mobile, Ala.

———

In early April 2008 I learned that Horton was coming to Huntsville to speak to a group formed for the sole purpose of hosting him and calling itself, "North Alabamians for Media Reform."

"Watchdogs or Lap Dogs?: Politics and the Alabama Press," was advertised as a one-man screed against the Alabama media, and chiefly, the Newhouse bad boys, the *Mobile Register* and *Birmingham News*. I asked to be permitted to give a short rebuttal at the end, remarking that any entity seeking to promote media reform would naturally wish to present both sides. The offer was rejected.

I decided to once again violate protocol. By this point I knew that Horton was to be a major actor in the book, figured I needed to see him in action, and made the seven-hour drive to the lion's den in Huntsville. Siegelman's hard-core support in Alabama is skin deep, but its alligator skin, and the crowd of about 200 represented the outer layer. Some of the true believers came from out of state to see the event.

Siegelman was there, as was Jill Simpson, and Pam Miles, a Huntsville activist and blindly devoted Siegelman backer who played a substantial role in the grassroots effort to drum up support for her hero. Glynn Wilson, the lone force behind the "Locust Fork," blog attended. To my disappointment, the Legal Schnauzer was a no show.

The area media was there in force, including at least one Huntsville television station.

I sat a few rows from the front. Siegelman, who received a standing ovation upon entering, was in the row behind me. Simpson, befitting her role as star, sat in the front row with Priscilla Duncan, her lawyer and my old friend.

Horton opened with his professorial survey of the Alabama media's failings after the Civil War; then during the Civil Rights Movement; and finally -- the state media's third epochal collapse and the reason we were all gathered – our coverage of the

Siegelman case. The crowd tittered in delight when Horton remarked that a recent story by one of the violators "tops anything I ever remember in the Soviet press."

Pravda under Stalin, concealing death camps and mass assassinations? Move over guys. Here comes the *Mobile Register* and the *Birmingham News* with stories about Don Siegelman!

After a stretch of this, and some business about the Newhouse organization, I was moved to stand up for Sy and my faraway masters in New York. I told Horton and the crowd that the Newhouse organization most assuredly had not directed me or anyone else at the paper to go after Siegelman.

Horton, all innocence, asked where I'd read that. He said he'd merely written that the state's papers were part of a "consolidated" media group. "That doesn't mean the Newhouse organization ordered its newspapers to go after him. That's ridiculous," he said.

That one left me speechless. Had I a photographic memory, there's no shortage of examples I could have reeled off. In column after column he'd accused the *Register* and *News* of joining forces to bring down Siegelman, and never failed to make the Newhouse connection. After Huntsville editorial page editor John Ehinger wrote disparagingly of Siegelman, Horton ripped the *Times* as well, not forgetting to link that paper to its two Newhouse cousins.

In a column printed in the *Anniston Star*, Horton wrote that if a "miscarriage of justice occurred, then the press in Alabama bears a large part of the blame. By press, I mean one media company, Newhouse Newspapers…"

It was these claims, not his backing of Jill Simpson, that brought the otherwise unknown *Harper's* writer to at the attention of the people at the *Register*, the *News*, and, after he started lumping them in with us, the folks at the *Huntsville Times* as well. The Anniston column prompted a response from Ehinger.

In, "Three state papers find themselves the targets of a N.Y. writer," he wrote that Horton "implies that joint ownership of the three papers somehow affects editorial policy, including editorial policy in the Siegelman case."

And then:

I find it "curious" -- to use Horton's term -- that although he claims to have studied press coverage of the case for two months he offers not a single editorial, news story, headline, paragraph or sentence in evidence. As a lawyer, would he limit his case to a jury to a summary of the evidence without presenting any actual evidence? I doubt it…

Scott Horton is a skilled writer and, I presume, a competent lawyer. Maybe the next time he'll provide some facts to support his claims and refrain from painting journalists he doesn't know with a brush so broad and, ultimately, so misleading.

But I had no such retort ready for Horton's willingness to run away from his own words and innuendo and stammered some lame response. He moved on, informing the audience that the *Register* published more than 100 stories on no bid contracts. He said reporters for the Mobile and Birmingham papers "knew what grand jury witnesses said" and that we were either "the hottest thing since Clark Kent" or had been fed secret grand jury testimony by the prosecutors.

Had he taken the time to ask me, Kim Chandler or Phil Rawls – the latter an AP reporter, with no fealty real or imagined to Si Newhouse -- we could have told him that we only knew what grand jury witnesses said when the witnesses told us, which they rarely did. If Horton had read the stories, he would have known that.

I let that one pass, but moved to correct his generalization about our stories. This did not sit well with the audience. I pointed back toward Siegelman and told Horton that the governor had thanked me for my stories on the G.H. Construction warehouse deal. I said my stories weren't just about no-bid contracts, but also reported, among other things, that Siegelman received more than $1.3 million in legal fees while governor; that he sold his house to a straw man for twice its value; and that his administration arranged to slash the hazardous waste fees at Emelle so Lanny Young could get paid $500,000 by Waste Management.

"Where's your question buddy? You're on a rant. We don't give a damn about your rant," howled a man behind me, and who'd been razzing me.

I told him I was correcting Horton because he had mischaracterized my stories. Horton said it "may be surprising to your fellow reporters" were they to hear me saying I wrote all the Siegelman pieces. He said I was not the only reporter at the *Register*. To which I told him, that, well, I did write the stories.

"I think y'all are afraid to hear an opposing viewpoint," I said. "You (Horton) never called the Newhouses or my paper because you don't like opposing viewpoints."

It was about then that the guy behind me pushed me -- not hard enough to knock me over, but a good nudge nonetheless. I turned around and told him, rather sternly, not to do that again, not knowing how in the world I would back up such a threat should he do it again.

One of the event organizers came to the front. She said that as a radical Democrat she, like others in attendance, have "had to sit in rooms and been berated for our positions ... If we're going to change this country then we have to have civil discourse on both sides…Until we can do that we are no better than those we oppose."

The woman, Yolanda McClain, said that "whether or not (I was) swayed or not from powers outside his control or directed" to write what I wrote was for others to decide.

She didn't mean it ugly, but that was the gist of the program -- that I and others with the *Register* and *Birmingham News* had willingly served as pawns for Republican politicians and prosecutors. Whether I was standing up for myself or once again revealing thin skin is a close call, but I told McLain it was "insulting to me to tell me I've been influenced by powers outside my control."

The scene – from my first objections, to the shouts for me to sit down to McLain's talk to the crowd – was posted on YouTube, though without the push. I saw it and, to my surprise, thought I did OK.

After the program McLain apologized for the behavior of the man behind me. She seemed a kind, intelligent woman, if misguided on this issue.

The evening's most interesting revelation followed a question from the audience. Horton was asked if he'd been questioned by the Judiciary Committee. He said he'd testified three times and expected to be called again.

If true – and again, the Judiciary Committee declined to respond to my inquiries – Congress needs to create a new committee, something along the lines of, "The U.S. House Committee for Standards in U.S. House Committee Reports."

Stories in the Huntsville and Decatur papers and the report by the Huntsville television station reported my objections to Horton's statements and the crowd's shouting me down. If nothing else, my presence helped give voice in those reports to a viewpoint other than that of the visiting expert from *Harper's*.

Ehinger, the Huntsville editor, had been there, and penned his second column on Horton. Of my contributions to the evening he wrote:

Alas, one person who apparently doesn't have a thick skin is Eddie Curran, a reporter for The Press-Register who has written extensively about the Siegelman case and other matters related to the former governor's administration. Curran, who is on leave from the Press-Register and is writing a book about Siegelman, was at UAH for Horton's talk.

… Curran objected to Horton's statement that he and others must have been fed confidential information by the attorneys prosecuting Siegelman. That might have turned into an interesting discussion but for the fact that when Curran tried to speak, he was repeatedly told by audience members to shut up and do other things. That's the passion I mentioned earlier -- passion and rudeness.

After the program, Jill Simpson told a Huntsville TV reporter that Siegelman "got destroyed by those individuals and it is very much a raw deal." She reached into the now familiar forensics bag of quotes, pointing to the ever-present Republican "fingerprints" on the Siegelman prosecution.

"They're smeared all over it," she said.

About a month earlier, and just a day or two before the 11th Circuit ruling that freed Siegelman, John Conyers asked the Justice Department to temporarily release Siegelman. Conyers wanted to bring Siegelman to Washington to testify about his prosecution and Rove's part in it.

A committee spokesperson told the Associated Press that Conyers felt Siegelman "would have a lot to add to the committee's investigation into selective prosecution." Conyers' request was revealed shortly after Siegelman's release, the upshot being that Siegelman was now free to come to Washington and testify.

Vince Kilborn told the *Birmingham News* that one of his client's "upcoming stops could be to Washington." He said Siegelman was "enthusiastic" about testifying before the committee.

It never happened. The last word on the subject was a letter from Artur Davis to Conyers in early April. The Alabama congressman urged Conyers not to seek Siegelman's testimony. Republicans would question Siegelman about his criminal case and his answers could be used against him by prosecutors, such as at a possible re-trial or basing new claims of obstruction of justice, Davis wrote.

Also, the minority members might "use the occasion to discredit (Siegelman) with the least flattering facts of the trial and his governorship ... and could call some of the cooperating witnesses who testified against Siegelman to further damage his credibility."

Davis declared that Siegelman's testimony was unlikely to reveal anything new on the committee's primary concern – whether political forces drove his prosecution. Here Davis was essentially conceding that Siegelman had no such information, in any event, nothing beyond Jill Simpson.

After Davis's letter, neither the Judiciary Committee, Siegelman or Kilborn spoke again of the former governor's enthusiastic desire to appear before the committee. That, however, did not stop Siegelman from continuing to rap on Rove for not testifying.

In a series of editorials over a year's time, the *Birmingham News* addressed Siegelman's relentless challenges that Rove testify while himself declining to do so. Among those was an August 2008 piece remarking that Rove's failure to testify "only makes it appear he has something to hide;" then remarked that it was "ironic for Siegelman to make an issue of this, since he hasn't exactly rushed forward to raise his right hand, either."

The editorial concluded:

At one point, remember, Siegelman was supposedly eager to do so. He was still in prison at the time, and members of Congress were clamoring for the government to allow him to come to Washington, D.C. But when he was released from prison and was free to go, Congress and Siegelman abruptly changed gears.

As Rove's refusal to testify raises questions, so, too, does the change of heart on the part of Siegelman and his congressional defenders. Are they serious about getting to the truth of this matter, or just playing politics themselves?

The allegations about Rove are serious business. Politics should play no role whatsoever in decisions about whom the federal government prosecutes.

Rove should cough up whatever information he has or say under oath there's nothing to say. Then again, so should Siegelman.

If Siegelman recognized this irony, he kept it to himself. It seemed hardly a day went by when he wasn't baiting Rove in some forum, be it talk radio, a lefty blog or, on a big day, a national news talk program, as on March 9, when he gave a lengthy interview to CNN's John Sanchez.

"Did Karl Rove politicize the Justice Department, actually have prosecutors doing the White House's handiwork?" began Sanchez, with the usual question that answers itself. "That is the accusation that a Judiciary Committee is going to be investigating. And this is serious stuff."

———

"Karl Rove could not have done it by himself, obviously," Siegelman told Sanchez. "But I think Karl Rove pressed this prosecution with the Department of Justice. This -- we have sworn testimony to that fact by a Republican lawyer who was -- who was part of the political machine -- the Republican political machine -- that was trying to get me out of the way."

That cog in the machine was of course Jill Simpson. Sanchez asked about her claim of following the then-governor on orders from Rove. Siegelman said she'd been asked to "find me in a sexually compromising position" and that "fortunately (Simpson) looked for several months and couldn't find anything."

Why, Sanchez, wondered, would Rove do something like that?

Siegelman explained that he was "the only viable Democrat in the state of Alabama." Furthermore, he was at the time thinking about "entering national politics in 2003, going into the 2004 elections."

Translation: Rove called upon secret agent Jill to prevent the doomsday scenario of a Democratic presidential nominee named Don Siegelman.

———

In August 2008, Siegelman attended the Democratic Convention in Denver. He spoke at churches, at the Denver Press Club, to a group of young Democrats, and at a breakfast gathering of the Colorado Democratic delegation. "In all of his appearances, Siegelman will deliver the same message – that he's an innocent man but Karl Rove isn't," reported Charles Dean of the *Birmingham News*.

Rove "will walk off into the sunset unless we hold him accountable for his role in this," he told the breakfast group, and lamented what he called "this let bygones be bygones" approach. Siegelman implored the Colorado delegates to contact their congressmen and urge them to put the Siegelman-Rove probe high on their agendas.

U.S. Rep. Ed Perlmutter, a Democrat from Colorado, didn't need urging. "This was a political witch hunt led by Karl Rove, and he will have to answer to his crimes," Perlmutter told the riled up crowd.

Siegelman stuck around after the breakfast, talked to his new Colorado fans, and signed autographs. "They treated him like a martyred celebrity," said Register cartoonist J.D. Crowe, who the paper sent to the convention.

In July 2009, Siegelman, Conyers and Judiciary Committee Democrats got what they'd been demanding for two years – Karl Rove on the hot seat, to face questions, under penalty of perjury, about his role in the firings of the eight U.S. Attorneys and the prosecution of Don Siegelman.

Rove wasn't put under oath, but that formality was unnecessary. It's a crime to lie to Congress, so his answers were subject to a possible perjury prosecution, oath or not.

The session lasted 12 hours over two days. The bulk of that time was used to question Rove about the prosecutor firings, and most of that regarded the 2006 dismissal of David Iglesias, the Bush-appointed U.S. Attorney in New Mexico.

The Siegelman case was the only so-called "selective prosecution" case about which Rove was really grilled (he was very briefly queried about two others.)

Questioning Rove was Elliot Mincberg, the Judiciary Committee's chief counsel for oversight and investigations. Mincberg repeatedly asked Rove if he had any communications with the Justice Department regarding the Siegelman case. As lawyers are wont to do, he asked the same question over and over, just changing the wording here and there. With some, he identified various personnel at Justice, including, in Montgomery, Leura Canary and the prosecutors in her office.

Lawyers, whether prepping clients for depositions or, in this case, congressional testimony, stress the need to be truthful but not to declare something as fact unless they are absolutely sure it's so. It would be dangerous for Rove, who has no doubt met or shaken hands or stood in pictures with tens of thousands of people, to declare as fact that he never met someone, only to have a picture or long-forgotten e-mail crop up and lead to calls for a perjury investigation. Rove, in keeping with such counseling, frequently gave the answers, "Not that I'm aware of," or, "Not that I recall."

But not always. For example, when asked if he ever communicated "about Governor Siegelman with anyone working at the Justice Department," he responded with a flat no.

The closest he came to conceding so much as a mention of Siegelman came when asked if he'd discussed the former Alabama governor with Bill Pryor or Bill Canary.

Rove said he's friends with both men and speaks to them on occasion. It was possible that over the four or five year period in question that the Siegelman situation could have come up in one of those chats, but if so, only because it was in the news. He said he couldn't rule out having such a discussion, but neither could he recall one.

Mincberg asked Rove if he'd ever spoken to Noel Hillman about anything – not just Siegelman, but anything at all. Rove said his only recollection of the name was from Hillman's 2006 appointment to the federal bench. (As described in an earlier chapter, the former head of the Justice Department's public corruption unit said he had never met nor communicated in any manner with Karl Rove.)

The recurring theme of Rove's testimony on the Siegelman case was indifference. During the period in question he was, after all, a senior advisor to the president of the United States. Don Siegelman was a defeated, scandal-tarred former Alabama governor, and a Democrat. To one question, Rove said it was his experience that it's "very unusual for defeated incumbent governors to come back from a defeat and get reelected again, particularly if they have a primary full of ambitious people who have won their last election."

That remark did not sit well with Mincberg. "In fact, you did have an interest in the Siegelman case, didn't you?" he demanded.

Rove's response suggested sarcasm but also the sort of perspective missing from this entire folly. He said he "had a lot more pressing things on my platter than the Alabama governor's race, and, as a result, a lot more significant things to worry about than the Don Siegelman case."

"Was I, as a student of Alabama politics or politics in general, you know -- I wouldn't say interested, but, you know, receive the information and process it? Yes. But the idea that I was somehow waiting on pins and needles for the outcome of a case in Alabama is -- which I think is sort of the implication of your use of the word 'interest,' is not accurate."

Mincberg had been hammering Rove on an issue upon which the Judiciary Committee had expended considerable effort and political capital, and hadn't scratched him. For the first time, he asked about Jill Simpson. Did Rove stand by his prior statements that he "had never met or spoken to Jill Simpson," and was he willing to say so, "under penalty of prosecution under 18 U.S. Code 1001?"

Rove said he had "no recollection of meeting her or talking to her."

Mincberg tried again, once more reciting the perjury code. Rove's lawyer, Robert Luskin, told the Judiciary Committee attorney to "stop the posturing" and "just ask questions." Mincberg cited the statute again, this time before asking Rove if he stood behind his testimony that he "had no communications relating to a possible investigation, prosecution, or illegal acts by Governor Siegelman?"

One of the Republican lawyers interjected to tell Mincberg that Rove had agreed to cooperate and didn't deserve to have questions loaded up with, "1950's House Un-American Activities Committee-style rhetoric and diction."

Unfazed, Mincberg again gave the perjury citation before asking if Rove stood by the testimony he'd given on the matter. Rove said him he stood by it.

In response to subpoenas, the Bush White House turned over documents related to the subjects under review. Most pertained to the prosecutor firings. The paucity of the evidence with which Mincberg had to work on the Siegelman matter was revealed in a series of questions about a publication called the *Southern Political Reporter*.

That's a newsletter which, as its name suggests, covers southern politics. Naturally, when the Siegelman case was in the news, it was also in the newsletter, as too were reports related to Riley, including the results of polls taken during the period. Out of an apparent abundance of caution, the White House furnished items from the newsletter when Riley or Siegelman was mentioned.

Mincberg pointed Rove to an item in the newsletter stating that the "other Democrat who might run is ex-Governor Don Siegelman;" and, down the page, a description of Siegelman as, "superb politician despite being dogged by several ethical clouds."

Did Rove remember seeing this?

No, came the answer.

After several such questions, Rove tried to explain why an item about Don Siegelman in the *Southern Political Reporter* might not have rocked his world. "That newsletter is produced, I believe, every week or every 2 weeks, and I received it for -- I have received it for 20 years," he said.

Rove said he was "not certain" that Mincberg should take his receipt of the *Southern Political Reporter* as "evidence that I read that (items about Riley and Siegelman) with a timely concern …"

To the extent the word applies, the most incriminating document turned over by the White House was a February 2005 e-mail sent to Rove by his assistant, Sara Taylor. She wrote, "We asked Kitty to do some digging, no word for sure, but sounds like probably Riley will run."

Kitty is Kelley "Kitty" McCollough, who had worked in Rove's consulting firm and was by then with the Republican National Committee. She'd spent time in Alabama and was known for having many contacts in the state.

Mincberg asked if the e-mail refreshed Rove's recollection about his communications with his assistant regarding Riley's plans. Rove said he didn't remember the e-mail and couldn't say if the "digging" directive came from him or someone else. He said it was possible that his interest was prompted by a request for President Bush to do a fund-raiser in Alabama.

In response to the request, McCollough contacted Riley chief of staff Toby Roth who reported back, via e-mail, that he thought his boss would seek re-election but that Riley "won't say."

At most, the e-mails revealed that Rove had some interest in whether Alabama's Republican incumbent was running for re-election. In all likelihood Rove – a political junkie to the core -- stayed abreast of governors races in states other than Alabama. Probably about 49 of them, though, as he told Mincberg, the White House was substantially more interested in congressional and Senate races than gubernatorial elections.

Rove was also asked about his relationship with Bill Canary – who Siegelman and others characterized as among the closest people on the planet to him. Rove said he met Canary when the latter was a (mid-level) aide to the first president Bush; and they became reacquainted in the mid-1990s, when Rove went to Alabama to work on campaigns to elect Republicans to the state Supreme Court.

He said that over the past seven or eight years he'd probably spoken to Canary, "maybe a half-dozen times, maybe a dozen times at most." Over the same period he'd seen Canary a handful of times, such as at fundraisers in Alabama and social events in Washington.

A case can be made that the "digging" directive – even assuming it originated with Rove -- supported his testimony on more crucial points. If he was such big pals with Rob and Bob Riley and Toby Roth, why didn't he just pick up the phone and call them or shoot them an e-mail? Or for that matter, his protégé, Bill Canary? And if he was so tight with the Alabama crowd, wouldn't he already know Bob Riley's plans? Also, Rove is widely known to be omniscient, so arguably wouldn't have needed to ask anyone about Riley's intentions.

Probably Rove didn't know if Riley was running because, as he testified quite reasonably, he "had a lot more pressing things on my platter than the Alabama governor's race."

Here again was Rove delivering some perspective -- you might call it basic common sense – that should have been obvious to those at the *New York Times*, *Time* magazine, "60 Minutes," the Judiciary Committee and elsewhere.

———

Siegelman's wish had come true. Karl Rove faced aggressive questioning, under penalty of perjury, from the best lawyer the Judiciary Committee could throw at him.

The transcript was made public in mid-August. Rove's fingerprints were not to be found on the Siegelman prosecution, nor will they ever be.

The best gauge of just how bad it was for Siegelman could be found – or not – in the *New York Times*.

Adam Cohen and the *Times'* opining team weighed in with an editorial called, "More Evidence of a Scandal."

The piece gamely tried to inflate the firing of one of the other eight prosecutors but declared -- I would say, conceded – that "some of the most disturbing revelations concern the firing of David Iglesias, the United States attorney in New Mexico."

The evidence and testimony -- little of it new, none of it earth-shaking -- showed that New Mexico Republicans complained to the White House about Iglesias. They claimed he wasn't prosecuting voting fraud cases – always a major Republican initiative – and not aggressively pursuing criminal cases against some Democratic legislators (at least one of whom was later prosecuted and pleaded guilty to all manner of slimy activities.)

As described earlier, it was that state's Republican senator Pete Domenici who did more than anyone to aggravate for Iglesisas' removal. He called the White House and -- far more seriously -- Attorney General Alberto Gonzales.

The evidence and testimony showed that Rove urged White House counsel Harriet Miers to contact the Justice Department and register the White House's complaints with Iglesias. However, Rove never himself called Justice. In fact, there is no evidence in any of the "Bush Justice" cases that Rover ever called, e-mailed or in any other fashion contacted anyone at the Justice Department.

It may bear repeating that U.S. Attorneys are appointed by presidents and serve at the pleasure of presidents.

Iglesias subsequently wrote a book, "In Justice: Inside the Scandal That Rocked the Bush Administration." In an interview after Rove's testimony, he said that he'd long suspected that Rove's "fingerprints were all over this."

Absent from the *Times'* editorial was the first mention of Don Siegelman.

The editorial page that had done so much to promote the Jill Simpson's tale – which had three times used the term "political hit" in relation to Rove and the Siegelman prosecution – pretended that Rove hadn't been asked about Siegelman.

And the news side, which at that point had published 23 stories about or relating to the Siegelman case since Jill Simpson's affidavit?

There, too, Siegelman was a no-show. A lengthy front-page piece by *Times'* reporters Eric Lichtblau and Eric Lipton was devoted almost entirely to the Iglesias firing. The reporters -- both of whom had bylines above stories about or relating to Siegelman -- were apparently unable to find anything even slightly incriminating in Rove's testimony about Siegelman. If they had, you can be sure it would have been in the story.

After all he'd written, Horton couldn't ignore Rove's testimony on Siegelman. But his offering, "Karl Rove's Convenient Memory Lapses," was, for him, an uninspired piece if, as usual, replete with errors and mischaracterizations. He wrote that documents produced as a result of the subpoenas (probably a reference to the *Southern Political Reporter* newsletters) showed that Rove, "took a keen interest in the case against Siegelman and fully appreciated the political impact of his prosecution – which was essential for Karl Rove's political plans in the Southland."

Lastly, he gave *Harper's* readers a link to the Legal Schnauzer's take on Rove's testimony. Horton touted it as a "careful review of Rove's non-denial denials relating to Siegelman."

———

A few days later, Schnauzer, writing about the same testimony, demonstrated the malleability of the conspiracy theorist.

Rove, as previously noted, had testified that, to the extent he kept up with Alabama politics, it was usually through his former employee, Kitty McCollough. Rove said McCollough sometimes talked to "a lawyer in Birmingham – or in Mobile, named McDonald, you know, friends."

It was an irrelevant piece of information. Schnauzer, though, seized upon it. In, "Karl Rove and His Mysterious Alabama 'Lawyer'," Roger Shuler aka Legal Schnauzer began by asking: "Who in the heck is this McDonald person?"

Schnauzer reported that a "source with strong knowledge of Alabama politics" told him it was Sid McDonald, the successful Arab, Ala., businessman, former legislator and, back when he was active, a prominent figure in state Republican politics.

Sid McDonald's connection to the conspiracy was established, at least for Schnauzer, through his former position as a University of Alabama trustee. Schnauzer posited that it was McDonald, acting at Rove's request, who arranged for Schnauzer to be fired from his job at the University of Alabama at Birmingham. This implies, among other things, that Rove, A) knows who Schnauzer is; B) cares; and C) that Sid McDonald could or would have someone fired if asked by Karl Rove.

Schnauzer suggested that Rove might be secretly controlling the University of Alabama board and that the university was being run by a "right-wing conspiracy."

"If it is Sid McDonald, will investigators check his phone and e-mail records to see what communication he might have had with Rove regarding the Siegelman case and other matters? Could Sid McDonald be called to testify before government investigators?"

The next day, Schnauzer wrote that he'd, uh, been wrong. In a second column, which he called, "Is this Karl Rove's 'Mystery McDonald,'" he unmasked Mobile lawyer Matt McDonald as the "Mystery McDonald."

This time he had it right. Matt McDonald, long active in the tort reform movement, does know Rove from the latter's involvement in the state Supreme Court campaigns in the 1990s.

Schnauzer admitted that linking Sid McDonald to his termination was, "off base." Then he launched into a second conspiracy theory, this one involving the real McDonald. He again urged investigators to subpoena the telephone and e-mail records from McDonald – Matt, not Sid.

The affair of the "Mystery McDonald," demonstrated, not that it needed to be, that all the likes of Schnauzer and Horton need is a name to set them off on a frenzied game of six degrees of separation.

———

A week after the *Times'* editorial, Rove wrote an op-ed in the *Wall Street Journal* asking the paper to apologize for, among other things, repeatedly claiming that he, "personally arranged for Alabama Governor Don Siegelman to be prosecuted."

Rove described Simpson – the *Times'* (and everyone else's) only source connecting him to the Siegelman case -- as "eccentric." He wrote that the Judiciary Committee staff "confided to me that they considered her an unreliable witness."

Simpson hit back. She wrote a letter purportedly addressed to Rove and Rupert Murdoch, whose company owns the *Wall Street Journal*. It wasn't published in the *Journal*, but rather, by the Legal Schnauzer.

Simpson rapped Rove for "completely distorting the truth," and the *Wall Street Journal* for publishing his "lies." She called Rove "delusional" and "a nut job."

The star of the "60 Minutes" investigative bonanza on the Siegelman case concluded by declaring that, with her letter, she had just "socked (Rove) in the nose with the truth."

Kaboom!

Chapter 48
Pardon me!

"This is an extraordinary case. It involves allegations of corruption at the highest levels of Alabama state government. Its resolution has strained the resources of both Alabama and the federal government.... Though the popular culture sometimes asserts otherwise, the virtue of our jury system is that it most often gets it right. This is the great achievement of our system of justice. The jury's verdict commands the respect of this court, and that verdict must be sustained if there is substantial evidence to support it. In our system, the jury decides what the facts are, by listening to the witnesses and making judgments about whom to believe. This they have done, and, though invited to do so, we shall not substitute our judgment for theirs."

-- March 6 decision by the 11th Circuit, upholding all the counts against Scrushy, five of seven counts against Siegelman, and in all likelihood setting in motion Siegelman's return to prison.

"I hope that (Holder) will take a look at some of the other cases that are buried on his desk."

-- Siegelman, expressing irritation with the attorney general after Holder dismissed the case against former Alaska senator Ted Stevens because of prosecutorial misconduct.

On December 9, 2008, the Atlanta-based 11th Circuit Court of Appeals entertained oral arguments on Siegelman and Scrushy's appeals of their convictions. Most of the reporters who covered the trial attended, as did I, having driven up from Mobile. Why, I'm not sure, considering the expense, but I wanted to see it. Adam Nossiter was there, Horton not.

Siegelman was accompanied by his wife and two children, as well as Kenneth "Maze" Marshall, the wheelchair bound veteran who almost never missed a day of trial. Scrushy wasn't permitted to leave prison for the hearing, though his wife Leslie attended. It appeared she'd let a plastic surgeon mess with her pretty face. She looked tougher and meaner, as if her face was uncomfortable from the stretching.

All sides retained ringers who specialize in appellate law. Washington D.C., attorney Sam Heldman argued for Siegelman, and Bruce Rogow, from Miami, for Scrushy. Alex Romano, a Justice Department lawyer who also specialized in appellate arguments, made the government's case.

The defendants had to be disappointed that neither of the two judges on the panel that ordered Siegelman released pending his appeal was on the three-judge panel picked to decide that appeal.

Each of the three somber, robed men was over 60, and two well over it. All were appointed by Republican presidents -- Chief Judge J.L. Edmondson by Ronald Reagan, and, flanking him, Judge Gerald Bard Tjoflat and Senior Judge James C. Hill, both Ford appointees.

The defense teams split duty. Heldman was to use Siegelman's time to argue that the government failed to prove the existence of an explicit quid pro quo between Siegelman and Scrushy regarding the lottery donation and the CON board appointment. Rogow devoted Scrushy's allotment to making the case for a mistrial based on juror misconduct by way of the e-mails. I was surprised that the defendants elected to spend half their allotted time on the juror e-mails, given how hopeless I considered this argument (as, indeed, it proved to be.)

The judges, as Siegelman himself noted after the hearing, had done their homework. With one notable exception they displayed considerable familiarity with the facts of the case and the arguments made in the briefings.

Siegelman's lawyer went first. He was only seconds into his no quid pro quo presentation when Edmondson, the chief judge, delivered a directive that had to send chills through all on the defense side of the courtroom.

"I don't think that's going to be your best argument today," said Edmondson, a lean, toothy man, and as impassive as he was authoritative.

It is said of oral arguments that the tenor and direction of the questions is often a poor guide to what the court is really thinking. But Edmondson's opening directive was just too strong to spin as anything other than bad news for Siegelman and Scrushy. Everyone seemed to immediately recognize that, at the very least, the chief judge had made up his mind on the bribery counts and was putting those in the government's column. Edmondson told the D.C. lawyer that he would be better off spending his time arguing the two "Tim Adams" charges against Siegelman.

Those were the counts, also in Scrushy's guilty column, regarding HealthSouth's hiring of and payments to CON board member Tim Adams. There had been, as Edmondson keenly noticed, no strong evidence tying Siegelman to that scheme.

The apparent good news that the chief judge seemed inclined to reverse those two counts against Siegelman was far outweighed by the implication that he seemed sold on the bribery counts.

One of the more discomforting colloquies for the defendants arose from an apparent error by Judge Hill.

Despite Edmondson's advice, Heldman didn't concede the quid pro quo argument. After all, it accounted for most of the counts against both defendants. In making that case, he belittled the import of Bailey's question to Siegelman -- the pivotal quote in which Bailey asked Siegelman what Scrushy was going to want "for that."

That, of course, was the $500,000 to the lottery foundation, with Siegelman's response, according to Bailey, being, "The CON board."

Hill corrected Heldman. The judge said Bailey's testimony was more ambiguous. He told Heldman that Bailey had actually testified to asking Siegelman, "What's he (Scrushy) going to want?"

The judge offered that if Bailey *had* added "for that" at the end of his question to Siegelman then it would have been far stronger evidence of a quid pro quo. Hill's correction seemed to perplex Heldman. The lawyer surely knew that he'd presented Bailey's testimony correctly. Bailey's actual testimony was: "What in the world is he going to want *for that?*"

But what was Heldman to do? Correct Hill, and in front of all, risk making the case of a quid pro quo against his client?

I wondered – and suppose Heldman did too – if Hill wasn't just messing with him to draw him into acknowledging the power of the statement against his client. Heldman elected not to correct Hill. He reluctantly accepted the gift horse, dead on its feet though it was.

Whether Hill was playing clever with Heldman or mistaken as to the wording of Bailey's question to Siegelman – and I think the latter – Heldman, his client and the rest of those on the defense side had to recognize the implication of Hill's question. Someone – his fellow judges, his law clerk -- was going to correct him, and, in all likelihood, remove for Hill the ambiguity of Bailey's question. (Three months later, when the 11th Circuit issued its opinion, Bailey's testimony – including the ending words, "for that" – was presented accurately and, for the defendants, damningly.)

Of the three judges, one – Tjoflat – said little. His only comment I caught did not portend well for the defendants, or in any event, Siegelman. Heldman was trying to explain for one of the other judges why the October 2001 meeting between Siegelman, Bailey and their two lawyers (when Siegelman wrote the check to Bailey for the rest of the motorcycle) did not constitute a cover-up.

Gruffly, almost under his breath, Tjoflat muttered words to the effect that he wasn't buying that tale.

The hearing lasted about 45 minutes. Out in the hall I asked Helen Hammonds, the "blogger lady" during the trial, what she thought. Helen tended to see things from the defense side and had good relations with Art Leach. She shook her head and smiled. It was, she said, a bad day for Siegelman and Scrushy. If Helen thought that, then indeed it had been.

In a line I suppose was intended to explain to readers why the *New York Times* went to the trouble of covering the hearing, Nossiter wrote that the Siegelman case "has become Exhibit A in the claims of Democrats that the Justice Department under President Bush was politicized."

If those words were true, then Nossiter and the *Times* had unwittingly cleared the Bush Justice Department of being "politicized."

It didn't take a crystal ball to see that Siegelman was in trouble. His appeal was doomed. The politician once again sought a political solution. Barack Obama had of course defeated John McCain in November. Starting in early 2009, there would be a Democrat running the Justice Department. Obama nominated Eric Holder, one of the top Justice Department officials in the Clinton years, to serve as attorney general.

Holder was –at this writing, continues to be – the focus of an intense public relations and lobbying effort, not just by Siegelman, but others as well, notably John Conyers, whose zeal to see the Siegelman case dropped cannot be overstated. Though not a pardon, a decision by Holder for Justice to dismiss the Siegelman case would have the same effect.

———

In January 2009, a month after the appeals hearing, Golden Flake made an appearance. He wrote an e-mail to citizens of Siegelman Nation. He instructed them to call the office of Pennsylvania Sen. Arlen Specter to ask Specter, then still a Republican, to lift his hold on Eric Holder's confirmation as U.S. Attorney General.

"As you know, there is much work to be done by the next Attorney General in investigating the firing of the U.S. Attorneys and Karl Rove's involvement in my prosecution," Siegelman wrote. "The new Attorney General will be able to facilitate the House Judiciary Committee's investigation of the use of the Department of Justice as a political weapon and those who abused their power."

Pardon my French, and my clichés too, but that's called *kissing ass*.

———

Two months later, Holder came to Selma for the 44th anniversary of the historic clash on the Edmund Pettis Bridge between civil rights marchers and bully club wielding law officers. The country's first black attorney general joined Jesse Jackson, Joseph Lowery, Georgia congressman John Lewis and other luminaries who led a crowd over the bridge, then gathered for a service in the Brown Chapel A.M.E. Church.

The day had nothing to do with Siegelman, but that didn't stop him from showing up and trying to steal the show. His supporters carried big red white and blue signs with the message, "Free Don," and chanted, "Free Don Siegelman."

Siegelman, quoted in most of the news stories on the day, said he didn't talk to Holder about his case. He hardly needed to, with his acolytes making a scene and he sitting on the second row in the church service.

A day devoted to the courageous sacrifice of civil rights marchers had instead become, at least to the extent he could make it, Don's day.

———

On March 6, 2009, the three 11th Circuit judges issued a unanimous opinion that kept Scrushy in prison and likely ensured Siegelman's return.

The court upheld all six counts against Scrushy. The judges killed off the two "Tim Adams" counts against Siegelman, but upheld the verdicts on the five remaining charges.

The 68-page opinion was in many ways a defense of the jury system's capacity to weigh circumstantial evidence when considering criminal cases, and, specifically, those involving bribery and public corruption.

In their appeals, Siegelman and Scrushy appeared to try to convince the court that under prevailing law, circumstantial evidence wasn't sufficient to bring much less convict on cases alleging bribery and extortion by public officials. They based that argument on their interpretation of a much-cited Supreme Court ruling on a West Virginia public corruption case called *McCormick*.

The defendants declared that, according to *McCormick*, "only express words of promise overheard by third parties or by means of electronic surveillance" can satisfy the evidentiary need for proving bribery.

Lawyers for Siegelman and Scrushy pointed out that there was no such recorded or first-person evidence presented to the jury. And they were right. There wasn't. They claimed that Bailey's testimony was the only evidence of an explicit *quid pro quo connecting the* $500,000 and Siegelman's appointment of Scrushy to the CON Board.

They argued that no reasonable juror could have concluded the existence of a criminal quid pro quo from the evidence at trial.

In its ruling, the 11th Circuit presented the defendants position, followed by: "We disagree."

Then, and not for the first or last time, the three judges launched into a vigorous defense of the right and ability of juries to weigh circumstantial evidence in such cases.

The judges rejected the defendants' interpretation of *McCormick*, writing that the ruling on the West Virginia case "does not impose such a stringent standard" of evidence in quid pro quo prosecutions.

They cited a 1992 case called *Evans*, decided since *McCormick*. In that case, U.S. Supreme Court Justice Anthony Kennedy wrote a concurring opinion declaring that there was no requirement that prosecutors present evidence of "an agreement memorialized in writing" or even first person testimony by someone who overheard a public official agreeing to an illegal quid pro quo pact.

Kennedy wrote that if that were the standard, then corrupt public officials and those bribing them could "escape criminal liability through 'knowing winks and nods.'"

In upholding the lottery foundation counts, the judges didn't limit their argument to a defense of the jury system. They also extolled the abundance and persuasiveness of the circumstantial evidence presented by the government in proving the CON Board scheme and, for Siegelman, the motorcycle/obstruction count.

The court was swayed by, among other things, the evidence showing the lengths to which both defendants went to conceal the two $250,000 contributions. On Scrushy's side, that entailed his threat to fire the investment banking firm UBS if it didn't contribute $250,000 to the foundation; and the eventual solution for the money to come from Integrated Health in Maryland.

The judges recited Mike Martin's testimony about a conversation with Scrushy in which the boss said that for HealthSouth to "have some influence or a spot on the CON Board," it had to help Siegelman raise money for the lottery campaign; and that if the company did contribute it "would be assured a seat on the CON Board."

The judges presented numerous portions of trial testimony, including Martin's statement that HealthSouth was "making a contribution . . . in exchange for a spot on the CON Board;" and Bill McGahan's testimony about being told by Martin and Scrushy that UBS had to donate to the Alabama foundation.

On several key points the 11th Circuit turned to the testimony of Darren Cline, the fundraising consultant hired by Siegelman to work on the lottery campaign. The court recited Cline's memorable line that, "if the governor wanted to get something done, then (Bailey) went ahead – blindly went ahead and did it."

It singled out Cline's testimony that Siegelman "called the shots" on the lottery campaign; that Siegelman told Cline that Scrushy arranged the $250,000 check from Integrated Health; and that Siegelman said another $250,000 would be coming later.

In the court's opinion, that and more buttressed Bailey's story that Scrushy agreed from the start to give $500,000, as opposed to $250,000 and, later, a separate decision to give the other $250,000. In other words, the two checks were parts of the same whole, and that wasn't just Bailey talking.

The judges emphasized the testimony showing how important it was for HealthSouth to have a seat on the CON board. Some of that came from Loree Skelton, who, as the court remarked, testified that she was "responsible for HealthSouth political donations" but was not told about the two $250,000 payments.

Skelton, the judges remarked, didn't learn about the $500,000 until 2002, and only then through the media.

The largely un-refuted evidence showing Siegelman's efforts to conceal the two $250,000 donations appeared to carry considerable weight with the court. The judges laid out the foundation's requirement to report its donations and expenditures to the Alabama secretary of state and its failure to abide by that requirement until more than two years later.

They remarked that the foundation only filed reports because, "Alabama newspapers questioned" the failure of the foundation and the Democratic Party to properly report their financial activities to the Alabama secretary of state office, prompting involvement by the attorney general's office.

(Not to correct the 11ᵗʰ Circuit, but "newspapers" should have been singular!)

The court made it abundantly clear that bribery charges can be brought in cases involving campaign contributions, regardless of whether a public official enjoys a personal financial benefit. Nevertheless, the 11ᵗʰ Circuit reminded the defendants that there was evidence of personal benefit in this case. The $730,789 loan to the foundation that was used to repay the Alabama Democratic Party was "personally and unconditionally guaranteed by Siegelman," the court noted.

"There was another personal guarantor, but each was individually liable."

The judges reminded the defendants that "the close relationship in time between the first check and Siegelman's appointment of Scrushy was also some evidence of *quid pro quo.*"

And then: "In sum, the evidence was sufficient such that a reasonable juror could have concluded that Siegelman and Scrushy explicitly agreed to a corrupt *quid pro quo*, thereby proving the bribery, conspiracy and the two related mail fraud counts."

The 11ᵗʰ Circuit was unmoved by the "juror misconduct" element of the appeal. The judges agreed with the government's argument that Fuller went to considerable lengths to investigate what were, after all, anonymously sent e-mails.

Nor was it swayed by Siegelman's defense on the obstruction count. That, the court noted, amounted to little more than an attack on the credibility of Nick Bailey and Lanny Young, and failed to explain away the multitude of checks and other evidence upon which the charge was based.

The judges meticulously laid out the documentary evidence – the $9,200 from Lanny to Nick to Siegelman by way of the check to Lori Allen – then offered excerpts of testimony by Bailey and Young. One regarded the meeting at the office of Siegelman lawyer Bobby Segall, where Bailey wrote Siegelman the $2,973.35 check as the purported balance on the sale of the motorcycle.

Government: *What was going on here?*
Bailey: *We made a decision to finalize the agreement we made regarding the motorcycle early on, and this was to finish that. We met at the Governor's attorney's office and with my attorney, and that's when I finished paying the Governor in full for the motorcycle to carry out the plan that we had entered into probably 12 to 18 months earlier.*
Government: *And what was that plan?*
Bailey: *To disguise the $9,200 from Lanny to the Governor.*

The judges then eviscerated Siegelman's obstruction appeal. They wrote that the jury was "entitled to infer from the sham check transaction in Bailey's lawyer's presence that Siegelman intended to mislead the lawyer into believing that the transaction was legitimate, that Bailey had, indeed, purchased the motorcycle from him, and that the check was final payment."

"As the 'unwitting third party,' the lawyer would be in a position factually to support the cover up since Siegelman clearly knew that there was a 'possibility' that the federal investigators would come asking."

Repeat: *Sham check transaction.* Those are the 11th Circuit's words, not Bailey's or Young's.

The court declared that Siegelman's argument against the obstruction charge mirrored those he "made against his convictions on virtually all the other counts – that the evidence in this case was not perfect, that it relied too heavily on circumstances and required the jury to draw inferences from those circumstances that might have been drawn differently by different jurors."

And then, this refutation of the basis of much of Siegelman's appeal:

"Siegelman's contention throughout his brief that 'there was no evidence' to support a particular inference too often meant merely that there was no evidence other than Bailey or Young's testimony," the court wrote. "While Siegelman may not approve that the testimony of coconspirators was sufficient to support the jury's findings of fact, the jury was free to disregard or disbelieve it.

They believed it.

———

I can't speak to the impact on appeals courts of egregious, nasty, unwarranted attacks on trial judges, but I doubt those made against Fuller by Scrushy's lawyers helped him or his co-defendant. Included in the Scrushy appeal was a request that the 11th Circuit order a new trial based on Fuller's failure to recuse because of his financial interest in Doss Aviation.

The judges wrote that the financial information about Fuller upon which the recusal motion was based had been "readily available" prior to trial from Fullers' required disclosures. Therefore, the recusal motion was "untimely."

Then, with apparent scorn, declared that Scrushy's post-trial demand had "all the earmarks of an eleventh-hour ploy based upon his dissatisfaction with the jury's verdict and the judge's post-trial rulings."

At some point you have to think: Either the lawyers are stupid, or their client is forcing them to be stupid, and they like the money too much not to go along with him.

"It's the story of my life," Siegelman told Adam Nossiter, who wrote the *Times'* story. "I end up in fights all the time. We're taking it to the next level."

It was Nossiter's final story on the Siegelman case. Several weeks later he took a new position, in Senegal, to oversee the *Times'* coverage of West Africa.

———

Because two of the counts against Siegelman were dismissed, he would need to be resentenced. Louis Franklin wrote federal probation officers recommending that Siegelman be sentenced to 20 years. As required, the probation office provided a copy of the letter to Siegelman's lawyers, who gave it to the Associated Press.

I considered their demand for 30 years on the first sentencing to have been a grave error, but this time, was indifferent. They knew there was no way Fuller was going to Siegelman to 20 years after sentencing him to seven when there were two more charges on the table.

I think Franklin and Feaga were making a point: That they felt the words and actions by Siegelman and his lawyers since the trial had been despicable, and they didn't give a damn about what the defendants and the national media and the Judiciary Committee and all the rest thought about them.

———

After the 11th Circuit ruling, lawyers for Siegelman and Scrushy requested a re-hearing before the entire court. Such appeals are commonly made but rarely granted. On May 15, the court denied the request. The *Birmingham News* reported the decision, as did the AP's Bob Johnson. Our paper, and presumably others, used Bob's wire story. To my knowledge, the only other paper in the country to produce its own story on the matter was the *New York Times*.

It was the paper's 21st news story on Siegelman in the two years since Jill Simpson's affidavit. It was written by John Schwartz, the *Times*' national legal correspondent, who wrote many of the Siegelman stories after Nossiter left and was, apparently, like-minded.

Of the three stories, only the New York paper looked outward for someone to say how awful a development was the 11th Circuit's ruling.

Here, readers, I will let you in on a little secret. When a reporter has a bias it is sometimes revealed at the very end of the story. One way: Find an "expert" or partisan who you know will agree with your take, and present his or her comments. It's a real give-away when a reporter concludes a story with such a quote. Nossiter was a practicioner of the art. So too Schwartz. He sought wrap-up commentary from the dependable Robert Abrams. Siegelman's old friend blasted away, railing on the prosecution request that Siegelman be sentenced to 20 years.

"This is another example of the outrageous and unfathomable conduct of the prosecutors in this case ... It is so crass that it openly displays the animus and partisan agenda in this prosecution," Abrams said.

End of story.

———

When the 11th Circuit declined to re-consider their appeals, lawyers for Siegelman and Scrushy announced their clients' intentions to appeal to the U.S. Supreme Court. They avowed that chances were good that the nation's highest court would consider the case because it hinged on an important point of law: What level of proof must a court and jury consider before finding guilt in a case involving campaign donations?

Siegelman asked that he be allowed to remain free pending the appeal to the Supreme Court. The 11th Circuit granted him that wish and ordered re-sentencing to be put on hold pending the appeal. Scrushy, however, had to remain in Beaumont.

———

On April 1, 2009, Attorney General Holder opened a new front for Siegelman, not that it was his intention to do so.

That day, Holder asked U.S. District Judge Emmet G. Sullivan to dismiss the case against former Alaska Senator Ted Stevens.

In October 2008, a Washington D.C. jury found the 85-year-old Stevens guilty of seven charges related to his receipt of some $250,000 in gifts and services from an oil services contractor. Stevens remained a candidate for re-election, but, saddled with a conviction, lost a close race in November to the Democratic mayor of Anchorage.

During and after trial, Judge Sullivan rebuked the Justice Department prosecutors for letting a witness leave town in mid-trial; submitting incorrect evidence; and failing to turn over some witness statements to Stevens' lawyers.

After the change in administrations, Holder appointed a new team of lawyers to the case for what should have been the fight to defeat Stevens' appeals. The new prosecutors discovered statements by a key witness that contradicted his trial testimony and which were not divulged to Stevens' lawyers.

Judge Sullivan was so disturbed that he took that he appointed a special prosecutor to investigate the Steven's prosecutors. Soon after, Holder asked the judge to dismiss the case against Stevens, which Sullivan quickly did.

In dismissing the charges, neither Holder nor the Justice Department was declaring that Stevens was innocent. In fact, the evidence suggests the jury got it right. However, the rules governing criminal prosecutions demand that prosecutors turn over potentially exculpatory evidence to defendants. This crucial requirement was violated and subsequently discovered. Thus, Stevens was set free.

You won't find Stevens among those victims of "Bush Justice" touted by the likes of Dan Abrams. Stevens wasn't merely a Republican – he was the longest serving Republican senator in United States history. He was indicted on the eve of a tough election battle, with Republicans desparately needing every senate seat. Everything about his case ran counter to the characterization of the Bush Justice Department as a tool to further Republican political interests.

If Stevens had been a Democrat, he, not Don Siegelman, would have been the "selective prosecution" poster boy.

Were Karl Rove to have wielded the influence over the Justice Department that the *New York Times*, the Judiciary Committee and others alleged, there never would have been a Ted Stevens case. Rove – heck, Bush himself -- would have ordered it stopped.

Team Siegelman's response to Holder's dropping the Stevens case was in its way impressive. It was as if the captain yelled all hands on deck, and everyone raced to their stations.

On the afternoon of Holder's decision, Siegelman gave an interview with Zachary Roth of the *TPM Muckracker*, the investigative arm of the reasonably respected and certainly well-known *Talking Points Memo* blog. Siegelman said the evidence of prosecutorial misconduct in his case would, "dwarf the allegations in the Stevens case."

The story ran under the whiny headline, "Siegelman: Stevens case is dropped, so why not mine?" This was a ridiculous proposition that TPM clearly endorsed.

Horton, nothing if not fast, posted a column that afternoon praising Holder. Then the *Harper's* writer declared that the misconduct in the Stevens' case was "trivial" to that which occurred in other "political prosecutions," he'd written about – namely, those of Siegelman and Mississippi trial lawyer Paul Minor, who, whether his supporters like to hear this or not, gave money to one of that state's many open-handed judges.

The next day, Legal Schnauzer chipped in with, "The Curious Juxtaposition of Ted Stevens and Don Siegelman."

It happened to Stevens, therefore it happened to Siegelman. That, in essence, was the new public relations/legal avenue applied by Siegelman and Scrushy. Various records indicate that Scrushy was funding most of the background research used by both men in their increasingly desperate legal briefs accusing the prosecutors, Judge Fuller, the jurors, secretaries, paralegals and pretty much every employee of the U.S. Attorneys Office of being evil gremlin co-conspirators.

All these efforts failed abysmally in court, where reality prevailed. But with left-wing Internet sites and the New York Times, they grew wings.

Scrushy, the more notorious and unlikable of the pair, was frequently left out or minimized in the media reports. It obvious that a win for Siegelman, regardless of how achieved, would bode well for the dour co-defendant.

Two days after Holder's request to drop the Stevens case, Vince Kilborn leapfrogged the entire Justice Department and for that matter, the federal court system, by going straight to the attorney general. Kilborn's letter laid out the purported evidence of prosecutorial misconduct in Siegelman's case and asked the nation's top law enforcement officer to do for Siegelman what he'd just done for Stevens.

John Conyers -- well on his way to filling up Holder's mailbox with pro-Siegelman letters and demands to investigate the latest red herring drummed up by Team Siegelman – parroted Kilborn's request with one of his own. It bore the seal of the House Judiciary Committee and was very official and authoritative.

The only reason anybody knew about Kilborn's letter was because Siegelman's people distributed it to the media, the court of public opinion, as always, their preferred forum.

It's one thing for desperate, say-anything defendants, their lawyers and partisan bloggers and politicians to torture logic. It's another when the country's leading newspaper tags along.

Editorial struck first, with, "Mr. Holder and the Ted Stevens Case," published on April 2, the day after Holder killed the Stevens' case. *Times'* opiners began by lavishing praise on the new attorney general for cashiering the Stevens prosecution, despite never before having agitated for it. Then -- the actual purpose of the piece? – the paper urged Holder not to "stop with this case."

"Don Siegelman, the former governor of Alabama, and Paul Minor, a prominent Mississippi trial lawyer, have charged that Justice Department prosecutors engaged in unethical behavior in cases that led to their convictions, Both men claim that they were singled out for prosecution because of their affiliation with the Democratic Party."

A reasonable interpretation: The Justice Department should re-examine and consider dropping every public corruption case in which defendants claim they were prosecuted for political reasons. Were that so, almost every public corruption conviction in the past the past 20 years would need to be reviewed. Claims of political martyrdom by public corruption defendants and their lawyers are *de rigueur,* to the point where a politician defendant could almost claim malpractice against a lawyer for not howling politics in the media.

On April 22, 2009, the *Times'* news side waded in with, "Review of Conviction Sought." Prompting this was the third but not final media splash by Robert Abrams, Grant Woods and Siegelman's other pals in the ex-attorneys general community. The number of signees had climbed to 75, up from 54 the last time around.

"We believe that if prosecutorial misconduct is found, as in the case of Senator Ted Stevens, then dismissal should follow in this case as well," the group declared in yet another letter bound for the harried Holder.

Kilborn was quoted saying that three top Justice Department officials who were held in contempt in the Stevens case participated in the Siegelman case. Their names -- Patty Stemler, William Welch and Brenda Morris -- were new to me, but apparently, simply by virtue of their positions, each had some minor supervisory role in the Siegelman case, as they no doubt had with hundreds of other Justice Department prosecutions throughout the country.

One rather substantial difference is that, in the Steven's case, the prosecutor's failings so enraged the trial judge that he took the extreme measure of appointing a prosecutor to investigate the prosecutors.

There were not – will never be – any such findings by the trial judge in the Siegelman case, by the Justice Department, or for that matter, the 11th Circuit. It doesn't matter how hard Siegelman and Scrushy's political researchers and private investigators try to dig up bogus affidavits and irrelevant red herrings; how loud howl the mouths of Siegelman and Kilborn; how many letters John Conyers writes to Eric Holder; or how many strident opinion pieces that the *New York Times* and Legal Schnauzer publish.

There was no prosecutorial misconduct. No judicial misconduct. No juror misconduct. The misconduct was, continues to be, by the defendants, their lawyers, and those in the employ of both.

Patty Stemler's sin in the Siegelman case?

She wrote the July 2008 letter disclosing to the defendants that postal inspectors had determined that the juror e-mails were frauds. Again, the postal inspectors review was sought by U.S. Marshals after the "e-mail bandit" sent the bogus e-mails to co-workers of jurors Katie Langer and Sam Hendrix, and both complained. It was a matter of court security, of protecting jurors from post-trial harassment.

"Here we are minding our own business and this Ted Stevens thing comes out — and some of the same cast of characters are in the Siegelman case, as it turns out," Kilborn told the *Times,* which actually used the quote.

God bless Vince Kilborn, and all the power to a hometown boy making it big with the *New York Times.* But somebody needs to tell the people at that paper up yonder that down here in the Heart of Dixie, Vince is regarded by reporters and certainly those in the legal community as a highly effective trial lawyer but, all the same, an inveterate blow-hard. Vince's charm is that he knows it. The *Times* does not.

The story did reflect that a *Times'* reporter asked Kilborn if he could cite any wrongdoing by William Welch or Brenda Morris in the Siegelman case, and reported his inability to do so.

That didn't stop the editorial page from swinging for the fences in the simply titled, "The Siegelman Case." It was the paper's 18th opinion piece since Jill Simpson's affidavit and second since Holder dropped the Stevens' prosecution. The editorial team led by Andrews Rosenthal cut straight to the chase:

Attorney General Eric Holder's recent decision to drop all of the charges against Ted Stevens, the former Republican senator from Alaska, because of prosecutorial misconduct raises an important question: What about Don Siegelman? A bipartisan group of 75 former state attorneys general has written to Mr. Holder asking him to take a fresh look at the former Alabama governor's case. He should do so right away.

The *Times* declared that "according to the Siegelman camp, at least three of the same officials who have been accused of prosecutorial misconduct in the Siegelman case were involved in Mr. Siegelman's prosecution."

"If true, this alone would seem to justify a thorough investigation of the case."

The piece recited the litany of complaints by Siegelman and his choir. Leura Canary and her husband, Bill – again referred to as a "Republican *operative*" -- took their 10,000[th] whack. Siegelman's insistence that "the case against him was politically motivated" was treated as if it were gospel. Also trotted out was the old saw that Siegelman was targeted because he "stood a good chance of once again being elected governor."

In topping off their argument that Holder should retroactively end the Siegelman prosecution, the *Times* presented by far the strongest piece of evidence linking Karl Rove to Siegelman's prosecution.

"A Republican lawyer in Alabama, Jill Simpson, has said that she heard Ms. Canary's husband, William Canary, say that he had discussed the prosecution with Karl Rove, the senior White House political adviser."

This was, mind you, April 2009. The authors of that editorial can be assumed to have watched on "60 Minutes" as Simpson told about bird-dogging Siegelman for naked pictures on Rove's behalf, and her follow-up performance on Dan Abrams show. Surely, given the attention to the case by the *Times* editorial staff, those writers working the Siegelman story read Simpson's testimony to the Judiciary Committee.

And still, the masters of the most important editorial page in the country if not the world were touting Jill Simpson as a viable witness for the conspiracy pitting Karl Rove and so many others against a washed-up former Alabama governor.

The problem isn't so much their ideology, it's their judgment. I'm tempted to question their intelligence but their resumes are quite impressive.

Epilogue

In December 2008, **Lanny Young** was released 11 months before the scheduled end of his two-year sentence. Louis Franklin asked Judge Fuller to free Young in part for safety reasons. Young, who was serving his time in an Arkansas prison, was placed in isolation after being threatened and extorted by gang members who learned of his cooperation with the government against Siegelman.

He was ordered to complete six months of home confinement and pay $389,781 in restitution to the state and to the Internal Revenue Service. In a story reporting Young's release, his lawyer declined to say where Young was living, and said his client was trying to put his troubled behind him.

Nick Bailey was released two months earlier after serving one year of his 18-month sentence. Stan Pate, the Tuscaloosa developer and Siegelman supporter, picked Bailey up at the penitentiary in Atlanta and took him to Birmingham, where Bailey served several months in a halfway house. Bailey, now 41, is again working for Pate – one of many reasons to believe that the Siegelman devotee is and will remain forever in the thrall of the former governor.

In the summer of 2009 **Paul Hamrick** left the Joe Perkins-led Matrix Group, where he'd been since leaving the Siegelman administration. He formed his own political consulting firm, called Paul Hamrick LLC.

Carrie Kurlander, after rising up the ranks at Alabama Power, is now a vice president of the utility's parent, the Southern Company, where she oversees the company's communications operations.

Rip Andrews, after graduating from Alabama law school with most of the top awards in his class, joined a leading Birmingham plaintiffs firm. If I ever see Rip's name on a ballot, and I hope I do, he will get my vote.

Ted Hosp returned to the Maynard Cooper law firm. His biography on the firm web-page now lists, "White Collar Criminal Practice," and, "Compliance and Investigations," among his areas of practice.

Scott Horton continues to write for *Harper's*, and contributes to other publications, including the *American Lawyer* and the *Daily Beast*, the web-site created by former *New Yorker* editor Tina Brown. He also remains a lecturer at Columbia Law School. If Siegelman's appeal to the Supreme Court fails and Eric Holder doesn't save his bacon, I would back an arrangement whereby Horton could serve Siegelman's time. That way, Siegelman could continue to entertain us with his zingers about Karl Rove's fingerprints and bloody gloves and Horton could take Siegelman's place as America's all-time top-ranked political prisoner.

On Aug.18, 2009, the long, lucrative and dodgy career of another player in the G.H. Construction scandal came to a crashing end. **Bill Blount** pleaded guilty to showering some $235,000 in bribes and gifts on Birmingham Mayor Larry Langford back when Langford was the chairman of the Jefferson County Commission. In turn, Langford made sure Blount's investment banking firm won placement on billions of dollars in county bond deals to fund sewer upgrades.

Blount Parrish collected $7.1 million in fees, much of it from the controversial, fee-laden "interest rate swap" bond deals blamed for Jefferson County's financial crisis. In August the county laid off 1,000 workers as part its last-ditch efforts to avoid filing the largest municipal bankruptcy in U.S. history.

With his plea, Blount admitted to funneling bribes to Langford through political consultant and lobbyist Al LaPierre. Like Blount, LaPierre is a former official with the state Democratic Party. He served as its executive director from 1982 to 1995.

Among other things, Blount agreed to testify that Langford approached him in 2003 with a request for $69,000. Blount wrote a check to LaPierre, who in turn paid Langford.

The seemingly hyperactive, say-anything mayor doesn't deny getting the money, but called it loans and gifts from friends. A not unsubstantial chunk of the Blount money was used to pay for debts rung up by Langford's in expanding his famously extravagant wardrobe. "I'm a kind of a clothes person. I like clothes," Langford told lawyers for the Securities and Exchange Commission in explaining his need for loans and gifts.

LaPierre, who Blount paid about $400,000 for his assistance, pleaded before Blount, presumably forcing Blount's hand. Blount fended off numerous investigations in his day, and his decision to plead guilty was a major state story.

He agreed to testify against Langford and repay $1 million in ill-gotten profits. In return, prosecutors agreed to recommend a maximum sentence of four years in prison.

Langford likened himself to Siegelman, saying the case against him was part of the Republican scheme to bring down leading Alabama Democrats. "It's obvious that's what it is," he said.

When considered along with the Siegelman scandals and the endemic corruption within the leadership of two-year system and the legislature, the cases arising from Jefferson County's sewer program – both the widespread bribery in the construction contracts as well as the financing – are more than enough to earn Alabama a number one ranking.

Scoot over, Louisiana, take a back seat New Jersey. Alabama has earned its number one ranking. Not in college football (though maybe that too), but public corruption. Almost without fail, it's been the party of the people – the Democrats – doing the stealing.

I wish it wasn't so, but the facts are what they are.

In June 2009, **John Conyers'** wife – Detroit city councilwoman Monica Conyers – pleaded guilty to extorting bribes in return for supporting companies with business before the city. She did it old style, taking cash hand-offs in a parking lot. News reports noted that John Conyers also provided assistance to a waste firm that was the source of some of that cash. Prosecutors insisted there was no evidence of criminal activity by the congressman, who lives separately from his wife and is rarely seen publicly with her.

The federal investigation lasted some two years, beginning when Bush was president. During those same two years, Conyers used his position as chairman of the House Judiciary Committee to hammer the Justice Department for "selective prosecution" of Democrats. The Siegelman case was of course lead dog in that farce.

In light of Monica Conyers' prosecution, the Judiciary Committee's overheated probe into "selective prosecution" seems tainted not just by bad facts and a reliance on the likes of Jill Simpson and Scott Horton, but a conflict on the part of the man leading it.

Katie Langer, that most abused of jurors, graduated magna cum laude from Montgomery's Jones School of Law School in 2009, finishing third out of her class of 76. In her senior year, she led a three-person team from Jones that finished second out of 187 teams in the National Appellate Advocacy Competition, which is run by the American Bar Association. She was named the fifth best advocate in the competition that included teams from the likes of Duke University. In October 2009, she won her first trial.

In August 2009, **Jill Simpson** parted ways with her lawyer, Priscilla Duncan, threw in the towel on two lawsuits and assumed representation of herself in a third, fairly straightforward debt case that will likely lead to a substantial judgment against her. If Simpson ever decides to tell the truth, it will be one helluva story.

In May 2009, **Richard Scrushy** returned home to Alabama, if not freedom, to testify in a lawsuit brought against him by HealthSouth shareholders. The plaintiffs were suing him for the entire $2.6 billion lost by the company in the wake of the accounting scandal.

On his best day Scrushy wasn't worth anything close to $2.6 billion, but even a partial victory by the plaintiffs was enough to break him.

Curiously, Scrushy agreed to a bench trial. The case, in state court, was heard and decided by Jefferson County Circuit Judge Allwin E. Horn. In an early ruling, back in 2006, Horn ordered Scrushy to pay back, with interest, the performance bonuses paid him based on the fraudulent profits. That came to $52 million.

It was, by all accounts, more subdued than the 2005 criminal trial. Scrushy's wife Leslie was a daily attendee, but the preacher-backers stayed away and the press coverage was lighter. Most of the testimony presented by the plaintiffs was through video depositions of the former HealthSouth officials who had pleaded guilty to participating in the fraud. There was little new, but a few fun facts emerged. The plaintiffs' lawyers played a video of 3rd Faze, the HealthSouth-funded girl group managed by Scrushy, and elicited testimony revealing that Scrushy had spent more than $4,000 in company money on breast enhancement surgery for one of the young singers.

"Are boob jobs for a girl band a violation of (HealthSouth's) compliance code?" plaintiffs' lawyer John Somerville asked Daryl Brown, a former HealthSouth board member and defense witness.

The plaintiffs' attorneys also played Judge Horn a video of the Scrushy-led, HealthSouth funded country music band, "Dallas County Line." This induced sniggers from the lawyer-dominated courtroom crowd.

The video was brilliantly described by Kyle Whitmire in the *Birmingham Weekly*: "In cutoff sleeves and a cowboy hat, Scrushy crooned 'Honk if You Love to Honky Tonk' with the same unabashed narcissism that's made eight seasons of American Idol possible and popular."

Birmingham News business reporter Michael Tomberlin used the occasion to interview Macey Taylor, a session musician hired to play in Scrushy's band and subsequently given a job at HealthSouth. Among Taylor's contributions to Scrushy lore: He told Tomberlin that during rehearsals, Scrushy arranged for video cameras and giant screen to be set up so the CEO singer could watch himself in real time.

After a trip to Nashville to record tracks, Scrushy became convinced that "his inability to sing the high notes was due to the high altitudes he experienced in his frequent plane trips," Tomberlin wrote.

"Richard had the pilot fly much lower than usual in order to protect his voice," Taylor said.

Anyone expecting a chastened, prison-weakened Scrushy to concede an iota of responsibility for the massive accounting fraud was disappointed. Under friendly questioning from his own lawyers, then rougher treatment from the plaintiffs' attorneys, Scrushy stuck with his story that he thought all was fine and dandy and that the company was kicking major ass until the FBI raided HealthSouth in 2003. Underlings, he said, hoodwinked him.

Scrushy told Horn it "was ridiculous what was done to this company" by his vice presidents and finance people. When asked about the breast job for the 3rd Faze singer, Scrushy said the girl became ill on tour as a result of complications from her previous implants. The new additions were a medical emergency, he said.

In mid-June 2009, Horn issued the ruling that promises to do to Scrushy's finances what the Siegelman case did to his freedom. He found that Scrushy participated in the accounting fraud. Additionally, Horn ruled that Scrushy funneled HealthSouth money to other companies with which he had a financial interest; profited from insider trading; and collected bonuses that would not have been available if not for the false profits created by the fraud.

"Scrushy knew of and actively participated in the fraud," wrote Horn. More than that, the judge found that Scrushy was "the CEO of the fraud."

Since Horn's ruling, it's been one indignity after another for Scrushy, with the plaintiffs' lawyers auctioning off his boats and houses and battling with him and his wife Leslie over assets missing, hidden or denied by the Scrushys.

HealthSouth shares rose 51 cents on the day of the Horn's ruling, to $13.02. The company, while smaller than in Scrushy's heyday, had returned to profitability, and that, too, is part of the Scrushy story. The rough-around-the-edges country boy from Selma spotted an unserved niche in the healthcare industry, created a business model to serve it, and that model has survived.

In mid-August 2009, and for the second year in a row, Siegelman appeared at Netroots, the national convention of **liberal bloggers**. Siegelman, treated like Moses, opened by telling the crowd that he'd just run into Valerie Jarrett, a senior advisor to President Obama. Siegelman reported telling Jarrett, "It's time for Dr. Obama to perform surgery on Rove appointed attorneys."

"That ended the discussion," said Siegelman, drawing laughs from the audience.

Jarrett, or in any event, according to Siegelman, told him that it was up to bloggers and Democratic activists to "bring it on" and build grassroots support for Siegelman. Siegelman told the Netroots crowd that he would do just that. He was good to his word, creating a link on DonSiegelman.Org called, **"FireRoveProsecutors.com."**

It was a letter ripping into Rove, the Canaries and – chutzpah time – Obama. The new president got it for not cleaning house at the Justice Department fast enough for Siegelman. The site provides supporters a means to forward the letter to Ms. Jarrett at the White House.

If reality is at all defined by the on-line encyclopedia **Wikipedia,** then give Jill Simpson and Scott Horton their due. The long entry on Siegelman provides the basics on his political career, but most of it devoted to the vast conspiracy, and from a decidedly pro-Siegelman point of view. High school and college students assigned term papers on Alabama's 51st governor are going to be outraged at what Karl Rove and those other Republicans did to him.

(These young impressionable readers will start off by getting his name wrong. Siegelman is the rare Don whose actual first name is Don. Not, in other words, Donald. Wikipedia shouldn't feel bad. The *New York Times* gets it wrong all the time.)

Some but my no means all of the conspiracy-related Wikipedia subheads are: "Partiality of the Jury," about the juror e-mails and other juror sins; "Testimony of Star Witness," a Horton-flavored take on Nick Bailey's testimony; "Federal Communications Commission Investigation," about the "60 Minutes" blackout; and "Public Reaction," which tells, among other things, about the support from all those former attorney generals.

The longest section, "Karl Rove connection," concludes:

Simpson's house burned down soon after she began whistleblowing, and Simpson's car was driven off the road by a private investigator and wrecked. As a result of the timing of these incidents, Simpson said, "Anytime you speak truth to power, there are great risks. I've been attacked," explaining she felt a "moral obligation" to speak up.

Scott Horton is the only journalist introduced by name, with Wikipedia presenting his take on the "60 Minutes," blackout.

The usual suspects are well represented in the, "References," and, "External Links," at the bottom of the entry. Those include links to Adam Zagorin's work for *Time*; the *New York Times* entire Siegelman oeuvre; the same for Horton's at *Harper's*; even three links to the reporting on the conspiracy by Larisa Alexandrovna and "Raw Story."

DonSiegelman.Org is the first "external link" given. The mean-spirited propagandists who authored Siegelman entry included, "The Dixie Mafia's Contract on America." That's the story on the web-site of John Caylor, "reporting" that Mark Fuller ran drugs for the Contras in the 1980s.

There is some self-reference going on here. If you go to DonSiegelman.Org, you will find a link to "One Shot Coverage," where people new to the scandal can find good summaries. These innocents directed to links leading to, "Rabbi Yonah's blog, *Wikipedia*, video at TPM (the Talking Points Memo web-site) and more."

In mid-August, **Siegelman** and **Scrushy** filed their appeals with the Supreme Court. Their arguments mirrored those made to and rejected by the 11th Circuit, chiefly: That circumstantial evidence is not sufficient to prove the bribery-related counts against the pair.

The greatest obstacle faced by Siegelman and Scrushy is the law of averages. Each year the Supreme Court receives some 7,000 appeals. Of those, about 100 are considered. The court generally takes cases only when the law and the facts are such that a decision could provide clarity to a law or set of laws that the nation's lower courts are struggling with.

Assuming that evidentiary standards in public corruption cases require clarifying – and there is some indication that they might -- it seems unlikely that the Supreme Court would choose this case to provide that clarity. For one thing, the 11th Circuit's dismissal of the appeal was powerfully written and argued.

As this goes to print, the government has yet to file a reply brief. In all likelihood Siegelman and Scrushy won't learn until early 2010 if the court will consider their appeal.

In late September, the **Robert Abrams** group struck for the fourth time and second in a matter of months. The tally had grown to 91 **former attorneys general,** each of whom signed a brief to the U.S. Supreme Court in support of Siegelman's appeal.

"It's an awesome statement," said Abrams. "Never before, in the history of this nation, have former attorneys general banded together in unity before the courts of this country in such great number."

Another perspective: Never before, in the history of the nation, have so many former attorneys general banded together in unity to support extortion and obstruction of justice.

About 4-5ths were Democrats, and – a sign that the numbers were thinning -- two of the signees had been convicted of crimes, and two others resigned in the midst of scandals.

There were, in the end, too many red herrings to address in this book, though one, I suppose, must be dealt with, if for no other reason than *Time*, the *New York Times*, John Conyers, Horton and Schnauzer made such a big deal out the allegations by Tamara Grimes, who in the past year supplanted Jill Simpson as a pro-Siegelman source and newsmaker.

Two lengthy investigations by Justice Department officials from out of state demolished her charges, most all of which were based on second, third or fourth-hand rumor and gossip, and none, even if true, were serious. The rumor that was treated as a big deal by Adam Nossiter and the *Times* was Grimes' claim that jurors sent notes to the prosecution during trial asking about an FBI agent who some of the jurors allegedly thought was cute.

The "note" rumor, it turned out, started after someone played a joke on the FBI agent, Keith Baker, telling him that some the jurors thought he was cute. By the time it got to Grimes – who was nowhere near the courthouse during the trial -- the joke had evolved to notes going from jurors to the prosecution asking if Baker was married. (He is, and has a big ring for all to see.)

"In summary, Ms. Grimes allegations have little basis in fact but, as rumors frequently do, grew from humble factual beginnings into unrecognizable detailed and distorted factual form," concluded department lawyers in a September 2008 report that should have been the end of the "Grimes whistleblower scandal."

Conyers demanded a second investigation into the case of the non-existent cute agent notes. The Justice Department was compelled to send in another team of out-of-state investigators who interviewed damn near everyone in the courthouse during the trial.

There had been no notes passed saying anyone was cute, or saying anything.

Grimes had worked in the civil division and been assigned for a matter of months to a warehouse where the Siegelman case records were maintained. It appears that she was upset about being pulled off the big case, having to return to her old job and then not being invited to a party held after sentencing.

While working on the case she made no claims against anyone. However, almost two years later, she made several, including one based on sexual harassment during her time at the warehouse. She made bizarre claims against the prosecutors on the trial team as well as many attorneys and employees who worked in other parts of the office, some of whom had been old friends.

One lawyer not on the Siegelman case was accused by Grimes of the crime of being "shy and introverted in the courtroom." She claimed that one hire by Leura Canary cost the government millions of dollars partly because of his "disdain for southern culture."

During mediation over her demand for $300,000, Grimes suddenly declared that she had tape-recorded some of the harassing comments. This concerned the office, since it appeared an employee was surreptitiously taping discussions held during a criminal investigation.

Grimes was confronted about the tapes and said she gave them to her lawyer. However, the lawyer told investigators he never received any tapes and Grimes – apparently after realizing that making such tapes could get her in trouble – changed her story. She had never made any tapes, she claimed.

Government investigators concluded that she'd invented the story about the tapes as a means of extorting a larger settlement.

Among Grimes' lawyers during this mess was Martin Adams.

He is the son-in-law of **... Richard Scrushy**, and was an attorney of record on Scrushy's defense team during the Siegelman case.

On June 9, 2009, the Justice Department fired Grimes. The *New York Times* reported this outrage in its 22nd story since Jill Simpson's affidavit. Reporter John Schwartz told readers Grimes' firing was "first reported on a Harper's Magazine blog."

The reasons for her firing were ignored by the reporter, thus leaving the reading public to make the conclusion most people make when they see that a "whistleblower" has been fired.

Grimes' nonsense was to find its way into motions by the defendants. She too wrote a long letter to Holder, an emotional plea for greater whistleblower protections.

In March, after the 11th Circuit upheld most of the charges against his client, **Vince Kilborn** said that if Siegelman's subsequent appeals failed, he would ask Judge Fuller not to send Siegelman back to prison.

"Nine months in a federal penitentiary is plenty," Kilborn said.

Given the long odds against the Supreme Court taking up Siegelman's appeal, it's reasonable to predict that, one final time, probably in spring 2010, that Siegelman and Kilborn will appear before Fuller. They will seek mercy.

Considering their behavior since the trial –attacks on the judge, jurors, prosecutors, really everyone – I don't think mercy from Fuller is in the cards for Siegelman.

Nor should it be. The judge has a responsibility to protect the process. Siegelman, Scrushy and their lawyers have run roughshod over that process.

If the above scenario pans out as predicted, Siegelman will likely return to prison in late spring 2010, probably spend about five or six more years behind bars and get out, in fine health, at about age 68.

At some point after Jill Simpson's affidavit -- late 2007 or early 2008 -- I got a call from Alex Koppelman, a New York-based reporter for **Salon,** the left-leaning on-line magazine. Years ago I was a regular reader, and when it switched for awhile to pay content, I subscribed. I moved on, but not because of any dissastisfaction with it. Just too much other stuff to read. Alex said he was doing a story on the Siegelman case, and it was immediately clear that he'd done his research. We talked several times, and it's my recollection that he'd interviewed Jill Simpson.

He was the only national reporter to call me, or, far as I can tell, any of the Alabama reporters, such as Kim Chandler and Brett Blackledge, who covered the Siegelman administration. In fact, the only Alabama journalists I ever saw quoted, such as in the *New York Times*, were editorials and editorial writers from the two or three papers, like Decatur's, that belonged in the Siegelman-Horton camp. If any of those editors ever attended a day of the trial, I'd be shocked, but they had their opinions and were free to express them.

I answered Koppelman's questions and freely gave him my take on the situation. We traded e-mails later, and he told me he had completed a lengthy story and that I was quoted. I was eager to read it. I still am.

It never ran. Alex wouldn't say it, but I don't think there's any question that his editors killed it for ideological reasons.

He had apparently told a story that his editors feared would upset *Salon's* customers – its left-center readers.

During one of our talks, Koppelman – I think to show me he was willing to write stories counter to the prevailing winds – suggested I read a piece he'd written about the two U.S. Border patrol agents prosecuted for shooting an unarmed drug dealer as he ran toward the border. The case became a cause célèbre of the right after CNN's Lou Dobbs, famous for his illegal immigration rants, took up the cause of the two agents, Ignacio Ramos and Jose Compean.

I don't know enough about the case to have an opinion one way or another. However, there was a brief passage at the top of Koppelman's story that struck me because, well, I agreed with it.

He wrote:

How did Ramos and Compean get reinvented as right-wing heroes? The answer lies in the way Americans get their information, from a fragmented news media that makes it easier than ever to tune out opposing views and inconvenient truths. When people seek 'facts' only from sources with which they agree, it's possible for demonstrable untruths to enter the narrative and remain there unchallenged.

An interesting perspective from a publication that later killed a story because – or so it appears -- the piece presented what would have been, to *Salon's* readers, some "inconvenient truths" about Siegelman and Karl Rove's non-role in that Democrat's prosecution.

In September 2009, *Register* editor Mike Marshall called with an ultimatum. My sabbatical (no pay, no benefits) was into its third year, and before that I'd worked part-time for a stretch. I still have a desk with pictures, files, and such but almost never go down there. Mike said they were doing the budget for the next year and he needed to know if I was coming back. If so, I would need to return in two weeks. It was a perfectly reasonable demand, but I wasn't finished with the book and now I've got to sell it.

I told him I couldn't return in two weeks and thus ended, on perfectly good terms, my relationship with the *Mobile Register*. I also told Mike that I had some misgivings about coming back, regardless of the date. Our paper, like those everywhere, is thinner. Ad revenues are down, which translates to less space, less money to pay a reporter who may go weeks or longer without a story. Many of the Siegelman stories were quite long, as were the many investigative series I've done going back 15 years.

The editor might say otherwise, but there is no way, under the current circumstances, that a reporter could have done the work I was doing when I left. Nothing would be more miserable than killing myself on a project, only to see it trimmed to nothing.

The media's role as a watch-dog over corruption and public spending has diminished and, I fear, will continue to do so.

As a political moderate and a reporter who lives in the conservative Deep South, I have frequently found myself alone when engaged in the "liberal media" argument. I believe, and still do, that the great majority of reporters are looking for a good story and seeking to tell it accurately, not to assist this or that party or further this or that ideology. I thought, for example, that the media, *New York Times* included, just could not have been tougher on Bill Clinton.

Nevertheless, after the research into what became the final portion of this book, I don't think I'll be able to summon as vibrant a defense of the "liberal media" charge. I just hope the *New York Times*, a paper I've always revered, doesn't get it this wrong this often, and for the reasons here -- and there's just no other explanation – the ideological leanings of its reporters and editors.

If there is one major failing with this book – and no doubt there are many – it's that I never made a strong enough effort to determine who fabricated and sent the juror e-mails. Nor have I told you enough about the mechanics of the Siegelman and Scrushy publicity machine, who and how it was paid for, and the role played by private investigators and political researchers. Nor did I clarify the part played by Scott Horton in the activities of the Judiciary Committee and other activities as well.

My defense is that this has been a complicated tale that has whipped my ass in a million ways, financially, physically, you name it. But I've got a web-page, and hopefully by the time you read this, or in any event before long, I'll be able to provide some clarity to those situations.

———

One more thing. In 1998, I voted for Siegelman over Fob James. If I had it to do again, and knowing what I know now, I'd still vote for Siegelman. In the long run you're probably better off having a governor who is corrupt but likes to govern than one who just likes to duck hunt.

———

Finally, after all these pages, all this work, it gives me great pleasure to say, to those of you still with me…on to the Acknowledgements!

(Please turn the page.)

Acknowledgements

I'm not being cheeky in acknowledging my gratitude to the inventors and/ or purveyors of various computer search engines and databases, without which many if not most of the discoveries revealed in my reporting would not have been made. Foremost among them, and in no particular order: Google; the federal courts search engine Pacer; Alacourt, a similar service for the state court system; Nexis, the grandest news search engine of them all; the Alabama Secretary of State web-site; Merlin, which is the *Mobile Register's* computerized library; and the state comptroller's computer system.

In the human department, those due gratitude, whether they want it or not, include my great friend, *Mobile Register* "layout artist" Chris Hall, for having to wait on my frequently late and too-long stories; Judi Rojeski, the sweet and beautiful guardian angel and island of calm in the newsroom; Sean Reilly, the paper's too-selfless Washington correspondent and formerly our Montgomery stalwart, who was always there with guidance and whose knowledge of the players in Montgomery was invaluable; *Register* managing editor Dewey English, who gave many of the stories their final read, never failing to improve them; the Montgomery correspondents during the time I covered the Siegelman administration – chiefly Bill Barrow, Jeff Amy and Sallie Owen – for letting me knock them off their computers when I was on deadline, giving me rides, and too many other favors to name.

Paul Cloos, my editor since I became a news reporter in 1994, is due a special debt of gratitude for his patience, sense of fairness, and the long hours and weekends he worked improving my stories. *Register* editor Mike Marshall stood behind me when other editors might not have, and for him I am also grateful.

There are too many other people at the paper to name, especially the many reporters, such as Gary McElroy, Willie Rabb, Jeb Schrenk and Steve Myers, who gave readers excellent stories day after day, thus allowing me to work weeks on the pieces that are the basis of this book.

The stories could not have been done without the many employees at state agencies and various courthouses who assisted me in procuring records. Alabama will miss Bob Childree, the since retired state comptroller, who believed public records were just that. Special thanks to members of Bob's staff, particularly Jeanne Brackin, for helping me navigate that office's ancient, unruly computer; and Myron Perdue, who went overboard locating the actual payment vouchers. Retired Finance Department lawyer Lee Miller would stick his neck out to make records public, and had to dodge some snakes doing it. I am also indebted to the ever-cheerful Dollie Burkhalter, in the public information office at the Alabama Department of Economic Affairs; and the dear women at the Ethics Commission, with special thanks to Joann Ward and Marie Malinowski, for retrieving long lists of ethics reports, always with a smile.

I can't over-emphasize my appreciation for my brother, Greg. Some years ago, Greg was recruited from one top Birmingham firm to another, Maynard, Cooper & Gale. During the Siegelman administration, Maynard Cooper was the state's and Siegelman's primary outside law firm, that being one smart hire the governor made. Despite Greg's assurances to the contrary, I know my stories made him uncomfortable. He never asked me to stop reporting or back off. I am also grateful to the firm for not asking him to intervene on Siegelman's behalf.

A wide-eyed thanks to the staff at Satori Coffee House, my office away from home, for letting me stay past closing on so many nights, and for their strong coffee and fine company. Random others deserving thanks include John Cleghorn, who gave me my first reporting gig, at Washington & Lee's student newspaper; and my sister Leslie, for racing to the courthouse in Birmingham when I had to have records, and pronto.

Extra special thanks to my "readers," those people on whom I foisted the book in its final stages, less to proof read than provide general feedback as to its readability. Chief among them are: high school chum Medford Roe; long-time friend and *Register* layout man Doug Dimitry; Mobile political junkie and writer of great elegance, Chip Drago; and Garry Mitchell, a great friend and for decades the Associated Press's one-man Mobile bureau.

My final reader was my father, Jerry Curran. He spent untold hours reading it, making notes, and going over the book with me page by page, and at a time when he was both working and caring for my mother in the final stages of her cancer. Thanks Daddy. I love you.

Ultimately, though, I was both writer and editor. There are, I'm sure, typos and grammatical errors, even, I fear, probably some errors of fact, though if so, not because of lack of effort. I ask that the above-named readers not be blamed. If anyone is at fault, it is Karl Rove.

A hearty thanks as well to the people at iUniverse. I have never published a book, and while I chose to self-publish, it wasn't without some trepidation. My research indicated that iUniverse was the best, and my experience with the company supports that 100 percent. Special thanks to Jade Council and those who worked with her in the production department. I felt like they really wanted my book to do well, and in part for them, I hope it does. A similar thanks to J. Arendall and Edward Herndon, the two-man operation at Mobile's Webjed, for going the extra mile to build the book's web-site and putting up with my constant changes.

In the unlikely event that I sell enough books to even recover my expenses, I will owe a debt of gratitude to "Republican operative" Jill Simpson, for keeping the story alive and helping it, as they say, "go national." On the flipside, her nonsense added an immense amount of work.

Whatever its strengths and weaknesses, there is no way this book or the reporting within could have been accomplished without my dear, beautiful wife Jana. She put up with my long hours at the *Register*, then supported me and our children, Jerry, Eva and Bud the Dog (there, Eva, I got Bud in the book), when I decided to leave the paper to write this. No one complained, or at least not much, about the piles and boxes of records strewn about the house.

Jana's paychecks kept us afloat, if barely, and her patience in the project that just would never end was more than I deserved.

I will never be able to thank her enough.

(Hey Jerry, it's finished. Leave me alone.)

Sources and end notes

Almost without fail, guides to writing non-fiction recommend avoiding a great degree of sourcing within the book because it can slow the, "narrative pace." I chose to take that risk, perhaps at my and the readers peril. I did this out of habit (my editors at the paper beat into me the need to source everything) and because I believed it suited the purpose of the book. More than anything, this is a book about journalism. As such, I considered the identities and work of other reporters to be part of the story.

Any shortcoming in these notes is, I hope, righted by the sourcing within the book.

This project arose out of my reporting on the Siegelman administration, which began in January 2001. A compendium of all the documents reviewed to write those stories would include citations for tens of thousands of pages of public records and hundreds of interviews, and hopefully is not deemed necessary here.

I chose consistency over accuracy in generally referring to the Mobile paper as the *Mobile Register*, both within the book and in these end notes. That was its name during the Siegelman administration. Subsequently, the name was changed to *The Press-Register*, with no Mobile in it. Maybe I just like the old name batter. In any event, some of the stories referred to as being published by the *Register* were actually published under the *Press-Register* banner.

Unless otherwise stated, "trial testimony" refers to testimony given during the 2006 trial of Siegelman and his three co-defendants. While not cited below, the court filings in the Siegelman case served as a chief source. That case, United States vs. Siegelman, is in the Middle District of Alabama, and bears the docket number: 2:05cr119-F.

The link to my investigative stories on the Siegelman administration is: http://www.al.com/specialreport/mobileregister/index.ssf?contracts.html

Most if not all the New York Times editorials and stories on the Siegelman case are at: http://topics.nytimes.com/topics/reference/timestopics/people/s/donald_siegelman/index.html

Many of the pieces by Scott Horton, the *Times*, and a slew of other resources are at: http://donsiegelman.org/

Introduction
"Personal and Confidential" letter, August 17, 2001, from Jim Buckalew to Howard Bronson.
Interview with Mack Roberts, summer 2006.

Preface: Fast Forward to Martyrdom
John Archibald, "Siegelman's blues insult true victims," Birmingham News, Dec. 19, 2006.
Court records regarding Dana Jill Simpson.
Affidavit of Terry Butts, Oct. 18, 2007.
July 17, 2007 letter from John Conyers to U.S. Attorney General Alberto Gonzales.
Scott Horton, "Justice in Alabama," Harper's web-site, June 24, 2007.

Chapter 1: Golden Flake
The Mobile Register paper (as opposed to computer) archives provided much of the information contained in this
*   chapter and pertaining to Siegelman's life and career before 1994. Most of the hundreds of stories, news items and*
*   editorials in those archives were written by Register or Associated Press reporters, with many of the latter re-writes*
*   of stories first published in the Birmingham News, Birmingham Post-Herald, and Montgomery Advertiser.*
Bill Barrow, "A lifetime of climbing," Mobile Register, Oct. 13, 2002.
Michael Sznajderman, "Siegelman at six months can count victories," Birmingham News, July 18, 1999.
Letter to Siegelman from Dr. Gerald Pohost, Nov. 26, 2001, Alabama State Archives.
Associated Press, "Alabama Republicans raise questions about about Siegelman's military record," Oct. 17, 1998.
Telephone interview with Cal Franklin, April 20, 2006.
Letter to Siegelman from Dr. Gerald Pohost, dated Nov. 26, 2001, Alabama State Archives.

Chapter 3: Off and Running
Bill Barrow, "A lifetime of climbing," Mobile Register, Oct. 13, 2002.
Trial testimony of Jim Allen.
Michael Sznajderman, "If it's bizarre, it must be Montgomery," Birmingham News, Feb. 16, 1997.
Michael Brumas, "'Tort Hell' is History,' Siegelman Promises," Birmingham News, June 23, 1999.
Sean Reilly, "Siegelman Honda meet proves pivotal," Mobile Register, May 8, 1999.

Chapter 4: Scrushy plays the lottery
John Helyar, "The Insatiable King Richard," Fortune, July 7, 2003.
Interview with Abe Beam, on Nov. 13, 2006
Kyle Whitmire, "Scrushy watch; fixed in the gaze," Birmingham Weekly, June 23, 2005.
Simon Romero, "Will the real Richard Scrushy please step forward?" New York Times, Feb. 17, 2005.
Trial and/or grand jury testimony of Bill McGahan, Taylor Pickett, Darren Cline, Nick Bailey, Mike Martin, Leif
*   Murphy and exhibits introduced during their testimony.*
Marlon Manuel, Peter Mantius, "Ala. Governor vows to try again after crushing lottery defeat," The Atlanta Journal
*   and Constitution, Oct. 13, 1999.*
Phillip Rawls, "Siegelman moves quickly to start Amendment One programs," Associated Press, Nov. 8, 2000.
Eddie Curran, "Future May brighten for state's Democrats," Mobile Register, Nov. 19, 2000.

Chapter 5: Honda
Ken Funderburke, memos produced in Eugene Crum vs. State of Alabama.
Eddie Curran, "No-bid job for Honda costs state $36 million," Mobile Register, Feb. 2001.
Interview with Mack Roberts, summer 2006.
Nick Bailey, trial testimony.
Eddie Curran, "Mercedes work may open up for bids," Mobile Register, Feb. 10, 2001.
Alan Choate, "Windom blames governor for bid-law loophole," Mobile Register, Feb. 7, 2001.

Chapter 6: Continuing Education
Eddie Curran, "No-bid Honda project costly," Mobile Register, Feb. 12, 2001.
Eddie Curran, "A point-by-point look at some Honda contract items," Mobile Register, Feb. 12, 2001.
Eddie Curran, "Governor selected building company," Mobile Register, Feb. 14, 2001.
Eddie Curran, "Gripes besiege Honda builder," Mobile Register, March 11, 2001.
Eddie Curran, "Record says governor's brother called about Honda contract," Mobile Register, Jan. 26, 2001.
Eddie Curran, "No-bid deal: Subcontractor did work for hired company," Mobile Register, Nov. 11, 2001.

Chapter 7: Lanny Landfill
April 2001 interview with Lanny Young.
Eddie Curran, "Trial to begin in lawsuit against Lanny Young, company," Mobile Register, Jan. 13, 2003.
Eddie Curran, "Young linked to state deals under scrutiny," Mobile Register, June 17, 2001.
Trial testimony of Phillip Jordan.
"DeKalb probate judge dies in apparent fall," Associated Press, June 24, 2004.
"DeKalb judge who died in fall named as go-between in bribery case," Associated Press, July 2, 2004.

Trial testimony of Nick Bailey.
Trial testimony of Claire Austin.
Dave Bryan, "McGregor withdraws plans as Jackson joins opponents of landfill," Associated Press, Aug. 23, 2000.
"Siegelman takes different tact toward friend's proposed landfill," Associated Press, Aug. 29, 2000.

Chapter 8: Seeds of Destruction
Trial testimony of Bill Blount.
Trial testimony of David Campbell.
G.H. Construction warehouse timeline produced by Ran Garver and introduced at trial.
Trial testimony of Ran Garver.
Eddie Curran, "Young linked to state deals under scrutiny," Mobile Register, June 17, 2001.
Eddie Curran, "Plea document tells of sending $100,000 to friend," Mobile Register, June 28, 2003.
Eddie Curran, "Testimony conflicts with past statements," Mobile Register, March 14, 2002.

Chapter 9: G.H. "Goat Hill" Construction
Phillip Rawls, "Engineering Executive had been at peak of career when indicted," Associated Press, Dec. 16, 2001.
Eddie Curran, "Testimony conflicts with past statements; Montgomery businessman in court to answer charges he bilked state in warehouse deal," Mobile Register, March 14, 2002.
Interviews with Roland Vaughan, Nick Bailey, and other administration officials in April 2001, and separately, with Lanny Young.
Henry Mabry, memo to Nick Bailey, Randall Smith and Don Siegelman, announcing halting of warehouse project, May 4, 2001.

Chapter 10: The Warehouse Stories
Eddie Curran, "Questions halt state project," Mobile Register, April 28, 2001.
Eddie Curran, "Unexplained bills lead to investigation of construction project," Mobile Register, April 29, 2001.
Eddie Curran, "Warehouse contract found, but public denied access," Mobile Register, May 1, 2001.
Jeff Amy, "Pryor announces investigation of warehouse construction deal," Mobile Register, May 2001.
Eddie Curran, "No answer at G.H. Builders," Mobile Register, May 2, 2001.
Eddie Curran, "Two contracts are released," Mobile Register, May 3, 2001.
C.C. "Bo" Torbert, Report on warehouse project, May 4, 2001.
Jeff Amy and Bill Barrow, "Siegelman fires construction firm," Mobile Register, May 5, 2001.
Eddie Curran, "State may face costs for halted G.H. deal," Mobile Register, May 9, 2001.
Eddie Curran, "Questions surround warehouse land sale," Mobile Register, May 12, 2001.
Eddie Curran, "Contract questions remain," Mobile Register, May 18, 2001.
Eddie Curran, "Investment experts: Warehouse deal bloated with fees," Mobile Register, May 27, 2001.

Chapter 11: Night on the Town
Robin DeMonia, "Liquor bottles raise questions at State House," Birmingham News, May 21, 1997.

Chapter 12: Siegelman Tax
Eddie Curran, "Is contract best deal the state could get?" Mobile Register, June 10, 2001.
Eddie Curran, "State gets refund for computer services," Mobile Register, Dec. 25, 2002.

Chapter 13: Friction
Eddie Curran, "Siegelman 'extremely disappointed' in friends involved in warehouse deal," Mobile Register, May 31, 2001.
Memo of May 10, 2001, cabinet meeting of Siegelman staff, Alabama State Archives.
Alan Choate, "Amid probe, governor moves head of agency," Mobile Register, June 7, 2001.
Bill Poovey, "Siegelman shakes up his cabinet," Associated Press, June 16, 2001.

Chapter 14: Siegelman's Big Score
Associated Press, "State Pays Family of Man Killed by Prison Van," Nov. 15, 1996.
Telephone interview with Cheryl and J.C. Cunningham, September 2006.
Phillip Rawls, "Governor makes more in legal fees than state salary," Associated Press, June 17, 2001.
Eddie Curran, "Siegelman tight-lipped over money," Mobile Register, July 22, 2001.
Eddie Curran, "Siegelman sought, then spurned, fees from USA tobacco lawsuit," Mobile Register, July 22, 2001.
Eddie Curran, "Lawyer: Siegelman sought pay based on name value," Mobile Register, July 26, 2001.
Eddie Curran and Jeff Amy, "Siegelman target of ethics charge," Mobile Register, July 27, 2001.
Kim Chandler and Brett J. Blackledge, "Siegelman settlement contains tobacco fees admission," Birmingham News, July 2, 2002.
David White, "Firm sends governor $800,000," Birmingham News, July 28, 2001.
Staff and wire report, "Siegelman: Former law firm paid him about $800,000 in severance," Mobile Register, July 28, 2001.
Eddie Curran, "Siegelman seeks to 'clarify' ethics form," Mobile Register, Aug. 3, 2001.

Chapter 15: The Phone Call
Felicity Barringer, "Governors' Limits on Press Raise Concerns," New York Times, Oct. 8, 2001.

Chapter 16: War
Jeb Schrenk, "Governor's staff bars interviews with investigative news reporter," Mobile Register, Sept. 21, 2001.
Jeff Amy, "Siegelman lawyer to screen all media document requests," Mobile Register, Sept. 26, 2001.
Sallie Owen, "Governor: New records policy not tied to Register reporter," Mobile Register, Sept. 27, 2001.
Jeff Amy, "Officials defend, amend policy," Mobile Register, Sept., 27, 2001.
Jeff Amy, "State agrees to produce some records," Mobile Register, Sept. 28, 2001.
Sallie Owen, "New state policy may target only certain record requests," Mobile Register, Sept. 28, 2001.
Jeff Amy and Jeb Schrenk, "Paper's rights said violated, " Mobile Register, Oct. 5, 2002.
Sallie Owen, "No written policy on records, says aide," Mobile Register, Oct. 5, 2002.
Eddie Curran, "State withholds documents on Mercedes plant project," Mobile Register, Oct. 7, 2001.
Jeb Schrenk, "Editor dismisses conspiracy claim involving reporter," Mobile Register," Oct. 5, 2002.
Jeff Amy, "New Siegelman policy on records," Mobile Register, Oct. 23, 2002.
Felicity Barringer, "Governors' Limits on Press Raise Concerns," New York Times, Oct. 8, 2001.
David White, "Suit filed to block Siegelman policy," Birmingham News, Sept. 28, 2001.
Carol Nunnelley and Ed Mullins, "Will Sept. 11 also reshape journalism?" Birmingham News, Oct. 14, 2001.

Chapter 17: Competition
Scott Horton, "There's no news in the B'ham News," Harper's web-site, July 25, 2007.
Brett J. Blackledge and Kim Chandler, "Unbid contracts go to firm tied to governor's friend," Birmingham News, June 24, 2001.
Brett J. Blackledge and Kim Chandler, "School inventory misses mark," Birmingham News, July 29, 2001.
Brett J. Blackledge, Kim Chandler and Mary Orndorff, "Governor pushed contract; $15 million no-bid deal for trooper equipment tied to two supporters," Birmingham News, Nov. 4, 2001.
Brett J. Blackledge and Kim Chandler, "Firms flourish under state's no-bid edict," Birmingham News, Nov. 25, 2001.
Eddie Curran, "ASD's demise: An inside look at computer deals in state," Mobile Register, Nov. 29, 2002.
Eddie Curran, "Public Safety officials were surprised to learn of ASD's termination," Mobile Register, Nov. 30, 2002.
Eddie Curran, "Firm gets OT despite protests," Mobile Register, Nov. 30, 2002.
Eddie Curran, "Who is Charlie Stephenson?" Mobile Register, Dec. 5, 2002.
Eddie Curran, "Perkins is said to be one of Gov. Siegelman's key policy advisors," Mobile Register, Dec. 2, 2001.

Chapter 18: Disarray
Letter to Siegelman from Dr. Gerald Pohost, Nov. 26, 2001. Alabama State Archives.
Nick Bailey resignation letter, Nov. 21, 2001, Alabama State Archives.
Jeff Amy, "Siegelman proposes contract reform," Mobile Register, Aug. 22, 2001.
Kim Chandler, "Ethics Legislation Going Nowhere," Birmingham News, Sept. 7, 2001.
Phillip Rawls, "Opponents want Siegelman judged by the company he keeps," Associated Press, Nov. 5, 2001.
Eddie Curran, "State may kiss $410,000 goodbye," Mobile Register, Dec. 21, 2001.
Eddie Curran, "G.H. officials don't respond to lawsuits," Mobile Register, Feb. 8, 2002.

Chapter 19: Landfill Lanny's Toxic Tax Cut
Eddie Curran, "Former owners to get chunk of huge profits," Mobile Register, Feb. 7, 1997.
Eddie Curran, "Waste firm paid consultant $500,000 after tax change," Mobile Register, July 27, 2002.
Editorial, "Waste Away Regulation Change Smells as bad as any landfill," Birmingham News, Aug. 2, 2002.
Trial testimony of Wade Hope and Nick Bailey.

Chapter 20: Selling a House, Siegelman style
Associated Press, "Siegelmans purchase home near Liberty Park," Jan. 13, 2002.
Eddie Curran, "Governor got high sale price for home," Mobile Register, Nov. 11, 2002.
Eddie Curran, "Letter says Vines' law firm paid Siegelman $50,000," Mobile Register, Nov. 16, 2002.
Editorial, "Dream Deal: Siegelman home sells for twice its appraised value," Birmingham News, Feb. 27, 2002.
Eddie Curran, "Papers show trial lawyer paid accountant for Siegelman house," Mobile Register, Nov. 11, 2002.
Records in U.S. Tax Court case, L.S. Vines v. Commissioner of Internal Revenue Service.
Jill Nolin, "Architectural Review Board decision saves historic home," Montgomery Advertiser, Nov. 20, 2008.
Jill Nolin, "Buyer found for former home of Montgomery, state leaders," Montgomery Advertiser," May 6, 2008.

Chapter 21: The $50,000 Fee
Eddie Curran, "Letter says Vines' law firm paid Siegelman $50,000," Mobile Register, Nov. 16, 2002.

Chapter 22: The Governor's Stockbroker
Brett J. Blackledge and Kim Chandler, "State investments benefit firm with ties to Siegelman," Birmingham News, Feb. 6, 2006.
Brett J. Blackledge and Kim Chandler, "Governor's staff urged broker hire, board says," Birmingham News, March 8, 2002.

Eddie Curran, "Governor held up pension contracts," *Mobile Register*, March 10, 2002.
Brett J. Blackledge and Kim Chandler, "Records show state staff favored broker administration," *Birmingham News*, March 15, 2002.
Eddie Curran, "Governor's stockbroker nets profits from state contracts," *Mobile Register*, March 15, 2002.
Eddie Curran, "Siegelman aide, personal broker did real estate deals," *Mobile Register*, March 15, 2002.
Brett J. Blackledge and Kim Chandler, "Siegelman got stock before friend's takeover try," *Birmingham News*, March 22, 2002.

Chapter 23: The Canary Canard
Jeff Amy and Eddie Curran, "State warehouse probe on fast track," *Mobile Register*, Oct. 26, 2001.
Stan J. Bailey and Brett J. Blackledge, "Grand jury indicts engineers in state warehouse probe," *Birmingham News*, Oct. 31, 2001.
Phillip Rawls, "Former Business Council of Alabama chairman indicted in warehouse scandal," *Associated Press*, Oct. 31, 2001.
Kim Chandler, "Construction president makes plea agreement in state warehouse case," *Birmingham News*, Jan. 12, 2002.
Brett J. Blackledge and Kim Chandler, "Siegelman's finances probed," *Birmingham News*, Feb. 10, 2002.
Tom Gordon, "GOP leaders find Pryor, Siegelman too friendly," *Birmingham News*, May 7, 2001.
Jay Reeves, "Governor hires top defense lawyer amid financial probe," *Associated Press*, Feb. 15, 2002.
Mark Niesse, "Siegelman attorney blames Republicans for investigation leaks," *Associated Press*, March 25, 2002.
Adam Zagorin, "Selective Justice in Alabama," *Time*, Oct. 4, 2007.
Tom Hamburger and David G. Savage, "Ex-governor says he was target of Republican plot," *Los Angeles Times*, June 26, 2007.
Paul Alexander, "Karl Rove destroyed my life," *The Daily Beast*, Dec. 27, 2008.
Karl Rove, testimony, U.S. House Committee on the Judiciary, July 29, 2009
Bill Canary, e-mails to the author, October 2009.
Kenneth Mullinax, "Lady Law: U.S. Attorney Leura Canary excels at the family business," *Montgomery Advertiser*, Oct. 14, 2007.
Eddie Curran, "Montgomery businessman in court to answer charges he bilked state in warehouse deal," *Mobile Register*, March 14, 2002.
Jeff Amy, "Montgomery engineer repeats claim that prosecution was politically motivated," *Mobile Register*, May 1, 2001.
Kim Chandler, "Travel probe sought proof of kickbacks," *Birmingham News*, Sept. 21, 2001.

Chapter 24: The Foundation Phantom
Eddie Curran, "Firm's PAC makes donation to now-dissolved lottery foundation," *Mobile Register*, March 12, 2002.
Eddie Curran, "Questions unanswered on lottery donation," *Mobile Register*, May 7, 2002.
Eddie Curran, "Lottery group failed to file tax return," *Mobile Register*, May 13, 2002.
Eddie Curran, "Democrats helped fund the last lottery campaign," *Mobile Register*, May 16, 2002.
Eddie Curran, "Pitt pledges to clarify party's lottery-related loan records," *Mobile Register*, May 17, 2002.
Eddie Curran, "Records reveal new mission for foundation," *Mobile Register*, May 26, 2002.

Chapter 25: A Scrushy Surprise
Eddie Curran, "Foundation records still unavailable," *Mobile Register*, July 17, 2002.
Eddie Curran, "Lawyer: Lottery foundation to show financial records," *Mobile Register*, July 25, 2002.
Eddie Curran, "Foundation received big donations ," *Mobile Register*, July 27, 2002.
Eddie Curran, "Alfa: Donation never meant for lottery," *Mobile Register*, July 28, 2002.
Eddie Curran, "Memo shows Siegelman sought revision of post-lottery foundation," Aug. 11, *Mobile Register*, 2002.
Eddie Curran, "Deductions incorrectly taken," *Mobile Register*, Aug. 22, 2002.
Eddie Curran, "Alfa officials questioned about gift to foundation," *Mobile Register*, Aug. 29, 2002.

Chapter 26: Ethics, Alabama Style
Kim Chandler and Brett J. Blackledge, "Siegelman settlement contains tobacco fees admission," *Birmingham News*, July 2, 2002.
Eddie Curran, "Some say commission ruling could lower ethics standards in Alabama," *Mobile Register*, June 2, 2002.
Eddie Curran, "Disclosure could pose problems for Siegelman," *Mobile Register*, Feb. 16, 2002.
Eddie Curran, "Siegelman reports law firm as largest source of income," *Mobile Register*, May 1, 2002.
Eddie Curran, "Panel to hear case against governor," *Mobile Register*, May 14, 2002.
Eddie Curran, "Hearing on Siegelman not yet a certainty," *Mobile Register*, May 15, 2002.
Eddie Curran, "Lawyers lay groundwork for case," *Mobile Register*, June 16, 2002.
Eddie Curran and Bill Barrow, "Siegelman scores important victory," *Mobile Register*, July 11, 2002.
Kim Chandler, "Siegelman contradicts lawyer on tobacco pay," *Birmingham News*, Aug. 7, 2002.
Eddie Curran, "Washington law firm paid Siegelman fees," *Mobile Register*, May 31, 2003.

Chapter 27: Siegelman v. Riley
Siegelman debate preparation memos, summer/fall 2002, Alabama State Archives.
Adam Cohen, "A Tale of Three (Electronic Voting) Elections," *New York Times*, July 31, 2008.
Eddie Curran, "State auditor looking into Group One contract with ADECA," *Mobile Register*, Sept. 1, 2002.

Eddie Curran

Eddie Curran, "Review faults ADECA, says Web designer performed duties," Mobile Register, Nov. 11, 2002.
Eddie Curran, "Feds blast state Web contract," Mobile Register, Nov. 20, 2002.
Eddie Curran, "Feds want state refund next week," Mobile Register, Feb. 7, 2003.
Mike Cason, "Campaign messages can come from strange places," Montgomery Advertiser, Sept. 29, 2002.
Editorial, "Cheap shots reflect on Siegelman, not Riley," Mobile Register, Aug. 31, 2002.
Sallie Owen, "BCA breaks tradition, backs Riley," Mobile Register, Aug. 9, 2002.
Phillip Rawls, "Heston aide says GOP shouldn't be surprised by endorsement," Associated Press, Sept. 23, 2002.
Thomas Spencer, "AG probing effort to air anti-Riley commercial," Birmingham News, Nov. 2, 2002.
Phillip Rawls, "Nasty tossup in Alabama's race for governor," Associated Press, Nov. 2, 2002.
Siegelman e-mail interview with Mark Crispin Miller, News from the Underground blog, April 10, 2008.
"Alabama governor begins recount process," United Press International," Nov. 8, 2002.
Phillip Rawls, "Alabama attorney general deals blow to governor's recount hopes," Associated Press, Nov. 8, 2002.
Mike Cason, "Riley goes to Supreme Court," Montgomery Advertiser, Nov. 15, 2002.
David White, "House Democrats urge Siegelman not to contest race," Birmingham News," Nov. 15, 2002.
Tom Gordon and Brett J. Blackledge, "Bow-out seen as beneficial; concession may keep door open to future runs," Birmingham News, Nov. 19, 2002.
Kyle Whitmire, "Spin Cycle: Courting public appeal," Birmingham Weekly, Jun 3, 2004.
John Archibald and Brett J. Blackledge, "Early printout was only source of wrong tally," Birmingham News, Nov. 10, 2002.
David White, "House Democrats urge Siegelman not to contest race," Birmingham News," Nov. 15, 2002.
Tom Gordon and Brett J. Blackledge, "Bow-out seen as beneficial; concession may keep door open to future runs," Birmingham News, Nov. 19, 2002.
Sallie Owen and Bill Barrow, "Siegelman concedes," Mobile Register, Nov. 19, 2002.

Chapter 28: The KKK Took My Election Away
Dana Jill Simpson, testimony, U.S. House Committee on the Judiciary, Sept. 14, 2007.
Dana Jill Simpson, affidavit, May 21, 2007.
Bob Johnson, "Aides of Siegelman contradict main part of Simpson affidavit," Associated Press, July 20, 2007.
Rip Andrews, written statement to media, July 19, 2007.
Affidavits of Terry Butts, Rob Riley and Matt Lembke.
Interviews with Rob Riley in 2008.
Bob Johnson, "3 deny being on GOP call to plot against Siegelman," Associated Press, June 2, 2007.
Kim Chandler, "Siegelman attorneys unaware of any deal; say he never mentioned offer to end inquiry," Birmingham News, Oct. 13, 2007.

Chapter 29: Warming the Bench
Mike Cason, "Governor's fund not totally private," Montgomery Advertiser, Feb. 28, 2002.
Eddie Curran, "Lori Siegelman billed travel costs to state, records show," Mobile Register, Feb. 23, 2003.
Editorial, "Using state charge card," Montgomery Advertiser, Feb. 24, 2003.
Bill Barrow, "Siegelman defends wife's travel bills," Mobile Register, March 1, 2003.
Eddie Curran, "State paid bill for Siegelman family's trip to Virgin Islands," Mobile Register, March 1, 2003.
Eddie Curran, "State paid bill for Siegelman family's trip to Virgin Islands," Mobile Register, March 1, 2003.
Eddie Curran, "Contingency fund records lack supporting documentation," Mobile Register, March 15, 2003.
Eddie Curran, "Auditor: Purpose of many expenditures still unexplained," Mobile Register, May 17, 2003.
Mitch Frank, "Alabama's most courageous politician," Time magazine, Aug. 15, 2003.
"A Profile in Courage," Governing magazine, November 2003 issue.
Eddie Curran, "Bailey, Young plead guilty," Mobile Register, June 25, 2003.

Chapter 30: The Bobo Debacle
Kim Chandler, "Bobo Tape: Funding had state support," Birmingham News, Oct. 5, 2001.
Kim Chandler, "Transcript: Bobo says he 'will low ball' competitors," Birmingham News, Oct. 4, 2001.
Jannell McGrew and John Davis, "Ex-governor denies bid-rigging claims," Montgomery Advertiser, May 28, 2004.
Brett J. Blackledge, "Poison Center funds traced Ex-Fire College chief routed $400,000 to foundation, $125,000 to a friend," Birmingham News, Aug. 10, 2006.
Brett J. Blackledge, "Firm has tied to earlier defense of Clemon," Birmingham News, Aug. 2, 2004.
Kim Chandler, "Judge: Siegelman can keep an attorney," Birmingham News, July 29, 2004.
Brett J. Blackledge, "Judge, U.S. have often squared off; family probe, lien once source of friction," Birmingham News, Aug. 1, 2004.

Chapter 31: The Crusades
Brett J. Blackledge and Kim Chandler, "Indictment casts doubt on testimony," Birmingham News, July 4, 2004.
Kim Chandler, "Grand jury eyes computer contracts from Siegelman era," Birmingham News, Aug. 23, 2005.
Kim Chandler, "Ex-aide to Siegelman appears before grand jury," Birmingham News, June 22, 2004.
Kim Chandler, "Grand jury hears about road project," Birmingham News, Sept. 22, 2005.
Letter from Brian McKee to Myron Thompson, March 17, 2004, from USA v. Faulk, et. al.
Eddie Curran, "Young faces new charges of bribing judge in landfill deal," Mobile Register, July 2, 2004.
Kent Faulk, "Strict Rules govern lobbyists release," Birmingham News, March 3, 2005.

Michael Tomberlin, "Scrushy backers got most of $1.9 million; Churches benefited from 2006 donations," *Birmingham News*, June 17, 2008.
Simon Romero, "Scrushy: Finding religion or saving self? Ex-hospitals chief a regular at church," *International Herald Tribune*, Feb. 18, 2005.
Dan Morse, Chad Terhune, Ann Carrns, "HealthSouth's Scrushy is acquitted," *Wall Street Journal*, June 29, 2005.
Kyle Whitmire, "Determined to find guilt, but expecting acquittal," *New York Times*, June 29, 2005.
Brian Grow, "Richard Scrushy's 'Amen Corner,'" *Businessweek*, Jan. 20, 2006.

Chapter 32: Indicted
Dana Beyerle, "The look of a candidate again," *The Times Daily*, Jan. 14, 2005.
Phillip Rawls, "Listening posts another sign Siegelman might run for governor," *Associated Press*, Jan. 11, 2005.
Eddie Curran, "Kilborn to defend Siegelman," *Mobile Register*, Feb. 11, 2006.
Thomas Spencer, "Though it's not official, Baxley says she's running," *Birmingham News*, Oct. 20, 2005.
Mike Cason, "Siegelman: Moore helps his re-election bid; says indictment likely an effort to thwart campaign," *Birmingham News*, Oct. 6, 2005.
Eddie Curran, Sallie Owen and Bill Barrow, "Siegelman indicted," *Mobile Register*, Oct. 27, 2005.
Eddie Curran, "Moore profits from book, speeches," *Mobile Register*, Nov. 26, 2005.
Kim Chandler, "Siegelman jury picked; will get directions today," *Birmingham News*, April 21, 2006.
Eddie Curran, "Attacks fly in Siegelman trial," *Mobile Register*, May 2, 2006.

Chapter 33: Nick and Lanny, Under Siege
Eddie Curran, "Attacks fly in Siegelman trial," *Mobile Register*, May 2, 2006.
Kyle Whitmire, "Trial of the 6-year-old century," *Birmingham Weekly*, May 4, 2006.
Bill Barrow, "Race issue makes appearance on first day as lawyers clash," *Mobile Register*, May 2, 2006.
Janet Guyon, "Richard Scrushy's chief believer," *Washington Post*, May 18, 2006.
Kim Chandler, "Trial set to begin for Siegelman, Scrushy, 2 others," *Birmingham News*, April 30, 2006.
Eddie Curran, "Siegelman ad troubles judge," *Mobile Register*, June 3, 2006.
Bob Johnson, "Siegelman sends letter to Riley on campaign donation charge," *Associated Press*, June 22, 2006.

Chapter 34: The Motorcycle
Kent Faulk, "Governor to ride 'hog' in Saturday motorcycle event," *Birmingham News*, September 14, 2001.
Trial testimony of Mona George, a Compass Bank records custodian.
Kim Chandler, "Lobbyist says gifts had price," *Birmingham News*, May 18, 2006.
Kent Faulk, "First Couple leads on Harley," *Birmingham News*, Sept. 16, 2001.
Brett J. Blackledge, "Man says he made payoffs for contracts; says $35,000 payment led to software deal," *Birmingham News*, Feb. 1, 2007.
Kyle Whitmire, "The Young and the reckless," *Birmingham Weekly*, May 25, 2006.
Phillip Rawls, "Tax records show Siegelman had motorcycle, trailer," *Associated Press*, Jun 26, 2003.

Chapter 35: Quid Pro Rico and the Absolute Agreement
Kim Chandler, "Neither side too pleased by pace," *Birmingham News*, May 12, 2006.
Bob Johnson, "Judge who took bribes testifies against Siegelman, Hamrick," *Associated Press*, May 23, 2006.

Chapter 36: Siegelman 17, Government 0
Grand jury testimony of Forrest "Mac" Macarto, as reported in, "Testimony: Scrushy bullied banking firm," *Curran/Mobile Register*, Jan. 21, 2006.
Phillip Rawls. "Toll bridge developer finds himself in political turmoil," *Associated Press*, April 10, 1999.

Chapter 37: Sudden Death Overtime
Bill Barrow, "Defense rests – with no defense," *Mobile Register*, June 13, 2006.
Jacque Kochak, "Auburn jury foreman: 'Sell out' by governor was unacceptable," *Auburn Villager*, July 13, 2006.
Topher Sanders, "Foreman describes deadlock," *Montgomery Advertiser*, July 1, 2006.

Chapter 38: Target: Jurors
Michael Tomberlin, "Scrushy, witness in picture; prosecutor says photo shows relationship," *Birmingham News*, Nov. 8, 2006.
Eddie Curran, "Lawyer grilled on juror contact," *Mobile Register*, Nov. 1, 2006.
Eddie Curran, "Siegelman jurors deny influence," *Mobile Register*, Nov. 18, 2006.
Mike Linn, "Siegelman juror wants to talk shop with prosecutors," *Montgomery Advertiser*, July 13, 2006
Adam Nossiter, "New twist in appeal of Ex-Alabama Governor," *New York Times*, Nov. 21, 2008.
Mary Orndorff, "Siegelman jury e-mails found forged," *Birmingham News*, July 24, 2008.

Chapter 39: The Dishonest Broker
Majority staff, U.S. House Committee on the Judiciary, "Allegations of Selective Prosecution in Our Federal Criminal Justice System," April 17, 2008.

Scott Horton's, "No Comment" columns on Harper's web-site, including "Javert's Wailings Grow Louder;" "More Responses to Javert;," "Javert's Amazing Pirouettes;" and, "A Brain Dead Press."
Scott Horton, April 22, 2008, presentation in Huntsville called, "Watchdogs or Lap Dogs?: Politics and the Alabama Press."

Chapter 40: Dana Jill
Lisa DePaulo, "Karl Rove likes what he sees," GQ magazine's web-site, April 2, 2008.
John Ehinger, "Don Siegelman wants people who can make nice about him," Huntsville Times, March 18, 2007.
Telephone interview with J. Holland.
"Political Campaign" fax from John Aaron to Dana Jill Simpson, Feb. 12, 2007.
Bryan Lyman, "Lawyer affidavit won't affect Siegelman appeal," Mobile Register, June 30, 2007.
Telephone interview with Ronnie Helton, March 2008.
Jill Simpson affidavit, dated May 21, 2007.
Eric Lipton, "Some ask if U.S. Attorney Dismissals Point to Pattern of Investigating Democrats," New York Times, April 30, 2007.
Adam Zagorin, "Rove named in Alabama controversy," Time, June 1, 2007.

Chapter 41: Hook Line and Sinker
Editorial, "Selective Prosecution," New York Times, Aug. 6, 2007.
Adam Zagorin, "Rove Named in Alabama Controversy," Time, June 1, 2007.
Edmund L. Andrews, "Ex-governor Says Affidavit Shows Politics in Bribe Case," New York Times, June 1, 2007.
Bob Johnson, "Lawyer links Rove to Alabama investigation," Associated Press, June 7, 2007.
Don Siegelman, "Live with Dan Abrams: Bush League Justice," MSNBC, April 7, 2008.
Carrie Johnson, "Former Ala. Governor turns tables on Justice Department," Washington Post, April 13, 2008.
Dana Siegelman, "Live with Dan Abrams: Bush League Justice," MSNBC, Feb. 27, 2008.
Paul Alexander, "Karl Rove destroyed my life," Dec. 27, 2008, The Daily Beast, Dec. 27, 2008.
Don Siegelman, interview with Thom Hartmann, April 2008.
Siegelman interview, "The Rachel Maddow Show," MSNBC, March 5, 2009.
Sam Stein, Huffington Post, March 28, 2008.
Kim Chandler and Mary Orndorff, "Two Siegelman advocates missed out on state contract," Birmingham News, June 9, 2007.
Scott Horton, "Abramoff and Justice in the Heart of Dixie," Harper's web-site, June 9, 2007.

Chapter 42: The Man in the Iron Mask
John Archibald, "Siegelman's blues insult true victims," Birmingham News, Dec. 19, 2006.
Kim Chandler, "All-American success stories gone-wrong come to the sentencing chapter," Birmingham News, June 25, 2007.
Bob Johnson, "Former Ala. Governor gets 7-plus years," Associated Press, June 29, 2007.
Adam Nossiter, "Ex-Governor Says Conviction Was Political," New York Times, June 26, 2007.
Bob Johnson, "Judge increases sentence ranger for Siegelman," Associated Press, June 28, 2007.
Helen Hammonds, "Courtroom Chronicles," WSFA web-site, June 28, 2007.
Kim Chandler and Charles J. Dean, "Both men leave court, are shackled, promise appeal," Birmingham News, June 29, 2007.
Kim Chandler, "Lawyers seek their clients' freedom," Birmingham News, June 30, 2007.
Telephone interview with Kyle Whitmire.
CBS News, "Did Ex-Alabama governor get a raw deal?" 60 Minutes, Feb. 24, 2008.
Telephone interview with Jess Seroyer.
Bob Johnson, "Former governor now lives in small cell 23 hours a day," Associated Press, July 10, 2007.
Staff and wire report, "Former attorneys general request probe of Alabama corruption case," Mobile Register, July 17, 2007.
Editorial, "Questions about a governor's fall," New York Times, " June 30, 2007.
Mary Orndorff, "Davis says Siegelman case may go to Congress 'Selective prosecution' cited in request for hearing," Birmingham News, July 7, 2007.
Bob Johnson, "Siegelman compares federal investigation to Watergate," Associated Press, April 21, 2007.
Jay Reeves, "Judge gives Bailey 18 months in jail," Associated Press, Aug. 30, 2007.
Scott Horton, "Javert in Alabama, Harper's web-site, July 2, 2008.
Scott Horton, "Siegelman in the Iron Mask," Harper's web-site, July 13, 2007.
Scott Horton, "Dana Jill Simpson issues press release," Harper's web-site, July 20, 2007.

Chapter 43: Creative Perjury
Dana Jill Simpson, testimony, U.S. House Committee on the Judiciary, Sept. 14, 2007.
Dana Jill Simpson affidavit, May 21, 2007.
Scott Horton, "2003 affidavit raises more serious questions about Siegelman judge," Harper's web-site, Oct. 16, 2007.
Brett J. Blackledge, Mary Orndorff and Kim Chandler, "Lawyer adds to her affidavit on Siegelman," Birmingham News, Oct. 10, 2007.
Interviews with Rob Riley in 2008 and 2009.
Telephone interview with Stewart Hall, July 30, 2008.
Scott Horton, "Judge Fuller: A Siegelman Grudge Match," Harper's web-site, Aug. 2, 2007.
Majority staff report of U.S. House of Representatives Committee on the Judiciary, "Allegations of Selective Prosecution in Our Federal Criminal Justice System," April 17, 2008.

Bill Barrow, "Riley's ratings are low: Governor would trail Moore, Siegelman in 2006 race," Mobile Register, Nov. 16, 2003.
"Alabama Governor '06: Two years and counting for Riley," The Hotline, June 7, 2004.
Bill Barrow, "Siegelman trails Moore, Riley in poll," Mobile Register, Jan. 23, 2005.
Bill Barrow, "Baxley leading Siegelman," Mobile Register, Jan. 30, 2005.
Bill Barrow, "Riley strong against Dems; survey shows surging governor with double-digit leads over Baxley, Siegelman," Mobile Register, Oct. 16, 2005.
David Prather, "Siegelman's guilty, relatively speaking," Huntsville Times, Nov. 7, 2007.
Scott Horton, "Siegelman Updates," Harper's web-site, Nov. 10, 2007.
Scott Horton, columns on Harper's web-site including, "Noel Hillman and the Siegelman case;" "Karl Rove linked to Siegelman Prosecution;" "The Noel Hillman connection;"
Telephone interview in 2006 with Noel Hillman.
Telephone interviews and e-mails to and from Noel Hillman, July and August, 2008.

Chapter 44: Dumb and Dumber

Adam Zagorin, "Selective Justice in Alabama," Time, Oct. 4, 2007.
Eddie Curran, "Pryor got boost from Young," Mobile Register, May 31, 2001.
Scott Horton, "Time reports on the political prosecutions in Alabama," Harper's web-site, Oct. 5, 2007.
Adam Zagorin, "Rove linked to Alabama case," Time, Oct. 10, 2007.
Philip Shenon, "Partisanship accusation expanded in Alabama," New York Times, Oct. 11, 2007.
Bob Johnson, "Simpson says Siegelman dropped challenge to avoid prosecution," Associated Press, Oct. 10, 2007.
Brett J. Blackledge, Mary Orndorff and Kim Chandler, "Lawyer adds to her affidavit on Siegelman," Birmingham News, Oct. 10, 2007.
Bob Johnson, "Conyers apologizes to Simpson for release of her statement," Associated Press, Oct. 26, 2007.
Scott Horton, "More from the Bama press," Harper's web-site, Oct. 22, 2007.
Adam Nossiter, "Democrats see politics in governor's jailing," New York Times, September 11, 2007.
Scott Horton, "More responses to Javert," Harper's web-site, Oct. 7, 2007.
Scott Horton, "The Argus-eyed University," Harper's web-site, Dec. 31, 2009.
Carrie Johnson, "Former Ala. Governor turns tables on Justice Department," Washington Post, April 13, 2008.
Adam Nossiter, "Freed ex-governor of Alabama talks abuse of power," New York Times, March 29, 2008.
Sean Reilly, "Former Siegelman attorney testifies," Mobile Register, Oct. 24, 2007.
Brett J. Blackledge, "Riley angered by Davis' remarks about GOP plot," Birmingham News, Oct. 25, 2007.
Scott Horton, "Riley protests too much," Harper's web-site, Oct. 27, 2007.

Chapter 45: Me v. Horton

Eddie Curran, "Judge, conduct of Siegelman trial defended," Montgomery Independent, Feb. 19, 2008.
Eddie Curran, "Eddie Curran's defense of Judge Fuller, Part 2," Montgomery Independent, Feb. 26, 2008.
Memorandum of Understanding between Jill Simpson and Thomas T. Gallion III, dated July 30, 2007.
Scott Horton, "Just Deserts," Montgomery Independent, Jan. 21, 2008.
Scott Horton, "Siegelman sentenced; Riley Rushes to Washington," Harper's web-site, June 28, 2007.
Scott Horton, "The Pork Barrel World of Mark Fuller," Harper's web-site, August 6, 2007.
Scott Horton, "Vote Machine: How Republicans hacked the Justice Department," Harper's magazine, March 2008 issue.
Larisa Alexandrovna, "Scott Horton under attack," Raw Story web-site, Feb. 22, 2008.

Chapter 46: "60 Minutes" Kicks Karl Rove's Butt

Scott Horton, "Searching for meaning in the 'B'ham News,'" Harper's web-site, Oct. 14, 2007.
Scott Horton, "CBS 60 Minutes Siegelman story to air on Sunday," Harper's web-site, Feb. 20, 2008.
Ben Evans, "Ex-Republican operative says Bush adviser Karl Rove pushed for dirt on Alabama's governor," Associated Press, Feb. 22, 2008.
Scott Horton, "Rove and Siegelman," Harper's web-site, Feb. 22, 1008.
Patricia McWhorter, "Canned fish swings TV vote in favor," Huntsville Times, Feb. 26, 2007.
Scott Horton, "CBS: More prosecutorial misconduct in Siegelman case," Harper's web-site, Feb. 24, 2008.
Editorial, "WHNT's technical glitches," New York Times, Feb. 27, 2008.
Jay Reeves, "Alabama TV station blames technical problem for blackout of '60 Minutes' story on Siegelman," Associated Press, Feb. 26, 2008.
Bill Carter, "Station says '60 Minutes' blackout was just technical," New York Times, Feb. 26, 2008.
Aman Batheja, John Moritz, "Newspaper learns hard way which Bass leans toward Democrats," Fort Worth Star-Telegram, March 9, 2008.
Ben Evans, "Alabama GOP disputes former campaign worker's claims on CBS show," Associated Press, Feb. 25, 2008.
Cynthia Tucker, "How to rout a pesky rival in Alabama," The Atlanta Journal-Constitution, March 2, 2008.
Dana Jill Simpson, "Live with Dan Abrams: Bush League Justice," MSNBC, Feb. 27, 2008.
Lisa DePaulo, "Karl Rove likes what he sees," GQ magazine's web-site, April 2, 2008.
Ben Evans, "Rove disputes allegations about Alabama governor," Associated Press, April 3, 2008.
"Statement by Alabama Republican Party Chairman Mike Hubbard on the Dana Jill Simpson Accusations Aired by CBS' 60 Minutes," Alabama Republican Party, Feb. 24, 2008.
CBS News, "The Prosecution of Don Siegelman; Don Siegelman released from prison after 60 Minutes story airs," 60 Minutes, April 6, 2008.

Chapter 47: 'Rappin on Rove
Sam Stein, "Siegelman on Rove: Probably the most devious, evil political operative in history," *Huffington Post*, May 27, 2008.
Brett Martin, "America's Most wanted," *GQ* magazine web-site, April Oct. 24, 2008.
Charles J. Dean, Kim Chandler and Stan Diel, ""Siegelman rejoins family after 9 months," *Birmingham News*, March 29, 2008.
Tom Gordon and Brett Blackledge, "Bow-out seen as beneficial concession; may keep door open to future runs," *Birmingham News*, Nov. 19, 2002.
"Live with Dan Abrams: Bush League Justice," *MSNBC*, March 28, 2008.
Adam Nossiter, "Freed ex-Governor of Alabama talks of abuse of power," *New York Times*, March 29, 2008.
Kyle Whitmire, "Did anyone ask about a yacht?" *Birmingham Weekly*, April 15, 2007.
CBS News, "The Prosecution of Don Siegelman; Don Siegelman released from prison after 60 Minutes story airs," *60 Minutes*, April 6, 2008.
Don Siegelman, "Live with Dan Abrams: Bush League Justice," *MSNBC*, April 7, 2008.
Michael Abramowitz, "Karl Rove: New rampart, old battles," *Washington Post*, June 23, 2008.
Mary Orndorff, "Rove's written reply denies any Siegelman role," *Birmingham News*, July 25, 2008.
Siegelman interview, "The Rachel Maddow Show," *MSNBC*, March 5, 2009.
The web-site, DonSiegelman.Org.
Majority staff, U.S. House Committee on the Judiciary, "Allegations of Selective Prosecution in Our Federal Criminal Justice System," April 17, 2008.
John Ehinger, "3 state papers find themselves the targets of a N.Y. writer," *Huntsville Times*, Aug. 26, 2007.
John Ehinger, "Watchdogs, lapdogs, and old dogs," *Huntsville Times*, April 27, 2008.
Dana Jill Simpson, interview with Greg Privett of NewsChannel 19 in Huntsville, April 24, 2008.
Bob Johnson, "Former governor is freed on bond," *Associated Press*, March 29, 2008.
Kim Chandler, "Siegelman leaving prison on appeal as Scrushy, once labeled flight risk, remains locked up," *Birmingham News*, March 28, 2008.
Charles Dean, Kim Chandler and Stan Diel, "Siegelman rejoins family after 9 months," *Birmingham News*, March 29, 2008.
Mary Orndorff, "Davis advises against Siegelman testifying," *Birmingham News*, April 1, 2008.
Don Siegelman, "Live with Dan Abrams: Bush League Justice," *MSNBC*, May 12, 2008.
Editorial, "Contempt for Karl Rove," *Birmingham News*, Aug. 5, 2008.
Patricia McCarter, "Sentencing Siegelman," *Huntsville Times*, June 25, 2007.
Charles J. Dean, "Siegelman busy pushing Rove's guilt, his innocence," *Birmingham News*, Aug. 26, 2008.
Karl Rove, testimony, U.S. House Committee on the Judiciary, July 29, 2009
Tom Hamburger and David G. Savage, "Ex-governor says he was target of Republican plot," *Los Angeles Times*, June 26, 2007.
Editorial, "More Evidence of a Scandal," *The New York Times*, Aug. 13, 2009.
Jason Leopold, "Iglesias 'long suspected Rove's fingerprints were all over' U.S. Attorney Firings," *The Public Record*, July 30, 2009.
Eric Lichtblau and Eric Lipton, "E-mail reveals Rove's key role in '06 dismissals," *New York Times*, Aug. 12, 2009.
Karl Rove, "Closing in on Rove," *Wall Street Journal*, Aug. 20, 2009.

Chapter 48: Pardon Me!
Adam Nossiter, "Appeal hearing in ex-governor's conviction," *New York Times*, Dec. 10, 2008.
Al Kamen, "Is Eric Holder one of those people who need people?" *Washington Post*, January 27, 2009.
Kim Chandler, "Former Alabama Gov. Don Siegelman, HealthSouth founder Richard Scrushy appeal convictions before 3-judge panel," *Birmingham News*, Dec. 10, 2008.
Bob Johnson, "Prosecutors ask for longer sentence for Siegelman," *Associated Press*, May 12, 2009.
John Schwartz, "Ex-Governor of Alabama loses again in court," *New York Times*, May 15, 2009.
Carrie Johnson and Del Quentin Wilber, "Holder asks judge to drop case against ex-Senator," *Washington Post*, April 2, 2009.
Zachary Roth, "Siegelman: Stevens case is dropped, so why not mine?" *TPM Muckraker*, April 1, 2009.
Scott Horton, "Justice on Stevens," *Harper's* web-site, April 1, 2009.
Editorial, "Mr. Holder and the Ted Stevens Case," *New York Times*, April 3, 2009.
John Schwartz and Charlie Savage, "Review of Governor's Conviction Sought," *New York Times*, April 22, 2009.
Editorial, "The Siegelman case," *New York Times*, April 25, 2009.

Epilogue
Shelly Sigo, "Blount pleads guilty; agrees to testify against Langford," *The Bond Buyer*, Aug. 19, 2009.
Jay Reeves, "SEC sues Birmingham mayor over benefits from bond firm," *Associated Press*, April 30, 2008.
Carrie Johnson and Alice Crites, "What Did Rep. Conyers Know?" *Washington Post*, July 5, 2009.
Wikipedia, entry for Don Siegelman.
Russell Hubbard, "Ex-CEO returns to jail after testimony," *Birmingham News*, May 23, 2009.
Russell Hubbard, "Scrushy to take stand next week," *Birmingham News*, May 16, 2009.
Michael Tomberlin, "Sour notes: Behind the music of Richard Scrushy at HealthSouth," *Birmingham News*, May 17, 2009.
George Altman, "AGs backing Siegelman mostly Dems," *Mobile Register*, Oct. 5, 2009.
Alex Koppelman, "The ballad of Ramos and Compean," *Salon*, Sept. 4, 2007.
John Schwartz, "Justice Dept. Whistle-Blower in Alabama Case Is Fired," *New York Times*, July 8, 2009.

Index

C

C&H Investments, 116-117, 130, 281

Café Louisa, 415, 461

Compass Bank, 422

Cahaba Trace Commission, 260

Camber Corp., 143, 145-146, 149

Campagna, Charles, ix, 79, 240, 242, 351

Campbell, David, 94, 98-99

Campbell, Richard, 273

Canary, Bill, xiv, xxiv-xxv, 51, 272, 275-278, 280, 342-348, 350, 390, 418, 487-488, 492, 496, 498, 500, 501-502, 503, 507-508, 510, 515, 517, 520, 529, 533-534, 536-537, 542, 567, 569, 571, 578-579, 592, 600, 603, 620

Canary, Leura, xiii, xxiii, xxv, 51, 272, 273-278, 280-281, 342, 350, 361, 386-387, 390, 399, 418, 487-488, 498, 500, 502, 507-508, 515, 517, 520-521, 533-534, 542, 567, 569, 571, 578, 600, 620, 628

C&H Investments, 116-117, 130, 281

Capital City Consultants, 20

Capstone Health Services, 377-379, 385

Carmichael, Leon, 403

Carr, Rob, 45

Carroll, John, 477

Carville, James, 13, 155

Cason, Mike, 331, 333, 352

Cassady, Joe, 560

Castano Group, 163

Castille, Ed, 67

Catalanello, Rebecca, 230

Caylor, John, 497, 626

CDG Engineers, 47, 87, 96, 100, 110, 112, 115, 116, 121-122, 128, 230, 440

Certificate of Need and Review Board (Also, CON board), 33, 34, 37, 246, 311, 313, 408, 432-433, 451, 561, 569-570, 608, 611-612

Chandler, Kim, xi, xxvi, 49, 154, 213-215, 218-219, 222-223, 227, 254, 266-267, 269, 271, 273, 284, 291, 322, 387-388, 391, 486, 508, 510, 541, 596, 629

Channel One, 510

Chemical Waste Management, 7, 234-236, 239, 331

Cherokee County (landfill and scandals), ix, xix, 79-80, 84-85, 89, 92, 386, 389-393, 417, 438-439

Cherry Givens (also, Cherry, Givens, Peters Lockett and Diaz.....), x, 161-164, 166, 168-182, 200-201, 206, 227, 315-316, 321-325, 401

Chez Soiree, 30, 587

Childers, Larry, 10-11, 101, 209, 327

Childree, Bob, 633

Children's First, 24

Cleghorn, John, 634

Clemon, Arnese, 381

Clemon, U.W., 376, 380-385, 528, 528

Cline, Darren, x, 28, 32, 37-38, 430-431, 621

Clinton, Bill, xxii, 3-6, 13, 155, 278, 380, 381, 487, 507, 545, 610, 630

Cloos, Paul, xi, 48, 123, 147, 150-151, 161-162, 191-193, 197, 200, 231, 251, 257, 284-286, 290, 293-296, 302, 308, 319, 375, 410, 633

Cloverdale, 106, 261, 415, 461

Old Cloverdale Association, 261

Cohen, Adam, xii, 326, 338, 368, 503-504, 573, 592, 603

Cole, Ray, 144-145

Collins, Alan, 461

Colonial Bank, 40-41, 79, 270, 301-301, 305, 333

Colorado MEDtech, 266, 271

Colsa, 216

Compass Bank, 422

Compean, Jose, 629-630

Comptroller's Office, 77, 89, 108-110, 146, 174, 246, 352, 633

Conference of Western Attorneys General, 354, 518

Connors, Marty, 196

ContemptForRove.com, 591

Conyers, John, xiv, xxiv-xxv, 276, 366, 517-518, 541, 547, 590-591, 597-598, 600, 610, 617, 619, 622-623, 627

Conyers, Monica, 622-623

Coody, Charles, 43, 587

Coogler, Scott, 382

Cooper, Melvin, 10, 319

Copeland, Susan, ix, 90-91, 95, 110, 238

Crain, Beth, 437-438

Crawford, Johnny, 87, 214, 235, 442

Crowe, J.D., iv, 53, 527, 364, 366-367, 369, 600

Crozier, Barbara, 164

Crozier vs. American Tobacco, 164-166, 178, 315-316, 321

Cumberland Law School, 477

Cunningham Bounds, 253

Cunningham, Bobo, 253

Cunningham, Cheryl, 49, 159-160

Cunningham, Harris & Associates, 28

Cunningham, J.C., 49, 159-160

Cunningham, Jim, 28, 40

Cunningham, Randall "Duke," 549

Cunningham, Todd, 49, 159-160

Curran, Bud, 634

Curran, Eddie, xv-xx, 16-21; 43; 58-78, 81-82; 87-93, 96. 100-142, 144-152, 154, 155-158, 160-162; 168-215; 217; 221-225; 229-232; 235-241; 244-270, 279, 283-314; 316, 319-325; 327-333, 346-348, 352-258, 361, 375; 388; 399-402, 406, 409, 413, 415, 436, 445, 451-455, 458, 461, 470-473, 486, 489, 485, 500, 504, 507, 512, 519-520, 536, 538, 544-546, 553-565, 567, 575-583, 585, 592-597, 607, 627, 629-635

Curran, Eleanor, v, 16, 100, 196, 634

Curran, Eva, v, 300, 634

Curran, Greg, 120, 634

Curran, Jana, v, 18, 375, 634

Curran, Jerry (author's son), v, 18, 189, 300, 375

Curran, Jerry (author's father), 4, 545, 634

D

E

F

P

Pacer, 89, 217, 254, 633
Parks, Rosa, 406
Parsons, Bobby Jo, 233-234
Parsons, James, 233-234
Patterson, Albert, 487
Patterson, Belknap, Webb & Tyler, 487
Pearce Family Investments LLC, 245-6, 248-249, 259, 261
Pearce, J. Wray, xi, 50, 244-259, 262, 264-265, 331
Pelley, Scott, xii, 279, 367, 568-572, 575-581, 583, 588
Peoples, Benny, 269
Perdue, Myron, 109, 633
Perkins, Giles, 38, 293
Perkins, Joe, xi, 154, 219, 223-225, 230, 252, 268, 270, 336, 621
Perlmutter, Ed, 600
Perrine, J.B., xii, 437
Peters, Chris, x, 53, 159, 164, 171, 173-174, 176-180, 186, 321-322, 485-486
Peters, Thomas Minott, 485
Pettagrue, Samuel, 397
Petranka, Joe, 261
Philip Morris, 163, 166
Pickett, Taylor, 36, 313
Pilger, Richard, xii, 508
Pitt, Redding, x, xiii, 11, 278, 291-294, 301-304, 387
Pitts, Chris, 88, 103, 126
Platinum Club, 417, 437
Pohost, Gerald, 231
Pool, James, 296-299, 304, 309
Pool, Sybil, 6
Poole, Phil, 379, 443-444
Poovey, Bill, 38, 39, 152, 153, 221
Porch Creek Indians, 510
Powe, Skip, 70
Poynter Institute, 139
Prather, David, 532
Press-Register (See *Mobile Register*)
Price, Charles, 159, 166
Pridgen, Dwight, 19
Pringle, Chris, 138
Project One, 394
Parkman, Jim, 396, 414
Provident Group Inc., 270
Pryor, Bill, xii, 86, 92, 120, 124-6, 130, 163, 165-166, 177, 272-274, 278, 282, 302, 307, 314, 316, 339, 361, 379, 382, 423, 518, 537-540, 545, 600
Public Integrity Section, xii-xiii, 361, 369, 386, 399, 533-535, 546, 548
Pugh, Mark, 96
Pylant, Stan, 573574

Q

Quality Research, 140, 142-146, 149,150, 156-157, 191, 216
quid pro quo, 429-431

R

Rabb, Willie, 633
Rabbi Yonah's blog, 626
Raby, Steve, 231
RaCON, 60-61, 63, 78
RainLine, xi, 393, 400, 441, 443, 445-450, 460, 462, 511
Ramos, Ignacio, 629
Rase, Kathy, 470
Rawls, Phil, xi, 60, 161, 168-169, 174, 181, 206, 224, 227, 229, 323, 334, 357, 388, 391, 409, 443-444, 596
Raw Story, 545-546, 562-563, 566, 580, 626
Ray, Alston, 288
Raymond James & Associates, 357
Reed, Joe, 398
Reed, Ralph, 510
Reese, Gene, 282
Reeves, Archie, 194
Reilly, Sean, 42, 633
Richard M. Scrushy Foundation, 394
"Rich Man's Dream," 31
Rick Renzi, 548
RICO (Also, the Rackateer Influenced Criminal Organization Act), 400, 429, 434-436, 462, 513
Riley, Bob
Riley, Rob, xiv, 326, 343-349, 494, 498, 502, 523-529, 531, 533, 535, 541, 546, 571-572, 592
Ring of Fire," xxi, 506
Robbins, Tony, 354
Roberts, Yolanda, 171
Roberts, Mack, ix, xi, xiii, xvii, xix, 12, 21-22, 25, 51, 60-67, 70, 74-75, 87, 143, 154, 157, 400, 409, 412-413, 415, 441-451, 453-454, 459, 511
Roden, Mark, 494
Roe, Medford, 634
Roberts, Jeff, 51, 367
Rogers, Nell, 510
Rogow, Bruce, 607-608
Rojeski, Judi, 633
Romano, Alex, 607
Rosenthal, Andrew, xii, 503-504, 619
Roth, Toby, 345, 509-510, 578, 602-603
Roth, Zachary, 617
Rowell, James "Jimmy," 142-145, 218
Rowland, John, 547
Rove, Karl, ii, xi-xiv, xxiii-xxv, 220, 276, 338, 342, 346-351, 359, 365-367, 369, 386, 390, 418, 420, 485, 487-488, 490, 492, 494-497, 499-500, 502-509, 512, 515, 517-518, 520-521, 523, 525, 530, 532-537, 540, 542, 545-546, 548-552, 557-560, 566-569, 571-578, 580-592, 597-606, 610, 617, 620-621, 625, 630, 634
Ryan, George, 547

Z

Y